Readings and Cases in International Human Resource Management and Organizational Behavior

Readings and Cases in International Human Resource Management and Organizational Behavior, 5th Edition examines cross-cultural interactions between people, cultures, and human resource systems in a wide variety of regions throughout the world.

This is truly a global collection.

Features include:
* new readings and case studies positioned alongside trusted "tried and true" readings and cases from past editions;
* a companion website featuring supplemental material and teaching notes to enhance instructors' abilities to use the readings and cases with their students.

Written to enable students to meet the international challenges that they face every day and to sensitize them to the complexity of human resource issues in the era of globalization, this text is a vital resource for all those studying international human resource management.

Günter K. Stahl is an Associate Professor of Organizational Behavior at INSEAD.

Mark E. Mendenhall is the J. Burton Frierson Chair of Excellence in Business Leadership at the University of Tennessee-Chattanooga.

Gary R. Oddou is a Professor at California State University-San Marcos. He teaches Leadership in a Global Context, Managing in Different Cultures, International Business Management, and International Human Resource Management.

Readings and Cases in International Human Resource Management and Organizational Behavior

Fifth Edition

Edited by

Günter K. Stahl,
Mark E. Mendenhall, and
Gary R. Oddou

Routledge
Taylor & Francis Group

NEW YORK AND LONDON

Fifth edition published 2012
by Routledge
711 Third Avenue, New York, NY 10017

Simultaneously published in the UK
by Routledge
2 Park Square, Milton Park, Abingdon, Oxon OX14 4RN

Routledge is an imprint of the Taylor & Francis Group, an informa business

First published 1991 by PWS Kent Publishing Company
Second and third editions published 1995 and 2000 by South-Western
College Publishing
Fourth edition published 2007 by Routledge

Library of Congress Cataloging in Publication Data
Readings and cases in international human resource management and
organizational behavior/edited by Günter K. Stahl, Mark E. Mendenhall,
and Gary R. Oddou.—5th ed.
    p. cm.
    Includes index.
    1. International business enterprises—Personnel management. 2. Personnel
    management—Cross-cultural studies. 3. Intercultural communication—Case
    studies. 4. Corporate culture—Cross-cultural studies. 5. Organizational
    behavior—Case studies. I. Stahl, Günter K., 1966– II. Mendenhall,
    Mark E., 1956– III. Oddou, Gary R.
    HF5549.5.E45R43 2011
    658.3—dc22
    2010054112

ISBN13: 978–0–415–89296–4 (hbk)
ISBN13: 978–0–415–89298–8 (pbk)
ISBN13: 978–0–203–81343–0 (ebk)

Typeset in Bell Gothic
by Florence Production Ltd, Stoodleigh, Devon

Printed and bound in the United States of America on acid-free paper
by Sheridan Books, Inc.

Contents

PART 4
People Issues in International Teams, Alliances, Mergers, and Acquisitions   **287**

PART 5
Global Business Ethics, Corporate Social Responsibility, and Management of Diversity   381

Illustrations

FIGURES

EXHIBITS

TABLES

Günter K. Stahl, Mark E. Mendenhall, and Gary R. Oddou

PREFACE: THE WHITE-WATER RAPIDS OF INTERNATIONAL HUMAN RESOURCE MANAGEMENT: ROBIN EARL'S DILEMMA

WELCOME TO THE FIFTH EDITION of *Readings and Cases in International Human Resource Management*. If you are a long-time user of this text, we would like to take a moment to thank you for using the book in your teaching or consulting endeavors. We originally put this book together because we couldn't find one ourselves, and we wanted such a book to use in our classes. Since then, with your help, the book has evolved and become a standby for teachers of international management/HRM/OB.

We think the best way to introduce the textbook is with an introductory reading/case. It sets the tone of the book, and, if you like, also makes an excellent reading assignment to begin class with. We call it "The White Water Rapids of Robin Earl."

READING AND CASE: THE WHITE WATER RAPIDS OF ROBIN EARL

Business leaders of the present—let alone the future—need to possess international business skills par excellence in order to survive the chaotic world of international business. It also goes without saying that human resource managers will face new, unforeseen obstacles. Peter Vaill uses the metaphor of "permanent white water" to describe the unpredictable, dynamic nature of doing business in the latter part of the twentieth century.

Most managers are taught to think of themselves as paddling their canoes on calm, still, lakes . . . They're led to believe that they should be pretty much able to go where they want, when they want, using the means that are under their control. Sure there will be temporary disruptions during changes of various sorts—periods when they will have to shoot the rapids in their canoes—but the disruptions will be temporary, and when things settle back down, they'll be back in a calm, still lake mode. But it has been my experience . . . that you never get out of the rapids! No sooner do you begin to digest one change than another one comes along to keep things unstuck. In fact, there are usually lots of changes going on at once. The feeling is one of continuous upset and chaos.[1]

This metaphor aptly illustrates the world of international business. As Vaill notes, in the world of international business, "things are only very partially under control, yet the effective navigator of the rapids is not behaving randomly or aimlessly. Intelligence, experience, and skill are being exercised, albeit in ways that we hardly know how to perceive, let alone describe" (p. 2). This book deals with the challenges that human resource managers will face in the twenty-first century. What will be the general nature of those challenges? Perhaps an example of a firm or individual would help illustrate these challenges. Let us consider the case of Robin Earl. Note that Robin Earl is a North American human resource manager in a North American company. However, she could just as easily be a manager in any medium-sized European, Asian, South or Central American, Australian or New Zealand, or African company. The issue is not her gender, her nationality, or the nationality of her firm, but rather the challenges she faces due to globalization.

ROBIN EARL'S "WHITE WATER RAPIDS"

Robin Earl is Director of Human Resources for BCN, a firm that, among other things, manufactures a line of semiconductors. BCN has been very successful in the last ten years. Sales have increased at an annual rate of 7 percent and profits have correspondingly grown.

BCN has had overseas sales offices for the last seven years, exporting its products from its local manufacturing operations to South America and Southeast Asia. Recently, BCN's top management has been mulling over the possibility of developing manufacturing and distribution capabilities in South America and Asia—and possibly even in Europe. Doing so would allow BCN to take advantage of cheaper labor rates in some of these countries and to avoid export barriers in others. In addition, it could be more responsive to local demand for its products, and in the age of globalization, move toward being a truly global firm.

Robin was asked by the firm's CEO to prepare an analysis (due on his desk in two weeks) of the human resource impact such moves would have on the firm. As Robin sat down at her desk, she began to jot down ideas. She found herself somewhat baffled by this global angle of HRM, as she had no experience or training in managing human resources internationally. The following are some of her thoughts as she attempted to create an outline for her report.

I. How Will International Assignments Fit into BCN's Business Strategy to Become a Truly Global Firm?

Do we have a clearly focused business strategy for becoming a multinational firm? She made a mental note to call John Fukumoto, the VP of Finance, to see how far the thinking of the top management team had progressed on that front. *How will the development of BCN's human resources fit into such a plan? I wonder why I am not on that planning team?* Robin wondered how she could insert herself into that process without being suspected of having ulterior motives.

What kind of perspective and experience should BCN's future top management have if they will be leading a true multinational firm? How will that experience be best obtained—through international assignments or by the use of consultants? Am I going to be responsible for educating management regarding international issues? If so, it's the blind leading the blind, she thought, for she would not even be sure how to evaluate the validity of an external consultant's proposals. *I could always hire experts to evaluate the bid proposals of consulting firms*, she thought, *but that would run into serious budget squeezes for my department.*

Who should we send—our high potentials that are destined to lead the company in the next 10 years or our non-designated personnel? How important will it be to have a global perspective at the top versus having one throughout the levels of the company?

Robin began to think about dual-career couple issues as well. *Just how hard will it be to attract our best people to go to a foreign country if their spouse has a good career here*, she wondered. She had heard about some firms that have formed a consortium in the foreign country to help provide employment for spouses of the repatriate. Working together, they had more flexibility than if they were trying to go it alone.

Will local managers—if we use local managers—desire to be promoted to US headquarters? Will top management desire that? Fifteen years from now what will, and what should, BCN's top management look like: an Asian managing a South American plant and a mixture of South Americans, Asians, Europeans, and Americans at headquarters? The cost of hiring the numbers of new workers—not to mention well-qualified managers—is not going to be loose change. I hope they aren't ignoring the cost of hiring well-qualified managers and retaining them in their financial analyses, Robin thought. *How will we retain the best and the brightest? What do Asians want in rewards? What do South Americans want? Is a good salary enough or are other factors involved?*

II. Which Countries Have Cultures that Best Fit BCN's Needs?

Robin remembered reading a newspaper article that mentioned that one of the factors important to Japanese firms locating in the US was finding compatible regional cultural norms. The Japanese liked the Southern US culture because of its regard for interpersonal relations in business settings, tradition, and respect for elders and persons in positions of authority. *Which countries have educational systems that would best support the knowledge base that our personnel will need? Which countries have social systems that favor unions more than management? Which cultures within these regions are most favorable to American expatriates and their families? Most importantly, which cultures promote a strong work ethic?*

Which countries have governments that are stable and are not likely to change and upset the equilibrium of our workers' and managers' work schedules? What about the possibility of terrorism? Will I have to devise a terrorism-prevention training program? Which countries are friendly to us, not just business-wise but in their perceptions of Americans and their right to manage the local residents? I wonder how much kidnap insurance costs? Robin's mind began to wander. She envisioned herself in a small, box-like hole covered with rusty iron bars. When would her kidnappers give her water? Her reverie was broken by a more practical concern that flashed across her mind.

III. Should We Send Our Own Personnel Overseas or Hire Locally?

Which countries in Asia, South America, or Europe have qualified personnel to staff manufacturing operations from top to bottom? Do some countries have laws that require hiring a certain percentage of local workers? Robin remembered meeting a man once at a professional convention who had worked for a mining company in Africa. He reported having had to hire local workers for all positions below middle management level, with the promise to phase out all Americans within ten years.

Can or should the subsidiary management come from BCN headquarters? If not, where would we find local managers to hire? The universities? Robin recalled reading once that, in France, the norm was to hire managers from the "Grand Écoles" and not from the universities. *If we send our personnel, who should go? How long should their assignments be? How expensive will it be to house an American family at their accustomed standard of living in the new country? How should we select the Americans to send? Should we base our decisions on experience in the company, adaptability potential, or desire to relocate? What if nobody wants to go?*

IV. How Will We Train Employees for Such Assignments?

How much training will they need before they go? How in depth will it need to be? Do they need language training or is English good enough? Robin thought that most business people around the world speak English, so maybe this was not really an issue. *Will the firm budget my department the resources necessary to do quality training or will I be left with a budget that will allow nothing more than bringing in a few local professors for a couple of hours each to do area briefings? Who can I call on to do the training?*

Robin felt somewhat relieved when she remembered reading about some cross-cultural training firms in the ad section of an HRM newsletter she reads. But her confidence ebbed when the following thought occurred to her: *How will I know if the training these external consultants provide is valid and helpful or just a dog and pony show? Can I, with my staff, develop my own training program? What kind of time and money will such an endeavor require?* As Robin began mentally planning a strategy to develop training programs with her staff, her mind switched to yet another problem.

V. What Are the Career Implications of Foreign Assignments?

Should the assignments be developmental or should slots simply be filled as they open up, regardless of whether or not the move will develop the employee? Robin was vaguely aware that companies such as IBM, Ciba-Geigy, and Philips view international assignments as an integral part of their management development for senior posts. *If the assignment is developmental, what will we do when the employee returns?* Robin wondered if the company would give her authority to dictate what position returning managers should receive . . . She doubted they would give her that authority. *But what would happen to these experienced internationalists if they didn't have a clear career path for them when they returned? How will we reintegrate these employees into BCN's home operations? We'll lose them,* Robin thought to herself, *if we can't offer them a good position when they return. How will the HRM department keep informed of the needs, concerns, performance, and evaluation of the overseas employees? By phone? Email? Teleconferencing? Site visits?* Robin wondered whether she could justify trips to the Far East as site visits. They may be necessary, but might be viewed by others as a new perk for the HRM department.

The re-entry part kept bothering Robin. Not only is there the position transition issue to plan for, but she wondered how they might best capture their learning about the foreign operations. *This could be really valuable*, she thought. *It could help us coordinate our efforts better, understand the challenges of our foreign operations, etc.*

VI. How Productive Will the Cheap Labor Be?

If we do opt to set up in a country where the labor rates are inexpensive, can we introduce our management systems into the manufacturing plants? Will those systems be in harmony with the work culture of that country? I wonder if we will run into transfer of technology problems? Probably. Okay, so, how do we train local workers to understand how we do things at BCN? Will I have to design those training programs too?

I wonder if our managers will have to develop unique incentive systems to get their subordinates to work. No, probably not . . . well, then again, maybe. After all, the people under me have different buttons that make them work harder—those buttons are not the same for everyone here in the US. Is it possible, Robin wondered, *for some cultures to have work norms that are antithetical to promotion and pay inducements? I think those would be universal motivators! Maybe this won't be a major problem. Maybe it will be more of a fine-tuning issue in terms of adapting our job design, incentive systems, and motivational techniques to the country where we decide to set up shop.* Then the thought occurred to her, *What about motivating and evaluating the Americans overseas?*

VII. How Should We Do Performance Evaluation?

Can we just use the same forms, procedures and, criteria, or is there something unique about a foreign assignment that requires unique performance evaluation systems? When should we evaluate people? Robin remembered reading in a professional newsletter that expatriate employees require at least six months to settle into their overseas assignments. *Would it be fair to evaluate employees before six months? When would it be valid? After eight, ten, or twelve months? This is getting very messy,* Robin sighed.

   Should the criteria by which to judge performance in Asia and other places be relative to the country in question, or should we use the same evaluation criteria everywhere? The last thing Robin felt like doing was overseeing the development of a new performance evaluation system! *We can get by with our current one,* she mentally noted. *Who should do the evaluating? Headquarters, the regional subsidiary superiors, peers, or a mixture of superiors and subordinates? Should the criteria revolve around bottom-line figures or personnel objectives? If financial-type performance criteria are emphasized, what happens if the dollar depreciates significantly against the local currency and wipes out the expatriate manager's cost savings and profits? How can the expatriate manager be evaluated, motivated, and rewarded under such conditions?*

   What about nationality differences in performance evaluation? If an American manager is being evaluated by a Peruvian subsidiary manager, will the evaluation be fair or is there potential for some sort of cultural bias? What if the American manager is a woman? Will we be able to put together an attractive, but not too costly, compensation package for our expatriates? I wonder what such a package would look like. We need to offer something good to entice the employee to go, especially if the employee might lose the spouse's income, yet if there's too great a difference in the package between the repatriate and local personnel, that will create "we–them" problems.

VIII. Will the Unions Be Trouble?

Robin's thoughts were now racing between problems. *I remember reading somewhere,* she mused, *that in order to shut down a manufacturing facility in France (or was it Germany or Sweden?), management had to give the workers a full year's notice, retrain them, and then find them new jobs!* She knew the top management of her firm would find such a contingency troubling at best. *Well, maybe the Asian labor markets are less unionized and won't be as problematic.* Then Robin recalled meeting a public relations spokeswoman for a toy firm at a party, and the nightmare she had described.

It seems that the U.S. management of her company had pressured the contract manufacturers in Hong Kong and the PRC to increase production dramatically in order to fill unforeseen demands during the Christmas season. The press had gotten hold of cases where female workers were working sixteen-hour days with no breaks; if the employees complained, they were terminated on the spot. Also, some of the women had miscarried. It was a public relations nightmare. *Maybe dealing with unions wouldn't be all bad ... maybe unions would protect us from questionable ethical nightmares,* Robin thought. But then she thought of codetermination laws in countries such as Germany and worker's representatives sitting on the local boards of directors—that would not be easy for American managers to stomach. *And what about managing people from other cultures? We have a hard enough time in our California and Texas plants, let alone overseas!* As Robin put down her pen, the obvious complexity of the report loomed before her. She had just scratched the surface of the basic human resources issues associated with "globalization" and there seemed to be no end to the potential permutations around each problem. *This will be no easy task,* she concluded. As she left her office and made her way to the parking garage, she wondered, *Where can I go for help?*

BCN's situation closely parallels the initial path on which virtually all companies must have had to tread in reaction to the issues, challenges, and opportunities associated with the globalization of business. Within the globalization context of business operations, many business decisions become critical. While some of those decisions pertain to a firm's financial or physical resources, the most neglected and perhaps most important decisions to be made concern the management of the firm's international human resources. One of the greatest problems is the lack of a global perspective on the part of a firm's managerial cadre. As a member of one culture, the manager tends to see life from that perspective, to judge events from that perspective, and to make decisions based on that perspective. In an increasingly global business environment, such a perspective breeds failure.

Our principal objective for this book is to sensitize the reader to the complex human resource issues that exist in the global business environment. With this primary objective in mind, as stated previously, we have attempted to represent many regions of the world balanced by the quality of information and discussion potential of the reading or case.

Most publishing companies are turning to online creation of packets of readings and cases. Although a good idea in theory, it requires a great deal of research in case repositories and online journal systems to design a supplemental text of one's own. Most instructors are too busy with other obligations to spend the time necessary to design and create supplemental texts online, particularly if there is a good alternative, and we believe a book such as this one is just that alternative. We believe there is a need for books to be published of "tried and true" cases and readings that provide stimulating and intellectually challenging material, yet written in ways that engage both the student and the instructor. If you are a new adopter of the book, we would like to thank you, and we look forward to your comments concerning your experience in using the book. Feel free to contact us with your feedback.

In this new edition of our book, we have kept the best cases from the previous editions and added new readings and cases that have the same type of "feel" as the old, "tried and true" ones. The format of the book has changed somewhat, as have the conceptual groupings of each major section of the book. We were reluctant to tamper with a conceptual format that so many people liked, but our field is dynamic, and in order to be current we have updated many of the readings and some of the cases. However, a few of these readings and cases seemed to us to be classics. That is, the issues they address seem to transcend time (and copyright date)! We chose to keep these in the book, since we like to teach from them, and we know that most of you do as well.

This book can be used in a variety of ways in human resource management, management, and organizational behavior courses. It can stand alone, if the instructor's preference is to teach predominately a case course. It can be used in tandem with other textbooks that have an IHRM, management, or organizational behavior focus, or as a supplement to them. Or the book can be used as a main text in human resource management or other related courses, and supplemented with other readings and texts with which the instructor is comfortable.

The instructor's manual is available on this book's website at Routledge. Contained in the instructor's manual are teaching notes for the cases, class discussion notes and guidelines for the readings, and in-class and out-of-class assignments for the cases and readings. Our goal is to support you as an instructor in all of your needs.

As stated earlier, our main objective for the book is simply this: to sensitize the reader to the complex human resource issues that exist in the global business environment. With this objective in mind, we have attempted to represent many regions of the world in terms of the locations in which the readings and cases are based: Bangladesh, Canada, China, France, Germany, Israel, Japan, Malaysia, Mexico, the Netherlands, Senegal, Sweden, the UK, and the US.

Additionally, our readings and cases involve cross-cultural interaction between people and cultures and human resource systems in the following combinations: UK–Israel, US–Japan, Senegal–France, Germany–US, Sweden–US, the Netherlands–Mexico, Canada–France, Sweden–China, Japan–France, China–US, Bangladesh–US, and Germany–China.

However, in providing for this diversity of location and interaction, we chose not to "force fit" something into the book for the sake of regional or geographic representation. We included what we and our editors felt were quality readings and cases in the field of international human resource management. We do not view this book as a North American HR text nor a European HR text. Our goal was to create a book of readings and cases that would focus on the points of confluence between cultures, human resource systems, and people in this era of globalization.

NOTE

1. Peter Vaill, *Managing as a Performing Art: New Ideas for a World of Chaotic Change* (San Francisco, CA: Jossey-Bass, 1989) p. 2.

Acknowledgments

W E WOULD LIKE TO THANK all those who have contributed to this book. Many of the authors willingly sent us cases, articles, manuscripts in progress, and bibliographies that they had developed over the years. We regret that we could not include all the sources offered to us.

We would like to express our appreciation to four people, for without their assistance and support this new edition of the book would not have occurred: our editor at Routledge, John Szilagyi, for his determined support and belief in this edition of the book and for his patience and flexibility in working with our needs; John's editorial assistant, Sara Werden, who was also very helpful in shepherding the project along; Charlotte Davis, who literally made this book "happen" because of her understanding of the field and attention to detail in preparing the final manuscript; and Christof Miska, who conducted an extensive search of the literature to help us identify new articles and cases that we believe are must-reads for those interested in international human resource management and organizational behavior.

A special thanks goes to our wives, Dorit, Janet, and Jane, for their untiring support of us over the years as we have pursued our fascination with "things international"—they make all we accomplish possible and our gratitude to them is eternal.

GÜNTER K. STAHL
Vienna, Austria

MARK E. MENDENHALL
Signal Mountain, Tennessee

GARY R. ODDOU
Oceanside, California

Contributors

Barbara Bakhtari
USA

Kristin Behfar
The Paul Merage School of
    Business
University of California, Irvine
Irvine, CA 92697–3125
949–824–7029
kbehfar@uci.edu

Allan Bird
313A Hayden Hall
Northeastern University
Boston, MA 02115–5000
617–373–2002
a.bird@neu.edu

Ingmar Björkman
Hanken School of Economics
Post Box 479
00101 Helsinki, Finland
+358–40 7040291
ibjorkma@hanken.fi

J. Stewart Black
INSEAD
Boulevard de Constance
77305 Fontainebleau
1 970 247 0621
stewart.black@insead.edu

David Bowen
Thunderbird School of Global
    Management
1 Global Place
Glendale, AZ 85306–6000
+1 (602) 978–7000
david.bowen@thunderbird.edu

Jeanne Brett
Kellogg School of Management
Jacobs Center Room 377
Northwestern University, USA
2001 Sheridan Rd
Evanston, IL 60208
847–491–3300
jmbrett@kellogg.northwestern.edu

Charlotte Butler
INSEAD
Boulevard de Constance
77305 Fontainebleau
+33 (0)1 60 72 40 00
charlotte.butler@insead.edu

David G. Collings
The University of Sheffield
Management School
9 Mappin Street
Sheffield, S1 4DT, United Kingdom
+44 114 222 3346
d.g.collings@shef.ac.uk

Henri-Claude de Bettignies
INSEAD, France and Singapore
Boulevard de Constance
77305 Fontainebleau
33 (0)1 60 72 42 92
hc.debettlgnies@insead.edu

Angelo S. DeNisi
GW I Rm 440F
Tulane University
New Orleans, LA 70118
504–865–5407
adenisi@tulane.edu

C. Brooklyn Derr
Brigham Young University
Provo, UT 84602
801–422–4636
brooke_derr@byu.edu

Joseph J. DiStefano
International Institute for
    Management Development (IMD)
Ch. de Bellerive 23
P.O. Box 915
CH–1001 Lausanne, Switzerland
+41 (0)21 618 0111
joe.distefano@imd.ch

Thomas Donaldson
The Wharton School
University of Pennsylvania
644 Jon M. Huntsman Hall
3730 Walnut Street
Philadelphia, PA 19104
215–898–6859
donaldst@wharton.upenn.edu

Peter W. Dorfman
New Mexico State University, USA
GU 113
P.O. Box 30001
Las Cruces, New Mexico,
    88003–8001
575–646–4086
pdorfman@nmsu.edu

Paul Evans
INSEAD
Boulevard de Constance
77305 Fontainebleau
33 (0)1 60 98 30 32
paul.evans@insead.edu

Stacey R. Fitzsimmons
Simon Fraser University
105–2572 Birch St.
Vancouver, British Columbia
+1–778–786–2101
sfitzsim@sfu.ca

Elizabeth Florent-Treacy
INSEAD
Boulevard de Constance
77305 Fontainebleau
+33 (0)1 60 72 40 00
elizabeth.florent-treacy@insead.edu

Roger Hallowell
The Center for Executive Development
420 Boylston St
Boston, Massachusetts
617–566–1970
rogerhallowell@comcast.net

Wes Harry
Bradford University School of
    Management
Emm Lane
Bradford, BD9 4JL, United Kingdom
01274 23 4346
W.E.Harry@bradford.ac.uk

Martin Hilb
University of St. Gallen
Dufourstrasse 40a
CH-9000 St. Gallen
+41 (0)71 224 23 70
martin.hilb@unisg.ch

Robert J. House
The Wharton School
University of Pennsylvania
644 Jon M. Huntsman Hall

3730 Walnut Street
Philadelphia, PA 19104
215–898–6183
robertjh@wharton.upenn.edu

Susan E. Jackson
Rutgers University
94 Rockafeller Road, Suite 216
Piscataway, NJ 08854
732–445–5447
sjackson@smlr.rutgers.edu

Mansour Javidan
Thunderbird School of Global
    Management
1 Global Place
Glendale, AZ 85306–6000
+1 (602) 978–7000
mansour.javidan@thunderbird.edu

Manfred F.R. Kets de Vries
INSEAD
Boulevard de Constance
77305 Fontainebleau
33 (0)1 60 72 41 55
manfred.ketsdevries@insead.edu

Mary C. Kern
Zicklin School of Business
Baruch College
One Bernard Baruch Way
New York, NY 10010
646–312–3673
Mary.Kern@baruch.cuny.edu

Carin-Isabel Knoop
Global Research Group
Harvard Business School
Boston, MA 02163
617–495–6000
Cknoop@hbs.edu

Kathrin Köster
Hochschule Heilbronn
Raum: G213

Max-Planck-Str. 39, 74081
    Heilbronn
+49(0)7131 504 340
kathrin.koester@hs-heilbronn.de

Carol T. Kulik
University of South Australia
City West Campus EM3–29
North Terrace, Adelaide
South Australia 5000 Australia
+61 8 830 27378
Carol.Kulik@unisa.edu.au

Philippe Lassere
INSEAD
1 Ayer Rajah Avenue
138676 Singapore
65 6799 5333
philippe.lasserre@insead.edu

Thomas Maak
Institute for Business Ethics
University of St. Gallen
Guisanstr. 11
CH-9010 St. Gallen
0041 71 224 2219
Thomas.Maak@unisg.ch

Mark E. Mendenhall
College of Business, University of
    Tennessee
300 Fletcher Hall
615 McCallie Avenue,
    Dept 6056
Chattanooga, TN 37403
(423) 425–4406
mark-mendenhall@utc.edu

Christof Miska
Vienna University of Economics
    and Business
Augasse 2–6
1090 Vienna, Austria
+43 1–313 36–4346
christof.miska@wu.ac.at

Michael J. Morley
Department of Management and
    Marketing
Kemmy Business School
Room: KB3–34
University of Limerick, Ireland
+353–61–202273
michael.morley@ul.ie

Evalde Mutabazi
EM Lyon Business School, France
23, av. Guy de Collongue
BP 174
69132 Ecully Cedex
France
33 (0) 4 78 33 78 00
mutabazi@em-lyon.com

Gary R. Oddou
California State University San
    Marcos
333 S. Twin Oaks Valley Rd.
San Marcos, CA 92096–0001
(760) 750–4236
goddou@csusm.edu

Asbjorn Osland
San José State University
College of Business
One Washington Square
San José, CA 95192–0070
(408) 924–3574
osland_a@cob.sjsu.edu

Joyce S. Osland
San José State University
College of Business
One Washington Square
San José, CA 95192–0070
408/924–3583
osland_j@cob.sjsu.edu

Nicola Pless
ESADE Business School
Avinguda Esplugues, 92–96
E-08034 Barcelona
34 932 806 162 Ext. 5560
nicola.pless@esade.edu

Vladimir Pucik
International Institute for
    Management Development (IMD)
Ch. de Bellerive 23
P.O. Box 915
CH–1001 Lausanne, Switzerland
+41 (0)21 618 0111
vpucik@gmail.com

Loriann Roberson
Columbia University
525 West 120th Street
New York, NY 10027
212–678–3336
lroberson@exchange.tc.columbia.edu

William H. Roof
Intellicheck Mobilisa, Inc.
191 Otto St.
Port Townsend, WA 98368
360–344–3233
info@icmobil.com

Randall S. Schuler
Rutgers University
Labor Education Center
George H. Cook Campus
    (Rutgers–New Brunswick)
50 Labor Center Way
New Brunswick, NJ 08901–8553
732–932–4636
schuler@rci.rutgers.edu

Hugh Scullion
J.E. Cairnes School of Business and
    Economics
National University of Ireland,
    Galway
University Road
Galway, Ireland
353 91 493079
hugh.scullion@nuigalway.ie

Günter K. Stahl
Vienna University of Economics and
    Business
Augasse 2–6
1090 Vienna, Austria
+43–1–31336–4434
guenter.stahl@wu.ac.at

and

INSEAD
Boulevard de Constance
77309 Fontainebleau Cedex
France
guenter.stahl@insead.edu

Mary Sully de Luque
Thunderbird School of Global
    Management
1 Global Place
Glendale, AZ 85306–6000
+1 (602) 978–7000
mary.sullydeluque@thunderbird.edu

Susan Taft
386 Henderson Hall
Kent State University
Kent OH–44240
330–672–8839
SusanSTaft@aol.com

Ibraiz Tarique
Pace University

New York City campus
Room W–492, 1 Pace Plaza
New York, NY 10038
212–618–6583
itarique@pace.edu

Soo Min Toh
University of Toronto, Canada
Room 207B Kaneff Centre
3359 Mississauga Road North
Mississauga, Ontario, Canada
L5L 1C6
905–569–4971
mgt.utm@utoronto.ca

Judith White
Santa Clara University
Management Department
500 El Camino Real
Santa Clara, CA 95053
408–554–4469
jwhite@scu.edu

Ming Zeng
Alibaba.com
Corporate Headquarters:
699 Wang Shang Road
Binjiang District
Hangzhou 310052
China
(+86) 571–8502–2088
mzeng@alibaba-inc.com

PART 1

The Context of IHRM: Challenges, Strategies, and External Forces

Paul Evans, Vladimir Pucik, and Ingmar Björkman

PUTTING THE CHALLENGES OF INTERNATIONAL HUMAN RESOURCE MANAGEMENT INTO PERSPECTIVE*

LIKE MANY OTHER COMPANIES, the Swedish–Swiss corporation ABB that was born out of a merger in 1988 wanted to be a fast-growing firm with a wide international presence. Percy Barnevik, its Swedish CEO, is notable for recognizing the dilemmas that this involved, adopting the now well-known corporate mantra of "acting local but thinking global." His vision was to create an international company that was able to deal effectively with three internal contradictions: being global and local, big and small, and radically decentralized with centralized reporting and control.[1] The key principle was local entrepreneurship, so most of the decision-making was to be done at the lowest possible level, in the 5,000 independent profit centers, the business units that became the foundation of the ABB organization.

Influential country managers controlled operations in countries within a matrix structure of regions and business segments. ABB also established business-steering committees and functional councils to coordinate the different units, exploit synergies, and help transfer knowledge and best practices across the network of local units. The firm developed a management information system called ABACUS that contained data on the performance of the profit centers. Barnevik and his team of top managers traveled extensively to ensure communication and knowledge-sharing across units, while international assignments helped instill all units with the corporate ethos that Barnevik was pursuing: initiative, action, and risk-taking.

However, after becoming one of the most admired companies in the world during its first 10 years, ABB encountered significant problems in its second decade. Hit by the economic downturn in Europe, limitations in the firm's management started to emerge. While flexible and responsive to local contexts, ABB had failed to achieve sufficient global synergies and efficiency. Conflicts between business areas and national units meant that many managers felt that decision-making was unclear. The local profit centers continued to operate their own human resources management (HRM) systems, which were, at best, aligned at national levels but not at regional or global levels.

Barnevik's successors between 1997 and 2005 tried to impose more clarity and discipline by eliminating the country managers and regions, giving more power to global businesses, also introducing centralized corporate processes to improve global control, coordination, and efficiency. However, these top-down initiatives further increased the complexity of the firm, and without country managers in place to coordinate local operations, the company verged on paralysis. Country managers were reintroduced, the structure was simplified by selling all businesses except for two (power and automation), and a new global ABB People Strategy was launched, aimed at linking HRM with the business. By 2005, ABB was profitable once again but had shrunk from 213,000 employees (in 1997) to 102,000. A new CEO, Fred Kindle, found a firm with a high degree of local entrepreneurship and innovation, but with limited coordination and still unsatisfactory global efficiency. Barnevik's contradictions were still on the table.

In this reading, we examine the challenges facing ABB from the historic perspective of internationalization of the firm and the concomitant evolution of HRM. The dilemmas faced by ABB have always existed. What has changed is the nature and speed of communication between a company's headquarters and its subsidiaries around the world. But the essential problems of being flexible and responsive to local market needs while promoting global efficiency, avoiding duplication, and coordinating and controlling diverse units and people remain.

As we will discuss, some modern firms have adopted a *multidomestic* strategy, with autonomous local operations that can respond readily to local needs, while others pursue a centralized *meganational* strategy to prevent duplication and make global operations more efficient. Their approach to human resource management is radically different.

However, both of these strategies have limitations, leading to the idea that contemporary global corporations have many contradictions, as ABB recognized. They have to be simultaneously local and global in scope, centralized and decentralized, capable of delivering short-term results while developing future assets, managing multiple alliances without full control, and responding to market pressures to do things better *and* cheaper *and* faster. In light of this, we examine the concept of the *transnational organization*, at the heart of which is the notion of contradiction,[2] and we explore the implications for people management.

EARLY INTERNATIONALIZATION

International business is not a recent phenomenon, nor is international HRM a product of the twentieth or twenty-first century. The Assyrians, Phoenicians, Greeks, and Romans all engaged in extensive cross-border trade. Roman organizations spanning Asia, Africa, and Europe are often heralded as the first global companies, in that they covered the whole of the known world.

The pioneers of international business were the sixteenth- and seventeenth-century trading companies—the English and Dutch East India companies, the Muscovy Company, the Hudson's Bay Company, and the Royal African Company.[3] They exchanged merchandise and services across continents and had a geographical spread to rival today's multinational firms. They signed on crews and chartered ships, and engaged the services of experts with skills in trade negotiations and foreign languages, capable of assessing the quality of goods and determining how they should be handled and loaded. These companies were obliged to delegate considerable responsibility to local representatives running their operations in far-away countries, which created a new challenge: how could local managers be encouraged to use their discretionary powers to the best advantage of the company? The trading companies had to develop control structures and systems to monitor the behavior of their scattered agents.

Formal rules and procedures were one way of exercising control, but this did not eliminate the temptations of opportunistic behavior for those far from the center. Other control measures were therefore developed, such as employment contracts stipulating that managers would work hard and in the interests of the company. Failure to do so could lead to reprimand or dismissal. Setting performance measures was the next step. These included the ratio of capital to tonnage, the amount of outstanding credit on advance contracts, whether ships sailed on time, and the care taken in loading mixed cargoes. There were also generous financial incentives, such as remuneration packages comprising a fixed cash component and a sizeable bonus. Such a mix of control approaches was not far off contemporary methods used to evaluate and reward managerial performance in large multinationals.

The Impact of Industrialization

The Industrial Revolution originated in Britain in the late eighteenth century. The emergence of the factory system in Europe and the US had a dramatic impact both on international business and on the management of people. The spread of industrialization in Europe and the US provided growing markets for minerals and foodstuffs and prompted a global search for sources of supply.

Cross-border manufacturing began to emerge by the mid-nineteenth century. But it was difficult to exercise real control over distant operations. The rare manufacturing firms that ventured abroad often used family members to manage their international operations. For example, when Siemens set up its St Petersburg factory in 1855, a brother of the founder was put in charge. In 1863, another brother established a factory to produce sea cables in Britain. Keeping it in the family was the best guarantee that those in distant subsidiaries could be trusted not to act opportunistically.

The international spread of rail networks and the advent of steamships in the 1850s and 1860s brought new speed and reliability to international travel, while the invention of the telegraph uncoupled long-distance communication from transportation. It became possible for firms to manufacture in large batches and to seek volume distribution in mass markets. The rapid growth in firm size provided a domestic platform from which to expand abroad, paving the way for a surge in international business activity in the last decades of the nineteenth century.[4]

The late nineteenth and early twentieth centuries saw a number of developments in international business and people-management practices. In parallel with developments in transport and communication, industrialization was having a significant impact on the organization of firms. They were being reshaped by new manufacturing techniques, by the increased specialization and division of labor, and by a change in the composition of the workforce from skilled tradesmen to unskilled workers, previously agrarian, who were unaccustomed to industry requirements such as punctuality, regular attendance, supervision, and the mechanical pacing of work effort—similar to the situation in labor-intensive industries in China during the last 30 years. Early personnel management practices were shaped in factories experiencing discipline and motivation problems, where entrepreneurs such as Robert Owen in Scotland (often referred to as the father of modern personnel management) began to pay more attention to working conditions and the welfare of employees.

The growth in international manufacturing sustained a flourishing service sector, which provided the global infrastructure—finance, insurance, transport—to permit the international flow of goods. All this led to a degree of internationalization that the world would not see again until it had fully recovered from the damage to the global economy created by two world wars. It was a golden age for multinationals, with foreign direct investment accounting for around 9 percent of world output.[5]

War and Economic Depression

The outbreak of World War I, followed by a period of economic depression and then World War II, transformed management practices and multinational activity in very different ways, stimulating the development of people-management practices but suppressing international trade.

The sudden influx of inexperienced workers (many of them women) into factories in 1915 to service war needs increased the pressure on managers to find ways to improve productivity rapidly. Tasks had to be simplified and redesigned for novices. To contain labor unrest, more attention had to be paid to working conditions and employee demands, which also meant training first-line supervisors. These initiatives centralized many of the aspects of employment relations previously discharged by individual line managers. In some progressive firms, employees began to be viewed as resources, and the alignment of interest between the firm and workers was emphasized. The 1920s also saw the development of teaching and research, journals, and consulting firms in personnel management.[6]

However, the Great Depression was the start of a bifurcation in employment practices in the US and Japan, the latter having gone through a period of rapid industrialization and economic growth. Leading firms in both the US and Japan were experimenting with corporate welfarism in the 1920s.[7] However, the depth of the Depression in the US in the 1930s meant that many firms had no option except to make lay-offs and repudiate the welfare arrangements that had been established in many non-unionized firms. They turned instead to a path of explicit and instrumental contracts between employee and employer, with wages and employment conditions often determined through collective bargaining.[8] Because of the militarization of the

Japanese economy, the impact of the Depression was much less severe on that side of the Pacific. Under legislation fostering "social peace" in the name of national unity, large firms maintained these welfare experiments, leading step-by-step to an HRM orientation built around implicit contracts (lifetime employment, corporate responsibility for the development of staff, and low emphasis on formalized performance evaluation). Endorsed by the strong labor unions that emerged in post-war Japan, these practices became institutionalized, reinforcing and reinforced by Japanese societal values.

In the West, World War II intensified interest in the systematic recruitment, testing, and assigning of new employees in order to leverage their full potential. Psychological testing used by the military spilled over into private industry.[9] In addition, the desire to avoid wartime strikes led the US government to support collective bargaining, strengthening the role of the personnel function as a result.

If these external shocks had some salutary consequences for the development of personnel practices, they had quite the opposite effect on multinational activities. The adverse conditions during the interwar years encouraged firms to enter cross-border cartels rather than risk foreign investments. By the late 1920s, a considerable proportion of world manufacturing was controlled by these cartels—the most notorious being the "seven sisters" controlling the oil industry.[10]

World War II dealt a crushing blow to these cartels, and after the war, the US brought in aggressive antitrust legislation to dismantle those that remained. While US firms emerged from the war in excellent shape, European competition was devastated, and Japanese corporations (known as *zaibatsu*) had been dismembered. The war had stimulated technological innovation and American corporations had no desire to confine their activities to the home market. A new era of international business had begun.

THE MODERN MULTINATIONAL

Although Europe had a long tradition in international commerce, it was the global drive of US firms after World War II that gave birth to the multinationals as we know them today. American firms that had hardly ventured beyond their home markets before the war now began to flex their muscles abroad, and by the early 1960s, US companies had built an unprecedented lead in the world economy.

American firms also found faster ways of entering new markets. Many moved abroad through acquisitions, followed by investment in the acquired subsidiary in order to benefit more fully from economies of scale and scope.[11] This was the approach taken by Procter & Gamble (P&G), who established a presence in Continental Europe by acquiring an ailing French detergent plant in 1954. An alternative strategy was to join forces with a local partner, as in the case of Xerox, which entered global markets through two joint ventures, with the English motion picture firm the Rank Organisation in 1956, and with Fuji Photo Film in Japan in 1962.

In professional services, McKinsey and Arthur Andersen scrambled to open their own offices in foreign countries through the 1950s and 1960s. Others, such as Price Waterhouse and Coopers & Lybrand, built their international presence through mergers with established national practices in other countries. For most others, the route was via informal federations or networks of otherwise independent firms.

Advances in transport and communications—the introduction of commercial jet travel, the first transatlantic telephone link in 1956, then the development of the telex—facilitated this rapid internationalization. More significant still was the emergence of computers. By the mid-1970s, computers had become key elements in the control and information systems of industrial concerns, paving the way for later complex integration strategies. Taken together, the jet plane, the new telecommunications technology, and the computer contributed to a "spectacular shrinkage of space."[12]

Alongside these technological drivers of internationalization, powerful economic and political forces were at work. Barriers to trade and investment were progressively dismantled with successive General Agreement on Tariffs and Trades (GATT) treaties. Exchange rates were stabilized following the Bretton Woods Agreement (July 1944), and banks started to play an international role as facilitators of international business. The 1957 Treaty of Rome established the European Community. US firms, many of which already perceived Europe as a single entity, were the first to exploit the regional integration. European companies were spurred by "the American challenge" (the title of a best-selling call-to-arms book by the French journalist and politician Jean-Jacques Servan-Schreiber in 1967), encouraging them to expand beyond their own borders.

Staffing for International Growth

In the decades following World War II, virtually all medium- and large-sized firms had personnel departments, typically with responsibility for industrial (union) relations and for the operational aspects of employment, including staffing subsidiaries abroad.[13] The newly created international personnel units focused on expatriation, sending home-country managers to foreign locations.

The largest 180 US multinationals opened an average of six foreign subsidiaries each year during the 1960s.[14] This rapid international expansion opened up new job possibilities, including foreign postings. While US firms in the immediate post-war period had been "flush with veterans who had recently returned from the four corners of the globe [and who] provided a pool of eager expatriates,"[15] more managers were now urgently needed. People had to be persuaded to move abroad, both those with much-needed technical skills and managers to exercise control over these expanding foreign subsidiaries. In most companies at the time, this meant paying people generously as an incentive to move abroad.

In the late 1970s, horror stories of expatriate failure gained wide circulation—the technically capable executive sent out to run a foreign subsidiary being brought back prematurely as a borderline alcoholic, with a ruined marriage, and having run the affiliate into the ground. Academic studies seemed to confirm this problem,[16] which for some companies became a major handicap to international growth. It was no longer just a question of persuading people to move abroad, it was a question of "how can we help them to be successful?" While the reluctance to move abroad was increasing, often for family reasons but also because of the mismanagement of re-entry to the home country, concern over the rising costs of expatriation was growing.

International business also became a subject of academic study during this period. In the early 1980s, the challenges of expatriation started to attract the attention of researchers, reinforced by the new-found legitimacy of HR, and the concern of senior managers anxious about growth prospects abroad. While it was too early to talk of an international HRM field, international growth was leading to new challenges beyond expatriation that were to shape this emerging domain.

Organizing for International Growth

Rapid international growth brought with it the problems of controlling and coordinating increasingly complex global organizations—where control refers to visible and hierarchical processes and structures while coordination signifies tools that facilitate alignment through lateral interactions such as cross-boundary project teams and informal social networks. The awareness that international HRM is crucial not just for international staffing but also for building corporate cohesion and inter-unit collaboration grew and matured between the 1960s and 1990s. It was becoming increasingly apparent that the traditional structures were not sufficient to cope with the growing complexities of managing international business.

Many firms selling a wide range of products abroad opted for a structure of worldwide product divisions, whereas those with few products but operating in many countries would typically organize themselves around geographic area divisions, as did IBM.[17] The tricky question was how to organize when the firm had many different products sold in many different geographic markets. It was not at all clear how companies should deal with this zone of maximum complexity.

In practice, two responses emerged. Some firms implemented matrix organizations involving both product and geographic reporting lines, others increased the number of headquarters staff in coordinating roles. Both of these routes were ultimately to show their limitations, but the two paths gave rise to a growing understanding of the potential role of HRM in dealing with the fundamental problems of cross-border coordination and control.

The Matrix Structure Route

By the early 1970s, several US and British companies (Citibank, Corning, Dow, Exxon, and Shell, among others) had adopted the idea of matrix as a guiding principle for their worldwide organization. Right from the start, some management scholars urged caution, pointing out that matrix is much more complex than reporting lines and structural coordination.[18] Matrix had to be built into leadership development, control and performance appraisal systems, teamwork, conflict resolution mechanisms, relationships, and attitudes, anticipating the later insight that matrix has more to do with HRM than it has to do with structure.[19] Few of the companies that opted for the matrix solution had such supporting elements in place.

A focus on *reporting lines,* the first dimension of coordination, was not sufficient. Attention also had to be paid to the second dimension of coordination, *social architecture*—the conscious design of a social environment that encourages a pattern of thinking and behavior supporting organizational goals. This includes interpersonal relationships and inter-unit networks, the values, beliefs, and norms shared by members of the organization, and the mindsets that people hold. ABB's Percy Barnevik was conscious of the importance of the social elements of the international firm, and thus the need for extensive communication, travel, and relocation of people across units.

Common management processes are a third element of coordination, including processes for managing talent (including recruitment, selection, development, and retention of key personnel), performance and compensation management, and knowledge management and innovation. As ABB's problems compounded, it became increasingly obvious to executives that they had to develop and implement global management processes, although it was less clear how to do this.

Many companies found matrix structures difficult. They led to power struggles, ambiguity over resource allocation, buck-passing, and abdication of responsibility. In theory, a manager reported to two bosses, and conflicts between them would be reconciled at the apex one level higher up. However, it was not unusual to find companies where managers were reporting to four or five bosses, so that reconciliation or arbitration could only happen at a very senior level. While matrix might ensure the consultation necessary for sound decision-making, it was painfully slow. By the time the firm had decided, for example, to build a new chemical plant in Asia, nimbler competitors were already up and running. By the early 1980s, many firms reverted to structures where accountability lay clearly with the product divisions, although some (such as ABB) retained a structure with many matrix features.[20]

But if matrix structures were gradually going out of fashion, the matrix problem of organization was more alive than ever. Practitioners and researchers argued that the traditional hierarchic tools of control (rules, standard operating procedures, hierarchical referral, and planning) could not manage the growing complexity of information processing.[21] Organizations required strong capabilities in two areas: first in information processing and second in coordination and teamwork. There was an explosion of interest in how to improve coordination while keeping the reporting relationships as clear and simple as possible.[22]

Gradually, it became clear that the matrix challenges of coordination in complex multinational firms were essentially issues of people and information technology (IT) management. Matrix, as two leading strategy scholars were later to say, is a "frame of mind" nurtured more than anything else by careful human resource management.[23]

The Headquarters Coordination Route

Most organizations took the well-trodden path of keeping control of international activities with central staff. This was particularly true for German and Japanese companies, but was also the dominant organizing pattern in Anglo-Saxon firms. As with matrix, this approach was initially successful but eventually led to inefficiencies and paralysis. Again, speed was shown to be the Achilles heel.

It took a long time to work through decisions in German *Zentralebereiche* (central staff departments), and particularly in Japanese *nemawashi*[24] (negotiation) processes of middle-up consultative decision-making. However, multinationals from both of these countries were largely export-oriented with sales subsidiaries abroad, and the disadvantages were initially outweighed by the quality of decision-making and commitment to implementation that accompanied the consensus-oriented decision-making. The complex consultative processes worked reasonably well as long as everyone involved was German or Japanese.[25]

The strains of staff bureaucracy began to show in the US in the early 1980s as companies started to localize, acquiring or building integrated subsidiaries abroad. With localization of the management of foreign units, the coordination of decision-making by central staff became more difficult, slowing down the process at a time when speed was becoming more important. Local managers in lead countries argued for more autonomy and clearer accountability, while the costly overhead of the heavy staff structures associated with central coordination contributed to the erosion of competitiveness.

Faced with the second oil shock and recession in the late 1970s, American firms were the first to begin the process of downsizing and de-layering staff bureaucracies, followed by Europeans in Nordic and Anglo-Saxon countries. The Japanese and Germans followed more slowly. After decades of post-war international growth, attention in HRM shifted to the painful new challenges of dealing with organizational streamlining and job redesign, lay-offs, and managing change under crisis.

Firms that had pursued the headquarters-coordination route came to the same conclusion as firms that had invested in a matrix structure: they had to develop non-bureaucratic coordination and control mechanisms by building lateral relationships facilitated by human resource management. The control and coordination problem became another important strand in the development of international HRM.

HRM Goes International

During the 1980s, the idea that HRM might be of strategic importance gained ground. The insight that strategy is implemented through structure had taken hold—and it was then logical to argue that strategy is also implemented through changes in selection criteria, reward systems, and other HR policies and practices. In turn, this challenged the notion that there might be a "best" approach to HRM—the approach would depend on the strategy.

Perhaps appropriate HRM practice also depends on cultural context? This question was prompted by the difficulties that expatriates had experienced in transplanting management practices abroad, and was supported by growing research on cultural differences, pioneered by Geert Hofstede's study based on the global IBM opinion survey. This showed significant differences in the understanding of management and organization.[26]

The emergence of "the Japanese challenge" in the 1980s as both threat and icon further highlighted the issue of cultural differences, as well as the strategic import-ance of soft issues such as HRM. Numerous studies attempted to explain how the Japanese, whose country was destroyed and occupied after World War II, had man-aged to rebound with such vigor, successfully taking away America's market share in industries such as automobiles and consumer electronics. How had they managed to pull this off with no natural resources apart from people? A large part of the answer seemed to lie in distinctive HRM practices that helped to provide high levels of skill, motivation, and collective entrepreneurship, as well as collaboration between organizational units.[27] This was a shock for Western managers, who suddenly realized that other approaches to management could be equally or even more successful.

New international human resource challenges were emerging. Many governments began to apply pressure on foreign firms to hire and develop local employees. Given the cost of expatriation, this persuaded some multinational firms to start aggressively recruiting local executives to run their foreign subsidiaries. This often required extensive training and development, but as one observer pointed out, "The cost must be weighed against the cost of sending an American family to the area."[28] At Unilever, for example, the proportion of expatriates in foreign management positions dropped from 50 percent to 10 percent between 1950 and 1970.[29]

However, there was a catch-22 in localizing key positions in foreign units: the greater the talent of local people, the more likely they were to be poached by other firms seeking local skills. Consequently, localization was a priority for only a minority of multinational firms until well into the 1990s, except for operations in highly devel-oped regions such as North America, Europe, and Japan.[30]

Some firms used expatriate assignments for developmental reasons rather than just to solve an immediate job need. In these corporations, high-potential executives would be transferred abroad in order to expose them to international responsibilities. The assumption was that with growing internationalization, *all* senior executives needed international experience, even those in domestic positions. For example, the vice president of P&G had already pointed out in 1963: "We never appoint a man simply because of his nationality. A Canadian runs our French company, a Dutchman runs the Belgian company, and a Briton runs our Italian company. In West Germany, an American is in charge: in Mexico, a Canadian."[31] This meant that P&G was able to attract the very best local talent, quickly developing an outstanding reputation around the globe for the quality of its management. For local firms in France, Singapore, Australia, and Brazil, P&G was the management benchmark, and not only in the fast-moving consumer goods sector. Other firms started to adopt the P&G approach, although this created new challenges for international HRM. How does one manage the identification, development, transfer, and repatriation of talent spread out across the globe?

The link between international management development and the problems of coordination and control was established by the landmark research of Edström and Galbraith. They studied the expatriation policies of four multinationals of comparable size and geographic coverage in the mid-1970s, including Shell.[32] The research showed that these companies had quite different levels and patterns of international personnel transfer.[33] There were three motives for transferring managers abroad. The first and most common was to meet an immediate need for particular skills in a foreign subsidiary. The second was to develop managers through challenging international experience. However, the study of Shell revealed a third motive for international transfers—as a mechanism for control and coordination. The managers sent abroad were steeped in the policies and style of the organization, so they could be relied on to act appropriately in diverse situations. Moreover, frequent assignments abroad developed a network of personal relationships that facilitated coordination.

It appeared that Shell was able to maintain a high degree of control and coordination while at the same time having a more decentralized organization than other firms. This suggested that appropriate HRM practices could allow a firm to be globally coordinated and relatively decentralized at the same time, avoiding the matrix and corporate staff traps. Global control and coordination, it appeared, could be provided through socialization, minimizing the necessity for centralized headquarters control or bureaucratic procedures.

These findings drew attention to expatriation, mobility, and management development as a vital part of the answer to the matrix/bureaucracy problem of coordination. In truth, the concept was not entirely new—the Romans had adopted a similar approach to the decentralization dilemma two millennia before, staffing far flung regions with trusted governors socialized to safeguard the interests of the Empire.

By the mid-1990s, with globalization deepening, surveys consistently showed that global leadership development was one of the top three HRM priorities in major US corporations.[34] In some companies in Europe and the US, international management development was seen to be so critical that this department was separated from the corporate HR function, and reported directly to the CEO.

ENTER GLOBALIZATION

By the end of the 1980s, the traditional distinction between domestic and multinational companies had started to become blurred. International competition was no longer the preserve of industrial giants; it was affecting everybody's business. Statistics from the 1960s show that only 6 percent of the US economy was exposed to international competition. By the late 1980s, the corresponding figure was over 70 percent and climbing fast.[35]

Globalization surfaced as the new buzzword at the beginning of the 1990s, though it has different meaning for different people, sometimes with strong negative overtones. Viewed as interdependence and interconnectedness, many of the ingredients of globalization had actually been around for several decades. The steady dismantling of trade barriers in Western Europe and in North and South America, the increasing availability of global capital, advances in computing and communications technology, the progressive convergence of consumer tastes, and, in particular, the universal demand for industrial products had all been underway for some time. What made a difference was that these trends now reached a threshold where they became mutually reinforcing.

Widespread deregulation and privatization opened new opportunities for international business in both developing and developed countries. The multinational domain, long associated with the industrial company, was shifting to the service sector, which by the mid-1990s represented over half of total world foreign direct investment. Problems of distance and time zones were further smoothed away as communication by fax gave way to email and fixed phone networks to wireless mobile technology. Globalization was further stimulated by the fall of communism in Russia and Eastern Europe. Together with China's adoption of market-oriented policies, huge new opportunities were opened to international business as most of the world was drawn into the integrated global economy.

Multinationals increasingly located different elements of their value-adding activities in different parts of the world. Formerly hierarchical companies with clean-cut boundaries were giving way to complex arrangements and configurations, often fluctuating over time. The new buzzword from GE was "the boundaryless organization."[36] With increasing cross-border project work and mobility, the image of an organization as a network was rapidly becoming as accurate as that of hierarchy. For example, a European pharmaceutical corporation could have international R&D partnerships with competitors in the US, and manufacturing joint ventures with local partners in China, where it also outsourced local sales of generic products to a firm strong in distribution.

Traditionally, the only resources that multinationals sought abroad were raw materials or cheap labor. Everything else was at home: sources of leading-edge technology and finance, world-class suppliers, pressure-cooker competition, the most sophisticated customers, and the best intelligence on future trends.[37] Global competition was now dispersing some of these capabilities around the world. India, for example, developed its software industry using a low-cost strategy as a means of entry, but then quickly climbed the value chain, just as Japan had done previously in the automobile industry. The implication of such developments was that multinational firms could no longer assume that all the capabilities deemed strategic were available close to home.

With the erosion of traditional sources of competitive advantage, multinationals needed to change their perspective. To compete successfully, they had to do more than exploit scale economies or arbitrage imperfections in the world's markets for goods, labor, and capital. Toward the end of the 1980s, a new way of thinking about the multinational corporation came out of studies of how organizations were responding to these challenges. The concept of the transnational organization was born.

The Road Map for Managing Globalization

If there is a single perspective that has shaped the context for our understanding of the multinational corporation and its HRM implications, it is Bartlett and Ghoshal's research on the transnational organization.[38] To this we can add Hedlund's related concept of heterarchy and Doz and Prahalad's studies on the multi-focal organization, all of which have origins in Perlmutter's geocentric organization.[39] These strategy and management researchers grew to believe that people management is perhaps the single most critical domain for the multinational firm. None of them had any interest in HRM by virtue of their training, but all were drawn to the HRM field by findings from their research.

Doz and Prahalad began to link the fields of multinational strategy and HRM when researching the patterns of strategic control in multinational companies.[40] As they saw it, multinational firms faced a central problem: responding to a variety of national demands while maintaining a clear and consistent global business strategy. This tension between strong opposing forces, dubbed local responsiveness and global integration, served as a platform for much subsequent research on multinational enterprises, and it was captured by Sony's "think global, act local" aphorism, also adopted by ABB as its guiding motto.

Bartlett and Ghoshal developed these concepts further in their study of nine firms in three industries (consumer electronics, branded packaged goods, and telephone switching) and three regions (North America, Europe, and Japan).[41] They discovered that these companies seemed to have followed one of three internationalization paths, which they called "administrative heritage":

- One path emphasized responsiveness to local conditions, leading to what they called a "multinational enterprise" and which we prefer to call multidomestic. This led to a decentralized federation of local firms led by entrepreneurs who enjoyed a high degree of strategic freedom and organizational autonomy. The strength of the multidomestic approach was local responsiveness to customers and infrastructure. Some European firms, such as Unilever and Philips, and ITT in the US, embodied this approach.
- A second path to internationalization was that of the "global" firm, typified by US corporations such as Ford and Japanese enterprises such as Matsushita and NEC. Since the term global is today applied like the term multinational to any large firm operating on a worldwide basis, we prefer to call such a firm the meganational firm. Here, worldwide facilities are typically centralized in the parent country, products are standardized, and overseas operations are considered as delivery pipelines to access international markets. The global hub maintains tight control over strategic decisions, resources, and information. The competitive strength of the meganational firm comes from efficiencies of scale and cost.
- Some companies appeared to have taken a third route, a variant on the meganational path. Like the meganational, their facilities were located at the center. But the competitive strength of these "international" firms was their ability to transfer expertise to less advanced overseas environments, while allowing local units more discretion in adapting products and services. They were also capable of capturing learning from such local initiatives and then transferring it back to the central R&D and marketing departments. The "international" enterprise was thus a tightly coordinated federation of local firms. Some American and European firms, such as Ericsson, fitted this pattern, heralding the growing concern with global knowledge management.

It was apparent to Bartlett and Ghoshal that specific firms were doing well because their internationalization paths matched the requirements of their industry. Consumer products required local responsiveness, so Unilever had been thriving with its multidomestic approach, while Kao in Japan—centralized and meganational in heritage—had hardly been able to move outside its Japanese borders. The situation was different in consumer electronics, where the centralized meganational heritage of Matsushita (Panasonic and other brands) seemed to fit better than the more localized approaches of Philips and GE's consumer electronics business. And in tele-communications switching, the international learning and transfer ability of Ericsson led its "international" strategy to dominate the multidomestic and meganational strategies of its competitors.

Perhaps the most significant of Bartlett and Ghoshal's observations was that accelerating global competition was changing the stakes. In all three industries, it was clear that the leading firms had to become more transnational in their orientation —more locally responsive *and* more globally integrated *and* better at sharing learning between headquarters and subsidiaries. What has been driving this change? Increasing competition was shifting the competitive positioning of these firms from *either/or* to *and*. The challenge for Unilever (like ABB in the opening story) was to maintain its local responsiveness, but at the same time to increase its global efficiency by eliminating duplication and integrating manufacturing. Conversely, the challenge for Matsushita was to keep the economies of centralized product development and manufacturing, but to become more local and responsive to differentiated niches in markets around the world.

The Transnational Solution

The defining characteristic of the transnational enterprise is its capacity to steer between the contradictions that it confronts. As Ghoshal and Bartlett put it:

> managers in most worldwide companies recognize the need for simultan-
> eously achieving global efficiency, national responsiveness, and the ability
> to develop and exploit knowledge on a worldwide basis. Some, however,
> regard the goal as inherently unattainable. Perceiving irreconcilable contra-
> dictions among the three objectives, they opt to focus on one of them, at
> least temporarily. The transnational company is one that overcomes these
> contradictions.[42]

However, it is not clear that all multinational firms are destined to move in a transnational direction. While all companies are forced to contend with the dimensions of responsiveness, efficiency, and learning, and intensified competition heightens the contradictory pressures, these features are not equally salient in all industries. Moreover, the pressures do not apply equally to all parts of a firm. One subsidiary may be more local in orientation, whereas another may be tightly integrated. Even within a particular function, such as marketing, pricing may be a local matter, whereas distribution may be controlled from the center. In HR, performance management systems may be more globally standardized, whereas reward systems for workers may be left to local discretion. Indeed, this differentiation is another aspect of the complexity of the transnational—one size does not fit all.

In many ways, the transnational concept drew its inspiration from the concept of matrix. But transnational is neither a particular organizational form nor a specific strategic posture. Rather, it is an "organizational model," a "management mentality," and a "philosophy."[43] The transnational challenge is therefore to create balanced perspectives[44] or a "matrix in the mind of managers."[45] The challenge for senior management is to build a common sense of purpose that will guide local strategic initiatives, to coordinate through a portfolio of processes rather than via hierarchic structure, and to shape people's attitudes across the globe.[46]

This leads international HRM researchers to examine the local–global tension in multinationals.[47] On the one hand there are pressures for HRM policies and practices to be adapted to fit local institutional rules, regulations, and norms, as well as the cultural context. Yet if the multinational decentralizes the responsibility for HRM to local units, this can result in duplication, excessive cost, and lack of regional or global-scale advantages within the HR function. Even more importantly, this may handicap inter-unit learning within the corporation while handicapping coordination. For example, a failure to address issues related to corporate social responsibility in a globally consistent manner can cost the company dear. Siemens experienced this when a corruption scandal erupted in 2007, as did Nike, severely criticized for not having tightly supervised labor practices across their global network of suppliers.

Capabilities and Knowledge as Sources of Competitiveness

Today, management, strategy, and international business scholars are increasingly focused on capabilities and knowledge as drivers of competitive advantage. A core organizational capability is a firm-specific bundling of technical systems, people skills, and cultural values.[48] To the extent that they are firm specific, such organizational capabilities are difficult to imitate because of the complex configuration of the various elements. The capabilities can therefore be a major source of competitive advantage (although their very success can also create dangerous rigidities).

The distinguishing feature of a capability is the integration of skills, technologies, systems, managerial behaviors, and work values. For example, FedEx has a core competence in package routing and delivery. This rests on the integration of barcode technology, mobile communications, systems using linear programming, network management, and other skills.[49] The capability of INSEAD or IMD in executive education depends on faculty know-how integrated with program design skills, marketing, relationships with clients, the competence and attitude of support staff, reward systems, and a host of other interwoven factors that have evolved over the years.

Another crucial source of competitive advantage comes from the firm's ability to create, transfer, and integrate knowledge.[50] At the heart of the surge of academic and corporate interest in management of knowledge lies the distinction between explicit and tacit knowledge. The former is knowledge that you know that you have, and in organizations explicit knowledge is often codified in texts and manuals.

The latter is personal, built on intuition acquired through years of experience, and hard to formalize and communicate to others. One of the main approaches to knowledge management is to build collections of explicit knowledge (customer contacts, presentation overheads, etc.) using software systems, and to make that knowledge available via an intranet. Another approach is to focus on building connections or contacts between people in the organization that can be used to transfer tacit knowledge.[51] Many professional firms have gone down this route, for instance by creating yellow-page directories that allow consultants to find individuals who have relevant experience and encouraging the development of informal relationships among people interested in a certain topic area. In a world where the retention of people is more difficult, it is particularly important to retain and transfer their knowledge.

These ideas about the source of competitive advantage are related to the *resource-based perspective* of the firm, which views it as a bundle of tangible and intangible resources. If such resources are valuable to the customer, rare, difficult to purchase or imitate, and effectively exploited, then they can provide a basis for superior economic performance that may be sustained over time. This view quickly attracted the attention of HRM scholars because its broad definition of resources could be applied to HRM-related capabilities, such as training and development, teamwork, and culture. Resource-based theory helped to reinforce the interrelationship between HRM and strategy. It provided a direct conceptual link between an organization's more behavioral and social attributes and its ability to gain a competitive advantage. This influential view, based largely on research on multinational corporations, has continued to play an important role in current strategy and HRM thinking.

THE EVOLUTION OF INTERNATIONAL HRM

As we have seen, the challenges of foreign assignments, adapting people management practices to foreign situations, and coordinating and controlling distant operations have existed since antiquity. It is only during the last 50 years that specialized personnel managers have begun to assume a responsibility for these tasks. With the acceleration of globalization, these and other international HRM issues have developed into a central competitive challenge for corporations. As Floris Maljers, former co-chairman of Unilever, put it: "Limited human resources—not unreliable or inadequate sources of capital—has become the biggest constraint in most globalization efforts."[52] Many scholars studying the multinational firm would agree.

The centrality of these HRM issues has increased over time. For example, as the bottom-line consequences became more visible, concern over expatriation broadened to include the understanding that it was not just about sending managers abroad but also about helping expatriates to be successful in their roles and future careers. The scope of expatriation has changed—today, expatriates come not only from the multinational's home country but also from other, third countries. Localization of staff in foreign units became a new imperative, leading to the complex task of tracking and developing a global talent pool. As globalization started to have an impact on local operations, for example in China, it also became clear that even local executives needed to have international experience. Globalization has raised awareness of the pivotal role played by managerial talent in implementing global strategies, and multinationals from different parts of the world are increasingly competing for talent from the same global talent pools.

As we enter the second decade of the twenty-first century, multinationals from high-growth emerging markets have become major global investors. Large international acquisitions by firms such as Tata Steel from India and CEMEX from Mexico, the world's largest building material company, have transformed industries that were traditionally dominated by firms from developed countries. The shift away from countries such as the US and Japan dominating lists of the world's largest companies is clear. Out of the world's 500 largest corporations, the US lost 26 of its 177 spots between 1999 and 2008, and Japan no less than 55 of its 81. The winners were emerging countries such as China (from 10 to 29), South Korea (12 to 14), India (1 to 7), Taiwan (1 to 6), Mexico (2 to 5), Brazil (3 to 5), and Russia (2 to 5).[53] Even Western scholars increasingly look to these emerging markets for new lessons in human resource management and building capabilities.[54]

As the ABB story illustrated, the failure of structural solutions to address the problems of coordination and control led to an increased focus on how HR practices might assist in providing cohesion to the multinational firm. HRM and strategy came together in the transnational concept, which helped to dissolve many of the traditional boundaries in organizational thinking. Today, the strategic importance of international HRM is widely recognized.

The increasing centrality of international HRM issues has blurred the boundaries between this domain of academic study and others. Once no more than an appendix to the field of personnel/HR management, international HRM has become a lens for the study of the multinational enterprise, the form of organization that dominates the world economy. Understanding the complex challenges facing today's global organizations calls for interdisciplinary work with scholars of strategy, institutional economics, organization, cross-cultural management, leadership, change management, organizational culture, and others.

NOTES

* Many of the observations in this reading are drawn from our recent book (Evans et al., 2011).

1. Barham and Heimer, 1998.
2. Bartlett and Ghoshal, 1989.
3. Carlos and Nicholas, 1988. On the other side of the world, southern Chinese clans spread their hold across Southeast Asia in the fourteenth and fifteenth centuries.
4. Wilkins, 1970.
5. Even by the early 1990s, foreign direct investment had only rallied to around 8.5 percent of world output (Jones, 1996). Recent data show the stock of FDI to be 22.4 percent of global GDP in 2007 (World Investment Report 2008, UNCTAD—available at www.unctad.org/Templates/WebFlyer.asp?intItemID=4700&lang=1).
6. Kaufman, 2007.
7. Moriguchi, 2000.
8. Kaufman, 2007.
9. Jacoby, 1985.

10. Sampson, 1975; Vernon et al., 1997. Similarly, in pharmaceuticals, electric light bulbs, steel, and engineering industries, elaborate arrangements were established among national champions, allowing them to focus on their home markets and to suppress international competition.
11. Chandler, 1990.
12. Vernon, 1977.
13. Kaufman, 2007.
14. Vaupel and Curhan, 1973.
15. Hays, 1974.
16. Tung, 1982.
17. Stopford and Wells, 1972.
18. Argyris, 1967.
19. Davis and Lawrence, 1977.
20. It would be misleading to say that matrix structure is dead. Some organizations introduced matrix organizations in the late 1980s and 1990s. The matrix structure that ABB employed until 1998 is perhaps the most well known example. Research suggests that matrix structure can be appropriate as a transition organization, facilitating the development of a "matrix culture," leading to different forms of multidimensional organization, facilitated by coordination mechanisms that the matrix introduced (Ford and Randolph, 1992; Galbraith, 2008).
21. Ford and Randolph, 1992; Galbraith, 1977.
22. Martinez and Jarillo, 1989.
23. Bartlett and Ghoshal, 1990.
24. The *nemawashi* process in Japanese firms is an informal process of consultation, typically undertaken by a high potential individual, involving talking with people and gathering support for an important decision or project.
25. Many German international firms had an unusual structure abroad, where the sales subsidiary was run jointly by a local general manager with a German commercial manager on a *primus inter pares* basis, facilitating this consensual approach.
26. Hofstede, 1980.
27. See Pucik and Hatvany, 1981 and Pucik, 1984. The success of Japan threw the spotlight on HR ingredients such as long-term employment, intensive socialization, team-based appraisal and rewards, slow promotion, and job rotation. Distinctive features of Japanese management that received attention in the West included continuous improvement, commitment to learning, quality management practices, customer-focused production systems, and consultative decision-making.
28. Oxley, 1961.
29. Kuin, 1972.
30. Even today, localization (how to develop the talent of local staff) remains one of the most neglected areas of international human resource management.
31. "Multinational companies: Special report," *BusinessWeek*, April 20, 1963, p. 76.
32. Edström and Galbraith, 1977.
33. "Three times the number of managers were transferred in Europe at [one company rather than the other], despite their being of the same size, in the same industry, and having nearly identical organization charts" (Edström and Galbraith, 1977, p. 255).
34. See the SOTA (State of the Art) surveys run annually since 1995 by the Human Resource Planning Society, reported each year in the journal *Human Resource Planning*; see also a survey undertaken in Fortune 500 firms by Gregersen et al., 1998.
35. Prescott et al., 1999.
36. Ashkenas et al., 1995.
37. Such clusters of critical factors helped particular nations to develop a competitive advantage in certain fields—such as German firms in chemicals or luxury cars, Swiss firms in pharmaceuticals, and US firms in personal computers, software, and movies.

38. Bartlett and Ghoshal, 1989.
39. See Hedlund, 1986; Prahalad and Doz, 1987; and Perlmutter, 1969.
40. Doz et al., 1981; Doz and Prahalad, 1984, 1986.
41. Bartlett and Ghoshal, 1989.
42. Ghoshal and Bartlett, 1998, p. 65.
43. Bartlett and Ghoshal, 1989.
44. Doz and Prahalad, 1986.
45. Bartlett and Ghoshal, 1989.
46. Ghoshal and Bartlett, 1997.
47. Rosenzweig and Nohria, 1994; Björkman and Lu, 2001.
48. Hamel and Prahalad, 1994; Leonard, 1995.
49. This example is taken from Hamel and Prahalad, 1994, who provide a more complete definition, emphasizing that core competences should be gateways to the future.
50. Kogut and Zander, 1992.
51. Polanyi, 1966; Nonaka and Takeuchi, 1995.
52. Cited by Bartlett and Ghoshal, 1992.
53. See http://money.cnn.com/magazines/fortune/global500/2008/full_list/.
54. For example, Cappelli et al., 2010 examine the lessons of business leaders in India.

REFERENCES

Argyris, C. (1967). "Today's problems with tomorrow's organizations." *Journal of Management Studies* 4(1): 31–55.

Ashkenas, R.N., D. Ulrich, T. Jick, and S. Kerr (1995). *The boundaryless organization: Breaking the chains of organizational structure.* San Francisco, CA: Jossey Bass.

Barham, K., and C. Heimer (1998). *ABB: The dancing giant.* London: Financial Times/Pitman.

Bartlett, C.A., and S. Ghoshal (1989). *Managing across borders: The transnational solution.* Cambridge, MA: Harvard Business School Press.

Bartlett, C.A., and S. Ghoshal (1990). "Matrix management: Not a structure, a frame of mind." *Harvard Business Review* (July–August): 138–45.

Bartlett, C.A., and S. Ghoshal (1992). "What is a global manager?" *Harvard Business Review* (September–October): 124–32.

Björkman, I., and Y. Lu (2001). "Institutionalization and bargaining power explanations of HRM practices in international joint ventures: The case of Chinese–Western joint ventures." *Organization Studies* 22(3): 491–512.

Cappelli, P., H. Singh, J. Singh, and M. Useem (2010). *The India way: How India's top business leaders are revolutionizing management.* Boston, MA: Harvard Business School Publishing.

Carlos, A.M., and S. Nicholas (1988). "Giants of an earlier capitalism: The chartered trading companies as modern multinationals." *Business History Review* 62 (Autumn): 398–419.

Chandler, A.D. (1990). *Scale and scope: The dynamics of industrial capitalism.* Cambridge, MA: Harvard University Press.

Davis, S.M., and P.R. Lawrence (1977). *Matrix.* Reading, MA: Addison-Wesley.

Doz, Y., and C.K. Prahalad (1984). "Patterns of strategic control within multinational corporations." *Journal of International Business Studies* 15(2): 55–72.

Doz, Y., and C.K. Prahalad (1986). "Controlled variety: A challenge for human resource management in the MNC." *Human Resource Management* 25(1): 55–71.

Doz, Y., C.A. Bartlett, and C.K. Prahalad (1981). "Global competitive pressures and host country demands." *California Management Review* 23(3): 63–74.

Edström, A., and J.R. Galbraith (1977). "Transfer of managers as a coordination and control strategy in multinational organizations." *Administrative Science Quarterly* 22(2): 248–63.

Evans, P., V. Pucik, and I. Björkman (2011). *The global challenge: International human resource management.* Boston, MA: McGraw-Hill.

Ford, R., and W. Randolph (1992). "Cross-functional structures: A review and integration of matrix organization and project management." *Journal of Management* 18(2): 267–94.

Galbraith, J.R. (1977). *Organization design*. Reading, MA: Addison-Wesley.

Galbraith, J. (2008). *Designing matrix organizations that actually work: How IBM, Proctor & Gamble, and others design for success*. San Francisco, CA: Jossey-Bass.

Ghoshal, S., and C.A. Bartlett (1997). *The individualized corporation*. New York: Harper-Business.

Ghoshal, S., and C.A. Bartlett (1998). *Managing across borders: The transnational solution*, 2nd ed. London: Random House.

Gregersen, H.B., A.J. Morrison, and S. Black (1998). "Developing leaders for the global frontier." *MIT Sloan Management Review* 40(1): 2–32.

Hamel, G., and C.K. Prahalad (1994). *Competing for the future*. Boston, MA: Harvard Business School Press.

Hays, R.D. (1974). "Expatriate selection: Insuring success and avoiding failure." *Journal of International Business Studies* 5(1): 25–37.

Hedlund, G. (1986). "The hypermodern MNC: A heterarchy?" *Human Resource Management* (Spring): 9–35.

Hofstede, G. (1980). *Culture's consequences. Comparing values, behaviors, institutions, and organizations across nations*. Beverly Hills, CA and London: Sage.

Jacoby, S.M. (1985). *Employing bureaucracy: Managers, unions and the transformation of work in American industry, 1900–1945*. New York: Columbia University Press.

Jones, G. (1996). *The evolution of international business*. London: Routledge.

Kaufman, B. (2007). "The development of HRM in historical and international perspective." In *The Oxford handbook of human resource management*, Eds. P. Boxall, J. Purcell, and P. Wright. New York: Oxford University Press.

Kogut, B., and U. Zander (1992). "Knowledge of the firm, combinative capabilities, and the replication of technology." *Organization Science* 3(3): 383–97.

Kuin, P. (1972). "The magic of multinational management." *Harvard Business Review* (November–December): 89–97.

Leonard, D. (1995). *Wellsprings of knowledge: Building and sustaining the sources of innovation*. Boston, MA: Harvard Business School Press.

Martinez, J.I., and J.C. Jarillo (1989). "The evolution of research on coordination mechanisms in multinational corporations." *Journal of International Business Studies* 20(3): 489–514.

Moriguchi, C. (2000). "Implicit contracts, the Great Depression, and institutional change: The evolution of employment relations in US and Japanese manufacturing firms, 1910–1940." Working paper. Harvard Business School, Boston.

Nonaka, I., and H. Takeuchi (1995). *The knowledge-creating company: How Japanese companies create the dynamics of innovation*. New York: Oxford University Press.

Oxley, G.M. (1961). "The personnel manager for international operations." *Personnel* 38(6): 52–8.

Perlmutter, H.V. (1969). "The tortuous evolution of the multinational corporation." *Columbia Journal of World Business* 4: 9–18.

Polanyi, M. (1966). *The tacit dimension*. London: Routledge & Kegan Paul.

Prahalad, C.K., and Y. Doz (1987). *The multinational mission: Balancing local demands and global vision*. New York: Free Press.

Prescott, R.K., W.J. Rothwell, and M. Taylor (1999). "Global HR: Transforming HR into a global powerhouse." *HR Focus* 76(3): 7–8.

Pucik, V. (1984). "White-collar human resource management in large Japanese manufacturing firms." *Human Resource Management* 23(3): 257–76.

Pucik, V., and N. Hatvany (1981). "An integrated management system: Lessons from the Japanese experience." *Academy of Management Review* 6(3): 469–80.

Rosenzweig, P.M., and N. Nohria (1994). "Influences on human resource management practices in multinational corporations." *Journal of International Business Studies* 25(2): 229–51.

Sampson, A. (1975). *The seven sisters: The great oil companies and the world they made*. London: Hodder & Stoughton.

Stopford, J.M., and L.T. Wells (1972). *Managing the multinational enterprise*. London: Longman.

Tung, R.L. (1982). "Selection and training procedures of US, European, and Japanese multinationals." *California Management Review* 25(1): 57–71.

Vaupel, J.W., and J.P. Curhan (1973). *The world's largest multinational enterprises*. Cambridge, MA: Harvard University Press.

Vernon, R. (1977). *Storm over the multinationals: The real issues*. Cambridge, MA: Harvard University Press.

Vernon, R., L.T. Wells, and S. Rangan (1997). *The manager in the international economy*. Englewood Cliffs, NJ: Prentice Hall.

Wilkins, M. (1970). *The emergence of multinational enterprise*. Cambridge, MA: Harvard University Press.

Randall S. Schuler, Susan E. Jackson, and Ibraiz Tarique

MANAGING GLOBAL TALENT CHALLENGES WITH GLOBAL TALENT MANAGEMENT INITIATIVES*

INTRODUCTION

BEGINNING IN THE LATE 1990S, firms around the world were confronted with a major threat to doing business: a demand for talented employees that far surpassed the supply (*McKinsey Quarterly*, 2008; Michaels et al., 2001). "Talent" and "talent retaining and talent management" became key expressions in global business. Firms faced many challenges, including having the right number of competent employees at the right place and at the right time. Increasingly, they also faced the challenges of needing to reduce the costs of operations, thus moving operations abroad, paying lower wages, and then having to find competent employees to staff the facility. Collectively, these challenges, because of their significant human capital issues, came to be known as "global talent challenges" and were dealt with through "global talent management" initiatives. These were composed of various HR actions depending upon the nature of the global talent challenge.

This reading describes these global talent challenges and global talent management initiatives. Some of our discussion reflects conditions that were present during recent economic and financial boom times (i.e. the years leading up to 2008), when worker shortages were a primary concern. Economic expansion is likely to return eventually, so labor shortages are likely to be of continuing concern. Nevertheless, in the near term, this concern may subside somewhat. Regardless of the size of the gap between the available and desired pool of talent globally, relocation and cost reduction through lower compensation levels are likely to remain major global talent challenges for the next several years.

GLOBAL TALENT CHALLENGES AND GLOBAL TALENT MANAGEMENT

In today's rapidly moving, extremely uncertain, and highly competitive global environment, firms worldwide are encountering numerous global talent challenges. *Global talent challenges (GTCs) are significant human capital issues that focus on managing a firm to ensure just the right amount of the right talent and motivation, at the right place, at the right price, during all economic and financial ups and downs in a very competitive world for the purposes of balancing the workforce with the needs of the firm in the short term, and positioning the firm to have the workforce needed in the long term* (Schuler et al., 2010).

To successfully address global talent challenges, firms of all sizes can and must take advantage of a wide variety of human resource management (HR) actions, which include the development of human resource policies and the design and implementation of specific HR practices (see Jackson et al., 2009). Conceptualized broadly, *global talent management (GTM) refers to the systematic use of HR actions (policies and practices) to manage the several global talent challenges that a firm confronts.* These can include HR policies and practices related to planning and forecasting, obtaining, selecting, motivating, developing, evaluating, retaining, and removing employees consistent with a firm's strategic directions, while taking into account the evolving concerns of the workforce and regulatory requirements (Schuler et al., 2010).

MAJOR FORCES AND SHAPERS OF THE GLOBAL TALENT CHALLENGES

Global talent management is carried out in the context of a dynamic environment. Among the many factors that shape the specific challenges and responses of particular firms are several major drivers, which include: (a) globalization, (b) changing demographics, (c) demand for workers with needed competencies and motivation, and (d) the supply of those needed competencies and motivation. Figure 1 depicts the linkage between these drivers and several HR actions used to manage global talent. We describe these drivers in more detail in the following paragraphs.

Globalization: World Trade, Competition, Customers, Individuals

Globalization is a concept that people use when referring to many different phenomena. Of particular relevance to our discussion are: expansion of world trade, intensified competition among firms, the potential to reach many more customers around the world, and the array of individuals worldwide who now comprise a global labor market.

World Trade

The value of world trade expanded from $89 billion in 1953 to more than $10 trillion in 2008. Although the contraction that occurred in 2009 may slow the rate of future

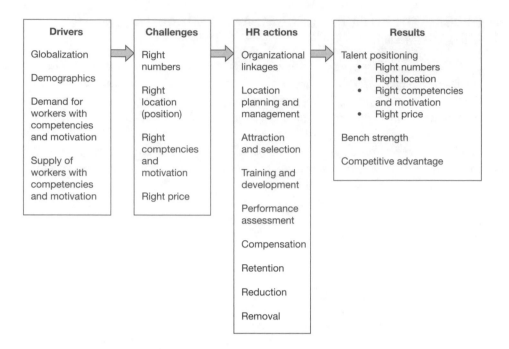

Drivers	Challenges	HR actions	Results
Globalization	Right numbers	Organizational linkages	Talent positioning <ul><li>Right numbers</li><li>Right location</li><li>Right competencies and motivation</li><li>Right price</li></ul>
Demographics	Right location (position)	Location planning and management	
Demand for workers with competencies and motivation	Right comptencies and motivation	Attraction and selection	Bench strength
Supply of workers with competencies and motivation	Right price	Training and development	Competitive advantage
		Performance assessment	
		Compensation	
		Retention	
		Reduction	
		Removal	

Figure 1. Framework for global talent challenges and management

expansion in the near term, the value of world trade may nevertheless reach $27 trillion by 2030. Foreign direct investment (FDI) went from $59 billion in 1982 to more than $1 trillion in 2008. The formal labor market expanded from 2 billion workers in 1990 to more than 3.5 billion in 2008. The global economy is projected to expand to $75 trillion by 2030, up from $10 trillion in 1970 and $40 trillion in 2008 (Kearney, 2008; Stephenson and Pandit, 2008). While such forecasts of specific values are only best estimates, most observers agree that the long-term trend is for continued expansion of world trade. Thus, while forecasts made early in 2009 pointed to a significant slowdown in FDI and world GDP that year (*The Economist*, February 21, 2009), by the end of the same year, forecasts for 2010 were projecting a modest upturn globally.

Competition

Competition has never been this intense and so multifaceted: it is fast developing, complex, extremely widespread, but also subject to the current global economic and financial crises (*The Economist*, February 21, 2009; Zakaria, 2008; Cairns and Sliwa, 2008; IBM, 2008; Hill, 2007). Global competition has forced many firms to improve quality and strive for innovation (often based on rapidly developed and more sophisticated technology), and increasingly global competition means that enhanced quality and innovation must be achieved while also keeping cost low. Thus, small and larger firms in almost every country are being forced to adapt and quickly respond as they compete with firms worldwide to gain and sustain global competitive advantage (*The Economist*, March 14, 2009; Engardio and Weintraub, 2008; Porter, 1985; IBM, 2008; Stephenson and Pandit, 2008; Palmisano, 2007; Schuler and Tarique, 2007; Gupta and Govindarajan, 2001). Globalization requires multinational companies to seek economies of scale and scope, find and take advantage of optimal locations while anticipating future relocations, adapt to local differences, learn continuously, and transfer knowledge more effectively than their competitors (Ghemawat and Houl, 2007; Porter, 1985; Krugman, 1979, 1981; Gupta and Govindarajan, 2001). A global competitive advantage awaits those firms that succeed in meeting these challenges (Daniels et al., 2007).

Customers

Customers in virtually all industries are demanding more, and often for less. The telecom industry is migrating rapidly from traditional fixed-line phone service to mobile smartphones. Companies such as BT are selling "experiences" more than telephone "hardware." Customers are demanding innovation and BT is responding by focusing on services and providing a social networking capability (Werdigier, 2008). And this applies to customers the world over, with some differences reflecting unique characteristics of the countries (Zakaria, 2008). Thus, for the typical company today, it is important to think and act global (IBM, 2008; Mendenhall et al., 2008; Dickmann and Baruch, 2010), which includes being where the customers are. Increasingly, companies such as Nokia, IBM, Tata, Caterpillar, and BT find that the growing customer base is in the BRIC countries (Brazil, Russia, India, and China) and in emerging economies throughout Asia, Latin America, and Eastern Europe.

Individuals

Individuals have been entering into the labor market in increased numbers over the past 15 years (Zakaria, 2008; Friedman, 2005). It has been estimated that more than 1.5 billion people have entered the global formal labor market during the past 15 years. Friedman (2005) argued that the development and spread of inexpensive technologies has flattened the world and facilitated the entry of all these workers into the workforce. One major consequence is the ability of firms to employ workers in the developing economies of the world at much lower wages than is possible in the developed economies of the world. Weekly wages in the developed economies are equivalent to monthly and even yearly wages in developing economies (US Department of Labor, 2008; Gomez-Mejia and Werner, 2008). The movement of work to an array of dispersed locations that may include both developed and developing economies is most likely to succeed when all employees have the needed competencies and motivations to do the work, when the work of dispersed employees is effectively coordinated, and when a firm's HR actions are consistent with the full array of relevant employment regulations in every location (Porter, 1985; Hill, 2007; World Bank, 2008; Palmisano, 2007). In addition to meeting these challenges, as multinational firms make decisions about workforce location and relocation, they also must address the challenges of developing an appropriate customer base, identifying and outmaneuvering competitors, managing transportation costs, reducing the possible consequences of political instability, protecting their intellectual property and rights, and so on (Porter, 1985; Daniels et al., 2007; World Bank, 2008; Palmisano, 2007).

Demographics

Worldwide demographics are another major driver of global talent management. In North America, Western Europe, Japan, and Australia, the age of retirement is being ushered in by the baby boomer generation. While this may be a relatively short-term phenomenon in North America (due to current birth and immigration rates), population shrinkage is a longer-term event in Western Europe and Japan (Strack et al., 2008). The long term-term outlook is grim: by 2025 the number of people aged 15–64 is projected to fall by 7 percent in Germany, 9 percent in Italy, and 14 percent in Japan (Wooldridge, 2007; *The Economist*, 2006).

"If you take into consideration the 70 million Baby Boomers expected to retire over the next 15 years (in the U.S.) and only 40 million workers expected to enter the workforce in the same period, you can plainly see that a shortage of workers is imminent" (Adecco, 2008: 9). "By 2010, it is expected the U.S. will face a shortage of more than 10 million workers" (Adecco, 2008: 10). And, according to Stephen Hitch, a human resource manager at Caterpillar in Peoria, Illinois: "We've got a global problem and it's only going to continue to get worse" (Coy and Ewing, 2007: 28). Of course, these pre-2008 projections are now being adjusted somewhat with more baby boomers extending their retirement dates due to significant depletions of their retirement savings as a consequence of the current economic and financial crises (Hansen, 2009a).

While the populations of many developed economies are aging and shrinking in size, the populations of developing and emerging economies are expanding and getting younger (Strack et al., 2008). Thus, there are major variations in demographic characteristics by age and by region that multinational firms need to know and consider in locating and relocating their operations internationally.

Demand for Workers with Competencies and Motivation

Although the pace of globalization has diminished greatly, new *jobs* are still being created that require higher levels of competencies, which are broadly defined as "basic and advanced skills, knowledge and abilities," or the "right know-how" (Daniels et al., 2007; Palmisano, 2007). For existing jobs, there is a growing need for employees who are willing to do the job under new and changing conditions that require the development of additional competencies (motivation). For skilled jobs, for example, there is a need for increased competencies to operate more sophisticated machinery, to interact with more demanding customers, and to use more advanced technology to perform the functions of the traditional skilled jobs (National Commission on Adult Literacy, 2008). And it appears that these increased competencies are being associated with almost all jobs traditionally performed in multinational firms around the world today (Price and Turnbull, 2007).

In addition to the increased need for basic skills and advanced skill levels for basic entry-level, front-line and skilled jobs, there are a rising number of jobs that involve "knowledge work" and thus there is increasing demand for "knowledge workers." This is true around the world, be it in China, India, Europe, or North America. By one estimate, 48 million of the 137 million workers in the US alone can be classified as knowledge workers. Knowledge work often requires competencies that are developed through extensive education and training, and it is generally work that is capable of having a significant impact on the success of the company (Jackson et al., 2003). Knowledge workers include managers, leaders, technicians, researchers, accountants, information specialists, consultants, and medical and pharmaceutical professionals. In multinational firms, knowledge workers such as these often work together in teams that cross cultural and geographic borders: "In the 21st century knowledge creation, integration and the leveraging of such 'new' knowledge are considered the *raison d'etre* of multinational firms" (Brannen, 2008). "The growing need for talented managers in China represents by far the biggest management challenge facing multinationals and locally owned businesses alike" (Lane and Pollner, 2008). Even if demand for managers and other knowledge workers has slowed significantly recently, the need for highly motivated and talented knowledge workers is likely to remain strong well into the future (Roach, 2009).

Just before the economic and financial crises began in 2008, the most prevalent question was: "Where are all the workers?" Although this is not the prevalent question today, it is likely to return sooner than later:

> Whether you can hear it or not, a time bomb is ticking in C-suites worldwide. Its shock waves will resonate for decades . . . Surveys conducted by the firm I work for (Egon Zehnder International) indicate that the number of managers in the right age bracket for leadership roles will drop by 30% in just six years. Factor in even modest growth rates, and the average corporation will be left with half the critical talent it needs by 2015.
>
> (Fernández-Aráoz, 2009: 72)

Just as the global economy began to slow in 2008, a study conducted by the global staffing agency Manpower Inc. found that nearly 40 percent of 37,000 companies across 27 countries were finding it a challenge to hire the people they needed (Manpower Inc., 2008a). A 2007 survey of more than 1,300 senior managers around the world found that the most significant trend expected to affect their business over the next 5 years was greater competition for talent worldwide (Price and Turnbull, 2007). More specifically, CEOs are searching for industry, technical, and particularly management skills to support geographic expansion. Many CEOs consider insufficient talent to be a significant barrier to global integration, surpassing the importance of regulatory and budgetary hurdles (IBM, 2008). In other words, most companies worldwide, regardless of size, are confronting and/or will soon confront their global talent challenge of talent shortage that, if ignored, will impact their global business strategies (Dunning, 2000; Manpower Inc., 2008b).

This global talent challenge appears to be a concern across many countries/ companies, and especially in India, China, and Brazil. According to a recent survey in China "88% of the Chinese executives said their globalization efforts were hindered by the scarcity of people with real cross-cultural knowledge or experience managing foreign talent; ninety-three percent said that Chinese companies would not achieve their global aspirations unless they developed suitable leaders more aggressively" (Dietz et al., 2008). For entry-level corporate positions, there seems to be a mismatch between the skills found among many Chinese graduates and the types of skills that are needed by local, regional, and multinational companies (Lane and Pollner, 2008).

The most frequently cited reasons for candidates being under-qualified include: poor English skills (which are needed to conduct international business), lack of experience working in teams, and a reluctance to assume leadership roles (*McKinsey Quarterly*, 2008). So while the graduation numbers of countries such as India, China, and Brazil are very impressive, those who are qualified to begin working in many companies are significantly less. For example, in India, the percentage of engineering graduates deemed qualified enough to hire is estimated to be 25 percent; in China the estimated portion is 10 percent; and in Brazil it is 13 percent (*McKinsey Quarterly*, 2008). McKinsey predicted that India would face a shortage of 500,000 staff capable of doing work for multinationals (Engardio, 2007). Clearly, the skills gap is threatening the technology boom in India (Sengupta, 2006). According to Jose Sergio Gabrielli, President of Petrobras, the state-run oil company in Brazil, "The lack of availability of technical ability may be a constraint on growth, no doubt about it" (Downie, 2008: C1, C5). The supply situation in other major countries around the world is largely the same as in India, China, and Brazil.

Supply of Workers with Competencies and Motivation

In developed economies such as North America, Western Europe, and Japan, there is also an expected shortage of competencies. According to a report from the US National Commission on Adult Literacy (2008), between 80 and 90 million American adults do not have the basic communication (also called people or "soft") skills to function well in the global economy or to earn family-sustaining wages. Unique among other advanced industrial countries, American 25 to 35 year olds are not as well educated as their parents. This same reality is also being found in Arab nations, where the younger generation sees that connections rather than education are often the route to career success (Harry, 2007). According to the US National Commission on Adult Literacy (2008), declining educational achievement now puts the US at a competitive disadvantage. The lack of technical knowledge workers continues to drive companies such as Microsoft, Cisco, and Wipro to plead with the US Congress to expand the number of H-1B visa permits granted each year (Preston, 2008; Herbst, 2009; Wadhwa, 2009).

Today the situation related to worker "shortages" is substantially different from the pre-economic and financial crises period described above, the period of time when "global talent management" became popular (*The Economist,* February 21, 2009). By late 2008, a majority of companies that had already begun to downsize were planning to continue making more cuts that year (McGregor, 2009). So, while the shortages described above are likely to return eventually, in the near term firms may find that there is a surplus of workers at all levels of competency and motivation worldwide. As the economic slowdown continues, it will result in reduced demand for goods and services worldwide, creating excess capacity in most firms and putting downward pressure on prices. The pressure for cost reduction may become intense and the use of workforce cost reduction may become irresistible (Mohn, 2009; *The Economist,* February 21, 2009). An increase in recent mergers and acquisitions to reduce capacity and costs suggests that workforce reductions are likely to continue in the next few years (*The Economist,* March 14, 2009). Competition among workers and countries is likely to result in more wage competition and more governmental support to encourage firms to bring jobs to their country.

Because these conditions will be with us for the near term, it seems appropriate to include them in our discussion and framework of global talent management (GTM). That is, we recognize that managing global talent is difficult in times of both talent shortages and talent surpluses. Because labor market conditions are always in flux, global talent management requires firms to stay focused on how actions they take in the near term might influence their ability to adapt to changing conditions in the longer term. Furthermore, we include the talent characteristics of location and price (wage level) in our treatment of GTM. For a more complete treatment of this approach and a review of the academic GTM literature, see Tarique and Schuler (2010).

Global Talent Challenges: Summary

Thus there are several global talent challenges that firms need to manage as effectively as possible, including:

- too little talent is available now when it is needed;
- too much talent is available now and it is not needed;
- the needed talent is available in the wrong place (or position); and
- the needed talent is available at the wrong price.

As a consequence of such conditions, firms may need to: (a) reduce/add workers and positions in their home country; (b) move to another country and establish new operations at lower cost levels; or (c) reduce/add workers, even in other countries. In addition, they may need to train and develop existing staff rather than hire new staff from the outside. They may also need to improve their performance management and compensation systems to ensure that the workers they have are as productive as they can be. In some situations, firms may need to reduce and remove workers from multiple locations. In other words, there are many HR actions that can be taken by firms, both to manage through the current environment of economic and financial crises, and to position themselves for the period of recovery after the crises. Appropriate HR actions taken to address the challenges of global talent management can enable a multinational firm to gain and sustain a global competitive advantage (Lane and Pollner, 2008; Porter, 1985; Stephenson and Pandit, 2008; Palmisano, 2007).

HR ACTIONS TO ADDRESS GLOBAL TALENT CHALLENGES

Due in part to the existence of many drivers of the global talent challenges, there are many possible HR actions that firms can use in their global talent management initiatives (Beechler and Woodward, 2009). Matching an accurate diagnosis of a company's talent management situation with possible HR actions is a first step in gaining and sustaining a global competitive advantage that may result from the successful implementation of the correct action. Several categories of possible HR actions that can be considered by multinational firms include:

- organizational linkages;
- location planning and management;
- attraction and selection;
- training and development;
- performance assessment;
- compensation;
- retention;
- reduction; and
- removal.

Organizational Linkages

Talent management actions can only gain and sustain a global competitive advantage if they are linked to the actions and strategies of the organization (Nag et al., 2007). Nokia decided to relocate to Cluji, Romania knowing that the labor force there was both competent and willing to work at substantially lower wages than the workforce in Bochum, Germany (Ewing, 2008). This move by Nokia fit well with their business strategy, which was to produce high-quality cell phones in a highly competitive market near a new marketplace. The HR action reflected a tight linkage between the firm's business strategy and its global talent management strategy. This linkage was possible because Nokia gathered extensive labor market information and then used it to make an informed decision about where to (re)locate their operations. The business strategy and talent management strategy development reflected a tight reciprocal linkage (Ewing, 2008).

Location Planning and Management

Multinational firms such as Nokia have been rapidly expanding and (re)locating around the world (Porter, 1985; Hill, 2007; Daniels et al., 2007; Ewing, 2008).

In a period of the past 3 years, IBM hired more than 90,000 people in Brazil, China, and India (Hamm, 2008). In 2001, Accenture had 250 employees in India; by 2007 it had more than 35,000 employees in India (Engardio, 2007). As a consequence of firms moving rapidly to India, India's seemingly unlimited skilled labor supply was nearly fully employed by 2008. Now, companies thinking about moving operations to India need to develop new talent management strategies in order to attract workers away from their existing employers, and then retain these same individuals. As the available supply of workers shrinks, decisions must be made about whether to locate elsewhere or perhaps develop training programs to train for the competencies that are needed, as Microsoft has done in China and Nokia did in Romania (Chen and Hoskin, 2007; McGregor and Hamm, 2008). To help ensure a supply of dependable labor at the right price when Chinese companies locate abroad, they also send many of their own employees (Wong, 2009).

Multinational firms that are now thinking of expanding or relocating operations confront a large number of questions that are the essence of location planning and management, including:

- Why go? Why move at all from where we are right now? Should we rather just outsource part of our existing operations, or offshore part of our existing operations?
- Where go? What locations should we move to? Have we done country assessments on the country locations on such issues as: compensation levels, workforce skills availability, employment legislation, and culture compatibility?

An extensive list of items composing a "country assessments for location management decisions for IHRM" is shown in Exhibit 1:

- How go? Shall we expand our operations by ourselves? Should we outsource some of our existing operations to others? Should we enter into a joint venture with a local partner? Should we use a merger or acquisition?
- When go? Do we need to go within a year? Do we have time to develop an image in a new country that will enable us to attract the best applicants (i.e. be perceived as "One of the Best Companies to Work for")? If we enter another country, will we need to develop new ways of managing the workforce? Will we have to change our practices of recruiting and training, for example, for the local employees? Will we want to create a common set of HR policies and practices for all our locations?
- How link? How do we link employees in multiple international locations with each other so as to gain efficiencies and transfer knowledge effectively?

Besides addressing these questions, multinational firms will likely need to also engage in more traditional human resource planning and forecasting (i.e. making estimates of the numbers of individuals and skills that will be needed in their various locations) using existing attrition and retirement data of the current employees in

EXHIBIT 1. Country assessments for location management decisions

Topic	Content	Example Websites
General facts about country	Size, location, population, infrastructure, country culture, customs, business etiquette, political systems, societal concerns, natural resources, educational system	• odci.gov/cia/publications/factbook • getcustoms.com; cyborlink.com • economist.com/countries • //news.bbc.co.uk/2/hi/country_profiles/default.stm • geert-hofstede.com • foreignpolicy.com • bsr.org • export.gov/marketresearch.html
Attractiveness of country to business	Familiarity of country; government support; favorable labor conditions; economic and political stability	• economist.com • doingbusiness.org • sustainability.org • bsr.com • //news.bbc.co.uk2/hi/business/5313146.stm • kpmg.com • orcworldwide.com
Competitiveness factors	Familiarity of country; government support; favorable labor conditions; economic and political stability	• economist.com • doingbusiness.org • sustainability.org • bsr.com • //news.bbc.co.uk2/hi/business/5313146.stm • kpmg.com • orcworldwide.com
FDI flows/levels	Amount of foreign direct investment coming into a country by other countries and companies establishing operations or buying operations	• economist.com • census.gov/foreign-trade/balance
Labor market	Regulations, size, competencies, ease of hiring /firing, costs, unemployment rates	• doingbusiness.org • manpower.com • adecco.com • atkearney.com • wfpma.org • pwc.com • mckinsey.com • ilo.org/public/English/employment/index.htm
HR policies (actual/likely)	Wage levels for several job classes; talent management; human resource planning; union qualities; T&D support; safety and health	• dol.gov; ilo.org • atkearney.com • economist.com/countries • businessweek.com • ft.com • iht.com • bcg.com • mckinsey.com • //jobzing.com

Note: Selected websites provided to access data on topics of interest.

© Randall S. Schuler, 2010, Rutgers University.

conjunction with the business plans of the firm. Of course, even traditional planning tools may benefit from modifications that take into account the fact that the past is not always a good predictor of the future, especially in these more uncertain and dynamic times (Cappelli, 2008). Under conditions of great uncertainty, scenario planning might be more prudent than the use of more traditional forecasting techniques (Courtney, 2008; Dye et al., 2009; *The Economist*, February 28, 2009).

Attraction and Selection

Today organizations are finding that they are having a much more challenging time finding the workers with the competencies they need to perform a wide variety of jobs, regardless of worldwide location (Scullion and Collings, 2006). In essence, workers at every level are more important than ever to multinationals that hope to be competitive, both globally and locally (Guthridge et al., 2008; Huselid et al., 2009). How firms navigate this challenge reflects assumptions they make about workforce management. Two philosophically distinct approaches to attracting and selecting talent are evident in the current literature. One approach assumes that some of a firm's employees are more valuable than others. Huselid et al. (2009) capture this approach with the use of alpha terminology, (e.g. Type "A" players, Type "B" players, and Type "C" players). They also assign these same letters to the positions in the firm. For positions, "A" indicates the most significant impact on the firm's strategy and its key constituencies and positions that offer the greatest variability in performance. For players (the employees), "A" indicates those employees who perform at the highest level of performance variability. The result of this categorization is that firms then would devote the most, but certainly not all, of their resources in their global talent management efforts to "A"–"A" combinations.

In contrast to what Huselid et al. (2009) refer to as their "differentiated workforce approach," companies such as the UK insurance company Aviva have developed a global talent management strategy that focuses on managing the "vital many" rather than risk alienating the bulk of its workforce by focusing exclusively on "highfliers" (the "A"–"A" combinations) (Guthridge et al., 2008).

From the premise that all employees are equally valuable (versus the differentiated approach in which some are treated as more important than others) flows a number of actions that help confront the talent management challenge. Rather than differentiate the workforce based on their value to the firm, the alternative approach leads a firm to create differentiated value propositions to attract and retain the full diversity of applicants and employees available in the labor market. For example, the UK retailer Tesco develops separate recruiting and selection tactics for applicants for frontline clerks depending upon whether they are straight from school, are working part-time, or are graduates wanting full-time work. There is a separate website whose materials and language are tailored to that group (*McKinsey Quarterly*, 2008). Tactics used for different groups are based on what the firm thinks will be most effective and valued by the applicants, not on the firm's view that some applicants are more valuable than others.

Although we have presented these two competing philosophies as if firms must choose one or the other, this is overly simplistic. Indeed, a better approach to thinking about who is included as "talent" may be to recognize that firms vary in their degree of inclusiveness, going from including everyone (high inclusiveness) to only the top 5 percent or so (low inclusiveness).

Training and Development

In locations where competencies fall short of what firms need, training and development programs can be used to improve the quality of talent available and at the same time increase a firm's appeal as an employer. In China, Microsoft uses development and recognition programs that appeal to first-time programmers. Development programs include a rotation to the US and recognition programs include being selected as a Silk Road Scholar (Chen and Hoskin, 2007).

Multinational firms such as Microsoft and Schlumberger also offer attractive career management opportunities. Schlumberger makes it possible for engineers to achieve recognition and compensation equivalent to managers while remaining on their engineering career track (*Schlumberger Annual Reports*, 2007, 2008). Applying this more broadly, multinational firms can be expected to emphasize internal markets even more (allowing employees to move around from job to job more freely), with rapid promotion for the superstars (Wooldridge, 2007).

To address the need for leaders and managers with a global mindset that is broader than knowledge about the details of local country operations, many Chinese companies have begun sending their best managers to intensive management-training programs, such as those offered through a corporate university or business school (Dietz et al., 2008).

Performance Assessment

Performance assessment is a key ingredient in successful global talent management (Varma et al., 2008). The performance assessment system at Novartis is central to its global talent management efforts (Siegel, 2008). At the heart of it is a system that grades employees on (a) business results (the "what") and (b) values and behaviors (the "how"). While the business results are unique to each business area, the values and behaviors (ten in all) are common across the entire firm. Combining these two performance dimensions results in a nine-box matrix for assessing employee performance. This assessment process takes place within the context of the business performance cycle, which begins with the strategic plan for the firm and cascades down to define "what" each business unit is expected to accomplish. Novartis employees receive quarterly performance feedback, participate in self-assessments, and engage in development planning and career discussions. Together, these practices are aimed at improving competencies, motivating talent, determining training needs, and establishing a basis for performance-based pay (Siegel, 2008).

Compensation

Compensation rates around the world reflect today's dynamic economic and competitive business conditions (US Department of Labor, 2008; Gomez-Mejia and Werner, 2008). In response to multinationals locating in their countries, local companies in China and India often must pay Western-level salaries (Wooldridge, 2007; Banai and Harry, 2005). Demands for compensation increases by workers in China caused some multinationals to move and/or consider moving operations to Vietnam and Bangladesh, in addition to keeping some of their operations in China, producing what is often referred to as "China plus one strategy" (Bradsher, 2008).

The recent global economic slowdown put more pressure on firms to move to lower-wage nations, and this trend may continue as global demand contacts and industries find themselves with excess capacity. Nevertheless, as long as the supply of qualified managers is limited in emerging economy nations, firms that wish to expand into those markets will need to offer high salaries in order to secure the talent they need.

At Novartis, pay-for-performance is an important component of their global talent management effort (Siegel, 2008). Using the results of an employee's performance assessment in the nine-box performance matrix, a bonus payout is calculated that recognizes both the individual's performance and the performance of their business unit. Because the market for employees such as those in research and development is global, firms such as Novartis set compensation rates at levels that reflect the global environment, even when that means paying salaries that are above the norm in some countries (Siegel, 2008). To help manage compensation costs, however, firms in this situation may locate their operations to second-tier (lower-cost) cities. Another tactic is to recruit talent that is currently under-employed (e.g. engineers who are temporarily working as taxi drivers because they have lost their jobs during the economic downturn).

Retention

Retaining talent is one of the biggest talent management challenges for global accountancy firms. Historically, annual turnover rates at these firms have been between 15 and 20 percent. In these accountancy firms, a variety of factors contribute to high turnover rates among early-career employees, including long hours, pressure to study during off-hours in order to pass professional certification exams, and an "up or out" partnership model (Harry, 2008). Jim Wall, the managing director of human resources at Deloitte, estimated that every percentage-point drop in annual turnover rates equated to a saving of $400–$500 million for the firm (*The Economist*, July 21, 2007). To stem the turnover tide among early-career accountants, some firms have attempted to increase long-term commitment by providing data to employees, showing that employees who stay at least 6 years with their first employer are likely to earn higher pay at other firms when they do eventually leave (*The Economist*, July 21, 2007). More likely to be effective are retention strategies that include characteristics such as: (a) top management making a strong commitment that talent management is a priority for all employees; (b) assessing the efficacy of current recruiting sources; (c) expanding the list of recruiting sources; (d) sourcing talent globally; (e) constantly monitoring labor markets worldwide; (f) establishing diversity programs; (g) establishing accountability among managers for retention goals; and (h) rewarding managers for improving talent retention (Guthridge and Komm, 2008; Caye and Marten, 2008; Holland, 2008).

Reduction and Removal

If global economic and financial conditions continue to deteriorate, unemployment will likely spread dramatically (*The Economist*, January 31, 2009; *The Economist*, March 14, 2009; Powell, 2009). The ILO estimated that more than 50 million jobs would be lost globally in 2009, and again in 2010. Because hiring usually lags behind economic recovery, low employment levels are expected to persist until at least 2012. Thus, the challenge of managing under conditions of surplus talent is likely to be with us for the next few years. Accordingly, "reduction and removal" HR actions are likely to dominate the global talent management agenda of many firms.

Reduction can involve the reduction of work hours, days, overtime, pay levels, pay increases, benefits, new hires and holidays, and also the increased use of attrition, unpaid leave, assignment for local volunteer work, sabbaticals, and contract employees and outsourcing (Mirza, 2008; Boyle, 2009). From these activities, firms can reduce their costs and existing employees can retain their jobs. In contrast, removal refers to the use of layoffs or other measures that result in permanent job loss (Hansen, 2009b). Firms have a great deal of choice in how they shrink their workforces, but their choices are not unlimited. For multinationals, decisions about which HR actions to use must reflect the concerns of various unions, governmental regulations, cultural norms, and corporate values.

INTEGRATED AND FLEXIBLE SYSTEMS OF HR ACTIONS FOR GLOBAL TALENT MANAGEMENT

As this brief summary of possible HR actions suggests, multinational firms must make an array of decisions about how to manage their global talent. Ideally, the HR actions they select reflect both the specific challenges facing the firm currently and consideration of the future challenges that are likely to arise as economic conditions change over time. Although the recent economic downturn has slowed business globally, firms still need to hire and manage their talent in anticipation of their future needs. Furthermore, the selection of particular HR actions is likely to be most effective in firms that adopt a systemic approach to global talent management. That is, HR actions need to be mutually supportive and internally consistent with each other, while also fitting firm characteristics such as top management leadership, vision, values, strategy, size, culture, and industry.

In a study entitled *The War for Talent* (Michaels et al., 2001), it was found that HR professionals spent a great deal of their time formulating and managing the traditional HR policies and practices such as recruiting, selecting, training, performance appraisal, and compensation. While these are important for addressing talent management challenges, their effectiveness results from being linked with the firm's strategies and directions, and this linkage was found to be lacking. "HR under-performs in companies where its capabilities, competencies, and focus are not tightly aligned with the critical business priorities" (Rawlinson et al., 2008: 23). Additionally, the study concluded that most HR professionals need to do a better job of measuring the impact of HR actions using metrics that are aligned with business strategies. Thus, for example, a firm might track the performance records of employees who have participated in global management training programs and compare them to those who have developed global skills on the job and/or compare them to people with no global exposure, using performance metrics that reflect desired strategic business outcomes such as revenue, profit targets, or retention of direct reports.

RESULTS OF EFFECTIVE GLOBAL TALENT MANAGEMENT

As shown in Figure 1, there are several potential results that are likely to follow from HR actions that successfully address a firm's global talent challenges. In particular, we have argued that addressing the challenge of global talent management improves the firm's success in having the right people at the right place at the right time with the needed competencies and motivation and at the right price at all levels and all locations (positions) of the firms (Lane and Pollner, 2008; Guthridge et al., 2008). In time, these effects accumulate and deepen the firm's bench strength (or future positioning) for all positions in the company, both anticipated and unanticipated, in all current and future locations around the world (Rawlinson et al., 2008).

In the short term, successful HR actions may provide a firm with a temporary advantage over competitors. In the long term, as the firm's global talent management system matures and as learning about how to management global talent becomes embedded in organizational systems, it may be possible for the firm to establish a sustainable global competitive advantage. Sustainability of competitive advantage is never assured, because the drivers of global talent management are likely to change continually (Porter, 1985; Daniels et al., 2007). Nevertheless, as firms gain experience and begin to develop the competencies needed for global success, they simultaneously position themselves to adapt as changing conditions require in the future. The development of such a virtuous cycle of effects seems more likely to occur in firms that take actions specifically designed to train and develop the firms' leaders and HR managers (Caye and Martin, 2008; Guthridge et al., 2008).

BARRIERS TO GLOBAL TALENT MANAGEMENT

It seems apparent that multinational firms have good reason to invest considerable resources in meeting the global talent challenges they face, but success in this endeavor remains elusive. Based on the responses of more than 1,300 executives worldwide, Guthridge et al. (2008) identified several barriers to the use of HR actions for global talent management. Many of these barriers to successful talent management exist for domestic firms, but they become more complex and difficult to overcome in global firms. The barriers include:

- the fact that senior managers do not spend enough time on talent management, perhaps thinking that there are other more pressing things to be concerned with;
- organizational structures, whether based regions, products, or functions, that inhibit collaboration and the sharing of resources across boundaries;
- middle- and front-line managers who are not sufficiently involved in or responsible for employees' careers, perhaps because they see these activities as less important than managing the business, and/or because they require such a long-term perspective;
- managers are uncomfortable and/or unwilling to acknowledge performance differences among employees—a step that is required in order to take actions to improve performance;
- managers at all levels who are not sufficiently involved in the formulation of the firm's talent management strategy, and therefore have a limited sense of ownership and understanding of actions designed to help manage the firm's global talent; and
- HR departments that lack the competencies needed to address the global talent challenge effectively, and/or lack the respect of other executives whose cooperation is needed to implement appropriate HR actions.

While there are many barriers to overcome, multinational firms such as IBM, Toyota, Procter & Gamble, Novartis, ThyssenKrupp, and Schlumberger have shown that success is possible with the commitment, leadership, and involvement of the top management (Farndale et al., 2010; Takeuchi et al., 2008; Lane and Pollner, 2008; Palmisano, 2007).

CONCLUSION

Many of the most pressing challenges facing global firms today are directly related to human capital challenges, and more specifically global talent challenges (Rawlinson et al., 2008; Adecco, 2008; Walker, 2007; Scott et al., 2007; Price and Turnbull, 2007; Scullion and Collings, 2006). These global talent challenges arise due to the ever-changing characteristics of the environment. In particular, among the major drivers are: enhanced globalization, evolving demographics, the need for more competencies and motivation, and the growing shortage/surplus of needed competencies and motivation. For firms throughout the world, the changing environment—particularly during volatile economic and financial periods of boom-and-bust such as those experienced in recent years—presents both global talent challenges and an opportunity to gain a sustainable global competitive advantage (Porter, 1985; Cairns and Sliwa, 2008). In this reading, we sought to provide a brief overview of possible HR actions that can be used to build an integrated and flexible system for global talent management, and described some of the barriers to success in this endeavor.

The greatest challenge may simply be the need for firms to be relentless in their efforts to effectively manage global talent, for even when success is achieved in the near term, new HR actions will soon be required simply to stay one step ahead of competitors. For the HR profession, an immediate challenge is to develop the supply of HR talent with the competencies and motivations required to understand the drivers that create global talent management challenges, develop systems that are tailored to address a particular firm's specific global talent needs, and work in partnership with the senior management team to ensure a close linkage between HR actions programs and the strategic objectives of the firm.

NOTE

* The authors wish to express thanks for preparatory comments and suggestions to Clemens Brugger, Dave Collings, Paul Sparrow, Mark Saxer, Hugh Scullion, Ken Smith, Rosalie Tung and Nadia Wicki. Supported by a grant from the School of Management and Labor Relations, Rutgers University. Adapted from our chapter in H. Scullion and D. Collings (Eds.), *Global Talent Management* (London: Routledge, 2010).

REFERENCES

Adecco (2008) *The next decade's talent war* (Geneva: Adecco).

Banai, M. and Harry, W. (2005). Transnational managers: A different expatriate experience. *International Studies of Management and Organization*, 34 (3): 96–120.

Beechler, S. and Woodward, I.C. (2009). Global talent management. *Journal of International Management* 15: 273–285.

Boyle, M. (2009). Cutting costs without cutting jobs, *Business Week*, March 9: 55.

Bradsher, K. (2008). Investors seek Asian options to costly china, *The New York Times*, June 18: A20.

Brannen, M.Y. (2008). What would it take for Japanese managers to be globally agile? Pressing concerns for Japanese talent management. Paper presented at the Academy of Management Annual Conference, August 9–13, Anaheim, CA.

Cairns, G. and Sliwa, M. (2008). *A very short, fairly interesting and reasonably cheap book about international business* (London: Sage).

Cappelli, P. (2008). *Talent on demand* (Boston, MA: Harvard Business School).

Caye, J-M. and Marten, I. (2008). *Talent management.* (Boston, MA: The Boston Consulting Group).

Chen, W. and Hoskin, J. (2007). Multinational corporations in China: Finding and keeping talent, *SHRM*, October: 1–4.

Coy, P. and Ewing, E. (2007). Where are all the workers? *Business Week*, April 9: 28–31.

Courtney, H. (2008). A fresh look at strategy under uncertainty: An interview, *McKinsey Quarterly*, December.

Daniels, J.D., Radebaugh, L.H., and Sullivan, D.P. (2007). *International business: Environment and operations* (Upper Saddle River, NJ: Pearson/Prentice-Hall).

Dickmann, M. and Baruch, Y. (2010). *Global career management* (London: Routledge).

Dietz, M.C., Orr, G., and Xing, J. (2008). How Chinese companies can succeed abroad, *McKinsey Quarterly*, May.

Downie, A. (2008). Wanted: Skilled workers for a growing economy in Brazil, *The New York Times*: C1, C5.

Dunning, J. (2000). The eclectic paradigm as an envelope for economic and business theories of MNE activity, *International Business Review*, 9: 163–190.

Dye, R., Sibony, O., and Viguerie, S.P. (2009). Strategic planning: Three tips for 2009, *McKinsey Quarterly*, April.

The Economist (2006) The battle for brainpower, *The Economist*: October 5.

The Economist (2007) Accounting for good people, *The Economist*, July 21: 68–70.

The Economist (2009) Swinging the axe, *The Economist*, January 31: 69–70.

The Economist (2009) Turning their backs on the world, *The Economist*, February 21: 59–61.

The Economist (2009) Managing in a fog, *The Economist*, February 28: 67–68.

The Economist (2009) When jobs disappear, *The Economist*, March 14: 71–73.

The Economist Intelligence Unit (2006) The CEO's role in talent management: How top executives from ten countries are nurturing the leaders of tomorrow. *The Economist* (London: The Economist Intelligence Unit).

Engardio, P. (2007). India's talent gets loads of TLC, *Business Week*, August 20 and 27: 52–53.

Engardio, P. and Weubtraub, A. (2008). Outsourcing the drug industry, *Business Week*, September 15: 49–53.

Ewing, E. (2008). Nokia's new home in Romania, *Business Week,* January.

Farndale, E., Scullion, H., and Sparrow, P. (2010). The role of the corporate HR function in global talent management, *Journal of World Business,* 46 (2).

Fernández-Aráoz, C. (2009). The coming fight for executive talent, *Business Week,* December.

Friedman, T.L. (2005). *The world is flat* (New York: Farrar, Straus & Giroux).

Ghemawat, P. and Hout, T. (2007). *Redefining global strategy* (Boston, MA: Harvard Business School Press).

Gomez-Mejia, L. and Werner, S. (2008). *Global compensation* (London: Routledge).

Gupta, A. and Govindarajan, V. (2001). Converting global presence into global competitive advantage, *Academy of Management Executive,* 15: 45–58.

Guthridge, M. and Komm, A.B. (2008). Why multinationals struggle to manage talent, *McKinsey Quarterly*, May: 1–5.

Guthridge, M., Komm, A.B., and Lawson, E. (2008). Making talent management a strategic priority, *McKinsey Quarterly*, January: 49–59.

Hamm, S. (2008). International isn't just IBM's first name, *Business Week*, January.

Harry, W. (2007). Employment creation and localization-the crucial human resources issues for the GCC, *International Journal of Human Resource Management*, 18 (1): 132–146.

Harry, W. (2008). Personal communication, October 1, 2008.

Hansen, F. (2009a). Downturn dilemma, *Workforce Management*, February 16: 29–30.

Hansen, F. (2009b). HR in the downturn, *Workforce Management*, February 16: 16.

Herbst, M. (2009). A narrowing window for foreign workers? *Business Week*, March 16: 50.

Huselid, M.A., Beatty, R.W., and Becker, B. (2009). *The differentiated workforce* (Boston, MA: Harvard Business School Press).

Hill, C.W.L. (2007). *International Business: Competing in the global marketplace,* 6th ed. (New York: McGraw-Hill/Irwin).

Holland, K. (2008). Working all corners in a global talent hunt, *The New York Times*, February 24: 17.

IBM (2008). *The enterprise of the future* (New York: IBM).

Jackson, S.E., Hitt, M.A., and DeNisi, A. (2003). *Managing knowledge for sustained competitive advantage* (San Francisco, CA: Jossey-Bass).

Jackson, S.E., Schuler, R.S. and Werner, S. (2009). *Managing human resourcess,* 10th ed. (Mason, OH: Cengage, Southwestern Publishing Company).

Kearney, A.T. (2008) *Globalization 3.0* (Boston, MA: A.T. Kearney).

Krugman, P. (1979). A model of innovation, technology transfer, and the world distribution of income, *The Journal of Political Economy,* 87 (2): 253–266.

Krugman, P. (1981). Intraindustry specialization and the gains from trade, *The Journal of Political Economy,* 89 (4): 959–973.

Lane, K. and Pollner, F. (2008). How to address China's growing talent shortage, *McKinsey Quarterly,* 3: 33–40.

McGregor, J. (2009). A pink-slip pandemic, *Business Week*, March 23 and 30: 14.

McGregor, J. and Hamm, S. (2008). Managing the global workforce, *Business Week*, January 28: 36–51

McKinsey Quarterly (2008) The war for talent, *McKinsey Quarterly*, 10 January.

Manpower Inc. (2008a) Borderless workforce survey, *Manpower White Paper.*

Manpower Inc. (2008b) Confronting the talent crunch, *Manpower White Paper.*

Mendenhall, M.E., Osland, J.S., Bird, A., Oddou, G.R., and Mazevski, M.L.G. (2008). *Global leadership: Research, practice and development* (London: Routledge).

Michaels, E., Handfield-Jones, H. and Axelrod, B. (2001). *The war for talent* (Boston, MA: Harvard Business School Press).

Mirza, B. (2008). Look at alternatives to layoffs, *SHRM On-line,* December 29.

Mohn, T. (2009). The long trip home, *The New York Times*, March 10: D1, D5.

Nag, R., Hambrick, D.C., and Chen, M-J. (2007). What is strategic management, really? Inductive derivation of a consensus definition of the field, *Strategic Management Journal*, 28: 935–955.

National Commission on Adult Literacy (2008) *Reach higher America: Overcoming crisis in the U.S. workforce* (Washington, DC: National Commission on Adult Literacy), June.

Palmisano, S. (2007). The globally integrated enterprise, *Foreign Affairs,* 85 (3): 127–136.

Porter, M. (1985). *Competitive advantage: Creating and sustaining superior performance* (New York: Free Press).

Powell, B. (2009). China's hard landing, *Fortune*, March 16: 114–120.

Preston, J. (2008). Visa application period opens for highly skilled workers, *The New York Times*, April 1: A5.

Price, C. and Turnbull, D. (2007). The organizational challenges of global trends: A McKinsey global survey, *McKinsey Quarterly,* May.

Rawlinson, R., McFarland, W., and Post, L. (2008). A talent for talent, *Strategy + Business,* Autumn: 21–24.

Roach, S. (2009). Testimony before the Chinese American Committee on Economic and Security, February 17.

Schlumberger Annual Reports (2007, 2008).

Schuler, R.S. and Tarique, I. (2007). International HRM: A North America perspective, a thematic update and suggestions for future research, *International Journal of Human Resource Management*, May: 15–43.

Scott, V., Schultze, A., Huseby, T., and Dekhane, N. (2007). *Where have all the workers gone?* (Chicago, IL: A.T. Kearney).

Scullion, H. and Collings, D. (2006). *Global staffing systems* (London: Routledge).

Sengupta, S. (2006). Skills gap threatens technology boom in India, *The New York Times,* October 17: A1, A6.

Siegel, J. (2008). Global talent management at Novartis, *Harvard Business School* (Case #9–708–486).

Stephenson, E. and Pandit, A. (2008). How companies act on global trends: A McKinsey global survey (Boston, MA: McKinsey).

Strack, R., Baier, J., and Fahlander, A. (2008). Managing demographic risk, *Harvard Business Review*, February: 2–11.

Tarique, I. and Schuler, R.S. (2010). Framework and review of global talent management and suggestions for future research, *Journal of World Business,* H. Scullion and D. Collings (special guest editors), 46 (2).

Takeuchi, H., Osono, E., and Shimizu, N. (2008). The contradictions that drive Toyota's success. *Harvard Business Review,* June: 96–104.

US Department of Labor (2008). *International comparisons of hourly compensation costs in manufacturing, 2006* (Washington, DC: Bureau of Labor Statistics).

Varma, A., Budhwar, P., and DeNisi, A. (2008). *Performance management systems* (London: Routledge).

Wadhwa, V. (2009). America's immigrant brain drain, *Business Week*, March 16: 68.

Walker, M. (2007). *Globalization 3.0* (Wilson Quarterly and reprinted by A.T. Kearney, 2008).

Werdigier, J. (2008). Retooling for a changing telecom landscape, *The New York Times*, March 8: C2.

Wong, E. (2009). China's export of labor faces growing scorn, *The New York Times,* December 21: A1–A9.

Wooldridge, A. (2007) The battle for the best, *The Economist: The World in 2007*, p. 104.

World Bank (2008). See the six indicators the World Bank uses to describe the extent of employment regulations in countries at www.doingbusiness.org.

Zakaria, F. (2008). *The post-American world* (New York: Norton).

Wes Harry and David G. Collings

LOCALISATION: SOCIETIES, ORGANISATIONS AND EMPLOYEES

INTRODUCTION

LOCALISATION HAS EMERGED as a key issue in the management of multinational corporations (MNCs). The concept is, however, often used in generic terms without specific definition. In this regard, Hideo Sugiura, the former vice chairman of Honda, distinguished between four types of localisation: localisation of products, profit, production and people (cited in Evans et al., 2002). Although the primary focus of this reading will be on people, we will also touch on some of the other concepts in setting the context for our later discussions. In this regard, a key debate centres on the extent to which MNCs' 'foreign affiliates (or subsidiaries) act and behave as local firms versus the extent to which their practices resemble those of the parent corporation or some other global standard' (Rosenzweig and Nohria, 1994: 229). Indeed, based on their work on patterns of strategic control in multinationals, Doz and Prahalad (1986) have argued that responding to a variety of national demands while maintaining a coherent strategy is a key strategic challenge facing MNCs. In a similar vein, Bartlett and Ghoshal (1998) call for organisations to maintain a 'dynamic balance' between globalisation (implementing globally standard practices) and localisation (adapting practices to account for the host environment) if they are to become truly transnational. The staffing orientations pursued by MNCs in their foreign affiliates are generally a key indicator of the firm's orientation in this regard. Specifically, firms that pursue an ethnocentric orientation are likely to fill key positions in subsidiary operations with parent country nationals or employees from the home country of the MNC. In contrast, MNCs that pursue a polycentric approach are significantly more likely to fill key positions at subsidiary level with host country nationals or employees from the country in which the subsidiary is located.

Localisation of labour (sometimes called labour nationalisation, host country national development or indigenisation) is defined as: 'the extent to which jobs originally filled by expatriates are filled by local employees who are competent to perform the job' (Selmer, 2004: 1094) and it is often considered one of the crucial drivers of the employment policies of many nation-states. It also influences the state's relationships with foreign organisations seeking to operate within their national boundaries. Evans *et al.* (2002) see localisation as systematic investment in the recruitment, development and retention of local employees, which is an important element in the globalisation strategy of multinationals. However, they also point to the differences between the rhetoric and the reality of many localisation strategies and the barriers to the implementation of localisation strategies will be considered below.

Demographics and cost concerns are often key drivers of localisation, particularly in the Gulf Cooperation Council countries (Bahrain, Kuwait, Oman, Qatar, Saudi Arabia and United Arab Emirates) and failure to solve the problems of ineffective localisation may have wide-ranging and long-term consequences (Yamani 2000). Debates around localisation are not restricted to managerial employees however, and also concern the employment of HCNs at lower levels in the organisational hierarchy. In this regard it might seem easy to create jobs for locals but in practice the creation of worthwhile productive jobs depends on an appropriate education system, suitable work ethic within the host population and willingness on the part of employers to make a sustained and genuine effort to support and transfer skills, attitudes and behaviours. As should be apparent from the proceeding introduction the localisation of human resources at managerial and staff levels is important not only in the context of developing the human resources of the host economy but also in building mutually beneficial, long-term relationships between the employing organisation and the host society. Further, lower profit margins in developing countries and a growing unwillingness among governments in poorer countries to allow key positions in foreign MNCs to be occupied indefinitely by expatriates are forcing more and more organisations to examine alternatives to traditional expatriate staffing methods (Sparrow *et al.*, 2004). In this reading we will first outline the key forces driving local responsiveness in international business. We then consider the business advantages and disadvantages of local responsiveness. Our discussion then focuses more specifically on the localisation of human resources and again the advantages and disadvantages of this will be outlined. After exploring the nature of localisation in practice, finally we consider the role of expatriates in the localisation process.

THE CHANGING MEANING OF LOCAL RESPONSIVENESS IN INTERNATIONAL BUSINESS

At one time organisations from developed countries could virtually afford to ignore local needs and wishes in servicing foreign markets, particularly those in developing countries. They generally had a monopoly, or near monopoly, of goods and services and so could impose on local markets whatever they wanted to sell. Some imposed, or tried to impose, their business practices and cultures in foreign operations (cf. Hertz, 2001). Some international organisations could even impose their will on sovereign states. The power of the companies was generally applied and monitored by expatriates, usually nationals of the parent country of their employer.

The imposition of products, services and people was resented, particularly for the colonialist attitudes which came with the imposition. Further, citizens from developing countries continue to resent expatriates holding high paid jobs, which they considered could be done by HCNs, and they often commented on the lack of commitment of expatriates to the local operations (Brewster, 1991). Since the 1960s, the desire to build nation-states and national economies has led to a strong move for nationalisation, local partnerships or at least significant investment within the host country (Sparrow *et al.*, 2004). In the following section we consider the business advantages and disadvantages of localisation.

THE BUSINESS ADVANTAGES AND DISADVANTAGES OF LOCALISATION

There are many sound economic and ethical reasons for MNCs to develop a localisation strategy. Such developments are not without some difficulties and disadvantages however and these are discussed below.

Advantages

There are four main advantages in developing localisation policies. First, localisation of human resources may improve relations between foreign investors and host country governments. Selmer (2004) has argued that this is the case in the Chinese context as the government favours the development of local employees. Indeed Lasserre and Ching (1997) have shown that central and provincial authorities there may view localisation to be an indication of foreign firms' commitment to the country. Thus from the MNC's point of view a localisation strategy may help to ensure foreign operations operate with minimum levels of conflict with the host authorities. Further it may assist the firm in gaining lucrative contracts or tenders with public sector organisations.

Second, localisation of human resources may improve communication, and, ultimately business performance in the host country. This is because communication local to local is usually more effective than foreigner to local. Human nature tends to favour the familiar rather than the strange. In this regard customers generally want to be served by those who understand their needs and it is most often fellow nationals and long-term residents who understand what these needs are. Successful organisations recognise that a shared language, with the local nuances, helps in communications and understanding. Further, HCNs may provide a valuable resource in developing local contacts in the host environment. While expatriate managers may have greater access to higher level institutional contacts, local employees will generally be in a better position to develop business relationships with lower levels of organisational and government hierarchies (Lasserre and Ching, 1997; Selmer, 2004). This is particularly important in some societies such as China where guanxi is vital for developing business contacts and opportunities.

Third, host country labour is generally a more reliable resource than temporary workers, who even if they work in the country for a long time, have divided loyalty (Black and Gregerson, 1992) and certainly see their ultimate destination as a different location. The loyalty of the foreign labour is purchased at a price that, with few exceptions, is more expensive than local labour. Harry and Banai (2005) have described the motivation of many senior expatriates and the costs of employing them – at rates much higher than most host country nationals. In a similar vein, it has been shown that expatriates operating in a Chinese context can be paid five times more than HCN comparators in total compensation (Economist Intelligence Unit, 1997; Selmer, 2004). Ruhs and Godfrey (2002) have shown that even for 'cheap' foreign labour, the costs, over the long term, are greater than most societies would willingly bear.

Finally, from an economic perspective, by responding to local needs, especially through investing capital and employing local labour, the organisation increases the wealth of the local population and so increases their ability to buy products and services sold by local businesses. Even if the market is small and poor, there can be good potential for growth and long-term profit (Prahalad, 2004). MNCs can create the capacity to consume by paying reasonable wages, training and developing staff and treating them well should be able to reap advantages from increased markets in the host country. Those organisations that develop local markets may gain a dominant market position, which latecomers will find hard to overturn.

Disadvantages

There are four main disadvantages in developing localisation policies. First, understanding local markets takes time and effort. Sometimes local management can make costly mistakes or events can occur outside their direct control that will cost the parent company heavily in financial terms, as companies such as Union Carbide in Bhopal India or Shell in Nigeria have found. The cost of educating customers who might not be familiar with a product or service, even those intended to meet apparent local needs, can be very high. So too can be the cost of adjusting the product or service to meet these local needs, for example smaller packets for those customers who cannot afford to buy enough to hold a stock of an item (Das, 1993) or different coloured materials to meet local preferences. On the basis of a cost-benefit analysis, organisations may feel that the costs associated with the adaptation of products to account for the local context may outweigh the benefits associated with such an action (Shenkar and Luo, 2004). Further, organisations may, on the basis of a user/need analysis of consumer needs, even decide not to introduce a popular product or service into a particular market (Shenkar and Luo, 2004: 419–20).

Second, there are disadvantages in having to make changes in the ways of working to meet local conditions. For example, the work patterns might be different from those expected or preferred, such as split shifts giving a long break at midday, or twelve-hour, six-day working with long vacations. Indeed, it has been argued (Nash, 2004) that the traditional Spanish siesta is coming under threat from globalisation as a growing number of MNCs are increasingly persuading executives that they cannot be absent from their desks for hours during the middle of the day. This indicates that these MNCs consider the siesta to be impractical in the modern globalised business environment. Thus, they are not prepared to sacrifice their traditional working time arrangements for what they consider to be an impractical and unworkable tradition that is at odds with their ideology for how the business enterprise should be run.

Third, managing without expatriates involves looser coordination from an HQ perspective and potentially greater problems in communicating with HQ from a subsidiary perspective. Indeed, empirical research has shown that the staffing decisions with regard to key executive appointments (with expatriates or locals) significantly impacted on the parent company's operational control of the host operations (Child and Yan, 1999). While more indirect methods of control have been effectively used to monitor subsidiary performance, a direct link with the subsidiary through a parent country national may aid in ensuring that communication lines between the HQ and the subsidiary are open and efficient. Without this link, the HQ may not have an accurate picture of how the subsidiary is performing. Specifically, while more indirect control methods such as financial reporting can provide HQ with a quantitative overview of subsidiary performance, some of the nuances of the subsidiary operation may be lost in the figures. For example, in some situations profit levels in the local market may not meet international levels or expectations but nonetheless they can still make a steady and potentially increasing contribution to the organisation's portfolio. Likewise, inefficiencies or financial problems could potentially be hidden in financial statements or other reporting procedures.

Fourth, a major concern of senior HQ managers with respect to localisation strategy is the fear of losing intellectual property rights, particularly in the emerging markets where the perception is that everything can be copied. Selmer (2004) describes this as an 'agency problem' and argues that expatriate presence may help to guard against local managers pursuing their personal self-interest in managing the subsidiary or making decisions that are incongruent with the organisation's global strategy. In this vein, Boisot and Child (1999) have noted that due to concerns over embezzlement in the Chinese context, many foreign firms have reserved the option of appointing their chief financial officers from within the organisation.

Having examined the advantages and disadvantages of local responsiveness in international management in a broader sense, we will now focus specifically on the localisation of human resources.

LOCALISATION OF HUMAN RESOURCES

In this section, we will consider the localisation of non-managerial staff in foreign subsidiaries. This is significant, as the number of non-managerial staff employed in subsidiaries is generally far in excess of those in managerial roles. This cohort of employees is generally neglected in the extant literature, however.

While globalisation appears to offer many advantages to international organisations, it does have the potential disadvantage that these organisations are judged not just as economic entities but as social creations that are expected, not least by customers and domestic pressure groups, to behave in a responsible and ethical manner – wherever they operate. Thus, localisation is not as straightforward a proposition as it may immediately appear. Hence, in this context a key ethical decision for international HR managers to consider is what to do when an employment practice that is illegal or even viewed as morally suspect in the home country is legal and acceptable in the host country (Briscoe and Schuler, 2004). Major international companies such as Shell, Union Carbine and Nike have found that their 'local' practices are judged by 'home' country ethical standards with the potential harm that does to reputation and sales (Litvin, 2003). Take, for example, the criticism Nike has received in recent years due to the conditions prevailing in its outsourced productions facilities in lower wage-cost countries (cf. Morris and Lawrence, 2003). In this regard, there are sound ethical reasons for developing local human resources (Hailey, 1999). These reasons include human rights in terms of employment and training opportunities not being linked to race and nationality but to capability, and with meeting the reasonable requirements of the whole stakeholder community and contributing to the greater human development.

It might seem straightforward to develop the skills required to localise many of the tasks required in large-scale industrialised operations and complex administrative services, but in the context of developing countries, it is important to note that the skills, attitudes, behaviours and methods of learning necessary in rural and small-scale industrial activities are not easily transferable to the large-scale and complex activities that characterise multinational investment. As most employees (and customers) will have little exposure to the requirements of industrialised and complex operations, it will take time, much training and expenditure to develop the workers to meet the organisation's needs.

We will now examine the benefits and barriers of localising human resources.

THE BENEFITS OF LOCALISING HUMAN RESOURCES

There are many benefits that arise from utilising local people rather than expatriates to fill key positions within foreign operations. Often these benefits are underestimated, particularly for senior positions, for reasons that are often based on racial or national stereotypes (Banai, 1992).

We have discussed above the advantages of provider and customer sharing a common language as well as common cultural communications and expectations. The impact of this sharing cannot be underestimated. As noted above, HCNs may provide a valuable resource in developing local contacts in the host environment. Specifically, we pointed to the fact that while expatriate managers may have greater access to higher level institutional contacts, local employees will generally be in a better position to develop business relationships with lower levels of organisational and government hierarchies (Lasserre and Ching, 1997; Selmer, 2004).

The cost of local employees is generally lower than that of expatriates. Expatriate costs are usually a multiple of the national employee, and expatriates are among the most expensive employees, even in home country terms (e.g. Brewster, 1991; Harry and Banai, 2005; Scullion and Brewster, 2001). Even the cost of administering the expatriate employees' conditions of service can be high, compared with that of the administration of host country nationals, with HR staff engaged in carrying out cost of living comparison studies, developing tax equalisation formulae and managing international careers (Dowling and Welch, 2004).

The lower costs of the host country staff and their longer-term employment means that the return on investment in recruiting and training these staff may be higher than for expatriates. Organisations that encourage the development and promotion of local staff are likely to see improved morale and greater retention rates of their best staff. These staff will stay for longer, ensuring that valuable knowledge and capability are retained within the organisation and thus making a potentially more valuable return from the investment in their recruitment and development than investing in expatriate staff. The long-term relationship between the local operation and the host population often means that the company is no longer seen as foreign but local. For example, Ford of Dagenham is now generally considered British and not American, and the Wellcome stores are generally considered a Hong Kong 'belonger' there.

As discussed earlier, the localisation of human resources may also have a positive political impact. Host country governments may view the localisation process as an indication of attachment or commitment to the host country and thus may aid or at least not greatly hinder the operation of the MNC in the host country. Even if there are no short-term political benefits, there are certainly long-term benefits, as Hailey (1999) and Litvin (2003) have shown, for taking an ethical stance not to exploit foreigners. In this regard, Sparrow et al. (2004: 133) posit: 'regulators and governments look at the behaviour of a company against local legal, socio-cultural and environmental norms'. Thus, ethical decisions in this regard are particularly complex, as not only must MNCs be cognisant of host norms in this regard, but also they are constrained by home norms and beliefs as discussed above. A final advantage of using local managers to run the foreign subsidiary is that this staffing approach allows the MNC to adopt a lower profile in sensitive political conditions than would be the case with expatriates in charge (Scullion, 1992).

The Barriers to Localising Human Resources

While it might seem to make economic, financial and ethical sense to localise human resources, there are many barriers that may mean the continued use of expatriates is more practical and sometimes preferable. In this section, we will outline some of the key challenges in this regard.

Most resistance to localising human resources is from the private sector organisations (national and international) where short-term costs are emphasised to the detriment of long-term benefits. In this section, we will outline the key challenges to the localisation of human resources with a particular focus on non-managerial employees. Specifically, we focus on: education and the workplace, jobs on offer that do not appeal, inappropriate selection methods, training and costs.

Education and the Workplace

Intelligence and potential are evenly spread in the human population, and no race or nationality lacks the ability to develop necessary skills, attitudes or behaviours required by modern organisations. However, whereas most developed countries have built up their skilled workforces and managerial systems, along with the educational support systems over many decades, in developing areas such as the Gulf Cooperation Council, China and Eastern Europe the pace of development has been very rapid. The pace has been so rapid that insufficient members of the host population have been educated to develop the capability needed by employers. For example, Warner (1985) noted that two in three Chinese managers had no qualifications beyond middle school in the mid-1980s. Further, their knowledge and skills in areas such as auditing, cost accounting, marketing and personnel were relatively weak. In a similar vein, Micklethwait (1996) posited that China was producing only 300 MBA graduates annually in 1995, when foreign joint ventures alone could have absorbed 240,000 of them.

The education systems in most developing countries are different from those in industrialised countries of the West. For most countries, education has focused on basic literacy (if that) and learning from an older generation how to undertake agricultural, small-scale repair or retail tasks. Even in Eastern Europe and states of the former Soviet Union, where the standards of education were high in terms of technical knowledge, there were considerable differences in terms of attitudes towards work and behaviour at work. Indeed, Kiriazov et al. (2000) posit that management training in Eastern European countries has traditionally focused on rote learning as opposed to action learning, thus limiting the potential contribution of these management graduates. Recently, organisations such as the Open University have begun to operate in these countries and Bennett (1996) reports some 7,000 annual enrolments in their courses in Russia alone. In many countries, little money has been spent on education in general and in education for the workplace in particular. In commenting on this issue in less developed international economies, a senior banking official commented: 'In countries like Vietnam and China, people are very keen to work for foreign multinational companies. The problem isn't getting people to come to work, the difficulty is with the government relations, *the language skills and standards of education*. You've got to support the employees with a lot of training' (quoted in Solomon, 1995: 64, emphasis added).

In these countries, significant resources have gone into educating the elite in tertiary education establishments at home or abroad and little spent on basic edu-cation for the mass of the population. For example, within Saudi Arabia the dropout rate after primary schooling is 30 per cent. In this regard, Yamani (2000) has demonstrated the wide gap between the expectations of the generation entering the workforce in Saudi Arabia and the reality of the workplace. Fewer than half of the 100,000 Saudis entering the employment market each year find a job (*The Economist,* 2002).

In the GCC, and many other countries, the emphasis in education is often on cultural or nation building rather than on ensuring employability in the workplace. In most countries, including in the developed world, technical subjects are shunned in favour of social sciences and other fields that might be useful in developing 'thinking skills' but are not immediately applicable in most work situations.

Jobs on Offer Do Not Appeal

In some countries, such as those of the GCC, even when young people are well educated and qualified, they may be reluctant to work in the type of jobs that are available. The socio-political elites who have access to the best education institutions are more likely to want to work in government or be entrepreneurs than to work for someone else. This is especially the case if the potential employer is a foreign organisation, although the prestige of a period in a well-known international organisation may be attractive at the beginning of a career.

Jobs that are not attractive to most HCNs, when they are wealthy enough to have a choice, include heavy manual work, domestic service and, in some parts of the Middle East, cash handling jobs including bank teller and jobs that involve providing direct service to a customer. Even poorly educated people will try to avoid such jobs. Thus, employers have a choice of bringing foreigners from poorer countries or of harnessing technology to change the nature of the manual work, or make changes in task design to make the job more attractive to HCNs. This is illustrated in many studies of the fast food sector where organisations such as McDonald's and Burger King regularly rely on cheap imported labour to fill jobs that are generally unattractive to large cohorts of the host population (see the various contributions in Royle and Towers, 2002).

Likewise, Kiriazov et al. (2000) argue that in Eastern European countries the move from the command economy towards capitalism poses serious challenges to many employees. Many of these employees were attached to the characteristics of the old command economy such as job security, guaranteed pay and highly structured jobs, as well as traditions such as nepotism and elements of the black economy that characterised the command economy (Kiriazov et al., 2000). For these reasons, combined with the fact that these employees would have witnessed a high number of business failures among inward-investing MNCs, local employees may not want to work for these MNCs and they may exhibit low levels of motivation if they are employed (ibid.).

In countries such as China, sometimes it is not the job but the supervision that makes locals reluctant to accept the work. The potential recruit may prefer not to work for a foreign supervisor, especially if from a country that is not well regarded by the hosts, or if there is a female supervisor of a male, or a younger supervisor of an older worker, or a supervisor from a different tribe or region. In this regard,

Gamble et al. (2003) provide some useful illustrations of reluctance to work under the supervision of Japanese expatriates in the retail sector.

Inappropriate Selection Methods

Even where there is a pool of available candidates seeking employment, MNCs may use inappropriate selection methods to select appropriate employees (Briscoe and Schuler, 2004; Sparrow, 1999). Selection methods utilised by the MNC may have been chosen based on their suitability in other cultures or are based upon the methods used for expatriates or other parent country nationals. Further, schools and other educational establishments generally fail to adequately prepare students for the methods used in selection and recruitment. Indeed, the concept of being interviewed is a challenge in many cultures. Paper-and-pencil tests might also be unfamiliar to many candidates. It is considered, in some societies, immodest to outline achievements and shameful to ask for a job. In the past, it is likely that a father or uncle would provide the employment and no application or selection was necessary.

This reliance on others to help find a job continues to be widely practised. The 'old school tie' may no longer work in the West but the network built up in business school, golf club or other gathering still helps executives find jobs. Weir and Hutchings (2006) have demonstrated in the Chinese context the significance of 'Guanxi' (the word 'Wasta' is used in a similar context in the Arab world) as the more usual methods used by local people to get jobs for themselves, their relations and friends. Capability is of much less importance than are connections. For a person with a role in selection, it is fully expected, in many places, that power to appoint will be used to give jobs to 'their' people rather than to 'other' people. So tribal or political affiliation, shared nationality (particularly among expatriates) and connections with customers or suppliers are all seen as crucial criteria when deciding who should be offered a job. While this nepotism may seem inappropriate in the global business context, it is important to note that empirical evidence in the European context has highlighted the importance of informal contexts in the selection of individuals for international assignments (see, for example, Harris and Brewster, 1999).

Training

A lack of appropriate training of HCNs is one of the crucial barriers in promoting successful localisation. As we have mentioned above, there are often gaps in the education system that mean employers have to make greater efforts in training than are necessary in societies where the education system and employment needs have been more closely aligned.

In many countries, the major task is not the issue of skills but rather attitudes and behaviours. The education system of the former Soviet Union, for example, produced people with good technical and professional skills but poor work attitudes, symbolised by the phrase 'Employers pretend to pay the staff and the staff pretend to work' (Harry, 2006). Likewise, Kiriazov et al. (2000) posit that the focus in training is on theory rather than application in Eastern European firms, resulting in poor quality levels and high scrap rates. Other examples are found in the GCC, where, culturally, students do not expect to work hard, and hence often resort to bullying of teachers and invigilators to pass and graduate (cf. Kapiszewski, 2001; Yamani, 2000). Students with these attitudes are poor at attending and concentrating on work and bring with them this undisciplined approach to work, so are unable to work at the standards required by most employers. Expatriates often use the lack of self-discipline on the part of the HCNs as a reason or excuse to resist localisation.

Costs

It is not only with regard to training costs that HCNs can be expensive in the short term, particularly for lower-level jobs. Where the number of capable local staff is lower than the labour market requires, local candidates will often be more expensive to employ than expatriates. Thus, in a country such as many of those in the GCC, which is resource and capital rich but labour poor, the HCN will be more expensive than the expatriates employed in similar jobs. This higher cost is driven by low remuneration rates expected by third country nationals (in this context, expatriates from poor countries) or those from countries with high income taxes, and by host governments providing social payments or alternative undemanding work, which makes working for a foreign employer unattractive unless for very high pay. In time, it can be expected that the high costs of locals in relation to expatriates in these atypical situations will decline as governments place more restrictions on the employment of expatriates and have less ability to offer high social security payments or undemanding jobs. Within the GCC, countries such as Bahrain, Oman and Saudi Arabia will soon reach a stage where local labour will be cheaper than that of the expatriates legally employed within the country.

The case study in Box 1 illustrates some of these points.

LOCALISATION IN PRACTICE

While the implementation of a localisation strategy may seem relatively straight-forward, research highlights the complexity of the process in practice.[1] Writing in this context, Gamble posits, based on his empirical study, 'localization is likely to proceed at a much slower pace than its main advocates may wish or anticipate, and that there are practical, cultural, and strategic factors which may, and perhaps should inhibit rapid localization' (Gamble 2000: 883).

Thus, in this section, we briefly outline some of the key stages an organisation should follow in designing a strategy for the localisation of human resources. In this regard, it is clear that the first step in implementing a successful localisation pro-gramme is the design of an appropriate strategy. At this stage, it is important to first weigh up the costs and benefits of implementing a localisation strategy. If localisation is seen as appropriate, then the MNC should formalise and codify clear localisa-tion objectives (Law et al., 2004; Wong and Law, 1999). In this context, it is important to be cognisant of a number of key points.

BOX 1. Case Study: Oman

Oman is one of the poorest of the Gulf Cooperation Council (GCC) States but has been host to many foreign workers, especially from South Asia. Prior to the 1970s, Omanis had mainly been engaged in agriculture and fishing with some trading. Omanis also worked as expatriates in other GCC States, especially in the military. During the 1980s, the government took a fairly casual attitude to localisation, believing that the employers of expatriate workers were committed to creating work for the growing numbers of Omanis, 44 per cent of whom were under 15 years of age (*The Economist*, 2002).

By the mid-1990s, the government had lost patience with the promise of localisation 'tomorrow'. The attempt at partnership between government and employers had not worked, as the employers had focused on short-term gains and preferred to use cheap and compliant foreign workers rather than the potentially more expensive, and probably less easily bullied, local population for a wide range of jobs. So the government used the legislation and regulation to force employers to create employment for Omanis as a requirement of operating within the country.

The banking sector had to rapidly replace expatriates with Omanis so that, by 2000, 95 per cent of clerical jobs and 75 per cent of senior- and middle-level positions had to be occupied by Omanis. Job categories such as human resource managers, bus drivers and delivery staff were to be reserved for Omanis and not only would no work permits be issued for these jobs but severe penalties would be imposed on those employers who did not comply.

Despite warnings from expatriates and employers' businesses, the picture was not of business failure. The banking sector did not collapse and, although they have been forced to invest more in staff and training, the long-term benefits to the country and to businesses have been considerable.

First, Selmer (2004) posits that implementing a process of localisation for purely cost-cutting reasons may be inadvisable. MNCs would be better to pursue localisation when such programmes fit with the strategic goals of the organisation. Thus, localisation should be driven by the search for strategic advantage as opposed to a forced compromise between home and host regimes (Taylor, 1999). Hence, it is important in completing the cost-benefit analysis of the merits of localisation that the MNC ensures that a localisation strategy is congruent with the company's strategic objectives. Empirical research, while highlighting the importance of supportive HR policies, suggests that the development of objectives and planning for localisation is the key stage in ensuring the success of localisation efforts in MNCs (Law et al., 2004).

The second key step in implementing a localisation programme is the *localising stage* (Wong and Law, 1999). During this stage, specific HR policies that support the localisation process should be adopted. However, while developing localisation policies is relatively easy, implementing them is not as simple, and indeed localisation driven from above is not sufficient because implementation of these policies must account for host conditions and requires the buy-in of both host and expatriate managers (Fryxell et al., 2004). Hence, in designing localisation policies, MNCs must provide opportunities and incentivise host managers to promote their development so that they can assume the roles held by expatriates (Law et al., 2004). In this regard, training of HCNs emerges as key. Indeed, Braun and Warner (2002) have demonstrated the significance of in-house training, assignments abroad and mentoring programmes in developing locals in the Chinese context. Significantly, however, Fryxell et al. (2004: 279) note that managers 'cannot expect simple recipes for successful localization'; rather, they must develop a programme based on a congruent package of policies and practices. Indeed, they argue that successful localisation efforts are driven by an appropriate combination of elements rather than a linear relationship between separate elements of the programme. A further key element of this stage is the development of incentives for managers to implement the localisation programme, and this will be considered in greater detail below.

The final stage in the localisation process is the *consolidation stage*, which occurs when HCNs have the necessary skills and competence to assume roles traditionally held by expatriates (Wong and Law, 1999). During this stage, the repatriation of expatriate managers emerges as a key factor. Specifically, if the MNC fails to adequately manage the repatriation process and offer incumbent expatriates attractive packages on repatriation, the whole localisation effort may be jeopardised (Law et al., 2004). This is because the self-interest of expatriates may dictate that they do not engage with the localisation process and perhaps even attempt to thwart efforts at localisation in an attempt to prevent repatriation and the associated career and personal issues associated with the process.

Thus, it should be apparent from the above discussion that localisation is, in practice, a relatively complex proposition. Nonetheless, empirical research in the Chinese context appears to support the view that MNCs who are truly committed to the localisation process are likely to plan for localisation and support the programme with appropriate human resource management policies and practices. Further, it is unlikely the localisation programmes will have much success without top management commitment, planning and goal setting and the implementation of appropriate HR policies and practices (Fryxell et al., 2004; Law et al., 2004). In the final section, we outline the role of expatriates in the localisation process.

THE ROLE OF EXPATRIATES IN THE LOCALISATION OF HUMAN RESOURCES

It has been argued that 'effective localization commences with the incumbent expatriates' (Selmer, 2004: 1094). Expatriates, perhaps because they can earn more abroad than at home, can also be serious obstacle to effective localisation. Expatriates' willingness and competence in developing competent HCNs as their own replacements is hugely significant in determining the success of the localisation process (Keeley, 1999; Law et al., 2004; Rogers, 1999; Selmer, 2004).

The many roles of expatriate assignments include filling skills gaps where skills are not available among host employees. In this regard, if localisation programmes are to be successful then, expatriate assignees must assume the roles of mentor and coach to host employees (Evans et al., 2002; Law et al., 2004). It is imperative that HCNs benefit from the knowledge and skills of the expatriate manager if they are to grow and develop and ultimately assume the responsibilities once held by the expatriate. This may be problematic for a number of reasons. First, expatriates may consider themselves unable to contribute to the localisation process (Selmer, 2004). Not all expatriates will be born mentors, nor will they necessarily have the skills required for developing their HCN managers (Lynton, 1999; Melvin and Sylvester, 1997). In addition, many expatriates may fail to promote localisation due to the short-term nature of their foreign assignment brief, which may promote the achievement of quantitative performance results such as return on investment or quality levels (Selmer, 2004). Further, there is growing evidence that the expatriate's individual self-interest may also potentially restrain localisation initiatives (Fuller, 2005).

Expatriates may give excuses about the locals not being hard working, not being interested nor capable, not trustworthy or too expensive to train and to employ. Empirical research (Selmer, 2004), however, indicates that unwillingness rather than inability tends to impede localisation. In addition, Furst (1999) found that some expatriates neglect their responsibilities for local staff development as soon as they are faced with the uncertainties associated with the repatriation process (Law et al., 2004).

Thus, the challenge for MNCs deploying expatriates and host country employers of international itinerants (Banai and Harry, 2004) in selecting, training and assigning expatriates with the aim of promoting localisation is to articulate the importance of HCN development, to provide training in mentoring skills to the employees and to design reward packages that recognise and promote the localisation of human resources. For those who are motivated by extrinsic rewards, incentive schemes offering a bonus for handing over to a host country national within a specific period can be effective. The role of intrinsic motivators should also be recognised. Many individuals get satisfaction from passing on skills to others, enjoy learning new skills themselves (such as how to improve capability of others in foreign lands) or have the self-satisfaction of a job well done (Banai and Harry, 2004). Thus, the challenge for the international HR manager is to develop a compensation system that accommodates these various motivators and encourages appropriate behaviours in expatriate employees. Further, as noted above, the significance of appropriate repatriation policies should be considered.

The expatriate's support is crucial to the success of the localisation process. Not only can expatriates transfer skills and knowledge, but they can also set an example and pass on attitudes, behaviours and standards that the locals will emulate. If the expatriate is resistant, cynical or incapable, then effective localisation will fail or be postponed. In contrast, if the expatriate is supportive, the localisation is much more likely to succeed (Selmer, 2004), particularly where there is a climate of trust between expatriate and HCN (Fryxell et al., 2004).

Expatriates may fulfil an important role as conduits in disseminating corporate structure and culture to subsidiary, host country employees (Gamble, 2000). They can be a very effective means of passing on knowledge and can greatly assist the process of localisation – or retard the process. Those expatriates linked to a parent organisation can act as champions for the host country nationals being developed. Independent expatriates find that their career path is boosted by the ability to train, to advise and to be consultants helping with localisation (cf. Banai and Harry, 2004). The most effective expatriates will realise that they are no longer employed as 'doers' but as supporters of those who have taken over as producers.

CONCLUSION

In this reading, we have outlined the key forces driving local responsiveness in international business. We then considered the business advantages and disadvantages of local responsiveness. Our discussion then focused more specifically on the localisation of human resources, and again the advantages and disadvantages of this were outlined. After exploring the nature of localisation in practice, we considered the role of expatriates in the localisation process. It should be apparent that localisation is not always the appropriate strategy for MNCs and should not be considered a panacea for problems in subsidiary operations. Nonetheless, what should be apparent from our discussions is that localisation is a complex process and that successful localisation begins with appropriate planning and the development of an appropriate strategy. The implementation of this strategy requires top management support and the development of congruent HR policies that fit with the strategy and the host context. If these conditions are met, localisation can represent an important element of an MNC's internationalisation strategy.

NOTE

1. The majority of this literature emanates from a Chinese context and thus this discussion is primarily based in this context. The potential for study on localisation in different economies is ample. In particular, research on localisation in MNCs in more developed countries would be welcome.

REFERENCES

Banai, M. (1992) 'The ethnocentric staffing policy in multinational corporations: a self-fulfilling prophecy', *International Journal of Human Resource Management*, 3(3): 451–72.

Banai, M. and Harry, W.E. (2004) 'Boundaryless global careers: the international itinerants', *International Studies of Management and Organization*, 34(3): 96–120.

Bartlett, C.A. and Ghoshal, S. (1998) *Managing Across Borders: The Transnational Solution*, 2nd edn, Boston, MA: Harvard Business School Press.

Bennett, D.R. (1996) 'The stalled revolution: business education in Eastern Europe', *Business Horizons*, 39(1): 23–9.

Black, J.S. and Gregerson, H.B. (1992) 'Serving two masters: managing the dual allegiance of expatriate employees', *Sloan Management Review*, 33(4): 61–71.

Boisot, M. and Child, J. (1999) 'Organizations as adaptive systems in complex environments: the case of China', *Organization Science*, 10: 237–52.

Braun, W.H. and Warner, M. (2002) 'Strategic human resource management in western multinationals in China: the differentiation of practices across different ownership forms', *Personnel Review*, 31: 533–79.

Brewster, C. (1991) *The Management of Expatriates*, London: Kogan Page.

Briscoe, D.R. and Schuler, R.S. (2004) *International Human Resource Management*, 2nd edn, London: Routledge.

Child, J. and Yan, Y. (2001) 'Investment and control in international joint ventures: the case of China', *Journal of World Business*, 34: 3–15.

Das, G. (1993) 'Local memoirs of a global manager', *Harvard Business Review*, 71(2): 38–47.

Dowling, P.J. and Welch, D.E. (2004) *International Human Resource Management: Managing People in a Multinational Context*, 4th edn, London: Thomson Learning.

Doz, Y. and Prahalad, C.K. (1986) 'Controlled variety: a challenge for human resource management in the MNC', *Human Resource Management*, 25(1): 55–71.

The Economist (2002) 'People pressure', *The Economist*, 21 March, www.economisl.com, accessed 23 March 2002.

Economist Intelligence Unit (1997) 'Local Heroes', *Business China*, 9: 1–3.

Evans, P., Pucik, V. and Barsouxm, J.L. (2002) *The Global Challenge: Frameworks for International Human Resource Management*, Boston, MA: McGraw-Hill.

Fryxell, G.E., Butler, J. and Choi, A. (2004) 'Successful localization in China: an important element in strategy implementation', *Journal of World Business*, 39: 268–82.

Fuller, T. (2005) 'Skilled help hard to find in China', *International Herald Tribune*, Beirut edition, 16 March.

Furst, B. (1999) 'Performance management for localization', in J. Lee (ed.) *Localization in China: Best Practice*, Hong Kong: Euromoney.

Gamble, J. (2000) 'Localizing management in foreign-invested enterprises in China: practical, cultural and strategic perspectives', *International Journal of Human Resource Management*, 11(5): 883–1004.

Gamble, J., Morris, J. and Wilkinson, B. (2003) 'Japanese and Korean multinationals: the replication and integration of their national business systems in China', *Asian Business and Management*, 2(3): 347–69.

Hailey, J. (1999) 'Localization as an ethical response to internationalization', in C. Brewster and H. Harris (eds) *International HRM*, London: Routledge.

Harris, H. and Brewster, C. (1999) 'The coffee-machine system: how international selection really works' *International Journal of Human Resource Management* 10(2): 488–500.

Harry, W.E. (2006) 'History and HRM in Central Asia', *Thunderbird International Business Review*, 48(1).

Harry, W.E. and Banai, M. (2005) 'International itinerants', in M. Michael, N. Heraty and D. Collings (eds) *International HRM and International Assignments*, Basingstoke: Palgrave Macmillan.

Kapiszewski, A. (2001) *Nationals and Expatriates*, Reading, UK: Ithaca Press.

Keeley, S. (1999) 'The theory and practice of localization', in J. Lee (ed.) *Localization in China: Best Practice*, Hong Kong: Euromoney.

Kiriazov, D., Sullivan, S.E. and Tu, H.S. (2000) 'Business success in Eastern Europe: understanding and customising HRM', *Business Horizons*, 43(1): 39–43.

Lasserre, P. and Ching, P-S. (1997) 'Human resources management in China and the localization challenge', *Journal of Asian Business*, 13(4): 85–100.

Law, K.S., Wong, C.S. and Wang, K.D. (2004) 'An empirical test of the model on managing the localisation of human resources in the People's Republic of China', *International Journal of Human Resource Management*, 15: 635–48.

Litvin, D. (2003) *Empires of Profit: Commerce, Conquest and Corporate Responsibility*, New York: Texere.

Lynton, N. (1999) 'Building a unified corporate culture', in J. Lee (ed.) *Localization in China: Best Practice*, Hong Kong: Euromoney.

Melvin, S. and Sylvester, K. (1997) 'Shipping out', *China Business Review*. May–June: 30–4.

Micklethwait, J. (1996) 'The search for the Asian manager', *The Economist*, 338(7956): S3–S5.

Morris, R.J. and Lawrence, A.T. (2003) 'Nike's dispute with the University of Oregon', in D.C. Thomas (ed.) *Readings and Cases in International Management: A Cross-cultural Perspective*, London: Sage.

Nash, E. (2004) 'Spanish suffer lack of sleep as globalisation ends siesta', *The Independent*, 20 December.

Prahalad, C.K. (2004) *The Fortune at the Bottom of the Pyramid: Eradicating Poverty Through Profits*, London: Wharton School Publishing/Pearson.

Rogers, B. (1999) 'The expatriates in China: a dying species?', in J. Lee (ed.) *Localization in China: Best Practice*, Hong Kong: Euromoney.

Rosenzweig, P.M. and Nohria, N. (1994) 'Influences in human resource management practices in multinational corporations', *Journal of International Business Studies*, 25(2): 229–42.

Royle, T. and Towers, B. (eds) (2002) *Labour Relations in the Global Fast-Food Industry*, London: Routledge.

Ruhs, M. and Godfrey, M. (2002) 'Cheaper labour on tap: wage and productivity trends in Kuwait', unpublished paper developed from ILO Migrant project.

Scullion, H. (1992) 'Strategic recruitment and development of the international manager: some European considerations', *Human Resource Management Journal*, 3(1): 57–69.

Scullion, H. and Brewster, C. (2001) 'Managing expatriates: messages from Europe', *Journal of World Business*, 36(4): 346–65.

Selmer, J. (2004) 'Expatriates' hesitation and the localization of Western business operations in China', *International Journal of Human Resource Management*, 15(6): 1094–107.

Shenkar, O. and Luo, Y. (2004) *International Business*, Hoboken, NJ: Wiley.

Solomon, C.M. (1995) 'Learning to manage host-country nationals', *Personnel Journal*, March: 60–7.

Sparrow, P. (1999) 'International recruitment, selection and Assessment,' in P. Joynt and B. Morton (eds) *The Global HR Manager: Creating the Seamless Organization*, London: Institute of Personnel and Development.

Sparrow, P., Brewster, C. and Harris, H. (2004) *Globalizing Human Resource Management*, London: Routledge.

Taylor, B. (1999) 'Patterns of control within Japanese manufacturing plants in China: doubts about Japanization in Asia', *Journal of Management Studies*, 36(6): 853–74.

Warner, M. (1985) 'Training China's managers', *Journal of General Management*, 11(2): 12–26.

Weir, D. and Hutchings, K. (2006) 'Guanxi and Wasta: a review of the traditional ways of networking in China and the Arab world and their implications for international business', *Thunderbird International Business Review*, 48(1).

Wong, C.S. and Law, K.S. (1999) 'Managing localization of human resources in the PRC: a practical model', *Journal of World Business*, 34: 26–40.

Yamani, M. (2000) *Changed Identities*, London: Royal Institute of International Affairs.

Ingmar Björkman

PETER HANSON: BUILDING A WORLD-CLASS PRODUCT DEVELOPMENT CENTRE FOR HI TECH SYSTEMS IN CHINA

INTRODUCTION

PETER HANSON, the Head of the Product Development Centre (PDC) of Hi Tech Systems in Shanghai had been in China for five months. He was the first person in the Product Development Centre when he arrived in Shanghai in April 2000. Thinking back at the period he had spent in China so far, he felt that things had gone quite well. The PDC was now up and running and today, on September 12, 2000, Peter welcomed its sixteenth employee.

Nonetheless, Peter still had a number of concerns. The PDC was still rather small and it was possible for him to interact with and influence all employees. As the PDC would grow significantly over the next year, he wanted to make sure to create a healthy and positive atmosphere and orientation towards work. His vision was to create a world-class PDC in Shanghai, but how to do that in a country that mainly was a recipient of technological know-how from abroad, and what measures should be taken to convince other parts of Hi Tech Systems to engage in joint development projects with his PDC? And even if he managed to develop the competencies needed to build a world-class PDC through careful recruitment and selection as well as good investments in training and development, how were they to retain the employees in a market where job hopping was common, money apparently an important reason why people switched jobs, and well-educated people had ample opportunities in other companies? Basically, his question was: would lessons on how to manage human resources obtained in North America and Europe apply also in the People's Republic of China?

PRODUCT DEVELOPMENT IN HI TECH SYSTEMS

Hi Tech Systems was established in Stockholm, Sweden, in 1976. By the late 1980s, it had become known as one of Europe's most innovative firms in its industry. The growth continued in the 1990s, with firm profitability remaining healthy. The company is currently one of the three largest firms in its industry. Hi Tech Systems' global manufacturing comprises six production facilitates in five different countries on three different continents. Approximately 45 percent of sales come from Europe, but Japan, China and, in particular, the United States have become important markets.

Product development is seen as key to the success of Hi Tech Systems. Almost 20 percent of Hi Tech Systems' employees are working in research and development. Hi Tech Systems has Product Development Centres (PDCs) in Sweden, the UK, the US, Japan, Hong Kong (China) and, most recently, mainland China. There is a global PDC management group headed by Johan Lind that consists of all the PDC heads, which convenes once a month. Johan Lind reports to the head of global product development in Hi Tech Systems, Anders Jonsson.

The responsibility for product development programs resides with the global business lines and the "platforms" (such as Japanese user interface). Research programs within the business lines that lead to actual products also draw on the work being done within the platforms. In each PDC, people work on projects related to both Hi Tech Systems business lines and platforms.

A full-grown PDC has some 400–500 employees, a variety of competencies, and is expected to have the capability needed to develop an entire new product. There are several reasons why the company has established a whole portfolio of PDCs. First, different areas differ in terms of technologies and standards relevant for the business. Therefore, it makes sense to locate research and development activities in locations where the technologies reside. Second, by dispersing PDCs to different parts of the world, the company can move product creation activities in response to environmental and market changes. Third, it enables Hi Tech Systems to draw on human resources not available in one location. Hi Tech Systems has traditionally done most of its product creation in Sweden, but as a result of growth there are not enough engineering students in the whole country to satisfy its needs. Fourth, products need to be local adapted and this is easier to carry out locally than in a distant PDC.

In a typical research program, most of the work on the key components of a new product is done within one single "core" PDC. Within each project, there is a fairly clear distribution of responsibilities across the PDCs involved. Other 'peripheral' PDCs are typically involved in developing locally adapted variances of the product. Most of the work has typically already been done in the core PDC before the other PDCs get involved (although, in order to ensure that the necessary local adaptations of the final product can be made at a later stage, people from each of the geographical regions are involved in steering groups during the conceptualization stage). The knowledge transfer mostly takes place through people from the PDCs who visit the core PDC for 1–3 months to work with the product development people before they return to their own units. At the point when the project has been established in the peripheral PDCs, the focal project leader reports to the global head of the focal product development project and to the head of their own PDC. Heavy emphasis is put on establishing and following up project milestones.

HI TECH SYSTEMS IN CHINA

The People's Republic of China started opening up to the outside world in 1979. In 1992, the Hi Tech Systems group established a representative office in Shanghai and, in 1995, a first joint venture was established. By the beginning of 2000, Hi Tech Systems already had four joint ventures and wholly owned subsidiaries in China. Hi Tech Systems had become a significant player in the rapidly growing Chinese market, where it was competing with other Western, Japanese, and also increasingly strong local competitors. China had become one of Hi Tech Systems' most important markets. Most of the products sold in China were produced in the firm's local factories.

However, Hi Tech Systems had so far no Product Development Centre in China. Towards the end of the 1990s, there was a growing consensus that this neglect had to be rectified. A decision to establish a PDC in Shanghai was made by Hi Tech Systems' management board in January 2000. Peter Hanson was chosen to head the PDC.

PETER HANSON

Peter Hanson was born in California in 1962. After graduating from college with a major in management, his first job was with a major US industrial firm. As a part of his job, in 1989–90 he spent 6 months in Hong Kong. During his assignment in Hong Kong, he fell in love with Asia and China. Since that moment he knew that he was going to return to Asia. Peter also met his future wife, who moved with him to the US. In 19991–93, Peter did an MBA and then started to work in a small start-up company. In late 1997, Peter was persuaded by one of his previous colleagues to join Hi Tech Systems. When joining Hi Tech Systems, Peter was appointed operations manager. After some months, he was asked to head the engineering unit of the new Product Development Centre that was built up in Philadelphia. Peter accepted the job, which meant that he would be responsible for the largest unit of the PDC. Peter and his new boss, Curtis O'Neill, soon became very close, with Peter acting as the second in charge of the PDC. Peter recalls:

> I learnt a lot from Curtis. He was very people-oriented. He would make sure that you get an opportunity to get into an environment where you either learn or you don't. He gave people lots of challenges, lots of learning opportunities, where they could prove themselves. He would also quite directly point to areas of improvement. He also underlined the importance of networking, how to build networks of people that you can draw on.

One of the things that Peter learned soon after joining Hi Tech Systems was the importance of having good personal contacts within the company. The Hi Tech Systems global product development worked, to a significant extent, through informal contacts across units and it was crucial to be well connected. His choice of the five product line managers in his department reflected this view. While people in the Philadelphia unit expected and pressured him to choose local people for the positions, he selected three expatriates and only two local employees:

> People thought I was taking promotions away from Philadelphia. I had my own views in mind – we needed to be connected to the other centers. If you're well connected people trust you to do a good job within a research program, and it is also easier to get technical help if needed. I then used lots of interviews with the candidates to convince people about their capabilities and to get some buy-in from the other managers. I also made sure to tell people that the objective was to fill the positions with local people in two-three years. In fact, the line managers had as an explicit objective to develop a local replacement of themselves.

During the next 18 months, Peter visited Sweden several times. He often took part in the global PDC group meetings as O'Neill's stand-in. The global PDC management also knew that he was interested in returning to Asia, something Peter had mentioned from the outset in his performance management discussions.

ESTABLISHING THE PRODUCT DEVELOPMENT CENTRE

During the summer of 1999, the global PDC management group decided that a feasibility study on the possible creation of a PDC in the People's Republic of China should be carried out. In October 1999, Peter was asked to become involved in the project. His task was to examine the data and write a report on whether or not a PDC should be established and, if so, where in China it should be located. By that time, Peter also knew that he would be the preferred candidate as head of the PDC (if approved). In January 2000, the Hi Tech Systems global management board approved the establishment of a PDC in Shanghai. One of the advantages of Shanghai was that the PDC would be able to use the existing Hi Tech Systems organization in the city. It would be easier to learn from the experiences of Hi Tech Systems' largest Chinese production and its China headquarters, both of which were located in Shanghai. In February, Peter went to China on a pre-visit mainly to meet with people in the Hi Tech Systems organization.

When it became clear that the PDC would be established, Peter started to look for people. There was no established policy for people management within the global product creation organization, but Peter was told to draw on the HR department at the Hi Tech Systems group in China for support. He thought he would initially need approximately ten positions for expatriates, and it would be of crucial importance to find suitable people for the key positions:

> It was networking all the way – the social networks were very important! There were many people who knew that I would do it and some of them

contacted me. I contacted and spoke to lots of people in all parts of the
Hi Tech Systems organization. I wanted the candidates to have experience
in launching Hi Tech Systems products in China. They should know the
Chinese environment and culture. This meant that there were only a very
small number of people who fulfilled my criteria. And they had to commit
to staying at least two or even three years, which is not usual in Hi Tech
Systems. Towards the end of the period they start hunting for another job
anyhow.

Peter finally identified four people that he wanted: one Swede, and three persons
from the People's Republic of China who had studied and worked for several years
abroad (two in the United States, one in Sweden). One of them he already knew in
advance, the others he had identified through his networking activities. All the Chinese
had a strong educational background, with degrees from top Chinese universities
before leaving the country for overseas graduate studies. Everybody had at least some
experience in leading their own teams:

I talked a lot to them. Have they thought about living in China? Were they
(the Chinese) conscious about the challenges involved in going back to China?
For instance, people may be jealous of them making much more money,
travelling abroad and having much higher positions than they themselves
had? Have they realized that it's going to be a start-up operation, and that
it may be difficult to get things started and people on board?

To persuade the people he wanted to accept relocating to China, Peter tried to
create a positive and challenging vision for the PDC. To date, Hi Tech Systems had
probably not done enough to meet the needs of the Chinese-speaking countries.
Did they want to become a part of the process of creating a world-class PDC in
China? The PDC would become responsible for the Chinese user interface platform
– did they want to participate in the challenge of its development? Being restricted
by the company's expatriate compensation policy, which was built on a standardized
job grading system, he was able to offer competitive but not exceptional salaries. He
finally managed to persuade all four candidates to accept a job in his PDC. They all
knew each other from their previous jobs. During the late spring of 2000, he found
some additional people in the global Hi Tech Systems organization who also agreed
to taking up jobs in Shanghai:

A part of my strategy was to get people from different Product Development
Centers. By having these people in my organization we are able to easily
reach into the other PDCs, which is particularly important in the beginning
as we are dependent on doing parts of larger projects in collaboration with
other centers. If we have good people who have credibility from each of the
other PDCs, we will be recognized and seen as trustworthy.

But Peter did not see technical competence as the only important criterion. In his view:

> 80 percent is attitude. It doesn't matter what you can do, if you lack drive. With drive you can always fill in the gaps ... Perhaps it has something to do with my own background. I have had to manage without an engineering education In an organization and industry that are extremely technology-intensive.

The PDC was to report to the Global PDC management and to the Hi Tech Systems China country management. As agreed upon with the Global PDC management group, PDC Shanghai would be responsible for product creation in the Chinese language area, including mainland China, Hong Kong, Singapore, and Taiwan. In the beginning, it would mostly do limited parts of larger products in collaboration with other global PDCs, working, for example, on software and on Chinese-specific applications. The long-term vision was eventually to have the competencies to be able to build new products in China.

THE START OF THE PRODUCT DEVELOPMENT CENTRE

Peter and his family finally arrived in Shanghai on April 12, 2000. The next employee arrived from overseas in May, and by September the unit had 16 employees, half of whom had been recruited from abroad. Peter's estimate was that, long term, 15–20 percent of the employees would be from overseas but that it would take 3–4 years to decrease the proportion of expatriates to that level:

> When you build a home, first you build the foundations. You need to make sure that the foundations are in place – the recruitment process, human resources management, finance. Then you need key managers to build the organization around.

In the recruitment of local employees, the PDC was collaborating closely with Hi Tech Systems' human resources (HR) department. After job descriptions and job grade levels had been determined by the PDC, the HR department would announce the position using both advertisements and the Hi Tech System home page, receive CVs, do a first screening of the candidates, and arrange for interviews and assessment of the applicants. The interviews were done by a minimum of two PDC managers, who also acted as observers in the assessment centers organized by the HR department. For the assessment of applicants in China, Hi Tech Systems used "The Space Shuttle." The Space Shuttle was a game where the applicants worked together in a group with the objective of reaching an agreement on how to build a space shuttle. By observing the applicants involved in a problem-solving situation where they also interacted with each other, the observers could draw their own conclusions about the applicants. Recruitment and selection of local employees largely resembled practices used elsewhere in the global Hi Tech Systems organization.

Some other Western firms had apparently made larger adjustments in their selection practices in China. For instance, Peter had heard that Shell had changed its selection practices based on an in-depth study of its existing Chinese managers and entry-level management trainees. Traditionally Shell focused on analytical and problem-solving abilities. However, when, for example, applicants were asked to identify the strengths and weakness of the Chinese educational system and then say what they would do to remedy deficiencies if they were the Minister of Education, if there were any responses at all they tended to be uniformly bland. It was also found that the kind of "Who would you throw out of the airplane?" question commonly used in the West also tended to engender a "learned helplessness effect" on the part of Chinese university graduates, who have excelled at clearly defined tasks in a familiar environment and who had "learnt" to respond to the unfamiliar by simple freezing. Shell's system identified the Chinese education system as the chief culprit. The educational system is hierarchical, extremely competitive and almost exclusively based on examination of rote learning. Problem-oriented interaction among strangers is unnatural and problematic for most Chinese. Therefore, to evaluate the decision-making skills, communication skills, analytical problem-solving abilities, and leadership capabilities of the applicants based on hypothetical cases solved in assessment situations may be very difficult. As a result, Shell's study recommended the use of real case studies rather than hypothetical questions.[1]

Competence development would probably be key to the success of the PDC, both in terms of localizing its operations and in producing good results. By mid-September, the new employees had mostly worked on small projects, such as setting up the IT system. A couple of people had also been sent to Hong Kong to work in the field with experienced engineers for 3 weeks. Formal training would be important, and the PDC would need to collaborate with Hi Tech Systems' HR unit on the course program offered to the PDC employees. To what extent should the Chinese employees receive the same content and delivery as Hi Tech Systems employees elsewhere? In China, the Confucian- and communist-influenced Chinese educational system in which the learner is a mostly passive receiver who is obedient to instructor tends to create linear rather than lateral thinking and precedent-based problem-solving where the focus in on getting the "right" answer.

Nonetheless, hands-on on-the-job coaching would be even more important for the development of the new employees. Most of the responsibility for coaching would obviously be on the experienced Hi Tech Systems employees but also important would be to bring in people from other PDCs for visits in Shanghai. Coaching on the part of the expatriates would be extremely important, Peter thought. He had already been discussing it at length with the managers that he had hired, but he was not sure whether or not that was enough, especially not when the unit would grow over the next couple of years. He certainly would not be able to coach all expatriates by himself.

In Hi Tech Systems' globally standardized performance management system, all employees should carry out performance management discussions with their superiors. Within this system, individual objectives are established and followed up. According to company policy, the individual's objectives must be specific and, if possible, measurable; key activities for how to reach the objectives shall be specified; criteria for how to evaluate the performance agreed upon; and, finally, development plans decided upon. Peter's aim was that every new employee would do their first performance management discussion within a month after they joined the organization. All Hi Tech Systems superiors in China were trained in how to use the system but there was still a question of how the "Western" system would be implemented In the Chinese culture characterized by respect for hierarchy, face, and harmonious personal relationships.

Peter had also given the question of the relationship between employee competence development and career progress quite a lot of thought. In Hi Tech Systems worldwide, people achieved high status by having excellent technological knowledge and skills rather than having made a successful career as a manager. However:

> In China especially the young people expect to get a new title every year; otherwise they had better start looking for another company. The speed of expected career progression clearly differs from the West. To develop the level of competence required for the next career step will be a challenge. Can they achieve it once a year? I think very few will.

The compensation of employees would follow the Hi Tech Systems policies. Managers and team leaders were compensated based on both business and individual performance. High-level executives and senior managers had a large business performance component in their bonus system, while the compensation of lower-level employees was mostly based on their individual performance. In the Shanghai PDC, individual performance would be evaluated based on 4–5 objectives. Peter required that the objectives had to be measurable on a ten-point scale. For instance, a manager's performance could be evaluated based on the manager's ability to fill positions in his/her group, employee satisfaction (as measured in company-wide surveys), employee turnover, the team's ability to stay within the budget, and some measure of quality (to be determined in discussions between the person and Peter). Each person's performance was evaluated every 6 months, and bonuses paid accordingly. The target bonus was 10 percent of the person's base salary, with 20 percent as maximum. People working on a specific development project were evaluated not every 6 months but the evaluation rather followed the milestones of the project. The bonus element was also somewhat larger for people working on projects than for other PDC members.

Peter believed that the compensation system would work well in China. Having clear objectives and rewards linked with their fulfillment would help send a clear message to the employees: your performance equals what you deliver – not the personal connections, or "*guanxi*," that you have! Nonetheless, at least in the start-up phase of the PDC it might be somewhat difficult to establish feasible objectives for the employees. Additionally, there had been reports from other foreign firms that there was a tendency among local employees to set objectives so that they would be reached by the subordinates.

LOOKING TOWARDS THE FUTURE

Analyzing the start-up phase of PDC, Peter found that many things had gone quite smoothly. For instance, the two Chinese "returnees" who had joined PDC so far (the third was still in Sweden but would relocate next month) seemed to do well. Although China had changed a lot since they left the country some 10 years ago, their interaction with the local employees seemed to go well.

Managing the growth would certainly be a challenge in the next couple of years, Peter thought. For instance, local employees would have to be taught to manage themselves and to take responsibility – behaviors not automatically understood and accepted in the Chinese environment. While the Hi Tech Systems culture was non-hierarchical and meritocratic, the Chinese culture is hierarchical, and the "face" of superiors could be at stake if subordinates made their own initiatives rather than waiting for orders from their superiors. Furthermore, since the communist regime from 1949, the Chinese have been discouraged from engaging in competitive and entrepreneurial behavior. The Chinese proverb "the early bird gets shot" aptly illustrates the reluctance on the part of Chinese employees to engage in the kind of innovative behavior that Peter wanted to see in the PDC. On the other hand, Peter had seen several Chinese changing their behavior significantly abroad. What should they do to promote this behavior also in the Shanghai PDC?

Peter was also looking for somebody to work closely with Hi Tech Systems' HR function. This person would work closely with him and the line managers to define future competence needs and how they could be met. "So far I guess I have fulfilled this role, but I'm afraid that neither me nor line managers will have time enough to pay sufficient attention to this issue in the future."

Finally, Peter was concerned about retention. "I have also been told by [a human resources expert] that a 1 renminbi salary difference may make a person switch job." Peter believed that money would not be key to retaining the employees, though. To create a positive, family-like atmosphere might help. Peter had started a tradition of everyone in his unit meeting for a snack on Monday mornings. He also made a conscious effort to spend time talking to people in the department. Furthermore, he had invited people out for lunch and dinner. To maintain a positive relationship between the foreign and local employees, he tried to coach the expatriates not to mention how much money they made, how they lived, and how cheap they found most things to be in Shanghai (say "reasonable" instead, was his advice). All this had apparently contributed to there starting to circulate rumors that "things are done a bit differently in PDC." He was now thinking of whether to involve the employees' families in some way. Formal team-building exercises should probably also be done.

There were so many things to do . . . Peter looked out of his window in one of the many new multi-story buildings in the Pudong area of Shanghai – where should he start?

NOTE

1.   The Economist Intelligence Unit (1998) *China on the Couch.* September 28, 3–4.

Evalde Mutabazi and
C. Brooklyn Derr

SOCOMETAL: REWARDING AFRICAN WORKERS

IT WAS A MOST UNUSUAL MEETING at a local cafe in Dakar. Diop, a young Senegalese engineer who was educated at one of Frances's elite engineering *grandes écoles* in Lyon, was meeting with N'Diaye, a model factory worker to whom other workers from his tribe often turned when there were personal or professional difficulties. N'Diaye was a chief's son, but he didn't belong to the union and he was not an official representative of any group within the factory.

Socometal is a metal container and can company. While multinational, this particular plant is a joint venture wherein 52 percent is owned by the French parent company and 48 percent is Senegalese. Over the last 20 years, Socometal has grown in size from 150 to 800 employees and it has returns of about 400 million FCFA (African francs) or $144 million. The firm is often held up as a model in terms of its Africanization of management policies, whereby most managers are now West African with only 8–10 top managers coming from France.

During the meeting, N'Diaye asked Diop if he would accept an agreement to pay each worker for 2 extra hours in exchange for a 30 percent increase in daily production levels. If so, N'Diaye would be the guarantor for this target production level that would enable the company to meet the order in the shortest time period. "If you accept my offer," he said with a smile, "we could even produce more. We are at 12,000 [units] a day, but we've never been confronted with this situation. I would never have made this proposal to Mr. Bernard but, if you agree today, I will see that the 20,000 [unit] level is reached as of tomorrow evening. I'll ask each worker to find ways of going faster, to communicate this to the others and to help each other if they have problems."

Mr. Olivier Bernard, a graduate of Ecole Centrale in Paris (one of France's more prestigious engineering schools), was the French production manager, and Diop was the assistant production manager. Mr. Bernard was about 40 and had not succeeded at climbing the hierarchal ladder in the parent company. Some report that this was due to his tendency to be arrogant, uncommunicative, and negative. His family lived in a very nice neighborhood in Marseille, and it was his practice to come to Dakar, precisely organize the work using various flowcharts, tell Diop exactly what was expected by a certain date, and then return to France for periods of 2–6 weeks. This time he maintained that he had contracted a virus and needed to return for medical treatment.

Shortly before Mr. Bernard fell ill, Socometal agreed to a contract requiring them to reach, in a short time, a volume of production never before achieved. Mr. Bernard, after having done a quick calculation, declared, "We'll never get that from our workers – *c'est impossible*!" After organizing as best he could, he left for Marseille.

Diop pondered what N'Diaye had proposed, and then he sought the opinions of influential people in different departments. Some of the French and Italian expatriates told him they were sure that the workers would not do overtime, but most agreed it was worth a try. Two days after his meeting with N'Diaye, Diop felt confident enough to take the risk. The next morning, N'Diaye and Diop met in front of the factory and Diop gave his agreement on the condition that the 30 percent rise in daily production levels be reached that evening. He and the management would take a final decision on a wage increase only after assessing the results and on evaluating the ability of the workers to maintain this level of production in the long run.

The reasons given by the French and Italian expatriates for why the Senegalese would not perform overtime or speed up their productivity are interesting. One older French logistics manager said, "Africans aren't lazy but they work to live, and once they have enough they refuse to do more. It won't make any sense to them to work harder or longer for more pay." And the Italian human resource manager exclaimed, "We already tried 2 years ago to get them to do more faster. We threatened to fire anyone caught going too slow or missing more than 1 day's work per month, and we told them they would all get bonuses if they reached the production target. We had the sense that they were laughing behind our backs and doing just enough to keep their jobs while maintaining the same production levels."

Four days after their first negotiation, the contract between Diop and N'Diaye went into action. Throughout the day, N'Diaye gave his job on the line to two of his colleagues in order to have enough time and energy to mobilize all the workers. The workers found the agreement an excellent initiative. "This will be a chance to earn a bit more money, but especially to show them [the French management] that we're more capable than they think," declared one of the Senegalese foremen. From its first day of application, the formula worked wonders. Working only 1 extra hour per day, every work unit produced 8 percent more than was forecast by Diop and N'Diaye. Over the next 2 months, the daily production level oscillated between 18,000 and 22,000 units per day – between 38 and 43 percent more than the previous daily production. It was at this production level, never experienced during the history of the company, that Mr. Bernard found things when he returned from his illness.

"I", said Diop, "was very happy to see the workers so proud of their results, so satisfied with their pay raise, and finally really involved in their work . . . In view of some expatriates' attitudes it was a veritable miracle ... But, instead of rejoicing, Mr. Bernard reproached me for giving 2 hours' pay to the workers, who were only really doing 1 hour more than usual. 'By making this absurd decision,' he said, 'you have put the management in danger of losing its authority over the workers. You have acted against house rules ... You have created a precedent too costly for our business. Now, we must stop this ridiculous operation as quickly as possible. We must apply work regulations.' And he slammed the door in my face before I had the time to say anything. After all, he has more power than me in this company, which is financed 52 percent by French people. Nevertheless, I thought I would go to see the managing director and explain myself and present my arguments. I owed this action to N'Diaye and his workers, who had trusted me, and I didn't care if it made Bernard any angrier."

In the meantime, the workers decided to maintain the new production level in order to honor their word to N'Diaye and Diop. A foreman and friend of N'Diaye stated, "At least he knows how to listen and speak to us like men."

The foreman indicated, however, that they might return to the former production level if Bernard dealt with them as he did before.

CASE DISCUSSION QUESTIONS

1. What are the underlying cultural assumptions for Mr. Bernard and how are these different from the basic assumptions of N'Diaye and Diop?
2. What would you do if you were Bernard's boss, the managing director?
3. In what ways is a reward system a cultural phenomenon? How might you design an effective reward system for Senegal?

Roger Hallowell, David Bowen, and Carin-Isabel Knoop

FOUR SEASONS GOES TO PARIS

Europe is different from North America, and Paris is very different. I did not say difficult. I said different.

A senior Four Seasons manager

THE LINKAGE BETWEEN SERVICE CULTURE AND COMPETITIVE ADVANTAGE

THE ENDURING SUCCESS of service organizations such as Southwest Airlines, the Walt Disney Company, Wal-Mart, and USAA (among others) is frequently attributed in no small degree to their corporate cultures. These companies have built and maintained organizational cultures in which everyone is focused on delivering high customer value, including service, and individuals behave accordingly. The culture influences how employees behave, which, in turn, shapes the value that customers receive, in part through the thousands of daily encounters between employees and customers.

Corporate culture has been linked to competitive advantage in companies, for better or worse,[1] and in service companies, in particular.[2] Culture is so important in service companies because of its effect on multiple factors affecting customer value, factors as critical as employee behavior and as mundane (but important) as facility cleanliness. These aspects are especially visible to customers, who often co-produce a service with employees. In many services, employee and customer interactions take place continually, in many parts of the organization, so that no realistic amount of supervision can ever exercise sufficient control over employee behavior. Under these circumstances, culture becomes one of management's most effective, if unobtrusive, tools to influence employee thoughts, feelings, and, most importantly, behavior.

UNDERSTANDING CORPORATE CULTURE

Our model of corporate culture, which uses Schein[3] as a point of departure, consists of the following four components: underlying assumptions, values, employee perceptions of management practices, and cultural artifacts.

Underlying Assumptions

These are basic assumptions regarding the workplace, such as the assumption that subordinates should fulfill their job requirements as a condition of employment.

Values

These are those things that are viewed as most important in an organizational setting, such as cost control, customer satisfaction, and teamwork.

Values exist in two forms in organizations. The first is what can be termed "espoused values," which are what senior managers or company publications say the values are.

The second form is "enacted values," which are what employees infer the values to be. Although enacted values, per se, are invisible, employees infer what they are by examining the evidence found in the next two components of culture: management practices and cultural artifacts. These two components are more readily observed than assumptions and values.

Employee Perceptions of Management Practices (Particularly Relating to Human Resources): Policies and Behaviors

Employees' views of practices such as selection, training, performance appraisal, job design, reward systems, supervisory practices, and so on shape their perceptions of what values are actually being enacted in a setting. For example, although customer service may be an espoused value, if job applicants are not carefully screened on service attitude, or if employees who provide great service are not recognized and rewarded, then employees will not believe that management truly values service. In short: culture is what employees perceive that management believes.

Cultural Artifacts

These include heroes, rituals, stories, jargon, and tangibles such as the appearance of employees and facilities. Again, given the espoused value of customer service, if jargon used to characterize customers is usually derogatory, then a strong service culture is unlikely to emerge.

In contrast, if espoused values are enacted – and thus reflected in policies, management behaviors, and cultural artifacts – then a culture may emerge in which senior management and employees share similar service-relevant thoughts, feelings, and patterns of behavior. This behavior has the potential to enhance customer value and contribute to competitive advantage.

EXPORTING CORPORATE CULTURE: CAN CULTURE TRAVEL ACROSS BORDERS?

If a company succeeds in creating a corporate culture that contributes to competitive advantage in its home country, can it successfully "export" that corporate culture to another country – particularly if that country's national culture is strongly distinct, as is the case in France?

The Issue of Flexibility Versus Consistency

Will an organization's *corporate* culture "clash" or "fit" with a different *national* culture? The key consideration here is what components of corporate culture link most tightly to competitive advantage and, as a consequence, must be managed *consistently* across country borders – even if they seem to clash with the culture of the new country. Alternatively, are there components of culture that are not critical to the linkage? If so, *flexibility* may enhance the competitiveness of the corporate culture given the different national culture.[4]

One way to frame this analysis is around whether the potential clash between corporate and national culture is over the corporate values themselves, i.e., *what* they are, or over the manner of their implementation, i.e., *how* they are enacted (specifically, management practices and cultural forms). Is there a clash between core corporate values and core country values? If so, and if those core values are critical to competitive advantage, then perhaps the company cannot be successful in that setting. If the clash is over how values are enacted, then some management practices or cultural forms can be modified in the new setting. However, this requires managers to ask which practices or forms can be modified, enhancing the competitive advantage of the corporate culture, and which practices, if modified, will undermine corporate culture.

In short, all of the elements of corporate culture can be thought of as the threads in a sweater: when a thread sticks out of a sweater, sometimes it is wisely removed, enhancing the overall appearance. However, sometimes removing a thread will unravel the entire sweater. Managers must determine which aspects of their corporate cultures will "stick out" in a new national environment and whether modifying or eliminating them will enhance the organization or weaken it.

FOUR SEASONS HOTELS AND RESORTS: OVERVIEW

In 2002, Four Seasons Hotels and Resorts was arguably the world's leading operator of luxury hotels, managing 53 properties in 24 countries. Being able to replicate "consistently exceptional service" around the world and across cultures was at the heart of the chain's international success and sustained advantage.

For Four Seasons, "consistently exceptional service" meant providing high-quality, truly personalized service to enable guests to *maximize the value of their time*, however guests defined doing so. Corporate culture contributed to the firm's success in two ways. First was through the values that the organization espoused.

For Four Seasons, these were personified in the Golden Rule: "Treat others as you wish they would treat you." Second was the set of behaviors that employees and managers displayed, in effect the enactment of the firm's values. The organizational capability of translating core values into enacted behaviors created competitive advantage at Four Seasons. Doing so required managers to address a central question as they expanded into new countries: what do we need to keep consistent, and what should be flexible, i.e., what should we adapt to the local market?

Performance

Four Seasons generally operated (as opposed to owned) mid-sized luxury hotels and resorts. From 1996 through 2000 (inclusive), Four Seasons increased revenues from $121 million to $347.5 million and earnings from $55.7 million to $125.8 million, a 22.6 percent compounded annual growth rate (CAGR). Operating margins increased from 58.8 percent to 67.9 percent during the same period. Four Seasons' 2001 revenue per room (RevPAR), an important hospitality industry measure, was 32 percent above that of its primary US competitors and 27 percent higher than that of its European competitors. Growth plans were to open five to seven new luxury properties per year, predominantly outside of North America.

Four Seasons entered the French market by renovating and operating the Hotel George V, a historic Parisian landmark. The hotel was renamed the Four Seasons Hotel George V Paris (hereafter, "F. S. George V").

International Structure

Each Four Seasons property was managed by a general manager responsible for supervising the day-to-day operations of a single property. Compensation was, in part, based on the property's performance. Hotel general managers had a target bonus of 30 percent of base compensation. 25 percent of the bonus was based on people measures (employee attitudes), 25 percent on product (service quality), and 50 percent on profit.

Four Seasons' management believed that the firm's regional management structure was a key component of its ability to deliver and maintain the highest and most consistent service standards at each property in a cost-effective manner. General managers reported directly to one of the 13 regional vice presidents or directly to one of the two senior vice presidents, operations. A regional marketing director, an area director of finance, and a regional human resources director completed each support team. The majority of these individuals were full-time employees of a Four Seasons-managed property, with a portion of their time devoted to regional matters, including both routine management and deciding how to customize Four Seasons' operating practice to the region.

Management

Four Seasons' top management team was noted for its longevity, many having been at the firm tor over 25 years. Characteristics that executives attributed to their peers included an international flair, a respect for modesty and compassion, and a "no excuses" mentality.

Italian in Italy, French in France

The firm's top managers were very comfortable in a variety of international settings. Antoine Corinthios, president, Europe, Middle East, and Africa, for example, was said to be "Italian in Italy, French in France." Born and educated in Cairo, Corinthios then spent 20 years in Chicago but described himself as a world citizen. He was as much of a cultural chameleon as he wanted Four Seasons hotels to be. "When I speak the language of the environment I am in, I start to think in the language I am in and adapt to that culture. If you are going global, you cannot be one way," he explained.

No Bragging, No Excuses

Modesty, compassion, and discipline were also important. A manager who stayed with Four Seasons from the prior management of the George V described the Four Seasons due diligence team that came to the property as "very professional and not pretentious; detail oriented; and interested in people. They did not come telling me that all I did was wrong," he remembered, "and showed a lot of compassion. The people are good, but still modest – many people in the industry can be very full of themselves." Importantly, excuses were not tolerated at Four Seasons. "Oh, but we have just been open a year" or "The people here do not understand" were not acceptable statements.

Strong Allegiance to the Firm

Both corporate and field managers often referred to the firm as a "family," complete with rules, traditions, and tough love. There was a strong "one-firm sentiment" on the part of managers in the field; they worked for the firm, not for the individual property to which they were assigned. For example, a general manager explained, "We are happy to let stars go to other properties to help them."

Service Orientation

Customer service extended to all levels in the organization. Managers sometimes assisted in clearing restaurant tables in passing. "If I see that something needs to get done," a manager explained, "I do it."

FOUR SEASONS' APPROACH TO INTERNATIONAL GROWTH

> Today, we have opened enough properties overseas that we can go into any city or town and pull people together to fulfill our mission.
>
> Isadore Sharp, Founder and CEO

Diversity and Singularity

One of the things Four Seasons managers were wary about was being perceived as an "American" company. They found it useful in Europe to position Four Seasons as the Canadian company it was. One noted, "The daughter of a property owner once told us, 'I do not want you to be the way Americans are.' She assumed that Americans say, 'Do it my way or take the highway.' Canadians are seen as more internationally minded and respectful of other value systems."

According to Corinthios, "Our strength is our diversity and our singularity. While the essence of the local culture may vary, the process for opening and operating a hotel is the same everywhere." He continued:

> My goal is to provide an international hotel to the business or luxury leisure traveler looking for comfort and service. The trick is to take it a couple of notches up, or sideways, to adapt to the market you are in. Our standards are universal, e.g., getting your message on time, clean room, good breakfast; being cared for by an engaging, anticipating and responding staff; being able to treat yourself to an exciting and innovative meal – these are global. This is the fundamental value. What changes is that people do it with their own style, grace, and personality; in some cultures you add the strong local temperament. For example, an Italian concierge has his own style and flair. In Turkey or Egypt you experience different hospitality.

As a result, "Each hotel is tailor made" and adapted to its national environment, noted David Crowl, vice president sales and marketing, Europe, Middle East, and Africa:

> Issy Sharp once told me that one of our key strengths is diversity. McDonald's is the same all over. We do not want to be that way. We are not a cookie cutter company. We try to make each property represent its location. In the rooms, we have 40 to 50 square meters to create a cultural destination without being offensive. When you wake up in our hotel in Istanbul, you know that you are in Turkey. People know that they will get 24-hour room service, a custom-made mattress, and a marble bathroom, but they also know that they are going to be part of a local community.

According to David Richey, president of Richey International, a firm Four Seasons and other hotel chains hired to audit service quality, "Four Seasons has done an exceptional job of adapting to local markets. From a design perspective, they are much more clever than other companies. When you sit in the Four Seasons in Bali, you feel that you are in Bali. It does not scream Four Seasons at you."

A manager explained Four Seasons' ability to be somewhat of a cultural chameleon with an analogy to Disney: "Unlike Disney, whose brand name is so strongly associated with the United States, Four Seasons' brand doesn't rigidly define what the product is. The Four Seasons brand is associated with intangibles. Our guests are not looking to stay in a Canadian hotel. Our product has to be 100 percent Four Seasons, but in a style that is appropriate for the country."

According to Crowl, Four Seasons learned from each country and property: "Because we are an international hotel company, we take our learning across borders. In Egypt, we are going to try to incorporate indigenous elements to the spa, but we will still be influenced by the best practices we have identified at our two spas in Bali."

Globally Uniform Standards

The seven Four Seasons "service culture standards" expected of all staff all over the world at all times are:

1. SMILE: Employees will actively greet guests, smile, and speak clearly in a friendly manner.
2. EYE: Employees will make eye contact, even in passing, with an acknowledgment.
3. RECOGNITION: All staff will create a sense of recognition by using the guest's name, when known, in a natural and discreet manner.
4. VOICE: Staff will speak to guests in an attentive, natural, and courteous manner, avoiding pretension, and in a clear voice.
5. INFORMED: All guest contact staff will be well informed about their hotel, their product, will take ownership of simple requests, and will not refer guests elsewhere.
6. CLEAN: Staff will always appear clean, crisp, well-groomed, and well-fitted.
7. EVERYONE: Everyone, everywhere, all the time, show their care for our guests.

In addition to its service culture standards, Four Seasons had 270 core worldwide operating standards (see Appendix 1 for sample standards). Arriving at these standards had not been easy; until 1998, there were 800. With the firm's international growth, this resulted in an overly complex set of rules and exceptions. The standards were set by the firm's senior vice presidents and Wolf Hengst, president, worldwide hotel operations, who explained, "We had a rule about the number of different types of bread rolls to be served at dinner and number of bottles of wine to be opened at lounges. But in countries where no bread is eaten at dinner and no wine is consumed, that's pretty stupid."

"While 270 standards might seem extensive," Richey noted, "if there are only 270, there are thousands of things that are not covered over which the general manager and local management team have a lot of control."

In addition, exceptions to the standards were permitted if they made local sense. For example, one standard stated that the coffee pot should be left on the table at breakfast so that guests could choose to refill their cups. This was perceived as a lack of service in France, so it was amended there. Standards were often written to allow local flexibility. While the standards require an employee's uniform to be immaculate, they do not state what it should look like. In Bali, uniforms were completely different from uniforms in Chicago. Managers underlined the fact that standards set *minimum expectations*. "If you can do something for a client that goes beyond a standard," they told staff, "do it." As a result, stories about a concierge taking a client to the hospital and staying with that person overnight were part of Four Seasons lore, contributing to cultural artifacts.

To evaluate each property's performance against the standards, Four Seasons used both external and internal auditors in its measurement programs. "Our standards are the foundation for all our properties," a senior manager noted. "It is the base on which we build." "When you talk to a Four Seasons person," Richey concluded, "they are so familiar with each of the standards, it is astonishing. With many managers at other firms this is not the case."

"We have been obsessed by the service standards," Hengst concluded. "People who come from the outside are surprised that we take them and the role they play in our culture so seriously. But they are essential. Talk to me about standards and you talk to me about religion." Another manager added, "Over time, the standards help to shape relationships between people, and those relationships contribute to building our culture."

Delivering Intelligent, Anticipatory, and Enthusiastic Service Worldwide

A manager stated, "We decided many years ago that our distinguishing edge would be exceptional, personal service – that's where the value is. In all our research around the world, we have never seen anything that led us to believe that 'just for you' customized service was not the most important element of our success." Another manager added, "Service like this, what I think of as 'intelligent service,' can't be scripted. As a result, we need employees who are as distinguished as our guests – if employees are going to adapt, to be empathetic and anticipate guests' needs, the 'distance' between the employee and the guest has to be small."

There were also tangible elements to Four Seasons' service quality. The product was always comfortable – so much so that at guests' requests, the company made its pillows, bedspreads, and mattresses available for sale. Guests could also count on a spacious bathroom, which was appreciated by the world traveler, especially in Europe where bathrooms tended to be small. "However, there are differences in the perception and definition of luxury," explained Barbara Talbott, executive vice president of marketing. "In the US, our properties have public spaces with a luxurious, but intimate, feeling. In the Far East, our properties have large lobbies enabling guests to see and be seen. People around the world also have different ways of using a hotel – restaurants, for example, are more important in hotels in Asia, so we build space for more restaurants in each property there."

Human Resources and the Golden Rule

Four Seasons' managers believed that human resource management was key to the firm's success. According to one senior manager, "People make the strength of this company. Procedures are not very varied or special. What we do is fairly basic."

Human resource management started and ended with "the Golden Rule," which stipulated that one should treat others as one would wish to be treated. Managers saw it as the foundation of the firm's values and thus its culture. "The Golden Rule is the key to the success of the firm, and it's appreciated in every village, town, and city around the world. Basic human needs are the same everywhere," Sharp emphasized. Appendix 2 summarizes the firm's goals, beliefs, and principles.

Kathleen Taylor, president, worldwide business operations, provided an example of how Four Seasons went about enacting the Golden Rule as a core value. "We give employees several uniforms so they can change when they become dirty. That goes to their dignity, but it is uncommon in the hospitality industry. People around the world want to be treated with dignity and respect, and in most organizational cultures that doesn't happen."

Managers acknowledged that many service organizations made similar statements on paper. What differentiated Four Seasons was how the chain operationalized those statements. Crowl noted, "A service culture is about putting what we all believe in into practice. We learn it, we nurture it, and most importantly, we do it."

In 2002, for the fifth year in a row, Four Seasons was among *Fortune* magazine's list of the top 100 best companies to work for in North America. While turnover in the hospitality industry averaged 55 percent, Four Seasons' turnover was half that amount.

GOING TO PARIS

However it developed its approach and philosophy, Four Seasons management knew that entering France would be a challenge.

The George V Opportunity

The six hotels in Paris classified as "Palaces" were grand, historic, and luxurious. Standard room prices at the F. S. George V, for example, ranged from $400 to $700. Most palaces featured award-winning restaurants, private gardens, and expansive common areas. For example, the Hotel de Crillon, a competitor to the F. S. George V, was an eighteenth-century palace commissioned by King Louis XV. The nine-story George V was designed in the 1920s by two famous French art deco architects. The property was located in one of Paris's most fashionable districts. For comparative data on Parisian palaces, please refer to Appendix 3.

Observers of the Paris hotel scene noted that by the 1980s and 1990s, the George V, like some of its peers, was coasting on its reputation. In December 1996, HRH Prince Al Waleed Bin Talal Bin Abdulaziz al Saud purchased the hotel for $170 million. In November 1997, Four Seasons signed a long-term agreement to manage the hotel. "We needed to be in Paris," John Young, executive vice president, human resources, explained, "We had looked at a new development, but gaining planning permission for a new building in Paris is very hard. Since we look for the highest possible quality assets in the best locations, the George V was perfect. It established us very powerfully in the French capital."

In order to transform the George V into a Four Seasons, however, an extensive amount of effort had to be placed into both the tangible and experiential service that the property and its people could deliver.

Physical Renovations

Four Seasons' challenge was to preserve the soul of the legendary, almost mythical, George V Hotel while rebuilding it for contemporary travelers. Four Seasons closed the hotel for what ended up being a two-year, $125 million total renovation. Because the building was a landmark, the facade had to be maintained. The interior of the hotel, however, was gutted. The 300 rooms and suites were reduced to 245 rooms of larger size (including 61 suites). Skilled craftsmen restored the facade's art deco windows and balconies, the extensive wood paneling on the first floor, and the artwork and seventeenth-century Flanders tapestries that had long adorned the hotel's public and private spaces.

The interior designer hired by Four Seasons, Pierre Rochon, noted, "My main objective was to marry functionality with guest comfort, to merge twenty-first-century technology with the hotel's 'French classique' heritage. I would like guests rediscovering the hotel to think that I had not changed a thing – and, at the same time, to notice how much better they feel within its walls."[5] The fact that the designer was French, Talbott pointed out, "signaled to the French that we understood what they meant by luxury."

While Four Seasons decided to build to American life-safety standards, it also had to adhere to local laws, which affected design and work patterns. For example, a hygiene law in France stipulates that food and garbage cannot travel the same routes: food and trash have to he carried down different corridors and up/down different elevators. Another law involved "right to light," stipulating that employees had the right to work near a window for a certain number of hours each day. As a result, employees in the basement spa also worked upstairs in a shop with a window for several hours a day, and as many windows as possible had to be programmed into the design.

The new Four Seasons Hotel George V opened on December 18, 1999 at 100 percent effective occupancy (occupancy of rooms ready for use). Managers credited extensive publicity, the millennium celebration, and the profile of the property for that success. The opening was particularly challenging because Four Seasons only took formal control of operations on December 1, in part due to French regulations. "The French are very particular about, for example, fire regulations, but the fire department would not come in and inspect until everything else was complete," a manager said.

BECOMING A FRENCH EMPLOYER

Entering the French hospitality market meant becoming a French employer, which implied understanding French labor laws, business culture, and national idiosyncrasies.

Rules

France's leaders remained committed to a capitalism that maintained social equity with laws, tax policies, and social spending that reduced income disparity and the impact of free markets on public health and welfare.[6] France's tax burden, 45 percent of GDF in 1998, was three percentage points higher than the European average – and eight points higher than the OECD average. A further burden on employers was the 1999 reduction of the work week to 35 hours. Unemployment and retirement benefits were generous. Importantly, Four Seasons' management was not unfamiliar with labor-oriented government policy. "Canada has many attributes of a welfare state, so our Canadian roots made it easier to deal with such a context," Young explained.

The country was known for its strong unions.[7] "In France, one still finds a certain dose of antagonism between employees and management," a French manager underlined. The political party of the Force Ouvrière, the union that was strongest at the F. S. George V, garnered nearly 10 percent of the votes in the first round of the 2002 French presidential election with the rallying cry, "Employees fight the bosses!"

"If you look at the challenges of operating in France," noted Corinthios, "they have labor laws that are restrictive, but not prohibitive. The laws are not the same as, for example, in Chicago. You just need to be more informed about them." The law did give employers some flexibility, allowing them to work someone a little more during peak business periods and less during a lull. A housekeeper, for example, might work 40-hour weeks in the summer in exchange for a few 30-hour weeks in the late fall. Furthermore, French employers could hire 10 percent to 15 percent of staff on a "temporary," seasonal basis.

A particularly tricky area of labor management in France involved terminations. "Wherever we operate in the world," a Four Seasons manager explained, "we do not fire at will. There is due process. There is no surprise. There is counseling. So, Paris isn't that different, except to have the termination stick is more challenging because you really need a very, very good cause and to document *everything* carefully. If you have one gap in the documentation, you will have to rehire the terminated employee."

National and Organizational Culture

Geert Hofstede's seminal work, *Culture's Consequences*,[8] indicates a great disparity between North American (US and Canadian) national culture and that of France. While Hofstede's work has been criticized for the construction of the dimensions along which cultures differ,[9] there is general agreement with the principle that cultures do differ. Further, Hofstede's work and that of other scholars indicate that the differences between North American and French organizational culture are large. Corinthios identified attitudes surrounding performance evaluation as one difference:

> European and Middle Eastern managers have a hard time sitting across from people they supervise and talking about their weaknesses. The culture is not

confrontational. It is more congenial and positive. It is very important to save face and preserve the dignity of the person being reviewed. Some Four Seasons managers using standard forms might even delete certain sections or questions or reprogram them in different languages.

For Didier Le Calvez, general manager of the F. S. George V and recently appointed regional vice president, another significant difference was the degree to which middle and front-line managers felt accountable. "The greatest challenge in France is to get managers to take accountability for decisions and policies," he said. "In the French hierarchical system there is a strong tendency to refer things to the boss."

Le Calvez was also surprised by managers' poor understanding of human resource issues. In France, when a manager has a problem with an employee, the issue generally gets referred to the human resources department. "We, at Four Seasons, on the other hand, require that operating managers be present, deal with the issue, and lead the discussion."

"Seeing is Believing"

When reflecting on their experiences with employees in France, several Four Seasons managers mentioned Saint Thomas ("doubting Thomas"). "They must see it to believe it," Le Calvez explained. "They do not take things at face value. They also tend to wait on the sidelines once they see that something works, they come out of their shells and follow the movement." A Four Seasons manager continued:

> Most of the workforce in France did not know what Four Seasons was all about. For example, they did not think we were serious about the Golden Rule. They thought it was way too American. Initially, there were some eyebrows raised. Because of this skepticism, when we entered France, we came on our tiptoes, without wanting to give anyone a lecture. I think *how* we came in was almost as important as *what* we did.

More Differences

For several Four Seasons managers, working in France required a "bigger cultural adjustment" than had been necessary in other countries. "In France, I always knew that I would be a foreigner," a manager explained. "It took me a while to adjust to the French way." "There is simply an incredible pride in being French," added another. "The French have a very emotional way to do things," an F. S. George V manager explained. "This can be good and bad. The good side is that they can be very joyous and engaging. On the bad side, sometimes the French temper lashes out."

According to Four Seasons managers, what was referred to in the cultural research literature as the French "logic of honor"[10] was strong. While it would be degrading to be "in the service of" (*au service de*) anybody, especially the boss, it was honorable to "give service" (*rendre service*), with magnanimity, if asked to do so with due ceremony. In this context, management required a great deal of tact and judgment.

Managing differing perceptions of time could also be a challenge for North Americans in France. North Americans have been characterized as having a "monochronic" culture based on a high degree of scheduling and an elaborate code of behavior built around promptness in meeting obligations and appointments.[11] In contrast, the French were "polychronic," valuing human relationships and interactions over arbitrary schedules and appointments. These differences created predictable patterns summarized in Appendix 4.

Specific areas where Four Seasons and French national culture differed often related to either (French) guest expectations of a palace hotel, including its physical structure and tangible amenities, or manager–employee relationships. For example, in France, hotel guests expected a palace hotel to have a world-class gastronomic restaurant. They also expected exquisite floral arrangements and to be wowed by the decor. In contrast, Four Seasons hotels generally have excellent, although not necessarily world-class, restaurants and are known for their understated, subtly elegant look. An example of differences in employee–manager relationships can be found in the French managerial practice of being extremely cautious in providing employee feedback to the degree that, according to Four Seasons' managers, the practice is unusual. In contrast, Four Seasons' management practice involved a great deal of communication, including feedback on an individual employee's performance, which managers believed critical to solving problems and delivering superior service.

Cultural Renovation at the F. S. George V

Awareness and management of French cultural patterns were especially important to Four Seasons managers in Paris because a significant portion of the former operator's management and staff remained. Young explained:

> When we explored options for refashioning the George V into a Four Seasons hotel, we realized that without being able to start from scratch, the task would be Herculean. The existing culture was inconsistent with ours. In a North American environment you can decide whom to keep after an acquisi- tion at a cost you can determine in advance on the basis of case law. In France, the only certainty is that you cannot replace the employees. You are acquiring the entity as a going concern. Unless you do certain things, you simply inherit the employees, including their legal rights based on prior service.

To be able to reduce headcount, by law an enterprise had to plan to be closed for over 18 months. Because the F. S. George V owner wanted the renovation to be complete in 12 months, staff were guaranteed a position with Four Seasons unless they chose to leave.[12] "Many of the best employees easily found other jobs, while the most disruptive were still there when the hotel reopened," Young said. "The number of people we really did not want was somewhere in the region of 40 out of 300 coming back on reopening."

Managers uniformly noted that the cultural renovation necessary to enable Four Seasons to be able to deliver its world-class service was on par with the extent of the physical renovation. Young provided an example. "During the due diligence process, the former general manager went to lunch with one of our senior staff. Even though guests were waiting, the maître d' immediately tried to escort the general manager and his party to the general manager's customary table. At Four Seasons this is seen as an abuse of privilege. For us, 'the guest always comes first.'"

Fortunately, in taking over The Pierre in New York, Four Seasons had been through a somewhat similar process. The scale of change necessary in each situation was enormous, as illustrated by this quotation from a senior Four Seasons manager: "Shortly after we bought The Pierre in 1981, a bell captain lamented that the times of the big steamer trunks were over. The staff had not adjusted to jet travel, despite its prevalence for two decades. This is the same kind of recalibration we had to do at the George V."

Apples and Oranges

Young described the firm's approach to cultural transformation in acquired properties with existing staffing:

> If we can achieve a critical mass of individuals among the workforce who are committed to doing things differently, to meeting our standards, that critical mass overcomes the resistance of what becomes a diminishing old guard. Progressively, that old guard loses some of its power. If one rotten apple can ruin the barrel, then you have to seed the organization with oranges that cannot be spoiled by the apples. As a result, a departing old-guard employee is very carefully replaced. Concurrently, individuals with the right culture and attitude are promoted. That creates a new culture, bit by bit by bit. At the F. S. George V, we also appealed to the national pride of our staff to help us restore a French landmark – to restore the pride of France.

"UN BOSS FRANCO-FRANÇAIS"

To effect this cultural change, Four Seasons picked Le Calvez to be general manager. Le Calvez was described as both demanding and "Franco-Français,"[13] an expression used in France to describe someone or something "unequivocably French." At the same time, Le Calvez brought extensive Four Seasons and North American experience. Prior to opening the Regent Hotel in Singapore, he spent 25 years outside France, including 11 years at The Pierre. "He is very international, yet also very French, very attached to his country and its culture," an executive explained. "He knows everyone and has an unbelievable memory for names and events (what happened to so-and-so's mother-in-law, etc.). He is very visible and accessible to the staff, eating in the staff cafeteria."

An F. S. George V manager noted, "The hotel's culture is embodied in the general manager – he shows a lot of love and respect for others and promotes social and cultural and ethnic integration." In a country where people typically referred to each other as Monsieur and Madame with their last name, Le Calvez encouraged the use of the first name. "It is more direct, relaxed, and straightforward. It represents the kind of relationship I want to have with my staff," he stated.

Young commented on the choice of Le Calvez: "The choice of senior leadership is absolutely critical. Adherence to our values and operational goals has to be extremely strong. Hotel openings require a lot of patience and tolerance because results are likely to be less positive as you manage through periods of major change."

The Task Force – "Culture Carriers"

To help Le Calvez and his team "Four Seasonize" the F. S. George V staff and ensure a smooth opening, Four Seasons assigned a 35-person task force, as it did to every new property. A manager noted:

> The task force helps establish norms. We help people understand how Four Seasons does things. Members listen for problems and innuendoes and communicate the right information to all, and squash rumors, especially when there are cultural sensitivities. The task force also helps physically getting the property up and running. Finally, being part of the task force exposes managers who may one day become general managers to the process of opening a hotel.

The task force, composed of experienced Four Seasons managers and staff, reflected the operating needs of each property. For example, if an experienced room service manager had already transferred to the opening property, those skills would not be brought in via the task force.

"The task force is truly a human resource, as well as a strong symbol," a manager explained. "The approach supports allegiance to the firm and not just one property – because members of the task force are not associated with one hotel. We are excited to participate, even if it means working long hours for weeks away from home." Most task force members, who typically stayed three weeks for an opening, stayed seven to eight weeks at the F. S. George V.

Strong Tides

After working 25 years abroad, Le Calvez admitted that he was hesitant to return to work in France in light of the general tension he sensed between labor and management. However, he was encouraged by what he had seen at The Pierre, where Four Seasons managers noted that they had fostered a dialogue with the New York hospitality industry union. Le Calvez felt he could do the same in Paris:

> When I arrived I told the unions that I did not think that we would need them, but since the law said we had to have them, I said 'Let's work together.'

I do not want social tensions. Of course, this is not unique to me; it is Four Seasons' approach. We have to be pragmatic. So we signaled our commitment to a good environment.

Le Calvez communicated this commitment by openly discussing the 35-hour work week, the Four Seasons retirement plan, and the time and attendance system, designed to make sure that staff would not work more than required.

At the outset of negotiations, in preparation for the reopening, Le Calvez took the representatives of the various unions to lunch. As work progressed, he organized tours of the site so that union representatives could see what was being done and "become excited" about the hotel. He noted that, "Touring the property in hard hats and having to duck under electric wires builds bonds. Witnessing the birth of a hotel is exciting." Managers stated that the unions were not used to such an inclusive approach in France.

Young felt that dealing with unions in France was easier than in New York: "In France, you are dealing with an institution backed by stringent, but predictable, laws. In the United States, you are dealing with individuals in leadership who can be much more volatile and egocentric."

Four Seasons' experience with The Pierre proved invaluable. According to Young:

In New York, we redesigned working spaces, and trained, and trained, and trained staff. But we also burned out a couple of managers. The old culture either wears you down or you wear it down. In an environment with strong labor laws, management sometimes gives up the right to manage. At some point, managers stop swimming against the tide. If that continues long enough, the ability to manage effectively is lost. The precedents in a hotel are those that the prior managers have permitted. If the right to manage has been given up, standards are depressed, productivity decreases, margins decrease, and eventually you have a bad business. Regulars are treated well, but many guests are not. Reversing this process requires enormous management energy. It is very wearing to swim against a strong tide. You are making decisions that you believe reasonable and facing reactions that you believe unreasonable.

The 35-Hour Work Week

Managers believed that Four Seasons' decision to implement the 35-hour work week at the F. S. George V to meet the letter and spirit of French law was a major signal to the unions and workforce about the way the company approached human resource issues. "When we hire staff from other hotels, they are always surprised that we obey the law," an F. S. George V manager noted. "They were working longer hours elsewhere."

A 35-hour work week yielded 1,820 annual workable hours per full-time staff equivalent. But since the French had more holidays and vacation than American employees, French employees provided 1,500 to 1,600 workable hours. This

Table 1. Employees-to-room ratios at selected Four Seasons properties

Property	Employees-to-Rooms Ratio
Four Seasons worldwide average	1.6
The Pierre New York	2.3
Four Seasons Hotel New York	1.6
Four Seasons Hotel George V Paris	2.5
Four Seasons Hotel Berlin	0.9
Four Seasons Hotel London	1.2
Four Seasons Hotel Canary Wharf, London	1.4
Four Seasons Hotel Milano	2.2

Source: Four Seasons.

compared to about 2,050 hours in the US for a full-time equivalent. The manager added, "We did not really understand the impact of the 35-hour work week. Each of our 80 managers has to have two consecutive days off a week, and each of the staff can work 214 days a year. Not 215. Not 213. But 214."

In 2002, 620 staff covered 250 rooms, or 2.5 staff per room. On average, Four Seasons hotels had 1.6 employees per room. Depending on food and banquet operations, that average could rise or fall significantly. Table 1 shows employees-to-room ratios at selected Four Seasons properties.

Young felt that labor laws explained about 15 percent of the need for increased staff ratios in Paris; vacations and holidays, 10 percent; with the rest explained by other factors including some logistics of the operation, e.g., a historic building, all compared to US norms. Corinthios elaborated:

> In Paris, you have six palaces competing for the same clients. It is a more formal operation. Guest expectations are very high, as is the level of leisure business (which requires higher staffing). People stay four to six days and use the concierge extensively. The concierge staffing at the F. S. George V is as big as anything we have in the chain. Then there is more emphasis on food and beverage. We have a fabulous chef and more staff in the kitchen for both the restaurant and room service – expectations of service in the gastronomic restaurant are very high.

RUNNING THE F. S. GEORGE V

Recruitment and Selection

Four Seasons wanted to be recognized as the best employer in each of its locations. In Paris, F. S. George V wages were among the top three for hotels. Salaries were advertised in help wanted ads, a first in the industry in Paris according to F. S. George V managers, who believed doing so would help them attract high-quality staff.

At the F. S. George V, as across the firm, every potential employee was interviewed four times, the last interview with the general manager. According to one executive, "In the selection process, we try to look deep inside the applicant. I learned about the importance of service from my parents – did this potential employee learn it from hers?" "What matters is attitude, attitude, attitude," Corinthios explained. "All around the world it is the same. Without the right attitude, they cannot adapt." Another manager added, "What we need is people who can adapt, either to guests from all over the world, or to operating in a variety of countries." One of his colleagues elaborated on the importance of hiring for attitude, and its challenges:

> You would think that you would have a lot of people with great experience because there are so many palace hotels in Paris. But because we hire for attitude, we rarely hire from the other palaces. We hire individuals who are still "open" and tend to be much younger than usual for palace hotels. Then we bet on training. Of course, it takes much longer to train for skills when people do not have them. We look for people persons, who are welcoming and put others at ease, who want to please, are professional and sincerely friendly, flexible, smiley, and positive. At the F. S. George V, people apply for jobs because they have friends who work here.

To spread the culture and "de-demonize" the US, the new F. S. George V management recruited staff with prior Four Seasons and/or US experience to serve as ambassadors. A manager noted, "Staff with US experience share with other staff what the United States is about and that it is not the terrible place some French people make it out to be." Several managers had international experience. About 40 individuals had prior US experience.

"Anglo-Saxon" Recognition, Measurement, and Benefits

Le Calvez and his team launched an employee-of-the-month and employee-of-the-year program. "This had been controversial at Disney. People said it could not be done in France, but we managed to do it quite successfully. It all depends how it is presented," Le Calvez noted. "We explained that the program would recognize those who perform. Colleagues can tell who is good at their job."

Le Calvez used the same spirit to introduce annual evaluations, uncommon in France:

> People said evaluations would be unpopular, but the system seems to work. We told the staff that it would be an opportunity for open and constructive dialogue so that employees can know at all times where they stand. This allows them to adapt when need be. We wanted to make clear that there would be no favoritism, but rather that this would be a meritocracy. Here your work speaks for itself. The idea that your work is what matters could be construed as very Anglo-Saxon!

In another "Anglo-Saxon" action, a "Plan d'Epargne d'Entreprise" was set up for George V employees. This was a combination tax-deferred savings account and 401(k)-type retirement plan. "This is totally new in France," Le Calvez claimed. Employees could contribute up to 4 percent of their salary, and the hotel would match it with 2 percent, to be raised based on profitability. The unions signed the agreement, although they were opposed to the principle of a non-government-sponsored retirement plan.

IMPLEMENTING THE GOLDEN RULE

The Golden Rule was at work at the F. S. George V, as its human resource director illustrated: "Cooks, before joining Four Seasons, used to have very long days starting in the morning to prepare for lunch, having a break during the afternoon, and coming back to prepare dinner. Today they work on either the morning or afternoon shift, enabling a better organization of their personal lives."

"All these gestures take time to work," Le Calvez summarized. "At first employees do not think we mean it. Some new hires think it's artificial or fake, but after a few months they let their guard down when they realize we mean what we say."

Managers believed that the effect of Four Seasons' human resource practices was reflected in customer satisfaction. Indeed, Le Calvez proudly reported that guest cards often included comments on how friendly and attentive the staff were. "All the other palace hotels in Paris are beautiful, but we believe that we have a special focus on friendly and personable service." He continued, "We offer friendly, very personal service. We have a very young and dynamic brigade with an average age of 26, spanning 46 different nationalities."

Communication

To promote communication and problem-solving, the F. S. George V management implemented a "direct line." Once a month, the general manager met with employees, supervisors, and managers in groups of 30. The groups met for three consecutive months so that issues raised could be addressed, with results reported to the group. Managers believed that the F. S. George V was the only palace hotel in France with such a communication process. It was important to note that the groups met separately – that is, employees met separately from supervisors – because subordinates in France did not feel comfortable speaking up in front of superiors.

French law mandated that a *comité d'entreprise* (staff committee) be established in organizations with more than 50 employees. It represented employees to management on decisions that affected employees (e.g., salaries, work hours). At the F. S. George V, Le Calvez chaired the committee's monthly meeting, which included union representatives. "We would do these things anyway, so it is easy to adjust to these laws," Corinthios said. "We do it in France because it is required by law. But we do the same around the world; it just has a different name."

Every morning, the top management team gathered to go over glitches – things that may have gone wrong the day before and the steps that had been, or were being, taken to address the problem. "Admitting what went wrong is not in the French culture," a French Four Seasons manager explained. "But the meetings are usually very constructive."

Finally, about three times a year, Le Calvez and his team hosted an open-door event, inviting employees and their families to spend some time at the hotel. "This is to break down barriers," he explained. "We take people around the hotel, into the back corridors. Try to remind people of a notion that is unfortunately being lost – that of the *'plaisir du travail'* – or enjoying one's work. Furthermore, we celebrate achievement. Good property rankings, for example, are recognized with special team celebrations."

The property also cultivated external communication with the press in a way that was culturally sensitive. Le Calvez and his team felt that they had been very open and responsive to the press (which they stated was unusual in France) and that as a result, "Not a single negative article had been written about Four Seasons Hotel George V since its opening". A colleague added, "The press appreciated that they were dealing with locals. It was not like Disney where everyone was American."

CULINARY *COUP D'ÉTAT*

In a significant diversion from typical Four Seasons practice, a non-Four Seasons executive chef was hired. "In France, having a serious chef and serious food is important," the F. S. George V food and beverage director noted. "You cannot be a palace hotel without that." "We knew that what mattered in Paris was food and decor," Talbott added. Although only 7 percent of room guests were French, most restaurant patrons were French.

Chef Philippe Legendre from the world-famous Parisian restaurant Taillevent was recruited. "Didier came to me through a common friend," Legendre explained. Legendre accepted Four Seasons' offer because "there was something exciting about being part of opening a hotel." He also liked their language, which he described as "optimistic" and "about creating possibilities."

Legendre felt that Four Seasons' real strength was around relationship management (with clients and among staff), which "is not something that we are that good at in France, or place particular emphasis on. We have a lot to learn in the social domain. Everything at Four Seasons is geared towards the needs of the guest. At first it was hard, especially the training. Perhaps because in France we think we know everything."

He continued, "After three years I might not talk the Four Seasons talk, I might not use the same words, but I have the same view and adhere to the same system."

Despite Legendre's success (earning two Michelin stars), a colleague added that, "bringing in such an executive chef was problematic. The challenge is that with this chef you have someone with extraordinary talent, but who must still adjust to the way service is delivered at Four Seasons." Coexistence was not always easy. Legendre described a situation illustrating miscommunication and cultural differences that required tremendous patience on the part of the restaurant, guests, and management:

> Recently a man ordered an omelet and his wife ordered scrambled eggs. The man returned the omelet because he decided he wanted scrambled eggs. We made them. Then he sent them back because they did not meet his expectations. Of course, we realize that our oeufs brouillés are different from scrambled eggs, which don't contain cream. Because we are Four Seasons we cooked the eggs as he wanted them, like American scrambled eggs, and didn't charge for them. But cooking is about emotion – if you want to please someone, you have to do it with your heart. *We live differently in France.*

RESULTS

A Cultural Cocktail

The F. S. George V was, in effect, a cultural cocktail. Le Calvez explained, "The F. S. George V is not *only* a French hotel – it is French, but it is also very international. We want to be different from the other palaces that are oh so very French. We want to project the image of a modern France, one that does not have to be dusty. We want to be a symbol of a France that is in movement, a European France, a France that stands for integration and equality."

The cultural cocktail also contained a number of elements unusual in France. At the time of the opening, journalists asked about the "American" smiling culture, which was referred to in France as "la culture Mickey Mouse." Le Calvez replied, "If you tell me that being American is being friendly and pleasant, that is fine by me. People tell me everyone smiles at the Four Seasons George V."

The spectacular flowers in the lobby of the F. S. George V (a single urn once contained 1,000 roses) were both very French and extremely international. "Paris is a city of fashion and culture, artistic and innovative," Le Calvez explained. "That is why, for example, we have the flowers we do. We can do that here." However, the flowers were designed by a young American. Another departure from French standard was the decision to hire women as concierges and men in housekeeping. These were viewed by managers as revolutionary steps in Paris.

Service Quality

Richey summarized the results of the first F. S. George V service-quality audit in October 2000, identifying some differences between French and North American business culture:

> Keep in mind that this occurred less than one year after opening, and it takes at least a year to get things worked out. There were three things we talked

to Four Seasons' executives about, mostly related to employee attitude. First, the staff had an inability to apologize or empathize. I think that could be construed as typically European, and especially French. Second, the team had a very tough time doing anything that could be described as selling. This is also typically European. For example: say your glass is empty at the bar. In Paris, they may not ask you if you want another drink. Third, the staff were rules and policy oriented. If something went wrong, they would refer to the manual instead of focusing on satisfying the guest.

Things had changed considerably by Richey's second audit in August 2001, when "they beat the competitive market set." The scores showed a significant improvement, raising the property to the Four Seasons' system average.

More good news came in July 2002 with the results of an Employee Opinion Survey, in which 95 percent of employees participated. The survey yielded an overall rating of 4.02 out of 5. The questions that ranked the highest were: "I am proud to work for Four Seasons Hotels and Resorts" (4.65) and "I would want to work here again" (4.61).

The property also received several industry awards, including Andrew Harper's Hideaway Report 2001 and 2002, World's Best Hotels and Resorts, Travel & Leisure Readers' Choice Awards 2001, #2 Best Hotel in Europe, and #5 World's Best Hotel Spa.

CONCLUSION: CULTURE, CONSISTENCY, AND FLEXIBILITY

The Four Seasons Hotel George V case illustrates how a service firm with a strong, successful organizational culture expanded internationally into a country with a distinct, intense national culture. When Four Seasons entered France, some elements of organizational culture were held constant, while others were treated flexibly. Managers never considered altering their *organizational values*, whether related to the service provided to guests, which had to be engaging, anticipating, and responding; the property, which had to be beautiful, luxurious, and functional; or how managers would treat employees, insisting that employees be treated as managers would like to be treated if they performed those jobs. While these values remained constant despite considerable differences in operating environments, the ways those values were enacted did sometimes change. This required changes in policies, management practices, and the use of cultural artifacts.

The tangible elements of service provide clear evidence of flexibility. Like all Four Seasons properties, the F. S. George V is luxurious. However, in France, the first floor of the hotel is adorned with gilt and seventeenth-century tapestries. No other Four Seasons property is decorated this way. The hotel elected to have a two-Michelin-star restaurant, despite the challenges of working with a famous chef in a country where there may be no more distinguished form of celebrity. More subtly, non-tangible elements of service quality changed, requiring changes in policies. For example, a coffee pot is never left on the table for guests to help themselves.

This change enables the hotel to meet the standard for service set by a Four Seasons' organizational value ("anticipatory") as interpreted in France, where one should not have to pour coffee oneself.

Management practices also changed. In order to have an engaging, anticipating, and responding staff, managers relied upon employee selection even more heavily than at other properties. In this way, management practice was intensified in response to a new national culture. However, the goal of those intensified selection efforts was to hire a less experienced staff than typical for other palace hotels and the chain. This was because of underlying, inflexible assumptions that many more experienced workers in France have about employment and how they should treat guests. Less experienced individuals are less set in attitudes and cultural stereotypes contrary to delivering the service for which Four Seasons is renowned. Management therefore focused more sharply on hiring based on attitudes rather than prior work experience. Thus, this management practice changed in France to enable Four Seasons to remain true to its organizational values.

The use of cultural artifacts also changed. While a typical Four Seasons property opening would be accompanied by information to the press on the world-renowned service for which the chain is famous, including legendary service stories, in France this was an afterthought to the glory of the property and the appropriateness of the renovations for a *French* architectural landmark.

Many management practices did not change upon arrival in France. Employee-of-the-month and -year recognition programs, feedback practices, and meetings to discuss problems were implemented despite a general belief that they would be found incompatible with the French environment. Yet, they were successful because of *how* they were implemented – using the words of one manager, "on tiptoes." Their more awkward (from a French perspective) elements were amended, and their purpose was communicated gently, but repeatedly. The individuals carefully selected into the Four Seasons' environment did not object to their use because they understood the intent of the practices, as well as their effect. The practices ultimately contributed to achieving the changes in organizational culture that Four Seasons managers believed were necessary, helping to ensure that the "oranges" (new employees) carefully selected into the property became the dominant culture carriers, overwhelming the leftover "apples" who refused to change, creating an environment in which those apples no longer fit comfortably.

Perhaps the most important element of management practice contributing to Four Seasons' success in France was management discipline. This took two forms, both of which can be viewed as contributing to the enactment of organizational values. First, discipline can be seen in the way Four Seasons managers lived the values they espoused; allowing guests to be seated first in the dining room; treating employees with dignity; and adhering to local labor laws and internal policies designed to protect employees. Second, Four Seasons managers had the discipline to insist that employees deliver outstanding service to guests. This occurred through adherence to the core service-culture standards and 270 operating standards (as occasionally amended). Meeting these standards has resulted in customer loyalty. Thus, discipline acts as a glue, ensuring that organizational values actually *drive* a culture, which in turn *contributes* to competitive advantage.

Managers in widely diverse service industries can benefit from Four Seasons' approach to global management when entering countries with distinct, intense national cultures. To do so, they must understand their own organizational culture: what are their (1) underlying assumptions, (2) values, (3) employee perceptions of management practices (policies and behaviors), and (4) cultural artifacts? Managers must then ask what elements of their culture, are essential to competitive advantage in existing environments, and how the new environment will change that linkage. When there is a change, does the element of culture itself need to change (coffee pot no longer left on the table), or does the way the element is implemented, the way a value is enacted, need to change, such as the implementation "on tiptoes" of an employee-of-the-month recognition program. In general, *values core to the organization's "value proposition" (what customers receive from the firm relative to what they pay for it) will not change, but elements of how they are enacted may.*

While organizations eventually come to understand how to operate in a new national environment, successful organizations cannot afford the type of negative publicity and poor financial performance that accompany blundering into a new national culture, as Disney discovered after opening Euro Disney in France. The Four Seasons case study is a single case, based on a single organization. As such, we do not claim that its findings are necessarily applicable to other firms. However, it illustrates an approach to global management that managers of other services may find useful, but which they must customize to their own organizational and cultural needs.

APPENDIX 1: SAMPLE CORE STANDARDS

Reservations

Mission: To provide crisp, knowledgeable, and friendly service, sensitive to the guest's time, and dedication to finding the most suitable accommodation.

- Phone service will be highly efficient, including: answered before the fourth ring; no hold longer than 15 seconds; or, in case of longer holds, call-backs offered, then provided in less than three minutes.
- After establishing the reason for the guest visit, reservationist automatically describes the guest room colorfully, attempting to have the guests picture themselves in the room.

Hotel Arrival

Mission: To make all guests feel welcome as they approach, and assured that details are well tended; to provide a speedy, discreet, and hassle-free arrival for business travelers; to provide a comforting and luxurious arrival for leisure travelers.

- The doorman (or first contact employee) will actively greet guests, smile, make eye contact, and speak clearly in a friendly manner.
- The staff will be aware of arriving vehicles and will move toward them, opening doors within 30 seconds.
- Guests will be welcomed at the curbside with the words "welcome" and "Four Seasons" (or hotel name), and given directions to the reception desk.
- No guest will wait longer than 60 seconds in line at the reception desk.

Hotel Departure

Mission: To provide a quick and discreet departure, while conveying appreciation and hope for return.

- No guest will wait longer than five minutes for baggage assistance, once the bellman is called (eight minutes in resorts).
- No guest will wait longer than 60 seconds in line at the cashier desk.
- Staff will create a sense of recognition by using the guest's name, when known, in a natural and discreet manner.

Messages and Paging

Mission: To make guests feel that their calls are important, urgent, and require complete accuracy.

- Phone service will be highly efficient, including: answered before the fourth ring; no longer than 15 seconds.
- Callers requesting guest room extensions between 1 am and 6 am will be advised of the local time and offered the option of leaving a message or putting the call through.
- Unanswered guest room phones will be picked up within five rings, or 20 seconds.
- Guests will be offered the option of voice mail: they will not automatically be routed to voice mail OR they will have a clear option to return to the operator.

Incoming Faxes and Packages

Mission: To make guests feel that their communications are important, urgent, and require complete accuracy.

- Faxes and packages will be delivered to the guest room within 30 minutes of receipt.

Wake-Up Calls

Mission: To make certain that guests are awakened exactly on time in a manner that gently reassures them.

- When wake-up calls are requested, the operator will offer a second reminder call.
- Wake-up calls will occur within two minutes of the requested time.

Guest Room Evening Service

Mission: To create a sense of maximum comfort and relaxation. When meeting guests, to provide a sense of respect and discretion.

- Guest clothing that is on the bed or floor will be neatly folded and placed on the bed or chair – guest clothing left on other furniture will be neatly folded and left in place; shoes will be paired.
- Newspapers and periodicals will be neatly stacked and left on a table or table shelf in plain view; guest personal papers will not be disturbed in any way.
- Guest toiletries will be neatly arranged on a clean, flat cloth.

Laundry and Valet

Mission: To provide excellent workmanship and make guests feel completely assured of the timing and quality of our service.

- Laundry service will include same-day service; express four-hour service; and overnight service (seven days per week).
- Dry cleaning service will include same-day service; express four-hour service (seven days per week).
- Pressing service will be available at any time, and returned within one hour; and can be processed on the normal laundry schedule.

Room Service

Mission: To provide a calm, competent, and thorough dining experience, with accurate time estimates and quick delivery.

- Phone service will be highly efficient, including: answered before the fourth ring; no hold longer than 15 seconds; or, in the case of longer holds, call-backs offered, then provided in less than three minutes.
- Service will be prompt and convenient; an estimated delivery time (an hour and minute, such as "nine-fifteen pm") will be specifically mentioned; and the order will be serviced within five minutes (earlier or later) than that time.
- Continental breakfast will be delivered within 20 minutes, other meals within 30 minutes, and drinks-only within 15 minutes.
- Table/tray removal instructions will be provided by a printed card, and tables will be collected within twelve minutes of guest call.

APPENDIX 2: FOUR SEASONS GOALS, BELIEFS, AND PRINCIPLES

Who We Are: We have chosen to specialize within the hospitality industry, by offering only experiences of exceptional quality. Our objective is to be recognized as the company that manages the finest hotels, resorts, residence clubs, and other residential projects wherever we locate. We create properties of enduring value using superior design and finishes, and support them with a deeply instilled ethic of personal service. Doing so allows Four Seasons to satisfy the needs and tastes of our discriminating customers, to maintain our position as the world's premier luxury hospitality company.

What We Believe: Our greatest asset, and the key to our success, is our people. We believe that each of us needs a sense of dignity, pride, and satisfaction in what we do. Because satisfying our guests depends on the united efforts of many, we are most effective when we work together cooperatively, respecting each other's contribution and importance.

How We Behave: We demonstrate our beliefs most meaningfully in the way we treat each other and by the example we set for one another. In all our interactions with our guests, business associates, and colleagues, we seek to deal with others as we would have them deal with us.

How We Succeed: We succeed when every decision is based on a clear understanding of and belief in what we do and when we couple this conviction with sound financial planning. We expect to achieve a fair and reasonable profit to ensure the prosperity of the company, and to offer long-term benefits to our hotel owners, our shareholders, our customers, and our employees.

APPENDIX 3: COMPARATIVE DATA ON PARISIAN PALACES

Property	Construction/Style	Capacity (Rooms and Suites)	Amenities	Price (Dollar/ Single Room)	Owner	Lessee/Operator
Bristol	Built in 1829/ Louis XV–XVI style	180	1 restaurant: Le Bristol 1 interior garden 1 swimming pool 1 fitness center 1 beauty salon	480–600	Société Oetker[c] (1978)	Independent
Crillon	Built in the 18th century/Louis XV– XVI style	152	2 restaurants: L'Ambassadeur and L'Obélix 1 fitness center Guerlain Beauty Institute	460–550	Groupe Hôtels Concorde[a] (1907)	Groupe Hôtels Concorde[a] (1907)
Four Seasons Hotel George V Paris	Built in 1928/ Art Deco style	245	1 restaurant: Le Cinq 1 swimming pool 1 fitness center 1 beauty salon	670	Prince Al Waleed Bin Talal[d] (1996)	Four Seasons Hotels and Resorts (2000)
Meurice	Built in the 18th century/Louis XV– XVI style	161	1 restaurant: Le Meurice 1 fitness center Caudalie Beauty Institute	470–550	The Sultan of Brunei (1997)	The Dorchester Group[b] (2001)
Plaza Athenée	Built in 1889/ Belle Epoque style	144	2 restaurants: Le Relais Plaza	490–508	The Sultan of Brunei (1997)	The Dorchester Group[b] (2001)
Ritz	Built in 1898/ Louis XV–XVI style	139	1 restaurant: L'Espadon Escoffier-Ritz cooking school 1 fitness center 1 beauty salon 1 swimming pool	From 580	Mohammed Al Fayed (1979)	Independent

[a] Groupe Hôtels Concorde was created in 1973 to regroup the luxury hotels such as the Crillon, the Lutetia, and the Hôtel Concorde Saint-Lazare (all in Paris) owned by La Société du Louvre. [b] The Dorchester Group, a subsidiary of the Brunei Investment Agency, was established in 1996 as an independent United Kingdom registered company to manage luxury hotels, including The Dorchester in London, The Beverly Hills Hotel California and the Hotel Meurice in Paris. [c] The Oetker Group is a German agribusiness group which owns four luxury hotels in addition to the Bristol: the Cap Eden Roc in Antibes, France; the Park Hotel in Vitznau, Switzerland; the Brenner's Park Hotel in Baden-Baden, Germany; and the Château du Domaine Saint-Martin in Vence, France. [d] Al Waleed Bin Talal owns 21.9 percent of Four Seasons' stocks. Investments by Prince Al Waleed in Four Seasons' properties include F. S. George V and Riyadh (100 percent); London (majority); Cairo, Amman, Alexandria, Sharm El Sheikh and Beirut (unspecified); and Aviara (minority).

Source: "Four Seasons Hotels and Resorts," Brian D. Egger et al., Crédit Suisse First Boston, April 5, 2002, page 21. http://meuricehotel.com, www.hotel-bristol.com, www.ritz.com, www.fourseasons.com/paris/vacations/index.html, www.plaza-athenee-paris.html, www.crillon.com. Accessed June 2002.

APPENDIX 4: PREDICTABLE PATTERNS OF MONOCHRONIC AND POLYCHRONIC CULTURES

Monochronic People (Americans)	Polychronic People (French)
Do one thing at a time	Do many things at once
Concentrate on the job	Can be easily distracted and manage interruptions well
Take time commitments (deadlines, schedules) seriously	Consider an objective to be achieved, if possible
Are low-context and need information	Are high-context and already have information
Are committed to the job	Are committed to people and human relationships
Adhere religiously to plans	Change plans often and easily
Are concerned about not disturbing others; follow rules of privacy and consideration	Are more concerned with those who are closely related (family, friends, close business associates) than with privacy
Show great respect for private property; seldom borrow or lend	Borrow and lend things often and easily
Emphasize promptness	Base promptness on the relationship
Are accustomed to short-term relationships	Have strong tendency to build lifetime relationships

Source: Adapted from Edward T. Hall, *Understanding cultural differences, German, French, and Americans*. Yarmouth: Intercultural Press, 1990.

NOTES

1. Kotter, J. P. and Heskett, J. L. 1990. *Corporate culture and performance*. New York: The Free Press.
2. Heskett, J. L., Schlesinger, L. A., and Sasser, W. E., Jr. 1997. *The service profit chain*. New York: The Free Press; Schneider, B. and Bowen, D. E. 1995. *Winning the service game*. Boston, MA: Harvard Business School Press; and Berry, L. L. 1995. *On great service*. New York: The Free Press.
3. Schein, E. H. 1990. Organizational culture. *American Psychologist*, 45(2): 109–19.
4. The theory behind this discussion finds its roots in the contingency work of scholars such as Lawrence and Lorch; see Lawrence, P. and Lorsch, J. 1967. *Organization and environment*. Boston, MA: Harvard Business School Press. Other scholars, including James Heskett, have used the contingency perspective as a starting point for theories of internationalization of services; see Loveman, G. 1993. *The internationalization of services*. Harvard Business School Module Note No. 9–693–103, Boston, MA: Harvard Business School Publishing. Heskett's views have influenced ours considerably. We are indebted to Professor Caren Siehl, Thunderbird, for much of the framework on managing the potential clash between organizational culture and country culture, which she developed for her organizational behavior MBA classes. In turn, Caren always acknowledges an intellectual debt to Professor Joanne Martin, Stanford University.
5. *Interior Design*, March 2000, p. S24.

6.   For example, maternity leave for a salaried employee's first child was 6 weeks of prenatal leave and 10 weeks of paid leave after birth; for a third child, it was 8 weeks off before and 18 weeks after birth.

7.   Communist-controlled labor union (Confédération Générale du Travail) or CGT, nearly 2.4 million members (claimed); independent labor union or Force Ouvrière, 1 million members (est.); independent white-collar union or Confédération Générale des Cadres, 340,000 members (claimed); Socialist-leaning labor union (Confédération Française Démocratique du Travail) or CFDT, about 800,000 members (est.). Source: www.Cia. gov/cia/publications/factbook/goes/fr.html, accessed June 10, 2002.

8.   Hofstede's work was based on a survey conducted by questionnaire with IBM employees in 50 different countries; see Hofstede, G. 1982. *Culture's consequences: international differences in work-related values*. Thousand Oaks, CA: Sage.

9.   Hofstede's approach has not been without its critics but, as Hickson comments, Hofstede had "frail data, but robust concepts;" see Hickson, D. 1996. The ASQ years then and now through the eyes of a Euro-Brit. *Administrative Science Quarterly*, 41(2): 217–28.

10.   See d'Iribarne, P. 1996/97. The usefulness of an ethnographic approach to the international comparison of organization. *International Studies of Management and Organisation*, 18(4): 32.

11.   Van der Horst, B. Edward T. Hall – a great-grandfather of NLP, www.cs.ucr.edu/gnick/ bvdh/print_edward_t_hall_great_htm, accessed April 20, 2002. The article reviews Hall, E. 1959. *The silent language*. New York: Doubleday.

12.   One alternative was to give the staff a significant enough severance package to encourage them to go. However, as Young explained, "The government deplores that approach."

13.   Usually used to describe a meal – say a first course of fromage de tête (pig's head set In jelly) or bouillabaisse (fish soup), followed by a main course of blanquette de veau (veal stew with white sauce) and rounded off with a plateau de fromage (cheese platter) or tarte aux pommes (apple tart).

PART 2

Cross-National and Global Leadership

Joyce S. Osland, Allan Bird, Mark E. Mendenhall, and Asbjorn Osland

DEVELOPING GLOBAL LEADERSHIP CAPABILITIES AND GLOBAL MINDSET: A REVIEW

W HAT MAKES GLOBAL LEADERS such as Carlos Ghosn (president of Nissan Motors, Ltd and Automotive News' 2000 Industry Leader of the Year) tick? Born in Brazil and educated in France, Ghosn served seven years as head of Michelin in the US and three years with Renault before becoming president and COO of Nissan. He is responsible for Nissan's renowned turnaround effort and cross-border alliance with Renault.

Although cultural differences exacted a toll on other cross-border automotive alliances, such as Daimler–Chrysler, Ghosn sees them as opportunities. "When you have taken the time to understand [that people don't think or act the same way] . . . and when you are really motivated and mobilized by a very strong objective, then the cultural differences can become seeds for innovation as opposed to seeds for dissention" (Emerson, 2001: 6). Ghosn contends that Europeans cannot call themselves "international" after working in Italy, Germany, or France: "you have to go to countries that have a totally different way of thinking, a totally different way of organization, and a totally different way of life" (Emerson, 2001: 7).

With the rise of globalization, managers such as Carlos Ghosn face complex challenges of leadership on a global scale. The nature of these challenges appears to be qualitatively different from those faced by international managers in the past. Consequently, there is a need to better understand what is required of these managers (Suutarl, 2002) and to identify the mindset and personal qualities essential to effective global leadership.

The context of leading globally is complex and fraught with disorienting challenges. The term "global" encompasses more than simple *geographic reach* in terms of business operations. It also includes the notion of *cultural reach* in terms of people and *intellectual reach* in the development of a global mindset. Lane and associates identify four aspects of the global context that combine to create significant challenges for global leaders (Lane et al., 2004):

- Multiplicity across a range of dimensions.
- Interdependence among a host of stakeholders, socio-cultural, political, economic, and environmental systems.
- Ambiguity in terms of understanding causal relationships, interpreting cues and signals, identifying appropriate actions, and pursuing plausible goals.
- Flux in terms of quickly transitioning systems, shifting values, and emergent patterns of organizational structure and behavior.

They maintain that the complexity of the global context can be addressed through attention to managing the following four *processes* (Lane et al., 2004):

- Collaborating. Working with others in relationships characterized by community, flexibility, respect, trust, and mutual accountability.
- Discovering. Transformational processes leading to new ways of seeing and acting, which, in turn, lead to the creation of new knowledge, actions, and things.
- Architecting. The mindful design of processes that align, balance, and synchronize organizational behavior.
- Systems thinking. Seeing and/or discovering the inter-relationship among components and levels in a complex system and anticipating consequences of changes in and to the system.

Rosen and associates (Rosen et al., 2000) took a different approach in delineating the context in which global leadership takes place. They sketched out the specifics of globalization forces by identifying a host of worldwide trends that affect how multinational corporations operate and how global managers lead. On the economic front, they argued that international mega-mergers, the rise of regional economic powers, continued privatization of government-owned corporations, the expanding economic integration of Europe, and China's growing economy and markets created new competitors and new consumers. On the social front, Rosen and associates pointed to increases in concern over the loss of national identities, increasing conflicts between the "haves" and the "have nots," ethnic strife, fundamentalist Islamic terrorists, a growing backlash against American influence and culture, significant demographic shifts due to rapidly aging populations in some countries, AIDS-devastated populations in some regions in the world, and escalating concerns about environmental degradation.

Within this context, corporate global leaders are often asked to accomplish near-Herculean tasks. To aid them, HR departments, consultants, coaches, researchers, and universities are attempting to define the parameters of global leadership and global mindset and determine how they can be developed in both individuals and organizations. Suutari's (2002) literature review concludes that developing global competence in leaders is acknowledged as a need and a high priority for firms.

For example, a US Fortune 500 survey found that 85 percent of the firms did not have an adequate number of global leaders, and 67 percent of existing leaders needed additional global skills and knowledge (Gregersen et al., 1998). Furthermore, the adoption of a global mindset has been viewed as a prerequisite to effectively manage transnational corporations (Bartlett and Ghoshal, 1992; Ohmae, 1989; Doz and Prahalad, 1991).

In order to gain a better understanding of the contributions of academe to the understanding of these pressing issues, we next summarize and identify general problems in the literature, and raise questions and suggestions to guide future research. Subsequently, we review literature on the development of global leadership and mindset and propose a non-linear framework to describe the process of global leadership development. The reading ends with implications for future research on developmental activities for both individuals and firms.

LITERATURE REVIEW OF GLOBAL MINDSET

How well individuals and firms observe and interpret the complex environment described in the introduction determines their success (Gupta and Govindarajan, 2002). Given Ashby's (1956) law of requisite variety, a complex global environment should be matched by internal complexity in the form of "managerial mindset" (Boyacigiller et al., 2004). Bartlett and Ghoshal (1989) claimed that mindset was more important than sophisticated structures and procedures. In this vein, for instance, the mindset of the chief executive is perceived as critical to a company's strategy (Paul, 2000). Rhinesmith (1993: 24) defines mindset as:

> a way of being rather than a set of skills. It is an orientation of the world that allows one to see certain things that others do not. A global mindset means the ability to scan the world from a broad perspective, always looking for unexpected trends and opportunities that may constitute a threat or an opportunity to achieve personal, professional or organizational objectives.

Maznevski and Lane (2004: 172) draw attention to the contextual application of Rhinesmith's "orientation to the world" when they define global mindset as 'the ability to develop and interpret criteria for personal and business performance that are independent from the assumptions of a single country, culture, or context; and to implement those criteria appropriately in different countries, cultures, and contexts.'

The concept of global mindset first appeared in Perlmutter's (1969) taxonomy of ethnocentric (home-country mindset), polycentric (host-country mindset), and geocentric (world mindset) MNCs. Bartlett and Ghoshal (1989) expanded geocentrism, calling it the transnational mindset. In the last decade, numerous articles have been published on global mindset (Begley and Boyd, 2003; Gupta and Govindarajan, 2002; Jeannet, 2000; Kedia and Mukherji, 1999; Kefalas, 1998; Maznevski and Lane, 2004; Paul, 2000; Rhinesmith, 1992, 1995; Srinivas, 1995) that are based either on consultants' experiences or academics' conceptualizations. Global mindset is assumed to correlate with strategic success in MNCs (Bartlett and Ghoshal, 1992; Ohmae, 1989; Doz and Prahalad, 1991), but there are few empirical studies on the topic (see Table 1).

There is also little agreement on how to define, measure, or develop global mindset (Bouquet et al., 2003). As a result, scholars have operationalized global mindset in a variety of different ways. For example, cognitive complexity (Wills and Barham, 1994), cognitive maps of CEOs (Calori et al., 1994), the international experience of top managers (Sambharya, 1996), judgments about international HR policies (Kobrin, 1994), cognitive orientation of top management teams (Levy, 2001), top management team (TMT) behavior (Bouquet et al., 2003), global orientation in managers (Nummela et al., 2004), and top management team global orientation (Beechler et al., 2004).

The dependent variables in these studies are measures of global strategy or performance, such as internationalization or international sales. Several studies prove that global mindset correlates with greater international scope (Calof and Beamish, 1994; Kobrin, 1994; Sambharya, 1996; Nummela et al., 2004), global strategic posture (Levy, 2001), and international financial performance (Nummela et al., 2004). In contrast, one study discovered that too much top management team attention to global issues (the authors' operationalization of global mindset) was as harmful to performance as too little attention (Bouquet et al., 2003). Global mindset also correlated with two internal measures – higher employee commitment and excitement about their job (Beechler et al., 2004). Due to the nature of their design, most of these studies cannot settle the question of causality. Murtha et al. (1998) found that global mindset increased during the implementation of a new global strategy. Some findings suggest that global mindset may follow strategy rather than the general assumption that strategy follows mindset (Levy et al., 1999). More research is needed to specify the contingencies that influence causality.

After reviewing how it has been used in the literature, Levy et al. (1999) have attempted to define the global mindset construct. They reached the following conclusion: global mindset is a cognitive structure composed of two constructs: cosmopolitanism (an enthusiastic appreciation of other cultures) (Merton, 1957; Hannerz, 1996) and cognitive complexity (the ability to perceive situations as highly differentiated and to integrate these differentiated constructs) (Weick, 1979; Bartunek et al., 1983). It remains to be seen whether or not this will be accepted as the standard definition of global mindset.

Problems with the global mindset research literature can be summarized in terms of three deficiencies. First, as of now there is no generally accepted definition of the construct, and it has been operationalized in numerous ways. Second, some studies use international work experience as a surrogate measure, but not all international assignments have the same result since some expatriates buffer themselves from the host culture and come home relatively unchanged without modifying their attitudes or worldview. Third, the global mindset research has focused on various levels of analysis – individual managers and CEOs, top management teams, and firms as a whole. Is global mindset in individuals the same construct as it is for firms? Are there different types of global mindsets in firms with different strategies or in different industries depending on varying levels of required global/cultural knowledge and involvement?

Significant further effort is called for in the addressing the following aspects of global mindset (GM) research:

- Further construct development or acceptance of the Levy et al. definition.
- Identification of different types of global mindset, perhaps at different levels of analysis.
- Creation and validation of a GM assessment instrument.
- Measurement of the impact of GM on performance outcomes.
- Identification of GM antecedents and clarification of causality.
- Determination of whether or to what extent GM can be developed in people.
- Identification of threshold personality characteristics, which can be used as selection criteria that identify GM or facilitate its development.
- Identification of the cognitive processes related to GM.
- Identification of organizational and team contingencies related to GM.
- Exploration of different forms of GM and their relationship to global strategies or industries.
- Identification of GM capability in both teams and organizations.
- Development of GM process models that include interaction with the environment.
- Antecedents of GM effectiveness.
- Delineation of the relationship between GM capability and organizational culture.
- Determination of what constitutes an adequate level of GM capability for organizational effectiveness.
- Outcomes of GM development training methodologies.

LITERATURE REVIEW OF GLOBAL LEADERSHIP

Within the field of management science, the construct of global leadership was born out of the needs of corporations in the 1990s to adopt global strategies, expand internationally, and compete in the global marketplace (Mendenhall and Osland, 2002; Von Glinow, 2001). Corporations realized that people with global capabilities were required to develop and implement their new strategic initiatives, and as a result, they created company-specific global leadership models to guide their management development efforts (Mendenhall and Osland, 2002). Because global leadership is a young field of study, many of these models and training programs, including those offered by universities and consulting companies, are not based on an extensive body of empirical research that identifies effectiveness in global leadership or global leadership training.

In this reading, global leadership is defined as a process of influencing the thinking, attitudes, and behaviors of a global community to work together synergistically toward a common vision and common goals (Adler, 2001; Festing, 2001). To date, most scholars have approached the global leadership construct by asking two questions: "What capabilities do global leaders need to acquire in order to be effective?" and

Table 1. A chronological list of empirical research on global mindset

Authors	Operationalization of Global Mindset	Method	Findings
Wills and Barham (1994)	Cognitive complexity	Interviews with 60 successful international managers in global organizations	Successful international managers were characterized by cognitive complexity, emotional energy, and psychological maturity, in addition to learned behaviors and skills
Calof and Beamish (1994)	Global mindset defined as geocentric	Surveys of 38 Canadian firms	Firms that characterized themselves as geocentric, rather than ethnocentric or polycentric, reported greater international sales and export intensity
Kobrin (1994)	International HR policies as indicators of geocentrism	Survey with geocentrism index on international HR policies administered to 68 US manufacturing firms	Geocentric mindset is related to geographic scope of firm, but not to global strategy
Calori et al. (1994)	Cognitive complexity of CEOs defined as number of constructs and density of links between constructs	Sample of 26 French and British firms in four industries	CEOs of international firms have more complex maps of their industry than other CEOs. Cognitive complexity of the CEOs correlates with the geographic scope of the firm and inter-organizational links, generally supporting "requisite variety"
Sambharya (1996)	Cognitive state of the top management team as measured by their international work experience	Sample of 54 US manufacturing firms	International experience of top management team correlates with international diversification

Study	Construct	Method/Sample	Findings
Murtha et al. (1998)	"Cognitive processes that balance competing country, business and functional concerns" in managers	Longitudinal survey administered to 370 managers in 13 country affiliates and US head office of an MNC	The change to a global strategy change resulted in a cognitive shift toward increased global mindset across all managers
Levy (2001)	"Cosmopolitanism and cognitive diversity" in top management teams	Content analysis of letters to shareholders of 69 US-based tech firms	Global mindset in top management were linked to a global strategic posture
Bouquet et al. (2003)	Top management team behaviors: global scanning, CEO foreign travel, communication with overseas managers, and discussions of globalization decisions	Questionnaires sent to 136 CEOs or presidents of MNCs	Global mindset is best explained by micro-level attention structures; too little or too much attention to global issues decrease firm performance
Nummela et al. (2004)	Global orientation attitude and international entrepreneurial behaviors	Web-based survey of 72 small Finnish information and communications technology companies	Managers' international work experience correlates with global mindset as does the globalness of their market; global mindset correlates with international financial performance
Beechler et al. (2004)	Global orientation of top management team	Surveys of 521 employees working in five countries of two Japanese MNCs	Employee perceptions of top management team's global orientation positively affected employee commitment and excitement about jobs

Table 2. A chronological list of empirical research on global leadership

Authors	Description	Method	Findings
Yeung and Ready (1995)	Identifies leadership capabilities in a cross-national study	Surveys of 1,200 managers from 10 major global corporations and 8 countries	Capabilities: articulate vision, values, strategy; catalyst for strategic and cultural change; empower others; results and customer orientation
Adler (1997)	Describes women global leaders in politics and business	Archival data and interviews with women global leaders from 60 countries	Women global leaders are increasing; they come from diverse backgrounds; are not selected by women-friendly countries or companies; use broad-based power rather than hierarchical power; are lateral transfers; symbolize change and unity; and leverage their increased visibility
Black et al. (1999)	Identifies capabilities of effective global leaders and how to develop them	Interviews of 130 senior line and HR executives in 50 companies in Europe, North America and Asia and nominated global leaders	Capabilities: inquisitive, character, duality, savvy; development occurs via: training, transfer, travel, teams
Kets de Vries and Forent-Treacy (1999)	Describes excellent global leadership	Case studies involving interviews with three global leaders	Identified best practices in leadership, structure, strategy, corporate culture
Ernst (2000)	Studies the impact of global leadership behavioral complexity on boss and subordinate perceptions of leadership effectiveness	Surveys of the bosses and subordinates of 174 upper-level managers from 39 countries working in 4 global organizations	Behavioral complexity variables were related to perceptions of leadership effectiveness; however, the relationships were not stronger for leaders in global versus local jobs

Rosen et al. (2000)	Identifies leadership universals	Interviews with 75 CEOs from 23 countries; 1058 surveys with CEOs, presidents, managing directors or chairmen; studies of national culture	Leadership universals: personal, social, business, and cultural literacies, many of which are paradoxical in nature
McCall and Hollenbeck (2002)	To identify how to select and develop global executives and understand how they derail	Interviews with 101 executives from 36 countries and 16 global firms nominated as successful global executives	Competencies: open-minded and flexible; culture interest and sensitivity; cognitively complex; resilient, resourceful, optimistic, energetic; honesty and integrity; stable personal life; value-added technical or business skills
Goldsmith et al. (2003)	To identify global leadership dimensions	Thought leader panels; focus and dialogue groups with 28 CEOs, and an unspecified number of current and future global leaders from various firms; interviews with 202 high potential next generation leaders; and 73 surveys from forum group members	Fourteen dimensions: integrity, constructive dialogue, shared vision, developing people, building partnerships, sharing leadership, empowerment, thinking globally, appreciating diversity, technologically savvy, customer satisfaction, maintaining competitive advantage
Kets de Vries et al. (2004)	Describes the development of 360-degree feedback instrument, GlobeInvent	Based on semi-structured interviews with a number of senior executives	Twelve dimensions/psychodynamic properties: envisioning, empowering, energizing, designing, rewarding, team-building, outside orientation, global mindset, tenacity, emotional intelligence, life balance, resilience to stress

"How can managers most effectively develop these characteristics?" The earliest publications on global leaders were either extrapolations from the domestic leadership literature, interviews, focus groups, or observations from the authors' consulting experiences (Kets de Vries and Mead, 1992; Tichy et al., 1992; Rhinesmith, 1993; Moran and Riesenberger, 1994; Brake, 1997). Two sources of current thinking, findings, and implications for future research are the *Advances in Global Leadership* volumes (Mobley et al., 1999; Mobley and McCall, 2001; Mobley and Dorfman, 2003) and the edited volume by Mendenhall et al. (2001). Additionally, *Human Resource Management* (vol. 39, 2000) published a special issue on global leadership, and Mendenhall and Osland (2002), Hollenbeck (2001), and Suutari (2002) conducted reviews of the literature.

The extant empirical studies on global leadership are described in Table 2. Empirical studies of global managers (e.g., Dalton et al., 2002; Leslie et al., 2002) and empirical work on comparative international leadership (e.g., the GLOBE project) exist in the field as well. From their extensive study of the impact of culture on leadership in 62 nations, the GLOBE project identified 21 universally accepted leader attributes and the transformational leadership style as generally advisable (House et al., 2004). Their subjects, however, were not global leaders, but middle managers and executives working in their own countries. These universal attributes may prove to be linked to effective global leadership; however, further research that tests for the presence of these attributes among successful global leaders is needed. As Adler noted, "A fundamental distinction is that global leadership is neither domestic nor multi-domestic; it focuses on cross-cultural interaction rather than on either single culture description or multi-country comparison (2001: 77). In our review of the literature, we include only studies with a specified focus on *global* leadership.

As shown in Table 2, the methodology utilized to study global leadership has been limited to surveys and/or interviews, with the exception of Kets de Vries and Florent-Treacy's (1999) initial case studies. Ernst (2000) went beyond interview or self-reported data to include 360-degree feedback from bosses and subordinates on behaviors, but his findings did not distinguish between domestic and global leadership. Using semi-structured interviews, Kets de Vries et al. (2004) developed an instrument to measure various psychodynamic properties associated with global leadership behavior. Black et al. (1999) and Goldsmith et al. (2003) also developed instruments to measure global leadership. Perhaps due to their recent development, as yet none of these instruments have been validated using commonly accepted standards for development of psychological assessment and testing instruments (Anastasi and Urbina, 1997; Nunnally and Bernstein, 1994). Several studies employed exploratory designs, which is appropriate in a nascent field of study. No one, however, has replicated Mintzberg's (1971) landmark observation of managerial behavior with global leaders or studied leader behavior directly. Although cognitive complexity is frequently mentioned as a global leadership competency, no research has directly measured the cognitive processes of expert global leaders (Osland and Bird, forthcoming).

The majority of the research findings in Table 2 were published in books; only three studies were published in peer-reviewed research journals or well-respected practitioner journals (e.g., Yeung and Ready, 1995; Gregerson et al., 1998; Kets de

Figure 1. Categorization of global leadership competencies in the empirical research

Vries et al., 2004). Consequently, it is more difficult to evaluate this research in terms of rigor.

While all of the global leader research in Table 2 makes a contribution to our understanding, and advances the field, the findings are not yet definitive. For example, the published research to date has not contributed much in the way of construct definition. No rigorous or collectively accepted definition of global leadership has emerged. In some studies, the definition of the construct was left up to interviewees; in other cases, the definition was merely assumed. As a result, there is conceptual confusion accompanied by enduring questions about whether there is a significant difference between global managers versus global leaders, or between global versus domestic leaders. In both sample selection and writing, the terms "global leader" and "global manager" are frequently used interchangeably, which is puzzling given the significant distinctions between managers and leaders in the leadership literature (Kotter, 1990).

Several studies asked global managers for their opinion about global leader capability without ensuring or clarifying whether they were, in fact, global leaders. Yeung and Ready (1995) used a global sample of 1,200 managers who chose among survey items to elicit their description of global leaders. After identifying 43 political and 38 businesswomen global leaders, Adler (2001) did content analysis using archival research and some interviews to describe their background, ascension, and use of power. Black et al. (1999) took a qualitative, exploratory approach. They asked 130 senior line and HR executives, as well as an unspecified number of nominated global leaders, for their opinion on global leadership capabilities and the methods of developing them. Rosen et al. (2000) interviewed 75 CEOs and surveyed 1,058 CEOs, presidents, managing directors, or chairmen about global leadership capabilities. Goldsmith and his colleagues took a three-pronged approach: (1) they asked the opinion of 18 well-known domestic leadership experts and futurists; (2) they held focus groups with 28 CEOs, an unspecified number of global managers, and 2,002 high-potential leaders of the "next" generation; and (3) they surveyed 75 forum members from various countries. McCall and Hollenbeck (2002) interviewed 101 executives from varied companies and countries who were nominated as successful global executives in high-level positions. They refer to their sample as global executives rather than leaders, although their sampling methods are similar to other global leader studies and they reviewed the global leadership literature prior to gathering data. Theirs is the only study to select all subjects solely on effectiveness, as perceived by others.

Black and his colleagues' subsample of nominated global leaders also took effectiveness into consideration. Kets de Vries and Florent-Treacy (1999) began their empirical work with case studies, utilizing a clinical orientation, of three global leaders who were acknowledged as highly successful global CEOs. As the basis of their subsequent research, an assessment instrument that measures global leader dimensions, they relied primarily on participants who attended INSEAD's senior executive seminar on Emotional Intelligence and Leadership and MBA program. This convenience sample, drawn from a prestigious school, may well be composed of global leaders, but their selection criteria, as well as most of the research reviewed here, assume that global managers are indistinguishable from global leaders. In contrast, we contend that all CEOs and global managers are not, by definition, global leaders. Given the limited amount of research in this field, more could be learned from exploratory research on global leaders who are effective. Both of these contentions argue for more careful selection criteria in global leadership research.

Mendenhall and Osland's (2002) review of the empirical and non-empirical literature yielded 56 global leadership competencies, a list too large to be useful. Noting that there were numerous areas of overlap across the various lists, they concluded that global leadership is a multi-dimensional construct with at least six core dimensions of competencies: cross-cultural relationship skills, traits and values, cognitive orientation, global business expertise, global organizing expertise, and visioning. This categorization seems applicable for the competencies identified in the empirical studies reviewed here, as shown in Figure 1.

One striking characteristic of the global leadership competency research is that it has, for the most part, taken a *content* approach. While such research is useful, it fails to explicate the process that global leaders utilize or to identify the contingencies that influence their behavior in specific contexts. Nor does it distinguish between essential and nonessential competencies. Are these competencies crucial at all times or important only in certain situations? Leadership requirements can vary by level, culture, and situation, as well as by functions and operating units, so competency lists might not apply across the board (Conger and Ready, 2004: 45).

The competency approach also fails to answer the conundrum of exemplary global leaders who succeed despite glaring weaknesses. In reality, few leaders live up to the idealized view of leadership that competency lists portray (Conger and Ready, 2004). McCall and Hollenbeck (2002) note that complex, high-level executive jobs are accomplished in various ways by executives with multiple forms of talent. Therefore, we would expect that global leaders can be effective without acquiring all competencies, but there is no research to prove or disprove this hypothesis.

Global leadership scholars may be distracted by the mythical lure of heroic leadership. The artist Andy Warhol stated, "In the future, everyone will be world-famous for 15 minutes." This may well describe some forms of global leadership. Leaders who accurately assess the shifting sands and rip tides of globalization may effectively harness the powers inherent in the situation and engage in "15 minutes" of global leadership. For that fleeting moment, their actions will be heroic. Do they then become heroes, destined like Spider-Man to repeatedly save us from evil, and become true global leaders? Probably not; 15 minutes may be more than most could hope for, as evidenced in the rise and fall of certain well-known global business leaders and in cases of domestic leaders who surprisingly rise to the challenge of a one-time global leadership role. Hence, another caveat is that scholars may well be reporting on episodic global leadership rather than finding subjects who act consistently as global leaders, contemporary examples of the archetypical heroic leader humankind so longs for. Our research needs to distinguish between global leaders and global leadership and between episodic and long-term global leadership behavior.

In summary, global leadership is an emerging field – reminiscent of the first stage of domestic leadership research – which also began by examining traits and subsequently evolved more complex theories. Furthermore, researchers have yet to focus on global leadership capability at the team or firm level, opting instead to study this topic only at the individual level of analysis. Future research is needed in the following global leadership (GL) topics:

- Construct definition for GL.
- Distinguish between the roles and behaviours of global managers and global leaders.
- Definitively answer the question of whether and how global leaders differ from domestic leaders.
- Determination of competencies that are threshold characteristics that should be used as selection criteria in development programs or promotion.
- Development and/or validation of GL assessment instruments.
- Identification of GL behaviors.
- Identification of GL thought processes and expert cognition.
- Identification of GL contingencies.
- Description of GL styles.
- Investigation of the relationship between global strategy and specific types of GL skills.
- Identification of GL capability in both teams and organizations.
- Development of GL process models that include interaction with the environment.
- Antecedents of GL effectiveness.

- Determination of how many global leaders firms need.
- Outcomes of GL development training methodologies.

The next literature review focuses on the development processes of global mindset and global leadership.

DEVELOPING GLOBAL MINDSET AND GLOBAL LEADERSHIP

One can develop attitudes, abilities, and knowledge through international assignments and global projects, but personality characteristics such as openness, flexibility, and reduction of ethnocentrism (which are closely related to cosmopolitanism and cognitive complexity) are, by definition, less amenable to change (Caliguiri and Di Santo, 2001). Therefore, selecting and promoting those who already have the desired personality characteristics is a critical aspect in developing both global mindset and global leadership.

Global Mindset Development

There are no extant empirical studies on global mindset development. However, based on research from cognitive psychology and knowledge development, Gupta and Govindarajan (2002: 120) assert that individual and organizational development of a global mindset are likely fostered by:

1. curiosity about the world and a commitment to becoming smarter about how the world works;
2. an explicit and self-conscious articulation of current mindsets;
3. exposure to diversity and novelty; and
4. a disciplined attempt to develop an integrated perspective that weaves together diverse strands of knowledge about cultures and markets.

They hypothesized that global mindset can be developed by (1) hiring diverse employees and managers, (2) providing opportunities such as cross-border teams and projects, short immersion experiences, and expatriate assignments, (3) holding meetings and business-unit headquarters in foreign locations, (4) fostering social networks across cultures, and (5) taking formal education courses (Gupta and Govindarajan, 2002). It has also been hypothesized that global mindset can be developed with a focus on global issues with structural positions (global jobs, champions, teams), meeting topics and speakers, and incentives and accountability for global performance (Bouquet et al., 2003).

Global Leadership Development

Few frameworks or models exist that describe the global leadership development process. (For a review of the literature on global leader development, see Suutari, 2002.) It is generally argued by scholars that the major challenges firms face in establishing global leadership development programs are: (1) establishing selection criteria, (2) agreeing on the competencies to develop and measure, (3) designing effective training programs, and (4) retaining their highly sought after "graduates."

Careful selection practices are essential. Certain personality characteristics that are desirable in global leaders – flexibility, ethnocentrism, openness – did not increase as a result of global assignments (Caliguiri and Di Santo, 2001). Caliguiri (2004) found that highly effective global leaders in one firm had significantly higher conscientiousness scores and significantly lower neuroticism than less effective ones. (They also had lived abroad with their families, had long-term international assignments, and were mentored by people from a different culture.) Therefore, certain threshold traits have to be these three characteristics, and others that have not yet been identified should constitute selection criteria. Furthermore, selection practices must avoid ethnocentrism and be inclusive since the traits, skills, and management styles that result in a superior track record in the home country may be counterproductive abroad (Mendenhall, 2001; Ruben, 1989; Osland and Taylor, 2001).

International assignments have been viewed as the most powerful development tool in facilitating global leadership competencies (Gregersen et al., 1998; Hall et al., 2001; Mendenhall et al., 2001), since they constitute a transformational experience that develops businesssavvy, continuous learning, cognitive complexity, behavioral flexibility, cross-cultural skills, and the ability to manage uncertainty (Osland, 2001). However, a multi-method approach is recommended (Osland and Taylor, 2001) that utilizes: international assignments, short-term developmental assignments, international teams, action learning groups/projects/task forces, international training and development programs, international meetings and forums, international travel (Oddou et al., 2000; Roberts et al., 1998), 360-degree evaluations that include input from foreign organizational members, and assessment centers (Stahl, 2001). All methods have to be used mindfully by tying them to company strategy and ensuring that the necessary developmental learning occurs.

Fulkerson (2002) summarizes practical advice for developing global leadership based, in part, on his research with international executives. McCall and Hollenbeck's (2002) research makes a major contribution to clarifying the development process of global executives from both an individual and organizational perspective. Their model consists of five components that lead to "the right stuff" in global managers (what they need to implement business strategy): talent, mechanisms, experience in a global context, catalysts, moderated by business strategy. They acknowledge several difficulties in assessing talent: identifying a common standard across cultures, country differences in assessing, promoting and developing managers, wide variability in global executive jobs, and the organization's openness to promoting executives from other nationalities (McCall and Hollenbeck, 2002: 185–186). The mechanism variable in their model consists of selection, succession, discovery, development, and recovery, which are elaborated in the following paragraphs.

Selection and succession refers, in part, to the organization's need to identify people who are ready to assume global positions when unexpected staffing needs arise – in other words, replacement planning for critical jobs. *Development* occurs by placing people in jobs that will expand their cultural or business skills, which is often done with people from a culturally diverse background who have a clear interest in international work. *Discovery* mechanisms provide parochial employees an opportunity early in their careers to ascertain whether they might have an interest in international work. *Recovery* pertains to the organization's efforts to integrate repatriates when they return home. Developmental *catalysts*, such as feedback, reward systems, etc., help executives learn. Finally, *business strategy* refers to a firm's specific development needs, which is based on their particular strategic intent and organizational design. Strategy and structure determine the number of international jobs, the types of global executives and their nationalities, and the skills they will need. Thus, McCall and Hollenbeck (2002) view business strategy as a moderator in their global executive development framework. They confirm the findings of other scholars that global experience is crucial to global leadership development.

GLOBAL LEADERSHIP DEVELOPMENT: A "NONLINEAR" PERSPECTIVE

The argument that global leadership is a process of personal transformation is an underlying theme in much of the literature. Assuming this thesis is cogent, it is likely that global leadership development is not a linear progression of adding competencies to an existing portfolio of leadership competencies, but rather a nonlinear process whereby deep-seated change in competencies and worldview takes places in the process of experiential overlays over time. This ongoing "experiential crucible" includes experiences over which the company may have little or no control. Consequently, traditional training cannot in and of itself be the primary tool through which global leadership competencies are inculcated within individuals. This process is akin to phenomena that are studied within the emerging field of nonlinear dynamics.

Traditional social scientific philosophy, methodology, and understanding are based on a core assumption: that relationships between variables in social phenomena are linear in nature (Capra, 1983, 1996). This cognitive and perceptual bedrock, which has been the center of socialization for thousands of doctoral students since the 1920s in North American universities, has produced the development of social scientific theories that are reductionistic, deterministic, and equilibrium-oriented in nature (Lichtenstein and Mendenhall, 2002). The superordinate goal of such social scientific theories is the prediction of human behavior (Capra, 1983, 1996; Hayles, 1991; Dooley, 1997; Lichtenstein and Mendenhall, 2002). This unconscious, ubiquitous paradigm is a lens through which managers, as well as academics, perceive reality. Wheatley (1992: 6) summarized the subtle effects of our socialization when she observed that:

> Each of us lives and works in organizations designed from Newtonian images of the universe. We manage by separating things into parts, we believe that influence occurs as a direct result of force exerted from one person to another, we engage in complex planning for a world that we keep expecting to be predictable, and we search continually for better methods of objectively

perceiving the world. These assumptions . . . are the base from which we design and manage organizations, and from which we do research in all of the social sciences.

One reason for the sustained permanence of this core assumption is that linearity does exist in the world. Many systems and laws in the universe are inherently linear in nature. An understanding of linearity has allowed humankind to transport astronauts to the moon and, on a more mundane note, to know what time it is at any given moment of the day.

An overarching characteristic of linear, deterministic systems is their proportionality, i.e., an input of x amount of force into a system results in a corresponding output, which proportionately reflects the amount of force (x). Lichtenstein and Mendenhall (2002) note that the implicit belief that predictable, closed mechanical systems are the norm for natural and social science modeling (Harding, 1986; Turner, 1997) was the basis for virtually all models of biological and social process (Bateson, 1980; Berman, 1984).

Over the past two decades, however, discoveries of nonlinearity in the natural sciences have led an increasing number of social scientists to explore the possibility that social phenomena have nonlinear elements within them (Capra, 1996; Eylon and Giacalone, 2000). Some social scientists, such as George Herbert Mead, Joseph Schumpeter, and Mary Parker Follett, saw and wrote about the relationship between nonlinearity and social phenomena in the 1920s and 1930s, but their voices were drowned out by the tide of logical positivism that emerged at that time, and has continued to the present, to be the foundational philosophy of social science (Lichtenstein and Mendenhall, 2002).

THE NATURE OF NONLINEARITY

Lichtenstein and Mendenhall (2002: 8) describe nonlinearity as "a common state of dynamic systems in which events and their outcomes are non-proportional." In the simplest sense, "nonlinear system Inputs are not proportional to the system's outputs; for example 140° F is not twice as pleasant as 70° F, and eight aspirin are not eight times as effective as one" (Goerner, 1994: 16). Another description of nonlinearity was provided by Meiss (1995: 1):

Nonlinear is defined as the negation of linear. This means that the result may be out of proportion to the input. The result may be more than linear, as when a diode begins to pass current; or less than linear, as when finite resources limit Malthusian population growth. Thus the fundamental simplifying tools of linear analysis are no longer available.

Some scholars have begun to theorize that global leadership development has nonlinear aspects and that firms need to understand this process better than they currently do in order to develop global leaders.[1] The multitudes of daily experiences that are encountered in a dynamic, intercultural milieu are not inherently linear.

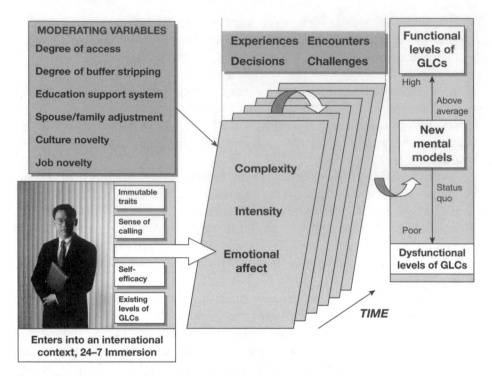

Figure 2. The Chattanooga Model of Global Leadership Development

Certain intercultural experiences trigger either functional or dysfunctional global competency development out of proportion to their importance to all other factors in the situation, or to the business context itself. Seemingly innocent or minor intercultural interactions can career out of control, causing global managers to internalize false or skewed intercultural understanding of "why" the event occurred and "what" the event means. In responding to these events, global managers continually create a new reality. Mary Parker Follett (1924: 62–63) argued that such social interaction was a nonlinear process:

> [an individual's] reaction is always reaction to a relating . . . I never react to you but to you-plus-me; or to be more accurate, it is I-plus-you reacting to you-plus-me . . . that is, in the very process of meeting, by the very process of meeting, we both become something different. It begins even before we meet, in the anticipation of meeting . . . It is I plus the-interweaving-between-you-and-me meeting you plus the-interweaving-between-you-and-me, etc., etc. If we were doing it mathematically we should work it out to the nth power.

Each intercultural situation that a global manager experiences – and there are myriad such experiences that occur daily – consist of "nonlinear relatings." That is, the creation of global leadership competencies is like an ongoing dance or tennis match with multiple partners. One is not independent of one's partners – the continual decisions and learning from decisions in response to continual behaviors enacted over time transform someone into either a competent or incompetent global leader – and all points in between. Lichtenstein and Mendenhall (2002) contend that components and behaviors in nonlinear dynamical systems cannot be separated, so independent forces do not bring about dependent outcomes. All elements in such systems are "mutually constituting" – they arise and evolve as an interconnected network (Capra, 1996). A cause does not have one and only one effect; therefore, the customary linear connection among antecedents and outcomes does not hold true. Instead, the "mutual causality" that characterizes this interdependence among variables constitutes a core principle of the new sciences (Briggs and Peat, 1988).

Based on the assumption that global leadership development in an individual is a nonlinear, mutually causal, emergent process moderated by a variety of key variables across time, we offer the following process model, depicted in Figure 2, as a first attempt to comprehend global leadership development through a nonlinear, paradigmatic lens. The model is termed, "The Chattanooga Model of Global Leadership Development" as it was developed in a think tank setting by global leadership scholars in Chattanooga, Tennessee in 2001 at the Frierson Leadership Institute.

At the left of the model, in the corner, an individual enters into a global/cross-cultural context and is immersed in it (24–7) over a significant period of time. The person enters with basic, core immutable personality traits, which includes fairly immutable competencies (ambition, desire to lead, sociability, openness, agreeableness, emotional stability, etc.) and cognitive processes (attribution flexibility, category width, tolerance for ambiguity, etc.). The individual also enters with existing levels of self-efficacy that are brought to bear on various aspects of living and working globally. The degree to which the individual perceives a "call to do this," or in other words, the degree to which people view themselves as global citizens and believe that this assignment fits "who they really are" inside is an important factor in their motivation to lead in a global situation. Finally, the person enters the global context with existing levels of global managerial/leadership competencies.

Each individual brings a unique configuration of these variables and brings this configuration to bear upon the multitude of daily experiences that are encountered in the new milieu. The "folders" or "pages" in Figure 2 represent experiences, interactions, and challenges the individual passes through over time. Each of these experiences differs in the degree to which they confront the individual with complexity, the degree to which they are important to the individual thus heightening the intensity of the experience for the individual. The combination of complexity and intensity contribute to the degree of emotional affect the individual experiences.

The recursive arrow in the model connotes the fact that a current experience can cause, through memory, an updating or reliving of past experiences. Thus, the global leadership development process is not based on independent experiences; rather, each experience is tied to past, multiple experiences and constitutes a sense-making process of learning and acquiring global leadership competencies. Bennis and Thomas (2002: 14) refer to the *gestalt* of these processes as constituting "crucibles," i.e., situations "characterized by the confluence of powerful intellectual, social, economic, or political forces" that severely test one's patience, and one's beliefs, and that produce a trans-formation in the individual, leaving him/her deeply different in terms of who they were before the crucible experience."

The nature of these various global/cross-cultural crucible experiences is critical to the formation of global leadership. The degree to which these experiences are buffered by organizational policies or the individuals themselves, or the degree to which access to these experiences is curtailed by companies (e.g., expensive housing that separates the global manager from interaction with the host society) moderates whether or not these potentially transforming experiences instead become shallow and non-catalytic in terms of global leadership development. Additionally, educational support systems, culture novelty, job novelty, and spouse/family adjustment can each enhance or detract from global leadership development.

Thus, a key factor in individual global leadership development is "access to high level challenges." Access to these challenges may produce, in some cases, solid global leadership competency development over time. However, such access also holds the potential to produce failure as well. Individuals may have the right kinds of experiences, but be unable to handle them or learn from them because they are over-whelming. New mental leadership models are indeed created within the individual; however, those models may be dysfunctional. It is important to note that though these mental models become apparent at the end of the process depicted in Figure 2, in actuality they are being created over and over again in response to each experience the individual has. Consequently, the developing framework is malleable, but it may harden into a dysfunctional systemic framework if experiences are not handled effectively over time.

In summary, the Chattanooga Model depicts the global leadership development process as emergent in nature, and constantly dynamic. If a person's immutable personality traits, access to powerful challenges, etc., are harmonious to working and learning in the global context, a functional global leadership process will ensue, and the individual will develop global leadership competencies. Similarly, other levels of global leadership, ranging from "status quo" to "dysfunctional" may result as a consequence of an individual's unique processual experiences. At any point in time, one's trajectory can rise, fall, or be moderated by the unique constellation of forces that impinge upon any given experience.

Much work remains to be done in the area of global mindset and leadership development. The Chattanooga Model and others need to be tested, and the effective-ness and costs of different types of developmental methods need to be compared. The organizational aspect of development cannot be overlooked; the alignment of HRM and the organizational culture with the firm's efforts to develop global leadership and global mindset also require more investigation. What is required are systemic analyses of the factors that promote or impede global leadership and mindset. The caveat remains, however, that efforts to understand development will be hamstrung by the lack of consensus on the definition and parameters of global leadership and global mindset. Finally, to avoid a western bias, future research on global mindset, leadership, and their development should include globally diverse subjects and settings.

NOTE

1.   A think tank of global leadership scholars met at the Frierson Leadership Institute, Chattanooga, Tennessee to discuss the nonlinear approach to global leadership development in 2001.

REFERENCES

Adler, N. J. 1997. Global leadership: Women leaders. *Management International Review*, 37(1): 171–196.

Adler, N. 2001. Global leadership: Women leaders. In M. Mendenhall, T. M. Kuhlmann, and G. K. Stahl (Eds.), *Developing global business leaders: Policies, processes, and innovations*, 73–97. Westport, CN: Quorum, and *Management International Review*, 1997, 37(1): 171–196.

Anastasi, A. and Urbina, S. 1997. *Psychological testing*, 7th ed. Upper Saddle River, NJ: Prentice-Hall.

Ashby, W. R. 1956. *An introduction to cybernetics*. New York: Wiley.

Bartlett, C. A. and Ghoshal, S. 1989. *Managing across borders: The transnational solution*. Boston, MA: Harvard Business School Press.

Bartlett, C. A. and Ghoshal, S. 1992. What is a global manager? *Harvard Business Review*, 124–131.

Bartunek, J. M., Gordon, J. R., and Weathersby, R. P. 1983. Developing complicated understanding in administrators. *Academy of Management Review*, 8(2): 273–284.

Bateson, G. 1980. *Mind and nature – a necessary unity*. New York: Bantam Books.

Beechler, S., O. Taylor, L. S., and Boyacigiller, N. 2004. Does it really matter if Japanese MNCs think globally? The impact of employees' perceptions on their attitudes. In A. Bird and T. Roehl (Eds.), *Advances in International Management*, 265–292.

Begley, T. M. and Boyd, D. P. 2003. The need for a corporate global mind-set. *Sloan Management Review*, 44(2): 25–32.

Bennis, W. G. and Thomas, R. J. 2002. *Geeks and geezers: How era, values, and defining moments shape leaders*. Boston, MA: Harvard Business School Press.

Berman, M. 1984. *The re-enchantment of the world*. New York: Bantam Books.

Black, J. S., Morrison, A., and Gregersen, H. 1999. *Global explorers: The next generation of leaders*. New York: Routledge.

Birkinshaw, J., Bouquet, C., and Morrison, A. 2004. Determinants and performance implications of global mindset: An attention-based perspective. Strategic and International Management Working Paper, 2004.

Boyacigiller, N., Beechler, S., Taylor, S., and Levy, O. 2004. The crucial but illusive global mindset. In H. Lane, M. Maznevski, M. Mendenhall & J. McNett (Eds.), *Handbook of global management*, 81–93. Oxford: Blackwell.

Brake, T. 1997. *The global leader: critical factors for creating the world class organization*. Chicago: Irwin Professional Publishing.

Briggs, J. and Peat, D. 1989. *Turbulent mirror*. New York: Harper & Row.

Calof, J. L. and Beamish, P. W. 1994. The right attitude for international success. *Ivey Business Quarterly*, 59(1), 105–110.

Caliguiri, P. 2004. *Global leadership development through expatriate assignments and other international experiences*. Paper presented at the Academy of Management, New Orleans, August.

Caliguiri, P. and Di Santo, V. 2001. Global competence: What is it and can it be developed through international assignment? *HR Resource Planning*, 24(3): 27–36.

Calori, R., Johnson, G., and Sarnin, P. 1994. CEO's cognitive maps and the scope of the organization. *Strategic Management Journal*, 15437–457.

Capra, F. 1983. *The turning point*. New York: Bantam Books.

Capra, F. 1996. *The web of life*. New York: Anchor Books.

Chattanooga think-tank on global leadership. 2001. Chattanooga, TN: Frierson Leadership Institute.

Conger, J. and Ready, D. 2004. Rethinking leadership competencies. *Leader to Leader*, 32: 41–48.

Dalton, M., Ernst, C., Deal, J., and Leslie, J. 2002. *Success for the new global manager: What you need to know to work across distances, countries, and cultures*. San Francisco, CA: Jossey-Bass and the Center for Creative Leadership.

Dooley, K. 1997. A complex adaptive systems model of organization change. Nonlinear dynamics. *Psychology and the Life Sciences*, 3: 230–249.

Doz, Y. and Prahalad, C. 1991. Managing DMNCs: A search for a new paradigm. *Strategic Management Journal*, 12145–164.

Emerson, V. 2001. An interview with Carlos Ghosn, President of Nissan Motors, Ltd. and Industry Leader of the Year (*Automotive News*, 2000). *Journal of World Business*, 36: 3–10.

Ernst, C. T. 2000. *The influence of behavioral complexity on global leadership effectiveness*. Unpublished dissertation, North Carolina State University.

Eylon, D. and Giacalone, R. 2000. Introduction: The road to a new management paradigm. *American Behavioral Scientist*, 43 (special issue): 1215–17.

Festing, M. 2001 The effects of international human resource management strategies on global leadership development. In M. Mendenhall, T. M. Kuhlmann, and G. Stahl (Eds.), *Developing global business leaders: Policies, processes, and innovations*, 37–56. Westport, CN: Quorum.

Follett, M. P. 1924. *Creative Experience*. New York: Peter Smith.

Fulkerson, J. 2002. Growing global executives. In R. Silzer (Ed.), *The 21st Century: Innovative Practices for Building leadership at the Top*. San Francisco, CA: Jossey-Bass.

Goerner, S. 1994. *Chaos and the evolving ecological universe*. New York: Gordon & Breach.

Goldsmith, M., Greenberg, C., Robertson, A., and Hu-Chan, M. 2003. *Global leadership: The next generation*. Upper Saddle River, NJ: Prentice Hall.

Gregersen, H. B., Morrison, A., and Black, J. S. 1998. Developing leaders for the global frontier. *Sloan Management Review*, 40(1): 21–33.

Gupta, A. K. and Govindarajan, V. 2002. Cultivating a global mindset. *Academy of Management Executive*, 16(1): 116–126.

Hall, D. T., Zhu, G., and Yan, A. 2001. Developing global leaders: To hold on to them, let them go! In W. Mobley and M. W. McCall, Jr. (Eds.), *Advances in Global Leadership*, vol. 2. Stamford, CT: JAI Press.

Hannerz, U. 1996. Cosmopolitans and locals in world culture. In U. Hannerz (Ed.), *Transnational connections: Culture, people, places*, 102–111. London: Routledge.

Harding, S. 1986. *The science question in feminism*. Ithica, NY: Cornell University Press.

Hayles, N. K. 1991. Complex dynamics in science and literature. In N. K. Hayles (Ed.), *Chaos and order: Complex dynamics in literature and science*. Chicago: University of Chicago Press.

Hollenbeck, G. P. 2001. A serendipitous sojourn through the global leadership literature. In W. Mobley and M. W. McCall, Jr. (Eds.), *Advances in Global Leadership*, vol. 2. Stamford, CT: JAI Press.

House, R. J., Hanges, P. W., Javidan, M., Dorfman, P., and Gupta, V. (Eds.) 2004. *Culture, leadership, and organizations: The GLOBE study of 62 societies*. Beverly Hills, CA: Sage.

Jeannet, J. 2000. *Managing with a global mindset*. London: *Financial Times*, Prentice-Hall.

Kedia, B. and Mukherji, A. 1999. Global managers: Developing a mindset for global competitiveness. *Journal of World Business*, 34(3): 230–250.

Kefalas, A. G. 1998. Think globally, act locally. *Thunderbird International Business Review*, 40(6): 547–562.

Kets de Vries, M. and Mead, C. 1992. The development of the global leader within the multinational corporation. In V. Pucik, N. M. Tichy, and C. K. Barnett (Eds.), *Globalizing management, creating and leading the competitive organization.* New York: John Wiley & Sons.

Kets de Vries, M. and Florent-Treacy, E. 1999. *The new global leaders.* San Francisco, CA: Jossey-Bass.

Kets de Vries, M., Vrignaud, P., and Florent-Treacy, E. 2004. The global leadership life inventory: development and psychometric properties of a 360-degree feedback instrument. *International Journal of Human Resource Management,* 15(3): 475–492.

Kobrin, S. J. 1994. Is there a relationship between a geocentric mind-set and multinational strategy? *Journal of international Business Studies,* 25(3): 493–512.

Kotter, J. 1990. What leaders really do. *Harvard Business Review,* 103–111.

Lane, H. W., Maznevski, M. L., Mendenhall, M. E., and McNett, J. (Eds.) 2004. *The Blackwell handbook of global management: A guide to managing complexity.* London: Blackwell.

Leslie, J. B., Dalton, M., Ernst, C., and Deal, J. 2002. *Managerial effectiveness in a global context.* Greensboro, NC: Center for Creative Leadership Press.

Levy, O. 2001. *The influence of top management team global mindset on global strategic posture of firms.* Paper presented at the Annual Meeting of the Academy of Management, Washington, DC.

Levy, O., Beechler, S., Taylor, S., and Boyacigiller, N. A. 1999. *What we talk about when we talk about "Global Mindset".* Paper presented at the Academy of Management Annual Meeting, Chicago, August 1999.

Lichtenstein, B. and Mendenhall, M. 2002. Non-linearity and response-ability: Emergent order in 21st century careers. *Human Relations,* 55(1): 5–32.

McCall, M. W. Jr. and Hollenbeck, G. P. 2002. *Developing global executives.* Boston, MA: Harvard Business School Press.

Maznevski, M. and Lane, H. 2004. Shaping the global mindset: Designing educational experiences for effective global thinking and action. In N. Boyacigiller, R. M. Goodman, and M. Phillips (Eds.), *Teaching and experiencing cross-cultural management: Lessons from master teachers.* London and New York: Routledge.

Meiss, J. D. 1995. Frequently asked questions about nonlinear science (version 1.0.9). Newsgroup sci.nonlinear: Department of Applied Mathematics at University of Colorado at Boulder, 1–31.

Mendenhall, M. E. and associates. 2001. *Chattanooga conference on global leadership.* Chattanooga, TN. March.

Mendenhall, M. 2001. Introduction: New perspectives on expatriate adjustment and its relationship to global leadership development. In M. Mendenhall, T. M. Kuhlmann, and G. Stahl (Eds.), *Developing global business leaders: Policies, processes, and innovations*: 1–16. Westport, CN: Quorum.

Mendenhall, M. and Osland, J. S. 2002. *An overview of the extant global leadership research.* Symposium presentation, Academy of International Business, Puerto Rico, June.

Mendenhall, M., Kuhlmann, T. M., and Stahl, G. (Eds.) 2001. *Developing global business leaders: Policies, processes, and innovations.* Westport, CN: Quorum.

Merton, R. 1957. Patterns of influence: Local and cosmopolitan influentials. In R. K. Merton (Ed.), *Social theory and social structure.* Glencoe, IL: Free Press.

Mintzberg, H. 1971. *The nature of managerial work.* New York: Harper & Row.

Mobley, W. and McCall, M. W. Jr. (Eds.) 2001. *Advances in global leadership,* vol. 2. Stamford, CT: JAI Press.

Mobley, W. and Dorfman, P. (Eds.) 2003. *Advances in global leadership,* vol. 3. Stamford, CT: JAI Press.

Mobley, W., Gessner, M., & Arnold, V. (Eds.) 1999. *Advances in global leadership,* vol. 1. Stamford, CT: JAI Press.

Moran, R. T. and Riesenberger, J. R. 1994. *The global challenge: Building the new worldwide enterprise.* London: McGraw-Hill.

Murtha, T. P., Lenway, S. A., and Bagozzi, R. P. 1998. Global mind-sets and cognitive shift in a complex multinational corporation. *Strategic Management Journal,* 19(2): 97–114.

Nunnally, J. C. and Bernstein, I. H. 1994. *Psychometric* theory, 3rd edn. New York: McGraw-Hill.

Nummela, N., Saarenketo, S., and Puumalainen, K. 2004. A global mindset – a prerequisite for successful internationalization? *Canadian Journal of Administrative Sciences*, 21: 51–65.

Oddou, G., Mendenhall, M., and Ritchie, J. B. 2000. Leveraging travel as a tool for global leadership development. *Human Resource Management*, 39(2, 3): 159–172.

Ohmae, K. 1989. Managing in a borderless world. *Harvard Business Review*, 67(3): 152–161.

Osland, J. 2001. The quest for transformation. In M. Mendenhall, T. M. Kuhlmann, and G. Stahl (Eds.), *Developing global business leaders: Policies, processes, and innovations*, 137–156. Westport, CN: Quorum.

Osland, J. and Taylor, S. 2001. Developing global leaders. *HR.Com*. February.

Osland, J. S. and Bird, A. (forthcoming). Global leaders as experts. In W. Mobley and E. Weldon (Eds.), *Advances in global leadership,* vol. 4. Stamford, CT: JAI Press.

Paul, H. 2000. Creating a mindset. *Thunderbird International Business Review,* 42: 187–200.

Perlmutter, H. V. 1969. The tortuous evolution of the multinational corporation. *Columbia Journal of World Business.* 4(1): 9–18.

Rhinesmith, S. H. 1992. Global mindsets for global managers. *Training & Development,* 63–68.

Rhinesmith, S. 1993. *A manager's guide to globalization.* Alexandria, VA: Irwin.

Rhinesmith, S. H. 1995. Open the door to a global mindset. *Training & Development,* 49(5): 35–43.

Roberts, K., Kossek, E. E., and Ozeki, C. 1998. Managing the global workforce: Challenge and strategies. *Academy of Management Executive,* 12(4): 93–106.

Rosen, R., Digh, P., Singer, M., and Philips, C. 2000. *Global literacies: Lessons on business leadership and national cultures.* New York: Simon & Schuster.

Ruben, B. D. 1989. The study of cross-cultural competence: Traditions and contemporary issues. *International Journal of intercultural relations,* 13: 229–239.

Sambharya, R. 1996. Foreign experience of top management teams and international diversification strategies of U.S. multinational corporations. *Strategic Management Journal,* 17(9): 739–746.

Srinivas, K. M. 1995. Globalization of business and the Third World: Challenge of expanding the mindsets. *Journal of Management Development,* 14(3): 26–49.

Stahl, G. 2001. Using assessment centers as tools for global leadership development: An exploratory study. In M. Mendenhall, T. M. Kuhlmann, and G. Stahl (Eds.), *Developing global business leaders: Policies, processes, and innovations*: 197–210. Westport, CN: Quorum.

Suutari, V. 2002. Global leader development: An emerging research agenda. *Career Development International,* 7(4): 218–233.

Tichy, N., Brimm, M., Charan, R., & Takeuchi, H. 1992. Leadership development as a lever for global transformation. In V. Pucik, N. Tichy, and C. K. Barnett (Eds.), *Globalizing management, creating and leading the competitive organization*: 47–60. New York: John Wiley & Sons.

Turner, F. 1997. Chaos and Social Science. In R. Eve, S. Horsfall, and M. E. Lee, (Eds), *Chaos, complexity, and sociology.* Thousand Oaks, CA: Sage.

Von Glinow, M. A. 2001. Future issues in global leadership development. In M. Mendenhall, T. M. Kulhmann, & G. Stahl (Eds.), *Developing global business leaders: Policies, processes and innovations*: 264–271. Westport, CT: Quorum Books.

Weick, K. E. 1979. Cognitive processes in organization. In B. Staw (Ed.), *Research in Organizational Behavior,* vol. 1: 41–74. Greenwich, CT: JAI Press.

Wheatley, M. 1992. *Leadership and the new science.* San Francisco, CA: Berrett-Koehler.

Wills, S. and Barham, K. 1994. Being an international manager. *European Management Journal,* 12(1): 49–58.

Yeung, A. and Ready, D. 1995. Developing leadership capabilities of global corporations: A comparative study in eight nations. *Human Resource Management,* 34(4): 529–547.

Mansour Javidan, Peter W. Dorfman, Mary Sully de Luque, and Robert J. House*

IN THE EYE OF THE BEHOLDER: CROSS-CULTURAL LESSONS IN LEADERSHIP FROM PROJECT GLOBE

EXECUTIVE OVERVIEW

Global leadership has been identified as a critical success factor for large multi-national corporations. While there is much writing on the topic, most seems to be either general advice (i.e. being open minded and respectful of other cultures) or very specific information about a particular country based on a limited case study (do not show the soles of your shoes when seated as a guest in an Arab country). Both kinds of information are certainly useful, but limited from both theoretical and practical viewpoints on how to lead in a foreign country. In this reading, findings from the Global Leadership and Organizational Behavior Effectiveness (GLOBE) research program are used to provide a sound basis for conceptualizing worldwide leadership differences. We use a hypothetical case of an American executive in charge of four similar teams in Brazil, France, Egypt, and China to discuss cultural implications for the American executive. Using the hypothetical case involving five different countries allows us to provide in-depth action-oriented and context-specific advice, congruent with GLOBE findings, for effectively interacting with employees from different cultures. We end the reading with a discussion of the challenges facing global executives and how corporations can develop useful global leadership capabilities.

IMPACT OF GLOBALIZATION

Almost no American corporation is immune from the impact of globalization. The reality for American corporations is that they must increasingly cope with diverse cross-cultural employees, customers, suppliers, competitors, and creditors, a situation well captured by the following quote:

> So I was visiting a businessman in downtown Jakarta the other day and I asked for directions to my next appointment. His exact instructions were: "Go to the building with the Armani Emporium upstairs—you know, just above the Hard Rock Cafe—and then turn right at McDonald's." I just looked at him and laughed, "Where am I?"
>
> Thomas Friedman, *New York Times,* July 14, 1997

Notwithstanding Tom Friedman's astonishment about the global world in Jakarta, the fact is that people are not generally aware of the tremendous impact that national culture has on their vision and interpretation of the world. Because culture colors nearly every aspect of human behavior, a working knowledge of culture and its influences can be useful to executives operating in a multicultural business environment. It is a truism by now that large corporations need executives with global mindsets and cross-cultural leadership abilities. Foreign sales by multinational corporations have exceeded $7 trillion and are growing 20 percent to 30 percent faster than their sales of exports.[1] But while the importance of such business grows, 85 percent of Fortune 500 companies have reported a shortage of global managers with the necessary skills.[2] Some experts have argued that most US companies are not positioned to implement global strategies due to a lack of global leadership capabilities.[3]

How can companies best use the available information for executive development and, moreover, what is the validity and value of such information? US and European executives have plenty of general advice available to them on how to perform in foreign settings. During the past few years, much has been written about global leadership, including several books.[4] Journals are also getting into the global action as seen in *The Human Resource Management Journal*, which recently published a special issue on global leadership.[5] Nevertheless, in a recent review of the literature, Morrison concluded that despite the importance of global leadership, "relatively little research has thus far been carried out on global leadership characteristics, competencies, antecedents, and developmental strategies."[6]

Advice to global managers needs to be specific enough to help them understand how to act in different surroundings. For example, managers with an overseas assignment are frequently exhorted to have an open mind and to show respect for other cultures.[7] They may also be told of the importance of cross-cultural relationship management and communication. Some will wrestle with the idea that they need to develop a global perspective while being responsive to local concerns.[8] Or they may wonder if they have the "cognitive complexity" and psychological maturity to handle life and work in a foreign setting. And they are likely to hear or read that they must "walk in the shoes of people from different cultures" in order to be effective.[9] There is nothing wrong with such advice, and the scholars and writers who proffer it have often been pioneers in the field. But it is insufficient for a manager who is likely to assume, mistakenly, that being open-minded in Atlanta, Helsinki, and Beijing will be perceived identically, or that walking in someone else's shoes will feel the same in Houston, Jakarta, and Madrid. Because of the lack of scientifically compiled information, businesspeople have not had sufficiently detailed and context-specific suggestions about how to handle these cross-cultural challenges. This is a particular problem for those in leadership positions.

Although there are universal aspects of leadership, information about which will be presented shortly, people in different countries do in fact have different criteria for assessing their leaders.[10] The issue for the American manager is whether the attributes that made him or her successful as a leader in the US will also lead to success overseas, be of no value, or, worst of all, cause harm in the foreign operation. Using the findings from an extensive research effort known as the Global Leadership and Organizational Behavior Effectiveness (GLOBE) Project, this reading provides a few answers to the questions about the universal and culture specific aspects of leadership. We will present specific information about key cultural differences among nations and connect the "dots" on how these differences influence leadership. This information should help a typical global executive better understand the leadership challenges s/he faces while managing operations outside the US. It will also provide suggestions on how to more effectively cope with such challenges.

To make the GLOBE findings come alive, we will follow a hypothetical American executive who has been given two years to lead a project based in four different countries: Brazil, France, Egypt, and China. This hypothetical project involves developing a somewhat similar product for the four different markets. The project team in each country is tasked with the marketing of a new technology in the telecommunications industry. The executive will work with local employees in each location. Success will be determined by two criteria: the executive's ability to produce results and to show effective leadership in different cultures and settings.

The four countries represent different continents and very diverse cultures. Brazil is the most populous and economically important South American country. France is the largest, most populous, and most economically developed Latin European country. Egypt is the largest and most populous Arab country. China is the fast-growing giant economy with unprecedented growth in its economic and diplomatic power in the world. We chose these countries to provide context-specific analysis leading to general recommendations for global executives. Our choice of countries was guided by our efforts to cover a wide range of cultures. Before turning to our hypothetical scenario, we will examine common cultural dimensions that characterize nations and discuss why these dimensions are important for the development of global leaders.

COMMON CULTURAL DIMENSIONS

To be open-minded and to understand the cultures of the different countries, managers need to be able to compare their own cultures with those of other countries. After a review of the available literature, especially the work of Hofstede, Trompenaars, and Kluckhohn and Strodt-beck,[11] GLOBE conceptualized and developed measures of nine cultural dimensions. These are aspects of a country's culture that distinguish one society from another and have important managerial implications. While a few of these dimensions are similar to the work of other researchers, the manner in which we conceptualized and operationalized them was different.[12] We reconceptualized a few existing dimensions and developed a few new dimensions. In all cases, the scales designed to capture and measure these cultural dimensions passed very rigorous psychometric tests. A brief description of each cultural dimension is provided below along with the basic research design of GLOBE. Further details can be found on GLOBE's website, www.thunderbird.edu/wwwfiles/ms/globe/.

It might be noted that the GLOBE Project has been called "the most ambitious study of global leadership."[13] Our worldwide team of scholars proposed and validated an integrated theory of the relationship between culture and societal, organizational, and leadership effectiveness. The 170 researchers worked together for ten years collecting and analyzing data on cultural values and practices and leadership attributes from over 17,000 managers in 62 societal cultures. The participating managers were employed in telecommunications, food, and banking industries. As one output from the project, the 62 cultures were ranked with respect to nine dimensions of their cultures. We studied the effects of these dimensions on expectations of leaders, as well as on organizational practices in each society. The 62 societal cultures were also grouped into a more parsimonious set of ten culture clusters (list provided in the next section). GLOBE studies cultures in terms of their cultural practices (the ways things are) and their cultural values (the way things should be). The nine cultural attributes (hereafter called culture dimensions) are:

- **Performance Orientation.** The degree to which a collective encourages and rewards (and should encourage and reward) group members for performance improvement and excellence. In countries such as the US and Singapore that score high on this cultural practice, businesses are likely to emphasize training and development; in countries that score low, such as Russia and Greece, family and background count for more.
- **Assertiveness.** The degree to which individuals are (and should be) assertive, confrontational, and aggressive in their relationships with others. People in highly assertive countries such as the US and Austria tend to have can-do attitudes and enjoy competition in business; those in less assertive countries such as Sweden and New Zealand prefer harmony in relationships and emphasize loyalty and solidarity.
- **Future Orientation.** The extent to which individuals engage (and should engage) in future-oriented behaviors such as delaying gratification, planning, and investing in the future. Organizations in countries with high future oriented practices such as Singapore and Switzerland tend to have longer-term horizons and more systematic planning processes, but they tend to be averse to risk-taking and opportunistic decision-making. In contrast, corporations in the least future-oriented countries such as Russia and Argentina tend to be less systematic and more opportunistic in their actions.
- **Humane Orientation.** The degree to which a collective encourages and rewards (and should encourage and reward) individuals for being fair, altruistic,

generous, caring, and kind to others. Countries such as Egypt and Malaysia rank very high on this cultural practice and countries such as France and Germany rank low.

- **Institutional Collectivism.** The degree to which organizational and societal institutional practices encourage and reward (and should encourage and reward) collective distribution of resources and collective action. Organizations in collectivistic countries such as Singapore and Sweden tend to emphasize group performance and rewards, whereas those in the more individualistic countries such as Greece and Brazil tend to emphasize individual achievement and rewards.

- **In-Group Collectivism.** The degree to which individuals express (and should express) pride, loyalty, and cohesiveness in their organizations or families. Societies such as Egypt and Russia take pride in their families and also take pride in the organizations that employ them.

- **Gender Egalitarianism.** The degree to which a collective minimizes (and should minimize) gender inequality. Not surprisingly, European countries generally had the highest scores on gender egalitarianism practices. Egypt and South Korea were among the most male-dominated societies in GLOBE. Organizations operating in gender egalitarian societies tend to encourage tolerance for diversity of ideas and individuals.

- **Power Distance.** The degree to which members of a collective expect (and should expect) power to be distributed equally. A high power distance score reflects unequal power distribution in a society. Countries that scored high on this cultural practice are more stratified economically, socially, and politically; those in positions of authority expect, and receive, obedience. Firms in high power distance countries such as Thailand, Brazil, and France tend to have hierarchical decision making processes with limited one-way participation and communication.

- **Uncertainty Avoidance.** The extent to which a society, organization, or group relies (and should rely) on social norms, rules, and procedures to alleviate unpredictability of future events. The greater the desire to avoid uncertainty, the more people seek orderliness, consistency, structure, formal procedures, and laws to cover situations in their daily lives. Organizations in high uncertainty avoidance countries such as Singapore and Switzerland tend to establish elaborate processes and procedures and prefer formal detailed strategies. In contrast, firms in low uncertainty avoidance countries such as Russia and Greece tend to prefer simple processes and broadly stated strategies. They are also opportunistic and enjoy risk-taking.

REGIONAL CLUSTERING OF GLOBE NATIONS

GLOBE was able to empirically verify ten culture clusters from the 62-culture sample. These culture clusters were identified as: Latin America, Anglo, Latin Europe (e.g. Italy), Nordic Europe, Germanic Europe, Confucian Asia, Sub-Saharan Africa, Middle East, Southern Asia, and Eastern Europe. Each culture cluster differs with respect to the nine culture dimensions (e.g. performance orientation). Table 1 shows a summary of how the clusters compare in terms of their scores on cultural practices.

Table 1. Cultural Clusters Classified on Societal Culture Practices (As Is) Scores

Cultural Dimension	High-Score Clusters	Mid-Score Clusters	Low-Score Clusters	Cluster-Average Range
Performance Orientation	**Confucian Asia** Germanic Europe Anglo	Southern Asia Sub-Saharan Africa Latin Europe Nordic Europe Middle East	**Latin America** Eastern Europe	3.73–4.58
Assertiveness	Germanic Europe Eastern Europe	Sub-Saharan Africa **Latin America** **Anglo** Middle East Confucian Asia Latin Europe Southern Asia	Nordic Europe	3.66–4.55
Future Orientation	Germanic Europe Nordic Europe	**Confucian Asia** **Anglo** Southern Asia Sub-Saharan Africa Latin Europe	**Middle East** **Latin America** Eastern Europe	3.38–4.40
Humane Orientation	Southern Asia Sub-Saharan Africa	**Middle East** **Anglo** Nordic Europe Latin America Confucian Asia Eastern Europe	**Latin Europe** Germanic Europe	3.55–4.71
Institutional Collectivism	Nordic Europe Confucian Asia	**Anglo** Southern Asia Sub-Saharan Africa Middle East Eastern Europe	Germanic Europe Latin Europe **Latin America**	3.86–4.88
In-Group Collectivism	Southern Asia Middle East Eastern Europe Latin America Confucian Asia	Sub-Saharan Africa Latin Europe	**Anglo** Germanic Europe Nordic Europe	3.75–5.87
Gender Egalitarianism	Eastern Europe Nordic Europe	**Latin America** **Anglo** Latin Europe Sub-Saharan Africa Southern Asia Confucian Asia Germanic Europe	**Middle East**	2.95–3.84
Power Distance		Southern Asia Latin America Eastern Europe Sub-Saharan Africa Middle East Latin Europe Confucian Asia **Anglo** Germanic Europe	Nordic Europe	4.54–5.39
Uncertainty Avoidance	Nordic Europe Germanic Europe	**Confucian Asia** **Anglo** Sub-Saharan Africa Latin Europe Southern Asia	**Middle East** **Latin America** Eastern Europe	3.56–5.19

NOTE: Means of high-score clusters are significantly higher ($p < 0.05$) than the rest, means of low-score clusters are significantly lower ($p < 0.05$) than the rest, and means of mid-score clusters are not significantly different from the rest ($p > 0.05$).

The clusters that are relevant to this reading are in bold. For instance, clusters scoring highest in performance orientation were Confucian Asia, Germanic Europe and Anglo (the US and the UK among other English-speaking countries). Clusters scoring lowest in performance orientation were Latin America and Eastern Europe. The Appendix shows the actual country scores for the six clusters in this reading.

MANAGING AND LEADING IN DIFFERENT COUNTRIES

Given the differences found in cultures around the globe, what does an effective American manager need to do differently in different countries? Everything, nothing, or only certain things? From a leadership perspective, we can ask whether the same attributes that lead to successful leadership in the US lead to success in other countries. Or are they irrelevant or, even worse, dysfunctional? In the following sections, we will answer these questions. We will examine some similarities and differences among cultures regarding management and leadership practices. We then assert that many of the leadership differences found among cultures stem from implicit leadership beliefs held by members of different nations.

Expatriate managers working in multinational companies hardly need to be reminded of the wide variety of *management* practices found around the world. Laurent, and more recently Trompenaars and Briscoe and Schuler,[14] document the astonishing diversity of organizational practices worldwide, many of which are acceptable and considered effective in one country but ineffective in another country. For instance, supervisors are expected to have precise answers to subordinates' questions in Japan, but less so in the US. As another example, the effectiveness of working alone or in a group is perceived very differently around the world; this would certainly influence the quality, aptitude, and fair evaluation of virtual teams found in multinational organizations.[15] An inescapable conclusion is that acceptable management practices found in one country are hardly guaranteed to work in a different country. Titus Lokananta, for example, is an Indonesian Cantonese holding a German passport, managing a Mexican multinational corporation producing Gummy Bears in the Czech Republic.[16] What management style will he be most comfortable with, and will it be successful with Czech workers and Mexican CEOs? How does he effectively manage if a conflict evolves between managing his workers and satisfying his supervisors?

Should we, however, conclude that cultural differences are so vast that common management practices among countries are the exception rather than the rule and will ever remain so? Not necessarily. Companies are forced to share information, resources, and training in a global economy. The best business schools educate managers from all over the world in the latest management techniques. Using academic jargon, the issue of common versus unique business and management practices is framed using contrasting perspectives embodied in the terms *cultural universals* versus *cultural specifics*. The former are thought to be found from the process of cultural convergence whereas the latter from maintaining cultural divergence. Perhaps not surprisingly, empirical research supports both views. For example, in their event management leadership research program Smith and Peterson found both commonalities and differences across cultures in the manner by which managers handled relatively routine events in their work.[17] All managers preferred to rely on their own experience and training if appointing a new subordinate, relative to other influences such as consultation with others or using formal rules and procedures. However, there were major differences in countries in the degree to which managers used formal company rules and procedures in contrast to more informal networks, and these differences co-vary with national cultural values.[18] As another example, Hazucha and colleagues[19] found a good deal of similarity among European countries regarding the importance of core management competencies for a Euromanager. Yet there were significant differences among countries in the perceived attainment of these skills. Javidan and Carl have recently shown important similarities and differences among Canadian, Taiwanese, and Iranian managers in terms of their leadership styles.[20]

Should we also expect that leadership processes, like management practices, are similarly influenced by culture? The answer is yes; substantial empirical evidence indicates that leader attributes, behavior, status, and influence vary considerably as a result of culturally unique forces in the countries or regions in which the leaders function.[21] But, as the colloquial saying goes "the devil is in the details," and current cross-cultural theory is inadequate to clarify and expand on the diverse cultural universals and cultural specifics elucidated in cross-cultural research. Some researchers subscribe to the philosophy that the primary impact of culture depends on the level of analysis used in the research program. That is, some view the basic functions of leadership as having universal importance and applicability, but the specific ways in which leadership functions are enacted are strongly affected by cultural variation.[22] Other researchers, including the contributors to this reading, question this basic assumption, subscribing more to the viewpoint that cultural specifics are real and woe to the leader who ignores them.

DO REQUIRED LEADERSHIP QUALITIES DIFFER AMONG NATIONS?

It has been pointed out that managerial leadership differences (and similarities) among nations may be the result of the citizens' implicit assumptions regarding requisite leadership qualities.[23] According to implicit leadership theory (ILT), individuals hold a set of beliefs about the kinds of attributes, personality characteristics, skills, and behaviors that contribute to or impede outstanding leadership. These belief systems, variously referred to as prototypes, cognitive categories, mental models, schemas, and stereotypes in the broader social cognitive literature, are assumed to affect the extent to which an individual accepts and responds to others as leaders.[24]

GLOBE extended ILT to the cultural level of analysis by arguing that the structure and content of these belief systems will be shared among individuals in common cultures. We refer to this shared cultural level analog of individual implicit leadership theory (ILT) as *culturally endorsed implicit leadership theory* (CLT). GLOBE empirically identified universally perceived leadership attributes that are contributors to or inhibitors of outstanding leadership. Project GLOBE's leadership questionnaire items consisted of 112 behavioral and attribute descriptors (e.g. "intelligent") that were hypothesized to either facilitate or impede outstanding leadership. Accompanying each item was a short phrase designed to help interpret the item. Items were rated on a 7-point Likert-type scale that ranged from a low of 1 (this behavior or characteristic greatly inhibits a person from being an outstanding leader) to a high of 7 (this behavior or characteristic contributes greatly to a person being an outstanding leader). Project GLOBE also empirically reduced the huge number of leadership attributes into a much more understandable, comprehensive grouping of 21 primary and then 6 global leadership dimensions. The 6 global leadership dimensions differentiate cultural profiles of desired leadership qualities, hereafter referred to as a CLT profile. Convincing evidence from GLOBE research showed that people within cultural groups agree in their beliefs about leadership; these beliefs are represented by a set of CLT leadership profiles developed for each national culture and cluster of cultures. For detailed descriptions of the statistical processes used to form the 21 primary and 6 global leadership dimensions and development of CLT profiles, see House et al.[25] Using the six country scenarios, in the last half of this reading we will show the range of leadership responses that should be effective in each cultural setting. The six dimensions of the CLT leadership profiles are:

1. **Charismatic/Value-Based.** A broadly defined leadership dimension that reflects the ability to inspire, to motivate, and to expect high performance outcomes from others on the basis of firmly held core beliefs. Charismatic/value-based leadership is generally reported to contribute to outstanding leadership. The highest reported score is in the Anglo cluster (6.05); the lowest score in the Middle East cluster (5.35 out of a 7-point scale).

2. **Team-Oriented.** A leadership dimension that emphasizes effective team building and implementation of a common purpose or goal among team members. Team-oriented leadership is generally reported to contribute to outstanding leadership (highest score in Latin American cluster (5.96); lowest score in Middle East cluster (5.47)).

3. **Participative.** A leadership dimension that reflects the degree to which managers involve others in making and implementing decisions. Participative leadership is generally reported to contribute to outstanding leadership, although there are meaningful differences among countries and clusters (highest score in Germanic Europe cluster (5.86); lowest score in Middle East cluster (4.97)).

4. **Humane-Oriented.** A leadership dimension that reflects supportive and considerate leadership but also includes compassion and generosity. Humane-oriented leadership is reported to be almost neutral in some societies and to moderately contribute to outstanding leadership in others (highest score in Southern Asia cluster (5.38); lowest score in Nordic Europe cluster (4.42)).

5. **Autonomous.** This newly defined leadership dimension, which has not previously appeared in the literature, refers to independent and individualistic leadership.

Autonomous leadership is reported to range from impeding outstanding leadership to slightly facilitating outstanding leadership (highest score in Eastern Europe cluster (4.20); lowest score in Latin America cluster (3.51)).

6. **Self-Protective.** From a Western perspective, this newly defined leadership dimension focuses on ensuring the safety and security of the individual. It is self-centered and face-saving in its approach. Self-protective leadership is generally reported to impede outstanding leadership (highest score in Southern Asia cluster (3.83); lowest in Nordic Europe cluster (2.72)).

Table 2 presents CLT scores for all 10 clusters. Analysis of Variance (ANOVA) was used to determine if the cultures and clusters differed with respect to their CLT leadership profiles. Results indicate that cultures (i.e. 62 societal cultures) and clusters (i.e. 10 groups consisting of the 62 societal cultures) differed with respect to all six CLT leadership dimensions ($p < .01$).

Table 3 presents summary comparisons among culture clusters to indicate which clusters are most likely to endorse or refute the importance of the six CLT leadership dimensions. Tables 2 and 3 may be used in combination to provide an overall view of how the different cultural clusters compare on the six culturally implicit leadership dimensions.[26]

CROSS-CULTURAL LEADERSHIP IS NOT ONLY ABOUT DIFFERENCES

The global and cross-cultural leadership literature is almost exclusively focused on cultural differences and their implications for managers. There is a basic assumption that leaders operating in different countries will be facing drastically different challenges and requirements. GLOBE surveys show that while different countries do have divergent views on many aspects of leadership effectiveness, they also have convergent views on some other aspects. From the larger group of leader behaviors, we found 22 attributes that were universally deemed to be desirable. Being honest, decisive, motivational, and dynamic are examples of attributes that are believed to facilitate outstanding leadership in all GLOBE countries. Furthermore, we found eight leadership attributes that are universally undesirable. Leaders who are loners, irritable, egocentric, and ruthless are deemed ineffective in all GLOBE countries. Table 4 below shows a few examples of universally desirable, universally undesirable, and culturally contingent leadership attributes.

Identifying universally desirable and undesirable leadership attributes is a critical step in effective cross-cultural leadership. It shows managers that while there are differences among countries, there are also similarities. Such similarities give some degree of comfort and ease to leaders and can be used by them as a foundation to build on. Of course, there may still be differences in how leaders enact such attributes. For example, behaviors that embody dynamic leadership in China may be different from those that denote the same attribute in the US. Current research currently under way by GLOBE team members is focused on this issue.

Table 2. CLT Scores for Societal Clusters

Societal Cluster	CLT Dimensions						
	Charismatic/ Value-Based	Team Oriented	Participative	Humane Oriented	Autonomous	Self-Protective
Eastern Europe	5.74	5.88	5.08	4.76	4.20	3.67
Latin America	5.99	5.96	5.42	4.85	3.51	3.62
Latin Europe	5.78	5.73	5.37	4.45	3.66	3.19
Confucian Asia	5.63	5.61	4.99	5.04	4.04	3.72
Nordic Europe	5.93	5.77	5.75	4.42	3.94	2.72
Anglo	6.05	5.74	5.73	5.08	3.82	3.08
Sub-Sahara Africa	5.79	5.70	5.31	5.16	3.63	3.55
Southern Asia	5.97	5.86	5.06	5.38	3.99	3.83
Germanic Europe	5.93	5.62	5.86	4.71	4.16	3.03
Middle East	5.35	5.47	4.97	4.80	3.68	3.79

NOTE: CLT leadership scores are absolute scores aggregated to the cluster level.

Table 3. Summary of Comparisons for CLT Leadership Dimensions

Societal Cluster	CLT Leadership Dimensions					
	Charismatic/ Value–Based	Team-Oriented	Participative	Humane Oriented	Autonomous	Self-Protective
Eastern Europe	M	M	L	M	**H**/H	H
Latin America	H	**H**	M	M	L	M/H
Latin Europe	M/H	M	M	L	L	M
Confucian Asia	M	M/H	L	M/H	M	H
Nordic Europe	H	M	H	**L**	M	**L**
Anglo	**H**	M	H	H	M	L
Sub-Sahara Africa	M	M	M	H	L	M
Southern Asia	H	M/**H**	L	**H**	M	H/**H**
Germanic Europe	H	M/L	**H**	M	H/**H**	L
Middle East	**L**	L	L	M	M	H/**H**

NOTES:
For letters separated by a "/", the first letter indicates rank with respect to the absolute score, second letter with respect to a response bias corrected score. H = high rank; M = medium rank; L = low rank. **H** or **L** (bold) indicates Highest or Lowest cluster score for a specific CLT dimension.

Table 4. Cultural Views of Leadership Effectiveness

The following is a partial list of leadership attributes with the corresponding primary leadership dimension in parentheses:

Universal Facilitators of Leadership Effectiveness

- Being trustworthy, just, and honest (integrity)
- Having foresight and planning ahead (charismatic–visionary)
- Being positive, dynamic, encouraging, motivating, and building confidence (charismatic–inspirational)
- Being communicative, informed, a coordinator, and team integrator (team builder)

Universal Impediments to Leadership Effectiveness

- Being a loner and asocial (self-protective)
- Being non-cooperative and irritable (malevolent)
- Being dictatorial (autocratic)

Culturally Contingent Endorsement of Leader Attributes

- Being individualistic (autonomous)
- Being status conscious (status conscious)
- Being a risk taker (charismatic III: self-sacrificial)

UNDERSTANDING CULTURALLY CONTINGENT LEADERSHIP

In this section, we will focus on those attributes of leadership that were found to be culturally contingent. These are attributes that may work effectively in one culture but cause harm in others. To provide an action-oriented analysis, we explore differences in effective leadership attributes among the four countries in our hypothetical scenario and discuss specific implications of these differences for our hypothetical American manager. Admittedly, we are being ethnocentric using the American manager as the focal person who finds himself/herself managing in a foreign culture. Obviously, expatriate managers are found from virtually all industrialized nations; however, there are over 200,000 US expatriates worldwide.[27] Nevertheless, expatriates from non-American and non-Western countries should be able to identify with cultural differences between their culture and that of the comparison countries. GLOBE cultural data for the five comparison countries can be found in Table 1 and the Appendix. Please note, the US, Brazil, and France are part of the Anglo, Latin American, and Latin European clusters, respectively. Egypt and China are part of the Middle East and Confucian Asia clusters, respectively.

Each section below begins with a summary of how each culture cluster fares with respect to the CLT profile. We then show how the countries of interest in this reading compare on specific leadership attributes that are culturally contingent. Next, we examine in detail what these differences mean and what they imply for the hypothetical American executive.

Brazil

Brazil is part of GLOBE's Latin American cluster. Viewing Tables 2 and 3, it is apparent that the CLT leadership dimensions contributing the most to outstanding leadership in this country cluster include charismatic/value-based and team-oriented leadership, followed by the participative and humane-oriented CLT dimensions. Autonomous and self-protective leadership are viewed as slightly negative. Table 3 shows that the Latin America cluster receives the highest rank for the team-oriented dimension, among the highest ranks for charismatic/value-based leadership, and ranks lowest with respect to the autonomous CLT leadership dimension. It occupies the middle ranks for the remaining CLT dimensions.

Figure 1 below contrasts the US and Brazil on the culturally contingent leadership items. Perhaps due to their high in-group collectivism, Brazilian managers intensely dislike the leaders who are individualistic, autonomous, and independent. A Brazilian sales manager working in the petrochemical industry recently reflected this, suggesting, "We do not prefer leaders who take self-governing decisions and act alone without engaging the group. That's part of who we are." While American managers also frown upon these attributes, they do not regard them as negatively as do the Brazilians. An American manager needs to be more cognizant to make sure that his/her actions and decisions are not interpreted as individualistic. He/she needs to ensure that the group or unit feels involved in decision-making and that others' views and reactions are taken into consideration.

On the other hand, Brazilian managers expect their leaders to be class- and status-conscious. They want leaders to be aware of status boundaries and to respect them. A manager in a large company in Brazil noted that blue- and white-collar workers from the same company rarely socialize together within and outside of work. They

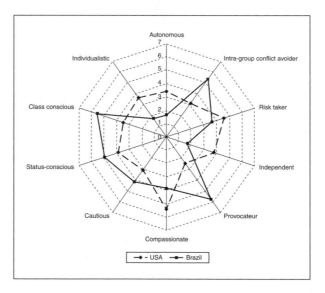

Figure 1. US versus Brazil

expect leaders to treat people according to their social and organizational levels. Perhaps due to their high power distance culture, Brazilians believe that people in positions of authority deserve to be treated with respect and deference. They prefer a formal relationship between the leader and followers. The same petrochemical sales manager told how Brazilian subordinates tend to stay outside of the perceived boundaries of their leaders and respect their own decision-making limitations. He added, "It's clear who has the most power in the work environment in Brazil, but in America this is not always the case." Americans tend to frown on status- and class-consciousness. Respect, to an American manager, does not necessarily mean deference but mutual respect and open dialogue. Americans tend to see formality as an obstacle to open debate. But what seems an open debate to an American manager may be viewed as aggressive and unacceptable behavior on the part of the subordinates by a Brazilian manager. So, while Brazilians do not like individualistic leaders, a typical American manager should be cautious using an open style of decision-making. While it may be a good idea in an American organization to directly contact anyone with the right information regardless of their level, such behavior may be seen as a sign of disrespect to those in formal positions in a Brazilian organization.

Another important difference is that American managers prefer a less cautious approach and a greater degree of risk-taking. In contrast, Brazilian managers prefer a somewhat more cautious and risk-averse approach. This is consistent with the finding that US culture is more tolerant of uncertainty than is Brazilian culture. Also, perhaps due to stronger assertiveness and performance orientation in American culture, US managers seem to favor a speedier decision-making process and a higher level of action orientation. Brazilians, on the other hand, may be more sensitive to group harmony and risk avoidance. A Brazilian account manager leading a four-company consortium working on a $200 million US contract with the Federal Department of Roads in Brazil realized this when a conflict occurred among the consortium players. He noted:

> Since our contract was a long-term relationship, we could not focus only on the particular moment. I had to find a way to motivate and to build a trusting environment. The only way to do so was to promote several meetings with all the consortium members trying to find a way to put all the members back together. By doing this, I assumed this was the best action to produce results, no matter how difficult it was or how much time it required.

Still another difference relates to the strong in-group collectivism dimension of the Brazilian culture. They expect their leaders to avoid conflict within the group to protect its harmony, but at the same time they like their leaders to induce conflict with those outside the group. A particularly successful executive working in Brazil told how Brazilians take pride in membership in small groups, especially families. In business, he said that people who are members of the same group expect special treatment (such as price discounts, exclusivity of contracts, etc.). In fact, without these group affiliations, attracting and conducting business can be difficult. American managers seem to dislike both these attributes, perhaps due to their stronger performance-orientation culture. Avoiding internal conflict, simply to maintain group harmony, even at the expense of results, is not a positive attribute to Americans. The typical American view of harmony is reflected in the following quote from the popular book *Execution* by Bossidy and Charan:[28]

> Indeed, harmony—sought out by many leaders who wish to offend no one— can be the enemy of truth. It can squelch critical thinking and drive decision making underground. When harmony prevails, here's how things often get settled: after the key players leave the session, they quietly veto decisions they didn't like but didn't debate on the spot. A good motto to observe is: "Truth over harmony."

Finally, an important and counter-intuitive finding is that American respondents have a much stronger desire for compassion in their leaders. They want their leaders to be empathetic and merciful. The Brazilian respondents, on the other hand, are quite neutral about this attribute. While this seems to go against the conventional stereotypes of Americans and Brazilians, it seems to be rooted in the fact that Brazil is reported to be a less humane culture than is the US. Confirming this finding, one manager stated that this reflects the expectation that people should solve their own problems, relying on help from their family or groups.

When in Brazil . . .

Here are a few specific ideas on what our hypothetical American manager needs to do when he starts working with his Brazilian team:

Very early on, he needs to spend time meeting with the key executives in the organization, even those who may not be directly relevant to his project. This is an important step because of high power distance and in-group collectivism in that culture. Being a foreigner and a newcomer, it is crucial to show respect to those in positions of power and to start the process of building personal ties and moving into their in-groups. Further, this step helps make sure that the other stakeholders do not view the manager's team as being insular, something that is likely to happen in high in-group cultures.

While it is important to work with the individual members of the team, it is also critical to spend as much time as possible with the team as a whole, both in formal work-related occasions and in informal settings. The families of the team members should also be invited to get together on many occasions. They are an important part of the relationships among team members. The high in-group culture facilitates the group working closely together, and the Brazilians' dislike for independent and individualistic leaders means that the leader is expected to treat the team and their close families as an extended family, spending much time together.

In developing a business strategy for the team's product, it is important to keep in mind Brazil's low scores on performance orientation and future orientation and its high score on power distance. The process of strategy development needs to allow for input from the employees, but the manager needs to be patient and to make an effort to encourage and facilitate the employees' participation. The Brazilian employees will not be as forthcoming with their ideas and input as typical American employees are. At the same time, the manager will need to make the final decision and communicate it. Brazilian employees are not used to strong participation in decision-making, but they also do not like leaders who simply dictate things to them. The strategy should not be seen as too risky or ambitious and should not have a long time horizon. Instead, it should consist of explicit short-term milestones. It should also focus on delivering short-term results to enhance employee understanding and support.

Due to the country's low score on institutional collectivism, employees will not be moved much by grand corporate strategies and visions. Instead, they would be more motivated by their individual and team interests, so the reward system should be based on both individual and team performance, although the team component should have the greater emphasis. The manager should also not be surprised if there are not many clear rules or processes and if the ones in existence are not followed very seriously. These are attributes of a society such as Brazil with low levels of rules orientation. Instead, the manager needs to make it very clear early on which rules and procedures are expected to be followed and why.

France

France is part of the Latin Europe GLOBE country cluster. The most desirable CLT dimensions in this cluster are charismatic/value-based and team-oriented leadership. Participative leadership is viewed positively but is not as important as the first two dimensions. Humane-oriented leadership is viewed as slightly positive, whereas autonomous leadership is viewed as slightly negative and self-protective is viewed negatively. Table 3 shows that the Latin Europe cluster is medium/high for charismatic/value-based leadership. It is in the middle rank for the remaining CLT leadership dimensions except the humane-oriented and autonomous dimensions where it ranks among the lowest-scoring clusters.

Figure 2 (p. 148) shows the contrast between French and American leadership on culturally contingent leadership attributes. The French culture is similar to the US on one cultural dimension, in that they both practice moderate levels of uncertainty avoidance. Although both cultures utilize predictable laws and procedures in business and society, characteristic of uncertainty avoidance cultures, France is much better known for its strong labor unions and bureaucratic formality. There are, however, significant differences between the French and American respondents on other cultural dimensions and leadership attributes. Both groups seem to like sincere and enthusiastic leaders who impart positive energy to their group, although American managers have much stronger preferences for these attributes. This may be a reflection of the finding that French culture is not as performance-oriented as US culture.

Besides their dislike for avoidance of conflict within the group (as discussed earlier), American managers have a clear dislike for cunning and deceitful leaders.

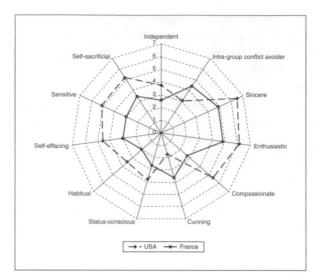

Figure 2. US versus France

The French, on the other hand, are neutral about both attributes. While Americans see these attributes as dysfunctional, the French see them as a part of the job that goes with the position of leadership. Compared to the US, in-group collectivism is more noted in French societies in the form of "favoritism" given to people from similar education, family, social, and even regional backgrounds. This is shown in the general tension that is perceived to exist between labor and management, as well and employees and clients.[29]

American managers seem to have a strong preference for compassionate and sensitive leaders who show empathy towards others. In contrast, French managers seem to have a distinctly negative view towards both these attributes. The CEO of an international audit firm expressed this in a quality audit of a French hotel stating, "The staff had an inability to apologize and empathize. I think that could be construed as typically European, and especially French."[30] These same behaviors would be expected from their leaders. Such a large contrast can perhaps be explained by the fact that the French culture is much less humane-oriented and much more power-oriented. To French managers, people in positions of leadership should not be expected to be sensitive or empathetic, or to worry about another's status because such attributes would weaken a leader's resolve and impede decision-making. Leaders should make decisions without being distracted by other considerations. Indeed, a very successful corporate executive in France noted that a leader should be able to handle change that affects the environment, but at the same time not change his/ her characteristics, traits, and skills that put the leader in that position. In other words, they should allow no distractions.

In contrast to Americans, French respondents have a negative view of leaders who are self-sacrificial and self-effacing. They do not like leaders who are modest about their role and forgo their own self-interest. The French executive added, "A leader must be clear about his role and vision. If a leader puts himself in a compromising situation, then doubt will arise in the followers' minds about the leader and that would affect their views of the roles the followers play in the broader picture." To them, the leader has an important role to play and important decisions to make, and s/he should not minimize that. They also do not like leaders who are habitual and tend to routinize everything because that diminishes the importance of their role. They do still prefer their leaders to work with and rely on others to get things done and do not like independent leaders. A French CEO known for his corporate turnaround finesse explained that leaders should not have too much independence from their followers because otherwise this would denote lack of character from the followers. He adds that a leader should guide without having too much power over the followers' thought processes, to ensure diverse thinking critical to conserve several solutions to the leader.

To sum up, a typical American executive taking on a leadership role in a French organization will face a more bureaucratic and formal work environment with higher levels of aggressiveness and lower levels of personal compassion and sensitivity than s/he is used to.

When in France . . .

The American manager in our scenario will face a very different experience with his or her French team. These managers will experience much more formal and impersonal relationships among the team members. The concept of visionary and charismatic leadership that is popular among American managers may not be as desirable to the French. They do not expect their leaders to play heroic acts and, due to their high power distance, have a more bureaucratic view of leaders. So, the American manager, in contrast to his experience in Brazil, needs to tone down the personal side of relationships and be much more business-oriented. The manager also has to be more careful and selective in contacting other executives and stakeholders. Their preference for maintaining high power distance may curb their enthusiasm about meeting with someone if they feel it is a waste of time and of no clear value to them. It is perhaps best for our American manager to make an offer to them and leave it to them to decide. Their low humane-orientation culture may mean that they are not particularly interested in being supportive of others, even in the same organization, especially if they are from separate in-groups.

Due to lower levels of future orientation and performance orientation, grand corporate strategies and visions may be of limited value to a French team. Any strong competitive language may be seen as typical American bravado. The manager needs to develop a process for making strategic decisions about the project and get the team members involved, but he needs to keep in mind that French employees may be best motivated by transactional forms of leadership where they see clear individual benefit in implementing the team's plans. The strategy and action plans need to be simple and well planned. So, the content and process of strategy development for the French team may have many similarities with the Brazilian team, even though they are different on many other dimensions.

Egypt

Egypt is part of the Middle East cluster. There are a number of striking differences in comparison to other clusters. While both charismatic/value-based and team-oriented leadership are viewed as positive, they have the lowest scores and ranks relative to those for all other clusters. Participative leadership is viewed positively, but again scores low compared with other clusters' absolute score and ranks. Humane-oriented leadership is perceived positively, but only about equally to other cluster scores. The self-protective CLT dimension is viewed as an almost neutral factor; however, it has the second-highest score and rank of all clusters.

Figure 3 below shows a contrast of leadership styles in the US and Egypt. The Egyptian culture is distinct by its emphasis on in-group and institutional collectivism, power distance, humane orientation, and male domination. In terms of leadership, American managers dislike autocratic leaders who want to make all the decisions themselves and micromanage their employees. They do not want their leaders to suppress others' ideas, even if they disagree with them. Egyptian managers have a more temperate view of such executives, perhaps due to their strong power distance culture.

A very important difference is the image of leaders in the Egyptian versus the American mind. Egyptian managers seem to have an elitist, transcendent view of their leaders. They view them as a distinct group and a breed apart. They want their leaders to be unique, superior, status- and class-conscious, individualistic, and better than the others in their group. They show strong reverence and deference toward their leaders. Americans, on the other hand, have a more benign and simplistic view toward their leaders. They do not see them as a breed apart or superhuman. They regard them as successful people but not extraordinary ones.

The country of Egypt has been ruled by dictators dating as far back as the time of the Pharaohs. Leaders were expected to lead by portraying a self-assured image.

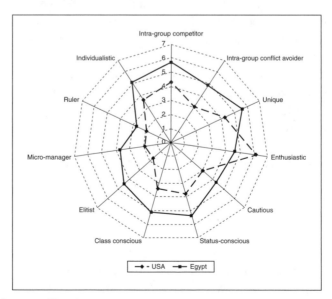

Figure 3. US versus Egypt

To maintain power, Egyptian leaders need to continuously be involved in making decisions. In the Arabic culture that is very much influenced by Islam, men do not wish to appear weak.

Despite such high level of respect for leaders, Egyptian employees, perhaps due to their very strong in-group collectivism, prefer their leaders to respect group harmony, avoid group conflict, and take caution in decision-making. It is rare to see leaders, especially political leaders, come out publicly and criticize a popular belief. They tend to avoid a conflict when it is not necessary, and they often use this collectivtism to build their influence and popularity.

The importance of family as kinship is the most significant unit of Egyptian society. An individual's social identity is closely linked to his/her status in the network of kin relations. Kinship is essential to the culture. Describing the tendency toward generosity and caring in their society, an Egyptian manager told of how early Islamic authorities imposed a tax on personal property proportionate to one's wealth and distributed the revenues to the needy. This type of government behavior left a certain culture of doing business in Egypt that has a strong emphasis on harmony with the environment, the industry, and the competition.

When in Egypt . . .

Our hypothetical American manager will find that his experience in Egypt will have both similarities and differences with his time in France and Brazil. First, what the manager may regard as a normal Informal leadership style in the US may be seen as weak and unworthy of a leader. This manager (typically a male) is expected to act and be seen as distinct from the others on the team and present an image of omnipotence. In the minds of his Egyptian team members, he needs to be seen as deserving of his leadership role and status. Addressing his role as a leader, a project manager from Egypt noted that being a leader brought with it great responsibility. He was in charge of disciplining anyone that did not follow the team rules. He noted, "In order to keep the team spirit up and focused on our goals, we can't afford to have individuals deviating from what we have set out to do." This is almost the opposite of his experience in France.

The American manager will also find that due to very strong in-group collectivism, various groups inside and outside the organization tend to show in-group/out-group phenomena in decision-making; i.e. strong participation by in-group members, little participation by out-group members, strong communication with in-group members, and little communication with out-group members. The extent to which Egyptians take pride in belonging to certain groups is immensely important. Families have endured through difficult times, requiring many of the members to stay together and work together. Family businesses tend to be passed from father to son without too many exceptions. Maintenance of the in-group is paramount in any decision. Leaders build their legitimacy not necessarily by accomplishing high performance but rather by forging loyalty to the group and group values. Furthermore, as a result of reliance on personal relationships, decision-making criteria and processes regarding any aspect of the organization tend to be informal and unclear.

Given such cultural underpinnings, the American manager needs to do even more than he did in Brazil to build and maintain group harmony. Many informal and formal meetings are needed, but there are three important differences compared with the experience in Brazil. First, to Egyptians, the team leader is more than just an executive; he is a paternal figure who will be rather autocratic but benign. He cares about them and their families. The relationship between the boss and employees is much more emotional and personal in Egypt. The Egyptian project manager described how he helped one of his employees who had experienced some personal difficulties. Explaining that the employee's behaviour was unacceptable, the manager added, "At the same time, I tried to understand if there were any personal issues that forced him to behave the way he did. I felt an obligation to try to help him." Second, due to very high humane orientation in Egypt, if the family of an employee has a problem, colleagues and the boss will quickly get involved to help. Taking care of friends in need is a major element of the culture and there is very little demarcation between colleagues and friends. Third, it is easier and more acceptable for the boss in Brazil to get to know the family members and spend time with them during social occasions. It is not, however, a good idea for him to try to do the same with Egyptian families. The contact should only be with and through the employee. Egyptian families tend to be more private and inaccessible to outsiders, possibly due to the intense in-group culture. People tend to stay close to their roots and develop a very strong sense of belonging. In short, even though the American manager will spend time building personal ties and maintaining in-group relationships both in Egypt and Brazil, the nature of his behavior will need to be somewhat different.

Like Brazil, the manager needs to pay his respects and call on the key executives in the Egyptian organization and start the process of building personal relationships. Unlike the French executives, the Egyptian executives will in all likelihood enjoy this approach and respond positively.

In developing a business strategy for the team, several cultural attributes need to be taken into consideration. The team will enjoy providing input but they expect decisions to be made by the leader. Family-related activities are always celebrated and employees are often excused from work to be able to properly plan such occasions. However, leaders also tend to use the friendly environment to maintain their control and build loyalty within their workforce. Egyptian employees expect their leaders to develop and communicate heroic and grand strategies. Due to their high institutional collectivism and performance orientation, it is helpful to design and communicate ambitious strategies and put them into the broader context of the corporation. Employees will resonate to ideas that would help the corporation and the unit achieve prominence in their competitive arenas. They also like strong rhetoric and get excited by the desire to be part of the winning team. In terms of the reward system, individual performance-based financial rewards, while helpful, are not the best motivators. The system should be seen to be humane to all; it should have a strong group-based component, and it should consist of a variety of benefits that are not typically offered in the US. Such benefits should be focused on the families of employees. For example, tuition assistance to employees' children, paid family vacation, and free or subsidized toys or home appliances could be very well received. As with other Middle East countries, although it is important for the individual to be successful, it is the family or group success that is more dominant.

China

China is part of the Confucian Asia cluster. The two CLT dimensions contributing to outstanding leadership are charismatic/value-based and team-oriented leadership, even though these scores are not particularly high. Humane-oriented leadership is viewed favorably, but it is not as important as the first two CLT dimensions. Although participative leadership is also viewed positively, it is about equal to the lowest-scoring clusters. Autonomous leadership is viewed neutrally, and self-protective leadership is seen as a slight impediment to effective leadership. Table 4 shows that compared to other GLOBE countries, the Confucian Asia cluster is ranked relatively low with respect to participative and relatively high with respect to self-protective leadership dimensions.

As shown in the Appendix, the US and Chinese cultures are similar in terms of their performance orientation, humane orientation, and power distance. The Chinese culture seems to be less future oriented, less assertive, more collectivist, both small group and socially, and more rules oriented.

Figure 4 below shows the comparison of culturally contingent leadership attributes between American and Chinese managers. Both American and Chinese managers like excellence-oriented leaders who strive for performance improvement in themselves and their subordinates. This is probably driven by the fact that both cultures share a strong performance orientation, as shown in the Appendix. They also both like leaders who are honest. However, the figure shows that the US scores on both these attributes are higher than the Chinese scores.

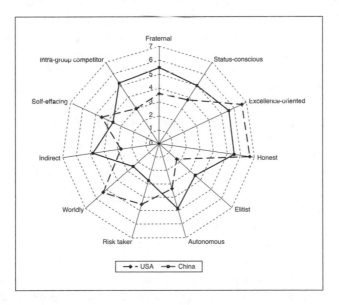

Figure 4. US versus China

Chinese managers seem to like leaders who are fraternal and friendly with their subordinates and who have an indirect approach to communication, using metaphors and parables to communicate their point. American managers have a neutral view of fraternal leadership and a negative view of indirect leadership. The difference can probably be explained by the fact that the US culture is much more assertive and less in-group oriented than that in China (see Appendix). In a less assertive culture such as China, people tend to use nuances and a context-rich language to communicate. They prefer indirect communication to avoid the possibility of hurting someone. Furthermore, in a highly group-oriented culture such as China, group harmony is critical and the leader's role is to strengthen group ties. As a result, leaders are expected to be supportive of their subordinates and act as good friends for them. They are expected to build emotional ties with their groups and their relationships with their subordinates go far beyond what is the norm in a country such as the US. The leader is seen as a paternal figure who should take care of his subordinates and their families.

American managers are not excited about leaders who are status conscious and are negative toward leaders who are elitist. In contrast, Chinese managers like the former type of leadership and are neutral toward the latter. This is reflective of the importance of hierarchy in the Chinese culture. Confucianism's "Three Bonds"— emperor rules the minister, father rules the son, and husband rules the wife—serve as the foundation of the Chinese society: "Chinese business structure can be directly linked to the history of patriarchy: the owner or manager plays the father's role, and the subordinates or employees play the son."[31]

Within such a hierarchical structure, the leader tends to be authoritative and expects respect and obedience and tends to make autonomous decisions. That is why Chinese managers do not admire leaders who are self-effacing, because such leaders do not emanate confidence. A group of American managers was recently in China to discuss a possible joint venture with a Chinese company. American managers expected to spend a few days working with their Chinese counterparts to brainstorm ideas and develop action plans. After a few frustrating days, they were told that they needed to find a Chinese agent to help them implement the deal. In conversations with the Chinese agent, they learned that the Chinese counterpart's expectation from the meetings was very different. They learned that the Chinese company wanted to use the meetings to help build personal ties among the Chinese and American managers and was upset that the Americans were asking aggressive questions and were focused solely on business rather than personal matters. They also learned that the top Chinese executive had no interest in sharing decision-making with anyone. Instead, he wanted to use private lunches and dinners with the head of the American delegation to make serious decisions and reach agreements.

Chinese managers are very negative toward worldly leaders who have a global outlook. In contrast, Americans admire such leaders. This could be explained by the fact that the two cultures are very different in terms of in-group collectivism. The Chinese culture is very high on this dimension, which means it is less interested in anything outside of their in-group. Perhaps they view the world as out-group compared to China and view it as less important.

When in China . . .

The Chinese culture is distinct by its high performance orientation, high institutional orientation, and high in-group collectivism. Building personal ties and relationships is reflected in the Chinese concept of "guanxi" whose loose English translation is networking. It is a manifestation of the fact that one's value and importance is embedded in his/her ties and relationships. As a result, "In China, the primary qualities expected in a leader or executive is someone who is good at establishing and nurturing personal relationships, who practices benevolence towards his or her subordinates, who is dignified and aloof but sympathetic, and puts the interests of his or her employees above his or her own."[32]

Much of Chinese life and culture is based on Confucian ideas, which emphasize the importance of relationships and community. Even the word "self" has a negative connotation.[33] Our hypothetical American manager needs to be careful about how his behavior and manners are perceived by the Chinese. Being polite, considerate, and moral are desirable attributes. At the same time, the American manager can get the Chinese employees excited by engaging their high performance culture. Developing an exciting vision is very effective. The relative high score on future orientation can also help the new manager get the employees motivated. But perhaps the most critical key success factor is how the manager goes about building personal ties and relationships with a wide network of individuals and groups. His "guanxi" will be the ultimate test of his success. In building guanxi with his employees, he needs to show high respect to the employees' families, keep them in mind when designing work schedules and reward systems, and make sure that employees see him and the organization as a strong supporter of their own guanxi. Perhaps a big challenge to the American executive is how to make sure his natural American assertiveness does not turn his Chinese employees and counterparts off and does not impede his efforts at building strong relationships.

EMBARKING ON A CROSS-CULTURAL LEADERSHIP JOURNEY

The existing literature on cross-cultural management is more useful at the conceptual level than at the behavioral level. Much of the advice offered to executives tends to be context-free and general such as "understand and respect the other culture." But the problems facing a typical global executive are context-specific; for example, how to understand and respect the Brazilian culture. In behavioral terms, understanding the Brazilian culture may be quite different from understanding and respecting the Egyptian culture because they are very different cultures.

In this reading, we have presented the cultural profiles of four countries based on a rigorous and scientific research project. We have also provided very specific ideas on the managerial implications of the different cultural profiles along with action-oriented advice on how an American manager can "put himself in the other culture's shoes" and be adaptable. Besides the culture specific ideas presented earlier, we propose a two-step process for any executive who is embarking on a new assignment in a new country. Regardless of the host country, these two steps help build a positive pathway towards cultural understanding and adaptability.

First, the executive needs to share information about his own, as well as the host country's, culture. Most of the advice that executives receive is about how they can adapt and adjust to other cultures. We propose a somewhat different approach. When people from different cultures come into contact, they usually have unstated and sometimes false or exaggerated stereotypes about the other side. While it is important that the executive learn about the host culture, it is not sufficient. Executives need to tell the host employees about their own cultures. For example, if these executives are in Egypt, then they should show the employees how the American and Egyptian cultures and leadership attributes compare. They should show both similarities and differences. In this reading, we showed that there is a set of leadership attributes that are universally desirable and universally undesirable. Similarities represent a fertile ground to build mutual understanding. The informed executive can then use the session to discuss their implications. What does integrity mean to a French manager? Or to a Brazilian manager? The executive can also compare the findings about his/her own culture with their perceptions of American culture to dispel any misunderstandings. This exercise in mapping and surfacing cultural attributes can go a long way to build mutual understanding and trust between the players. For example, our findings show that American culture is reported to be more moderate on many cultural dimensions than it is stereotypically believed to be. One of the unique features of GLOBE is that we have taken several steps to ensure that the reports by country managers are not confounded by such things as methodological problems and represent the true broader culture of their societies.

Second, the global manager needs to think about how to bridge the gap between the two cultures. Much of the advice executives receive seems to suggest, explicitly or implicitly, that the executive needs to become more like them. We do not necessarily subscribe to this viewpoint. While it is important to understand the other culture, it does not necessarily mean that one should automatically apply their approach. For example, leaders are seen as benign autocrats in Egypt. If an American manager does not like this approach, then he should educate the employees on his approach to leadership; why it is not dictatorial, and why he prefers it. Managers need to make sure the employees understand that their approach is not a sign of weakness, but a more effective style for the manager and for the team's and organization's success. It is a judgment call to say it is a "more effective" style than what the team is used to, but it is one that they should employ with the team. The global manager needs to tell the employees what managerial functions they are willing to change and what team functions they would like the employees to change so that the team can work from, and succeed on, common ground incorporating both cultures. The manager then needs to seek their help on both approaches; i.e. each culture making changes to accommodate and strengthen the other. Both approaches can take place at the same time and with respect to both cultures, as long as the manager gets the employees involved in the process. In other words, instead of a solitary learning journey for the executive, managers can create a collective learning journey that can be enriching, educational, and productive for both sides.

ATTRIBUTES OF GLOBAL LEADERS

The essence of global leadership is the ability to influence people who are not like the leader and come from different cultural backgrounds. To succeed, global leaders need to have a global mindset, tolerate high levels of ambiguity, and show cultural adaptability and flexibility. This reading provides some examples of these attributes. In contrast to a domestic manager, the hypothetical manager discussed in this reading needs a global mindset because s/he needs to understand a variety of cultural and leadership paradigms, and legal, political, and economic systems, as well as different competitive frameworks.[34] We used GLOBE findings to provide a scientifically based comparison of cultural and leadership paradigms in the five countries. We showed that countries can be different on some cultural dimensions and similar on others. Brazil and Egypt are both high on in-group collectivism, but different on performance orientation. France and the US are both moderate on uncertainty avoidance but differ on power distance. China and the US are both high on performance orientation but very different on in-group collectivism. Furthermore, there are similarities and differences in the countries' leadership profiles. While a leadership attribute such as irritability is universally undesirable, another attribute such as compassion is culturally contingent, i.e. it is much more desirable in the US than in France.

Tolerance of ambiguity is another important attribute of a global leader. Every new country that s/he has to work in represents a new paradigm and new ways of doing things. This is typically an uncomfortable position for many people to be in because it requires learning new ideas quickly and letting go of what has already been learned. Of course, in the four scenarios, we showed that there are things in common across cultures and there are portable aspects of cultural learning. But we also showed that there are differences as well. Figuring out which one is which and what to do represents potentially stressful ambiguity to an expatriate manager.

Cultural adaptability refers to a manager's ability to understand other cultures and behave in a way that helps achieve goals and build strong and positive relations with local citizens. In the country scenarios, we showed that while in France the manager should not emphasize grand and ambitious corporate strategies, he can do this in China. Cultural adaptability refers to the mental and psychological ability to move from one situation and country to another. It means the ability to do a good job of developing personal relationships while in Egypt and then doing it very differently in France. The dexterity to adjust one's behavior is a critical requirement. Not everyone can do this; to many people it may bring into question one's own identity. In some ways, it is reminiscent of acting but the difference is that the global manager, unlike the actor, lives and works among real people and not other actors, so his task is more complicated.

DEVELOPING GLOBAL LEADERS

As mentioned earlier in this reading, a large majority of *Fortune* 500 corporations report a shortage of global leaders. Devising programs that would develop a global mindset in leaders has been called "the biggest challenge that looms in the new millennium for human resource managers."[35] There are a variety of ways that companies can enhance their pool of global leaders. To start with, they can make a large volume of information on cross-cultural and global issues and country-specific reports available to their managers. We have already referred to several books on this topic. In addition to the special issue of the *Human Resource Management Journal* mentioned earlier, there are special issues of other journals.[36] There are also a variety of software packages such as a multimedia package called "Bridging Cultures," a self-training program for those who will be living and working in other cultures. In addition, several services such as CultureGrams (www.culturegram.com) provide useful information about many countries. There are also a few websites providing useful information to managers[37] such as www.contactcga.com, belonging to the Center for Global assignments, the CIA World Fact Book at www.odci.gov/cia/publications/facxtbook/, and Global Dynamics Inc.'s www. globaldynamics.com/expatria.htm.

Formal education and training can also be helpful in developing global leaders. A recent survey showed that a large majority of firms were planning to increase funding for programs that would help globalize their leaders.[38] But despite its prevalence among multinational corporations, there is general consensus among experts that it is not a highly effective source of developing global leaders.[39] It is generally best used as a component of a comprehensive and integrated development program. Work experience and international assignment is by far the most effective source for developing global leadership capabilities.[40] Some experts view long-term international assignments as the "single most powerful experience in shaping the perspective and capabilities of effective global leaders."[41] Increasingly, companies such as GE, Citigroup, Shell, Siemens, and Nokia are using international assignments of high-potential employees as the means to develop their managers' global leadership mindsets and competencies.

APPENDIX 1: COUNTRY SCORES ON CULTURAL PRACTICES

Anglo Cultures	Latin Europe	Middle East Cultures	Confucian Asia	Latin America

Performance Orientation

Anglo Cultures	Latin Europe	Middle East Cultures	Confucian Asia	Latin America
USA 4.49	France 4.11	Egypt 4.27	China 4.45	Brazil 4.04
Canada 4.49	Israel 4.08	Kuwait 3.95	Hong Kong 4.80	Bolivia 3.61
England 4.08	Italy 3.58	Morocco 3.99	Japan 4.22	Argentina 3.65
Ireland 4.36	Portugal 3.60	Qatar 3.45	Singapore 4.90	Colombia 3.94
New Zealand 4.72	Spain 4.01	Turkey 3.83	South Korea 4.55	Costa Rica 4.12
South Africa (W) 4.11	Swiss (French) 4.25		Taiwan 4.56	Ecuador 4.20
Australia 4.36				El Salvador 3.72
				Guatemala 3.81
				Mexico 4.10
				Venezuela 3.32

Anglo Cultures	Latin Europe	Middle East Cultures	Confucian Asia	Latin America

Future Orientation

Anglo Cultures	Latin Europe	Middle East Cultures	Confucian Asia	Latin America
USA 4.15	France 3.48	Egypt 3.86	China 3.75	Brazil 3.81
Canada 4.44	Israel 3.85	Kuwait 3.26	Hong Kong 4.03	Bolivia 3.61
England 4.28	Italy 3.25	Morocco 3.26	Japan 4.29	Argentina 3.08
Ireland 3.98	Portugal 3.71	Qatar 3.78	Singapore 5.07	Colombia 3.27
New Zealand 3.47	Spain 3.51	Turkey 3.74	South Korea 3.97	Costa Rica 3.60
South Africa (W) 4.13	Swiss (French) 4.27		Taiwan 3.96	Ecuador 3.74
Australia 4.09				El Salvador 3.80
				Guatemala 3.24
				Mexico 3.87
				Venezuela 3.35

APPENDIX 1 — continued

Anglo Cultures	Latin Europe	Middle East Cultures	Confucian Asia	Latin America
Assertiveness Orientation				
USA 4.55	**France 4.13**	**Egypt 3.91**	**China 3.76**	**Brazil 4.20**
Canada 4.05	Israel 4.23	Kuwait 3.63	Hong Kong 4.67	Bolivia 3.79
England 4.15	Italy 4.07	Morocco 4.52	Japan 3.59	Argentina 4.22
Ireland 3.92	Portugal 3.65	Qatar 4.11	Singapore 4.17	Colombia 4.20
New Zealand 3.42	Spain 4.42	Turkey 4.53	South Korea 4.40	Costa Rica 3.75
South Africa (W) 4.60	Swiss (French) 3.47		Taiwan 3.92	Ecuador 4.09
Australia 4.28				El Salvador 4.62
				Guatemala 3.89
				Mexico 4.45
				Venezuela 4.33

Anglo Cultures	Latin Europe	Middle East Cultures	Confucian Asia	Latin America
Societal Collectivism				
USA 4.20	**France 3.93**	**Egypt 4.50**	**China 4.77**	**Brazil 3.83**
Canada 4.38	Israel 4.46	Kuwait 4.49	Hong Kong 4.13	Bolivia 4.04
England 4.27	Italy 3.68	Morocco 3.87	Japan 5.19	Argentina 3.66
Ireland 4.63	Portugal 3.92	Qatar 4.50	Singapore 4.90	Colombia 3.81
New Zealand 4.81	Spain 3.85	Turkey 4.03	South Korea 5.20	Costa Rica 3.93
South Africa (W) 4.62	Swiss (French) 4.22		Taiwan 4.59	Ecuador 3.90
Australia 4.29				El Salvador 3.71
				Guatemala 3.70
				Mexico 4.06
				Venezuela 3.96

APPENDIX 1 — continued

In-Group Collectivism

Anglo Cultures	Latin Europe	Middle East Cultures	Confucian Asia	Latin America
USA 4.25	**France 4.37**	**Egypt 5.64**	**China 5.80**	**Brazil 5.18**
Canada 4.26	Israel 4.70	Kuwait 5.80	Hong Kong 5.32	Bolivia 5.47
England 4.08	Italy 4.94	Morocco 5.87	Japan 4.63	Argentina 5.51
Ireland 5.14	Portugal 5.51	Qatar 4.71	Singapore 5.64	Colombia 5.73
New Zealand 3.67	Spain 5.45	Turkey 5.88	South Korea 5.54	Costa Rica 5.32
South Africa (W) 4.50	Swiss (French) 3.85		Taiwan 5.59	Ecuador 5.81
Australia 4.17				El Salvador 5.35
				Guatemala 5.63
				Mexico 5.71
				Venezuela 5.53

Humane Orientation

Anglo Cultures	Latin Europe	Middle East Cultures	Confucian Asia	Latin America
USA 4.17	**France 3.40**	**Egypt 4.73**	**China 4.36**	**Brazil 3.66**
Canada 4.49	Israel 4.10	Kuwait 4.52	Hong Kong 3.90	Bolivia 4.05
England 3.72	Italy 3.63	Morocco 4.19	Japan 4.30	Argentina 3.99
Ireland 4.96	Portugal 3.91	Qatar 4.42	Singapore 3.49	Colombia 3.72
New Zealand 4.32	Spain 3.32	Turkey 3.94	South Korea 3.81	Costa Rica 4.39
South Africa (W) 3.49	Swiss (French) 3.93		Taiwan 4.11	Ecuador 4.65
Australia 4.28				El Salvador 3.71
				Guatemala 3.89
				Mexico 3.98
				Venezuela 4.25

APPENDIX 1—continued

Power Distance

Anglo Cultures	Latin Europe	Middle East Cultures	Confucian Asia	Latin America
USA 4.88	France 5.28	Egypt 4.92	China 5.04	Brazil 5.33
Canada 4.82	Israel 4.73	Kuwait 5.12	Hong Kong 4.96	Bolivia 4.51
England 5.15	Italy 5.43	Morocco 5.80	Japan 5.11	Argentina 5.64
Ireland 5.15	Portugal 5.44	Qatar 4.73	Singapore 4.99	Colombia 5.56
New Zealand 4.89	Spain 5.52	Turkey 5.57	South Korea 5.61	Costa Rica 4.74
South Africa (W) 5.16	Swiss (French) 4.86		Taiwan 5.18	Ecuador 5.60
Australia 4.74				El Salvador 5.68
				Guatemala 5.60
				Mexico 5.22
				Venezuela 5.40

Gender Egalitarianism

Anglo Cultures	Latin Europe	Middle East Cultures	Confucian Asia	Latin America
USA 3.34	France 3.64	Egypt 2.81	China 3.05	Brazil 3.31
Canada 3.70	Israel 3.19	Kuwait 2.58	Hong Kong 3.47	Bolivia 3.55
England 3.67	Italy 3.24	Morocco 2.84	Japan 3.19	Argentina 3.49
Ireland 3.21	Portugal 3.66	Qatar 3.63	Singapore 3.70	Colombia 3.67
New Zealand 3.22	Spain 3.01	Turkey 2.89	South Korea 2.50	Costa Rica 3.56
South Africa (W) 3.27	Swiss (French) 3.42		Taiwan 3.18	Ecuador 3.07
Australia 3.40				El Salvador 3.16
				Guatemala 3.02
				Mexico 3.64
				Venezuela 3.62

APPENDIX 1—*continued*

Anglo Cultures	Latin Europe	Middle East Cultures	Confucian Asia	Latin America
Uncertainty Avoidance				
USA 4.15	France 4.43	Egypt 4.06	China 4.94	Brazil 3.60
Canada 4.58	Israel 4.01	Kuwait 4.21	Hong Kong 4.32	Bolivia 3.35
England 4.65	Italy 3.79	Morocco 3.65	Japan 4.07	Argentina 3.65
Ireland 4.30	Portugal 3.91	Qatar 3.99	Singapore 5.31	Colombia 3.57
New Zealand 4.75	Spain 3.97	Turkey 3.63	South Korea 3.55	Costa Rica 3.82
South Africa (W) 4.09	Swiss (French) 4.98		Taiwan 4.34	Ecuador 3.68
Australia 4.39				El Salvador 3.62
				Guatemala 3.30
				Mexico 4.18
				Venezuela 3.44

NOTES

* **Mansour Javidan** is professor and director of the Garvin Center for the Cultures and Languages of International Management at Thunderbird, The Garvin School of International Management in Arizona. He is on the board of directors of the GLOBE (Global Leadership and Organizational Behavior Effectiveness) research program. Contact: javidanm@t-bird.edu.
Peter W. Dorfman is a full Professor in the Department of Management, New Mexico State University. Contact: pdorfman@nmsu.edu.
Mary Sully de Luque is an Assistant Professor of Management and a Research Fellow at Thunderbird, The Garvin School of International Management. Contact: sullym@t-bird.edu.
Robert J. House holds the Joseph Frank Bernstein endowed chair of Organizational Studies at the Wharton School of the University of Pennsylvania. Contact: house@wharton.upenn.edu.

1. House, R. J., Hanges, P. J., Ruiz-Quintanilla, S. A., Dorfman, P. W., Javidan, M., Dickson, M., et al. 1999. Cultural influences on leadership and organizations: Project GLOBE. In W. F. Mobley, M. J. Gessner, and V. Arnold (Eds.), *Advances in global leadership* (vol. 1, pp. 171–233). Stamford, CT: JAI Press.
2. Gregersen, H. B., Morrison, A. J., and Black, J. S. 1998. Developing leaders for the global frontier. *Sloan Management Review*, Fall: 21–32.
3. Hollenbeck, G. P. and McCall, M. W. 2003. Competence, not competencies: Making global executive development work. In W. Mobley and P. Dorfman (Eds.), *Advances in global leadership* (vol. 3). Oxford: JAI Press.
4. Black, J. S., Morrison, A. J., and Gergersen, H. B. 1999. *Global explorers: The next generation of leaders*. New York: Routledge; Rhinesmith, S. H. 1996. *A manager's guide to globalization*. Chicago: Irwin; Osland, J. S. 1995. *The adventure of working abroad: Hero tales from the global frontier*. San Francisco, CA: Jossey-Bass; Black, J. S., Gergersen, H. B., Mendenhall, M. E., and Stroh, L. K. 1999. *Globalizing people through international assignments*. Reading, MA: Addison-Wesley; Mobley, W. H. and Dorfman, P. W. 2003. *Advances in global leadership*. In W. H. Mobley and P. W. Dorfman (Eds.), *Advances in global leadership* (vol. 3). Oxford: JAI Press.
5. Gergerson, H. B., Morrison, A. J., and Mendenhall, M. E. 2000. Guest editors. *Human Resource Management Journal*, 39, 2&3, 113–299.
6. Morrison, A. J. 2000. Developing a global leadership model. *Human Resource Management Journal*, 39, 2&3, 117–131.
7. Kiedel, R. W. 1995. *Seeing organizational patterns: A new theory and language of organizational design*. San Francisco, CA: Berrett-Koehler.
8. Pucik, V. and Saba, T. 1997. Selecting and developing the global versus the expatriate manager: A review of the state of the art. *Human Resource Planning*, 40–54.
9. Wills, S. 2001. *Developing global leaders*. In P. Kirkbride and K. Ward (Eds.), *Globalization: The internal dynamic*. Chichester: Wiley, 259–284.
10. Bass, B. M. 1997. Does the transactional-transformational leadership paradigm transcend organizational and national boundaries? *American Psychologist*, 52(2), 130–139.
11. Hofstede, G. 1980. *Culture's consequences: International differences in work-related values*. Newbury Park, CA: Sage; Hofstede, G. 2001. *Culture's Consequences: Comparing values, behaviors, institutions, and organizations across nations*, 2nd ed. Thousand Oaks, CA: Sage; Trompenaars, F. and Hamden-Turner, C. 1998. *Riding the waves of culture*, 2nd ed. New York: McGraw-Hill; Kluckhohn, F. R. and Strodtbeck, F. L. 1961. *Variations in value orientations*. New York: Harper & Row.
12. House, R. J., Hanges, P. J., Javidan, M., Dorfman, P. W., and Gupta, V., and GLOBE Associates. 2004. *Leadership, culture and organizations: The globe study of 62 societies*. Thousand Oaks, CA: Sage.
13. Morrison, A. J. 2000. Developing a global leadership model. *Human Resource Management Journal*, 39, 2&3, 117–131.

14. Laurent, A. 1983. The cultural diversity of western conceptions of management. *International Studies of Management and Organization*, 13(2), 75–96; Trompenaars, F. 1993. *Riding the waves of culture: Understanding cultural diversity in business.* London: Breatley; Briscoe, D. R. and Schuler, R. S. 2004. *International human resource management,* 2nd ed. New York: Routledge.

15. Davis, D. D. and Bryant, J. L. 2003. Influence at a distance: Leadership in global virtual teams. In W. H. Mohley and P. W. Dorfman (Eds.), *Advances in global leadership* (vol. 3, pp. 303–340). Oxford: JAI Press.

16. Millman, J. Trade wins: The world's new tiger on the export scene isn't Asian; it's Mexico. *Wall Street Journal,* p. A1. May 9, 2000.

17. Smith, P. B. and Peterson, M. F. 1988. *Leadership, organizations and culture: An event management model.* London: Sage.

18. Smith, P. B. 2003. Leaders' sources of guidance and the challenge of working across cultures. In W. Mobley and P. Dorfman (Eds.), *Advances in global leadership* (vol. 3, pp. 167–182). Oxford: JAI Press; Smith, P. B., Dugan, S., and Trompenaars, F. 1996. National culture and the values of organizational employees: A dimensional analysis across 43 nations. *Journal of Cross-Cultural Psychology*, 27(2), 231–264.

19. Hazucha, J. F., Hezlett, S. A., Bontems-Wackens, S., and Ronnqvist, G. 1999. In search of the Euro-manager: Management competencies in France, Germany, Italy, and the United States. In W.H. Mobley, M.J. Gessner, and V. Arnold (Eds.), *Advances in global leadership* (vol. 1, pp. 267–290). Stamford, CT: JAI Press.

20. Javidan, M. and Carl, D. 2004. East meets West. *Journal of Management Studies,* 41:4, June, 665–691; Javidan, M. and Carl, D. 2005. Leadership across cultures: A study of Canadian and Taiwanese executives, *Management International Review,* 45(1), 23–44.

21. House, R. J., Wright, N. S., and Aditya, R. N. 1997. Cross-cultural research on organizational leadership: A critical analysis and a proposed theory. In P. C. Earley and M. Erez (Eds.), *New perspectives in international industrial/organizational psychology* (pp. 535–625). San Francisco: The New Lexington Press.

22. Chemers, M. M. 1997. *An integrative theory of leadership.* London: Lawrence Erlbaum Associates; Smith, P. B. and Peterson, M. F. 1988. *Leadership, organizations and culture: An event management model.* London: Sage.

23. Shaw, J. B. (1990). A cognitive categorization model for the study of intercultural management. *Academy of Management Review,* 15(4), 626–645.

24. Lord, R. G. and Maher, K. J. 1991. *Leadership and information processing: Linking perceptions and performance* (vol. 1). Cambridge, MA: Unwin Hyman.

25. House, R. J., Hanges, P. J., Ruiz-Quintanilla, S. A., Dorfman, P. W., Javidan, M., Dickson, M., et al. 1999. Cultural influences on leadership and organizations: Project GLOBE. In W. F. Mobley, M. J. Gessner, and V. Arnold (Eds.), *Advances in global leadership* (vol. 1, pp. 171–233). Stamford, CT: JAI Press.

26. In addition to the aggregated raw (i.e. absolute) scores for CLTs provided in Table 2, we also computed a response bias corrected measure as an integral part of the analysis strategy. We referred to this measure as the relative measure because of a unique property attributed to this procedure. These relative CLT scores indicate the relative importance of each CLT leadership dimension within a person, culture, or culture cluster. This procedure not only removed the cultural response biases, but it also had the advantage of illustrating the differences among the cultures and the clusters. Along with ranking the clusters with absolute CLT scores, we used this relative measure to compare the relative importance of each CLT dimension among cultures. Ranking of clusters using both types of scores are presented in Table 3. We should point out that the correlation between the absolute and relative measures is close to perfect—above .90 for all of the CLT leadership dimensions. Computational procedures for this measure are detailed in House et al., 2004.

27. Cullen, J. B. 2002. *Multinational management: A strategic approach* (2nd ed.). Cincinnati, OH: South-Western Thomson Learning.

28.   Bossidy, L. and Charan, R. 2002. *Execution: The discipline of getting things done.* New York: Crown Business Books. p. 103.
29.   Hallowell, R., Bowen, D., and Knoop, C. 2002. Four Seasons goes to Paris, *Academy of Management Executive,* 16(4), 7–24.
30.   Ibid.
31.   Dayal-Gulati, A. 2004. *Kellogg on China: Strategies for success,* Evanston, IL: Northwestern University Press.
32.   De Mente, Boye Lafayette. 2000. *The Chinese have a word for it: The complete guide to Chinese thought and culture.* Chicago: Passport Books.
33.   Rosen, R. *Global Literacies.* Simon & Schuster, 2000.
34.   Black, J. S. and Gergersen, H. B. 2000. High impact training: Forging leaders for the global frontier. *Human Resource Management Journal,* 39 (2&3), 173–184.
35.   Oddou, G., Mendenhall, M.E., and Ritchi, J. B. Leveraging travel as a tool for global leadership development. *Human Resource Management Journal,* 39, 2&3, 159–172.
36.   Dastmalchian, A. and Kabasakal, H. 2001. Guest editors, special issue on the Middle East, *Applied Psychology: An International Review.* vol. 50(4); Javidan, M. and House, R. Spring 2002 Guest editors, special Issue on GLOBE, *Journal of World Business,* Vol. 37, No. 1; Peterson, M. F. and Hunt, J. G. 1997. Overview: International and cross-cultural leadership research (Part II). *Leadership Quarterly,* 8(4), 339–342.
37.   For more information, see Mendenhall, M.E. and Stahl, G. K. Expatriate training and development: Where do we go from here? *Human Resource Management Journal,* 39, 2&3, 251–265.
38.   Black, J. S., Morrison, A. J., and Gergersen, H. B. 1999. *Global explorers: The next generation of leaders.* New York: Routledge.
39.   Dodge, B. 1993. Empowerment and the evolution of learning, *Education and Training,* 35(5), 3–10; Sherman, S. 1995. How tomorrow's best leaders are learning their stuff. *Fortune,* 90–106.
40.   Conner, J. 2000. Developing the global leaders of tomorrow. *Human Resource Management Journal,* 39, 2&3, 147–157.
41.   Black, J. S., Gergersen, H. B., Mendenhall, M. E., and Stroh L. K. 1999. *Globalizing people through international assignments.* Reading, MA: Addison-Wesley.

Stacey R. Fitzsimmons, Christof Miska and Günter K. Stahl

MULTICULTURAL INDIVIDUALS: WHAT CAN THEY BRING TO GLOBAL ORGANIZATIONS?

GLOBAL BUSINESSES are fast-moving places with technologies that enable people to be more mobile than ever. Not only do individuals travel more frequently and connect with people from societal cultures that are different from their own, but as globalization dissolves geographical barriers, more and more individuals find themselves identifying with not only one culture but with two or even more. Immigration statistics indicate that this demographic is both large and growing. In 2006, 12 percent of the population in OECD countries were foreign-born (OECD, 2009), and multicultural individuals are becoming so important that UNESCO discussed their impact in a recent report (*Investing in Cultural Diversity and Intercultural Dialogue*, 2009).

Indra Nooyi and Carlos Ghosn could be poster children for multiculturalism. Indra Nooyi, CEO and chair of PepsiCo, ranked the #1 most powerful woman by Fortune Magazine from 2006 to 2009 (Fortune, 2009), draws on her multicultural identity to shape PepsiCo as a global company. Nooyi moved to the US to complete her Master's degree at Yale, after degrees at the Indian Institute of Management and Madras Christian College. Under her watch, PepsiCo ramped up its international sales, and she has turned PepsiCo into a corporation that truly appreciates and derives benefit from its diverse employees. She also speaks out – sometimes controversially – in favor of working globally:

Although I'm a daughter of India, I'm an American businesswoman ... Graduates, as you aggressively compete on the international business stage, understand that the five major continents and their peoples – the five fingers of your hand – each have their own strengths and their own contributions to make. Just as each of your fingers must coexist to create a critically important tool, each of the five major continents must also coexist to create a world in balance. You, as an American businessperson, will either contribute to or take away from, this balance.

(Indra Nooyi, as cited in *Business Week*, May 20, 2005)

Carlos Ghosn, another well-known multicultural, is president and CEO of both Renault and Nissan. He speaks five languages, was born in Brazil, spent time in Lebanon as a child, graduated with engineering degrees from Paris, and is a French citizen. When he merged Renault with Nissan, he drew on his Brazilian–Lebanese–French background in order to succeed in Japan, a country that was completely foreign to him at the time.

In contrast to monoculturals, multiculturals possess considerable experience in two or even more cultural settings. Because they take part concurrently in several cultural contexts, multiculturals develop cultural awareness and knowledge about the habits, norms and values of several cultures. They understand and apply the rules of their cultures and are usually fluent in the respective languages, which helps them operate within and between their cultures (David, 2006). In other words, multiculturals have deeply internalized more than one culture (Nguyen and Benet-Martinez, 2007), making them potentially valuable in the world of international business and global organizations, where cultural fluency is both a necessity and a challenge.

Yet, few global organizations are truly aware of multicultural individuals' potential. One reason might be that there is more than one way to be multicultural (Nguyen and Benet-Martinez, 2007), making it challenging for organizations to identify multicultural employees. Alternatively, organizations may not be aware of the particular skills their multicultural employees possess, may be threatened by people of mixed cultural identity or may see them as a source of problems. Even organizations that consider a multicultural workforce an asset may lack the necessary processes to leverage the distinct skills of multiculturals (e.g. selection processes to place them in positions where they can realize their full potential). In order to understand how organizations can best use their multicultural employees' skills, it is important to first understand what multicultural employees contribute to international business.

HOW CAN MULTICULTURAL EMPLOYEES CONTRIBUTE TO GLOBAL BUSINESS?

Next, we explore multiculturals' impact on five international business activities – international teams, intercultural negotiations, international assignments, mergers and acquisitions, global leadership and ethics – illustrated with examples about Indra Nooyi and Carlos Ghosn.

Multiculturals' Impact on Teams

When you have a very diverse team – people of different backgrounds, different culture, different gender, different age, you are going to get a more creative team – probably getting better solutions, and enforcing them in a very innovative way and with a very limited number of preconceived ideas.

(Ghosn, April 11, 2008)

I look at the amazing diversity of our Executive Committee. We have 29 people in the Executive Committee. We have a Sudanese leading Europe, a North American as a vice chair, an Italian who is leading North American beverages, a Middle Easterner runs Asia, and I don't even want to talk about the CEO. That diversity is what keeps our company grounded and helps us make market-based, sensible decisions.

(Nooyi, 2009)

Indra Nooyi and Carlos Ghosn have both harnessed the power of diverse teams to drive innovation at PepsiCo and Nissan-Renault. Ghosn, in particular, is known for using cross-cultural and cross-functional teams whenever possible. "Competing in the global marketplace requires the contributions of multitalented, multicultural people working together to achieve success" (Carlos Ghosn, as cited in Rivas-Micoud, 2007). In the future, Nooyi's list of the cultures represented on her executive committee might include more hyphenated cultures: Sudanese–French, Italian–American or Chinese–Canadian. As businesses move from teams where each individual has only one culture to teams where each individual has two or more cultures, we propose two ways multicultural individuals might influence team effectiveness: they might act as bridges across cultural faultlines, and reduce the process time required to tap multiple perspectives.

First, global teams are usually multicultural. Divisions within groups – also known as faultlines – often develop along cultural lines, promoting disharmony, dissatisfaction and poor performance (Lau and Murnighan, 2005; Polzer et al. 2006). Faultlines develop along cultural lines when the group's composition emphasizes cultural divisions. For example, American–Chinese teams often develop faultlines, because it is obvious who is Chinese and who is American. In order to avoid faultlines and the tendency of culturally diverse teams to divide into *factions based on nationality*, managers can make subgroup divisions less obvious by including multicultural individuals (e.g. Chinese–Americans) on the team (Gibson and Vermeulen, 2003). When team members straddle the cultural divide, and belong in both groups, they become bridges across the faultline, reducing its effect (Lau and Murnighan, 2005). Multiculturals can bridge faultlines through language, cultural knowledge or by explaining the opposing subgroup's behavior. Also, team members are less likely to categorize multiculturals into specific national or cultural groups (e.g. "she's typically Chinese"), which reduces "us versus them" thinking, intergroup hostility and stereotyping. Overall, we predict that when multicultural individuals are part of teams that cross cultures, those teams will be less likely to develop cultural faultlines and dysfunctional team dynamics than cross-cultural teams using only monoculturals.

Second, multicultural individuals may benefit teams by speeding up the process of tapping diverse perspectives in a multicultural team. The most common reason to purposefully build multicultural teams is to benefit from new ideas drawn from different cultural perspectives, but the most common drawback is that multicultural teams take longer to perform tasks, because of conflict, misunderstandings or differences in values (called process time) (DiStefano and Maznevski, 2000; Schippers et al., 2003). Multicultural individuals may bring new ideas to the team, because they have multiple cultural perspectives, and are able to access more than one simultaneously, but are less likely to produce team conflicts and misunderstandings, because they also share cultures with their teammates. For example, experiments showed that Asian–American multiculturals developed more creative dishes from both Asian and American ingredients, rather than from all Asian or all American ingredients (Cheng et al., 2008). We predict that multicultural employees can contribute the most to internationally focused creative team activities, such as global product development, scenario planning and the design of a locally adapted marketing strategy.

Overall, when teams are made of individuals from multiple cultures, it usually takes longer for those individuals to understand one another than for members of a monocultural team (DiStefano and Maznevski, 2000; Thomas, 1999). When the team's multiculturalism comes from multicultural individuals instead of monoculturals from different cultures, the team may be able to work together faster, because faultlines may be weakened and because multiculturals are more likely to be curious about other cultures, as evidenced by Carlos Ghosn's comments in this reading. Multicultural individuals may be most useful in teams that are expected to perform complex, internationally focused tasks.

Multiculturals' Impact on Intercultural Negotiations

As CEO of PepsiCo, Indra Nooyi negotiates with businesses all over the world. Among her biggest negotiations were the merger with Quaker Oats Company in 2000, and her negotiations with the Indian media and government in 2006 about Pepsi's health standards in India. She was able to draw on her own cultural norms and bargaining strategies in both cases, adding to the ease of negotiations. It is a different situation in China, where she has very little experience, but her experience seeing the world through multiple cultural frames taught her to look for opportunities for integrative deals, based on cultural differences. For example, she took a two-week trip to China because she wanted to get a better feel for the country. "What are its issues? What makes it tick? I didn't want to come here clueless as to what was going on" (Indra Nooyi, as cited in Einhorn, 2009). Her experience demonstrates several ways multicultural negotiators can improve negotiations.

Good negotiators find a balance between maximizing individual objectives and common goals simultaneously. It is therefore important that negotiators understand their counterparts' goals, expectations, and negotiation strategies, which in a cross-cultural setting frequently turn out to be an obstacle. When negotiators share a culture, they usually share common expectations about acceptable negotiation strategies, behavior, and the sequence of the bargaining process. However, when negotiators from different cultures meet, they are often used to different cultural norms and standards (Cohen, 1997). For example, Argentineans, French and Indians prefer top-down approaches, from general to specific principles, whereas Mexicans, Japanese and Brazilians prefer building agreement from bottom up (Salacuse, 2005). Because of these types of differing expectations, same-culture negotiations, such as US–US or Japanese–Japanese, tend to have better outcomes than cross-cultural bargaining, (Brett and Okumura, 1998). We propose two ways multiculturals may be able to mitigate some of these intercultural negotiation challenges.

First, multicultural negotiators might appreciate differences in perspectives and negotiation strategies more than monoculturals, rather than seeing dissimilarities as obstacles. Multiculturals may develop this skill because they are constantly confronted with diverse or even contradicting realities, so they learn how to deal with such situations and how to make the best of them (Tadmor et al., 2009). Especially if negotiations are complex and require creative solutions, multicultural experience may be an advantage. Galinsky et al. (2008) found that perspective-taking (the ability to consider the world from another person's viewpoint) helped negotiators identify creative bargaining solutions. Multiculturals, because of their multiple cultural backgrounds, are likely to possess good perspective-taking abilities and thus have an advantage in negotiations that require considering different views. In fact, Nooyi identifies this ability as her key negotiating strength: "I always look at things from their point of view as well as mine" (Indra Nooyi, as cited in Hobbs, 2008).

Second, multicultural negotiators may be able to positively influence their negotiation partners' communication experience. Research shows that although cross-cultural negotiations are often fraught with tensions and misunderstandings, international negotiations can produce higher joint gains than same-cultural negotiations when the communication experience is pleasant for both parties (e.g. when both parties feel comfortable and make efforts reciprocating and adapting to the other party's norms and expectations) (Liu et al., 2010). When both partners feel at ease and the negotiation takes place in an atmosphere of trust and respect, intercultural negotiators may be able to leverage their multiple perspectives for increased creativity, creating joint gains. Together, these mechanisms indicate that in international negotiations, multiculturals may be at an advantage because they are better able to take both perspectives and positively influence their negotiation partners' communication experience.

Multiculturals' Impact on Expatriation

As a larger number of organizations become increasingly global, it will become gradually more necessary for employees to move internationally. In fact, international job rotations may be among the most effective talent development tools (Stahl et al., 2009). Yet, international assignments are fraught with failure. Some return home early, while others are merely ineffective; all are costly to the organization. Multicultural individuals may be more successful in international assignments than monoculturals because they possess certain skills and knowledge that help them adjust to a different cultural environment.

Brannen et al. (2009) found that multicultural individuals have higher cultural metacognition than monoculturals, a key aspect of cultural intelligence. This aspect of cultural intelligence is essential in situations where international assignees are not familiar with the host culture, because it facilitates cross-cultural adjustment and cultural learning (Thomas et al., 2008). When Carlos Ghosn took positions in France and Brazil, he identified with the cultures, and knew how to work effectively in both locations. In contrast, when he moved to the US and Japan, he had no prior experience with the cultures, and had to learn how to be effective as he went along. As a multicultural individual, he had the mindset and skills necessary to be effective in cultures he knew well, and in those he did not. As he says in his book, when choosing an expatriate, "I wouldn't pick a person who'd never lived abroad, . . . who'd never demonstrated an ability to work in a different culture from his own, and send him into such a situation. I had the 'ideal' background." (Ghosn and Riès, 2005)

However, multiculturalism's impact on expatriation success is not straight-forward. Expatriates are not only faced with the challenges associated with adapting to a different culture and work environment, but must also act as liaisons between the foreign subsidiary and the home office. In this capacity, they must demonstrate strong commitment to the head office, and make sure that the company's global policies are carried out locally – a situation that has been termed the *dual allegiance* dilemma (Black and Gregersen, 1992; Vora et al., 2007). Dual allegiance refers to the fact that expatriates are often torn between their allegiance to the home office, and their allegiance to the local subsidiary.

There are four ways expatriates resolve the dual allegiance dilemma: by remaining primarily loyal to their home-country environment (*hearts at home*); by priori-tizing local needs over the needs of head office (*gone native*); by caring primarily about their own careers, over and above the needs of head office or the local subsidiary (*free agents*); or by remaining highly committed to both the parent firm and the local subsidiary, and trying to reconcile the often conflicting demands and expectations of both organizations (*dual citizens*) (Black and Gregersen, 1992). Although each of these patterns may have some benefits, the first three patterns tend to be detrimental to the firm: Hearts-at-home expatriates sometimes force head office ideas on to subsidiaries, regardless of their local effectiveness; gone-native expatriates sometimes fight head office to a degree that impedes global coordination; and free agents have lost their allegiance to the parent firm, without making any attempts to adjust to the local environment. By contrast, dual citizens tend to excel at coordinating between head office and the local subsidiary, and they have a higher probability of completing the international assignment successfully (Vora et al., 2007). They are also better than the others at transferring knowledge.

Multicultural individuals may solve the dual allegiance dilemma differently than monoculturals, because they have experience managing two or more sometimes-conflicting identities. People such as Carlos Ghosn are more strongly linked to a global identity, rather than to individual countries, so they may be less likely to take on either the hearts-at-home or gone-native positions, and more likely to become dual citizens. However, a potential danger of a multicultural orientation is that managers may be prone to become "free agents", i.e. they may lack a strong commitment to either the parent firm or the local organization. When Ghosn was working for Michelin, he was willing to travel to any location, with any company. He saw himself as a global citizen, first and foremost, and as such may have had lower loyalty to any one country or organization. This example illustrates a challenge that is unique to multicultural employees.

Multiculturals' Impact on Ethics and Leadership

Indra Nooyi faced a particularly thorny ethical dilemma starting in 2003, when PepsiCo India was accused of allowing pesticides from local groundwater into their soft drinks, and of using up scarce water for an unnecessary commodity. The nation was appalled, protestors defaced ads, several Indian states banned soft drinks altogether and sales crashed. In addition, the government debated imposing strict new standards on soft drink companies. They would bring Indian standards in line with Europe's, but would make it difficult to operate profitably in the country. By 2006, when Nooyi took over as PepsiCo's CEO, things had not improved. Nooyi had to act quickly to convince India that Pepsi's products were safe and that they were protecting India's water supply.

Executives and businesspeople working in the global arena must decide whether to use their own ethical principles, or to adopt the local ethical principles. For example, when working in countries where bribery is common, some managers refuse to take part because bribery is universally wrong, while others accept some level of bribery – such as "facilitation payments" – as normal in that context. These two perspectives are called universalist and relativist ethical perspectives, respectively, and they represent two broad categories of ethical argumentation across cultures (Windsor, 2004). Ethical universalism assumes that the situation does not influence what is ethical; only universal rules determine what is ethical. The most famous example is Kant's categorical imperative, where right and wrong are based on rules that apply at all times, regardless of circumstances or consequences (White and Taft, 2004). In contrast, ethical relativism assumes that each culture has the right to determine its own set of rules about right and wrong. Visitors must respect the local customs and adapt to them (Tasioulas, 1998).

Multicultural employees may be able to reconcile these seemingly conflicting perspectives because they have more complex cognitive schemas associated with ethical decision making – particularly in cross-cultural contexts – and can use their multicultural identities to strike the appropriate balance between global consistency and local sensitivity – what ethics scholars Donaldson and Dunfee have described as "a need to retain local identity with the acknowledgement of values that transcend individual communities" (1999, p. 50). Frame switching gives multiculturals experience seeing the world from more than one perspective, and as a consequence, potentially increases their ability to determine when different is different and when different is simply wrong.

PepsiCo's Indra Nooyi, for example, endorses ethical relativism while at the same time adhering to universal standards and maintaining the ability to make decisions that are in the best interest of the whole organization. Nooyi's response to Pepsi's problems in India was universalist and reflected the company's global commitment to environmental sustainability and safety: "One thing I should have done was appear in India three years ago and say: Cut it out. These products are the safest in the world, bar none. And your tests are wrong." Despite these strong words, she also adopted some relativist behaviors, by reducing water usage to one quarter of previous levels. "We have to invest, too, in educating communities in how to farm better, collect water, and then work with industry to retrofit plants and recycle" (Indra Nooyi, as cited in Brady, 2007).

Multiculturals' ability to balance global consistency and local flexibility in ethical decision making has important implications for multinational corporations. If a company (e.g. from the US) wants to enforce a bribery ban when working abroad, then it might be better served by monocultural employees from the parent country, who are less likely to be responsive to local needs and expectations. If a company wants to recognize that different environmental standards exist across their operations, staffing key positions with local managers who lack a strong global orientation might be the best choice. Companies that have adopted a transnational approach to business ethics, which requires managers to be responsive to both global and local imperatives, might be best served by multicultural employees, whose ability to see complex ethical situations from multiple perspectives should be useful in this context.

Multiculturals' Impact on Cross-Border Alliances, Mergers and Acquisitions

Alliances, mergers and acquisitions are notoriously difficult to implement successfully. In mergers and acquisitions (M&A), special emphasis is usually placed on the strategic and financial goals of the deal, while the cultural and people implications rarely receive as much attention. However, research shows that the failure of M&A that otherwise have a sound strategic and financial fit is often due to problems integrating the different cultures and workforces of the combining firms (Marks and Mirvis, 2001; Pucik et al., 2010). Problems are exacerbated when M&A occur between companies based in different countries. In addition to obstacles created by differences in the institutional environments, cultural chauvinism, differences in management styles and business norms, and the often-unanticipated challenges inherent in communicating across long distances can all undermine the success of M&A. For example, the poor performance of DaimlerChrysler, one of the most talked-about mergers of the past decade, is often attributed to a culture clash that resulted in major integration problems (Vlasic and Stertz, 2000).

Strategic alliances tend to be more successful than mergers, but they are difficult to manage – especially across borders. In 1999, Carlos Ghosn led the alliance between Nissan and Renault. From an outside perspective, the cultural and language barriers seemed insurmountable. Nissan was in a desperate financial situation, and Renault had only recently pulled out of its own slump. Yet, the alliance's success was due, in part, to the fact that neither firm had enough power to control the other. Instead of forcing Nissan to change, Ghosn had to rely on building strong relationships across the organizational and cultural boundaries. In hindsight, this looks like brilliant strategizing, but it was likely also influenced by Ghosn's uniquely multicultural identity. He explains, "It's imperative for each side to preserve its own culture while at the same time making an effort to understand the other's culture and to adapt to it. We've chosen a way based on mutual respect and the acknowledgement of two enterprises and two identities" (Ghosn and Riès, 2005).

In cross-border alliances and M&A, multicultural managers may influence outcomes in several important ways and at different stages of the process. A key asset of multiculturals is their greater cultural empathy, perspective-taking skills and ability to bridge cultural gaps. These skills are important before the alliance or merger takes effect, during the due diligence and negotiation stages. The purpose of cultural due diligence is to evaluate factors that may influence the organizational fit, to understand the future cultural dynamics as the two organizations merge, and to prepare a plan for how cultural issues should be addressed if the deal goes forward. Questions of this nature require the due diligence team to probe into the normative structure, core values and assumptions, and the core philosophy of the company itself in order to understand the company from a holistic cultural perspective. In addition, the culture of the target company or partner reflects the industry, national and regional cultures in which it is embedded (Schneider and Barsoux, 2003). Thus, the cultural due diligence team must understand and assess not only the company itself but also the context in which the company exists, particularly its national culture. Managers with a multicultural background, who have a thorough understanding of both the acquiring firm's and the target's (or partner's) culture, and the environment in which it is embedded, can play a key role in the evaluation of the cultural fit and the development of the integration strategy.

Strategic alliances and M&A require some degree of interdependence and integration, and the integration is always a delicate and complicated process. There will be inevitable culture clashes and questions will arise about which identity will dominate when corporate cultures are combined. Instead of melting everyone together, senior executives must capitalize on the differences in culture. Carlos Ghosn discussed this point as follows:

> People will not give their best efforts if they feel that their identities are being consumed by a greater force. If any partnership or merger is to succeed, it must respect the identities and self-esteem of all the people involved . . . Two goals – making changes and safeguarding identity – could easily come into conflict. Pursuing them both entails a difficult, yet vital balancing act.
> (Carlos Ghosn, as cited in Stahl, 2004, p. 5)

To pull off this balancing act, companies are increasingly turning to dedicated integration managers supported by transition teams (Ashkenas and Francis, 2000). It seems likely that individuals who are well versed in both companies' cultures are better able to serve as integration managers or members of transition teams because they understand the vulnerabilities on both sides and are able to come up with culturally appropriate solutions that preserve the identity and dignity of all the people involved.

TYPES OF MULTICULTURAL INDIVIDUALS

This reading has so far focused on potential skills and abilities of multicultural employees as a group, but there is more than one way to be multicultural (Table 1). Each one is associated with its own unique set of benefits and challenges, and it is important for organizations to understand the differences, so they can avoid assuming all multiculturals share the same perspective. This is not an exhaustive list of ways to be multicultural, but the following four types are useful when considering how multicultural individuals can contribute to international business activities.

Marginals are people who have more than one culture, but who feel disassociated with both or all of them. Marginalization is psychologically difficult. For example, a survey of 5,366 immigrant adolescents across thirteen countries found that marginalized immigrants fared the worst, both psychologically and socioculturally (Berry et al., 2006). Even though Berry and colleagues' study demonstrates that this pattern is common among multicultural individuals, business people often do not talk openly about feeling marginalized, perhaps because of the negative implications of this pattern. However, there may be some benefits to being marginal. In particular, marginalized individuals may feel free to choose activities that are unconventional to both cultures (Rudmin, 2003). Because they have an in-depth knowledge of, yet are somewhat detached from, the cultures they represent, they may be able to make unpopular or even painful decisions, for example regarding layoffs and pay cuts, in a culturally appropriate manner.

Marginals may be more likely to employ a universalist ethical perspective, because they are less likely to switch cultural frames. Even though marginals have deeply internalized cultures, their cultural frames remain relatively stable, so they may be more likely to see ethics as a relatively stable construct, and may be more likely to endorse ethical universalism as a consequence. With respect to expatriation, and based on similarities with their cultural identity structures, we propose that marginals may be most likely to become free agents. Marginals have weak links to their own cultures, so may be more likely to also see themselves as weakly linked to their organizations.

Cosmopolitans, on the other hand, identify with many cultures (Hannerz, 1990). They are usually frequent travelers, and have lived in several different countries (Thompson and Tambyah, 1999). Cosmopolitans such as Carlos Ghosn tend to do well psychologically, with evidence that they are highly adaptable and are able to think in complex ways (Tadmor et al., 2009). Their multiple identities also make them especially resilient to identity threats (Binning et al., 2009). For example, if a South African-Dutch-German person felt like her Dutch identity was being threatened, she could switch to South African or German identities momentarily, to cope with the threat. This could explain why cosmopolitans tend to have better psychological outcomes than other types of multiculturals.

Table 1. Multicultural Types

Multicultural Type	Description	Example
Marginals	Marginals have more than one culture, but feel disassociated with both or all of them	**April Raintree, Métis character in a Native Canadian novel:** "It would be better to be a full-blooded Indian or full-blooded Caucasian. But being a half-breed, well, there's just nothing there." (Mosionier, 1999, p. 142; Pucik et al., 2010)
Separated	Separated multiculturals keep their cultural identities apart and identify with one or the other depending on the context	**Andrea Jung, CEO of Avon, and Chinese-American:** "I've definitely become more assertive ... It really was critical to have that *Western* versus *Eastern* aspect, and still feel like I never had to change who I am." ("Women@Google: Andrea Jung," 2009)
Integrated	Integrated multiculturals merge their cultures together, resulting in a new, hybrid culture	**Eric Liu, former speechwriter for President Clinton, and Chinese–American:** "I could never claim to be Chinese at the core. Yet neither would I claim, as if by default, to be merely 'white inside.' I do not want to be white. I only want to be integrated." (Liu, 1998)
Cosmopolitans	Cosmopolitans identify with many cultures, are usually frequent travelers, and have lived in several different countries	**Carlos Ghosn, President and CEO of Renault and Nissan, and French–Brazilian–Lebanese:** "He is the quintessential global executive." (Najjar, 2008, August) "When you are an outsider and you cannot be categorized into one culture, it makes people feel that you are unlikely to be biased." (Ghosn, 2008, August)

Both marginals and cosmopolitans may be at risk of becoming free agents during expatriation, and of preferring universalist ethics over relativist ethics. Marginals are only weakly identified with their cultures, while cosmopolitans identify more strongly with a global identity, over their individual countries. As a result, both types may take a similar approach with their organizations, and also see themselves as weakly linked to both parent and local organizations. Marginals and cosmopolitans also have relatively stable cultural frames, so they may be more likely to see ethics as a stable construct, and endorse ethical universalism as a result. Cosmopolitans alone may have an advantage during negotiations, over other types of multiculturals, because they have broader cultural experience than other multiculturals.

Separated and *integrated multiculturals* are related types, because they both identify with two cultures, although they mentally organize those cultures differently (Hong et al., 2000). Separated multiculturals keep their cultural identities apart. They identify with one or the other, depending on the context, resulting in two unique sets of cultural values. Integrated multiculturals merge their cultures together, resulting in a new, hybrid culture.

Research suggests that integrated multiculturals seem to have a lot of benefits, including lower stress, better social integration across cultures, and more creativity than separated individuals (Cheng et al., 2008; Mok et al., 2007). However, separated multiculturals seem to have higher levels of cognitive complexity, perhaps because they spend more time switching back and forth between cultural lenses.

Separated and integrated multiculturals may be more likely to use a relativist ethical perspective, because they switch frames in response to the cultural environment (Cheng et al., 2006). Frame-switching increases their experience seeing the world from more than one perspective, and as a consequence, potentially increases their endorsement of ethical relativism. Separated multiculturals may be most likely to take on either the hearts-at-home or gone-native positions, because they find it difficult to feel strong allegiance to two organizations, especially when their interests are in conflict with each other. For similar reasons, integrated multiculturals should be most likely to become dual citizens, and have bigger creative potential because they are used to combining differences and contradictions. These relationships are likely to hold because individuals take on whichever cultural identity pattern feels most natural to them, indicating that they're more likely to use an organizational identity pattern that reflects their cultural identity pattern. Now that it is clear that multicultural individuals as a group have unique skills to contribute to international business, and that different types of multiculturals may contribute different skills, we suggest how organizations can tap these skills.

MANAGING A MULTICULTURAL WORKFORCE: IMPLICATIONS FOR ORGANIZATIONAL CULTURE DEVELOPMENT AND HUMAN RESOURCE MANAGEMENT

Multicultural employees have the potential to add value in the five key areas described above, but only when organizations implement the procedures necessary to use their skills (for example, selection processes and career development practices to place

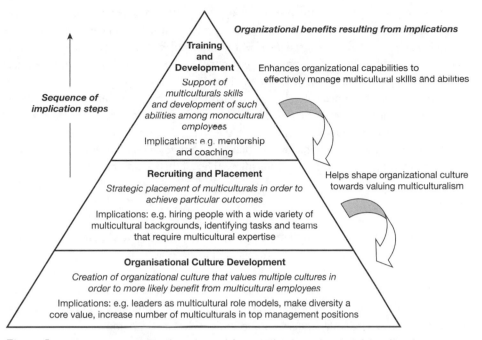

Figure 1. Managing a Multicultural Workforce: The Organizational Implications Pyramid

them in positions where they can be most useful). Given that multinational organizations often fail to take advantage of the knowledge, skills and experiences of their global employees, organizations with the right processes in place have an opportunity to get ahead of their competitors. Ahead, and illustrated in Figure 1, we propose steps organizations can take in order to leverage the distinct skills and abilities of their multicultural employees. Organizations should first develop an organizational culture that encourages diversity of thought and perspectives; next, place value on hiring people with multicultural backgrounds, and place them strategically so they can use their unique skills; and, finally, train and develop multicultural employees to further enhance their skills with respect to the organization's requirements.

Organizational Culture Development

Organizations that value multiple cultures are more likely to benefit from cultural diversity (Jackson et al., 2003), because when they don't, they risk suppressing employees' multicultural identities, and suppressing the skills and abilities that emerge from being multicultural as a consequence (Ely and Thomas, 2001). Organizational contexts that suppress multicultural identities could have especially strong organizational cultures, and value one particular way of thinking. They train employees to think, behave and react similarly to one another, resulting in a cohesive workforce, but one that misses out on the unique benefits of its multicultural employees (Jackson et al., 2003). Therefore, organizations should create visible signs that the company values employees with a multicultural background, and that international experience and a cosmopolitan orientation will improve one's career advancement within the organization. For example, leaders could create multicultural role models by promoting multiculturals to top management positions, or by instituting international experiential programs, explained ahead. Ideally, these initiatives should originate from the top-down, in order to stress their strategic importance, and to shift organizational culture. By shaping the organizational culture towards one that values multiculturalism, companies can provide the necessary context to leverage multiculturals' potential. Simply hiring multicultural employees is not enough; it is also essential to set up the conditions that allow their skills to emerge.

Staffing

Companies should develop systems that identify multiculturals' potential for both recruiting and placement. Multiculturals should be placed in positions where they can be most useful, otherwise their unique skills will be wasted. For example, the leadership and ethics section of this reading discussed strategically placing multicultural employees, in order to achieve particular outcomes and ensure global consistency in responsible leadership and ethical decision-making.

According to our analysis, multiculturals are most likely to contribute to the success of diverse teams when they are working on complex tasks requiring creativity. Therefore, organizations should identify tasks and teams with these characteristics, and try to place multicultural employees on those teams. For example, multicultural employees are more likely to benefit an international coordination team, rather than a team focused on coordinating with a stable, local supplier (DiStefano and Maznevski, 2000).

Since it is not practical to measure how much individuals identify with their cultures for recruitment purposes, we recommend hiring people with a wide variety of multicultural backgrounds, and placing them strategically once more is known about their particular skill sets. This approach will also help shift the organizational culture in the right direction.

Training and Development

We recommend using corporate training and development programs to achieve two goals: supporting multiculturals to become more conscious of their skills and abilities, and developing similar skill sets among monocultural employees. On average, monoculturals are not likely to develop these skills to the same degree as multiculturals, even with training, but they can be developed in order to close the gap. Mentorship and coaching are best suited to achieving the first goal, while global experiential programs could achieve both.

For example, Pless et al. (forthcoming) studied a global experiential program at PricewaterhouseCoopers, where high-potential employees work with local partners in developing countries for eight weeks. The program helped managers acquire skills similar to those of multiculturals. Experiencing the heightened ambiguity, competing tensions and challenging ethical dilemmas associated with working in a foreign culture can trigger a transformational experience and produce new mental models in managers. Evidence shows that this program helped participants broaden their horizons, reduce stereotypes and prejudices, learn how to perceive the world through the eyes of people who are different, and work effectively with a diverse range of stakeholders – qualities similar to those of multicultural employees – which are essential for leading responsibly in a global and interconnected world. If a program like this one is not feasible because of cost or time constraints, then organizations could use short-term field experiences to expose employees to sub-cultures within their own countries (for example, by looking after homeless people, working with juvenile delinquents, or living with immigrants seeking asylum) to provide significant cultural immersion experiences and perspective-taking skills (Mendenhall and Stahl, 2000).

Overall, organizations can create visible signs that the company values multicultural employees by hiring and placing employees to maximize their ability to use their skills, mentoring new multicultural employees by senior-level multicultural role models, and developing all employees for multicultural skills, using experiential programs. Together, these steps should create the conditions that allow multicultural employees to shine.

CONCLUSION

Multicultural individuals may contribute valuable skills to teams, negotiations, alliances, mergers and acquisitions, international assignments, ethics and leadership. Although this discussion has focused primarily on multiculturals' overall contributions, their experiences are not universal, and organizations are at risk of alienating their multicultural employees unless they consider the different ways to be multicultural. The next step is for companies to take advantage of the potential in their multicultural employees by staffing, training and leading with these benefits in mind.

REFERENCES

Ashkenas, R. N. and Francis, S. C. (2000). Integration managers: Special leaders for special times. *Harvard Business Review, 78*(6), 108–116.

Berry, J. W., Phinney, J. S., Sam, D. L. and Vedder, P. (2006). Immigrant youth: Acculturation, identity and adaptation. *Applied Psychology: An International Review, 55*, 303–332.

Binning, K. R., Unzueta, M. M., Huo, Y. J. and Molina, L. E. (2009). The interpretation of multiracial status and its relation to social engagement and psychological well-being. *Journal of Social Issues, 65*, 35–49.

Black, J. S. and Gregersen, H. (1992). Serving two masters: Managing the dual allegiance of expatriate employees. *Sloan Management Review, 33*(4), 61–71.

Brady, D. (2007, June 11). Pepsi: Repairing a poisoned reputation in India. *BusinessWeek.*

Brannen, M. Y., Garcia, D. and Thomas, D. C. (2009). *Biculturals as natural bridges for intercultural communication and collaboration.* Paper presented at the International Workshop on Intercultural Collaboration, Palo Alto, CA.

Brett, J. and Okumura, T. (1998). Inter- and intracultural negotiation: U.S. and Japanese negotiatiors. *Academy of Management Journal, 41*, 495–510.

BusinessWeek (May 20, 2005). Indra Nooyi's graduation remarks. *BusinessWeek,* from www.businessweek.com/bwdaily/dnflash/may2005/nf20050520_9852.htm.

Cheng, C.-Y., Lee, F. and Benet-Martínez, V. (2006). Assimilation and contrast effects in cultural frame switching: Bicultural identity integration and valence of cultural cues. *Journal of Cross-Cultural Psychology, 37,* 742–760.

Cheng, C.-Y., Sanchez-Burks, J. and Lee, F. (2008). Connecting the dots within: Creative performance and identity integration. *Psychological Science, 19,* 1178–1184.

Cohen, R. (1997). *Negotiating Across Cultures.* Washington, DC: United States Institute of Peace.

David, E. J. R. (2006). Biculturalism. In Y. Jackson (Ed.), *Encyclopedia of Multicultural Psychology.* Thousand Oaks, CA: Sage.

DiStefano, J. J. and Maznevski, M. L. (2000). Creating value with diverse teams in global management. *Organizational Dynamics, 29,* 45–63.

Donaldson, T. and Dunfee, T. W. (1999). When ethics travel: The promise and peril of global business ethics. *California Management Review, 41*(4), 45–63.

Einhorn, B. (2009, July 2). Pepsi's Indra Nooyi focuses on China. *BusinessWeek.*

Ely, R. J. and Thomas, D. A. (2001). Cultural diversity at work: The effects of diversity perspectives on work group processes and outcomes. *Administrative Science Quarterly, 46,* 229–273.

Fortune. (2009). 50 Most Powerful Women. Retrieved January 22, 2010, from http://money.cnn.com/popups/2006/fortune/mostpowerfulwomen/1.html.

Galinsky, A. D., Maddux, W. W., Gilin, D. and White, J. B. (2008). Why it pays to get inside the head of your opponent: The differential effects of perspective taking and empathy in negotiations. *Psychological Science, 19,* 378–384.

Ghosn, C. (2008, August). Carlos Ghosn tells students to embrace diversity. Retrieved July, 2010, from www.aub.edu.lb/news/archive/preview.php?id=74360.

Ghosn, C. (April 11, 2008). The transcultural leader: Carlos Ghosn, CEO of Renault, Nissan. from http://knowledge.insead.edu/ILSTransculturalLeaderGhosn080501.cfm?vid=45.

Ghosn, C. and Riès, P. (2005). *Shift: Inside Nissan's historic revival* (J. Cullen, trans.). New York: DoubleDay.

Gibson, C. B. and Vermeulen, F. (2003). A healthy divide: Subgroups as a stimulus for team learning behavior. *Administrative Science Quarterly, 48,* 202–239.

Hannerz, U. (1990). Cosmopolitans and locals in world culture. In M. Featherstone (Ed.), *Global culture: Nationalism, globalization and modernity.* London: Sage.

Hobbs, S. (2008, June). Indra Nooyi: Simon Hobbs meets the CEO and chairman of PepsiCo. *CNBC Business.*

Hong, Y.-Y., Morris, M. W., Chiu, C.-Y. and Benet-Martínez, V. (2000). Multicultural minds: A dynamic constructivist approach to culture and cognition. *American Psychologist, 55,* 709–720.

Investing in Cultural Diversity and Intercultural Dialogue (2009). UNESCO (United Nations Educational, Scientific and Cultural Organization).

Jackson, S. E., Joshi, A. and Erhardt, N. L. (2003). Recent research on team and organizational diversity: SWOT Analysis and implications. *Journal of Management, 29,* 801–830.

Lau, D. C. and Murnighan, J. K. (2005). Interactions within groups and subgroups: The effects of demographic faultlines. *Academy of Management Journal, 48,* 645–659.

Liu, E. (1998). *The Accidental Asian.* Toronto: Random House.

Liu, L. A., Chua, C. H. and Stahl, G. K. (2010). Quality of communication experience: Definition, measurement, and implications for intercultural negotiations. *Journal of Applied Psychology, 95*(3), 469–487.

Marks, M. L. and Mirvis, P. H. (2001). Making mergers and acquisitions work: Strategic and psychological preparation. *Academy of Management Executive, 15*(2), 80–92.

Mendenhall, M. and Stahl, G. (2000). Expatriate training and development: Where do we go from here? *Human Resource Management, 39,* 251–265.

Mok, A., Morris, M. W., Benet-Martínez, V. and Karakitapoglu-Augün, Z. (2007). Embracing American culture: Structures of social identity and social networks among first-generation biculturals. *Journal of Cross-Cultural Psychology, 38,* 629–635.

Mosionier, B. C. (1999). *In Search of April Raintree.* Winnipeg, Canada: Portage & Main Press.

Najjar, G. (2008, August). Carlos Ghosn tells students to embrace diversity. Retrieved July, 2010, from www.aub.edu.lb/news/archive/preview.php?id=74360.

Nguyen, A.-M. D. and Benet-Martinez, V. (2007). Biculturalism unpacked: Components, measurement, individual differences, and outcomes. *Social and Personality Psychology Compass, 1,* 101–114.

Nooyi, I. (2009, May 12). Address to the Economic Club of Washington, from www.pepsico.com/Download/IKN_Economic_Club.pdf.

OECD (2009). Society at a Glance 2009: OECD Social Indicators. Paris: OECD.

Pless, N., Maak, T. and Stahl, G. (forthcoming). Developing responsible global leaders through International Service Learning Programs: The Ulysses experience. *Academy of Management Learning & Education.*

Polzer, J. T., Crisp, C. B., Jarvenpaa, S. L. and Kim, J. W. (2006). Extending the faultline model to geographically dispersed teams: How colocated subgroups can impair group functioning. *Academy of Management Journal, 49,* 679–692.

Pucik, V., Bjorkman, I., Evans, P. and Stahl, G. (2010). Human resource management in cross-border mergers and acquisitions. In A.-W. Harzing and J. van Ruysseveldt (Eds.), *International Human Resource Management* (3rd ed.). London: Sage.

Rivas-Micoud, M. (2007). *The Ghosn Factor: 24 lessons from the world's most dynamic CEO.* New York: McGraw-Hill.

Rudmin, F. W. (2003). Critical history of the acculturation psychology of assimilation, separation, integration, and marginalization. *Review of General Psychology, 7,* 3–37.

Salacuse, J. W. (2005). *Leading Leaders: How to manage smart, talented, rich and powerful people.* New York: AMACOM.

Schippers, M. C., Den Hartog, D. N., Koopman, P. L. and Wienk, J. A. (2003). Diversity and team outcomes: The moderating effects of outcome interdependence and group longevity and the mediating effect of reflexivity. *Journal of Organizational Behavior, 24,* 779–802.

Schneider, S. and Barsoux, J. L. (2003). *Managing Across Cultures.* London: Prentice Hall.

Stahl, G. K. (2004). Getting it together: The leadership challenge of mergers and acquisitions. *Leadership in Action, 24*(5), 3–6.

Stahl, G. K., Chua, C. H., Caligiuri, P., Cerdin, J.-L. and Taniguchi, M. (2009). Predictors of turnover intentions in learning-driven and demand-driven international assignments: The role of repatriation concerns, satisfaction with company support, and perceived career advancement opportunities. *Human Resource Management, 48,* 89–109.

Tadmor, C. T., Tetlock, P. E. and Peng, K. (2009). Acculturation strategies and integrative complexity: The cognitive implications of biculturalism. *Journal of Cross-Cultural Psychology, 40,* 105–139.

Tasioulas, J. (1998). Consequences of ethical relativism. *European Journal of Philosophy, 6,* 172.

Thomas, D. C. (1999). Cultural diversity and work group effectiveness. *Journal of Cross-Cultural Psychology, 30,* 242–263.

Thomas, D. C., Stahl, G., Ravlin, E. C., Poelmans, S., Pekerti, A., Maznevski, M., et al. (2008). Cultural Intelligence: Domain and Assessment. *International Journal of Cross Cultural Management, 8*(2), 123–143.

Thompson, C. J. and Tambyah, S. K. (1999). Trying to be cosmopolitan. *Journal of Consumer Research, 26,* 214–241.

Vlasic, B. and Stertz, B. A. (2000). *Taken for a Ride: How Daimer-Benz drove off with Chrysler.* New York: Wiley.

Vora, D., Kostova, T. and Roth, K. (2007). Roles of subsidiary managers in multinational corporations: The effect of dual organizational identification. *Management International Review, 47*, 595–620.

White, J. and Taft, S. (2004). Frameworks for teaching and learning business ethics within the global context: Background of ethical theories. *Journal of Management Education, 28*, 463–477.

Windsor, D. (2004). The development of international business norms. *Business Ethics Quarterly, 14*, 729–754.

Women@Google: Andrea Jung. (2009). Mountain View, CA: Google.

Martin Hilb

COMPUTEX CORPORATION

Goteborg, May 30, 1985

Mr Peter Jones
Vice President – Europe
Computex Corporation
San Francisco
USA

The writers of this letter are the headcount of the Sales Department of Computex Sweden, AS, except for the Sales Manager.

WE HAVE DECIDED to bring to your attention a problem, which, unsolved, probably will lead to a situation where the majority among us will leave the company within a rather short period of time. None of us want to be in this situation, and we are approaching you purely as an attempt to save the team for the benefit of ourselves as well as Computex Corporation.

We consider ourselves an experienced, professional, and sales-oriented group of people. Computex Corporation is a company that we are proud to work for. The majority among us have been employed for several years. Consequently, a great number of key customers in different areas of Sweden see us as representatives of Computex Corporation. It is correct to say that the many excellent contacts we have made have been established over years; many of them are friends of ours.

These traits give a very short background because we have never met you. What kind of problem forces us to such a serious step as to contact you?

Problems arise as a result of character traits and behavior of our General Manager, Mr Miller.

First, we are more and more convinced that we are tools that he is utilizing in order to "climb the ladder." In meetings with us individually, or as a group, he gives visions about the future, how he values us, how he wants to delegate and involve us in business, the importance of cooperation and communication, etc. When it comes to the point, these phrases turn out to be only words.

Mr Miller loses his temper almost daily, and his outbursts and reactions are not equivalent to the possible error. His mood and views can change almost from hour to hour. This fact causes a situation where we feel uncertain when facing him, and consequently are reluctant to do so. Regarding human relationships, his behavior is not acceptable, especially for a manager.

The extent of the experience of this varies within the group due to our location. Some of us are seldom in the office.

Second, we have experienced clearly that he has various means of suppressing and discouraging people within the organization.

The new "victim" now is our Sales Manager, Mr Johansson. Because he is our boss, it is obvious that we regret such a situation, which to a considerable extent influences our working conditions.

There are also other victims among us. It is indeed very difficult to carry through what is stated in our job descriptions.

We feel terribly sorry and wonder how it can be possible for one person almost to ruin a whole organization.

If this group consisted of people less mature, many of us would have left Computex Corporation already. So far, only one has left the company due to the above reasons.

From September 1, two new Sales Representatives are joining the company. We regret very much that new employees get their first contact with the company under the present circumstances. An immediate action is therefore required.

It is not our objective to get rid of Mr Miller as General Manager. Without going into details, we are thankful for what he has done to the company from a business point of view. If he could control his mood, show some respect for his colleagues, keep words, and stick to plans, we believe that we can succeed under his leadership.

We are fully aware of the seriousness of contacting you, and we have been in doubt whether or not to contact you directly before talking to Mr Miller.

After serious discussions and considerations, we have reached the conclusion that a problem of this nature unfortunately cannot be solved without some sort of action from the superior. If possible, direct confrontation must be avoided. It can only make things worse.

We are hoping for a positive solution.

Six of your Sales Representatives in Sweden

Peter Jones let out a long sigh as he gazed over the letter from Sweden. "What do I do now?" he thought, and began to reflect on the problem. He wondered who was right and who was wrong in this squabble, and he questioned whether he would ever get all the information necessary to make a wise decision. He didn't know much about the Swedes, and was unsure whether this was strictly a work problem or a "cross-cultural" problem. "How can I tease those two issues apart?" he asked himself, as he locked his office and made his way down the hallway to the elevator.

As Peter pulled out of the parking garage and on to the street, he began to devise a plan to deal with the problem. "This will be a test of my conflict management skills," he thought, "no doubt about it!" As he merged into the freeway traffic from the on-ramp and began his commute home, he began to wish that he had never sent Miller to Sweden in the first place. "But would Gonzalez or Harris have done any better? Would I have done any better?" Few answers seemed to come to him as he plodded along in the bumper-to-bumper traffic on Interstate 440.

Joseph J. DiStefano

JOHANNES VAN DEN BOSCH
SENDS AN EMAIL

Professor Joe DiStefano prepared this mini-case as a basis for class discussion rather than to illustrate either effective or ineffective handling of a business situation.

The mini-case reports events as they occurred. The email exchanges in both cases are reported verbatim, except for the names, which have been changed. Professor DiStefano acknowledges with thanks the cooperation of "Johannes van den Bosch" in providing this information and his generous permission to use the material for executive development.

AFTER HAVING HAD SEVERAL email exchanges with his Mexican counterpart over several weeks without getting the expected actions and results, Johannes van den Bosch was getting a tongue-lashing from his British MNC client, who was furious at the lack of progress. Van den Bosch, in the Rotterdam office of Big Five Firm, and his colleague in the Mexico City office, Pablo Menendez, were both seasoned veterans, and van den Bosch couldn't understand the lack of responsiveness.

A week earlier, the client, Malcolm Smythe-Jones, had visited his office to express his mounting frustration. But this morning he had called with a stream of verbal abuse. His patience was exhausted.

Feeling angry himself, van den Bosch composed a strongly worded message to Menendez, and then decided to cool off. A half hour later, he edited it to "stick to the facts" while still communicating the appropriate level of urgency. As he clicked to send the message, he hoped that it would finally provoke some action to assuage his client with the reports he had been waiting for.

He reread the email, and as he saved it to the mounting record in Smythe-Jones' file, he thought, "I'm going to be happy when this project is over for another year!"

Message for Pablo Menendez
Subject: IAS 1998 Financial statements
Author: Johannes van den Bosch (Rotterdam)
Date: 10/12/99 1:51 p.m.

Dear Pablo,

This morning I had a conversation with Mr Smythe-Jones (CFO) and Mr Parker (Controller) re: the finalization of certain 1998 financial statements. Mr Smythe-Jones was not In a very good mood.

He told me that he was very unpleased by the fact that the 1998 IAS financial statement of the Mexican subsidiary still has not been finalized. At the moment he holds us responsible for this process. Although he recognizes that local management is responsible for such financial statements, he blames us for not being responsive on this matter and informing him about the process adequately. I believe he also recognizes that we have been instructed by Mr Whyte (CEO) not to do any hand-holding, but that should not keep us from monitoring the process and inform him about the progress.

He asked me to provide him tomorrow with an update on the status of the IAS report and other reports pending.

Therefore I would like to get the following information from you today:

• What has to be done to finalize the Mexican subsidiary's IAS financials;
• Who has to do it (local management, B&FF Mexico, client headquarters, B&FF Rotterdam);
• A timetable when things have to be done in order to finalize within a couple of weeks or sooner;
• A brief overview why it takes so long to prepare and audit the IAS f/s;
• Are there any other reports for 1998 pending (local gaap, tax), if so the above is also applicable for those reports.

As of today I would like to receive an update of the status every week. If any major problems arise during the finalization process I would like to be informed immediately. The next status update is due January 12, 2000.

Mr Smythe-Jones also indicated that in the future all reports (US GAAP, local GAAP and IAS) should be normally finalized within 60 days after the balance sheet date. He will hold local auditors responsible for monitoring this process.

Best regards and best wishes for 2000,

Johannes

Manfred F.R. Kets de Vries and Elizabeth Florent-Treacy

CARLOS GHOSN: LEADER WITHOUT BORDERS

(A) THE ROAD THAT LED TO NISSAN

IN LATE 2004, after five years at the head of Nissan in Japan, Carlos Ghosn* was hotter than a new Nissan Z350, a 1970s icon recreated by Nissan in 2000. He was probably the most recognized and revered *gaijin* (foreigner) in Japan— hounded by autograph seekers, star of a *manga* comic book, greeted at the airport like a rock star. In Lebanon, some people thought he should run for president. But the French-educated, Lebanese–Brazilian Ghosn was about to shift into even higher gear, to become CEO of both Nissan and its French partner, Renault. Renowned for his transparency, listening and analytical skills, and for having the "subtlety of a chainsaw,"[1] as of 2005 he would lead an automative alliance operating on three continents, with all the production issues, personnel challenges, and currency fluctuations contingent to the job. Ghosn was typically confident but pragmatic about it: "The only power a CEO has is to motivate. The rest is nonsense."[2]

Nissan-Renault: A Marriage of Reason

Before Carlos Ghosn took over at Nissan, the company had long been the number two manufacturer in Japan behind Toyota. Nissan had suffered a string of loss-making years in the 1990s. Mismanagement and complacency had saddled it with huge debt, production overcapacity, and an uninspiring model line-up. Yet it was a solidly established company with a strong brand reputation, in the center of a traditional *keiretsu*—several European car manufacturers saw potential horsepower in the unimpressive chassis. Pursuing a strategy of global presence, they were beginning to look eastward, towards Asia. Japan was a missing link; Nissan looked like the right partner to fill the gap.

Figure 1. Ghosn presents the new Z350

The first to approach Nissan was Daimler, the giant German car manufacturer, maker of the famous Mercedes Benz luxury cars. In 1998, Daimler completed its acquisition of Chrysler, the smallest of the big three American manufacturers. The new DaimlerChrysler was now one of the largest companies in the world in its sector. However, after weighing the advantages and disadvantages of a Nissan deal—and after months of discussion and due diligence—DaimlerChrysler walked away.

In March 1999, Louis Schweitzer, chairman and CEO of Renault, offered $5.4 billion for a controlling stake in Nissan. Renault was an industry leader in Europe but a second-rung player on the world stage—perhaps not the ideal suitor, but Nissan, now near bankruptcy, could not afford to turn down the offer. Outside observers, however, were very skeptical. Renault did not seem to have the muscle to redress the fortunes of Nissan and, after all, the giant DaimlerChrysler had given up on the deal.

Undaunted, several months later Schweitzer sent Carlos Ghosn, an executive who was little known outside France, to head the new alliance. Ghosn would not languish in anonymity for long; his very visible presence at Nissan would eventually project him into the global spotlight and propel him to superstardom in Japan. By early 2004, the charismatic Ghosn had returned Nissan to profitability, nearly erased all debt, and launched a fleet of new models. In the process, his spectacular success was quickly becoming the stuff of legend; he was *the* hot ticket in business schools around the world.

Then Renault announced that Ghosn would be leaving Japan to become CEO of Renault (retaining his title as CEO of Nissan). Now, with the benefit of hindsight,

Table 1. Production of cars in 2000

Manufacturer	Cars (millions)
Toyota	4.9
Nissan	2.3
Renault	2
Mitsubishi	1

it would be easier to sort fact from fiction and deconstruct the success of Nissan's renaissance. Was Ghosn leaving Nissan with the structures and people necessary for continued growth under a Japanese leader? Had Ghosn's leadership style made a difference, or was he simply in the right place at the right time? What characteristics of Carlos Ghosn the man had influenced Carlos Ghosn the CEO? Was he truly a global leader, able to adapt wherever he landed? The answers to these questions would more accurately establish the legacy of a leader who was undoubtedly talented but also, arguably, lucky.

The Brazilian–Lebanese–French–American Way

Carlos Ghosn was born in Porto Velho, Brazil, into an emigrant Lebanese family of Maronite Christian origin. His grandparents had come to Brazil in one of the successive waves of migration that carried Lebanese expatriates far across Africa, Latin America, and Asia. Bichara, Carlos's grandfather arrived in Brazil at the beginning of the twentieth century with little money. Although the Lebanese readily describe themselves as easy-going, fun-loving, and not particularly hard-working, this tongue-in-cheek characterization bears little resemblance to Lebanese emigrant communities, least of all Bichara. Through hard work and persistence, he established himself as a successful businessman. His four sons and four daughters were all born in Brazil.

Carlos' father Jorge inherited his father's successful air transport business. On one of the family's frequent trips to Lebanon, Jorge met and married Rose, who was also from an emigrant family. Carlos was the second-born of their four children. When Carlos was six years old, Rose moved back to Lebanon with her children so they could study there, leaving her husband to earn a living in South America.

Carlos was a student at the prestigious Notre Dame secondary school in Beirut, which was run by Jesuits. Raised as a Maronite Christian, openness and tolerance were an essential part of his religious education. Jesuit priests, however, have a deserved reputation for intellectual rigor. Carlos was a brilliant but rebellious student, and was often in trouble with his Jesuit professors. But the strict discipline finally paid off; at the age of 17, he passed the French *baccalauréat* exam and was sent to the exclusive Lycée Saint Louis in the heart of the Latin Quarter in Paris. His talent for mathematics primed him for the tough *classe préparatoire* at Saint Louis.[3] Ghosn did well in the highly selective *grandes écoles* entrance exam and was admitted to *Polytechnique*, one of the top engineering schools in France. The French-speaking

Lebanese–Brazilian would soon become a graduate of the highly elitist *grandes écoles* system, and as a result certain doors would open wide.

A Lucky Break? The Michelin Years

In March 1978, while finishing his studies, Ghosn received an early morning phone call asking if he would be interested in going to Clermont Ferrand, a city in central France, for a job interview. Michelin, the tire company, was looking for French-trained engineers who knew Brazil and spoke Portuguese. Ghosn fitted the bill perfectly.

Despite misgivings about leaving the *Quartier Latin* for the isolated *Massif Central* region, the possibility of eventually returning to Rio de Janeiro was a powerful incentive. His emotional attachment to the country was still strong.[4] Ghosn accepted the offer.

At that time, Michelin was led by François Michelin, the founder's grandson. It was still a closely held family firm but was making an important transition from a French company to a multinational competitor. François Michelin had been at the helm for 30 years. He had an austere and simple, but tasteful, style. He was a "people-person," favoring direct contact and conversation over paperwork.[5]

The company had a reputation for being a conservative, slightly paternalistic organization. Ghosn discovered it also had a strong culture of technical innovation and quality. He was given a degree of responsibility early on, which was greater than he had expected.

After working on the factory floor for a few months, Ghosn was promoted to team leader in Le Puy en Velay, where Michelin manufactured tires for construction equipment. There, he got his first taste of leadership. Working closely with his team, he learned the importance of communication and coaching. Even the best ideas, he saw, were worthless if people could not be convinced to accept and use them.[6] After further stints in Germany, then in Tours (France), Ghosn was again promoted, to production group leader in Cholet, France.

In 1981, at the age of 27, he returned to Le Puy en Velay, this time as director of the entire factory. He was the youngest member of the factory's management team and was now managing people who had been his superiors just three years earlier. He handled this by making sure he got to know all his subordinates and establishing a sense that they were on the same team. His duties were strictly defined by head office, leaving him little latitude to improvise. His main task was to organize production within a narrow band of parameters. He delivered.

After two more assignments in France in 1983 and 1984, Ghosn finally embarked for Rio, in June 1985, as country manager for Brazil. His assignment was the culmination of a seven-year training program that had seen him cover a variety of responsibilities across Europe. (Shortly before moving to Brazil, he married Rita, a young woman of Lebanese origin, who had been studying pharmacology in Lyon.)

In the mid-1980s, Brazil was in transition from military to civilian rule. The country was in dire economic straits: inflation hit occasional peaks of more than 1,000 percent per year, with interest rates up to 35 percent. Workers suffered greatly and there were regular riots against price increases. On top of this, the government was prone to micromanaging in the business world in an attempt to solve the economic problems.

Michelin's head office in Clermont-Ferrand was very concerned by the situation in Brazil and kept their operations there under tight control. Although Ghosn had respected head office dictates for many years, one of his top priorities when he arrived in Brazil was to reduce this interventionism. His message to headquarters was, "Let us do our job, and judge us on our results." His second priority was to build a cohesive team from the disparate groups of people—in finance, sales, operations, and so on—with whom he had to work.

Most of the problems in the Brazilian subsidiary were internal. Business practices had been imposed with little regard for local business customs. Ghosn adapted operations to create a more rational series of management, financial, and operational controls. By 1989, four years after his arrival, Brazil was one Michelin's most profitable global operations. Ghosn's success caught the eye of François Michelin himself, and Ghosn was soon on to his next challenge: the integration of a new acquisition, Uniroyal-Goodrich, into the Michelin group in the US.

Uniroyal-Goodrich was a good match for Michelin in the North American market. They were of similar size (about 10 percent market share) and their market strengths were complementary: Michelin was strong on factory-fitted tires and Uniroyal-Goodrich on replacements. One of the most critical tasks in the integration was merging the two very different cultures. Michelin North America remained very French, despite the presence of a few North American executives. It was a family firm with a long-term perspective in terms of strategy, product, quality, and investment. Uniroyal-Goodrich, on the other hand, was controlled by an investor, focused on short-term returns, and market-oriented. Ghosn's solution to this dilemma was to maintain Uniroyal-Goodrich as a separate business unit.

While in the US, Ghosn was directly exposed to the American way of doing business. Competition was much stronger than in France or in Brazil, and he had to take the market into consideration far more than before, notably by establishing a joint sales network between Michelin and Uniroyal-Goodrich.[7] As a tire manufacturer, he was able to observe close up the operations of a number of major car companies such as the American big three (GM, Ford and Chrysler); Japanese such as Toyota and Nissan; and the European brands in the US market. He also met legendary characters such as Bob Lutz and Lee Iaccoca of Chrysler. Michelin executives were pleased with Ghosn's results in the US. In 1995, he was called back to head office in Clermont Ferrand.

At the young age of 42, Ghosn was now very close to the top job at Michelin. Unfortunately for him, he could never become CEO. The Michelin family wanted Francois' successor to be a member of the Michelin family, and would soon name Edouard, François' son. A man with Ghosn's ambition could never be satisfied with such a situation and he began to consider options outside the company.

Moving On, Moving Up: The Renault Years

In April 1996, a headhunter called with the news that Louis Schweitzer of Renault was looking for someone to fill a top executive position. After a few meetings, in July 1997 Ghosn agreed to join Renault.

Renault had been founded at the beginning of the twentieth century by Louis Renault.[8] The company grew rapidly and was a renowned industrial concern by the start of World War I. During World War II, Louis found himself on the wrong side of history and his company was later nationalized by the French government as a punishment for being an "instrument of the enemy." Always a stronghold of the powerful labor movement in France, Renault workers continued this tradition for more than 50 years after coming under state control.

Ownership of the company finally returned to private hands in 1996, but by then Renault had developed a culture of rigidly separated "silos" among which there was little communication. It was a typical French firm with a highly centralized, hierarchical culture. Interminable meetings were characterized by seemingly unproductive discussions. High costs and quality problems were endemic. The company was also still trying to recover from by its successive international faux pas with AMC and Jeep in the US, and Volvo in Sweden.[9] Notwithstanding, the organization possessed some remarkably talented people, able to mobilize for great causes.

Carlos Ghosn was named vice president in charge of purchasing, R&D, engineering, and production programs. He also oversaw Renault operations in the Mercosur region (Argentina, Brazil, Paraguay, and Uruguay). Renault had just initiated a plan to reduce the average production cost of each new car by €460. Ghosn suggested to Schweitzer that they go further and adopt a €3 billion cost-reduction plan, to be carried out without any compromises on technology or quality, which would effectively triple the cost savings on each car. Schweitzer gave his approval.

One of Ghosn's cost-saving measures caused major political fallout. Having established that Renault had excess production capacity and that it should close one of its factories, the site at Vilvorde in Belgium, where 3,000 people were employed, was chosen. The decision was leaked by the Belgian Prime Minister, who opposed the closure. Seeing the conflict as a showdown between the old forces of union activism and the pressing requirements of modern capitalism, Schweitzer refused to budge, and eventually Renault (and Ghosn) rode out the storm. Ghosn earned the sobriquet "le cost killer," but defended his actions, arguing that all executives, especially those in the car business, had to keep a close eye on costs.

As an outsider with little experience at a carmakers, and (*quelle horreur*) not even a Frenchman, his position in terms of internal Renault politics was far from favorable. Ghosn was conscious of this but chose to disregard the initial skepticism and hostility,[10] insisting, "I am not a man of conflict. I don't create disturbances. I am firm, but I'm not aggressive."

In March 1999, after eight months of discussions, Renault announced its intention to purchase a 35 percent stake in Nissan for $5.4 billion. Ghosn, who had actively participated in the negotiations between the two companies, was named COO of Nissan. He moved with his family to Tokyo and immediately set to work.

Although there were numerous skeptics at the time, Schweitzer and Ghosn were outwardly confident that they would succeed. Schweitzer was convinced that it was the right move, and, as the CEO who had brought Renault out of near-bankruptcy only a few years earlier, he had the experience (at least in Europe) on which to base his decision. But the "lynchpin" in his strategy, Schweitzer later said, was Carlos Ghosn. Schweitzer felt Nissan was a good company but badly managed, and he was convinced that Ghosn had the ability and charisma to lead the transformation of the Japanese organization. He and Ghosn presented a turnaround plan to Nissan's then-CEO months before the alliance was announced. Thereafter, as Schweitzer later remarked, they did exactly what they had promised.[11]

Ghosn on Nissan

Ghosn felt that he was an obvious candidate for the job, given his prior experience in turnaround situations, but he was initially less confident than Schweitzer about his own potential for success. Nissan had been struggling for years to turn a profit. He would subsequently observe that, "It is remarkable how in a company going through a bad time, nobody feels responsible . . . I found everybody accommodating to the situation as the ship went down."[12] The challenges appeared all but insurmountable: low profit margins, little brand recognition in the US, purchasing costs up to 25 percent higher than at Renault, production overcapacity, and huge corporate debt. As he said, "This was literally a do-or-die situation. Either we'd turn the business around, or Nissan would cease to exist:"[13]

> The Japanese wanted to know, "How can a company like Renault help us? How is Ghosn going to help us?" At first I was received in Japan with curiosity tainted with scepticism. The European media made a big deal about le Cost Killer coming to Japan. I was even scared myself by the description! It was all very caricatural. I was the "Big Bad Wolf," and no one was even sure if I was the right kind of wolf. But we were able to use that curiosity, to say, "We're going to be very transparent; we're going to make commitments, and you [Nissan employees] are going to be able to measure our performance."
>
> I started with the facts: (1) Nissan was the most indebted company in the car industry in 1999; (2) the eight previous years, including 1999, had been unprofitable; and (3) Nissan was losing market share.
>
> How do you get out of a situation like this? You do it by asking: "Why are we here? What happened?" You begin with a diagnosis, then explore solutions to turn around the challenges, and then you create specific action plans.
>
> A lot of transformation attempts are undermined by feelings, or thoughts, or subjective analysis. If you want to mobilize 130,000 people in different countries and cultures, you have to be precise, basing everything you say on evidence people can measure.

Leadership starts with transparency, especially in situations of crisis. Nothing [about our turnaround plan] was fuzzy. Everything was very precise, with commitments and a timeline behind it. And we said, "Frankly, if we're not successful, then we're out."

Was I sure I would be successful? Not at all. It is a part of the game that you are always wondering, "Am I going to make it or not?" This keeps you open, keeps you attentive . . . it keeps your eye on the ball. But I was confident about my past experience— in Brazil, North America, and in the turnaround of Renault France in 1996— so I felt I was well prepared for this.[14]

Soon after his arrival in Japan in 1999, Carlos Ghosn identified five key reasons why Nissan was in such a bad state:[15]

- **Loss of focus on profits.** Nissan management had neither the necessary data nor metrics to measure the performance of their company. For instance, of the 43 models sold by Nissan, only 4 were profitable. Under these circumstances, it was very difficult for the company to be profitable.
- **Loss of focus on the customer.** There was no clear understanding of which models were aimed at what type of client, or why. Cars were usually developed in reaction to what the competition was doing. Even worse, the company paid only lip service to the concept of "client focus," and seemed to be mired in complacency.
- **No sense of urgency.** Despite the difficulties of the company, there was little sense of a need to move quickly. Decisions often took an inordinately long time. This was partly due to the "comfort zone" created by being in a prosperous country where the culture promoted consensus and discouraged challenging others.
- **Existence of silos.** Nissan's team culture was so strong that it discouraged transversal collaboration.
- **No vision.** Although the lack of a clear strategy is quite common in Japanese companies, it prevented the people of Nissan from sharing an understanding of where their company would be 5 or 10 years down the road.

Another issue invoked by Ghosn was the seniority system. The longer an employee had been with the firm, the more responsibility and pay they received. This further encouraged complacency and prevented the company from promoting promising young talent faster. In Japanese companies, where the group is typically important, responsibility may often be shared. This promotes teamwork but in a crisis it can mean that responsibility is diffused and no individual has a duty to make the final decision. (Ultimate responsibility lies with the head of the company, who is often a figurehead and quite incapable of leadership. Rather, he is elected through consensus for his coordination skills.) This was also true, to a certain degree, at Nissan.

Revival

On October 20, 1999, six months after his arrival at Nissan, Carlos Ghosn made a very high profile speech at the Tokyo Motor Show in which he announced the "Nissan Revival Plan," and the measures that he would take to turn the company around.

Figure 2. Revival Plan speech

These included:

* Elimination of 21,000 jobs by March 2002, and reduction of production capacity by 30 percent.
* Production of models using only 15 platforms instead of 24, and sharing of platforms with Renault. Nissan and Renault expected to produce 1 million units a year using a single platform.
* Reduction in number of suppliers from 1,145 to 600 within 3 years so that suppliers could spread costs over larger volumes.
* Sale of unrelated and/or unprofitable investments.

By appearing in person at such a high-profile event, where he was guaranteed maximum exposure, Ghosn sent a clear signal to investors, customers, and employees: Nissan had to make a clear break with the past. By making such a public announcement, not only did he show that he was highly determined, he also ensured that Nissan would be closely watched. In establishing clear targets and a sense of direction for personnel, he removed their ability to hide from responsibilities. It was a risky move.

If his turnaround strategy had proved unsuccessful, the company would undoubtedly have suffered from a media backlash and public derision.

Ghosn ended with an astonishing declaration: he and his team would leave Nissan if the company was not profitable within a year:

> Our commitment was: (1) during the first year of the plan, a return to profit-ability; (2) debt would be reduced by half after three years; (3) profitability would improve over the next three years. If any one of these objectives was not met, I was out, and with me all the members of the executive committee. As it became apparent that our results would be even greater than we'd promised, [opinion] began to turn around.[16]

The team Ghosn brought with him from France gave him support and a bridge to Renault, but was small enough to prevent an expatriate silo effect. He chose his team members according to four criteria: they had to be (1) open-minded, (2) experts in their fields, (3) experienced coaches, and (4) willing, even eager, to go to Japan. Once in Japan, Ghosn was careful to avoid giving the impression that the Renault people formed a separate clan within the company. There were no Renault meetings, and each French executive integrated a Nissan team. Renault would not save Nissan, Nissan would save Nissan:[17]

> People would rather be with other people like themselves. It's more comfort-able. The problem is, you only learn from people who are different. But this is a basic problem of management: How do you make people *like* difference? How do you drive people to understand that difference is the basis of innovation?
>
> The motivation is identity. If you don't know who you belong to, or what your company is about, then forget about going the extra mile. You have to maintain identity and get people to work together. That's what we're trying to do in the Nissan-Renault alliance.[18]

Cross-functional teams (CFTs) were a crucial aspect of Carlos Ghosn's approach to breaking silos and instilling cross-company cooperation. He had used them several times before at Michelin and Renault. Nissan CFTs were first used by Ghosn to define his revival plan and later for day-to-day operations. By using the teams to help define the turnaround plan, he ensured that there would be an early sense of ownership and buy-in throughout the organization.

A typical CFT was made up of 10 people, generally drawn from the ranks of middle managers. These were supplemented by sub-teams, which include members of the main team plus other external managers. Each team was led by two senior managers from different divisions or functions who served as sponsors, helping to give authority to the team's operations. The real work, however, was done by the 10 regular members. It was led by a predesignated pilot. The senior managers would take a "back seat" and did not necessarily attend all meetings.

Each team was given a mandate and objectives to propose and implement change. The team had broad powers to investigate all aspects of the company's operations. Although they had no decision powers per se, the team reported to and advised the senior management. Various functions—for example, purchasing, engineering, manufacturing, and finance—were represented in each team to ensure cross-functional cooperation.

The CFT teams were a powerful lever to engage managers. This system gave them responsibility and freedom to perform. Several teams even exceeded the ambitious targets set by senior management. In addition, their proximity to frontline operations made them far more effective at finding opportunities for change.

Ghosn knew that despite all the measures taken to improve Nissan's performance, the company's fortunes would not improve unless consumers wanted to buy its cars. For this to happen, it had to produce a large number of attractive models. In one of his most important decisions, Ghosn decided to hire away top designer Shiro Nakamura from Isuzu in 1999. Nakamura was given unprecedented authority over the design process.[19] Within five years, Nissan was recognized as a leader in car design.[20]

Carlos Ghosn's rise to power in Nissan was progressive. When he arrived in Japan, he was named chief operating officer, a position that traditionally does not exist in Japanese firms. In March 2000, he replaced Yoshikazu Hanawa as president. Hanawa remained as chairman and CEO. In March 2001, Ghosn gained direct control over sales operations in Japan and direct management control over the alliance between Nissan and Renault. In June 2003, Hanawa resigned as chairman and Carlos Ghosn became co-chairman with executive vice president Itaru Koeda.

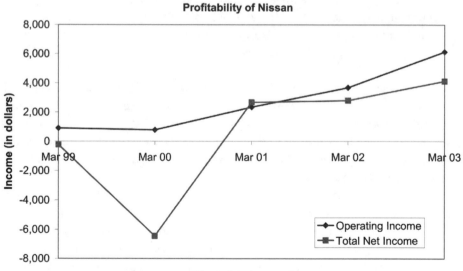

Figure 3. Profitability under Carlos Ghosn

By the middle of 2001, it was becoming obvious that Nissan's fortunes were changing.[21] A loss of ¥684 billion in 2000 was converted into a profit of ¥331 billion in 2001.[22] By 2004, Nissan was one of the most profitable car manufacturers in the world, with an 11.1 percent operating margin at end of financial 2003.[23] It launched a new plan, called Value-Up, which aimed to raise its annual sales by 37 percent to 4.2 million cars in 2008.

(B) THE MAN AT THE WHEEL

When asked in 2004 to look back and reflect on why he sent Ghosn to Nissan, Schweitzer replied:

> I was convinced Carlos was the man I wanted. He has something quite striking—intelligence, extraordinary stamina, and vitality. On top of that, he has an enormous ability to learn . . . and to listen.
>
> Carlos was clearly in charge. He put his head on the block and his job on the line . . . There was clarity . . . People knew that what was being done was for the good of Nissan . . . It was clear that Ghosn was working for Nissan . . . We couldn't have done this turnaround without Carlos.[24]

It should be pointed out that not only was Ghosn very capable, but he also had an excellent mentor. Louis Schweitzer's professional path was very different from Ghosn's. Although he was also a product of a French *grande école* (*Ecole Nationale d'Administration*), Schweitzer spent many years as an aide to Laurent Fabius, former budget minister and prime minister of France. As such, his promotion to CFO of Renault was a classic example of the close ties between politics and business in France. His political connections notwithstanding, Schweitzer was very successful at the helm of Renault and one of the most respected business leaders in France. His leadership of Renault was crowned in September 2004 when the market value of Renault reached that of General Motors.[25] Some of this value was attributed to the partnership with Nissan, and by extension, credited to Carlos Ghosn.

From his early days as a young manager at Michelin, Ghosn attracted the trust and confidence of top organizational leaders. In particular, Schweitzer and Ghosn quickly developed a close personal alchemy. Schweitzer never showed any resentment of Ghosn's media success;[26] both men were quick to give credit to each other. Schweitzer gave free rein to Ghosn in managing Nissan and apparently never tried to keep his deputy under close control. His approach paid off.

Ghosn said that he built trust and confidence with his superiors and his employees by being consistent and transparent, and by listening to their feedback:

> I think the first job of the CEO is to bring light to the company. The CEO is not the owner; he is the enlightener. The CEO helps people to acknowledge the evidence, then to act on it.
>
> Confusion is the first sign of trouble. I hate ambiguity. When I say something, it's always clear . . . Leadership starts with transparency and with evidence, especially in situations of crisis.

If you are afraid to fail, you will collect mistakes; if you correct a mistake, it won't become a failure. To correct mistakes, ask for feedback. Listen to negative comments. Positive comments are refreshing, but not helpful. You learn from bad news.[27]

Indeed, when people in Renault and Nissan were asked about their first impression of Carlos Ghosn, "clear," "good communicator," "open," "transparent," and "decisive" were frequent responses.[28] Although his direct reports often felt stretched and pushed very hard, they described their working relationship as one of deep respect and affection. When asked about his weaknesses, they tended to see them as being the flipside of his strengths, or as one executive said, "If you want the quiet life with no challenges—the civil servant's life—you really should not work for Ghosn."

Transparency, Consistency, Simplicity

When trying to convince Renault managers of the need to change, Ghosn communicated simple and clear facts about Renault internally. For example, in 1996 Renault was the only main European carmaker not to have experienced any real major (above market trend) growth for 10–20 years. Renault people probably already knew the facts but had never focused on the situation until Ghosn called it to their attention. As a former Renault manager explained, "It was a shock to people and created a challenge for them." Ghosn's conclusion was that Renault was not structured for growth and that this would have to change.

Ghosn was perceived as being open and transparent all the time. When Nissan's executive committee met to make important decisions, they often discussed issues for an entire 12-hour day. Nevertheless, it was always Ghosn who made the final decision, even if the majority had an opposing view. The point of the discussions was to ensure that the decision-making process was transparent. It also served as a model for decision-making for executives in their own departments.

As one vice-president at Nissan said, "There is a huge consistency both inside and outside the company. Even in a one-on-one meeting, Ghosn will say the same thing as he has said to the press—barring confidential facts. There can never be a 'betrayal' of his real thoughts because he always speaks freely." Another executive said, "Ghosn always tries to make things simple; if a subject is complex he will try to cut it into simple slices." To be sure people understood him clearly, Ghosn would repeat himself (in slightly different ways), often using images to illustrate a point.

Informal Formality

Ghosn had a tendency to keep his distance from people. French associates at Nissan addressed him as "Monsieur Ghosn" and used the formal "vous." But as one executive at Renault recounted, "Although Ghosn might have a tough reputation in some quarters, he is never initially aggressive with people; rather he tries hard to get them to express themselves. He has a simple contact style. While it is not overtly friendly, it is very professional and open. You are encouraged to say what you think."

Ghosn explored all available hard data from different angles, but also took people's convictions and emotions into consideration. He observed body language (very important in Japan), and was a good listener, whether with a factory operator or a vice president. "Ghosn always concentrates when talking to people, listening intently to, and questioning the meaning of, people's words," explained his chief of staff. "When Ghosn is listening to somebody he often reformulates what the person is saying. For example, 'What you mean is . . .' There are no taboo subjects, but people have to prove their point. His subordinates greatly appreciate this openness and knowing where they stand."

Specific Actions and Clear Timelines

Ghosn's subordinates knew that although there was some flexibility in the system, essentially commitments and targets had to be met. A direct report at Nissan confirmed that, "Ghosn is not patient, but he is realistic. He is very good at making priorities if someone is overloaded."

His chief of staff described how "Ghosn certainly uses benchmarking as a way to avoid 'reinventing' things. He only wants to innovate when there is no applicable benchmark." For Nissan during the early 2000s, as with most car manufacturers, Toyota was the basic benchmark, but Ghosn never expected Nissan to "out-Toyota" Toyota. His aim, rather, was to achieve the same target but in the *Nissan* way.

Ghosn did not invent the motto "Planning is 5 percent and implementation 95 percent," but it became a mantra for his managers. People were sometimes surprised by how rapidly he made a decision— if he agreed with the logic—and how quickly he expected the approved plan to be implemented. If people were unprepared or had no opinion, Ghosn expressed his impatience in no uncertain terms.

Realistic Ambitions, Fair Rewards, and Stretch Goals

Ghosn was extremely wary of complacency and bureaucracy, particularly after several successful years at Nissan. To avoid stagnation, he actively challenged people. As one vice president at Renault explained, "Ghosn tends to always push people harder, but not unthinkingly. He pushes them to do better than they thought was possible." Many of his staff recall the experience of being pushed beyond what they thought were their limits and realizing that, in fact, they *were* capable of more.

Nevertheless, Ghosn was realistic about people's capabilities. For example, his former chief of staff recounted, "After Ghosn arrived at Nissan, targets for sales in Japan were always aggressive. In the first two years, the objectives were not met [by a large margin]. In the third year, ambitious objectives were set again, but Ghosn ensured that they could be successfully achieved."

Other executives pointed out that Ghosn could be very demanding and was sometimes critical when goals were not met. For example, a Nissan executive explained, on one occasion when a new Nissan team missed their mid-term investment targets despite their best efforts, "The initial criticism from Ghosn was taken very badly; he had to backtrack and explain it wasn't meant to be personal." Ghosn's staff occasionally described working for him as "endless"—reaching an important milestone and thinking they could finally relax, only to see Ghosn come along with the next step. As a Renault executive put it, "The problem is that he is personally quite strong, and you feel you simply have to follow him."

Ghosn required his direct reports "to start by improving themselves," said one of his former subordinates. "If someone has the basics, then it becomes a virtuous circle of stretching and improvement based on their skills and (Ghosn's) ambition."

Essentially, Ghosn pushed people to excel because he believed that if individuals never succeed, they give up. But he was also convinced that high returns should be rewarded with high salaries. Many of the questions at Nissan's 2004 stockholders' meeting[29] related to compensation packages and the use of stock options, which Ghosn defended.

Hands-On Delegation

Ghosn was very hands-on and close to operations. A Nissan executive noted that, "Ghosn has an ability to get to a level of detail that others simply cannot." He headed committees (manufacturing, purchasing, R&D, etc.) and made decisions across a very wide number of functions. At the same time, he pushed delegation very far down in the organization. As a Renault executive described it, "If Ghosn has confidence in someone or an organization, he delegates by setting clear targets, and then meeting regularly with the person. If he is not confident in someone's ability, he will go deeper and deeper into the problem and will not fully delegate until he has confidence in the person." A Nissan executive put it another way: "Ghosn wants managers to make as many decisions as possible, but they should make them openly, with Ghosn having full knowledge of the decision." Because responsibilities were delegated with clear objectives, Ghosn had more time to meet with the CFTs, *Genba* (plant/shop floor in Japanese) regional representatives, visit dealerships, and drive Nissan cars—he was one of the first Nissan executives to do so.

Work/Life Balance

Although one of his nicknames was "7–11," referring to the hours he put in at the office, Ghosn made it a rule not to take work home. He was not available for meetings on the weekend, when he was often seen at places like Tokyo Disneyland with his wife and younger children. His leadership philosophy reflected his family values; if people do not achieve a balance between work and home, they will become demotivated and eventually both their personal and professional selves will suffer.[30]

Global Leadership

Perhaps one of Carlos Ghosn's greatest attributes at Nissan was his cultural and corporate uniqueness. A Renault executive explained, "He is not a Renault guy. He is not a Polytechnique guy, usually. He is not French in terms of business or political networks, although he shows some elements of French culture. He is not American, although he has some American business styles." Indeed, Ghosn entitled his auto-biography *Citizen of the World*. As one of his chief designers neatly summarized it, "Ghosn is not Japanese, clearly, but he is not Brazilian or French, either. He is a leader."[31]

Simply put, Ghosn drew on all his experiences. He frequently encountered Japanese, French, and Americans, and many other nationalities. Not only was he comfortable in five languages, but he was also able to manage different styles of communication as well. For example, Ghosn was clearly at ease with Americans and moved at a faster pace with them. Although he often re-phrased a point he wanted to make, he was less likely to do this with French people who might be offended by the implication they didn't understand the first time. With Japanese people he was careful not to be overly critical.

This ability to survive and thrive was not simply a chameleon-like reflection of local color; rather, Ghosn developed a leadership style that was flexible but consistent and coherent across different cultures. Ultimately, as a Nissan executive explained, "Ghosn is always the same with everyone: frank, clear and transparent."

Before the Renault team's departure for Japan, there was a great deal of discussion about whether, or how, they should adapt to Japanese culture. Several consultants advised Ghosn that, "things have to be done 'the Japanese way'" (move slowly, avoid making lay-offs, and so on). His former chief of staff recalled that, "Ghosn never did things the 'Japanese way' and resolved to avoid talking to consultants for the first year at Nissan." Having said that, he continued, "It is not that Ghosn did not make concessions to the Japanese way of doing business. He always tried to be respectful of major Japanese cultural norms to avoid unnecessarily hurting feelings and to show his respect."

Ghosn cleverly used the Japanese media to his and Nissan's advantage, perhaps alerted to the possibilities by the "rock star" welcome he received as he stepped out of his plane on one of his first trips to Japan. It proved to be a win-win situation; his co-operation with the Japanese media gave them something interesting to report about the first *gaijin* (foreigner) to head a large Japanese company, and allowed Ghosn to polish Nissan's image. One Nissan executive said, "People will always remember Ghosn. After 10 years of recession in Japan, what Renault achieved at Nissan gives Japanese people hope." Others remembered visiting dealerships with Ghosn: "Women, men, and children would stop and shout 'Ghosn-san!' when they saw him in the street." Interestingly, Ghosn's media image—as "le cost killer"—had been quite negative in Europe. There seemed to be a mutual reserve, Ghosn once refusing to answer a question about his marital status with, "No personal questions." Yet in Japan he was willing to discuss his relationship with his daughter on national television. Ghosn often reminded his staff that a "high media profile in Japan was a necessity." According to his former chief of staff, "Nissan's media image was definitely calculated. Ghosn was very interested in his image and the connection between his image and Nissan's. He studied it carefully through regular surveys. He understood different elements of his image and tried to adjust Nissan's communication plan accordingly."

His staff concurred that it was important to portray Nissan in a positive light in the Japanese media. Nevertheless, they also agreed that at a later point it became difficult to separate the leader from the company. As one Renault executive pointed out, "Nissan needed to be warm and sympathetic. Ghosn's image was therefore clearly measured and adjusted to drive Nissan's image in Japan and the US. This brought huge benefits to Nissan in both markets."

Shifting into Higher Gear

Ghosn took over from Louis Schweitzer as CEO of Renault in mid-2005, while retaining his position as CEO of Nissan. (His successor at Nissan, one of the company's top Japanese executives, would be COO, and would probably succeed Ghosn as CEO at a later date.) As of late 2004, Nissan had become the most profitable carmaker in the world, with an operational margin of more than 11 percent. The challenge for Ghosn would be formidable, with Renault topping out at an operational margin of 5 percent.[32]

The challenge was twofold: Ghosn would have to shift his eagle-eyed focus from Nissan to the bigger picture at Renault, and at the same time ensure that Nissan's engine continued to purr. Although he had delegated a great deal of responsibility to subordinates at Nissan, he rarely delegated strategic decisions. Whether this centralization was due to his leadership style or the specific requirements of a turnaround situation is unclear, but the essential question remained: how would Nissan fare without the charismatic Ghosn?

In Nissan's dark days in the mid-1990s, many of the organization's best people had left. Not surprisingly, Nissan had trouble attracting highly qualified talent during that period. Ghosn himself did not make many changes in the existing executive teams upon his arrival and some therefore felt Nissan might suffer from a depleted pool of potential leaders. One of Ghosn's options was to promote young stars—although this went against the traditional Japanese system—but once he returned to Renault it would be quite a challenge to maintain the momentum for change within Nissan.

By late 2004 many Nissan executives already felt they were living "life after Ghosn." They moved on to different responsibilities in Nissan and Renault and no longer reported to him directly. They all admitted missing the excitement and discussion about Nissan's targets and future and, as one manager said, no longer "being part of the process where Ghosn gets the best out of people and stretches them while getting them to set their own challenges."

There was clearly a certain intensity involved in working directly for Carlos Ghosn. This meant that there was a limit to how long and how closely a person could work for him. At the end of the experience, it was clear that people had grown immensely, even if there may have been cases of overstretch. Everyone talked about not being the same person as before (and being better for it). As one manager put it, "He is tough, but you do it with pleasure!"

After the turnaround at Nissan, Carlos Ghosn's image in Japan was much better than his reputation in France. Japan can be very forgiving of foreigners, and in any case Nissan was not in a position to be choosy when Ghosn arrived. In many ways, Renault would be a more difficult assignment than Nissan. Ghosn was not a true product of the French establishment (from a French point of view), and he would have to deal with the challenges raised by the spicy Gallic blend of politics and business on his plate at Renault. He would also have to orchestrate the complicated alliance between Nissan and Renault, develop synergies within the partnership, and, at the same time, foster competition between the two brands in some markets. In addition, Renault hoped to be back in the US market some time after 2010. With no imminent crisis at Renault, would Carlos Ghosn's transformational leadership style—and his frankness and openness—be enough to take Renault from admirable to awe-inspiring at a global level?

NOTES

* (Rhymes with *bone*).

1. Bremner, Brian et al. (2004), "Nissan's boss," *Business Week*, October 4, Issue 3902, pp. 50–57.
2. Ibid.
3. In the French education system, *baccalauréat* graduates enter a two-year course to prepare for a competitive exam. Depending on their results, they can then enter a number of engineering schools, of which the most prestigious is the *Ecole Polytechnique*. Many Polytechnique graduates finish their education in other top engineering schools such as the *Ecole des Mines*. The system is ruthlessly meritocratic, but also a powerful vector for integration. It is not possible to enter the best schools other than by passing the exam with a score in the top percentile.
4. Ghosn, Carlos and Philippe Riès (2003), *Citoyen du monde*, Grasset, pp. 63–64.
5. Ibid., pp. 82–83.
6. Ibid., pp. 78–79.
7. Ibid., pp. 120–121.
8. Renault web site, www.renault.fr.
9. Renault enjoyed a brief stint of success in the early 1980s in the US market with the Alliance, a car produced with American Motors Corporation (AMC). However, America's taste for French cars proved to be short lived and, after large losses, Renault sold its stake in AMC to Chrysler in 1987. AMC was also the producer of the Jeep range. Renault and Volvo attempted a failed merger, which was finally dismantled in 1993 after it was opposed by Volvo institutional shareholders. The alliance had initially been motivated by a desire to join forces to compete against bigger competitors. The failure of the merger was blamed on political suspicions over the intentions of the French state regarding the merger.
10. Ghosn and Riès (2003), pp. 159–160.
11. Peterson, Thane (ed.) "How Renault Jump-started Nissan", *Business Week Online*, Newsmaker Q&A, October 1, 2004.
12. Carson, Iain (2002) "Nissan's Napoleon", *World Link*, July/August, 15:4, p 38.
13. Ghosn, Carlos (2002), "Saving the business without losing the company", *Harvard Business Review*, January, pp 37–45.
14. From Global Leadership Series speech, INSEAD, September 24, 2002 (permission granted to use excerpts).
15. Ghosn and Riès (2003).
16. From Global Leadership Series speech, INSEAD, September 24, 2002.
17. Ghosn and Riès (2003), pp. 217–218.
18. From GLS speech, INSEAD.
19. Magee, David (2003), *Turnaround. How Carlos Ghosn rescued Nissan*, HarperCollins, pp. 117–119.

20. "Inspired by Japan, the copycats are now the copied", *New York Times,* October 25, 2004.
21. For greater detail on the turnaround process at Nissan, see INSEAD case study "Redesigning Nissan (A): Carlos Ghosn Takes Charge," and "Redesigning Nissan (B): Leading Change" (Manzoni, J.F., Hughes, K., and Barsoux, J.L., 2003).
22. "Halfway down a long road", *The Economist,* vol. 360, Issue 8235, August 18, 2001, p. 51.
23. "Nissan's net rises as sales gain", *Asian Wall Street Journal,* April 27, 2004, p. A3.
24. Peterson, Thane (Ed.), Interview with Louis Schweitzer, CEO of Renault: "How Renault Jump-Started Nissan," *Business Week Online,* www.businessweek.com, October 1, 2004.
25. "Renault vaut désormais autant que General Motors en Bourse," *Le Monde,* September 14, 2004.
26. Carlos Ghosn was featured in a multipart comic book series in Japan, "The true story of Carlos Ghosn". He wrote two books, *Renaissance* and *Citoyen du Monde.* Both were bestsellers. *Renaissance* even outsold Jack Welch's book in Japan.
27. Global Leadership Series speech, INSEAD.
28. All anonymous comments and observations on Ghosn's leadership in this section were taken from Mark Mildon's series of interviews with senior managers (past or present direct reports to Carlos Ghosn) at Nissan and Renault, Tokyo and Paris, July and August 2004.
29. Item 3 – Proposed Items, 105th Ordinary Shareholders Meeting, Tokyo, June 23, 2004.
30. Anonymous, "The family—seeking stronger bonds", *The Daily Yomiuri,* January 8, 2005, p. 4.
31. *Fortune,* February 18, 2002, p. 37.
32. "Carlos Ghosn, futur pilote redouté de Renault", *Challenges,* September 23, 2004.

PART 3

Training, Performance Management, Appraisal, and Compensation Issues for Global Managers

David G. Collings, Hugh Scullion and Michael J. Morley

CHANGING PATTERNS OF GLOBAL STAFFING IN THE MULTINATIONAL ENTERPRISE: CHALLENGES TO THE CONVENTIONAL EXPATRIATE ASSIGNMENT AND EMERGING ALTERNATIVES*

ABSTRACT

WE ARGUE THAT MANY MNCs continue to underestimate the complexities involved in global staffing and that organisations and academics must take a more strategic view of staffing arrangements in an international context. We suggest that the context for the management and handling of the international assignment has altered significantly, leading in some quarters to a fundamental reassessment of the contribution of, and prospects for, the international assignment as conventionally understood. We explore a variety of supply side issues, cost issues, demand side issues and career issues as triggers to this reassessment. Alongside the conventional expatriate assignment, we point to the emergence of a portfolio of alternatives to the traditional international assignment including short-term assignments, commuter assignments, international business travel and virtual assignments. In the context of these developments, we argue that a standardised approach to international assignments is untenable and that it is essential to develop HR policies and procedures that reflect differences in the various forms of emerging alternative international assignments and their associated complexities. Here, recruitment and selection, training, reward, and occupational health and safety issues and implications are all explored.

1. INTRODUCTION

The topic of international assignments has an established pedigree in the international management literature and has, in particular, dominated the research agenda of international human resource management (IHRM) for over three decades. While the research focus of those investigating the IHRM field has expanded significantly in recent years, expatriate management issues remain a critical concern (Collings and Scullion, 2006; Lazarova, 2006; Stahl and Björkman, 2006).

Staffing issues are complex in the international environment (Torbiorn, 1997), something that is attested to by a stream of research highlighting international alliances: the importance of effective staffing strategies for the successful implementation of international business strategies, especially strategic alliances and cross-border mergers in emerging and culturally distant markets; the decision points relating to different approaches to international staffing; the problem of shortages of international managers, particularly in emerging markets, where there is often fierce competition between MNCs and local organizations to recruit and retain high quality staff; the requisite supports necessary in order to ensure a satisfactory outcome from the organisational and individual perspective; and the management and utilisation of knowledge flows that may accrue (cf. Evans *et al.*, 2002; Minbaeva and Michailova, 2004; Schuler *et al.*, 2004).

However, research suggests that many MNCs continue to underestimate the complexities involved in global staffing (Tung, 1998). Concomitantly, the context for the managing of the international assignment has altered significantly, leading in some quarters to a fundamental reassessment of the contribution of, and prospects for, the international assignment as conventionally understood. The importance of this reassessment has been signalled by those who have questioned why multinationals continue to use conventional expatriate assignments to the extent that they do due to the high costs and continuing problems associated with such assignments (Morley and Heraty, 2004; Scullion and Brewster, 2001), and by the increasing prominence of alternative forms of international assignments and the emergence of a portfolio of assignments within the international firm (Fenwick, 2004; Roberts *et al.*, 1998).

We build on this emerging body of literature through exploring the issues surrounding the ongoing utility of the conventional expatriate assignment and the key issues around alternative forms of international assignments. The reading contributes to our understanding of international assignments by critically exploring the current context for international assignments in MNCs. First, we critically re-examine the reasons advanced for the utilisation of expatriates in the traditional assignment (usually three to five years and involving the relocation of the expatriate and their family) in view of changing patterns of global staffing. Much of the research on the management of expatriates available in the international literature until fairly recently has been drawn from research focused on North American MNCs. In this journal, Scullion and Brewster (2001) advocated that research be conducted on countries other than in the US in order to develop a broader understanding of expatriation. This is reflected in our reading, which draws heavily on recent research in Europe and elsewhere and we take up the challenge of developing this broader understanding by contributing to a deeper appreciation of the importance of the context in which staffing takes place. Finally, our reading critically examines the growing importance of alternative forms of international assignments in the light of recent research, which suggests that long-term assignments may become less dominant as new patterns of global staffing emerge (Scullion and Collings, 2006a). In particular, we focus on four key questions with regard to these assignments, namely: (1) how can we classify alternative forms of international assignments?; (2) in what circumstances are alternative forms of international assignments considered appropriate?; (3) what evidence is there on levels of use of alternative forms of international assignments?; (4) what operational issues emerge in the context of managing these assignments?

2. WHY DO ORGANISATIONS USE EXPATRIATES?

Before considering the challenges associated with the traditional expatriate assignment, it is important to briefly outline the key strategic reasons why MNCs use expatriates, as the literature is characterised by a number of well-articulated advantages associated with the deployment of expatriates in the staffing of international subsidiaries and operations.

Indeed, it has been argued that entrepreneurs have recognised the importance of physically relocating managers to foreign locations where business operations are based since approximately 1900 BC. Indeed, even at this stage, locals were viewed as inferior and restricted to lower-level jobs while parent country nationals (PCNs) were afforded superior conditions, similar to modern day expatriates (Moore and Lewis, 1999: 66–67). Owners of international organisations thus realised the benefits of utilising people known to them and socialised into the organisation in minimising the agency problems (Jensen and Meckling, 1976) associated with managing spatially diverse organisations from an early stage. This is because these individuals had built a level of trust with their superiors and thus were considered to be more likely to act in the best interests of the organisation, relative to local managers from the host country who were largely an unknown quantity. Thus, expatriates were used as a means of addressing agency issues as a result of the separation of ownership and management and their amplification through distance.

In their landmark study, Edström and Galbraith (1977) proposed three motives for using expatriates. First, as *position fillers* when suitably qualified host country nationals (HCNs) were not available. Second, as a means of *management development*, aimed at developing the competence of the individual manager. Third, as a means of *organisational development*, aimed at increasing knowledge transfer within the MNC and modifying and sustaining organisational structure and decision processes. Although it is important to note that assignments generally have more than one rationale (Sparrow et al., 2004), Edstrom and Galbraith's typology provides a useful point of departure for the consideration of why MNCs use expatriates.

More recently, Harzing (2001) identified three control specific roles of expatriates, namely: the bear, the bumblebee and the spider.

Bears act as a means of replacing the centralisation of decision-making in the MNC and provide a direct means of surveillance over subsidiary operations. The title highlights the degree of dominance these assignees have over subsidiary operations. *Bumblebees* fly "from plant to plant" and create "cross-pollination between the various offshoots" (Harzing, 2001: 369). These expatriates can be used to control subsidiaries through socialisation of host employees and the development of informal communication networks. Finally, *spiders*, as the name suggests, control through the weaving of informal communication networks within the MNC.

Harzing's study is significant because it goes beyond the basic question of why MNCs use expatriates and sheds light on the potentially more significant question of whether these roles are equally important in different situations. Significantly, Harzing (2001) argues that although expatriates generally appear to perform their role as *bears* regardless of the situation, the study suggests that their roles as *spiders* and *bumblebees* tend to be more context specific. Specifically, the *bumblebee* and *spider* roles appeared to be more significant in longer-established subsidiaries (longer than 50 years) while the *bumblebee* role appeared to be important in newly established subsidiaries also. Significantly, the level of localisation of subsidiary operations and further lower levels of international integration, in that the subsidiary was not greatly reliant on the HQ for sales and purchases, were positively related to the likelihood of expatriates performing the *bumblebee* and *spider* roles. Perhaps unsurprisingly, *bumblebees* and *spiders* were also more prevalent in greenfield than brownfield acquisitions.

3. THE EXPATRIATE ASSIGNMENT IN RETREAT?

Linked to the debates reviewed above, there is a growing debate over the issue of the continued utility and viability of the conventional expatriate assignment (Dowling and Welch, 2004). We identify five key aspects of this debate, i.e. supply side issues, demand side issues, expatriate performance and expatriate "failure," performance evaluation, costs and finally career dynamics. Some of these (expatriate failure, costs and performance evaluation) can be considered *older challenges*, in that they have been associated with the field since the early academic studies emerged on the topic. Others (demand issues surrounding emerging markets and requirements for expatriates in a broader range of organizations; supply issues around career issues and specifically dual careers, the impact of 9/11, etc.), however, can be considered *newer challenges*, in that they have gained increasing importance in recent years. Broadly, we discuss these issues in order of significance based on our rating.

3.1. Supply Side Issues

The first key challenge to the traditional expatriate assignment is the supply side issue of availability, which has emerged as a key strategic HR issue facing MNCs (Scullion and Starkey, 2000). There is growing recognition that shortages of international managers are a significant problem for international firms and frequently constrain the implementation of global strategies in these firms (Evans *et al.*, 2002; Scullion,

1994). Research indicates that the demand for experienced and competent global managers is growing rapidly and is greater than the current supply (Caligiuri and Cascio, 1998; Quelch and Bloom, 1999). Indeed, it has been argued that for US MNCs, the current international climate and continued concerns about terrorist attacks, post-9/11, mean that potential international assignees will remain reluctant to travel and relocate overseas in the future (Konopaske and Werner, 2005). Yet despite continued uncertainties and anxieties prevailing in the current international climate, MNCs must more than ever before encourage staff to work abroad to better understand the global markets and to develop the skills required to work effectively across cultures.

Under the heading of supply side issues, as they relate to the availability of expatriate employees, we highlight four key trends – dual careers issues, the limited participation of women in international management, repatriation issues and weaknesses of talent management systems at the international level. Broadly, these issues can be grouped as issues concerning the recruitment and retention of potential expatriate employees.

3.1.1. Issues Related to Recruitment of Potential Expatriate Employees

The increasing significance of dual-career couples emerges as a key constraint on the ability of MNCs to attract and retain international management talent (Harvey, 1998). Due to increasing female participation rates in the labour force, particularly in developed countries, those targeted for expatriate assignments are no longer necessarily male sole-breadwinners, with spouses who are willing, and able, to follow their partners abroad for the period of the assignment. There is some evidence to suggest that families are less willing to accept the disruption of personal and social lives associated with international assignments than was the case in the past (Forster, 2000). In addition, dual-career problems and disruption to children's education are seen as major barriers to future international mobility in many different countries and pose considerable restrictions on the career development plans of multinationals (Mayrhofer and Scullion, 2002). This is now considered a worldwide trend that is posing a major dilemma for both multinationals and employees alike (Black *et al.*, 2000; Harvey, 1998).

A second key problem is that the participation of women in international management remains relatively low (Adler, 2002; Tung, 2004) despite growing shortages of international managers. Studies indicate a significant growth in female expatriates since the 1980s, when only about 3 per cent of expatriates were female (Adler, 1984), to around 12–15 per cent in the mid 1990s (Tung, 1998). The most recent available data, however, suggest that the female expatriate population has not risen significantly over the past decade and remains at approximately 10 per cent (PricewaterhouseCoopers, 2005). The apparent lack of willingness to recruit and develop women as international managers is somewhat paradoxical, as recent research conducted on the outcome of women's global assignments has indicated that female expatriates are generally successful in their global assignments (Caligiuri and Tung,

1999; Napier and Taylor, 2002; Tung, 2004). Yet, as global competition intensifies, competition for global leaders to manage overseas operations will steadily intensify and MNCs must develop new ways to identify, attract and retain new pools of international executive talent (Black *et al.*, 2000; Mayrhofer and Scullion, 2002).

3.1.2. *Issues Related to Retention of Expatriate Employees*

The retention of expatriate employees is a major international talent management challenge for MNCs (Scullion and Collings, 2006c), yet research suggests that many MNCs continue to adopt an ad hoc approach toward the repatriation process and that many expatriate managers continue to experience the repatriation process as falling far short of expectations (Stroh *et al.*, 2000). Repatriation has been identified as a major international HRM problem for multinational companies in Europe and North America (Stroh and Caliguiri, 1998). There is growing recognition that where companies are seen to deal unsympathetically with the problems faced by expatriates on re-entry, managers will be more reluctant to accept the offer of international assignments (Lazarova and Tarique, 2005; Scullion, 2001). North American research indicates that 20 per cent of all managers who complete foreign assignments wish to leave their company on return. Yet, while it is generally accepted that retention of expatriates is a growing problem and that the costs of expatriate turnover are considerable (Dowling and Welch, 2004), many international firms have failed to develop repatriation policies or programmes which effectively assist the career progression of the expatriate (Black *et al.*, 2000).

In the European context, the repatriation problem has become particularly acute because internationalisation had often taken place at the same time as downsizing of the domestic business that reduced opportunities for expatriate managers on re-entry (Scullion, 1994). Empirical studies confirm the requirement for MNCs to develop a more strategic approach to repatriation and international career management (Stroh and Caliguiri, 1998), which is becoming increasingly necessary in order to retain valuable employees and to encourage the acceptance of international positions (Forster, 2000).

A final constraint on the supply of international management talent in many MNCs is the weaknesses of talent management systems, which may be defined as approaches to recruit, retain, develop and motivate a competent cohort of managerial talent with appropriate international experience in the global business environment (Briscoe and Schuler, 2004; Scullion and Collings, 2006b). In this context, Scullion and Starkey (2000) demonstrated that a key integration role for the corporate HR function in the international firm was the strategic management of talent on an international basis. However, despite the rhetoric and hype about talent management, there is little evidence to suggest that many companies practice talent management in a co-ordinated and efficient way (Cohn *et al.*, 2005). Recent research highlighted that many MNCs are frequently unaware of where their best talent is located (Evans *et al.*, 2002) and, in addition, many MNCs have difficulties in identifying their high performers (Michaels *et al.*, 2001).

In this section, we highlighted the key supply side issues that impact on the landscape of international assignments in the international firm. We now turn to the impact of the significant costs attached to the international assignment, which we consider the next most significant challenge to the traditional expatriate assignment.

3.2. Costs

As noted above, a major challenge for the continued use of expatriate assignments is the cost associated with them. While Sparrow *et al.* (2004: 139) conclude on the basis of empirical study that few organisations had a true grasp of the costs associated with expatriate assignments, they also highlighted that generally MNCs had little knowledge of the benefits accruing from the various types of international assignments. Given this limitation, however, it is generally estimated that the cost associated with the international assignment is between three and five times an assignee's home salary per annum (Selmer, 2001).

A key challenge for both international HRM professionals and academics is to understand and develop methodologies for accurately measuring the relative costs and benefits associated with international assignments. Indeed, a recent study found that three quarters of organisations studied had identified cost reduction in expatriate assignments as a priority issue (either important or very important) in the development of international assignment practices (PricewaterhouseCoopers, 2005: 9). A second study (GMAC, 2005) found that only 14 per cent of respondents measured return on investment (ROI) of international assignments, which is surprising given that the same survey reported that 65 per cent of respondents reported that their organisations were making an effort to reduce costs associated with assignments. This reinforces the requirement for more research to better understand how expatriate assignments can add value in different contexts.

In attempting to explain this paradox of the limited emphasis on measuring return on investment on international assignments, it has been argued in more generic terms that the main focus in the strategy process has been on strategy formulation, with often a relative lack of attention to implementation issues (Tahvanainen and Suutari, 2005). As we argue below, this is also applicable in the context of expatriate assignments. A failure of strategic planning at the operational level is often reflected in a failure to develop HR policies and practices aimed at ensuring congruence between employees' work behaviours and the organisational strategy (see also Torraco and Swanson, 1995). So while organisations may have a well-designed and articulate strategy with regard to staffing their foreign operations, they have often failed to monitor the performance of international assignees to accurately measure their performance and contribution to the bottom line.

In advancing the debate, McNulty and Tharenou (2004) have developed a theoretical model of expatriate return on investment. This more business-focused approach may help managers to effectively evaluate the utility of expatriate assignments through illuminating the contribution of expatriates to firm performance by looking beyond traditional historical cost analyses and measurements of failure. In developing a theoretical foundation for the consideration of expatriate ROI, McNulty and Tharenou (2004) call for a strategic approach to calculating ROI on expatriate assignments, which ensures that items included in the ROI calculation are based on a link between the costs and benefits of the assignment and the objective of the assignment itself. They argue that, when an international assignment has clearly defined objectives and is carefully planned, the MNC is likely to display a set of congruent HR policies to support the assignment. Thus, they posit the link between the assignee's performance and the objectives of the assignment are easier to determine.

Further, it is proposed that by examining the effect of the entire bundle of IHRM practices used during the assignment, organisations will be better able to accurately determine rates of return on the costs of expatriate assignments. In considering the true costs and benefits of expatriate assignments ROI type analysis represent a useful model for the managers of MNCs, and have the potential to build on the work on bundles of HRM and performance in the domestic setting.

3.3. Demand Side Issues

Alongside costs and supply side issues, there are also a number of key challenges around demand issues in MNCs. For example, the rapid growth of emerging markets such as China, India and Eastern Europe has had a significant impact on both the demand and supply of international managers. Indeed, the recent wave of EU accession countries from Central and Eastern Europe (CEE) and countries such as India and China have been identified as "hot spots" for inward FDI in the period 2004–7 by the UNCTAD (2004). In this regard, the growth of these markets leads to an increasing demand for managers with the distinctive competences and the desire to manage in these culturally and economically distant countries. It also results in greater competition between MNCs for managers with the context specific knowledge of how to do business successfully in these emerging markets (Björkman and Xiucheng, 2002; Michailova and Worm, 2003).

In addition, there is an increasing demand for expatriate employees in a far wider range of organisations than the traditional large MNC, partly due to the rapid growth of small and medium enterprise (SME) internationalisation (Anderson and Boocock, 2002) and international joint ventures (IJVs) (Schuler et al., 2004). Research highlights the importance of staffing and the top management team's international experience to the performance of international SMEs (Monks et al., 2001).

Arguably, therefore, a relatively small recruitment pool for global assignments is being further diluted by an expanding number of firms and locations competing for scarce international management talent. Even when an organisation does find suitably competent managers to take up expatriate assignments, however, there are a number of other factors which make their performance problematic and which organisations must address in considering the utility of the traditional expatriate assignment.

3.4. Expatriate Performance and Expatriate "Failure"

Traditionally, a key issue in the global staffing literature is expatriate failure, which represents a significant issue for MNCs due to the high costs of expatriate failure which are both direct (e.g. salary, training costs, travel and relocation expenses) and indirect (damaged relations with host country organisations and loss of market share) (Dowling and Welch, 2004). Research suggests that the latter should be considered as the most significant costs by multinationals, as damage to reputation in key strategic foreign markets or regions could be highly detrimental to the prospects of successfully developing international business in particular regions (Schuler *et al.*, 2002). The debate over the magnitude of the expatriate failure problem has been led by Harzing (1995, 2002) who questions the reported high expatriate failure rates In the US literature and highlights the lack of reliable empirical work in this area. She suggests that there is little empirical evidence for the claims of very high expatriate failure and claims that the myth of high expatriate failure rates has been perpetuated by careless and inappropriate referencing of Tung's (1981, 1982) seminal work. There has been growing debate in recent years on the measurement of expatriate failure and a number of authors have called for a broader conceptualisation of expatriate failure (Briscoe and Schuler, 2004; Scullion and Collings, 2006b).

If firms can take a broader view of the success or failure of expatriate assignments, they are more likely to gain a better understanding of the utility of such assignments than they can with narrow definitions of failure. In summary, we suggest that in the future expatriate performance, rather than expatriate failure, should be the key focus for both HR practitioners and academics. We now develop this theme.

3.5. Expatriate Performance

Managing the performance of individual expatriate employees emerges as the penultimate challenge for MNCs in the context of the traditional expatriate assignment cycle. Mendenhall and Oddou (1985) point to the complexity added to this process by the fact that expatriates must meet the often conflicting expectations of HQ management and subsidiary colleagues. Indeed, it has been argued that there are a number of factors which impact on the performance of expatriate employees. These include technical knowledge, personal (and family) adjustment to the foreign culture, and environmental factors (political and labour force stability and cultural distance from one's home culture) (Cascio, 2006; Oddou and Mendenhall, 2000). It is important to note, however, the potential problems that would result from a primary focus on technical competence, which lacks adequate consideration of cultural factors. Other factors that emerge as significant include the peculiarities of the host environment and the level of support provided by the headquarters (Cascio, 2006; Oddou and Mendenhall, 2000).

Designing performance management systems for international assignees involves taking into account a number of key factors including: the impact of exogenous factors such as foreign exchange fluctuations on the performance of business operations (Black *et al.*, 1999); the clear articulation of the performance objectives of the assignee and ensuring that the appraisal measures the same things in different countries; and identifying the persons best placed to evaluate the performance of the assignee. Briscoe and Schuler (2004) postulate that the key to the success of managing the performance of expatriates is recognising the need to adapt the appraisal system to take into account the host context, and they demonstrate the limitations of operating with standardised systems.

3.6. Career Issues

The final challenge we consider in the context of traditional international assignments is the changing nature of careers in the international context. Changing attitudes toward careers are included in our discussion, as these shifts may affect willingness both to accept assignments and conditions under which assignments are accepted, as well as retention after assignment. In this regard we point to two key trends. The first of these is the changing nature of careers in the labour force and in particular the increasing emphasis placed by employees on career mobility and decreasing commitment to specific organisations. Second, we point to the emerging emphasis placed on self-initiated international assignments or assignments initiated by individuals without organisational support (cf. Inkson et al., 1997; Suutari and Brewster, 2000).

In considering the former, there is a growing body of research that indicates international assignees perceive the value of the assignment to be in developing individual competence, which can be transferred across organisations and is valued in the external labour market (DeFillippi and Arthur, 1996; Parker and Inkson, 1999; Stahl et al., 2002). Indeed, Dickman and Harris (2005: 400) posit: "the link between an IA [international assignment] and the organization's benefits in career capital augmentation is ... tenuous", which further reflects the fact that international assignments may be more beneficial from an individual career perspective and in building individual social capital than in building organizational capital. This literature resonates with the emerging literature on the boundaryless career (Arthur and Rousseau, 1996). As Thomas et al. (2005: 341) note:

> The boundaryless careerist . . . is the highly qualified mobile professional who builds his or her career competencies and labor market value through transfer across boundaries. He or she is explicitly and implicitly contrasted with more staid careerists pursuing traditional organizational careers, who, it is implied, are at risk in a rapidly changing society because their career-relevant skills and networks are associated with single organizations vulnerable to unexpected change.

Thus, in ensuring their employability, individuals are increasingly concerned with enhancing their social capital, marketability and employability in the broader labor market rather than limiting their progression to the organisation within which they work. The implications of boundaryless careers for organisations are two-fold. First, it is becoming progressively more evident that individuals value more generic skills that have transferability to other organisations and this, rather than developing skills that may be more relevant to the employing organisation, may be their primary focus in terms of development while on assignment. Second, it may call into question ongoing organisational loyalty, reflected, for example, in the high levels of expatriate turnover on repatriation that emerge in the literature.

A second key theme with regard to the changing nature of careers in global context is the emergence of self-initiated expatriate assignments, which is also relevant in the context of boundaryless careers (Thomas *et al.*, 2005). By this, we are referring to those whose international experience is not initiated by an international transfer within an organisation but rather those who relocate abroad without organisational assistance and of their own accord, a topic first explored by Inkson *et al.* (1997) and later termed self-Initiated foreign work experience (SFE) (Suutari and Brewster, 2000).

They argue that these SFEs may have different motivations than traditional assignees and are generally self-financing and assume responsibility for establishing themselves in the new environment. In addition, SFEs are more likely to have a more heterogeneous skill set and may range from those at the margins of the labour market who travel abroad to work in low-level jobs to those at the higher end of the labour market, particularly in developing countries, who go abroad to take advantage of career opportunities (the *brain drain*). The key implication of the increasing number of SFEs who are joining the global labour market is that MNCs can make use of these employees to fill key positions in subsidiary operations at a lower cost than expatriates. However, there is a dearth of empirical research both on the individual issues faced by SFEs seeking re-entry and on the HR issues facing organisations who seek to employ them.

Having reviewed the reasons that MNCs traditionally used expatriate assignments and the current climate of such assignments with a particular focus on the challenges to their continued utility, we now examine the alternatives to traditional international assignments available to MNCs.

4. ALTERNATIVE FORMS OF INTERNATIONAL ASSIGNMENTS

The discussion above may suggest the demise of traditional expatriate assignment in MNCs. However, research suggests there is little evidence of a significant decline in the use of long-term assignments but does identify the growing use of alternative forms of international assignments (cf. Dowling and Welch, 2004; Fenwick, 2004; Mayerhofer *et al.*, 2004; PricewaterhouseCoopers, 2005; Scullion and Collings, 2006c; Tahvanainen *et al.*, 2005). A recent survey reported that 62 per cent of respondents suggested that their organisations were seeking alternatives to long-term assignments (GMAC, 2005). This suggests that what is happening is the emergence of a portfolio of international assignments within the MNC (Roberts *et al.*, 1998). The emergence of these alternative assignments has been driven in large part by the problems associated with the traditional expatriate assignment discussed above.

In the portfolio of emerging alternatives, we examine short-term assignments, international business travellers (IBT), rotational assignments and international commuter assignments, and virtual assignments.[1] We now identify the circumstances under which the different types of alternative forms of international assignments are considered appropriate, examine the evidence relating to their level of usage and identify operational issues that emerge in the context of managing these alternative forms of international assignments.

4.1. Short-Term International Assignments

It has been argued that short-term assignments are the most popular form of non-standard assignment (Tahvanainen et al., 2005). There is some variation in how short-term assignments are defined by organisations and Tahvanainen et al. (2005) have called for further empirical work on this topic. In this reading, we highlight a number of key characteristics that are associated with a classic short-term international assignment. Typically, what constitutes "short-term" is company specific, but it could be considered an assignment longer than a business trip but shorter than a year's duration. Further, the assignee's family often remain in the home country, while salary, pension and social security benefits are also handled there (Peltonen, 2001; PricewaterhouseCoopers, 2002, 2005; Tahvanainen et al., 2005). Thus, we define a short-term international assignment as a temporary internal transfer to a foreign subsidiary of between one and twelve months duration. We argue that the relocation of family and remuneration issues are of secondary importance in terms of definition, although they may have significant operational implications for the MNC and personal implications for the assignee. Although there is limited evidence available on the actual extent of utilisation of short-term international assignments in MNCs, we can point to some key trends. PricewaterhouseCoopers (2005) report that over 50 per cent of companies surveyed expect the use of short-term assignments to increase in their operations in the future, with the emerging markets of Asia and Eastern Europe coming to the fore as significant destinations for such assignees.

These assignees can be suitable for organisational, or to a lesser degree individual, development objectives, which could be achieved at a fraction of the costs associated with traditional expatriate assignments (Scullion and Collings, 2006c). Based on their exploratory empirical study, Tahvanainen et al. (2005: 665) identify the following situations in which short-term assignments are used in MNCs: (1) problem-solving or skills transfer; (2) for control purposes; and (3) for managerial development reasons. Other rationales that emerge include: temporarily importing the talent necessary to train the local workforce, to handle needs on a project basis, to eliminate the cost and disruption of relocating entire families (Melone, 2005). We suggest that the circumstances in which short-term assignments are used merits further empirical research, and that an exploration of the variables that impact on their usage would be particularly useful.

Key advantages associated with short-term international assignments include increased flexibility, simplicity and cost effectiveness (Tahvanainen et al., 2005: 667–668). Alongside these benefits, common disadvantages include: (1) taxation issues particularly for assignments over six months duration, (2) the potential for side-effects such as alcoholism and marital problems, (3) failure to build effective relationships with local colleagues and customers and (4) work visas and permits (Tahvanainen et al., 2005).

4.2. Frequent Flyer Assignments

Another alternative international staffing option is the use of frequent flyer assignments, or international business travellers. The IBT has been defined as "one for whom business travel is an essential component of their work" (Welch and Worm, 2006: 284), which has the advantage of avoiding the relocation of the expatriate and their entire family to a foreign country. Some researchers have argued that IBTs do not come under the remit of alternative forms of international assignments, as they do not involve physical relocation to a different country (Welch and Worm, 2006). However, following Fenwick (2004) we include them in our discussion because the evidence suggests that they are an important alternative to the traditional expatriate assignment for MNCs (Michailova and Worm, 2003). IBTs provide the advantage of face-to-face interaction in conducting business transactions without the requirement for their physical relocation. Welch and Worm (2006) argue that IBTs are particularly appropriate in developing markets or volatile countries where people would be reluctant to relocate. Arguably, they are also particularly appropriate in the European and South East Asian contexts, where many capitals can be reached with a short flight (1–3 hours). There is little available evidence on the extent of utilisation of IBTs in MNCs, although anecdotal evidence suggests that the level of business travel remains relatively high despite recent high-profile terrorist attacks. For example, a UK survey found that the number of business flights taken by executives is likely to increase by 12 per cent before 2015 (Barclaycard, 2006), however given the wide range of people involved in business travel it is a significant challenge for MNCs to establish an accurate account of the number of IBTs in their organisations (Welch and Worm, 2006).

IBTs are most appropriate for conducting irregular specialised tasks, such as annual budgeting meetings or production scheduling in MNCs but more crucially they can develop important networks with key contacts in foreign markets. Further, they are useful in maintaining a personal touch in managing subsidiary operations without the need for relocation. However, there is a dearth of empirical research on the main issues and challenges faced by IBTs and research on these issues would be timely.

IBTs offer a number of advantages to MNCs and individuals. First, they allow for face-to-face interaction with subsidiary employees, which develops their social capital without the need for their physical relocation and thus minimises interruption to the individual's careers and reduce costs to the MNC. They also minimise the impact of international work on dual-career couples, however they are not without their difficulties. For example, the stress and other health issues of frequent business travel are well documented in the literature (cf. De Frank et al., 2000; Welch and Worm, 2006). Further, the impacts on family life should not be underestimated. Indeed, Welch and Worm (2006) suggest that many short trips that followed one upon the other created more serious family problems than more infrequent yet longer absences. There is also evidence that many firms underestimate the impact of frequent business travel on individuals' workloads and fail to allow time for IBTs to catch up on the work backlog when they return to the office. In a similar vein, there can be significant pressure to cram a huge amount of work into a business trip (Scullion and Collings, 2006c).

4.3. Commuter and Rotational Assignments

Commuter assignments and rotational assignments have grown in importance in recent years (Scullion and Collings, 2006c). The former are defined as where an assignee commutes from their home base to a post in another country, generally on a weekly or bi-weekly basis (PricewaterhouseCoopers, 2005). While the latter are defined as where staff commute from their home country to a workplace in another country for a short period followed by a period of time off in the home country (Welch and Worm, 2006). This latter type of assignment is common on oil rigs. In both of these instances, family do not generally relocate with the assignee. PricewaterhouseCoopers (2005: 17) report a small increase in the use of rotational assignments in recent years, reflected in the fact that 11 per cent of organisations had written policies for them. They report particular success of this approach in the Chinese context, although they also point to the complexities of using such assignments due to issues around compensation, taxation and social security. Mayrhofer and Scullion (2002) cite the example of German quality engineers with managerial and technical responsibilities in the clothing industry who travelled frequently in several countries in Eastern Europe, returning regularly for briefings and to spend weekends with their families. It has been suggested that the geographic situation in Europe means that Euro-commuting and frequent visiting is a viable alternative to expatriate transfers (Mayrhofer and Brewster, 1997). However, a recent review raised a note of caution on commuter assignments concluding, "there are serious concerns about the viability of commuter arrangements over an extended period of time due to the build up of stress from intensive travel commitments and the impact on personal relationships" (Dowling and Welch, 2004: 68).

4.4. Global Virtual Teams

As a result of increasing decentralisation and globalisation of work processes, many organisations have responded to their dynamic environments by introducing global virtual teams, in which members are geographically dispersed and coordinate their work predominantly with electronic information and communication technologies. This trend has accelerated since the late 1990s due to the growth of the Internet and other communication technologies (Hertel *et al.*, 2005). In global virtual teams, staff do not relocate to a host location but have a responsibility to manage international staff from the home base (Dowling and Welch, 2004) and generally lead to some sort of jointly achieved outcome involving a degree of intercultural interaction. There is limited evidence on the utilisation of virtual assignments in MNCs, which is surprising given that some 25 per cent of organisations surveyed by PricewaterhouseCoopers (2005: 17) considered virtual assignments to be a key part of their international HR policy development. Interestingly, though, the number of organisations utilising such assignments had fallen from 7 per cent in the 2002 survey to only 4 per cent in 2005. Thus, it appears that organisations have not yet begun to fully utilise the benefits of virtual assignments. The academic literature associated with this type of assignment is largely located within the global virtual teams literature and recently there has been a rapid growth in interest in global virtual teams, which are being utilised to help global firms to use the best talent wherever it is located (Maznevski *et al.*, 2006). It has been argued that virtual assignments are most appropriate for relatively routine activities and that there are certain circumstances where face-to-face communication is indispensable (Hertel *et al.*, 2005; Maznevski *et al.*, 2006). Further research on the use and effectiveness of virtual assignments in organisations is needed and could focus on the circumstances in which such assignments would be appropriate and the key factors which contribute to their effectiveness. We now turn to considering the HR implications of managing alternative forms of international assignments.

4.5. The HR Implications of Managing Alternative Forms of International Assignments

There is little doubt that a significant challenge for international HR managers in managing a broader portfolio of international assignments is the need to develop a range of IHRM policies and practices to take account the different types, objectives and different circumstances surrounding each type of assignment.

4.5.1. Policies Surrounding Alternative Forms of International Assignments

It is important to highlight at the outset that a growing portfolio of types of international assignments is likely to result in a greater administrative burden in some areas for international HR managers. Not least of these challenges will be tracking and accounting for this increasingly diverse group of internationally mobile employees, particularly in relation to tax, social security, visa and legal requirements of the various countries (PricewaterhouseCoopers, 2005). In this regard, estimates of the development of written policies for traditional expatriate assignments range from less than 50 per cent (Fenwick, 2004) to as high as 71 per cent (GMAC, 2005). The Internet emerges as a key outlet for the dissemination of such policies. Research indicates that over 50 per cent of respondents followed a single policy for both long- and short-term assignments (PricewaterhouseCoopers, 2005). This would seem a weakness, as it fails to account for the obvious differences in requirements of long- and short-term assignments and it is possible that many of these individuals would fall outside traditional expatriate policies and thus create difficulties for international HR managers. Arguably, this observation is reflected in the finding that over 80 per cent of respondents to the same survey believed that changes to their policies were necessary. On balance, the literature points to the limited development of appropriate HR policies to support IBTs and virtual assignments. In the latter case, this has been attributed to the fact that they still tend to be relatively uncommon assignment options in MNCs (cf. Fenwick, 2004). The former tend to be covered by the MNC's business travel policies. While these polices may cover some of the pertinent issues, it is unlikely that they have been developed to account for people who travel internationally with the organisation on a very regular basis. For example, the shift toward low-cost carriers (Barclaycard, 2006) may be appropriate for individuals who travel for business on an irregular basis on short-haul flights, but arguably they are much less appropriate for those who travel longer distances on a regular basis. The danger for organisations and assignees in failing to develop appropriate policies is that their international assignment will fall outside the traditional remit of the international HR function and thus they will not receive the level of organisational support required. The challenge for the international HR function is to develop appropriate policies to support the IBTs in the most effective way.

On the other hand, while research has emphasised the importance of support for traditional international assignments (Tung, 2000), recent research has highlighted the lack of HR support for alternative international assignees and suggested that the burden of managing these assignments is largely left with employees and their families (Mayerhofer et al., 2004). Recent research highlighted the use of personal initiative by alternative international assignees working in Eastern Europe for German clothing manufacturers (Mayrhofer and Scullion, 2002) and it has been suggested that, more generally, staff involved in alternative international assignments play a proactive role in their adjustment and use their networks and contacts to meet the challenges they face (Mayerhofer et al., 2004). It has also been argued that more of the personal cost of this type of assignment is born by employees and their families than in the case of traditional expatriate assignments and that non-traditional assignments would be more successful for both the organisations and individuals if HRM policies and practices focused more on family friendly staffing policies (Mayrhofer and Scullion, 2002; Mayerhofer et al., 2004).

4.5.2. Recruitment and Selection

The importance of effective recruitment and selection for the success of traditional expatriate assignments and for enabling international firms to compete effectively in international business has long been recognised (Tung, 1981, 1982). Indeed, effective recruitment and selection is also key for successful completion of alternative forms of international assignments. However, recent research on short-term assignment indicates that formal selection for short-term assignments was rarely practised among respondents (Tahvanainen et al., 2005). This resonates with earlier research, which highlighted the importance of personal recommendations and informal methods for selecting expatriates (Brewster, 1991). Recent research on the selection of traditional expatriate assignees further reinforced the importance of informality in expatriate selection systems (Harris and Brewster, 1999). It has been argued that if MNCs do not improve their recruitment and selection practices, critical shortages of international managers may become even more significant (Tahvanainen et al., 2005). Thus, in selecting assignees for alternative forms of international assignments, MNCs should be aware of the limitations associated with more traditional forms of international assignments and should work toward more sophisticated recruitment and selection techniques. The majority of international firms continue to rely on technical skills and domestic track record as the most important selection criteria and many organisations still undervalue the importance of the "soft skills" of international management (Morley and Flynn, 2003; Sparrow et al., 2004).

Finally, when seeking to develop selection criteria for alternative international assignees, it should be recognised that selection criteria for international managers need to change to reflect changes in the purposes of international assignments (Scullion and Collings, 2006c).

4.5.3. Training

The value of cross-cultural training in increasing the probability of success of international assignments is relatively well documented in the extant literature (cf. Parkinson and Morley (2006) for an overview). However, the requirements for cross-cultural training to support alternative forms of international assignments are less well explored. Recent research highlights the lack of HR support for international assignees and suggests that managers are often expected to assume responsibility for their own training and development (Mayerhofer *et al.*, 2004). The practitioner literature suggests that expatriates on short-term assignments and IBTs do not have the same time as traditional expatriates to adjust to a new culture. Indeed, it has been argued that their experience of culture shock is similar to traditional assignees but in "fast forward" (Melone, 2005). However, there is a dearth of empirical research in this area. The available evidence suggests that cross-cultural issues are at least as important in non-traditional international assignments as in traditional ones (Mayerhofer *et al.*, 2004). In a similar vein, cultural awareness and cross-cultural communication training would be an important consideration for those involved in virtual assignments, as would issues around the application of technology to the process. Paradoxically, empirical evidence suggests that these assignees are not provided with the same degree of country-specific and cross-cultural training as traditional expatriates (Tahvanainen *et al.*, 2005). This is a significant weakness, and MNCs should introduce cross-cultural training programmes appropriate to particular assignments in their organisation.

4.5.4. Reward

Given the fact that cost reduction is identified as a key factor driving the shift towards alternative forms of international assignments in MNCs, impacts around reward are likely to emerge as a key consideration for MNCs. In this regard IBTs' remuneration tends to be limited to *per diem* with hardship allowances for locations considered to be dangerous or volatile. In addition, however, IBTs tend to be rewarded indirectly through travelling business class, retaining their frequent flyer miles for personal use and staying in high-class hotels that add to the costs of such assignments. There is little available evidence on commuter assignments. On balance, it appears that salary payments remain in the home country for short-term assignments (Pricewaterhouse Coopers, 2005; Tahvanainen *et al.*, 2005). In a similar vein, short-term assignees are generally awarded a *per diem* allowance and, when necessary, a hardship allowance is paid. Further, in situations where the cost of living in the host country is higher than the assignee's home country, a cost-of-living adjustment may apply (Tahvanainen *et al.*, 2005). Further, accommodation in the host is generally arranged by and paid for by the MNC (ibid.). This is not straightforward, however, and Melone (2005) points to the high cost of temporary housing as opposed to longer-term alternatives. Thus, while a hotel may be suitable for relatively short stays, for IBTs or short-term assignments lasting less than a month or two, serviced apartments may be more suited to longer stays. These options may, however, be significantly more expensive than longer-term options.

4.5.5. Occupational Health and Safety

A final substantive area of HR practice that is emerging as significant in the context of alternative forms of international assignment is occupational health and safety. Although often excluded in discussions of this nature, we feel it is necessary to highlight the importance of this area. This is particularly the case with regard to IBTs, as there is a growing body of literature that highlights the health issues associated with business travel (De Frank et al., 2000; Neck, 2000; Welch and Worm, 2006). These issues can range from a lack of emphasis and decline of physical fitness (Neck, 2000), to increased alcohol consumption, to significantly increased stress levels related to business travel (De Frank et al., 2000; Welch and Worm, 2006). While these issues have significant implications for the individuals concerned, it is without doubt that health issues could potentially have significant implications for organisational performance (Quick, 2000). It is not only the health issues associated with IBTs that should be of concern to MNCs. It is also possible, due to the fact that their families will not accompany them, that those on short-term and commuter assignments may work excessive hours and fail to manage their work/life balance, which can lead to stress, burnout and poor performance. MNCs must be aware of these potential issues and proactively develop HR policies accordingly. Indeed, the area of work/life balance among traditional expatriates and those undertaking alternative forms of international assignments remains under explored in the literature and there is significant potential for further study in this area.

5. CONCLUSION

The literature demonstrates that expatriate assignments do offer a number of potential benefits as well as the well-documented costs to MNCs in staffing their foreign operations. The challenges associated with such assignment have resulted in international assignments gaining a degree of critical attention from scholars in the field. In this regard, we argue that both international organisations and academics must take a more strategic and holistic view of staffing arrangements in the international context. The first key decision to be made by top managers in MNCs is whether or not a traditional expatriate assignment best meets the organisational requirements on a case-by-case basis. In other words, could the proposed objectives be achieved through an alternative means? Academics could advance the theoretical literature in the field by developing taxonomies or models that aid practitioners' decision-making in this area.

We argue that multinational companies, in response to cost pressures and growing problems of staff shortages and resistance to international mobility are making greater use of a range of alternative or non standard forms of international assignment such as short-term assignments, commuter assignments, international business travel and virtual assignments (see Dowling and Welch, 2004). In this regard, the literature suggests the emergence of a portfolio of forms of international assignment within the MNC as opposed to the demise of the traditional assignment (Roberts *et al.*, 1998).

A key challenge for practitioners in MNCs will be to develop effective international HRM policies and practices to ensure the effective implementation of alternative international assignments. Our review suggests that a standardised approach to international assignments would not be effective and that it would be essential to develop HR policies and procedures that reflect differences in the various forms of alternative international assignment.

Recent research on short-term international assignments suggests that attention should be paid to staff selection, pre-departure cross-cultural training, compensation, performance management, repatriation and family issues (Tahvanainen *et al.*, 2005; Welch *et al.*, 2003). This would be a good starting point for researchers and practitioners interested in the broader area of alternative forms of international working. There are also implications for the role of the HR function, as it has been suggested that the more that non-standard forms of international assignments are used relative to traditional expatriate assignments, the greater the need for a more structured and centralised approach to their management. Indeed, it has been suggested that as HR staff are required to broaden their focus to develop policies and practices for non-standard assignments, this may necessitate a redefinition of the international HR role (Tahvanainen *et al.*, 2005).

Our reading also highlights some HR implications of alternative forms of international assignments that may be of particular interest to both IHRM specialists and line managers in MNCs. We highlight that alternative forms of international assignments can often provide solutions to some of the complex global staffing challenges facing multinational companies by providing the required skills and developing international capabilities simultaneously (Tahvanainen *et al.*, 2005). Alternative forms of assignments can also be utilised as an effective way of developing younger high potential international managers by exposing them to different experiences in a variety of foreign markets, which also augments their social capital (Mayrhofer and Scullion, 2002).

Our review also points to the need for researchers and practitioners to pay more attention to family issues relating to alternative forms of international assignment. Little is known about the impact of alternative forms of international assignment on the family and the employees' work/life balance. One the one hand, it has been argued that an advantage of short-term international assignments is that they do not directly affect the career of the partner or children's education. On the other hand, there is some evidence that short-term assignments can lead to negative impacts such as stress and burnout for some short-term international assignees (Brewster *et al.*, 2001). More research is needed to guide researchers and practitioners in devising HR policies to respond to and anticipate some of the little understood side effects of alternative forms of international assignments.

It is important to note that there are a number of alternative international assignments that can be used by MNCs in staffing foreign operations (Tharenou and Harvey, 2006). These require firms to explore alternatives to traditional expatriate pools. For example, it has been argued that the employment of third country nationals in key positions could result in significant cost savings for MNCs. In this regard, self-initiated expatriates could also potentially reduce the costs of expatriate assignments. A further option available to MNCs is the localisation of key positions traditionally held by expatriates (cf. Harry and Collings, 2006). The utilisation of both TCNs and self-initiated expatriates in MNCs would reduce the costs associated with relocation.

When the organisation decides that a traditional expatriate assignment is the best alternative in a given situation, we argue that the key to success is a more strategic focus. In this regard, the challenge is not just strategy formulation, which many organisations do relatively well (Tahvanainen and Suutari, 2005), but also to translate strategic planning to the operational level, through the development of HR policies and practices aimed at ensuring congruence between employees' work behaviours and the organisational strategy. Specifically, we argue that international HR managers, in conjunction with line managers, must begin by defining appropriate objectives for the expatriate assignment. The achievement of these objectives will be improved if the individual expatriate is selected and supported through a congruent set of HR policies throughout the expatriate cycle. This begins with appropriate selection criteria and techniques that expand on simple measures of technical competence that have been shown empirically to be poor indicators of managers' performance while they are on assignment. Further, appropriate compensation and performance management systems and, particularly significantly, repatriation policies will aid in the achievement of the assignment's objectives. In other words, the challenge for IHRM practitioners is to ensure that each international assignment has clearly defined goals and in this context to continue the advancement of techniques aimed at measuring the return of investment on international assignments. Thus, in measuring the utility of such assignments, MNCs and scholars alike must take the objective of the assignment as their starting point and must evaluate the contribution of expatriate assignments in this context. The utilisation of congruent HR policies should result in a *virtuous* circle whereby successful completion of expatriate assignments and repatriation into the home organisation will result in employees becoming more amenable to being sent on assignment and organisational experience will mean increasing competence within the MNC in managing expatriation. This suggests that IHRM scholars need to undertake further work on bundles of IHRM practices and their contribution to business performance in the international context with a specific emphasis on supporting international assignments. There is also the need for academics to develop more sophisticated theory to help better explain the staffing choices selected by MNCs (Tarique et al., 2006), and we suggest scholars build on the agency and transaction cost theories used in this context by researchers such as Harvey *et al.* (2000) and Tan and Mahoney (2004), which highlight the importance of the MNEs' environment in influencing strategic staffing choices.

The key implications of the preceding discussion for IHRM practitioners include the importance of clearly identifying and articulating HR planning requirements in foreign subsidiaries. Following this, they must determine the extent to which PCN expatriates actually represent the most appropriate staffing option for the particular role. If this does prove to be the case then the challenge is to develop clearly defined performance objectives for the role and to select an appropriate candidate on the basis of the objectives of the assignment. Supporting HR policies should be premised on supporting these objectives and finally the return on the investment should be evaluated on this basis also.

NOTES

* The authors are grateful to the editor Rosalie Tung, Mila Lazarova and the anonymous referees for their comments on earlier drafts of this reading. Any errors remaining are our own.

1.   Other alternatives include localisation of managerial positions whereby positions initially filled by expatriates are filled with host country nationals (cf. Harry and Collings, 2006 for a discussion) or inpatriation where host country nationals are transferred to the home country of the MNC on a permanent or semi-permanent basis (Harvey *et al.*, 1999), provided they return to the home country. A further option available to MNCs is the permanent transfer of the individual to the host country payroll, which would eliminate most additional costs. A discussion of these options is, however, beyond the scope of the current reading.

REFERENCES

Adler, N. (1984). Women in international management: Where are they? *California Management Review, 26*(4): 78–89.

Adler, N. (2002). Global managers: No longer men alone. *International Journal of Human Resource Management, 13*: 743–760.

Anderson, V. and Boocock, G. (2002). Small firms and internationalisation: Learning to manage and managing to learn. *Human Resource Management Journal, 12*: 5–24.

Arthur, M. B. and Rousseau, D. M. (eds). (1996). *The boundaryless career: A new employment principle for a new organizational era.* Boston, MA: Cambridge University Press.

Barclaycard. (2006). *The Barclaycard Business Travel Survey 2005/2006.* Barclaycard Business, Stockton-on-Tees.

Björkman, I. and Xiucheng, F. (2002). Human resource management and the performance of western firms in China. *International Journal of Human Resource Management, 13*: 853–864.

Black, J. S., Morrison, A. and Gregersen, H. B. (2000). *Global explorers: The next generation of leaders.* New York: Routledge.

Black, J. S., Gregersen, H. B., Mendenhall, M. E. and Stroh, L. K. (1999). *Globalizing people through international assignments.* Reading, MA: Addison Wesley.

Brewster, C. (1991). *The management of expatriates.* London: Kogan Page.

Brewster, C., Harris, H. and Petrovic, J. (2001). Globally mobile employees: Managing the mix. *Journal of Professional Human Resource Management, 25*: 11–15.

Briscoe, D. R. and Schuler, R. S. (2004). *International human resource management* (2nd edn). London: Routledge.

Caligiuri, P. and Cascio, W. (1998). Can we send her there? Maximising the success of Western women on global assignments. *Journal of World Business, 33*: 394–416.

Caligiuri, P. M. and Tung, R. (1999). Comparing the success of male and female expatriates from a US based company. *International Journal of Human Resource Management, 10*: 763–782.

Cascio, W. F. (2006). Global performance management systems. In G. K. Stahl and I. Björkman (eds), *Handbook of research in international human resource management*. Cheltenham, UK: Edward Elgar.

Cohn, J. M., Khurana, R. and Reeves, L. (2005). Growing talent as if your business depended on it. *Harvard Business Review, 83*(10): 62–71.

Collings, D. and Scullion, H. (2006). Global staffing. In G. K. Stahl and I. Björkman (eds), *Handbook of research in international human resource management*. Cheltenham, UK: Edward Elgar.

DeFillippi, R. and Arthur, M. (1996). Boundaryless contexts and careers: A competency-based perspective. In M. B. Arthur and D. M. Rousseau (eds), *The boundaryless career: A new employment principle for a new organizational era*. New York: Oxford University Press.

De Frank, R. S., Konopaske, R. and Ivancevich, J. M. (2000). Executive travel stress: Perils of the road warrior. *Academy of Management Executive, 14*(2): 58–71.

Dickman, M. and Harris, H. (2005). Developing career capital for global careers: The role of international assignments. *Journal of World Business, 40*(4): 399–420.

Dowling, P. and Welch, D. (2004). *International human resource management: Managing people in a global context* (4th edn). London: Thomson Learning.

Edström, A. and Galbraith, J. R. (1977). Transfer of managers as a coordination and control strategy in multinational organizations. *Administrative Science Quarterly, 22*: 248–263.

Evans, P., Pucik, V. and Barsoux, J. L. (2002). *The global challenge: Frameworks for international human resource management*. Boston, MA: McGraw-Hill.

Fenwick, M. (2004). On international assignment: Is expatriation the only way to go? *Asia Pacific Journal of Human Resources, 42*: 365–377.

Forster, N. (2000). The myth of the international manager. *International Journal of Human Resource Management, 11*: 126–142.

GMAC Global Relocations Services (2005). *Global relocation trends: 2005 survey report*, New Jersey, GMAC.

Harris, H. and Brewster, C. (1999). The coffee-machine system: How international selection really works. *The International Journal of Human Resource Management, 10*: 488–500.

Harry, W. and Collings, D. G. (2006). Localisation: Societies, organisations and employees. In H. Scullion and D. Collings (eds), *Global staffing*. London: Routledge.

Harvey, M. (1998). Dual-career couples during international relocation: The trailing spouse. *International Journal of Human Resource Management, 9*: 309–331.

Harvey, M., Speier, C. and Novicevic, M. M. (1999). The role of inpatriation in global staffing. *International Journal of Human Resource Management, 10*: 459–476.

Harvey, M. G., Speier, C. and Novicevic, M. M. (2000). A theory based framework for strategic human resource staffing policies and practice. *International Journal of Human Resource Management, 12*: 898–915.

Harzing, A. W. K. (2001). Of bears, bees and spiders: The role of expatriates in controlling foreign subsidiaries. *Journal of World Business, 26*: 366–379.

Harzing, A. W. K. (1995). The persistent myth of high expatriate failure rates. *International Journal of Human Resource Management, 6*: 457–475.

Harzing, A. W. K. (2002). Are our referencing errors undermining our scholarship and credibility? The case of expatriate failure rates. *Journal of Organizational Behaviour, 23*: 127–148.

Hertel, G., Geister, C. and Konradt, U. (2005). Managing virtual teams: A review of current empirical research. *Human Resource Management Review, 15*: 69–95.

Inkson, K., Arthur, M. B., Pringle, J. and Barry, S. (1997). Expatriate assignment versus overseas experience: Contrasting models of human resource development. *Journal of World Business, 32*: 351–368.

Jensen, M. C. and Meckling, W. H. (1976). Theory of the firm: Managerial behaviour, agency costs and ownership structures. *Journal of Financial Economics, 3*: 305–360.

Konopaske, R. and Werner, S. (2005). US managers' willingness to accept a global assignment: Do expatriate benefits and assignment length make a difference. *International Journal of Human Resource Management, 16*: 1159–1175.

Lazarova, M. B. (2006). International human resource management in global perspective. In M. J. Morley, N. Heraty and D. G. Collings (eds), *International HRM and international assignments*. Basingstoke, UK: Palgrave Macmillan.

Lazarova, M. and Tarique, I. (2005). Knowledge transfer upon repatriation. *Journal of World Business, 40*: 361–373.

McNulty, Y. and Tharenou, P. (2004). Expatriate return on investment. *International Studies of Management and Organization, 34*(3): 68–95.

Mayerhofer, H., Hartmann, L. C., Michelitsch-Riedl, G. and Kollinger, I. (2004). Flexpatriate assignments: Neglected issue in global staffing. *International Journal of Human Resource Management, 15*(8): 1371–1389.

Mayrhofer, W. and Brewster, C. (1997). Ethnocentric staffing policies in European multinationals. *International Executive, 38*: 749–778.

Mayrhofer, W. and Scullion, H. (2002). Female expatriates in international business: Empirical evidence from the German clothing industry. *International Journal of Human Resource Management, 13*: 815–836.

Maznevski, M., Davison, S. C. and Jonsen, K. (2006). Global virtual team dynamics and effectiveness. In G. Stahl and I. Björkman (eds), *Handbook of Research in International Human Resource Management*. London: Edward Elgar.

Melone, F. (2005). *Changing with the times: Creative alternatives to long-term international assignments*, online resource, downloaded from www.gmacglobalrelocation.com/insight_support/article_archive.asp, last accessed on 10 May 2006.

Mendenhall, M. and Oddou, G. (1985). The dimensions of expatriate acculturation: A review. *Academy of Management Review, 10*: 39–47.

Michaels, E., Handfield-Jones, H. and Axelrod, B. (2001). *The war for talent*. Boston, MA: Harvard Business School Press.

Michailova, S. and Worm, V. (2003). Personal networking in Russia and China: Blat and Guanxi. *European Management Journal, 21*(4): 509–519.

Minbaeva, D. B. and Michailova, S. (2004). Knowledge transfer and expatriation in multinational corporations: The role of disseminative capacity. *Employee Relations, 26*: 663–680.

Monks, K., Scullion, H. and Creaner, J. (2001). HRM in the international firm: Evidence from Ireland. *Personnel Review, 30*: 536–553.

Moore, K. and Lewis, D. (1999). *Birth of the multinational*. Copenhagen: Copenhagen Business Press.

Morley, M. and Flynn, M. (2003). Personal characteristics and competencies as correlates of intercultural transitional adjustment among U.S. and Canadian Sojourners in Ireland. *International Management, 7*(2): 31–46.

Morley, M. and Heraty, N. (2004). International assignments and global careers. *Thunderbird International Business Review, 46*: 633–646.

Napier, N. and Taylor, S. (2002). Experiences of women professionals abroad: Comparisons across Japan, China and Turkey. *The International Journal of Human Resource Management, 13*: 837–851.

Neck, C. P. (2000). The fit executive: Exercise and diet guidelines for enhancing performance. *Academy of Management Review, 14*(2): 72–83.

Oddou, G. and Mendenhall, M. E. (2000). Expatriate performance appraisal: Problems and solutions. In M. E. Mendenhall and G. Oddou (eds), *Readings and cases in international human resource management* (3rd ed.). Cincinnati, OH: South-Western.

Parker, P. and Inkson, K. (1999). New forms of career: The challenge to human resource management. *Asia Pacific Journal of Human Resources, 37*: 76–85.

Parkinson, E. and Morley, M. (2006). Cross cultural training. In H. Scullion and D. G. Collings (eds), *Global staffing*. London: Routledge.

Peltonen, T. (2001). *New forms of international work: An international survey study. Results of the Finnish survey*. University of Oulu and Cranfield School of Management.

PricewaterhouseCoopers. (2002). *International assignments: Global policy and practice, Key trends 2002*. PricewaterhouseCoopers.

PricewaterhouseCoopers (2005). *International assignments: Global policy and practice, Key trends 2005*. PricewaterhouseCoopers.

Quelch, J. A. and Bloom, H. (1999). Ten steps to global human resource strategy. *Strategy and business* (First Quarter, pp. 1–6).

Quick, J. C. (2000). Executive health: Building strength, managing risks. *Academy of Management Review, 14*(2): 34–44.

Roberts, K., Kossek, E. and Ozeki, C. (1998). Managing the global workforce: Challenges and strategies. *Academy of Management Executive, 12*(4): 93–106.

Schuler, R. S., Budhwar, P. S. and Florkowski, G. W. (2002). International human resource management: Review and critique. *International Journal of Management Reviews, 4*: 41–70.

Schuler, R. S., Jackson, S. E. and Luo, Y. (2004). *Managing human resources in cross-border alliances*. London: Routledge.

Scullion, H. (1994). Staffing policies and strategic control in British multinational. *International Studies of Management and Organization, 4*(3): 18–35.

Scullion, H. (2001). International human resource management. In J. Storey (ed.), *Human resource management*. London: International Thompson.

Scullion, H. and Brewster, C. (2001). Managing expatriates: Messages from Europe. *Journal of World Business, 36*: 346–365.

Scullion, H. and Collings, D. G. (2006a). Introduction. In H. Scullion and D. G. Collings (eds), *Global staffing*. London: Routledge.

Scullion, H. and Collings, D. G. (2006b). International talent management. In H. Scullion and D. G. Collings (eds), *Global staffing*. London: Routledge.

Scullion, H. and Collings, D. G. (2006c). Alternative forms of international assignments. In H. Scullion and D. G. Collings (eds), *Global staffing*. London: Routledge.

Scullion, H. and Starkey, K. (2000). In search of the changing role of the corporate human resource function in the international firm. *International Journal of Human Resource Management, 11*: 1061–1081.

Selmer, J. (2001). Expatriate selection: Back to basics? *International Journal of Human Resource Management, 12*: 1219–1233.

Sparrow, P., Brewster, C. and Harris, H. (2004). *Globalizing human resource management*. London: Routledge.

Stahl, G. K. and Björkman, I. (eds). (2006). *Handbook of research in international human resource management*. Cheltenham, UK: Edward Elgar.

Stahl, G. K., Miller, E. and Tung, R. (2002). Toward the boundaryless career: A closer look at the expatriate career concept and the perceived implications of an international assignment. *Journal of World Business, 37*: 216–227.

Stroh, L. K. and Caliguiri, P. M. (1998). Increasing global competitiveness through effective people management. *Journal of World Business, 33*: 1–16.

Stroh, L. K., Gregerson, H. B. and Black, J. S. (2000). Triumphs and tragedies: Expectations and commitments upon repatriation. *International Journal of Human Resource Management, 11*: 681–697.

Suutari, V. and Brewster, C. (2000). Making their own way: International experience through self-initiated foreign assignments. *Journal of World Business, 35*: 417–436.

Tahvanainen, M. and Suutari, V. (2005). Expatriate performance management in MNCs. In H. Scullion and M. Linehan (eds), *International human resource management: A critical text*. Basingstoke: Palgrave.

Tahvanainen, M., Welch, D. and Worm, V. (2005). Implications of short-term international assignments. *European Management Journal, 23*: 663–673.

Tarique, I., Schuler, R. and Gong, Y. (2006). A model of multinational enterprise subsidiary staffing Composition. *International Journal of Human Resource Management, 17*: 207–224.

Tharenou, P. and Harvey, M. (2006). Examining the overseas staffing options utilized by Australian headquartered multinational corporations. *International Journal of Human Resource Management, 17*: 1095–1114.

Thomas, D. C., Lazorova, M. B. and Inkson, K. (2005). Global careers: New phenomenon or new perspectives? *Journal of World Business, 40*: 340–347.

Torbiorn, I. (1997). Staffing for international operations. *Human Resource Management Journal, 7*(3): 42–51.

Torraco, R. J. and Swanson, R. A. (1995). The strategic role of human resource development. *Human Resource Planning, 18*(4): 10–12.

Tung, R. (2000). Human resource management international. In R. Tung (ed.), *The IEBM handbook of international business*. London: International Thomson Business Press.

Tung, R. L. (1981). Selection and training of personnel for overseas assignments. *Columbia Journal of World Business, 16*: 68–78.

Tung, R. L. (1982). Selection and training procedures of U.S., European and Japanese multinationals. *California Management Review, 25*: 57–71.

Tung, R. L. (1998). American expatriates abroad: From neophytes to cosmopolitans. *Journal of World Business, 33*: 125–144.

Tung, R. L. (2004). Female expatriates: A model for global leaders? *Organizational Dynamics, 33*: 243–253.

Welch, D., Worm, V. and Fenwick, M. (2003). Are virtual assignments feasible? *Management International Review, 43*: 95–114.

Welch, D. E. and Worm, V. (2006). International business travellers: A challenge for IHRM. In G. K. Stahl and I. Björkman (eds), *Handbook of research in international human resource management*. Cheltenham, UK: Edward Elgar.

Gary R. Oddou and
Mark E. Mendenhall

EXPATRIATE PERFORMANCE APPRAISAL: PROBLEMS AND SOLUTIONS

FOR MORE AND MORE COMPANIES, gaining a competitive edge increasingly means making decisions that reflect an acute understanding of the global marketplace – how other countries utilize and view marketing strategies, accounting and financial systems, labor laws, leadership, communication, negotiation and decision-making styles. Gaining a knowledge of these components is most directly accomplished by sending managers to work in an overseas subsidiary and utilizing them on re-entry.

Our research shows clearly that expatriates develop valuable managerial skills abroad that can be extremely useful to their development as effective senior managers. Based on current research on expatriates, including our own surveying and interviewing of more than 150 of them, probably the most significant skills expatriates develop as a result of their overseas assignments include the following:

- Being able to manage a workforce with cultural and subcultural differences.
- Being able to plan for, and conceptualize, the dynamics of a complex, multi-national environment.
- Being more open-minded about alternative methods for solving problems.
- Being more flexible in dealing with people and systems.
- Understanding the interdependencies among the firm's domestic and foreign operations.

These skills are the natural outgrowth of the increased autonomy and potential impact expatriates experience in their international assignment. In fact, in our study, 67 percent reported having more independence, and they also indicated they had more potential impact on the operation's performance than in their domestic position. With increased decision-making responsibilities in a foreign environment, expatriates are subjected to a fairly intense working environment in which they must learn the ropes quickly.

The skills expatriate managers gain are obviously crucial to effectively managing any business operation, particularly at the international and multinational level. Nightmares abound in the business press of the inept decisions sometimes made by top management due to ignorance of cross-cultural differences in business practices. The ability to plan and conceptualize based on the complex interdependencies of a global market environment with significant cultural differences is required of top management in MNCs.

In short, expatriates can become a very valuable human resource for firms with international or multinational operations. However, one of the most serious stumbling blocks to expatriates' career paths is the lack of recognition of the value of expatriation and the informality with which firms accurately evaluate their expatriates' overseas performance. Although the attributes expatriates gain overseas can and do translate into concrete advantages for their firms, a quick glance at the skills previously listed indicates intangibles that are often difficult to measure and usually are not measured – or are measured inaccurately – by present performance evaluation methods. Hence, it is critical to more closely examine this potential stumbling block to expatriates' careers and to make specific recommendations to improve the process and accuracy of such reviews.

APPRAISING THE EXPATRIATE'S PERFORMANCE

Several problems are inherent to appraising an expatriate's performance. First, an examination of those who evaluate an expatriate's job performance is relevant. Those evaluators include the host national management and often the home office management.

Host National Management's Perceptions of Actual Job Performance

That local management evaluates the expatriate is probably necessary; however, such a process sometimes is problematic. Local management typically evaluates the expatriate's performance from its own cultural frame of reference and set of expectations. For example, one American expatriate manager we talked to used participative decision-making in India but was thought of by local workers as rather incompetent because of the Indian notion that managers, partly owing to their social class level, are seen as the experts. Therefore, a manager should not have to ask subordinates for ideas. Being seen as incompetent negatively affected local management's review of this expatriate's performance, and he was denied a promotion on return to the US. Local management's appraisal is not the only potential problem, however. In fact, based on our research with expatriates, local management's evaluation is usually perceived as being more accurate than that of the home office.

Home Office Management's Perceptions of Actual Job Performance

Because the home office management is geographically distanced from the expatriate, it is often not fully aware of what is happening overseas. As a result, for middle and upper management, home office management will often use a different set of variables than those used by local management. Typically, more visible performance criteria are used to measure the expatriate's success (for example, profits, market share, productivity levels). Such measures ignore other, less visible variables that in reality drastically affect the company's performance. Local events such as strikes, devaluation of the currency, political instability, and runaway inflation are examples of phenomena that are beyond the control of the expatriate and are sometimes "invisible" to the home office.

One expatriate executive told us that in Chile he had almost singlehandedly stopped a strike that would have shut down their factory completely for months and worsened relations between the Chileans and the parent company in the US. In a land where strikes are commonplace, such an accomplishment was quite a coup, especially for an American. The numerous meetings and talks with labor representatives, government officials, and local management required an acute understanding of their culture and a sensitivity beyond the ability of most people. However, because of exchange rate fluctuations with its primary trading partners in South America, the demand for their ore temporarily decreased by 30 percent during the expatriate's tenure. Rather than applauding the efforts this expatriate executive made to avert a strike and recognizing the superb negotiation skills he demonstrated, the home office saw the expatriate as being only somewhat better than a mediocre performer. In other words, because for home office management the most visible criterion of the expatriate's performance was somewhat negative (sales figures), it was assumed that he had not performed adequately. And though the expatriate's boss knew a strike had been averted, the bottom-line concern for sales dollars overshadowed any other significant accomplishments.

The expatriate manager must walk a tightrope. He must deal with a new cultural work group, learn the ins and outs of the new business environment, possibly determine how to work with a foreign boss, find out what foreign management expects of him, and so on. He must also understand the rules of the game on the home front. It is difficult, and sometimes impossible, to please both. Attempting to please both can result in a temporarily, or permanently, railroaded career. So it was with an individual who was considered a "high potential" in a semiconductor firm. He was sent to an overseas operation without the proper product knowledge preparation and barely kept his head above water because of the difficulties of cracking a nearly impossible market. On returning to the US, he was physically and mentally exhausted from the battle. He sought a much less challenging position and got it because top management then believed they had overestimated his potential. In fact, top management never did understand what the expatriate was up against in the foreign market.

In fact, expatriates frequently indicate that headquarters does not really understand their experience − neither the difficulty of it nor the value of it. One study found that one-third of the expatriates felt that corporate headquarters did not understand the expatriate's experience at all. In a 1981 Korn/Ferry survey, 69 percent of the managers reported they felt isolated from domestic operations and their US managers. It is clear from others' and our own research that most US senior management does not understand the value of an international assignment or try to utilize the expatriate's skills gained abroad when they return to the home office. The underlying problem seems to be top management's ethnocentricity.

Management Ethnocentricity

Two of the most significant aspects of management's inability to understand the expatriate's experience, value it, and thereby more accurately measure his or her performance are (1) the communication gap between the expatriate and the home office and (2) the lack of domestic management's international experience.

The Communication Gap

Being physically separated by thousands of miles and in different time zones poses distinct problems of communication. Not only does the expatriate have difficulty talking directly with his manager, but usually both the US manager and the expatriate executive have plenty of other responsibilities to attend to. Fixing the day-to-day problems tends to take precedence over other concerns, such as maintaining contact with one's boss (or subordinate) in order to be kept up to date on organizational changes or simply to inform him or her of what one is doing. Most of the expatriates in our research indicated they had very irregular contact with their home office and that often it was not with their immediate superior. Rarely did the boss initiate direct contact with the expatriate more than once or twice a year.

The Lack of International Experience

The old Indian expression "To walk a mile in another man's moccasins" has direct meaning here. How can one understand what another person's overseas managerial experience is like – its difficulties, challenges, stresses, and the like – without having lived and worked overseas oneself? According to one study, more than two-thirds of upper management in corporations today have never had an international assignment. If they have not lived or worked overseas, and if the expatriate and US manager are not communicating regularly about the assignment, the US manager cannot evaluate the expatriate's performance appropriately.

Of course, how the US manager and foreign manager perceive the expatriate's performance will depend partly on the expatriate's actual performance and partly on the managers' *perceptions* of the expatriate's performance. Up to now, we have discussed the managers' perceptions of the expatriate's performance. Let's now turn our attention to what usually composes the expatriate's *actual* performance to better understand why evaluating it is problematic.

Actual Job Performance

As repeatedly mentioned by the expatriates in our study and in other research, the primary factors relating to the expatriate's actual job performance include his or her technical job know-how, personal adjustment to the culture, and various environmental factors.

Technical Job Know-How

As with all jobs, one's success overseas partly depends on one's expertise in the technical area of the job. Our research indicates that approximately 95 percent of the expatriates believe that technical competency is crucial to successful job perform-ance. Although common sense supports this notion, research shows that technical competence is not sufficient in itself for successful job performance. For example, an engineer who is an expert in his or her field and who tends to ignore cultural variables that are important to job performance will likely be ineffective. He or she might be less flexible with local personnel, policies, and practices because of his or her reliance on technical know-how or because of differences in cultural views. As a result, the host nationals might become alienated by the expatriate's style and become quite resistant to his or her objectives and strategies. A less experienced engineer, with less technical competence, might be more willing to defer to the host country's employees and their procedures and customs. A shade of humility is always more likely to breed flexibility, and in the long run, the less experienced engineer might develop the trust of the foreign employees and might well be more effective than the experienced engineer.

We have been given numerous examples by expatriates, in fact, where this has been the case. One expatriate who represented a large construction firm was sent to a worksite in India. The expatriate was an expert in his field and operated in the same fashion as he did in the US. He unintentionally ignored local work customs and became an object of hatred and distrust. The project was delayed for more than six months because of his behavior.

Adjustment to a New Culture

Just as important as the expatriate's technical expertise is his or her ability to adapt to the foreign environment, enabling him or her to deal with the indigenous people. Nearly every expatriate in our survey felt understanding the foreign culture, having an ability to communicate with the foreign nationals, and being able to reduce stress were as – if not more – important to successful job performance than was technical competence. Regardless of how much an expatriate knows, if he or she is unable to communicate with and understand the host nationals, the work will not get done.

An expatriate's adjustment overseas is also related to at least two personal variables: (1) one's marital and family status (that is, whether accompanied by a spouse and children) and (2) the executive's own personal and the family's pre-disposition to acculturation. Research clearly indicates that expatriates who have their family abroad are often less successful because of the stress on the family of being in a foreign environment. The stress on the spouse negatively affects the employee's concentration and job performance. With an increasing number of dual-career couples being affected by expatriation, the problems are even keener. A number of expatriates reported that their formerly career-positioned spouse suffered from depression most of the time they were overseas. Moving from experiencing the dynamics of a challenging career to having no business-world activity and being unable to communicate the most basic needs is a grueling transition for many career-oriented spouses.

Company variables affecting cultural and work adjustment also come into play. The thoroughness of the company's expatriate selection method and the type and degree of cross-cultural training will affect expatriate adjustment and performance. In other words, if the firm is not selective about the personality of the expatriate or does not appropriately prepare the employee and dependents, the firm may be building in failure before the manager ever leaves the US.

All these factors influence the expatriate's learning curve in a foreign business environment. More time is thus required to learn the ins and outs of the job than for the expatriate's domestic counterpart who might have just taken a comparable position stateside. In fact, most expatriates say it takes three to six months to even begin to perform at the same level as in the domestic operation. Hence, *performance evaluations at the company's normal time interval may be too early to accurately and fairly reflect the expatriate's performance*.

A SUMMARY OF FACTORS AFFECTING EXPATRIATION PERFORMANCE

In summary, an expatriate's performance is based on overseas adjustment, his or her technical know-how, and various relevant environmental factors. Actual performance, however, is evaluated in terms of perceived performance, which is based on a set of fairly complex variables usually below the evaluator's level of awareness. Much of the perceived performance concerns perceptions of the expatriate and his or her situation. Depending on whether the manager assessing the expatriate's performance has had personal overseas experience or is otherwise sensitive to problems associated with overseas work, the performance appraisal will be more or less valid. *The bottom line for the expatriate is that the performance appraisal will influence the promotion potential and type of position the expatriate receives on returning to the US*. Because expatriates generally return from their experience with valuable managerial skills, especially for firms pursuing an international or global market path, it behooves organizations to carefully review their process of appraising expatriates and the evaluation criteria themselves.

GUIDELINES ON HOW TO APPRAISE AN EXPATRIATE'S PERFORMANCE

Human Resource Personnel: Giving Guidelines for Performance Evaluation

Human resources departments can do a couple of things to help guide the evaluator's perspective on the evaluation.

A basic breakdown of the difficulty level of the assignment should be done to properly evaluate the expatriate's performance. For example, working in Japan is generally considered more difficult than working in England or English-speaking Canada. The learning curve in Japan will take longer because of the very different ways business is conducted, the language barrier that exists, and the isolation that most Americans feel within the Japanese culture. Major variables such as the following should be considered when determining the difficulty level of the assignment:

- Operational language used in the firm.
- Cultural "distance," based often on the region of the world (for example, Western Europe, Middle East, Asia).
- Stability of the factors affecting the expatriate's performance (for example, labor force, exchange rate).

Many foreigners speak English, but their proficiency does not always allow them to speak effectively or comfortably, so they rely on their native language when possible. In addition, they usually do not speak English among themselves because it is not natural. In Germany, for example, one expatriate said that while relying on English allowed a minimum level of work to be performed, the fact that he did not speak German limited his effectiveness. Secretaries, for example, had very limited English-speaking skills. German workers rarely spoke English together and therefore unknowingly excluded the expatriate from casual and often work-related conversations. And outside work he had to spend three to four times the amount of time to accomplish the same things that he did easily in the US. Most of the problem was because he could not speak good enough German, and many of the Germans could not speak good enough English.

Although sharing the same language facilitates effective communication, it is only the surface level of communication. More deep-rooted, cultural-based phenomena can more seriously affect an expatriate's performance.

Countries or regions where the company sends expatriates can be fairly easily divided into categories such as these: (1) somewhat more difficult than the US, (2) more difficult than the US, and (3) much more difficult than the US. Plenty of information is available to help evaluate the difficulty level of assignments. The US State Department and military branches have these types of ratings. In addition, feedback from a firm's own expatriates can help build the picture of the varying level of assignment difficulty.

Rather than having the manager try to subjectively build the difficulty level of the assignment into his or her performance appraisal, human resources could have a built-in, numerical difficulty factor that is multiplied times the quantity obtained by the normal evaluation process (for example, somewhat more difficult = ×1.2; more difficult = ×1.4; much more difficult = ×1.6).

Evaluator: Trying to Objectify the Evaluation

Several things can be clone to try to make the evaluator's estimation more objective:

1. Most expatriates agree that it makes more sense to weight the evaluation based more on the on-site manager's appraisal than the home-site manager's notions of the employee's performance. This is the individual who has been actually working with the expatriate and who has more information to use in the evaluation. Having the on-site manager evaluate the expatriate is especially valid when the on-site manager is of the same nationality as the expatriate. This helps avoid culturally biased interpretations of the expatriate's performance.

2. In reality, however, currently the home-site manager usually performs the actual written performance evaluation after the on-site manager has given some input. When this is the case, a former expatriate from the same location should be involved in the appraisal process. This should occur particularly with evaluation dimensions where the manager is trying to evaluate the individual against criteria with which he or she is unfamiliar relative to the overseas site. For example, in South America the dynamics of the workplace can be considerably different from those of the US. Where stability characterizes the US, instability often characterizes much of Latin America. Labor unrest, political upheavals, different labor laws, and other elements all serve to modify the actual effects a supervisor can have on the productivity of the labor force in a company in Latin America. A manager who has not personally experienced these frustrations will not be able to evaluate an expatriate's productivity accurately. In short, if production is down while the expatriate is the supervisor, the American boss tends to believe it is because the supervisor was not effective.

3. On the other hand, when it is a foreign on-site manager who is making the written, formal evaluation, expatriates agree that the home-site manager should be consulted before the on-site manager completes a formal terminal evaluation. This makes sense because consulting the home-site manager can balance an otherwise hostile evaluation caused by an intercultural misunderstanding.

One expatriate we interviewed related this experience. In France, women are legally allowed to take six months off for having a baby. They are paid during that time but are not supposed to do any work related to their job. This expatriate had two of the three secretaries take maternity leave. Because they were going to be coming back, they were not replaced with temporary help. The same amount of work, however, still existed. The American expatriate asked them to do some work at home, not really understanding the legalities of such a request. The French women could be fired from their jobs for doing work at home. One of the women agreed to do it because she felt sorry for him. When the American's French boss found out one of these two secretaries was helping, he became very angry and intolerant of the American's actions. As a result, the American felt he was given a lower performance evaluation than he deserved. When the American asked his former boss to intercede and help the French boss understand his reasoning, the French boss modified the performance evalution to something more reasonable to the American expatriate. The French manager had assumed the American should have been aware of French laws governing maternity leave.

Performance Criteria

Here again, special consideration needs to be given to the expatriate's experience. Expatriates are not only performing a specific function, as they would in their domestic operation, they are also broadening their understanding of their firm's total operations and the inherent interdependencies thereof. As a result, two recommendations are suggested:

1. Modify the normal performance criteria of the evaluation sheet for that particular position to fit the overseas position and site characteristics.

Using the Latin American example referred to before might serve to illustrate this point. In most US firms, maintaining positive management–labor relations is not a primary performance evaluation criterion. Stabilizing the workforce is not highly valued because the workforce is already usually a stable entity. Instead, productivity in terms of number of units produced is a highly valued outcome. As such, motivating the workforce to work faster and harder is important. In Chile, however, the workforce is not so stable as it is in the US. Stability is related to constant production – not necessarily to increasing production – and a stable production amount can be crucial to maintaining marketshare. In this case, if an expatriate is able to maintain positive management–labor relations such that the workforce goes on strike only two times instead of twenty-five times, the expatriate should be rewarded commensurately. In other words, while the expatriate's US counterpart might be rated primarily on increases in production, the expatriate in Chile should be rated on stability of production.

How can such modifications in the normal performance criteria be determined? Ideally, returned expatriates who worked at the same site or in the same country should be involved in developing the appropriate criteria or ranking of the performance criteria or both. Only they have first-hand experience of what the possibilities and constraints are like at that site. This developmental cycle should occur approximately every five years, depending on the stability of the site – its culture, personnel, and business cycles. Re-evaluating the criteria and their prioritization periodically will make sure the performance evaluation criteria remain current with the reality of the overseas situation. If expatriate availability is a problem, outside consultants who specialize in international human resource management issues can be hired to help create country-specific performance evaluation forms and criteria.

2. Include an expatriate's insights as part of the evaluation.

"Soft" criteria are difficult to measure and therefore legally difficult to support. Nevertheless, every attempt should be made to give the expatriate credit for relevant insights into the interdependencies of the domestic and foreign operations. For example, if an expatriate learns that the reason the firm's plant in India needs supplies by certain dates is to accommodate cultural norms – or even local laws – such information can be invaluable. Previously, no one at the domestic site understood why the plant in India always seemed to have such odd or erratic demands about delivery dates. And no one in India bothered to think that their US supplier didn't operate the same way. If delivering supplies by specific dates asked for by their Indian colleagues ensures smoother production or increased sales and profits for the Indian operation, and if the expatriate is a critical link in the communication gap between the US and India, the expatriate should be given credit for such insights. This should be reflected in his or her performance review.

To obtain this kind of information, either human resource or operational personnel should formally have a debriefing session with the expatriate on his or her return. It should be in an informal interview format so that specific and open-ended questions can be asked. Questions specific to the technical nature of the expatriate's work that relate to the firm's interdependencies should be asked. General questions concerning observations about the relationship between the two operations should also be included.

There is another, even more effective way this aspect of performance review can be handled. At regular intervals, say, every three to six months, the expatriate could be questioned by human resource or operational personnel in the domestic site about how the two operations might better work together. Doing it this way helps maximize the possibility of noting all relevant insights.

CONCLUSION

With the marketplace becoming increasingly global, the firms that carefully select and manage their internationally assigned personnel will reap the benefits. Today, there is about a 20 percent turnover rate for expatriates when they return. Such a turnover rate is mostly due to firms not managing their expatriates' careers well. Firms are not prepared to appropriately reassign expatriates on their re-entry. This obviously indicates that firms do not value the expatriate's experience. This further carries over into the lack of emphasis on appropriately evaluating an expatriate's performance. Appropriately evaluating an expatriate's performance is an issue of both fairness to the expatriate and competitive advantage to the firm. With the valuable experience and insights that expatriates gain, retaining them and effectively positioning them in a firm will mean the firm's business strategy will be increasingly guided by those who understand the companies' worldwide operations and markets.

Soo Min Toh and Angelo S. DeNisi

A LOCAL PERSPECTIVE TO EXPATRIATE SUCCESS: EXECUTIVE OVERVIEW

M ANY EXPATRIATE HUMAN RESOURCE (HR) policies, particularly in the area of compensation, remain rooted in the past because they continue to favor the expatriate over local staff and do not take into account the increasing qualifications and aspirations of these local employees. Inequitable treatment leads to low commitment and poor work performance among local staff. More importantly, inequitable treatment creates tension between local and expatriate employees and causes the local staff to be less willing to be cooperative or supportive of the expatriates with whom they have to work. Without local support, expatriates may experience greater difficulty adjusting to their new jobs and the new environment, which is a contributing factor in the failure of expatriates. To minimize these problems, HR practices of expatriating organizations should focus on providing more equitable compensation for local and expatriate employees, selecting expatriates who are truly worthy of the higher pay, and increasing the transparency of pay practices so that local employees can see the linkage between work inputs and compensation more clearly. Managers at the local organization should emphasize favorable referents for local staff, breed organizational identification among the employees, prepare the local staff for incoming expatriates, and encourage them to assist and mentor incoming expatriates. It is critical that multinational companies (MNCs) are aware that some existing HR practices have potentially unintended negative consequences and that neglecting the impact of these practices on local employees hurts the effectiveness of the organization as well as the ability of expatriates to succeed in their assignment.

A LOCAL PERSPECTIVE TO EXPATRIATE SUCCESS

With increasing foreign revenues, MNCs' need for expatriate assignments shows little signs of slowing down. Maintaining an expatriate is a costly and often complicated process – and if the expatriate fails in his or her assignment, the expatriate exercise becomes even more costly for all involved. Losses and damages resulting from expatriate failure include loss of business and productivity, damage to other employees and relationships with customers, suppliers, and host government officials, as well as the financial and emotional costs borne by the expatriate and his or her family.[1] Given these potential costs, it is imperative that expatriate assignments are managed effectively.

A recent survey released by the US National Foreign Trade Council reported failure to adjust to the foreign cultural environment as a key reason for expatriate failure.[2] MNCs' records for providing sufficient pre-departure training for expatriates and their families have been poor. Expatriates often complain that they are not well prepared for the challenges they face on the assignments. Selection practices have also frequently been criticized for emphasizing technical competence and neglecting critical success factors such as relational skills and cross-cultural competence. Therefore, in addition to providing attractive expatriate packages, many MNCs have worked to improve training and orientation programs for expatriates, and to fine-tune the selection criteria to better match identified critical success factors.

Clearly, the onus for completion of a successful assignment has been primarily on the expatriate, as well as the parent company, whose responsibility has been to engage in various activities that are deemed to facilitate the adjustment of expatriates. Whereas these efforts have been met with measured success, many MNCs have overlooked the potential of yet another important avenue to facilitate adjustment. This potential lies in the local or host country staff with whom the expatriates work closely while on assignment. Traditionally, local employees were the expatriate's subordinates, but they are increasingly the co-workers and supervisors of expatriate assignees as well. As we will discuss in the present reading, local staff could be the expatriate's best on-site trainers as expatriates wade in possibly treacherous cultural waters. In the same vein, local staff could also seriously jeopardize the expatriate's ability to carry out his or her assignment by engaging in various counter-productive behaviors at work. Yet, with few exceptions, multinationals overlook the socializing potential of local staff in aiding expatriates in their adjustment and are not cognizant of how the very practices meant to ensure the success of expatriates can also inadvertently lead to their failure.

Given the potential importance of local staff to any multinational, the present reading has three main objectives. First, we identify the HR practices in MNCs that may adversely affect the organizations' effectiveness. Certain types of expatriate HR practices, especially ethnocentric ones, can be perceived as inequitable by local staff and create unforeseen (and unwanted) effects on the local staff's work attitudes and behaviors. Lowered commitment and job satisfaction, as well as counterproductive work behaviors such as absenteeism and turnover, are potential outcomes of ethnocentric HR practices, and can ultimately hurt the effectiveness of the multinational. Second, we demonstrate how violating equity between local and expatriate employees is detrimental to expatriate adjustment. The fates of the two groups of employees are often inextricably linked – the expatriates cannot be successful if their host country counterparts are not. In fact, it seems obvious that expatriates will find it much more difficult to succeed in their assignments without the support of local staff. Unfortunately, ethnocentric HR practices do not create the conditions that would cause such support to be forthcoming. Finally, we propose several alternative interventions adopted by companies that have been relatively successful at managing expatriate assignments, which multinationals should consider as means to motivate and retain local staff as well as to better harness the important socializing potential that local staff can offer to expatriates. Hence, our recommendations for the design of HR practices consider their larger effects on all employees in the organization and not merely on any particular subset of employees in the organization. Throughout, we highlight real-life issues faced by multinationals, provide real-life solutions adopted around the globe, and report relevant findings of organizational research.

LOCAL EMPLOYEES ARE IMPORTANT TOO

A critical factor often considered by MNCs when making decisions about where to locate overseas subsidiaries is the availability of qualified local workers. MNCs depend on a qualified local workforce to be effective and this dependence amplifies significantly if it is the MNC's aim to completely localize its overseas subsidiaries. Siemens AG, for example, locates itself worldwide and relies heavily on local workers to achieve its goals – in the US alone it employs over 60,000 Americans, and hires more than 20,000 personnel in China. New research also suggests that local managers can offer more control to the MNC than expatriates can in situations where cultural asymmetries between the headquarters country and the host country are high and the operating environment is risky.[3] Furthermore, if the market that the MNC enters is one where its existing personnel have little relevant knowledge or expertise to effectively run the local subsidiary, local human capital would be especially useful because the local managers speak the local business language and also understand the country's culture and political system better than most expatriates sent to the perform the job. Local staff are thus often better equipped than expatriates to penetrate the target market. The experience of MNCs in China, for example, has demonstrated that capable local managers and professionals are indispensable for the success of MNCs because expatriates continue to flounder in unfamiliar territory. Hence, there is little dispute that capable local employees are strategic assets to an MNC.

It is also in host countries such as China that we find much discontent among local staff and resentment towards expatriates because often inept expatriates are ostensibly treated as superior relative to the locals in terms of their compensation, benefits, and developmental opportunities.[4] This is especially so when expatriates do not have a clear advantage over the local employees in terms of work qualifications, expertise, or experience. Local staff may feel that they are treated like second-class citizens when working alongside expatriates in their own country, and may resent that fact. They may also perceive expatriates as being sent to be "watchdogs" for headquarters instead of value-added resources. Clearly, this mistrust of and dissatisfaction with the expatriate and the multinational set the stage for a whole host of negative consequences for the multinational, such as lowered productivity and effectiveness and higher rates of turnover and absenteeism. When resentment is high, more extreme counterproductive work behaviors may also ensue, such as theft and sabotage. It is clear that multinationals truly cannot afford to be insensitive to the feelings and opinions of the local staff in their organization.

However, local staff have yet another important part to play. It lies in their potential significance as a valuable socializing agent and facilitator of the expatriate's role in the host unit organization. Most of us are probably able to recall that time when we first started a new job: adjusting to the new environment, new responsibilities, and new relationships were probably made easier if we had received some guidance and support from someone in the early transition stages of our job. This person (or persons) probably had more experience and greater knowledge of the job and environment we were entering into than we did. This person was also often someone holding a similar or higher post than us, who had been in the organization longer than us, and had sufficient history with the organization to understand how things worked or how best to get things done. Organizational research corroborates these experiences by showing very clearly that the stresses related to starting a new job can be assuaged by supportive relationships within the work organization (e.g., coworker, supervisor, mentor). Hence, many organizations apply this principle by adopting mentoring and buddy systems to orient new employees in domestic opera-tions, and the effects have often been very positive. For example, Sun Microsystems Inc. in Palo Alto, California pairs newcomers with more experienced "SunVisors," while the New York office of PriceWaterhouseCoopers uses a buddy system, as well as more senior coaches, to supplement their formal training and orientation programs. In some companies, peers and designated mentors are also put through training programs to become effective coaches, and hiring managers attend workshops on getting ready for new employees joining the unit. A US-based company, National City Corp., uses a similar training program where managers are trained to communi-cate effectively and create supportive environments, and reports that the training is highly successful. Specifically, they report decreased turnover and absenteeism rates and higher productivity, which resulted in annual savings of over a million dollars after implementing the program.[5]

The same principles could and should be applied more widely to the context of the host unit organization where an expatriate assignee needs to learn the ropes of being a new member of the host subsidiary despite possibly having had experience in the parent company. He or she must also quickly become proficient in the perform-ance of his or her job, while at the same time adapting to the unfamiliar surroundings and culture. MNCs such as SAS Institute and Intel recognize the importance of expatriates gaining the cooperation of their local counterparts, loyalty from their subordinates, and the trust of their supervisors. Instead of placing the onus solely on the expatriate to develop effective working relationships and strong bonds with the local staff, these organizations adopt buddy systems where local peers act as ad hoc trainers for the expatriate. They also encourage and prepare the receiving managers and local teammates of the expatriate to ensure that the newcomer expatriates are assimilated quickly. Intel, for example, trains managers who are about to receive an expatriate. The training emphasizes ways to integrate and work with groups of people of other cultural backgrounds. With this training, local managers are better equipped to interact with expatriates and are less likely to find expatriates foreboding. Faced with more approachable local counterparts, expatriates are less likely to be isolated by the local staff, and have greater opportunities to learn from them and develop effective work relationships with them.

We will return later to other steps MNCs can employ to help insure that local employees contribute more fully. Before we do, however, we need to address how local staff can contribute to the adjustment and success of expatriates through the informational support, cooperation, and emotional support they provide to those expatriates.

Informational Support

Expatriates face substantial uncertainty regarding their new role in the organization when they first arrive in their new location. They must figure out how things work and what the best way is to approach problems that they may encounter. Any information the expatriates gain regarding the new job, the organization, and the larger cultural environment will help them learn what to expect, how to interpret various stimuli they encounter day-to-day, and what the appropriate behavior is in a given situation. In most situations, expatriates need to have a working knowledge and good understanding of the cultural mores of the organization and the national context in order to be effective. This need is especially critical when the job is novel and challenging for the expatriate, when the culture of the organization and the country is unfamiliar, or when sources of information that the expatriate relied upon in his or her home country are not readily available.

Informational support is also important if the expatriates are sent to host subsidiaries to acquire knowledge and gain cultural competence. Such assignments are increasingly popular as MNCs recognize the importance of gaining international experience among their employees. For example, ABB (Asea Brown Boveri) rotates about 500 managers around the world to different countries every few years to develop a cadre of managers with a global outlook.[6] Similarly, expatriates who are sent to the host location to set up "greenfield" operations will also need to acquire rich local knowledge in order to find sources for raw material, human resources, potential business associates, and potential customers. This necessity has been encountered by many companies that have tried to set up shop in China and found it to be a culturally challenging environment and impossible without local "guanxi," because these social networks are also very rich informational networks. The expatriates may be left out of important decisions and information if they are unable to penetrate existing informational networks.[7]

Of course, the local employees at the host organization would have these different types of information. By virtue of being born and raised in the host country and having been members of the host organization longer than the expatriate, local staff possess the additional experience and understanding of the culture and the organization, and also have developed the necessary network of relationships that could facilitate the conduct of many of the expatriates' tasks. The local staff's advantage is even greater in new markets for the multinational where expatriates are likely to be treading in unfamiliar political, economic, and social waters. If local staff are willing to share their intimate local knowledge with the expatriates, expatriates can set up shop in the host country or learn what they were sent to learn much more successfully. Local staff also possess critical information regarding the cultural mores of the workplace.[8] For example, many Western managers in Beijing report the Chinese culture as being quite incomprehensible and they have great difficulty operating effectively in the Chinese context. Sharing insights about the cultural norms and idiosyncrasies with fledgling expatriates will help them better establish the necessary networks within the organization and facilitate their adjustment to the new organizational and national culture. Knowing what is culturally acceptable and appropriate behavior is also critical for expatriates to avoid offending local co-workers, subordinates, and supervisors. As in the case of a *Fortune* 100 company, it was reported that its expatriates across 19 worldwide locations demonstrated greater adjustment to their work and social interactions when they had access to on-site host country mentors.[9] Clearly, the informational support from local staff is integral to an expatriate's ability to succeed.

Paradoxically, informational support from local staff most critical to the successful experience of the expatriate is also likely to be more difficult to gain. Many local staff have traditionally expected to learn from expatriates, because the expatriates are often viewed to be the experts with specialized knowledge, sent to the host unit to lead local staff rather than to learn from them. When these expectations are coupled with the fact that expatriates often earn much more than the local staff, the local employees may feel resentful. This resentment may be expressed by shutting out expatriates from informational networks since they may feel that doing so, and helping expatriates out, are not really part of their job requirement. As a result, the expatriates and the organization lose a valuable source of country and organizational information. Thus, it is important that the practices of the multinational do not breed resentment, but encourage the sharing of information between local staff and expatriates.

Cooperation

Expatriates sent to lead subsidiaries in various capacities will find gaining the local staff's cooperation indispensable to the performance of their job. Without the following of local subordinates and the cooperation of other local managers – neither of which expatriates should erroneously take for granted – expatriates may find their leadership role seriously frustrated and undermined. Those sent to manage local employees quickly lose credibility if they appear to have little local understanding or lack endorsement from other local staff managers. Also, if expatriates do not become part of the social network, decisions may be made without the full input and acceptance of the local employees. With the increased use of teams, expatriates who are not well integrated and accepted by their local staff colleagues are less likely to perform the job well or be satisfied with work relationships within the team. In the case of expatriates sent to transfer knowledge and expertise to local staff and train future local managers, these expatriates will not be successful if local staff are not receptive to their presence in the host organization and are unwilling to learn from them.

Poor expatriate–local relations may also lead to other counterproductive work behaviors ranging from tardiness and absenteeism to more extreme behaviors such as insubordination, withholding of vital information, and even sabotage. For example, local American executives admit that they would continue to produce data with errors because they are not willing to work around the clock to make it error free no matter what their Japanese bosses say; and local Chinese managers deliberately exclude the expatriate manager whom they view as an outsider, in the making of major decisions.[10] A top manager from a Swedish–Swiss MNC recounts how Singaporean employees deliberately did not alert an expatriate manager of a bad decision because the expatriate simply "should know better." These problems could have been avoided if expatriates had been able to gain the local staff's cooperation or if the organization had ways in which to encourage and reward cooperation.

Emotional Support

Whereas the importance of the spouse's emotional and moral support has been recognized in research and practice, the role of local staff as a source of emotional support for expatriates has not been widely regarded as important. However, research in newcomer adjustment finds unequivocal evidence for the importance of supportive work relationships as well. Emotional support helps a person to believe that he or she is cared for, esteemed, valued, and belongs to a network of communication and mutual obligation.[11] It includes the friendships that provide emotional reassurance, or instrumental aid in dealing with stressful situations. No doubt, being a newcomer in a new organization or a newcomer in a foreign country can be a highly stressful experience. But with the support of others in the organization, the newcomer can better make the transition to the new job and situation. We see evidence of this in a group of expatriates in Hong Kong, where expatriates' level of adjustment was significantly higher when support was available from their local co-workers than if such support was not available.[12]

According to existing research, even if actual support is not needed or sought after, the mere knowledge of the existence and availability of such support for the newcomer can be quite reassuring, and in turn can reduce the level of stress experienced by the individual. Thus, although the expatriate may never encounter the need to confide in local staff, just knowing that local staff are available and willing confidants alleviates some of the stress the expatriate faces. Furthermore, having supportive relationships in the organization can create a stronger sense of belonging for expatriates. Expatriates feel like they "fit in" with their local colleagues better and thus enjoy greater levels of work satisfaction and commitment to the host organization. The lack of such support could, on the other hand, hinder the expatriate's adjustment. Expatriates in US- and Europe-based multinationals reported lower levels of commitment and adjustment when they felt that they were being ostracized by their local colleagues.[13] The lack of deep friendships is especially disappointing for expatriates of more relationship-oriented cultures. For example, Korean expatriates in the US find their American counterparts friendly on a superficial level, but quite unwilling to develop stronger relationships. This often results in hurt feelings, disappointment, and a sense of isolation. The expatriates, in turn, become reluctant to socialize with the native-born Americans because they feel that they do not understand them and therefore seek solace through the friendships with the other expatriates.[14] The distancing of expatriate groups ultimately hurts the overall adjustment of expatriates, and also negatively affects their job performance and their ability and willingness to learn from their local counterparts.

However, just as is the case with informational support and cooperation, providing care and support to another employee is not usually specified in one's job description. Forming supportive relationships or friendships with the expatriates they work with is not required by local staff's jobs and would have to occur on their own initiative. Given suitable circumstances, local staff may be willing to go out of their way to support expatriates and help socialize them during their time of transition along the dimensions discussed. Unfortunately, several conditions are prevalent in multinational organizations that could cause local staff to be unwilling socializing agents. We discuss these factors next, and highlight how HR policies can inadvertently discourage the socializing role of local staff.

HR PRACTICES THAT DISCOURAGE THE SOCIALIZING ROLE OF LOCAL EMPLOYEES

What would determine whether local staff chose to exhibit or withhold critical socializing behaviors? Empathy is a critical driving force for an employee's decision to help a fellow co-worker.[15] Employees who like and care about their co-worker are more likely to provide help on their own accord, whenever help is needed by the co-worker. Employees in cohesive work groups, or groups with enhanced positive relationships among members, are more likely to spontaneously help out than employees in less cohesive groups. Similarly, local staff who empathize and have positive feelings towards their expatriate co-workers will be more willing to help expatriates in the course of their work if expatriates appear to need it.

Many HR practices adopted by MNCs have the potential to indirectly hurt the establishment of cohesiveness and rapport between expatriates and local staff. Ethnocentric HR practices that favor the expatriate over local staff, whether intentionally or unintentionally, send a message to local staff that they are less valued than the expatriates. As a result, local staff are less likely to feel friendly or supportive towards expatriates who receive favorable treatment for reasons that may not always seem obvious or acceptable. The inequitable treatment also draws clear lines between local staff and expatriates, creating an intergroup mentality where local staff view expatriates as "outsiders" and expatriates remain in their exclusive expatriate cliques. The clear differentials could reinforce us-versus-them stereotypes, increase friction and frustration, and could create further misunderstandings and conflict.[16] All of these factors would make it unlikely that local staff will feel empathetic towards their expatriate counterparts or go out of their way to help them out when needed. These differentiating HR practices, which we will discuss, include compensation, selection and promotion, and training.

Compensation

A potentially long-standing sore point between expatriates and local staff has been the way both parties are compensated relative to each other. Many multinational organizations seek to minimize expatriate failure by providing expatriates with enough incentives to take on and remain on the assignment until the task is completed. When expatriates are transferred to the host country organization, they expect that the relocation will not be disadvantageous to them in any way, and may in fact be beneficial to their future with the company. According to the 1997–98 North American Survey of International Assignment Policies and Practices published by Organization Resources Counselors Inc. (ORC), the most popular approach to compensating expatriates is still the "balance-sheet approach." The balance-sheet approach sets salary according to the base pay and benefits of their home country, plus various allowances (e.g., cost-of-living, housing standard, hardship) and tax equalization. With the inclusion of the various allowances and benefits, the relocation usually results in a financial gain for expatriates, especially if the relocation involves moving to a host location with a higher cost of living.

Even though the balance sheet approach has several advantages, it is particularly problematic for maintaining internal equity among local staff and expatriates in the host unit organization. Expatriates who come from a country of higher standards of living are likely to have a base pay that is much higher than that of the local staff, in addition to the various allowances and incentives awarded to the expatriates for taking on the assignment. When expatriates are moved to a destination with a high cost of living such as Tokyo or London, MNCs usually make significant adjustments to the expatriates' total compensation package to allow the expatriate to maintain a standard of living comparable to that which they would have enjoyed in their home country.

Few companies attempt to replicate local peers' pay in the assignment location, and expatriates are often lavishly rewarded with various perks that are not available to the locals. Consequently, it is not unusual to find cases of differentiation where a local manager's total compensation forms only a fraction of the expatriate's pay package.[17] For example, expatriates of a German chemical company in China are paid an average of $300,000 a year, including salary, housing, education of children, and other benefits, but the local managers are paid only 10–20 percent as much.[18] Such significant wage discrepancies will not be viewed as justified by the local staff if they do not view the expatriates as being more qualified and deserving of higher pay. These discrepancies can lead to strained relationships between the two groups of employees, making it unlikely that the local staff will go out of their way to help out an expatriate who may be having difficulties adjusting to the new job and environment. Worse, these discrepancies can result in resentment, leading the local staff to be unwilling to cooperate with the expatriate on any aspect of the assignment, and potentially frustrating the expatriate's efforts to be successful. Thus, the very compensation practices often put in place to help ensure expatriate success may actually jeopardize it instead.

Selection, Promotion, and Training

Ethnocentric HR practices can also be found in selection, promotion, and training. In many MNCs, the staffing of top positions in overseas units continues to be reserved for individuals from the parent country company. This is especially true when headquarters believes that having a parent country expatriate at the helm has some strategic value. Frequently, for control purposes, parent companies prefer their own nationals to hold those positions whether or not they are the necessarily the best-qualified persons for the job. It becomes frustrating for local staff when they view expatriates getting choice positions while a similarly qualified local gets passed over. Singaporean managers, for example, often report being disadvantaged when competing against parent company expatriates for opportunities in training and promotion.[19] Local managers in Japanese corporations' overseas subsidiaries recognize that they would have to be exceptional to be selected over a Japanese manager for a high-level post. Such ethnocentric practices often come at the expense of the promotion and development of capable local staff, further perpetuating the large wage discrepancies between local staff and expatriates and creating resentment among them.[20] Feeling like they have little future in an organization that treats them as second-class citizens, local staff display little loyalty towards the host organization and are more likely to leave when better job opportunities arise elsewhere.

SO WHAT HAS CHANGED?

The HR practices we have described have generally been in place for quite some time, yet they have not always resulted in the negative consequences we are suggesting in this reading.[21] The reason for this is that many aspects of globalization have changed, but the HR practices have not changed accordingly. One thing that has changed is the relative competence of expatriates versus local staff.

The basis for much of the global economy has it roots in colonialism. From the earliest days of colonization, the home country was significantly more developed and had superior resources relative to the overseas host (colony) destinations. This easily led to the practice whereby managers from Western multinationals were sent to Asia, South America, and other locations to fill needs in foreign operations that could not be satisfied with local labor, and provide a source of much-desired control over the foreign operations. Local staff would have been unlikely to view themselves as comparable to expatriates because of the vast differences in backgrounds, qualifications, and experience. Thus, local staff were more accepting of expatriates being managers and of the privileges they enjoyed.[22] They may also have already been quite satisfied with the relatively favorable remuneration they received compared to their previous job or their present alternatives. One study found that Chinese managers felt fairly treated by their organization because they perceived themselves to be better off compared to other locals in the same company or in other international joint ventures, even though they were worse off than the expatriates in their organization.[23] We also find this situation outside multinational organizations – in universities, for example, among professors and trainers who are sent to places such as Asia to team-teach courses where they receive much higher salaries than their local counterparts.[24]

The new reality, however, presents quite a different scenario. Popular host countries in the Asia Pacific region, such as China, India, Malaysia, and Singapore, are no longer merely sources of cheap labor, but the homes of some of the most competitive workforces in the world with high work aspirations.[25] The gap between the parent and host countries in terms of level of economic development has narrowed and the local staff are often trained in many of the same institutions as the expatriates. They are increasingly similar to expatriates in qualifications, and thus are more often co-workers, rather than merely subordinates, of expatriates. These locals are progressively more fluent in English, are trained in the West or in Western managerial ideology, and on top of that have an advantage over expatriates with their intimate understanding of the local culture and practices.[26] They are also less likely to encounter the adjustment and commitment issues faced by expatriates. Accordingly, their perceptions and expectations of how they should be treated by the organization change. Many Russian managers feel that they are generally better educated and cultured than their Western peers and expect to be treated similarly to the expatriates. As a result, the acute pay discrepancies that traditionally occur are now quite unacceptable in far more situations than before.

In addition, international assignments are increasingly treated by MNCs as a key developmental activity for their personnel and future executives. Expatriates are posted overseas to gain international experience and learn new processes that are unique to the host organization.[27] This could be a form of on-the-job training for expatriate managers as they learn how to operate effectively in a different environment. Thus, these expatriates are sent to learn from the local staff. When local staff perceive expatriates as not possessing any unique or specialized skill above what they themselves possess, or may in fact know more about the task that the expatriates and end up being the person the expatriate has to lean on to perform the expatriate's job, the large wage discrepancies between them quickly become objectionable.[28] In other words, if expatriates are viewed to be less qualified than the local staff in the organization, the extra privileges awarded to them will be viewed by the local staff as unfair and unacceptable.

Interestingly, despite the changes that have been occurring, we find that cultural differences sometimes mitigate the problems we highlight in this reading, i.e. the reaction to inequity is not universal. Cultures differ in their sensitivity to inequity. Fairness is defined differently by people of different cultures. Some cultures, such as many Asian and Latin cultures, prefer rewards to be allocated based on seniority or need, rather than equity.[29] The importance and value placed on various forms of rewards also differs. Monetary rewards are often not necessarily the most valued. Thus, salary differences, per se, may not be as important to local staff as significant differences in status or other benefits such as housing, medical, and transportation. In certain economies, such as that of Russia, where commodities are often more valuable than money, differentials in salaries are likely to be less undesirable and offensive than differentials in prized commodities. In collective societies, harmony may take precedence over pay equity. We often find that the assumed ''same job same pay'' mentality is not prevalent among local staff in the organizations of various host countries. As such, local staff's reactions to compensation differentials and differences in treatment and opportunities vary according to the cultural values that they hold and the problems that we suggest to result from differential treatment are not necessarily universal.

WHAT CAN ORGANIZATIONS DO?

Thus far, we have described a situation where expatriates need the help and support of local staff, but where multinational HR policies may be working to reduce the willingness of the local staff to do so. Although there may be exceptions, as noted above, any such unwillingness on the part of local staff will certainly be unacceptable in the long run. But, even in cases where local staff are sensitive to pay differentials, there are some steps a multinational firm could take to minimize this problem. Specifically, we propose seven recommendations for MNCs to consider (see Table 1): (1) change existing compensation practices; (2) select expatriates more carefully; (3) use transparent procedures to determine pay and promotion; (4) emphasize favorable comparative referents; (5) breed organizational identification; (6) prepare local staff; and (7) use and reward local staff buddies or mentors. We will discuss each of these in greater detail.

Change Existing Expatriate Compensation Practices

As noted, many multinational firms have adopted HR practices that serve to differentiate expatriates from local staff, which are often inequitable from the perspective of the local staff. Clearly, if a firm minimizes the differential treatment between expatriates and local staff, the perceptions of inequity are likely to diminish. However, less than generous incentives for expatriates may deter employees from taking on overseas assignments, and thus expatriate packages are quite resistant to change. Many of the large MNCs, such as the traditional manufacturing enterprises, have become too large, complex, and entrenched in their existing practices to effect changes to compensation policies easily. Thus, even though the benefits of a more flexible approach are widely recognized, a 2000 PriceWaterhouseCoopers survey of 270 European multinational organizations reported that only 7 percent of the companies surveyed adopted such an approach. Furthermore, expatriates still tend to expect favorable compensation packages for their relocation. For example, expatriate managers of 49 Taiwanese multinationals reported that the compensation package was the most important factor in deciding whether or not to relocate internationally.[30] Without favorable remuneration, organizations will have trouble finding enough interested employees to take on overseas postings.

In time, change should become easier as expatriates come to view overseas assignment as a valuable part of their portfolio and become willing parties to the assignment even without lavish compensation packages. However, many expatriates still have concerns over their career progression while they are away on assignment, as well as having a suitable job and promising career upon repatriation.[31] The truth of the matter is, most multinationals do not guarantee a job upon return and do not counsel repatriates when they come home.[32] Hence, we find that employees sometimes view

Table 1. How to Improve Expatriate–Local Relations

At the headquarters of the organization:

1. **Change Existing Compensation Policies** – Pay expatriates salaries more in line with local employees. But, in order to do this, the organization should:
   a. Develop better plans for repatriation to assure expatriates that they will get comparable jobs upon return.
   b. If overseas assignments are truly valued as a developmental activity, include procedures so that they can be rewarded.
   — In the end, the real question is "Will managers still accept expatriate assignments?" If the answer is "no," then the organization must consider alternatives.

2. **Select More Carefully** – Ensure that expatriates are qualified to perform the jobs expected of them at a level consistent with the pay they will receive. But this will require the organization to:
   a. Make sure that expatriate managers have social as well as technical skills needed.
   b. See if there are local employees who are equally qualified. If so, are they paid comparably?
   c. Communicate performance expectations and criteria for success clearly to the expatriate.
   — There will be fewer problems if host country nationals can see clear evidence that the expatriate is "worth" what he or she is paid.

3. **Use Transparent Pay and Promotion Policies** – Develop pay policies that are viewed as fair and that are clear to all involved. But this requires the organization to:
   a. Actually develop pay policies that can stand scrutiny by local employees as well as by home country employees.
   b. Communicate pay policies as well as the basis for expatriate compensation rates (clear statement of hardships and barriers to overcome).
   — If host country nationals come to see that the fact that they are paid less than expatriates is based on fair procedures, they will be less resentful.

At the host country site:

4. **Emphasize Favorable Referents** – Identify alternative referent persons for host country national comparisons instead of the expatriate manager. But this requires that the organization should:
   a. Determine that such reasonable comparison others exist and make them public.

b.   Work to make expatriates less salient as referents.

—   If host country nationals can be convinced to compare their pay (and treatment) to other employees in their country, instead of expatriates, they will be more satisfied with their conditions.

5.   **Breed Organizational Identification** – Build a single organizational identity instead of allowing an "us vs. them" mentality to develop. But, for this to happen, the organization must:

a.   Develop a superordinate corporate identity strong enough to overcome identification based on nationality.

b.   Insure that host country nationals have access to various organizational "symbols" such as a company car or parking spaces.

c.   Increase the number and frequency of experiences that expatriates and host country national share.

d.   Develop common goals for host country nationals and expatriates to work towards.

—   If host country nationals develop a strong corporate identity they will work harder towards company goals and be less concerned about comparisons within the company.

6.   **Prepare Local Staff** – The local employees should be trained and oriented to deal with the incoming expatriates in much the same way as expatriates are often trained to deal with locals. But this would require the company to:

a.   Spend resources on training and orientation for employees who usually do not receive such attention.

—   The entire expatriate assignment process requires adjustment and consideration on the part of everyone involved, and if local employees could be trained to know more about the culture of incoming expatriates, this would make the process easier.

7.   **Use and Reward Local Mentors** – Identifying mentoring expatriates as part of the local employee's job, and then rewarding such behavior will make it more likely to occur. But this would require the company to:

a.   Recognize the important role local staff play in the success of expatriates.

b.   Recognize that, normally, local staff behavior aimed at helping expatriates adjust, is exhibited on a purely voluntary basis.

c.   Actually reward local staff for behaviors that help expatriates succeed.

—   This lies at the heart of our arguments about the importance of local employees. They are critical to expatriate success, but this fact must be recognized by organizations and encouraged as well as rewarded.

overseas assignments as a career graveyard, and that organizations are forced to provide attractive incentives to convince employees to accept long-term overseas assignments. If, however, MNCs develop better strategies for managing the careers of expatriates, including specific plans for repatriation prior to the assignment, expatriates may be more willing to forego lavish compensation packages and view assignments as a benefit by itself.

More companies have also turned to paying expatriates at host country levels (localization) or adopting more flexible approaches for compensating their employees in order to reduce their wage bills and lower pay discrepancies between expatriates and locals.[33] Many companies, such as Nokia Asia Pacific, localize their expatriate employees after a certain number of years in the host country whereby the employee takes on the same pay package as would a local employee. Companies such as Deloitte & Touche, National Semiconductor, and Towers Perrin have also started on paying for performance programs, varying compensation packages based on assignment length and type, and using more sophisticated measures to calculate cost-of-living differences.[34] As a result, discrepancies between expatriates and local staff may be reduced. Also, more and more multinational companies are using short-term assignments and extended business trips, as opposed to long-term expatriate assignments, thus avoiding the need to pay excessive benefits and adjustments to the expatriate. We see this trend as being quite positive, and as having the potential to truly reduce resentment among the local staff.

Yet, we recognize that there is only so much an organization can do to adjust these HR policies, especially in the short run, since most organizations must still somehow induce managers to accept overseas assignments, or at least assure them that they will not suffer as a result of those assignments. Eventually, salary localization policies and increased reliance upon short-term assignments may make it easier to adopt HR practices that treat expatriates and local staff the same. Expatriates sent overseas for developmental reasons should not necessarily expect a significant pay adjustment since the stint is usually short-term and potentially beneficial for the employee. For now, though, expatriate HR practices, especially in the area of compensation, will probably continue to favor expatriates over local staff. As such, MNCs must turn to other means to overcome the negative effects of internally inequitable expatriate compensation packages.

Select More Carefully

One alternative to changing compensation practices in order to reduce problems caused by perceived inequity is to ensure that the expatriates MNCs send overseas are in fact suitably qualified to perform the job in question and deserving of any higher pay they receive. As noted, expatriates encounter resentment if they are viewed as overpaid by local staff (i.e. being equally or under-qualified for the position they hold in the host unit, but at the same time being paid more than a local holding the same position). If expatriates demonstrate competence worthy of higher pay, local staff will be less dissatisfied. Many experts suggest that it is important to select expatriates who not only have the technical knowledge, but also the social and cultural skills needed to be effective in a different culture. Expatriates equipped with good communication skills will be able to integrate themselves better into the new culture and work more effectively with local staff. The European division of ICI, a British chemicals company, selects individuals who are good at getting along with colleagues at home because this is usually a good predictor of how much effort they will put in building understanding and trust with local staff.[35] Thus, adopting selection techniques that take into consideration these "soft skills" and prepare expatriates adequately for the assignment and all the challenges that it entails is a highly pertinent measure that MNCs could take.

At the same time, MNCs should make the criteria and procedures for selecting candidates to hold high-level positions in the host unit as clear as possible. Unambiguously stated criteria and procedures could reduce perceptions of nepotism. Seeking and utilizing input from local staff in making assignment decisions can be helpful for selecting the appropriate candidate, and could increase the legitimacy of the expatriate assignee in the local staff's eyes. Where suitable, other qualified local staff should also be allowed to compete for promotions alongside expatriates. This creates opportunities for local staff to gain desirable jobs within the organization and debunk any views of favoritism in the organization. Local staff who do compete for the promotion should be kept informed throughout the process. Transparency of the selection and promotion procedures is especially important if the local employee is not selected because local staff might feel that they have been unfairly rejected. In such instances, it is especially imperative that management treats the rejected applicant with much sensitivity and dignity to avoid hurt feelings or misunderstandings.

Use Transparent Procedures to Determine Pay

In addition to using open and rigorous selection procedures, MNCs should also ensure that the procedures used to determine pay packages for expatriates and local staff be transparent and fair. If local staff view the procedures used to arrive at the pay packages (and selection, promotion, and training decisions) as legitimate, receive reasonable explanations and justifications for the discrepancies, and feel that their concerns and needs are treated with care and sensitivity by the organization, their dissatisfaction with any inequity may be reduced.[36] Local staff often do not realize the challenges faced and sacrifices made by expatriates. To that effect, multinational organizations should be proactive in explaining the purpose of sending expatriates, and establishing and communicating clear and fair procedures to local staff. If reward discrepancies have to persist, then it is imperative that organizations make an extra effort to be sensitive to the reactions of the local staff and also to treat them with the necessary dignity and respect.

Emphasize Favorable Comparative Referents

Organizations can also reduce the negative perceptions held by local staff by emphasizing the ways in which local staff are better off compared to other groups of employees. As mentioned earlier, one study found that locals in a Hong Kong joint venture were not disturbed by having lower wages than expatriates because they were cognizant of how much better off they were compared to other Chinese employed by local firms. Often, even though local staff feel disadvantaged relative to the expatriates in their organization, they may still regard their higher wages, greater autonomy, and better opportunities for career development as very attractive aspects of being employed by an MNC. Furthermore, if expatriates are a less prominent comparative referent in local staff's minds, and local staff are satisfied with other aspects of their jobs, local staff react less negatively to the inequity between themselves and the expatriates. MNCs can redirect local staff's attention away from expatriates by publishing statistics that emphasize the advantages these employees have in terms of their pay packages, investments in training and development, and other employee benefits relative to employees of other local organizations or other industry competitors. In general, MNCs have access to a large pool of resources to make more investments in their human resources, which are not matched by local enterprises. Clearly, some careful impression management goes a long way in helping multinational organizations avoid the negative consequences we have suggested.

Breed Organizational Identification

Us-versus-them perceptions by local staff can be minimized by emphasizing the corporate identity to local staff so that expatriates are viewed less as outsiders, but fellow members of the larger, more inclusive organizational group. This process is known as "recategorization," where enhancing the prominence of an overarching identity reduces the prominence of a lower level group identity. In the case of the host unit, emphasizing organizational identity over national identity may reduce the local staff's likelihood of viewing an expatriate in the organization as someone they are competing against for organizational rewards.[37] Emphasizing the superordinate identity has another advantage of raising organizational commitment, and drawing attention away from contentious tendencies within the organization to focus on extra-organizational referents, such as the organization's competitors. In other words, intergroup comparisons can be diverted to occur across organizations (e.g. industry competitors), rather than within the organization between the local staff and the expatriates. As far as possible, organizations should minimize referring to expatriates as a separate group from local staff. Distinctions in day-to-day operations should be avoided and expatriates integrated to the local unit as much as possible so that they are perceptibly less different from the local staff. Organizational symbols, such as office space, parking spaces, common cafeterias, and informal socializing grounds act as subtle yet strong signals to local staff about how much distinction the organization makes between the two groups, and thus should be minimized.

Organizational identification can also be developed by putting both local staff and expatriates together in orientation and training programs. The shared experiences help develop a sense of cohe-siveness. Examples of this type of socialization include McDonald's policy of having all restaurant managers attend Hamburger University, or joint training exercises for NATO military units. In each case, the process builds a strong corporate identity that could transcend other types of group identities (e.g. nationality) by putting employees through similar socialization experiences.

Increasing the interactions between expatriates and local staff as well as emphasizing common work goals can also breed organizational identification and minimize the perception of expatriates as outsiders. By having more frequent interactions with their expatriate colleagues, local staff have more opportunities to learn about each expatriate personally and develop more accurate understanding of the expatriates with whom they work. In this way, pre-existing stereotypes may be refuted and the locals can come to view expatriates more as "one of us" rather than "one of them." Organizing expatriates and local staff in teams, working together to achieve common objectives, can help local staff and expatriates be more attuned to a common fate shared between them. When local staff perceive themselves and the expatriates to be working towards the same overarching goal(s), the prominence of the national boundaries may diminish and the perception of expatriates as part of the organization may heighten. As local staff begin to view expatriates as part of their in-group, they will also be more likely to support and cooperate with them.

Prepare Local Staff

MNCs should also provide both expatriates and local staff adequate training in cross-cultural communication and understanding. Being able to communicate effectively with each other is a key step in developing supportive relationships. Local staff, as well as the expatriates, need to be equipped with the necessary knowledge and skills to interact and work effectively with foreign nationals. Research suggests that large cross-cultural differences pose significant obstacles to the effective transfer of knowledge between locals and expatriates.[38] Thus, when Tellabs acquired Helsinki-based Martis Oy, all foreign executives underwent training on conducting business meetings, developing supervisory-subordinate relationships, and communicating effectively. Many Finnish engineers were also sent to headquarters to learn how to interface with their American colleagues and other employees.[39]

People make assumptions about an individual's intelligence, competence, and even social class based on how the individual speaks and carries him or herself. Cultural sensitivity training will help avoid misunderstandings, educate both local staff and expatriates on the appropriate behaviors, and dispel whatever negative stereotypes and assumptions they have about each other. In an experimental study of American host country managers confronted with Japanese managers, it was found that the extent to which the American managers' expectations of the Japanese managers' behaviors were met influenced subsequent intentions to trust them and to associate with them.[40] The researchers concluded that it is important to equip receiving local managers with realistic expectations of foreign managerial behavior in order for more positive relationships to be developed between them.

Some MNCs make the mistake of not carrying out cultural training based on the fact that the host country and the expatriates share the same language. However, even if expatriates and local staff speak the same language, misunderstandings can still occur. The director of an international provider of international assignment support programs recounts how a Texan in the UK came across to her British colleagues as arrogant and vulgar because she talked too loud and slowly, and was prematurely familiar with her colleagues both verbally and in her body language.[41] As a result, she was unable to fit in with her work group. It is important that organizations do not overlook the significance of preparing both the expatriates and the local staff for cross-cultural encounters at work.

Use and Reward Local Buddies or Mentors

As noted before, there is often no formal requirement or reward for local staff to facilitate the adjustment of expatriates and thus helping expatriates out or being cooperative needs to stem from their own initiative. To avoid leaving such behaviors to chance, MNCs could provide formal incentives to local staff for displaying cooperative and supportive behaviors towards expatriates. MNCs could pair up expatriates with local staff for a period of time and reward local staff involved in socializing newcomer expatriates, or for participating in some sort of buddy program that facilitates the expatriate's entry to the host unit. In this way, local staff's socializing behaviors are formalized and rewarded, and the help that expatriates need from local staff is better ensured. MNCs should also make efforts to involve local staff in the planning and facilitation of an expatriate's transition. This not only boosts local staff morale but also improves the chances of expatriate success.[42] Getting the local staff involved in the process also increases the transparency of the policies surrounding expatriation and the local staff who themselves are interested in developing their international experience could gain from being in continuous contact with incoming expatriates. This informational exchange greatly benefits both parties.

To ensure that information is shared with expatriates, SAS Institute's regional headquarters in Heidelberg, Germany assigns insider buddies to expatriate newcomers to help the newcomer to be self-sufficient and reach high levels of productivity as quickly as possible. These buddies are volunteers with no explicit or formal obligations. They help listen and answer simple questions expatriates may have, offer simple advice, and help point expatriates in the right direction on work and non-work matters. Similarly, at Korean multinational semiconductor manufacturer Samsung's Texas computer memory chip factory, each incoming expatriate is paired with an American counterpart upon arriving at Austin. These "buddies" help the Korean expatriates with work and with their downtime. The locals take the Korean workers on nights out, lunch meetings, and weekend trips.[43] With the help of local staff who are willing to share information with expatriates, the expatriates enjoy greater success in their efforts to adjust to their work demands and cultural challenges.[44]

THE LOCAL PERSPECTIVE

In this reading, we have discussed how HR practices designed to help and encourage expatriates can produce negative reactions by the local staff. We believe that this possibility has been largely overlooked because multinationals have tended to focus more on the expatriates than on the locals. We also believe, however, that the changing competitive landscape, the development of human capital in local markets, and the importance of cooperation and teamwork in a global economy, all point to a need to increase the attention paid to the local workforce. No global organization can hope to be truly competitive unless it fully utilizes its entire workforce. Furthermore, as we have pointed out in this reading, local staff are important, not only in their own right as potentially productive members of the organization, but also as a source of support and help for expatriate managers sent to their country.

What does this mean? It means that multinational organizations must pay attention to and gather information on the attitudes, goals, and feelings of the local staff. It also means that organizations need to develop programs to increase the motivation and commitment of those local employees. Many managers of MNCs view local staff as dispensable – perhaps more so now than before. Local staff are still likely to believe that the multinational pays better and treats employees better than the alternatives, and would still be motivated and committed to the organization. However, we believe that a local perspective means that the MNC will no longer take those things for granted. Instead, the MNC will recognize that the local staff have alternatives in third-party countries, or with other MNCs, and that the organization needs to work at motivation and commitment of the local staff. Of course, this perspective would also require the MNC to consider the impact upon local staff of any proposed policy, and weigh this impact when deciding whether or not to implement these programs. We believe it is critical that MNCs adopt such a perspective in order to be successful in the future.

CONCLUSIONS

The present reading represents a call for attention to be paid to local staff. We began by pointing out how, although local staff employees are increasingly well-trained and well-educated, many HR policies for expatriates still favor expatriates over local staff, and so do not recognize these accomplishments. We also discuss how local staff could compare their outcomes to those of the expatriates and how this could result in local staff believing they are being treated unfairly. These beliefs could then result in those local employees withholding advice and support, which, while not required as part of the local employee's job, are important for the ultimate success of the expatriate.

But, as we also note, a number of global companies are coming to recognize the importance of local staff, and are implementing programs designed to improve commitment and perceptions of fairness by those local employees. We also suggest a number of other interventions and programs that might help local staff feel appreciated, fairly treated, and committed to the larger organization. Several of these suggestions mirror those implemented by some more innovative multinationals, and we discuss these examples as well.

Therefore, we end by reiterating the message that local staff is important and must be recognized as such by MNCs. We believe that many organizations are coming to recognize this and act accordingly, but we also believe that there is much more that can be done. We believe that it is increasingly clear that the effective management of local staff will be a key component of effective competition in the coming years.

ACKNOWLEDGEMENTS

We thank the editor Bob Ford, Jim Wilkerson, Sonia Chainini, and the two anonymous reviewers for their input.

NOTES

1. Vatikiotis, M., Clifford, M., & McBeth, J. 1994. The lure of Asia. *Far Eastern Economic Review*, 157(5): 32–34.
2. Cited from Swaak, R. A. 1995. Expatriate failures: Too many, too much cost, too little planning. *Compensation and Benefits Review, 27*(6): 47–55. Over 90 percent of the respondents cited failure to adjust as the key reason for expatriate failure.
3. Volkmar, J. A. 2003. Context and control in foreign subsidiaries: Making a case for the host country national manager. *Journal of Leadership and Organizational Studies*, 10(1): 93–105.
4. Li, L., & Kleiner, B. H. 2001. Expatriate-local relationships and organizational effectiveness: A study of multinational companies in China. *Management Research News*, 24(3/4): 49–55.
5. Hammers, M. 2003. Quashing quick quits. *Workforce*, 82(5): 50.
6. Deresky, H. 2002. *Global management: Strategic and interpersonal*. Upper Saddle River, NJ: Prentice Hall.
7. Bjorkman, I., & Schaap, A. 1994. Outsiders in the Middle Kingdom: Expatriate managers in Chinese–Western joint ventures. *European Management Journal*, 12(2): 147–153.
8. Black, J. S., Mendenhall, M., & Oddou, G. 1991. Toward a comprehensive model of international adjustment: An integration of multiple theoretical perspectives. *Academy of Management Review*, 16(2): 291–317.
9. Feldman, D. C., & Bolino, M. C. 1999. The impact of on-site mentoring on expatriate socialization: A structural equation modeling approach. *International Journal of Human Resource Management*, 10(1): 54–71.
10. Li & Kleiner, op. cit.; Bjorkman & Schaap, op. cit.
11. Fisher, C. D. 1985. Social support and adjustment to work: A longitudinal study. *Journal of Management*, 11(3): 39–53; Kirmeyer, S. L., & Lin, T. R. 1987. Social support: Its relationship to observed communication with peers and superiors. *Academy of Management Journal*, 30(1): 138–151.
12. Aryee, S., & Stone, R. J. 1996. Work experiences, work adjustment and psychological well-being of expatriate employees in Hong Kong. *International Journal of Human Resource Management*, 7(1): 150–162.
13. Florkowski G. W., & Fogel, D. S. 1999. Expatriate adjustment and commitment: The role of host-unit treatment. *International Journal of Human Resource Management*, 10(5): 783–807.
14. Solomon, C. M. 1997. Destination USA. *Workforce*, April: 18–22.
15. Barr, S. H., & Pawar, B. S. 1995. Organizational citizenship behavior: Domain specifications for three middle range theories. *Academy of Management Best Paper Proceedings*, 302–306.
16. Schneider, S. C., & Barsoux, J-L. 2003. *Managing across cultures*, 2nd ed. Harlow: England. Prentice Hall.

17.   For more on expatriate pay policies, how they are developed and what they mean for pay differentials, see Beamish, P. 1998. Equity joint ventures in China: Compensation and motivation. *Ivey Business Quarterly*, 63(1): 67–68; Dowling, P., Welch, D. E., & Schuler, R. S. 1999. *International human resource management: Managing people in a multi-national context*. Cincinnati, OH: South-Western College; Hodgetts, R. M., & Luthans, F. 1993. U.S. multinationals' expatriate compensation strategies. *Compensation & Benefits Review*, 25(1): 57–62; Peters, S. 1994. Expatriates' pay exceeds nationals' in Central and Eastern Europe. *Personnel Journal*, 73(5): 19 20.

18.   Hagerty, B. Executive pay (A special report) – Asian scramble: Multinationals in China hope lucrative compensation packages can attract the local executives they desperately need. *Wall Street Journal*, April 10, 1997, R12.

19.   Hailey, J. 1996. The expatriate myth: Cross-cultural perceptions of expatriate managers. *The International Executive*, 38(2): 255–271.

20.   Further discussions of multinational policies regarding opportunities for local staff versus expatriates can be found in Geringer, J. M., & Hebert, L. 1989. Control and perform-ance of international joint ventures. *Journal of International Business Studies*, 20(2): 235–254; Hamill, J., & Hunt, G. 1996. Joint ventures in Hungary: Criteria for success. In Arch G. Woodside and Robert E. Pitts (Eds.) *Creating and managing international joint ventures*, pp. 77–106. Wesport, CT: Quorum Books; and Shenkar, O., & Zeira, Y. 1987. Human resources management in international joint ventures: Directions for research. *Academy of Management Review*, 12(3): 546–557.

21.   Leung, K., Smith, P. B., Wang, Z., & Sun, H. 1996. Job satisfaction in joint ventures hotels in China: An organizational justice analysis. *Journal of International Business Studies*, 27(5): 947–962.

22.   Hailey, op. cit.

23.   Chen, C. C., Choi, J., & Chi, S. C. 2002. Making justice sense of local-expatriate compensation disparity: Mitigation by local referents, ideological explanations, and interpersonal sensitivity in China-foreign joint ventures. *Academy of Management Journal*, 45(4): 807.

24.   Bates, R. A. 2001. Equity, respect, and responsibility: An international perspective. *Advances in Developing Human Resources*, 3(1): 11–25.

25.   For example, Delisle, P., & Chin, S. 1997. Remunerating employees in China: The complicated task faced by foreign firms. *Benefits & Compensation International*, 24(2): 16–20.

26.   Hailey, op. cit.; Vatikiotis et al., op. cit.

27.   For example, Carpenter, M. A., Sanders, W. G., & Gregersen, H. B. 2001. Bundling human capital with organizational context: The impact of international assignment experience on multinational firm performance and CEO pay. *Academy of Management Journal*, 44(3): 493–511; Hailey, op. cit.; Solomon, C. M. 1995. Global compensation: Learn the ABCs. *Personnel Journal*, 74(7): 70–75; Torbiorn, I. 1994. Operative and strategic use of expatriates in new organizations and market structures. *International Studies of Management and Organizations*, 24(3): 5–17.

28.   Semeneko, I. 2002. Study: Expat managers ethical but big headed. *Moscow Times*; Hailey, op. cit., 263.

29.   Clearly, the relationship between culture and fairness models is more complicated than we can discuss here. More extensive treatments of the relationship between fairness models and nationality are provided by Kim, K. I., Park, H-J., & Suzuki, N. 1990. Reward allocations in the United States, Japan, and Korea: A comparison of individualistic and collectivistic cultures. *Academy of Management Journal*, 33(1): 188–198; and Mueller & Clarke, op. cit. A more detailed discussion of culture and sensitivity to differential outcomes is provided by Chen, C. C. 1995. New trends in rewards allocation preferences: A Sino-US comparison. *Academy of Management Journal*, 38(2): 408–428; Chen, C. C., Meindl, J. R., & Hui, H. 1998. Deciding on equity or parity: A test of situational, cultural

and individual factors. *Journal of Organizational Behavior*, 19(2): 115–129; Chen, Y., Brockner, J., & Katz, T. 1998. Toward an explanation of cultural differences in in-group favoritism: The role of individual versus collective primacy. *Journal of Personality and Social Psychology*, 75(6): 1490–1502. Several other authors have addressed cultural differences in the importance attached to inputs versus outcomes for deciding upon fairness. These include Beamish, op. cit.; Huo, Y. P. & Steers, R. M. 1993. Cultural influences on the design of incentive systems: The case of East Asia. *Asia Pacific Journal of Management*, 10(1): 71–85; Leung et al., op. cit.

30.   Huang, L-Y. 2003. Attitudes toward the management of international assignments – A comparative study. *Journal of American Academy of Business*, 3(2): 336–344.

31.   Yan, A. M., Zhu, G., & Hall, D. T. 2002. International assignments for career building: A model of agency relationships and psychological contracts. *Academy of Management Review*, 27(3): 373–391.

32.   GMAC Global Relocation Services. 2002. *Global relocation trends 2002 survey report.* February 2002.

33.   Milkovich, G. T., & Bloom, M. 1998. Rethinking international compensation. *Compensation and Benefits Review*, 30(1): 15–23.

34.   Mervosh, E. M. 1997. Managing expatriate compensation. *Industry Week*, 246(14): 13–16; and Barton, R., & Bishko, M. 1998. Global mobility strategy. *HR Focus*, 75(3): S7-S9.

35.   Schneider & Barsoux, op. cit.

36.   Chen, et al., op. cit.; Kickul, J., Lester, S. W., & Finkl, J. 2002. Promise breaking during radical organizational change: Do justice interventions make a difference? *Journal of Organizational Behavior*, 23(4): 469–488.

37.   Toh, S. M., & DeNisi, A. S. 2003. Host country national (HCN) reactions to expatriate pay policies: A proposed model and some implications. *Academy of Management Review*, 28(4): 606–621.

38.   Bhagat, R. S., Kedia, B. L., Harveston, P. D., & Triandis, H. C. 2002. Cultural variations in the cross-border transfer of organizational knowledge: An integrative framework. *Academy of Management Review*, 27(2): 204–221.

39.   Solomon, C. 1995. Learning to manage host-country nationals. *Workforce*, 74(3): 60–67.

40.   Thomas, D. C., & Ravlin, E. C. 1995. Responses of employees to cultural adaptation by a foreign manager. *Journal of Applied Psychology*, 80(1): 133–146.

41.   Melles, R. 2003. "They speak the same language so I'll be ok." Not so fast. *Canadian HR Reporter*, September, 23, 11–12.

42.   Ashamalla & Crocitto, op. cit.

43.   Gallaga, O. M. Welcome to Austin: Samsung helps new employees feel at home. *Austin American Statesman*, 6 August 1997, D1.

44.   Aryee, S., & Stone, R. J. 1996. Work experiences, work adjustment and psychological well-being of expatriate employees in Hong Kong. *International Journal of Human Resource Management*, 7(1): 150–162.

J. Stewart Black

FRED BAILEY: AN INNOCENT ABROAD*

FRED GAZED OUT THE WINDOW of his 24th floor office at the tranquil beauty of the Imperial Palace amid the hustle and bustle of downtown Tokyo. It had only been six months ago that Fred had arrived with his wife and two children for this three-year assignment as the director of Kline & Associates' Tokyo office. Kline & Associates was a multinational consulting firm with offices in nine countries worldwide. Fred was now trying to decide if he should simply pack up and tell the home office that he was coming home or whether he should try to somehow convince his wife and himself that they should stay and try to finish the assignment. Given how excited Fred thought they all were about the assignment to begin with, it was a mystery to him as to how things had gotten to this point. As he watched the swans glide across the water in the moat that surrounds the Imperial Palace, Fred reflected back on the past seven months.

Seven months ago, the managing partner, Dave Steiner, of the main office in Boston asked Fred to lunch to discuss "business." To Fred's surprise, the "business" was not the major project that he and his team had just successfully finished, but was instead a very big promotion and career move. Fred was offered the position of managing director of the firm's relatively new Tokyo office, which had a staff of 30, including 7 Americans. Most of the Americans in the Tokyo office were either associate consultants or research analysts. Fred would be in charge of the whole office and would report to a senior partner (located in Boston) who was over the Asian region. It was implied to Fred that if this assignment went as well as his past, it would be the last step before becoming a partner in the firm.

How could Fred go back now? Certainly going back early would be the kiss of death for his career in Kline. But Jenny was not in a mood to discuss things. As far as she was concerned, there was nothing to discuss. She hated Japan. She felt the company and Fred had oversold the country and how "well they would be looked after." Fred worked 80+ hours a week because of all the after-hours socializing that he had to do with clients. He was never home and "had no idea what life was really like in Japan." Jenny had given Fred an ultimatum: either they packed up together or she went home alone. That things had escalated this far just didn't seem possible to Fred. What was he supposed to do? Sacrifice everything he had worked for over the years? His Harvard MBA would no doubt get him another job, but he had a real future at Kline if he could just hit even a double in this assignment. But if he walked away from the plate now, his career was over. On the other hand, he loved his wife and children and did not want to lose them. What had gone wrong?

FRED AND JENNY

Fred and Jenny met during their last year in college in a senior seminar class on business ethics. Fred was instantly attracted to Jenny's warm smile and flair for fashion. Jenny recognized in Fred ambition and a kind heart. The two started dating only a week after the class started.

Jenny came from a well-to-do family in Connecticut. Her father was a senior executive with a major firm headquartered in New York. She had majored in fashion merchandising as a way of combining her interest and talent for fashion and her father's advice about studying something practical.

Fred was the oldest of six children and was the first to go to college. His father was a construction worker and his mother a beautician. Fred had worked hard in high school and graduated second in his class. Even with a partial scholarship and loans, tuition help from his parents put a real financial burden on them. Fred was determined to take advantage of the opportunity he was being given and make his parents proud.

Fred and Jenny were married on a warm June afternoon. Although skeptical at first, Jenny's parents gradually came to recognize in Fred what Jenny saw from the beginning. Fred was bright and determined but his humble background sparked in him a genuine interest in others that put them at ease whenever Fred was around.

Before and after getting married, Fred and Jenny talked at length about careers and family. Fred wanted to go back and get his MBA after a couple of years of work. He had landed a great job with American Express after graduation and hoped with two years experience in a name-brand company, his stellar college grades, and good GMAT scores he could get into a top MBA program. Jenny wanted to be a buyer for a major store such as Saks Fifth Avenue and later have her own shop. They both wanted children but thought they would wait until Fred finished his MBA before starting a family. At that point, Jenny would take a few years off and then start her own small clothing store once the kids were in school. They both thought that owning her own shop would give Jenny the flexibility and time to spend with their children that she wanted.

Everything had gone according to plan up until the offer to go to Japan.

THE OFFER

Fred joined Kline right after graduating from Harvard. He had a couple of other offers, but including expected performance bonuses, the job at Kline paid 20 percent more than any of the others. Fred took it and immediately was put on the San Francisco team of one of the hardest-charging young consultants at Kline.

Rick Savage was one year away from the magical "up or out" decision concerning partnership. This decision typically happened about the seventh year of employment for typical MBA hires. Rick had been given a very high profile assignment with Kline's largest client. Success here would guarantee a partnership. Fred felt his life must be charmed to have landed on Rick's team out of the gate.

That first project and nearly every other project Fred had been part of were successes in his first three years at Kline. In his fourth year, he was given a major assignment and led a team of seven consultants and associates. Fred had just completed this 10-month assignment when Dave asked him to lunch.

Fred was stunned by the Tokyo offer. The Tokyo office was opened in part to serve major US clients' operations in Japan. From the same base, Kline would begin to develop relationships with Japanese firms. Once the relationships were formed, Kline would be able to service the Japanese multinational's American operations from their established offices in seven major cities in the US. The strategic significance of the office and the offer did not escape Fred.

Fred's predecessor in Japan had opened the office a year ago. George Woodward was a partner with a mixed reputation. George had friends at the very top of Kline, but he also had enemies all along the way. Fred wasn't sure why George had been suddenly transferred to the UK. Because the transfer to England was taking place "right away," Dave told Fred that he and his family had about three weeks to get prepared for the move.

When Fred told his wife about the unbelievable opportunity, he was shocked at her less-than-enthusiastic response. Jenny thought that it would be rather difficult to have the children live and go to school in a foreign country for three years, especially when Christine, the youngest, would be starting first grade next year. Besides, now that the kids were in school, Jenny wanted to open her own clothing store.

Fred explained that the career opportunity was just too good to pass up and that the company's overseas package would make living in Japan terrific. The company would pay all the expenses to move whatever the Baileys wanted to take with them. The company had a very nice house in an expensive district of Tokyo that would be provided rent-free. Additionally, the company would rent their house in Boston during their absence. The firm would provide a car and driver, education expenses for the children to attend private schools, and a cost of living adjustment and overseas compensation that would nearly double Fred's gross annual salary. After two days of consideration and discussion, Fred told Mr Steiner he would accept the assignment.

PREPARING FOR THE MOVE

Between getting things at the office transferred to Bob Newcome, who was being promoted to Fred's position, and the logistic hassles of getting furniture and the like ready to be moved, neither Fred nor his family had much time to really find out much about Japan, other than what was in the encyclopedia.

Kline handled many of the logistical and relocation details internally. Unfortunately, a number of things went wrong. For example, when the packers came, they were totally unprepared for the fact that some of the Baileys' stuff was going into storage and some was being shipped to Japan. On a "look see visit" a week after Fred had accepted the assignment, Jenny saw the house in Japan where they were to live and instantly knew that not even a third of their belongings would fit. In fact, none of the antiques would fit through the door, let alone in the house.

FRED'S EARLY EXPERIENCES

When the Baileys arrived in Japan, they were greeted at the airport by one of the young Japanese associate consultants and the senior American expatriate. Fred and his family were quite tired from the long trip and the two-hour ride back to Tokyo was a rather quiet one. After a few days of just settling in, Fred spent his first full day at the office.

Fred's first order of business was to have a general meeting with all the employees of associate consultant rank and higher. Although Fred didn't really notice it at the time, all the Japanese staff sat together and all the Americans sat together. After Fred introduced himself and his general ideas about the potential and future directions of the Tokyo office, he called on a few individuals to get their ideas about how things for which they were responsible would likely fit into his overall plan.

From the Americans, Fred got a mixture of opinions with specific reasons about why certain things might or might not fit well. From the Japanese, he got very vague answers. When Fred pushed to get more specific information, he was surprised to find that a couple of Japanese simply made a sucking sound as they breathed and said that it was "difficult to say." Fred sensed the meeting was not meeting his objectives, and so he thanked everyone for coming and said he looked forward to their all working together to make the Tokyo office the fastest growing office in the company.

After they had been in Japan about a month, Fred's wife complained to him about the difficulty she had getting certain products such as maple syrup, peanut butter, and quality beef. She said that when she could get it at one of the specialty stores, it cost three and four times what it would cost in the US. She also complained that the washer and dryer were much too small and so she had to spend extra money by sending things out to be cleaned. On top of all that, unless she went to the American Club in downtown Tokyo, she never had anyone to talk to. After all, Fred was gone 10–16 hours a day. Unfortunately, at the time Fred was preoccupied, thinking about his upcoming meeting between his firm and a significant prospective client – a top 100 Japanese multinational company.

The next day, along with the lead American consultant for the potential contract, Ralph Webster, and one of the Japanese associate consultants, Kenichi Kurokawa, who spoke perfect English, Fred met with a team from the Japanese firm. The Japanese team consisted of four members – the VP of administration, the director of international personnel, and two staff specialists. After shaking hands and a few awkward bows, the Japanese offered to exchange business cards. Fred's staff had prepared his cards in advance with Japanese on one side and English on the other. Fred handed his cards to each Japanese with the English side up.

After the card exchange, Fred said that he knew the Japanese gentlemen were busy and he didn't want to waste their time so he would get right to the point. Fred then had Ralph Webster lay out Kline's proposal for the project and what the project would cost. After the presentation, Fred asked the Japanese what their reaction to the proposal was. The Japanese did not respond immediately and so Fred launched into his summary version of the proposal thinking that the translation might have been insufficient. But again, the Japanese had only the vaguest of responses to his direct questions.

The recollection of the frustration of that meeting was enough to shake Fred back to reality. The reality was that in the five months since the first meeting, little progress had been made and the contract between the firms was yet to be signed. "I can never seem to get a direct response from Japanese," he thought to himself. This feeling of frustration led him to remember a related incident that happened about a month after his first meeting with this client.

Fred had decided that the reason not much progress was being made with the client was that he and his group just didn't know enough about the client to package the proposal in a way that was appealing to the client. Consequently, he called in the senior American associated with the proposal, Ralph Webster, and asked him to develop a report on the client so the proposal could be re-evaluated and changed where necessary. Jointly, they decided that one of the more promising Japanese research associates, Tashiro Watanabe, would be the best person to take the lead on this report.

To impress upon Tashiro the importance of this task and the great potential they saw in him, they decided to have the young Japanese associate meet with both Fred and Ralph. In the meeting, Fred had Ralph lay out the nature and importance of the task, at which point Fred leaned forward in his chair and said, "You can see that this is an important assignment and that we are placing a lot of confidence in you by giving you this assignment. We need the report this time next week so that we can revise and re-present our proposal. What do you think?" After a somewhat pregnant pause, the Japanese responded somewhat hesitantly, "I'm not sure what to say." At that point Fred smiled, got up from his chair and walked over to the young Japanese associate, extended his hand, and said, "Hey, there's nothing to say. We're just giving you the opportunity you deserve."

The day before the report was due, Fred asked Ralph how the report was coming. Ralph said that since he had heard nothing from Tashiro that he assumed everything was under control, but that he would double check. Ralph later ran into one of the American research associates, John Maynard. Ralph knew that John was hired because of his language ability in Japanese and that unlike any of the other Americans, John often went out after work with some of the Japanese research associates, including Tashiro. So, Ralph asked John if he knew how Tashiro was coming on the report. John then recounted that last night at the office Tashiro had asked if Americans sometimes fired employees for being late with reports. John had sensed that this was more than a hypothetical question and asked Tashiro why he wanted to know. Tashiro did not respond immediately and since it was 8:30 in the evening,

John suggested they go out for a drink. At first Tashiro resisted, but then John assured him that they would grab a drink at a nearby bar and come right back.

At the bar, John got Tashiro to open up. Tashiro explained the nature of the report that he had been requested to produce. Tashiro continued to explain that even though he had worked long into the night every night to complete the report that it was just impossible and that he had doubted from the beginning whether he could complete the report in a week.

At this point, Ralph asked John, "Why the hell didn't Tashiro say something in the first place?" Ralph didn't wait to hear whether John had an answer to his question or not. He headed straight to Tashiro's desk.

The incident just got worse from that point. Ralph chewed Tashiro out and then went to Fred explaining that the report would not be ready and that Tashiro didn't think it could be from the start. "Then why didn't he say something?" Fred asked. No one had any answers and the whole thing just left everyone more suspect and uncomfortable with each other than ever.

There were other incidents, big and small, that had made especially the last two months frustrating, but Fred was too tired to remember them all. To Fred, it seemed that working with Japanese both inside and outside the firm was like working with people from another planet. Fred felt he just couldn't communicate with them, and he could never figure out what they were thinking. It drove him crazy.

JENNY'S EARLY EXPERIENCES

Jenny's life in Japan was equally frustrating. Jenny was determined at first to make an adventure of living in Japan. During the first week, she went down to the local grocery store to buy some food and basic household supplies. However, not being able to read the labels had its drawbacks. She had mistakenly bought a bluish colored bathroom cleaning liquid believing it was mouthwash and only discovered the mistake after "swishing," "gargling," and nearly choking to death on the stuff.

After about a month, Jenny tried to take the Tokyo subway system from her house to the American Club. What was supposed to be a 15-minute ride turned into a 4-hour ordeal. Jenny missed her stop but didn't discover it for several more. Then, when she did, she got off the train, only to discover she had no idea how to get to the other side of the tracks and head back the opposite way. She exited the station and tried to ask how to get to the other side. Finally, someone in broken English pointed out some stairs that led to a tunnel that went under the tracks to the other side. However, arriving there, she found that she had no idea how much a ticket would cost to the stop she wanted and she had no change on her, only yen bills.

At this point she was so frustrated and broke into tears as she saw little grade school kids buy tickets and go through the turnstile. She saw a pay phone and tried to call Fred with the prepaid phone card she had been given. After a couple of times of the phone spitting the card back out, she realized she was inserting it in upside down. When she finally got through to Fred, she was crying and he seemed irritated at being called out of a meeting because she was lost on the subway system.

After a brief discussion, Fred and Jenny reasoned that she should take the escalator up out of the subway and hail a taxi. Fortunately, the Japanese taxi driver understood "American Club please" and Jenny arrived just as the group Jenny was supposed to meet was breaking up.

Two in the group were more than sympathetic to Jenny's ordeal and could not say enough about the "stupid" things they encountered in "this most backward of all developed countries." As part of this cathartic complaint session, Jenny related her "mouthwash" incident. After they all had a good laugh, one of the women told Jenny about National Azabu, a small but American grocery store. "At least there you can get decent food," she said.

THE BOMBSHELL

For Jenny, these incidents were only the tip of the iceberg. She wanted to go home, and yesterday was not soon enough. Even though the kids seemed to be doing OK, she was tired of Japan – tired of being stared at, of people trying to touch her hair, of not understanding anybody or being understood, of not being able to find what she wanted at the store, of not being able to drive and read the road signs, of not having anything to watch on TV, of not being involved in anything. She wanted to go home and she could not think of any reason why they shouldn't. After all, she reasoned they owed nothing to the company because the company had led them to believe this was just another assignment, like the two years they spent in San Francisco, and it was anything but that!

Fred tried to reason with her, but the more he countered, the more determined she became. Suddenly, she dropped the bombshell on him: either they could go home together or he could stay here alone.

THE DECISION

Fred looked out the window once more, wishing that somehow everything could be fixed, or turned back or something. What had gone wrong? Why was Jenny being so unreasonable? Did he dare call Dave and explain the situation? Dave was very old fashioned and had once made a derogatory comment about a promising young consultant whose future looked dimmer and dimmer because he "couldn't control his complaining wife."

Looking down again, Fred could see traffic backed up down the street and around the corner. Though the traffic lights changed, the cars and trucks didn't seem to be moving. Fortunately, in the ground below, one of the world's most advanced, efficient, and clean subway systems moved hundreds of thousands of people about the city and to their homes.

NOTE

* This case was written by Professor J. Stewart Black as a basis for class discussion rather than to illustrate either effective or ineffective handling of an administrative situation. Revised December 12, 1996.

William H. Roof and Barbara Bakhtari

RECRUITING A MANAGER FOR BRB ISRAEL

B RB INC., a multinational electronics corporation, plans to establish a new subsidiary in Israel. The firm's base is in Los Angeles, California, with a second overseas headquarters in England. The US office staffs and operates six North American divisions and three South American subsidiaries. The UK office is responsible for operations in Europe and Asia. The Israeli venture is the company's first business thrust in the turbulent Middle East.

During the past 10 years, BRB's phenomenal growth resulted largely from its ability to enter the market with new, technically advanced products ahead of the competition. The technology mainly responsible for BRB's recent growth is a special type of radar signal processing. With Fourier transforms, BRB's small, lightweight, and inexpensive radar systems outperform the competitions' larger systems in range, resolution, and price. It is this type of lightweight, portable radar technology that has enormous potential for Israel during conflicts with the Arab States.

BRB's human resource functions in the US and Europe each boast a vice president. John Conners is the vice president of human resources in the US, and Francis O'Leary is the vice president of human resources in the UK. Paul Lizfeld, the CEO of BRB, contacted the two vice presidents and told them to recruit a general manager for the Israeli operation. "I don't care who finds him, but he better be right for the job. I cannot afford to replace him in six months. Is that clear!" Lizfeld told them to look independently and then coordinate together to select the right person. They knew that their jobs could be in jeopardy with this task.

The two human resource operations were independent, and each was managed individually. Recruiting processes differed between US and UK operations. Each had different organizational structures and corporate cultures. The only link between the two was Lizfeld's strong micromanagement style, which emphasized cost control.

US OPERATIONS

John Conners has worked for BRB for the past 20 years. He started with a degree in engineering and worked in the engineering department. After earning his MBA in human resource management from UCLA, he transferred to the human resource department. Management felt that someone with an engineering background could hire the best technical employees for BRB. With BRB's high turnover rate, they felt that someone who could relate to the technical side of the business could better attract and screen the right people for the organization. BRB promoted Conners to vice president three years ago, after he hired the staffs for the subsidiaries in Peru and Brazil. Except for the general managers, they were all correct fits. Conners felt that the problem with the general managers was an inability to work with Lizfeld.

John Conners looked at many different strategies to determine how to begin recruiting for the Israeli position. He wanted to be sure he found the right person for the job. The first step in choosing the ideal candidate was to determine the selection criteria.

Conners defined the task in Israel to include control and management of BRB's Israeli operations. The GM must work with the Israeli government both directly and indirectly. The political unrest in Israel also requires the GM to conduct sensitive transactions with the Israeli government. This person would also work directly with Lizfeld, taking direction from him and reporting regularly to him.

As with many countries in the Middle East, Israel was in turmoil. Conners actually knew very little about the Israeli culture, but decided to ask different associates who had past dealings with Israel. He knew that the threat of war constantly hung over Israel. The country was also suffering from high inflation rates and troubled economics. Lately, he also learned that the country had become divided over certain political and cultural issues. The person accepting this job needed nerves of steel and extraordinary patience.

Conners decided the selection criteria that would be important for the candidate included technical skill, cultural empathy, a strong sense of politics, language ability, organizational abilities, and an adaptive and supportive family. He also felt that the GM would have to have the following characteristics: persuasiveness, ability to make decisions, resourcefulness, flexibility, and adaptability to new challenges. Now all he needed to do was find a person who had all these attributes.

He decided to begin his search for candidates within the organization. He knew this route had both advantages and disadvantages. Since BRB was still in the beginning stages of internationalization in Israel, a "home country" presence might prove to be very helpful. Lizfeld would appreciate this. The disadvantages would be many. It might be very difficult to find someone willing to relocate in Israel. The increased cost of living and the political unrest make it a tough package to sell. Conners knew of the "Israeli mentality." He also knew he would have to take care in sending someone who might either overpower the Israelis or break under their aggressive business style. Conners knew that Lizfeld wanted to have the home country atmosphere in Israel and planned to be very active in the management of Israeli operations.

The second option Conners had was to recruit from outside the company. The ideal candidate would have both domestic and international experience. Conners could recruit either by contacting an employment agency or by placing an ad in the *Wall Street Journal*. He thought he could find a person with the right qualifications, but he also knew it would be difficult to find someone Lizfeld liked outside the company. Conners had hired two managers for the South American offices, and Lizfeld had driven them over the edge within six months. Conners knew that he had to be extra careful. One more "unqualified" candidate might put his own job on the line.

Conners found three potential candidates for the Israeli position. One candidate, Joel Goldberg, was a recommendation from the headhunter Conners had commissioned. Goldberg had 35 years of electronics and radar experience. He had been CEO of Radar Developments Incorporated, a major electronics corporation in New York. Goldberg had taken control of Radar Developments Incorporated in 1981. By 1986, the company had tripled sales and increased profits five-fold. Goldberg had the technical knowledge to perform the job. He also had the necessary individual characteristics Conners felt would be important for this position. Goldberg had studied in Israel on a kibbutz for two years after college, spoke fluent Hebrew, and was a practicing Jew. He wanted to retire in Israel in a few years. Conners worried that Goldberg would not stay with the company long enough to establish a solid organization. Goldberg also liked running his own show, and that created a potential problem with Lizfeld.

The next candidate was Robert Kyle, vice president of BRB's radar electronics department. Kyle had been with BRB for more than 20 years and headed two other international divisions for BRB in Japan and Canada. Kyle was familiar with the international process and the BRB corporate culture. Lizfeld had given him excellent reviews in the other two international positions. He had strong management skills and was highly respected both within the organization and in the industry. Kyle received his PhD from MIT in electrical engineering and his MBA from Dartmouth. He had the technical expertise and was familiar with the company and its procedures. Conners was afraid of Kyle's cultural acceptance in Israel since he did not speak the language and was not familiar with Israeli attitudes. He could require Kyle to participate in extensive cultural training, but Conners still had some reservations about sending a gentile to head operations in Israel.

The last candidate was Rochelle Cohen, an Israeli who relocated to the US in 1982. She originally relocated to assist the head of the electronics division of Yassar Aircraft, an Israeli company that opened its first international office in 1978. Cohen did very well and brought Israeli thoroughness and assertiveness to the US operations. She now wanted to move back to Israel to be with her family. Additionally, her fiancé recently relocated in Israel, and she wanted to return to marry and raise a family. Cohen had experience in the international circuit, having worked in the US, UK, and Israel, but Conners was still worried about hiring her. Although she had the political knowledge and the proper connections in the Israeli government, the problems were her young age, lack of technical expertise, and sex.

Conners contacted O'Leary to see what progress he had made. Knowing the consequences that would come from this decision, Conners realized it was going to be a difficult one to make.

UK OPERATIONS

Francis O'Leary reflected on his past eight years with BRB. His rise from the strife-torn east side of Belfast to BRB's corporate vice president for human resources was extraordinary. While most Irish business careers in large English firms peak at middle management, O'Leary's actually began at that point. He proved his capabilities through hard work, constant study, and an astute ability to judge the character and substance of people on first sight. His task of finding a suitable general manager for the new division in Israel offered a challenge he readily accepted.

O'Leary excelled at recruiting and hiring innovative employees who brought technical ideas with them to BRB. The management structure at BRB in England did not support internal growth of technology and innovation, so new ideas and techno-logical advances were not rewarded with commensurate fiscal incentives. As such, turnover of experienced innovators forced O'Leary to recruit and hire innovation on a "rotating stock" basis. It was this success in hiring innovators that broke him from the shackles of middle management and thrust him to the top of the corpora-tion. Four years ago, through a well-planned and well-executed recruiting program, O'Leary hired Rani Gilboa, a young Israeli engineer and former Israeli army officer. For Gilboa, the need for lightweight, inexpensive battlefield systems drove a desire to approach the problem from a new aspect: signal processing. After graduate study in this field, Gilboa sought and found a company that would support his concepts. That company was BRB. Gilboa's subsequent contributions to BRB's profits secured his and O'Leary's positions atop their respective disciplines within the firm.

Since that time, O'Leary had other successes hiring innovators from Israel. This stemmed largely from his tireless self-study of Israeli culture. With a feel for the Israeli people rivaling that of an "insider," O'Leary enjoyed success in pirating established innovators from Israeli firms. Now, he faced the task of recruiting and hiring a general manager for the newly established electronics division near Haifa.

Selecting the right manager would be more difficult than expected. With his knowledge of the Israeli culture, O'Leary knew intuitively that an Israeli should head the new division. Acceptance by the division's employees, ability to speak Hebrew, spousal support, and knowledge of Israeli government regulations and tax structures were vital to the success of the new division. Unfortunately, BRB's CEO preferred home country presence in the new division and directed O'Leary to recruit with that as the top priority. After O'Leary presented a strong case, however, the CEO agreed to review all candidates. Another potential problem arose when Lizfeld, the CEO, announced a hands-on management style with plans to participate actively in the management of the Israeli division. To O'Leary, this meant that Western values, along with the current innovative recruiting strategy practiced in England, would extend to Israel as well.

Until recently, O'Leary's recruiting for management positions concentrated on internal promotions. A known performer from within was a better bet than an outsider. When current employees could not meet the job requirements, O'Leary typically turned to newspapers as his primary source of candidates, The recent emergence of reputable executive placement services in England gave him an additional sourcing tool. At times, O'Leary had turned to social contacts, job centers, and the internal labor market as candidate sources, but the percentages of good leads from these were comparatively low.

After months of reading résumés, introductory letters, and job applications, three candidates emerged for the position in Israel. It was now up to O'Leary to decide the candidate he would recommend to Lizfeld.

Michael Flack worked for BRB for more than 19 years. After graduating from Cambridge College with a degree in general engineering, Flack joined the company as a mechanical engineer. Initially, he worked in the mechanical design group of the radar division. After five years, BRB promoted Flack to engineering section manager. While in this position, he enjoyed various successes in radar miniaturization design. During his eleventh year, BRB again promoted Flack to department head in the manufacturing engineering group. Emphasis in this position shifted from design to production. During his seventeenth year, he became director of engineering design, where he was responsible for managing 43 engineers' efforts in new-product design.

Flack had no international experience, and he was a reputed "tinkerer." He liked to spend time in the labs designing mechanical components along with his engineers. This generated tremendous esprit within his department but often resulted in inattention to his administrative responsibilities.

Rani Gilboa thought his friend Yair Shafrir was perfect for the position. Shafrir was currently vice president of engineering at Elta Electronics in Israel. Elta is one of Israel's top radar firms, with several products proven in actual combat during the last Arab–Israeli conflict. Shafrir received his degree in electrical engineering from the University of Jerusalem. He had spent his professional career in Israel, usually changing companies to accept promotions. He had been with four companies since graduating from the university 19 years ago. Shafrir was a strong-willed, organized individual who took pride in his record of technical management accomplishments. He had been able to complete projects on schedule and within budget over 70 percent of the time, a rare feat for an Israeli company. This record resulted mainly from the force of his personal leadership and strength of will. With his entire career spent in Israeli companies, O'Leary had little doubt that Shafrir could manage BRB's new electronics division. Culturally, he was perfect for the job. O'Leary had concerns, however, about Paul Lizfeld's injection of Western culture through his active management plan. The obstinate Shafrir, with no international business experience, might resent the interference.

A well-placed advertisement in *The Times'* employment section drew a number of responses. One of the three final candidates responded to the ad about four weeks after it appeared in *The Times*.

Harold Michaelson was an English citizen of Jewish faith. Michaelson's family fled Poland in 1938 when Harold's father insisted that the "Nazi madman" would never attack England, especially after Prime Minister Chamberlain's successful visit to Munich. Harold was born to the newly naturalized couple in 1940. Later, he attended college in the US, where he earned both bachelor's and master's degrees in electrical engineering at Georgia Tech. After graduating, Harold spent two years with General Electric until his father's illness forced him to return to England. He accepted an engineering position with Marconi, and he has remained with that company. Shortly after his return, his father died. Michaelson continued to take care of his mother for the next year. Mrs Michaelson had always dreamed of living in the Jewish homeland – a dream not shared by her husband. One year after his death, she joined her sister's family in Haifa. Harold had readily accepted a position with Marconi in Israel to work on the new Israeli defense fighter, LAVI. Unfortunately, cancellation of the LAVI program also canceled his chances to work in Israel for Marconi. At the time of the interview, Harold was vice president of engineering for Marconi's air radio division. He was also the youngest vice president in the corporation. His background in engineering and administrative functions, coupled with his ability to speak Hebrew, made Harold a strong candidate for the position. During the interview, he mentioned his mother's failing health and her refusal to leave Israel. He intended, if selected, to take care of her there. O'Leary wondered if that was Harold's main reason for wanting to live in Israel. Would he still want to live and work there if he lost his mother? O'Leary was anxious to discuss his candidates with John Conners.

Günter K. Stahl and
Mark E. Mendenhall

ANDREAS WEBER'S REWARD FOR SUCCESS IN AN INTERNATIONAL ASSIGNMENT: A RETURN TO AN UNCERTAIN FUTURE*

ANDREAS WEBER'S MIND would not stop racing. Normally, an intense run in the evening had the effect of dissipating his worries, but tonight this did not work. The further he jogged along his standard route on the banks of the Hudson River, the more he could not get out of his mind the letter he knew he must write tomorrow. "How had it all come to this?" he wondered. This thought triggered his memory back seven years, to the initial event that had set in motion the process that led to his current trouble.

ANDREAS' DECISION TO PURSUE AN INTERNATIONAL CAREER

Andreas remembered the occasion clearly; Herr Görner, the managing director, had walked into his office at the Frankfurt headquarters of his bank, and offered him the chance to participate in a company-wide international leadership development program. Herr Görner explained that the program involved an international assignment with the intention of fostering the professional development of young, aspiring managers. After their overseas assignments, the trainees would constitute a pool of internationally experienced young managers with the potential for senior management positions at corporate headquarters. Andreas accepted the offer on the spot, with pride. He had worked very hard since joining the bank and felt that his efforts had finally paid off.

The program started with a one-week seminar at a leading business school in the US. The CEO had flown in from Frankfurt, demonstrating the commitment of top management to this program. In his speech to the participants, the CEO stressed that the major challenge and "number one" priority for the bank in the future was globalization. He made it clear that international experience was a key value and a prerequisite for promotion into the ranks of senior management. Andreas felt confident that he had made the right decision in accepting the offer and in pursuing an international career.

Shortly after the program started, an unexpected vacancy opened up in the bank's New York branch and Andreas was asked if he was interested. He discussed the prospect of a three-year assignment to New York with his wife, Lina. The offer looked very attractive from all angles, and they quickly agreed that Andreas should accept it. Two months later, he was transferred to New York.

ASSIGNMENT NEW YORK: THE FIRST YEAR

Andreas remembered the day of his arrival as if it were yesterday. He arrived at JFK Airport early in the afternoon. Since his only contact point about the job assignment was corporate HR in Frankfurt, he assumed that they had made all the necessary arrangements with the New York office for his arrival. However, no one came to the airport to pick him up. He took a taxi and went directly to the New York branch of the bank. When he arrived, he was not sure where he should go. He had not been informed about whom he should contact after his arrival, so he went straight to the office of the head of the corporate finance department where he was supposed to work. When he entered the office and told the secretary that he was the new manager from Germany, she looked at her notebook, shook her head, and told him that they were not expecting anybody. Confused, Andreas rushed to the HR department and soon found that several misunderstandings had occurred. First, it was not the corporate finance department but the credit department that had requested his transfer. Second, contrary to what he was told in Frankfurt, there was only a non-management position vacant. They were looking for a credit analyst, basically the same job that he had done in Germany.

Andreas shook his head in reaction to the memory: "There I stood, in what was supposed to be my new office, with three pieces of luggage on the desk, and wondering whether I should stay or take the next plane home!"

Why he decided to stay in New York, he could never quite figure out. In retrospect, it was probably just a split-second decision to make the best of the situation. The whirl of images of the next two months flashed across his memory: rushed days and nights trying to learn the ropes of a new office with new procedures, looking for a place to live, meeting new people, and exploring new places. Then a clear memory intervened the collage of memories of those first two months – Lina's arrival. Lina, his wife, and their three-year-old daughter, Anne-Marie, followed Andreas to New York two months after his arrival. They moved into a small house in the outskirts of New York. Lina knew New York pretty well, as she had worked there for a couple of months as an intern at a reinsurance company. She arrived excited to re-discover her favorite restaurants, art galleries, and museums.

Except for occasional attacks of homesickness, Lina was satisfied with her new life. The week after they had moved into their new house, they received a dinner invitation from a young married couple next door. To their surprise, their American neighbors quickly embraced the Webers. Since Lina was not able to get a work permit, she joined her new acquaintance in doing volunteer work at a local art museum. Anne-Marie spent every second afternoon at a local kindergarten, which gave Lina plenty of time to pursue her own interests. At the end of their first year in the US, a second daughter, Elena, was born. By then, the Webers had already made several more new friends, both Americans and other expatriates. When the Webers stepped off the plane at JFK after their first home leave to Germany, it felt more like they were coming home than returning to a temporary assignment.

ANDREAS' FAST-TRACK CAREER AS AN EXPATRIATE

Professionally, things had gone extremely well during this time period. The New York branch of the bank had been right at the start of a boom-phase that lasted for several years. Throughout the boom, the bank's staff increased significantly. After eight months of working in the back office, Andreas was promoted to supervisor of a group of credit analysts. Then, one year after his first promotion, a position opened up at the senior management level. The deputy head of the rapidly expanding corporate finance department – a German expatriate – had unexpectedly left for a job at one of their American competitors, and the bank had to fill his position with a manager who spoke fluent German, was familiar with the finance departments of a number of German and other European companies, and was instantly available. Andreas was asked if he was willing to extend his foreign service contract for another three years and accept the position as deputy head of the corporate finance department. After discussing it with Lina, Andreas accepted.

In the fifth year of his assignment, Andreas made another step upward in his career. His boss retired, and Andreas was promoted to head of the corporate finance department. He was now one of five managing directors in the branch. When Andreas signed his new contract, it was agreed that he would stay with the New York branch of the bank for another three years and would then return to the bank's German headquarters.

These were warm memories, memories that somewhat buffered the intensity of Andreas' frustration and anger over his current situation. But as he continued running, the warmth of the past dissipated into the turmoil of the present.

"It all started with that promotion," he muttered to himself. As head of the corporate finance department, Andreas' professional and private lives had unexpectedly changed. He was now responsible for a huge area – his business activities no longer concentrated on North American subsidiaries of foreign-based companies, but included their headquarters in Europe and East Asia. In the first six months of his new job, Andreas had traveled almost 100,000 miles, mainly on business flights to Europe. His extensive traveling was hard on Lina. She felt alone, and was concerned about their children's education. Their eldest daughter, Anne-Marie, was now nine years old and had spent most of her life outside of Germany. Lina was also concerned about her missing out on a German high school education. Anne-Marie's German language skills had gradually deteriorated over the last two years, and that troubled Lina as well. Their second daughter, Elena, was attending kindergarten, and except for the yearly home leave, she had no contact with other German children. Elena's German was quite poor. In fact, both Anne-Marie and Elena considered themselves Americans.

Lina also started to be more and more discontented with her life as a housewife. Obtaining a work permit in the US remained impossible, and it was not easy for her to find new volunteer activities to quench her interests. To make things worse, Lina's father fell ill and died in that same year, leaving her mother alone. Andreas remembered the long conversations he had had with Lina during this period of time, many of which were by telephone from hotel rooms in far away places. When he was home, they spoke often in the quiet of their living room, and on long walks – Andreas lost count of the multitude of times they had talked as they walked through the same park he was now running through.

ANDREAS' DILEMMA: STAYING IN NEW YORK OR RETURNING HOME TO AN UNCERTAIN FUTURE

"It was an extremely difficult situation," Andreas remembered, "not so much for the children, but for Lina and I . . . From a professional standpoint, my assignment to New York was the best thing that could ever happen to me: I worked in the financial center of the world; I loved my job, the freedom of being away from the bureaucracy at corporate headquarters, the opportunities to travel; I became a member of the senior management team at a very young age – impossible if I stayed in Germany. Personally, we were also happy: our children felt at home in New York; we were quickly embraced by our neighbors and the expatriate community; we had many friends . . . The question we continually wrestled with was: 'Does it make sense to give all these up for a return to an uncertain future in Germany?' In principle, the answer would clearly have been: 'No.' But on a long-term basis, moving back to Germany appeared to be the best solution for our children. After all, we felt responsible for their future."

After several weeks of consideration and discussion, Lina and Andreas decided to move back to Germany. This was about a year ago. Immediately after the decision was made, Andreas contacted the bank's corporate headquarters and informed the human resource executive in charge of international assignments about his decision. Three weeks later, Andreas received a short letter from him, stating that there were currently no positions available in Germany at his level. Part of the problem, Andreas was told, was due to the current economic downturn in Europe, but since several new branches were due to be opened in the eastern part of Germany over the course of the next year, he was told that chances were good that the company would be able to find him a suitable return assignment within the next six months. Since then,

Andreas had several meetings with executives at corporate headquarters, as well as with managers of domestic branches of the bank, but he still had not been offered any re-entry position.

Lina gradually became discouraged. She had told her mother that they were coming home immediately after they made their decision to return to Germany, but eight months had passed, and her mother kept asking when they were coming. Andreas' parents were persistent in their queries as well. Finally, last week, Andreas received a telephone call from the corporate HR department, in which he was informed that they had found what they called a "challenging" return assignment. They offered him the position of deputy head of a medium-sized branch of the bank in the Eastern part of Germany. Andreas was told that a letter explaining the details of the position offer had already been sent.

THE OFFER

The memory of opening that letter and reading it, and the resulting emotions of anger, betrayal, disbelief, and frustration all came back to him. He stopped running, and sat down on a park bench alongside the jogging trail. "Not only will I earn little more than half the salary that I currently make in New York, I will not be able to use the skills and experiences that I gained during my overseas assignment, I will be out of touch with all the important decisions being made at headquarters, and on top of that, I will be posted to this God-forsaken place!" he thought, bitterly.

With all the frustrations and anger welling up in his chest, Andreas thought, cynically, "The bank's promotion policy – if there ever was any rational policy – is to punish those who are really committed to the organization. They assign you to one of those programs for high-fliers and send you abroad, but there is no career planning whatsoever. If there just happens to be a job vacant when you return, you are lucky. If not, they let you wait and wait and wait, until you finally accept the most ridiculous job offer ... Their slogan that international experience is a key value and a prerequisite for promotion into the ranks of senior management is garbage! If you look at the actual promotion and career development practices in this organization, it becomes clear it's only lip service ... and lies! ... In this bank, the better you perform overseas, the more you get screwed when you come back."

He began to wonder if he should accept the offer. Perhaps they should just stay in New York and make their home here. But then, images of Lina, Lina's mother, Anne-Marie, Elena, and his parents, and all of their combined needs enveloped him.

Leaning back on the park bench, he blankly stared down the path that would lead out of the park and into the street, and then home.

NOTE

* This case was prepared by Günter K. Stahl, Assistant Professor of Asian Business at INSEAD and Mark E. Mendenhall, J. Burton Frierson Professor of Leadership at the University of Tennessee. It is intended to be used as a basis for class discussion rather than to illustrate either effective or ineffective handling of an administrative situation. Financial support for the project "Expatriate Careers" (INSEAD research grant # 2010-502 R) is gratefully acknowledged.

PART 4

People Issues in International Teams, Alliances, Mergers, and Acquisitions

Readings

- Jeanne Brett, Kristin Behfar, and Mary C. Kern
  MANAGING MULTICULTURAL TEAMS

- Susan E. Jackson and Randall S. Schuler
  CULTURAL DIVERSITY IN CROSS-BORDER ALLIANCES

- Vladimir Pucik, Paul Evans, and Ingmar Björkman
  HUMAN RESOURCE MANAGEMENT ISSUES IN INTERNATIONAL MERGERS
  AND ACQUISITIONS

Cases:

- Philippe Lassere
  A MARRIAGE OF REASON: RENAULT AND NISSAN GLOBAL STRATEGIC
  ALLIANCE

- Kathrin Köster and Günter K. Stahl
  LENOVO-IBM: BRIDGING CULTURES, LANGUAGES, AND TIME ZONES

- Ingmar Björkman and Ming Zeng
  GUANGDONG ELECTRONICS

Jeanne Brett, Kristin Behfar, and Mary C. Kern

MANAGING MULTICULTURAL TEAMS*

Teams whose members come from different nations and backgrounds place special demands on managers – especially when a feuding team looks to the boss for help with a conflict.

WHEN A MAJOR INTERNATIONAL software developer needed to produce a new product quickly, the project manager assembled a team of employees from India and the US. From the start the team members could not agree on a delivery date for the product. The Americans thought the work could be done in two to three weeks; the Indians predicted it would take two to three months. As time went on, the Indian team members proved reluctant to report setbacks in the production process, which the American team members would find out about only when work was due to be passed to them. Such conflicts, of course, may affect any team, but in this case they arose from cultural differences. As tensions mounted, conflict over delivery dates and feedback became personal, disrupting team members' communication about even mundane issues. The project manager decided he had to intervene – with the result that both the American and the Indian team members came to rely on him for direction regarding minute operational details that the team should have been able to handle itself. The manager became so bogged down by quotidian issues that the project careened hopelessly off even the most pessimistic schedule – and the team never learned to work together effectively.

Multicultural teams often generate frustrating management dilemmas. Cultural differences can create substantial obstacles to effective teamwork – but these may be subtle and difficult to recognize until significant damage has already been done. As in the case above, which the manager involved told us about, managers may create more problems than they resolve by intervening. The challenge in managing multicultural teams effectively is to recognize underlying cultural causes of conflict, and to intervene in ways that both get the team back on track and empower its members to deal with future challenges themselves.

We interviewed managers and members of multicultural teams from all over the world. These interviews, combined with our deep research on dispute resolution and teamwork, led us to conclude that the wrong kind of managerial intervention may sideline valuable members who should be participating or, worse, create resistance, resulting in poor team performance. We're not talking here about respecting differing national standards for doing business, such as accounting practices. We're referring to day-to-day working problems among team members that can keep multicultural teams from realizing the very gains they were set up to harvest, such as knowledge of different product markets, culturally sensitive customer service, and 24-hour work rotations.

The good news is that cultural challenges are manageable if managers and team members choose the right strategy and avoid imposing single-culture-based approaches on multicultural situations.

THE CHALLENGES

People tend to assume that challenges on multicultural teams arise from differing styles of communication. But this is only one of the four categories that, according to our research, can create barriers to a team's ultimate success. These categories are direct versus indirect communication; trouble with accents and fluency; differing attitudes toward hierarchy and authority; and conflicting norms for decision-making.

Direct Versus Indirect Communication

Communication in Western cultures is typically direct and explicit. The meaning is on the surface, and a listener doesn't have to know much about the context or the speaker to interpret it. This is not true in many other cultures, where meaning is embedded in the way the message is presented. For example, Western negotiators get crucial information about the other party's preferences and priorities by asking direct questions, such as, "Do you prefer option A or option B?" In cultures that use indirect communication, negotiators may have to infer preferences and priorities from changes – or the lack of them – in the other party's settlement proposal. In cross-cultural negotiations, the non-Westerner can understand the direct communications of the Westerner, but the Westerner has difficulty understanding the indirect communications of the non-Westerner.

An American manager who was leading a project to build an interface for a US and Japanese customer-data system explained the problems her team was having this way: "In Japan, they want to talk and discuss. Then we take a break and they talk within the organization. They want to make sure that there's harmony in the rest of the organization. One of the hardest lessons for me was when I thought they were saying yes but they just meant 'I'm listening to you.'"

The differences between direct and indirect communication can cause serious damage to relationships when team projects run into problems. When the American manager quoted above discovered that several flaws in the system would significantly disrupt company operations, she pointed this out in an email to her American boss and the Japanese team members. Her boss appreciated the direct warnings; her Japanese colleagues were embarrassed, because she had violated their norms for uncovering and discussing problems. Their reaction was to provide her with less access to the people and information she needed to monitor progress. They would probably have responded better if she had pointed out the problems indirectly – for example, by asking them what would happen if a certain part of the system was not functioning properly, even though she knew full well that it was malfunctioning, and also what the implications were.

As our research indicates is so often true, communication challenges create barriers to effective teamwork by reducing information sharing, creating interpersonal conflict, or both. In Japan, a typical response to direct confrontation is to isolate the norm violator. This American manager was isolated not just socially but also physically. She told us, "They literally put my office in a storage room, where I had desks stacked from floor to ceiling and I was the only person there. So they totally isolated me, which was a pretty loud signal to me that I was not a part of the inside circle and that they would communicate with me only as needed."

Her direct approach had been intended to solve a problem, and in one sense it did, because her project was launched problem-free. But her norm violations exacerbated the challenges of working with her Japanese colleagues and limited her ability to uncover any other problems that might have derailed the project later on.

Trouble with Accents and Fluency

Although the language of international business is English, misunderstandings or deep frustration may occur because of non-native speakers' accents, lack of fluency, or problems with translation or usage. These may also influence perceptions of status or competence.

For example, a Latin American member of a multicultural consulting team lamented, "Many times I felt that because of the language difference, I didn't have the words to say some things that I was thinking. I noticed that when I went to these interviews with the US guy, he would tend to lead the interviews, which was understandable but also disappointing, because we are at the same level. I had very good questions, but he would take the lead."

When we interviewed an American member of a US–Japanese team that was assessing the potential expansion of a US retail chain into Japan, she described one American teammate this way: "He was not interested in the Japanese consultants' feedback and felt that because they weren't as fluent as he was, they weren't intelligent enough and, therefore, could add no value." The team member described was responsible for assessing one aspect of the feasibility of expansion into Japan. Without input from the Japanese experts, he risked overestimating opportunities and underestimating challenges.

Non-fluent team members may well be the most expert on the team, but their difficulty communicating knowledge makes it hard for the team to recognize and utilize their expertise. If teammates become frustrated or impatient with a lack of fluency, interpersonal conflicts can arise. Non-native speakers may become less motivated to contribute, or anxious about their performance evaluations and future career prospects. The organization as a whole pays a greater price: its investment in a multicultural team fails to pay off.

Some teams, we learned, use language differences to resolve (rather than create) tensions. A team of US and Latin American buyers was negotiating with a team from a Korean supplier. The negotiations took place in Korea, but the discussions were conducted in English. Frequently the Koreans would caucus at the table by speaking Korean. The buyers, frustrated, would respond by appearing to caucus in Spanish – though they discussed only inconsequential current events and sports, in case any of the Koreans spoke Spanish. Members of the team who didn't speak Spanish pretended to participate, to the great amusement of their teammates. This approach proved effective: it conveyed to the Koreans in an appropriately indirect way that their caucuses in Korean were frustrating and annoying to the other side. As a result, both teams cut back on sidebar conversations.

Differing Attitudes Toward Hierarchy and Authority

A challenge inherent in multicultural teamwork is that by design, teams have a rather flat structure. But team members from some cultures, in which people are treated differently according to their status in an organization, are uncomfortable on flat teams. If they defer to higher-status team members, their behavior will be seen as appropriate when most of the team comes from a hierarchical culture; but they may damage their stature and credibility – and even face humiliation – if most of the team comes from an egalitarian culture.

One manager of Mexican heritage, who was working on a credit and under-writing team for a bank, told us, "In Mexican culture, you're always supposed to be humble. So whether you understand something or not, you're supposed to put it in the form of a question. You have to keep it open-ended, out of respect. I think that actually worked against me, because the Americans thought I really didn't know what I was talking about. So it made me feel like they thought I was wavering on my answer."

When, as a result of differing cultural norms, team members believe they've been treated disrespectfully, the whole project can blow up. In another Korean–US negotiation, the American members of a due diligence team were having difficulty getting information from their Korean counterparts, so they complained directly to higher-level Korean management, nearly wrecking the deal. The higher-level managers were offended because hierarchy is strictly adhered to in Korean organizations and culture. It should have been their own lower-level people, not the US team members, who came to them with a problem. And the Korean team members were mortified that their bosses had been involved before they themselves could brief them. The crisis was resolved only when high-level US managers made a trip to Korea, conveying appropriate respect for their Korean counterparts.

Conflicting Norms for Decision-Making

Cultures differ enormously when it comes to decision-making – particularly how quickly decisions should be made and how much analysis is required beforehand. Not surprisingly, US managers like to make decisions very quickly and with relatively little analysis by comparison with managers from other countries.

A Brazilian manager at an American company who was negotiating to buy Korean products destined for Latin America told us, "On the first day, we agreed on three points, and on the second day, the US-Spanish side wanted to start with point four. But the Korean side wanted to go back and re-discuss points one through three. My boss almost had an attack."

What US team members learn from an experience like this is that the American way simply cannot be imposed on other cultures. Managers from other cultures may, for example, decline to share information until they understand the full scope of a project. But they have learned that they can't simply ignore the desire of their American counterparts to make decisions quickly. What to do? The best solution seems to be to make minor concessions on process – to learn to adjust to and even respect another approach to decision-making. For example, American managers have learned to keep their impatient bosses away from team meetings and give them frequent, if brief, updates. A comparable lesson for managers from other cultures is to be explicit about what they need – saying, for example, "We have to see the big picture before we talk details."

FOUR STRATEGIES

The most successful teams and managers we interviewed used four strategies for dealing with these challenges: adaptation (acknowledging cultural gaps openly and working around them), structural intervention (changing the shape of the team), managerial intervention (setting norms early or bringing in a higher-level manager), and exit (removing a team member when other options have failed). There is no one right way to deal with a particular kind of multicultural problem; identifying the type of challenge is only the first step. The more crucial step is assessing the circumstances – or "enabling situational conditions" – under which the team is working. For example, does the project allow any flexibility for change, or do deadlines make that impossible? Are there additional resources available that might be tapped? Is the team permanent or temporary? Does the team's manager have the autonomy to make a decision about changing the team in some way? Once the situational conditions have been analyzed, the team's leader can identify an appropriate response (see Exhibit 1).

Adaptation

Some teams find ways to work with or around the challenges they face, adapting practices or attitudes without making changes to the group's membership or assignments. Adaptation works when team members are willing to acknowledge and name their cultural differences and to assume responsibility for figuring out how to live with them. It's often the best possible approach to a problem, because it typically involves less managerial time than other strategies; and because team members participate in solving the problem themselves, they learn from the process. When team members have this mindset, they can be creative about protecting their own substantive differences while acceding to the processes of others.

An American software engineer located in Ireland who was working with an Israeli account management team from his own company told us how shocked he was by the Israelis' in-your-face style: "There were definitely different ways of approaching issues and discussing them. There is something pretty common to the Israeli culture: they like to argue. I tend to try to collaborate more, and it got very stressful for me until I figured out how to kind of merge the cultures."

The software engineer adapted. He imposed some structure on the Israelis that helped him maintain his own style of being thoroughly prepared; that accommodation enabled him to accept the Israeli style. He also noticed that team members weren't just confronting him; they confronted one another but were able to work together effectively nevertheless. He realized that the confrontation was not personal but cultural.

In another example, an American member of a post-merger consulting team was frustrated by the hierarchy of the French company his team was working with. He felt that a meeting with certain French managers who were not directly involved in the merger "wouldn't deliver any value to me or for purposes of the project," but said that he had come to understand that "it was very important to really involve all the people there" if the integration was ultimately to work.

A US and UK multicultural team tried to use their differing approaches to decision-making to reach a higher-quality decision. This approach, called fusion, is getting serious attention from political scientists and from government officials dealing with multicultural populations that want to protect their cultures rather than integrate or assimilate. If the team had relied exclusively on the Americans' "forge ahead" approach, it might not have recognized the pitfalls that lay ahead and might later have had to back up and start over. Meanwhile, the UK members would have been gritting their teeth and saying "We told you things were moving too fast." If the team had used the "Let's think about this" UK approach, it might have wasted a lot of time trying to identify every pitfall, including the most unlikely, while the US members chomped at the bit and muttered about analysis paralysis. The strength of this team was that some of its members were willing to forge ahead and some were willing to work through pitfalls. To accommodate them all, the team did both – moving not quite as fast as the US members would have on their own and not quite as thoroughly as the UK members would have.

Structural Intervention

A structural intervention is a deliberate reorganization or reassignment designed to reduce interpersonal friction or to remove a source of conflict for one or more groups.

EXHIBIT 1. Identifying the right strategy

The most successful teams and managers we interviewed use four strategies for dealing with problems: adaptation (acknowledging cultural gaps openly and working around them), structural intervention (changing the shape of the team), managerial intervention (setting norms early or bringing in a higher-level manager), and exit (removing a team member when other options have failed). Adaptation is the ideal strategy because the team works effectively to solve its own problem with minimal input from management – and, most importantly, learns from the experience. The guide below can help you identify the right strategy once you have identified both the problem and the "enabling situational conditions" that apply to the team.

Representative Problems	Enabling Situational Conditions	Strategy	Complicating Factors
• Conflict arises from decision-making differences • Misunderstanding or stone-walling arises from communication differences	• Team members can attribute a challenge to culture rather than personality • Higher-level managers are not available or the team would be embarrassed to involve them	Adaptation	• Team members must be exceptionally aware • Negotiating a common understanding takes time
• The team is affected by emotional tensions relating to fluency issues or prejudice • Team members are inhibited by perceived status differences among teammates	• The team can be subdivided to mix cultures or expertise • Tasks can be subdivided	Structural Intervention	• If team members aren't carefully distributed, sub-groups can strengthen preexisting differences • Subgroup solutions have to fit back together
• Violations of hierarchy have resulted in loss of face • An absence of ground rules is causing conflict	• The problem has produced a high level of emotion • The team has reached a stalemate • A higher-level manager is able and willing to intervene	Managerial Intervention	• The team becomes overly dependent on the manager • Team members may be sidelined or resistant
• A team member cannot adjust to the challenge at hand and has become unable to contribute to the project	• The team is permanent rather than temporary • Emotions are beyond the point of intervention • Too much face has been lost	Exit	• Talent and training costs are lost

This approach can be extremely effective when obvious subgroups demarcate the team (for example, headquarters versus national subsidiaries) or if team members are proud, defensive, threatened, or clinging to negative stereotypes of one another.

A member of an investment research team scattered across continental Europe, the UK, and the US described for us how his manager resolved conflicts stemming from status differences and language tensions among the team's three "tribes." The manager started by having the team meet face-to-face twice a year, not to discuss mundane day-to-day problems (of which there were many) but to identify a set of values that the team would use to direct and evaluate its progress. At the first meeting, he realized that when he started to speak, everyone else "shut down," waiting to hear what he had to say. So he hired a consultant to run future meetings. The consultant didn't represent a hierarchical threat and was therefore able to get lots of participation from team members.

Another structural intervention might be to create smaller working groups of mixed cultures or mixed corporate identities in order to get at information that is not forthcoming from the team as a whole. The manager of the team that was evaluating retail opportunities in Japan used this approach. When she realized that the female Japanese consultants would not participate if the group got large, or if their male superior was present, she broke the team up into smaller groups to try to solve problems. She used this technique repeatedly and made a point of changing the subgroups' membership each time so that team members got to know and respect everyone else on the team.

The subgrouping technique involves risks, however. It buffers people who are not working well together or not participating in the larger group for one reason or another. Sooner or later, the team will have to assemble the pieces that the subgroups have come up with, so this approach relies on another structural intervention: someone must become a mediator in order to see that the various pieces fit together.

Managerial Intervention

When a manager behaves like an arbitrator or a judge, making a final decision without team involvement, neither the manager nor the team gains much insight into why the team has stalemated. But it is possible for team members to use managerial intervention effectively to sort out problems.

When an American refinery-safety expert with significant experience throughout East Asia got stymied during a project in China, she called in her company's higher-level managers in Beijing to talk to the higher-level managers to whom the Chinese refinery's managers reported. Unlike the Western team members who breached etiquette by approaching the superiors of their Korean counterparts, the safety expert made sure to respect hierarchies in both organizations.

"Trying to resolve the issues," she told us, "the local management at the Chinese refinery would end up having conferences with our Beijing office and also with the upper management within the refinery. Eventually they understood that we weren't trying to insult them or their culture or to tell them they were bad in any way. We were trying to help. They eventually understood that there were significant fire and safety issues. But we actually had to go up some levels of management to get those resolved."

Managerial intervention to set norms early in a team's life can really help the team start out with effective processes. In one instance reported to us, a multicultural software development team's lingua franca was English, but some members, though they spoke grammatically correct English, had a very pronounced accent. In setting the ground rules for the team, the manager addressed the challenge directly, telling the members that they had been chosen for their task expertise, not their fluency in English, and that the team was going to have to work around language problems. As the project moved to the customer-services training stage, the manager advised the team members to acknowledge their accents up front. She said they should tell customers, "I realize I have an accent. If you don't understand what I'm saying, just stop me and ask questions."

Exit

Possibly because many of the teams we studied were project-based, we found that leaving the team was an infrequent strategy for managing challenges. In short-term situations, unhappy team members often just waited out the project. When teams were permanent, producing products or services, the exit of one or more members was a strategy of last resort, but it was used – either voluntarily or after a formal request from management. Exit was likely when emotions were running high and too much face had been lost on both sides to salvage the situation.

An American member of a multicultural consulting team described the conflict between two senior consultants, one a Greek woman and the other a Polish man, over how to approach problems: "The woman from Greece would say, 'Here's the way I think we should do it.' It would be something that she was in control of. The guy from Poland would say, 'I think we should actually do it this way instead.' The woman would kind of turn red in the face, upset, and say, 'I just don't think that's the right way of doing it.' It would definitely switch from just professional differences to personal differences.

"The woman from Greece ended up leaving the firm. That was a direct result of probably all the different issues going on between these people. It really just wasn't a good fit. I've found that oftentimes when you're in consulting, you have to adapt to the culture, obviously, but you have to adapt just as much to the style of whoever is leading the project."

Though multicultural teams face challenges that are not directly attributable to cultural differences, such differences underlay whatever problem needed to be addressed in many of the teams we studied. Furthermore, while serious in their own right when they have a negative effect on team functioning, cultural challenges may also unmask fundamental managerial problems. Managers who intervene early and set norms; teams and managers who structure social interaction and work to engage everyone on the team; and teams that can see problems as stemming from culture, not personality, approach challenges with good humor and creativity. Managers who have to intervene when the team has reached a stalemate may be able to get the team moving again, but they seldom empower it to help itself the next time a stalemate occurs.

When frustrated team members take some time to think through challenges and possible solutions themselves, it can make a huge difference. Take, for example, this story about a financial-services call center. The members of the call-center team were all fluent Spanish-speakers, but some were North Americans and some were Latin Americans. Team performance, measured by calls answered per hour, was lagging. One Latin American was taking twice as long with her calls as the rest of the team. She was handling callers' questions appropriately, but she was also engaging in chitchat. When her teammates confronted her for being a free rider (they resented having to make up for her low call rate), she immediately acknowledged the problem, admitting that she did not know how to end the call politely – chitchat being normal in her culture. They rallied to help her: using their technology, they would break into any of her calls that went overtime, excusing themselves to the customer, offering to take over the call, and saying that this employee was urgently needed to help out on a different call. The team's solution worked in the short run, and the employee got better at ending her calls in the long run.

In another case, the Indian manager of a multicultural team coordinating a company-wide IT project found himself frustrated when he and a teammate from Singapore met with two Japanese members of the coordinating team to try to get the Japan section to deliver its part of the project. The Japanese members seemed to be saying yes, but in the Indian manager's view, their follow-through was insufficient. He considered and rejected the idea of going up the hierarchy to the Japanese team members' boss, and decided instead to try to build consensus with the whole Japanese IT team, not just the two members on the coordinating team. He and his Singapore teammate put together an eBusiness road show, took it to Japan, invited the whole IT team to view it at a lunch meeting, and walked through success stories about other parts of the organization that had aligned with the company's larger business priorities. It was rather subtle, he told us, but it worked. The Japanese IT team wanted to be spotlighted in future eBusiness road shows. In the end, the whole team worked well together – and no higher-level manager had to get involved.

NOTE

* **Jeanne Brett** is the DeWitt W. Buchanan, Jr., Distinguished Professor of Dispute Resolution and Organizations and the director of the Dispute Resolution Research Center at Northwestern University's Kellogg School of Management in Evanston, Illinois. **Kristin Behfar** is an assistant professor at the Paul Merage School of Business at the University of California at Irvine. **Mary C. Kern** is an assistant professor at the Zicklin School of Business at Baruch College in New York.

Susan E. Jackson and
Randall S. Schuler

CULTURAL DIVERSITY IN CROSS-BORDER ALLIANCES

A MAJOR DETERMINANT of the success of cross-border alliances such as international joint ventures (IJVs) and international mergers and acquisitions (IM&As) is how well managers are able to address the cultural differences present in their new organization. In this reading, we use the term *culture* to refer the unique pattern of shared assumptions, values, and norms that shape the socialization, symbols, language, narratives and practices of a group of people. Culture provides a context—a mindset—for interpreting events and assigning meaning.

Cultures develop in large and small groups of people. Some cultural differences become most evident when comparing large geographic regions, while others can be found at the level of countries, regions within countries, industries, organizations, occupational groups, demographic groups within a country, and so on. For any particular international joint venture, merger, or acquisition, cultural differences at many or all of these different levels are likely to be relevant.

NATIONAL CULTURES

Depending on the cultural distance between the national cultures involved in a cross-border alliance, managing differences in country cultures or regional cultures may be of relatively great or only minor significance. In some cross-border alliances, such as those between US and Canadian business, differences in country cultures are *relatively* small. In others, however, cultural differences in such key areas as leadership styles and decision-making procedures can be substantial (Brodbeck et al., 2000). Even when an alliance occurs between companies within a single country, cultural differences may be significant due to regional differences. A study of more than 700 managers in large cities in each of China's six major regions suggests that there are at least three distinct subcultures in China: one in the southeast, another in the northeast, and a third covering much of the central and western parts of the country. The subculture of the southeast region is the most individualistic, whereas the subculture of the central and western areas is the most collectivistic. The culture of the northeast region falls between these two extremes. Thus, cultural diversity may create just as great a challenge for an alliance between companies from different regions in China as it would for other cross-border alliances (Ralston et al., 1996).

Variations (or similarities) in the institutional environments of the alliance partners may further complicate (or help to alleviate) the challenge of managing differences due to national cultures. For example, the European Union, the Asia-Pacific Economic Cooperation, and the North American Free Trade Agreement all represent institutional arrangements that seek to provide a common framework or perspective that can be used to guide some relationships between companies in the member countries. As these institutional arrangements become more established, it is likely that cross-border alliances within an economic trade region will become easier despite significant differences in national cultures. Nevertheless, even within economic trade zones, differences in institutional arrangements among countries result in differences in the functioning of corporate boards and top management teams, as well as approaches to managing an organization's human resources (Brewster, 1995; Glunk et al., 2001; Mayer and Whittington, 1999).

INDUSTRY CULTURE

Similarly, differences in industry cultures may be important in some cross-border alliances and nearly irrelevant in others. Industry cultures are likely to be relatively unimportant when an alliance is created between companies within an industry, but when organizations from distinct industries attempt to form an alliance, such differences may be as significant as differences in country culture. Industries boundaries are both fuzzy and unstable, so the question "What industry are we in?" isn't always easy to answer. Furthermore, some companies compete by constantly pushing at the boundaries of the industry and, eventually, redefining the industries in which they compete. Nevertheless, at any point in time, the relevant industry for most organizations is comprised of a group of companies that offer similar products and services. Companies within an industry experience similar patterns of growth and eventually a common industry culture may develop. Generally, companies within the same industry are a firm's most significant competitors, as well as their most likely partners in strategic alliances, including international mergers, acquisitions and joint ventures.

Unfortunately, there is very little empirical research evidence available to use in understanding industry-based cultural differences. An exception is the work of Hofstede (1997), who suggested that industry cultures can be described using four dimensions: see Box 1.

These dimensions build on Hofstede's earlier work on organizational cultures, described below.

BOX 1. Four Dimensions of Industry Culture

Employee-oriented: Concern focuses on the people sharing the work	⟷	*Job-oriented:* Concern focuses on getting the job done
Parochial: Employees identify with the organization in which they work	⟷	*Professional:* Employees Identify with the type of work they do or their profession
Open system: Many types of people can feel comfortable in the organization	⟷	*Closed system:* The type of person who fits is narrowly specified; it takes time for employees to feel at home
Loose control: Codes of conduct allow for much variation among employees	⟷	*Tight control:* Written and unwritten rules exert tight control over behavior

---

ORGANIZATIONAL CULTURES

As is true for industry cultures, describing differences in organizational cultures can be difficult because there has been little empirical work directed at understanding the nature of these differences and how they are manifested across different countries. Here we describe three approaches for describing organizational cultures.

One popular typology for describing organizational cultures uses two dimensions to create a typology of four cultures, with each culture characterized by different underlying values. In this typology, one dimension reflects the *formal control orientation*, ranging from stable to flexible. The other dimension reflects the *focus of attention*, ranging from internal functioning to external functioning. When these four dimensions are combined, they form a typology of four pure types of organizational cultures: *bureaucratic, clan, entrepreneurial,* and *market* (Quinn and Rohrbaugh, 1983; Hooijberg and Petrock, 1993).

Another popular approach to describing organizational cultures is based on Hofstede's research in ten companies located in three European countries. Hofstede proposed using six dimensions to conceptualize organizational cultures (Hofstede, 1991): *process versus results orientation; employee versus job orientation; parochial versus professional; open versus closed system; loose versus tight control; and normative versus pragmatic*. Rather than reflecting different values, these dimensions reflect differences in management practices (see also Peterson and Hofstede, 2000).

Using yet a third approach to conceptualizing organizational culture, the GLOBE Project (Dickson et al., 2000; House et al., 1999) has made the assumption differences in organizational cultures can be understood using the same dimensions that differentiate among national cultures.

DOMESTIC CULTURAL DIVERSITY

In any organization, differences in values, beliefs, and behavioral styles contribute to domestic workforce diversity. Other forms of domestic diversity are associated with membership in various demographic groups. Regardless of which other forms of cultural diversity exist in cross-border alliances, *domestic* cultural diversity is always an issue.

When the firms of Davidson and Marley entered into an international joint venture (IJV), the Dutch workforce hired at the manufacturing plant shared a societal culture, but other forms of domestic diversity proved challenging nevertheless. Recruitment and selection practices intentionally sought to represent the demographic diversity (gender, age, and so on) of the Dutch labor market within the plant. Additional diversity was introduced unintentionally, however, because employees were hired in two distinct waves. All employees who were hired had to meet the same technical skill requirements, but different personalities were sought during these two hiring waves. In selecting the first 100 employees, they sought people who were willing to contribute to building up the firm in its pioneering phase. Good problem-identification and problem-solving abilities were needed. In addition, they looked for employees with an international orientation because these employees would be traveling to the US or the UK to receive training.

Differences found among demographic groups within a country are shaped by the country's national culture. For example, gender differences appear to be more pronounced in some countries than others, as do the relationships between men and women (Best and Williams, 2001; Williams and Best, 1990). In North America, gender differences in verbal and nonverbal communication, influenceability, interpersonal styles and leadership styles are well documented (e.g. see Eagly and Johnson, 1990; Tannen, 1990). Also well documented are age and cohort differences in work attitudes and values (e.g. Rhodes, 1983).

Presumably, differences among ethnic and language groups within countries tend to mirror cultural differences between the host country and the original home country of an ethnic group. The historical political and economic relationship between employees' countries of origin as well as differences in cultural values combine to create many unique forms of workforce diversity found in organizations.

UNDERSTANDING HOW CULTURAL DIVERSITY INFLUENCES BEHAVIOR

Scholars who study culture at different levels of analysis disagree about how to describe cultures, the social levels of analysis at which it is appropriate to apply the concept of culture, and many other issues that are beyond the scope of this reading. Without attempting to either summarize or resolve these debates, in this reading we make some simplifying assumptions about the nature of "culture."

One assumption is that our understanding the consequences of cultural diversity in cross-border alliances can move ahead without resolving the question about how best to assess the "content" of culture. We do not intend to suggest that specific aspects of the cultures involved are unimportant. However, a complete understanding of the ways that the cultures of various subgroups are similar or different from each other is not needed in order to begin to understand how the presence of cultural differences—in whatever form they take—shapes behavior in organizations.

We also assume that the behavior of an individual is influenced by multiple cultures, which are associated with the person's multiple memberships in and identification with a variety of overlapping and intersecting social entities (societies, organizations, professions, ethnic populations, and so on). These multiple cultures provide the individual with a variety of value systems (which need not be consistent with each other) for interpreting and responding to events in the environment. Depending on the social setting, some of the value systems available to an individual become more salient and important in guiding behavior.

A MODEL FOR UNDERSTANDING CULTURAL DIVERSITY AND ITS CONSEQUENCES

Jackson et al. (1995) developed a model to illustrate how domestic diversity influences behavior in organizations. Here, we have adapted their model to illustrate how many aspects of cultural diversity can combine to influence the behavior of employees in cross-border alliances. First, we describe the model shown in Exhibit 1, and briefly review some of the evidence used to develop it. Then we illustrate its implications for understanding the dynamics of managing cultural diversity in cross-border alliances.

THE MANY FORMS OF CULTURAL DIVERSITY

The model shown in Exhibit 1 recognizes that the cultural context includes several layers or levels. To some extent, these layers of culture are nested, with the more inclusive levels of culture operating as constraints around the "lower" levels of culture. For example, the organizational cultures of single-business domestic firms tend to be constrained by and reflect their country and industry cultures. We do not intend to imply that the more inclusive levels of culture determine the cultures of more delimited social systems, however. Nor do we intend to suggest that a lower-level social system is fully nested within only one higher-level social system. Indeed, for cross-border alliances, this is definitely not the case—instead, at least some individuals (e.g. the top management team) within any organization formed by a cross-border alliance are embedded in multiple organizational and country cultures, and perhaps also multiple industry cultures.

EXHIBIT 1. The Dynamics of Cultural Diversity in Cross-Border Alliances

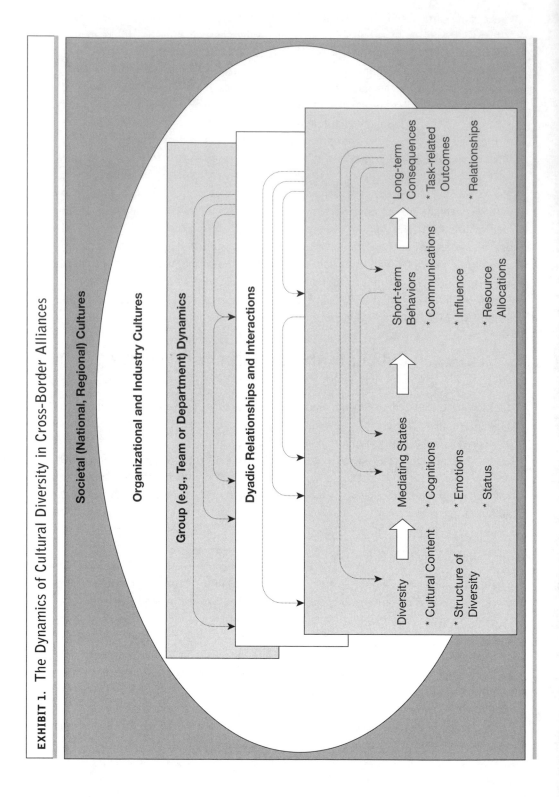

Recognizing that cultural diversity can be created in many ways, the model shown in Exhibit 1 organizes constructs into four general categories that are linked as follows: cultural diversity → mediating states and processes → short-term behavioral manifestations → longer term consequences. The model can be used to analyze the behavior of individuals, dyads, and larger social units, such as work teams or departments.

Beginning on the left, the content and structure of cultural diversity are viewed as partial determinants of the way people feel and think about themselves and each other. The *content* of cultural diversity simply refers to the specific values, norms, language, and other elements of a culture. As already noted above, multiple levels of cultural content will be relevant in most situations. For cross-border alliances, societal, organizational, and industrial cultures are likely to be particularly salient. However, demographic cultures also are likely to play a role in shaping the interactions between individuals and groups within the organization.

The *structure* of cultural diversity refers to how cultural differences are distributed within the focal unit (e.g. IJV, IM&A, management team, business unit). The specific circumstances of a particular cross-border alliance mean that both the structure and content of cultural diversity may be somewhat unique to each alliance. For example, in the combination phase of IM&As, the structure of organizational diversity within the integration teams is likely to be balanced (or, some might describe it as polarized), especially if the partners try to merge the cultures of the two companies. If each of the partners is a domestic firm with little societal-level diversity represented, then the integration team also will be balanced in terms of societal cultural diversity. In this situation, the alignment of societal and organizational membership reinforces the cultural divide between the subgroups within the team, creating a cultural fault-line (Lau and Murnighan, 1998).

Next, consider the example of an IJV that is located outside the countries of the two parents and staffed completely with local talent. In that case, there may be little societal diversity within the IJV. Nevertheless, if employees were hired from the local external labor market, a great deal of organizational and industry-based diversity may be present. If the local labor market for jobs is demographically diverse, and if employment practices encourage hiring across the full range of the labor force, then demographic diversity will also be present in the workforce. Under this scenario, the expectation might be that the structure of diversity should not create a strong fault-line or polarization between any two groups. Nevertheless, cultural fault-lines and polarization may arise even under this type of scenario.

In the Davidson-Marley IJV, a cultural fault-line was inadvertently created among employees in the Dutch manufacturing plant. The fault-line developed because employees were hired in two distinct waves. The first group of 100 employees who were hired worked in a start-up operation and were deeply involved in working out the details of how the operation was run. After the new plant was established and growing, the IJV hired 200 more employees. For this wave of hiring, they sought people who were willing to accept and adjust to the management practices of the now-thriving operation, and who could work well in teams. Thus, differences in the job tenure of employees were aligned with differences in personality. Furthermore, due to the timing of the hires, these two waves of employees found themselves working under different employment contracts. And, due to the seniority differences in the two groups, those who were hired first were always assigned to more advanced job categories and received higher pay. As a result, a fault-line was created, which roughly divided employees into two groups: the early hires had more seniority tended to be more individualistic and worked under one type of employment contract, while the second group tended to work well in teams, had less seniority, and generally were paid less. This divide within the workforce created unexpected conflicts, and in retro-spect, the HR manager realized that it would have been better to hire on a continuous basis rather than two distinct groups of employees who did not see themselves as all being part of the same company culture (van Sluijs and Schuler, 1992).

The *content* of cultural differences has received the most attention in past research. However, research on group dynamics clearly shows that the *structure* of cultural diversity has important consequences. For example, inter-group conflict is almost inevitable when cultural fault-lines are present, regardless of the cultural values or norms that separate the groups. In contrast, when differences are more broadly distributed and diffuse, problems of coordination may be more problematic than overt conflict, especially in the early stages of a group's development. However, given enough time, very diverse multinational teams in which there is no opportunity for nationality-based cliques to form can overcome these problems and outperform more homogeneous teams in the long run (Earley and Mosakowski, 2000).

HOW CULTURAL DIVERSITY INFLUENCES EMPLOYEES' THOUGHTS AND FEELINGS

The forms of diversity present in an organization can influence how people think and feel. Eventually, their thoughts and feelings are translated into observable behaviors. Attraction, discomfort, admiration, stereotyping, perceptions of status and power—all of these thoughts and feelings are influenced by cultural diversity.

Emotional Reactions

Regardless of the basis for identifying people as similar or dissimilar (e.g. commonality of national, industry, organizational and/or demographic culture), people tend to feel more comfortable with and positive about others who they perceive to be similar. Loyalty and favoritism characterize interactions with similar others while distrust and rivalry characterize interactions with those who are dissimilar. The tendency to be attracted to and biased in favor of similar others is so pervasive that it operates even when people judge their similarity based on meaningless information (such as randomly determined group membership).

For work teams and larger organizational units, feelings of attraction or liking among members translate into group cohesiveness. Although there has been little research on the effects of shared societal, industry, or organizational cultures on group cohesiveness, there is a great deal of evidence showing this effect of similarity for other background characteristics, including age, gender, race, education, prestige, social class, attitudes, and beliefs (Jackson et al., 1995). As will soon become apparent, this similarity(attraction(cohesiveness dynamic can have important consequences for the emotional landscape within which members of cross-border alliances conduct their work.

Cognition

Cultural diversity also shapes the cognitive landscape of cross-border alliances. In order to simplify and make manageable a world of infinite variety, people naturally rely on stereotypes to inform their evaluations of others, guide their behavior towards others, and predict the behavior of others. Mental models are another cognitive short-cut for making sense of a complex world and deciding how to act. In work organizations, the mental models of employees may include beliefs about the priority assigned to various performance objectives (e.g. speed versus friendliness in customer inter-actions) as well as beliefs about how cause-and-effect relationships (e.g. what a group should do if it wants to increase speed). The content of stereotypes and mental models reflect past experiences, and are almost inextricably bound up with the content of a culture. This point is illustrated by cross-cultural research on negotiations and conflict resolution. Mental models of negotiation and conflict resolution appear to be some-what culture bound. Although mental models in various cultures tend to share some common objectives, such as minimizing animosity, differences become apparent when one considers the beliefs people hold about how best to achieve this objective (Leung, 1997).

Another ubiquitous mental model that appears to vary across cultures is the model of personal and environmental influences people use as explanations for their own and others' behaviors. For example, whereas North Americans explain behavior as due to a person's disposition, Hindu Indians tend to view forces in the environment as more important determinants of behavior (Miller, 1987).

Stereotypes and mental models do not simply reflect past experience; they influence what aspects of the environment people attend to and they guide the actions people take. Thus, they can either contribute to or interfere with coordinated action. When cultural diversity results in greater diversity of stereotypes and mental models, misunderstandings among employees are more likely, so more time and effort will be needed to avoid or correct the harm that such misunderstandings may cause.

Status

Even in the flattest and most egalitarian social systems, some groups enjoy more status than others. In cross-border alliances, status hierarchies may reflect differences in the sizes and reputations of the organizations involved, as well as the specific circumstances of the alliance. Although we know of no research that has investigated status dynamics within joint ventures or mergers, anecdotal evidence suggests that employees of acquired firms experience feelings of lost or lower status. Status relationships may also be shaped by an acquiring firm's use of the absorption approach to managing cultural diversity, in which the culture of the acquired firm is subsumed or obliterated and the culture of acquiring firm becomes dominant.

Although cultures differ in the role that status plays in shaping interactions, status differences are recognized in all cultures. The dysfunctional effects of status differences are likely to be greatest when low status individuals have resources or expertise that the work group needs to perform their task, and high status people do not. Compared to those with lower status, higher status persons display more assertive non-verbal behaviors during communication; speak more often, criticize more, state more commands, and interrupt others more often; have more opportunity to exert influence, attempt to exert influence more, and actually are more influential. Consequently, lower status members participate less. Because the expertise of lower-status members is not fully used, status differences inhibit creativity, contribute to process losses, and interfere with effective decision-making.

Status characteristics also create dissatisfaction and discomfort. Initially, group members behave more positively toward higher status members. Low-status team members often elicit negative responses from others and because of their low status they must absorb the negative reactions rather than respond and defend their positions.

In newly formed cross-border alliances, observed conflicts often are attributed to disagreements that reflect an ongoing contest over the establishment of a status hierarchy among the members of the organization. In the case of acquisitions, the status hierarchy is perhaps most quickly established, with higher status going to members in the acquiring firm. In deals described as mergers, however, power-sharing structures may be set up to communicate the message that employees from the two firms are to be accorded equal status. Such structures seldom endure, however, and a clear status hierarchy eventually emerges. Similarly, joint ventures often are structured to communicate a message of equality among the partner firms. Inevitably, however, status hierarchies emerge and become established within the joint venture firm (e.g. see Yan and Luo, 2001).

SHORT-TERM BEHAVIORAL REACTIONS TO CULTURAL DIVERSITY

Short-term behavioral reactions to cultural diversity refer to observable interactions between people, including communications, resource sharing, and influence attempts.

Communication

Cultures shape the way people communicate in a variety of ways, and because different cultures use different languages and communication styles, misunderstandings are common when people from different cultures attempt to communicate. Despite careful planning for the Davidson-Marley IJV, the American engineers who designed the Dutch manufacturing plant sent measurements calculated in feet, inches and US gallons, which meant that local Dutch engineers had to convert all of the measurements before letting contracts and gaining approval from government officials.

Low-fidelity communication and misunderstandings are not the only short-term manifestations of cultural diversity—and they may not be the most important. Cultural diversity also shapes who speaks with whom, how often and what they speak about. That is, cultural diversity shapes the structure of communication as well as the content. Although they are not well documented, these same dynamics are likely to shape communication networks in cross-border alliances.

Through their communications, employees exercise influence over each other. Influence attempts made for the purpose of changing the attitudes, values, beliefs, and behaviors of others are viewed as particularly potent short-term manifestations of cultural diversity. Ultimately, the meaning that organizational members assign to such influence attempts is likely to determine how effectively the organization uses its resources—including its human resources.

Resource Allocation

Two categories of communication prevalent in organizations are task-related communication and relations-oriented communication, or instrumental and social exchanges. Through task-related communication, members of an organization seek, offer, and negotiate for work-related information and resources. Each person's access to information and resources, in turn, has important consequences for the individual's performance, as well as the group's performance.

Social Influence

The basic dynamics of social influence include attempts aimed at changing the attitudes and behaviors of others as well as the responses made to such attempts. Social influence processes appear to be a universal aspect of group behavior that is found in most cultures (Mann, 1980). Nevertheless, the specific influence tactics used and the means through which conformity is expressed are somewhat culture bound. Comparative studies of social influence reveal a variety of differences among national cultures (Smith, 2001). For example, in collectivist cultures, people are relatively more responsive to influence attempts, and managers from different cultural backgrounds use different influence tactics in their attempts to influence subordinates (Sun and Bond, 1999). Findings such as these suggest that the contours of cultural diversity in an organization are likely to shape how, and how effectively influence is wielded.

LONG-TERM CONSEQUENCES OF CULTURAL DIVERSITY

So far, we have argued that the cultural diversity present in cross-border alliances has important implications for employees' emotions, cognitions, and interpersonal behaviors. In this section, we describe the longer-term consequences that are the reasons why cultural diversity is important for organizations to understand and learn to manage.

Several published reviews of the extensive literature addressing this topic suggest that cultural diversity can affect organizations and individuals in a variety of ways

—some effects are potentially beneficial and others may be detrimental; some are directly relevant to the organization's performance and others are personally relevant to individual employees. (For more details, see Jackson et al., 2003; Jackson and Joshi, 2010).

Potential Benefits of Cultural Diversity

In alliances that adopt either a blending approach or a new organization approach, it is likely that the executives who promoted the alliance believed that (a) the creation of an alliance would enable the partners to learn from their differences, and/or (b) the new organization would approach issues in new and innovative ways that were less likely to be found in either of the partner organizations.

As we noted above, cross-border alliances are often viewed as learning opportunities—partners may hope to learn from each regarding new technologies, new markets, new industries and so on. The establishment of NUMMI by Toyota and General Motors is a well-known example of a US automaker's attempt to learn about the lean manufacturing methods that were being used so successfully in Japan. Conversely, Toyota was able to gain access that enabled them to learn about the competitive strategies of their partner and to more easily monitor developments within the US auto industry (Doz and Hamel, 1998).

When learning is cited as an objective for alliances, the learning process often is depicted as one partner learning something that the other partner already knows. In other words, learning is viewed as knowledge transfer. For knowledge transfer opportunities to be valuable, the two partners must have different knowledge bases— for example, one partner may hope to acquire knowledge that the other partner has about a national market and its culture, a different industry, or a different technology or management system, etc. This view of learning may understate the value of diversity in alliances where learning is a key objective, however, because it ignores the potential value of diversity as a catalyst for creativity and innovation.

Creativity often arises when new problems are identified or new solutions are developed to address well-known problems. Generating *new* knowledge and new understanding are the heart of creativity. For teams working on tasks that require developing new and creative solutions to problems, diverse perspectives seem to be beneficial on several counts. During the environmental scanning that occurs in the earliest phase of problem-solving, people with diverse perspectives can provide a more comprehensive view of the possible issues that might be placed on the group's agenda. Subsequently, discussion among members with diverse perspectives can improve the group's ability to consider alternative interpretations and generate creative solutions that integrate their diverse perspectives. As alternative courses of action and solutions are considered, diverse perspectives can increase the group's ability to foresee a wide range of possible costs, benefits, and side-effects. Finally, diversity can enhance the group's credibility with external constituencies, which should improve their ability to implement their creative solutions (Jackson, 1992).

It seems reasonable to assume that the presence of diversity creates opportunities for learning—including learning that occurs through knowledge transfer and learning that is associated with creativity and innovation. Unfortunately, however, there has been very little research on how individuals or larger organizations can take advantage of such learning opportunities. In fact, there are many reasons to believe that organizations often are not able to take advantage of the learning opportunities that diversity presents because cultural diversity also generates conflict and turnover.

Detrimental Effects of Cultural Diversity

Cultural diversity seems to interfere with the development of cohesiveness among members of an organization. An important caveat to note is that this conclusion is based almost exclusively on research investigating the cultural diversity associated with demographic differences. Nevertheless, the pattern of greater diversity resulting in lower levels of cohesiveness has been found for diversity in age, gender, race, education, prestige, social class, attitudes and beliefs.

Low levels of cohesiveness can be detrimental to both organizations and individual employees. The positive feelings of attraction to co-workers that is present in a cohesive organization promote helping behavior and generosity, cooperation, and a problem-solving orientation during negotiations. Cohesiveness may also translate into greater motivation to contribute fully and perform well as a means of gaining approval and recognition. If cultural diversity reduces these positive social behaviors, the performance of individuals as well as the organization as a whole is likely to suffer.

In addition to lowering feelings of attraction and cohesiveness among coworkers, dissimilarity often promotes conflict, which may influence one's decision to maintain membership in a group or organization. This was illustrated in a study of 199 top management teams in US banks. During a 4-year period, managers in more diverse teams were more likely to leave the team compared to managers in homogeneous teams. This was true regardless of the characteristics of the individual managers, and regardless of how similar a manager was to other members of the team. Simply being a member of a diverse management team increased the likelihood that a manager would leave (Jackson et al., 1991). Presumably, more diverse teams experienced greater conflict and were less cohesive, creating feelings of dissatisfaction and perhaps increasing the perceived desirability of other job offers. Several other studies have examined the relationship between team diversity and team turnover rates, and most results support the assertion that demographic diversity is associated with higher turnover rates.

GUIDELINES FOR MANAGING CULTURAL DIVERSITY IN CROSS-BORDER ALLIANCES

Organizations that engage in cross-border alliances do so for a variety of reasons. Regardless of their motives behind such alliances, companies need to pay attention to culture up front in order to effectively manage the many forms of cultural diversity present in the new organization. Ideally, the employees who participate in cross-border alliances leverage their differences for the benefit of the organization while at the same time enriching their own experiences. But how can this ideal be achieved, given all of the interpersonal challenges that diversity creates? Here are some guidelines to consider:

GUIDELINE: Before committing to a cross-border alliance, be vigorous in assessing the many types of cultural diversity that are likely to be present in the organization created by the cross-border alliance.

Cultural audits conducted during the process of soft due diligence that precedes alliance formation are perhaps the widely used tools for anticipating cultural differences in the new organization. If cultural differences between partners are judged to be too great, a deal may be halted. More typically, the soft due diligence process is used to develop a plan for changing current management practices or instating new ones. Although a similar approach could be used when planning IJVs, usually formal cultural audits are not conducted before an agreement is reached.

Even when cultural differences are accurately anticipated, they can be difficult to manage. Nevertheless, several principles have proved to be effective for reducing cultural prejudice and its consequences. The following principles were first offered by Allport (1954), and they have since been validated by hundreds of subsequent studies: (see Pettigrew, 1998). Specifically, managers should ensure that participants in the alliance:

1. Create a shared understanding of the objectives for the alliance.
2. Recognize that each partner contributes to the success of the alliance, and thus is deserving of equal esteem and respect.
3. Establish an organizational culture that rewards cooperation between members of different cultural groups, and penalizes behavior that appears to be biased or prejudicial.
4. Provide opportunities for members of different cultural groups to learn about and from each other.
5. Provide opportunities for members of different cultural groups to develop personal friendships.
6. Support activities that encourage everyone to reflect on their own values and gain insights into how their values influence both their own behaviors and the ways that they interpret the behaviors of others.

To maximize the probabilities of success, participants in cross-border alliances need to consider the implications of these six principles for managing each type of diversity present in the alliance and at each evolutionary stage of the alliance. Following these principles is likely to improve the chances of success of all types of cross-border alliances.

As described next, a variety of human resource management practices may be helpful for organizations that wish to follow these principles. Although we describe the role of each area of human resource practice separately, we do not intend to imply that each practice works in isolation of the others. As is true for effectively managing human resources in any organization, a coherent and integrated system of practices is required to achieve the desired results. Together, the entire set of practices should communicate a single message to employees (e.g. see Jackson et al., 2009). For example, Fiat, an Italian automobile company, undertook organization-wide programs that included the reevaluation of international positions as well as organizational culture change. Their approach moved beyond the use of a single intervention—such as new staffing techniques or a training program—to include a systematic, large-scale effort to evaluate and adjust all aspects of how employees were treated (Schneider and Barsoux, 1997).

Work and Organization Design

GUIDELINE: Whenever possible, rely on teams (not individuals) to conduct the activities involved in planning and implementing cross-border alliances.

Throughout all evolutionary stages of alliance formations, teams are a basic form of organization. Prior to alliance formation, teams typically serve to ensure that the perspectives of all alliance partners are represented when key decisions are made. During the early stages of evolution, teams may be used to assess cultural similarities and differences between the partners and plan for their integration. As an alliance evolves, teams may continue to be used to facilitate coordination on daily activities and ensure transfer of learning. In the DaimlerChrylser merger, for example, over 100 integration teams were used to handle coordination between the various functional areas and the different management levels in the organization (Charman, 1999). Most of the practices described below apply to the management of all the various teams and task forces likely to be present in cross-border alliances.

Staffing

GUIDELINE: When making staffing decisions, gather reliable information about how employees' respond to cultural differences. Competencies related to managing diversity should be given at least as much weight as technical competencies.

Throughout the lives of a joint venture or merger, numerous staffing decisions must be made, including decisions regarding who to hire, who to promote, and perhaps who to let go. In addition to ensuring that an alliance is staffed with people who have the technical proficiencies required, staffing practices can improve the organization's effectiveness by identifying individuals who are more likely to be effective working amidst cultural diversity. Staffing practices also should be sensitive to the composition of teams (i.e. the content and structure of cultural diversity).

Staffing for Cross-Cultural Competency

Based on their experiences and a review of the literature, Schneider and Barsoux (1997) proposed a set of behavioral competencies needed for effective intercultural performance. These included: linguistic ability; interpersonal (relationship) skills;

cultural curiosity; ability to tolerate uncertainty and ambiguity; flexibility; patience; cultural empathy; ego strength (strong sense of self); and a sense of humor. When evaluating employees for staffing decisions, competency models such as this one provide useful guidance that can increase an organization's ability to staff its alliances with employees who easily adjust to and enjoy cultural diversity. However, it should be noted that competency models for cross-cultural adjustment often are developed based on the experiences of expatriates. While expatriate assignments may share some similarities with jobs within an international joint venture or merger, there are many differences. Much more research is needed to identify the personal characteristics most likely to contribute to success in these setting. When an organization's strategy requires that it participate in a large number of IJVs and IM&As, it has the opportunity to conduct such research. Doing so can help it further refine its understanding of how various personal characteristics relate to the performance of employees in culturally diverse organizations.

GUIDELINE: When staffing teams and larger work units, avoid creating situations in which strong cultural fault-lines are likely to create unmanageable conflicts.

Staffing for Composition

As we have noted, cross-cultural alliance partners often establish teams to ensure the airing of multiple perspectives prior to decision-making. Especially during the early stages of the alliance's evolution, these teams often are staffed with equal numbers of representatives from each partner involved in the alliance. For example, following a merger, this tactic might be used ensure that the two companies have equal representation in the new top management team. This tactic also is likely to be used when forming the board that oversees an alliance, when staffing integration and transition teams, and so on.

While representational staffing has many benefits, it may inadvertently lead to unnecessary conflict, divisiveness and turnover if it creates teams characterized by strong fault-lines. Fault-lines can be avoided if staffing decisions take into consideration the structure and content of diversity created by a combination of people selected to staff a team. In other words, selecting the "best" people for a team assignment involves more than evaluating the performance potential of individuals— it requires evaluating the performance potential of the team as a whole.

In addition to avoiding the creation of teams or departments with clear faultlines, staffing decisions also need to consider the status dynamics that are likely to arise within a team or organizational unit. When members of a group perceive a clear status hierarchy, lower participation and involvement can be expected from those at the lower rungs of the hierarchy, regardless of their actual expertise and knowledge.

Training and Development

GUIDELINE: Offer training designed to improve employees' skills in managing their diversity, but don't ignore training in technical and business skills.

Training and development activities can address a number of challenges created by the cultural diversity present in IJVs and IM&As. Training to improve cultural awareness and competencies may seem the most relevant form of training for improving inter-cultural relations, but appropriate business training should also be helpful.

Cultural Awareness and Competency Training

Perhaps most obviously, cultural awareness and competency training can quickly teach employees about cultural similarities and differences, and perhaps diminish their reliance on inaccurate stereotypes. Although stereotypes can be resistant to change, they can be modified with sufficient disconfirming evidence.

As implied by our earlier discussion of the many types of cultural diversity present in some IJVs and IM&As, awareness training should not be limited to learning about national cultures—employees may also benefit from information about differences (and similarities) due to regional locations, industries, organizations and membership in various demographic groups. Besides imparting knowledge, effective training provides employees with opportunities to practice and hone their interpersonal skills. Nor should awareness training be viewed as a one-time event. Educational briefings may be helpful initially, but as the alliance evolves, more intensive team-building workshops and joint problem-solving sessions will likely be needed as employees experience the many implications that cultural diversity has for their daily interactions.

Business Training

The potential benefits of cultural awareness training seem obvious, but business training also can improve the alliance's ability to manage its cultural diversity. Business training can help to establish two of the conditions that enable diverse groups to reap the benefits of their diversity: an understanding of shared goals and mutual respect. Unless participants in an alliance believe they share the same interests, they may assume a competitive relationship exists between the alliance partners. Furthermore, unless they understand why the capabilities and resources of each partner are needed to succeed in achieving their shared goal, they may perceive that the contributions of one partner are more important, more valuable, and thus more deserving of respect. Through business training, employees in an alliance can develop an appreciation for how the capabilities and resources of each partner can contribute to success. For example, if IJV partners enter a relationship that is not based on a 50–50 equity relationship, employees in the venture may assume that higher equity partner will ultimately have more influence and control, placing the lower equity partner in a position of lower status. Yet, in such a venture, it is likely that the intangible resources of the lower equity partner are essential to the venture's success (Yan and Gray, 1994). Thus, teaching employees about the complementary value of capital and intangible resources provides employees with a solid foundation for developing mutual respect.

Performance Management

For any organization, performance management is an important and very complex aspect of human resource management. For IM&As, creating a unified performance management system is perhaps the greatest challenge faced by organizations that seek to blend two disparate cultures (Fealy et al., 2001). For IJVs, a major challenge is creating a performance management system that aligns the interests of managers in the venture with those of the parents (Evans et al., 2002). In addition to contributing to employee's performance in the technical aspects of their jobs, performance management systems can improve cross-cultural relations by ensuring that employees' efforts are directed toward shared goals, providing them with feedback that provides insights about how people from other cultures interpret their behaviors, and rewarding them for developing the competencies required to be effective in a culturally diverse organization.

GUIDELINE: Use the performance management system as a communication tool that provides guidance and direction for achieving shared goals and objectives.

Training programs can inform employees about the shared goals of alliance partners, but performance management systems must convince employees that the rhetoric is also the reality. Ideally, at each evolutionary stage, all employees involved will understand how their performance is assessed and how performance assessments relate to the goals for the alliance. Rewards and recognition for performance that contributes to achieving the alliance goals serve to reinforce the message.

GUIDELINE: Use feedback procedures that are sensitive to the cultural norms of the person receiving the feedback.

The norms that govern giving and receiving feedback in various cultures differ greatly, yet in any culture giving and attending to feedback is necessary for maintaining effective relationships. Cultural differences mean that feedback communications are particularly prone to misunderstandings and misinterpretations. One response to such problems is to avoid giving feedback to people from other cultures. Well-designed performance management practices can ensure that employees receive the feedback they need in a culturally appropriate way.

GUIDELINE: Use rewards and recognition to encourage employees to develop their cultural competencies.

Often organizations provide training but do not mandate full participation nor do they reward employees who apply the training lessons in their work. According to a study involving several hundred US organizations, the success of domestic diversity interventions was enhanced when supporting sanctions were in place. Requiring everyone to attend cultural awareness and competency training communicates their importance, as does providing rewards to employees who provide evidence of improvement.

Organizational Development and Change

GUIDELINE: When developing management practices for the formal organization, consider their consequences for the informal organization, and then monitor these consequences systematically.

Organizational development and change activities can serve many purposes during the formation and subsequent management of cross-border alliances. Here we focus on organization development aimed at developing the informal organization. Research and anecdotal evidence alike point to the important role of personal friendships in the success of cross-cultural alliances. For example, in explaining the factors that resulted in a successful joint venture between an Italian and US firm, managers pointed to the strong friendship between the two chairmen of the parent companies. Conversely, the lack of personal friendships between employees at FESA—a joint venture between Japanese Fujitsu and Spanish Banesto—made it difficult for them to develop the level of trust that was required in order for learning and knowledge transfer to occur (Yan and Luo, 2001).

Due to the many forms of cultural diversity that often are present in cross-border alliances, employees may find it more difficult than usual to develop close personal relationships with their colleagues from other cultural backgrounds. Yet, the positive feelings associated with one close friendship with someone from an ''out-group'' culture (e.g. the joint venture partner) are likely to generalize to the entire group (Pettigrew, 1997). Thus, organizational development activities that help employees develop even a few friendships may be quite beneficial to an alliance. As is true for all HRM practices, however, a major challenge is designing activities that have the intended effects across all segments of the organization. Within culturally diverse organizations, this is particularly challenging, because the same assumptions, values and believes will not be shared by all employees.

CONCLUSION

As businesses globalize, they will continue to use cross-border alliances as a means to expand and grow their both operations and knowledge base. To succeed, such businesses must effectively manage the many forms of cultural diversity inherent in such organizations. Although IJVs and IM&As represent only two types of cross-border alliances, our discussion illustrates how cultural diversity can affect alliances of other types. The challenge of managing cultural diversity involves much more than assessing the degree of cultural fit between alliance partners and creating plans to close (or otherwise manage) the cultural gap, for example, by designing a new HRM system. Creating alignment among the formal systems is a necessary first step, but additional efforts are needed to ensure that organizational structures do not create additional barriers to cross-cultural collaboration and to develop a workforce with the competencies needed to work effectively amid cultural diversity.

REFERENCES

Allport, G. W. (1954). The nature of prejudice. Reading, MA: Addison-Wesley.

Best, D. L. and Williams, J. E. (2001). Gender and culture. In D. Matsumoto (Ed.), *The handbook of culture and psychology* (pp. 195–219). Oxford: Oxford University Press.

Bloom, H. (2002). Can the United States export diversity? *Across the Board,* March/April, 47–51.

Brewster, C. (1995). Towards a European model of human resource management. *Journal of International Business Studies, 26,* 1–21.

Brodbeck, F. C. et al. (2000). Cultural variation of leadership prototypes across 22 European countries. *Journal of Occupational and Organizational Psychology, 73,* 1–29.

Charman, A. (1999). Global mergers and acquisitions: The human resource challenge *international focus.* Alexandria, VA: Society for Human Resource Management.

Dickson, M. W., Aditya, R. M., and Chhokar, J. S. (2000). Definition and interpretation in cross-cultural organizational culture research: Some pointers from the GLOBE research program. In N.M. Ashkanasy, C. P. M. Wilderom, and M. F. Peterson (Eds.), *Handbook of organizational culture and climate* (pp. 447–464). Thousand Oaks, CA: Sage.

Doz, Y. L. and Hamel, G. (1998). *Alliance advantage: The art of creating value through partnering.* Boston, MA: Harvard Business School Press.

Eagly, A.,H. and Johnson, B. T. (1990). Gender and leadership style: A meta-analysis. *Psychological Bulletin,* 90: 1–20.

Earley, P. C. and Mosakowski, E. M. (2000). Creating hybrid team cultures: An empirical test of international team functioning. *Academy of Management Journal, 43,* 26–49.

Evans, P., Pucik, V., and Barsoux, J.-L. (2002). *The global challenge: Frameworks for international human resource management.* Boston, MA: McGraw-Hill.

Fealy, E., Kompare, D., and Howes, P. (2001). Compensation and benefits in global mergers and acquisitions. In C. Reynolds (Ed.), *Guide to global compensation and benefits,* 2nd ed. (pp. 25–54). San Diego, CA: Harcourt.

Glunk, U., Heijltjes, M. C., and Olie, R. (2001). Design characteristics and functioning of top management teams in Europe. *European Management Journal, 19,* 291–300.

Hofstede, G. (1991). *Cultures and organizations: Software of the mind.* London: HarperCollins.

Hofstede, G. (1997). *Culture and organizations: Software of the mind* (Rev. Ed.). New York: McGraw-Hill.

Hooijberg, R., and Petrock, F. (1993). On cultural change: Using the competing values framework to help leaders execute a transformational strategy. *Human Resource Management, 32,* 29–50.

House, R. J., Hanges, P. J., Ruiz-Quintanilla, S. A., Dorfman, P. W., Javidan, M., Dickson, M., Gupta, V., and 170 country investigators (1999). Cultural influences on leadership and organizations: Project GLOBE. In W. Mobley, J. Gessner, and V. Arnold (Eds.), *Advances in global leadership,* vol. 1 (pp. 171-234). Stamford, CT: JAI Press.

Jackson, S. E. (1992). Team composition on organizational settings: issues in managing an increasingly diverse work force. In S. Worchel, W. Wood, and J. A. Simpson (Eds.), *Group process and productivity* (pp. 204–261). Newbury Park: Sage.

Jackson, S. E. and Joshi, A. (2010). Work team diversity. In S. Zedeck (ed.), *APA Handbook of industrial and organizational psychology,* vol. 2. Washington, DC: American Psychological Association.

Jackson, S. E., Joshi, A., and Erhardt, N. L. (2003). Recent research on team and organizational diversity: SWOT Analysis and Implications. *Journal of Management, 29,* 801–830.

Jackson, S. E., May, K. E., and Whitney, K. (1995). Understanding the dynamics of diversity in decision making teams. In R. A. Guzzo and E. Salas (Eds.), *Team effectiveness and decision making in organizations,* pp. 204–261. San Francisco, CA: Jossey-Bass.

Jackson S. E., Schuler R. S., and Werner, S. (2009). *Managing Human Resources,* 10th ed. Mason, OH: South-Western Cengage Learning.

Jackson, S. E., Brett, J. F., Sessa, V. I., Cooper, D. M., Julin, J. A., and Peyronnin, K. (1991). Some differences make a difference: individual dissimilarity and group heterogeneity as correlates of recruitment, promotions, and turnover. *Journal of Applied Psychology, 76,* 675–689.

Lau, D. C. and Murnighan, J. K. (1998). Demographic diversity and faultlines: The compositional dynamics of organizational groups. *Academy of Management Review.*

Leung, K. (1997). Negotiation and reward allocation across cultures. In P. C. Earley and M. Erez (Eds.), *New perspectives on international industrial/organizational psychology* (pp. 640–675). San Francisco, CA: New Lexington.

Mann, L. (1980). Cross-cultural studies of small groups. In H. C. Triandis and R. W. Brislin (Eds.), *Handbook of cross-cultural psychology*, vol. 5. (pp. 155–209). Boston, MA: Allyn & Bacon.

Mayer, M. C. J. and Whittington, R. (1999). Strategy, structure, and systemness: National institutions and corporate change in France, Germany, and the UK, 1950–1993. *Organization Studies, 20,* 933–959.

Miller, J. G. (1987). Cultural influences on the development of conceptual differentiation in person description. *British Journal of Developmental Psychology, 5,* 309–319.

Peterson, M. F. and Hofstede, G. (2000). Culture: National values and organizational practices. In N. M. Ashkanasy, C. P. M. Wilderon, and M. F. Peterson (Eds.), *Handbook of organizational culture and climate* (pp. 401–416). Thousand Oaks, CA: Sage.

Pettigrew, T. F. (1998). Intergroup contact theory. *Annual Review of Psychology,* 49: 65–85.

Quinn, R. E. and Rohrbaugh, J. (1983). A spatial model of effectiveness criteria: Toward a competing values approach to organizational analysis. *Management Science, 29,* 363–377.

Ralston, D. A., Kai-Cheng, Y., Wang, X., Terpstra, R. H., and Wei, H. (1996). The cosmopolitan Chinese manager: Findings of a study on managerial values across the six regions of China. *Journal of International Management, 2,* 79–109.

Rhodes, S. R. (1983). Age-related differences in work attitudes and behavior: A review and conceptual analysis. *Psychological Bulletin,* 93: 328–367.

Schneider S. C. and Barsoux, J. (1997), *Managing across cultures.* London: Prentice Hall.

Smith, P. B. (2001). Cross-cultural studies of social influence. In D. Matsumoto (Ed.), *The handbook of culture and psychology* (pp. 361–374). Oxford: Oxford University Press.

Sun, H. and Bond, M. H. (1999). The structure of upward and downward tactics of influence in Chinese organizations. In J. C. Lasry, J. G. Adair, and K. L. Dion (Eds.), *Latest contribution to cross-cultural psychology* (pp. 286 – 299). Lisse, The Netherlands: Swets & Zeitlinger.

Tannen, D. (1990). *You just don't understand: Men and women in conversation.* New York: Ballantine.

van Sluijs, E. and Schuler, R. S. (1994), As the IJV Grows: Lessons and Progress at Davidson-Marley BV. *European Management Journal 12*(3): 315–321.

Williams, J. E. and Best, D. L. (1990). *Measuring sex stereotypes: A multination study.* Newbury Park, CA: Sage.

Yan, A. and Gray, B. (1994). Bargaining power, management control, and performance in United States-China joint ventures: A comparative case study. *Academy of Management Journal 37,* 1478–1517.

Yan, A. and Luo, Y. (2001). *International joint ventures: Theory and practice.* Armonk, NY: Sharpe.

Vladimir Pucik, Paul Evans, and Ingmar Björkman

HUMAN RESOURCE MANAGEMENT ISSUES IN INTERNATIONAL MERGERS AND ACQUISITIONS*

THE M&A PHENOMENON

UNTIL THE 1980S, international mergers and acquisitions (M&As) were relatively rare: governments in many countries did not look fondly on foreigners acquiring local assets. Since then, liberalization of foreign direct investment resulting from multilateral trade agreements has greatly accelerated the M&A phenomenon. And while global mega-deals continue to grab the headlines, more and more cross-border acquisitions take place among small- and medium-sized firms. Understanding the logic of such internationalization strategies, their human resources implications, and mastering their implementation, is therefore becoming one of the HRM competences required of managers worldwide.

The Drivers of International M&A

There are a number of reasons why companies pursue cross-border mergers and acquisitions. Achieving economies of scale and scope, or increasing market share by adding capacity, brands, or distribution channels are probably the most important reasons behind many cross-border M&As.[1]

Larger firms aim to gain market power while at the same time reduce the overcapacity that characterizes many mature industries. Or they pursue large-scale mergers or acquisitions strategies to leapfrog their competitors—who then try to catch up through their own mergers. Smaller firms resort to cross-border deals to leverage their niche competences in new markets more quickly than they could through organic expansion. For these firms, the primary opportunities for value creation are likely to arise from cross-selling existing products or services and from accessing new markets. M&As are also increasingly used to gain fast access to new technologies.

People issues dominate the management agenda in many of these M&As. Indeed, an increasing number of acquisitions are motivated by the need to access talented people and their know-how. The employees may be more valuable than the company's product—price per engineer drives the cost of such deals. In contrast, the strategic driver in other deals is consolidation and cost cutting. There the focus is on workforce reduction, which in some countries may be as tricky as the retention of Silicon Valley entrepreneurs.

How Successful Are Mergers and Acquisitions?

Extensive research has been conducted on the performance of M&As. Early studies reported that only a minority of the deals achieved the promised financial results.[2] Recent academic research and consulting reports are more positive, but even there the contribution of M&As to the value of the acquiring firm is on average close to zero.[3] Sellers virtually always emerge as winners as the buyer typically pays a significant premium for the target.[4] And when buyer overpays, no amount of post-merger integration skills can bring back the value lost when the deal was signed.

However, there is some evidence that the success rate of cross-border deals may be higher than for purely domestic transactions.[5] Several reasons have been suggested for this surprising finding. One explanation is that there tend to be greater complementarities between the parties in international acquisitions.[6] Cross-border acquirers often buy companies in related industries—familiar businesses to which they can add value and, conversely, from which they can gain value by accessing local markets, new products, and local know-how. Further, it appears that there may be less conflict between the parties in international M&As. Domestic acquisitions of competitors are often accompanied by a history of fierce rivalry that is difficult to overcome. Also, the level of integration tends to be lower in cross-border than in domestic acquisitions, leading to less tension between employees in the two units. Finally, it may be that the more overt cross-cultural dimensions of such deals lead buyers to pay more attention to the softer, less tangible, but critical HRM aspects of M&A management.[7]

A Framework for Thinking About M&As

The appropriate approach to integrating the two organizations will depend on the strategic driver behind the acquisition. Each acquisition must be managed in a different way. A simple framework developed by Killing[8] provides a useful overview of different types of acquisition integration (see Figure 1).

Stand-Alone

Sometimes the main rationale behind the merger is to get hold of talented management or other soft skills and capabilities (such as speed of product development).

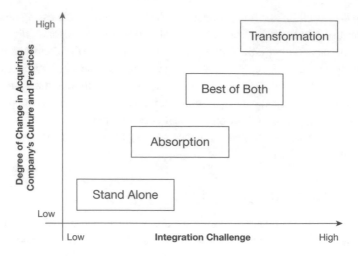

Figure 1. Four Types of Acquisition Integration

Source: Adapted from J.P. Killing (2003), "Improving acquisition integration: Be clear on what you intend and avoid 'best of both' deals," *Perspectives for Managers*, no. 97, 1.

Integration into the acquiring firm can work against this, aggravating the challenges of retention. In this case, the key to success is to protect the new subsidiary from unwarranted and disruptive intrusions from the buyer, though this can be hard to ensure. Even with the best of intentions, there is a danger of creeping assimilation, as the buyer encourages the new unit to work in its way, and to develop systems and processes that match those of the parent organization.

A fundamental question associated with the stand-alone strategy is how the buyer can create value through the acquisition to offset the premium that it has paid for the target. A single booster shot of functional knowledge soon after the closing is one possible approach to create operational synergies and efficiencies. Normally stand-alone is a temporary phenomenon, lasting until conditions change and the acquired unit can be more fully assimilated into the new parent.[9]

Absorption

This kind of acquisition is fairly straightforward, and is most common when there are differences in size and sophistication between the two partners. The acquired company conforms to the acquirer's way of working. Such deals are common when the target company is performing poorly.

Most of the synergies come from cost cutting, along with improvements in systems and processes brought in by the acquiring firm. The key to success is to choose the target well, and to move fast to eliminate uncertainty and capture the available benefits.

The logic of absorption is simple. However, companies are sensitive to public perceptions of being a foreign bully, and they are often hesitant to declare their objective of absorbing the target, fearing that it may compromise the deal. But this often creates confusion and mistrust that make the process more difficult. In contrast,

GE Capital, the financial services arm of General Electric, offers blunt advice to the management of acquired firms: "If you do not want to change, don't put yourself up for sale." GE makes it very clear that the acquired company must now play by GE's rules, and it provides a framework in which to do so.

Best of Both

The option of best of both is pursued in what is often presented as a merger of equals. In theory, best practices are taken from both firms and integrated. There are, however, few genuine mergers of equals. The merger of the German car manufacturer Daimler and its US competitor Chrysler in late 1990s was presented as a merger of equals. In reality, Daimler was larger and clearly the more powerful of the two. Daimler executives soon took control of the whole merged organization.

The scarcity of examples of best of both attests to its difficulty. Putting together the "best" parts of both sides may lead to inconsistencies in the two firms. Another danger is that the integration approach may become too political and time consuming. Who decides what is "best" and based on what criteria? During the integration process, many decisions are interpreted politically, and in the absence of explicit criteria and objective evaluation, the choice of what constitutes best is often viewed as biased.

Saying best of both, without acting accordingly, is likely to backfire as the target employees will view the buyer as untrustworthy.[10] When the Swedish bank Nordbanken and the Finnish bank Merita were combined in a "merger of equals" in the late 1990s, the Finnish employees coined the phrase "Best practices are West practices" ("West" meaning "Swedish," as Sweden is located west of Finland).[11]

Transformation

In contrast to best-of-both acquisitions, which take existing organizational practices as they come, both companies in a transformation merger hope to use the merger to make a clean break with the past. Merger or acquisition can be the catalyst for doing things differently, or reinventing the organization.

For a long time, the creation of ABB through the merger of Asea and Brown Boveri was considered an archetype for transformational mergers. More recently, the merger of pharmas Astra and Zeneca into AstraZeneca could be described as a case of transformation through M&A, as was Lenovo's acquisition of IBM's PC business. The main challenge is always how to manage radical change on top of the integration process.

This kind of merger is complex and difficult to implement. It requires full commitment, with focus and strong leadership at the top to avoid getting trapped in endless debates while the ongoing business suffers. Speed is essential, with top management in the merging companies using the time period immediately after the merger announcement to carry out major changes. Like the best-of-both strategy, the transformation strategy has a better chance of success if key people from both parties are excited by the vision of creating a leading company with superior capabilities.[12]

Key Human Resources Issues

There is no shortage of empirical evidence that attention to "soft" factors or people issues is one of the most critical elements in making an acquisition strategy work. In a pioneering McKinsey study of international M&As, the top-ranked factors identified as contributing to acquisition success are all people related:

- Retention of key talent (identified by 76 percent of responding firms).
- Effective communication (71 percent).
- Executive retention (67 percent).
- Cultural integration (51 percent).[13]

According to another study, published a decade later, the problems remained the same. Differences in organizational culture (50 percent) and people integration (35 percent) were top of the list of M&A challenges—four of the six top issues were people related.[14]

It is hard to find an acquisition where people issues do not matter. When the objective is to establish a new geographic presence, then managing cross-cultural, language, and communication issues heads the list of priorities. When the aim is to acquire new technology or competences, retaining key technical staff or account managers is the principal challenge. When the objective of the deal is consolidation, dealing effectively with redundancies at all levels is the dominant concern.

Based on these observations, it may seem natural that the HR function should play a significant role in all phases of an acquisition. Yet the overall influence of HR during the acquisition process as a whole is patchy. In addition many companies have neither the resources nor the know-how to give the HR domain the priority it merits.[15]

When Should HR Get Involved?

As we noted earlier, the scope and importance of people issues depends on the type of acquisition—transformational acquisitions demand far more attention to HRM than stand-alone acquisitions. But regardless of the type, the HR function can make a substantial contribution at all stages of the acquisition process.

However, the reality is often different. HR does not get involved until relatively late in the process. According to a Towers Perrin/SHRM study, HR was fully involved in the M&A planning in less than a third of responding firms.[16] HR involvement is marginally higher during the negotiation stage, but it is only after the deal is signed that 80 percent of firms see HR as fully engaged. It is obviously not easy for HR to ensure the smooth implementation of the deal when it has little or no part in shaping it. US-based companies seem to put rather more emphasis on early HR involvement than their European counterparts.

One reason for keeping HR out of the room is the secrecy surrounding most acquisitions before the bid or agreement is announced. In many companies, communication about pending acquisitions is treated as strictly confidential, for commercial as well as regulatory reasons and HR is not seen as indispensable. A determining factor is whether the top HR executive is a member of the senior management team and a full participant in the strategy planning process. HR is unlikely to be involved if is not already perceived as a valuable contributor to business and strategy development.

FROM PLANNING TO CLOSING

A typical cross-border acquisition starts with the development of the acquisition strategy and the selection of a target—a process often led by a dedicated acquisition team. An integral part of the selection process is the evaluation of the target—due diligence. The due diligence process should cover all the important HRM considerations, including a human capital audit and a cultural assessment. This examination moves to center stage when formal negotiations begin with the target or when a hostile takeover bid is launched.

Setting Up the Acquisition Team

Some multinationals have a special acquisition unit that is involved in the planning and execution of every transaction.[17] Much of what is done during the planning and negotiation stage requires specialized and often highly technical financial and legal expertise. However, such units should not work in isolation from the managers who will have the responsibility for implementing the strategy and/or managing the acquisition. In some firms, such as GE, the future business leader and the designated HR manager are part of the acquisition team from the very beginning.

An important component of acquisition planning is making sure that the company has the appropriate leadership team in place. When Renault considered acquiring a 37 percent stake in Nissan, Renault's Chairman Louis Schweitzer commented: "If I didn't have Mr. Ghosn [sent by Renault to Tokyo to become president of Nissan], I would not have done the deal with Nissan. That means I sent him in because I had the absolute confidence in his ability."[18]

In international acquisitions, the approach toward human resources cannot be separated from the cultural and social context. Often the company may not have any expertise in the particular geographical area, so early planning on how to mobilize the necessary resources to guide the firm through unfamiliar territory is important. It is also important at any early stage to orient the members of the due diligence team, who are likely to be selected for their analytical and technical skills rather than for their familiarity with the culture and environment of the target firm. When CEMEX based in Mexico acquired RMC in Europe, more than 300 people received training on what to look for in the environments and cultures where RMC operated.

HR can serve as a valuable resource and sounding board here. No one can expect HR to have all the information on the quality of human assets and the characteristics of the organizational culture readily available. In the words of a GE HR manager who participated in planning a number of acquisitions: "Even if you know the industry, each acquisition is different: different culture, legal framework, management team in place. We are at the table not because we have all the answers, but we certainly know the questions that we have to ask."

HR Due Diligence

Good acquisition planning is not possible without good data, and HR due diligence is no exception. However, in cross-border acquisitions, the acquisition team must be sensitive to the fact that attitudes toward acquisition due diligence vary from country to country.[19] Under Anglo-Saxon practice, lawyers and their clients expect comprehensive due diligence before the acquisition is completed. In other countries, due diligence may be interpreted as intrusive at best, or as a sign of mistrust or bad intentions on the buyer's part. Getting information about the people side of the business, such as the quality of the management team, requires particular care.

Where does this information come from? Former employees, industry experts, consultants, executive search firms, and customers who know the company are usually good sources of information. Cultivating some of these sources on a longer-term basis helps to mediate the constraints of confidentiality. Some of these data may be in the public domain, and Web-based search engines can speed up finding information. Once the agreement to close the deal is reached, HR records and interviews with managers in the target company can be used to supplement and verify the assessment.

The transparency and accessibility of this information varies from country to country. Companies often bemoan lack of information when in fact the real issue is lack of familiarity with local sources. However, HR due diligence is not just about collecting data to avoid potential financial landmines or to prepare for harmonizing the policies and practices quickly after the deal. It is more important to understand the impact of the HR system on the values, norms, and behaviors of the company to be acquired. It is not easy to do this well, even in domestic acquisitions. Less then a third of US HR professionals consider that HR was effective in the due diligence phase of acquisitions.[20]

An important component of due diligence process is talent identification. Talent identification has a number of important facets: ensuring that the target company has the talent necessary to execute the post-acquisition strategy; identifying which individuals are critical to sustaining the value of the deal; and assessing any potential weaknesses in the management cadre. It is also important to understand the motivation and incentive structure, and to highlight factors that may impact retention.

Cultural Due Diligence

In 2008, 670 executives from multinationals from around the world participated in a survey of cross-border M&As and identified organizational cultural differences as the most significant issue in recent M&As.[21] Despite this, culture assessment is generally not given much priority *before* the deal is done. In one survey of European executives actively involved in mergers and acquisitions, assessment of cultural fit came close to the bottom of the list.[22] It is therefore not surprising that culture clashes often are a source of difficulties *after* the deal is done.

The purpose of cultural assessment is to evaluate factors that may influence organizational fit, to understand the future cultural dynamics as the two organizations merge, and to plan how the cultural issues should be addressed if the deal goes forward. Cultural assessment can be formal or informal, based on a variety of potential sources, such as market intelligence, external data, surveys, and interviews. It is important to have at least a rudimentary framework that helps to organize the issues and draw the proper conclusions.[23]

Some companies use cultural assessment as an input into a stop/go decision about an acquisition. For example, Cisco avoids buying companies with cultures that are substantially different from its own, recognizing that it would be difficult to retain key staff if they cannot decide how a business should be run. On the other hand, GE Capital is less concerned with retention, and is more aggressive in Its approach— cultural assessment is also a "must" but mainly as a tool to plan integration. It is impossible to say that one approach is better than the other, but both companies are clear about what is important and how they want to get there.

Cultural assessment is not just a question of assessing the other company's culture, it is also a matter both of having a clear culture oneself and understanding it. The "know thyself" adage applies equally well to companies as it does to people. The criteria used in cultural assessment of the target will to a great extent reflect the cultural attributes of the buyer.

Conventional wisdom suggests that companies should avoid any deal where cultural differences might be a problem. This is rooted in the assumption that cultural differences are largely unmanageable and will undermine the success of a deal. However, the empirical evidence suggests that the fear of cultural differences may be exaggerated. For example, results from a recent study suggest that cross-border acquisitions may perform better in the long run if the acquirer and the target come from countries that are culturally more disparate.[24]

The research on this topic offers two important conclusions. First, it is important to distinguish between differences in organizational and national culture. Second, the nature of the deal matters.[25] For example, in a related acquisition that needs higher levels of business integration, cultural differences can create tensions that make integration more difficult. However, these differences are more likely to be due to differences in organizational than national culture. In addition, cultural differences were actually found to be positively associated with post-acquisition performance in M&As that required lower integration, probably due to increased opportunities for mutual learning.[26]

In today's global business environment, companies have to manage the risks, disaggregating imprecisely defined cultural issues into discrete, manageable elements. Strategic imperatives drive many potential M&A deals forward, and firms no longer have the luxury of avoiding potential deals on the grounds of cultural issues.

Closing the Deal

Until the agreement to acquire is signed (or a hostile tender offer is announced), much of the vital HR involvement In the acquisition process will go on behind the scenes. Immediately after the deal is signed the scope of the HRM agenda expands rapidly. Companies often wait until closing before considering people issues because the period between the signature of the agreement and implementation can be anywhere from several months to a year. This time should not be wasted.

The first priority is to complete the due diligence, now with full access to data. This is a sensitive period, and the first impressions of the new foreign owners may last for a long time. For example, when interviewing, opinions should be solicited from everyone, not just those who speak the new owners' language. In many countries, union consent is desirable, if not essential, if the transaction is to go ahead. As in all labor relations, honest and open communication with union representatives is most effective.

The people you hire to work on your behalf may tell local employees a great deal about your intentions and capabilities. A European pharmaceutical firm made a friendly offer to buy one of its large but struggling Japanese distributors. To facilitate the transaction, the company retained a local HR consulting group that, unknown to the Europeans, had a reputation for a confrontational approach to post-merger restructuring. The result: employees with outside opportunities headed for the door, while the rest set up a union with the aim of blocking the acquisition. Faced with unexpected resistance, the offer had to be withdrawn.

As discussed before, the acquiring company needs to have the key components of the HRM implementation blueprint in place by the time the acquisition is ready to close. This includes the organizational structure and reporting relationships, the composition of the new team, timeline for action on specific HRM issues, and so on. The final element of pre-closing activity is the selection of the integration manager and the transition team who will be charged with the responsibility for combining the organizations.

THE POST-MERGER INTEGRATION PROCESS

People often talk about "the first 100 days" of a merger, and how this sets the tone for the longer task of integration. During this time, it is the responsibility of HR to ensure a sharp focus on people and leadership issues, making sure that transitional organization and teams are in place on day one, fully prepared to deal with the complexities of a cross-cultural deal. The next step is staffing—who will stay and who will go? The evaluation of talent that was initiated before closing the deal continues, but it is not easy to assess people quickly in a foreign setting.[27] And finally, what kind of policies and practices should be introduced in the acquired firm? Human resource management provides a subtle means of control by which a parent company can influence the acquired unit, so the choice of HRM approach is intrinsically linked to the overall strategy for integration.

Managing the Integration Process

The pressure of additional work created by the need to manage integration, on top of everyone's day job, can be formidable. If you add to this the risk of intercultural misunderstanding, natural tendency to resist change, and the shortage of qualified managers, you have a recipe for an overstressed, underperforming organization. Unsurprisingly, the difficulties surrounding the integration process are frequently blamed for acquisition performance falling short.

As all acquisitions require some degree of integration (even stand-alone deals generally require the integration of financial reporting systems), it is important to tailor integration to the purpose of the acquisition and the characteristics of the companies involved. The integration process requires engaged leadership and often a dedicated integration manager working with a transition team. In most cases, moving with speed is an advantage. A critical part of the process is focusing on the areas where the acquisition can create new value, while maintaining the ongoing business.

Leading the Integration Process

The signing of the deal is often followed by the appointment of new leadership. Who should head the acquired organization? Ideally, it should be someone familiar with both sides, for example, a local executive already in a leadership position with the buyer or another foreign company—but these executives are usually in short supply.

In our research, lack of clear vision and the leadership style of top management consistently topped the list of factors contributing to failed acquisitions. Three capabilities are seen as fundamental to the effectiveness of the top leadership: a credible new vision, a sense of urgency, and effective communication.[28] In interviews for a study of M&As in Japan, respondents indicated again and again that creating a sense of urgency around implementing the vision and maintaining momentum in driving change are the keys to success.[29] The ability to articulate vision must be accompanied by soliciting feedback and engaging in two-way communication.

Another critical factor is getting leadership selection right at the outset. Instability in the top management team seems to be correlated with failed integration. When Vodafone bought J-Phone—a Tokyo-based mobile telecom company—the top position in J-Phone was occupied by four executives in three years. Although the business strategy remained nominally the same, expectations changed as the company moved from expatriate to local leadership and back again, leading to confusion and instability. Differences in leadership and communication style between each generation of executives only enhanced tensions already existing in the organization. At the end of three years, the company—by now deep in the red—was sold to a local competitor, Softbank, which brought it back to profitability within six months.

The Role of the Integration Manager

The integration of the acquired company with the new parent is a delicate and complicated process. After closing the deal, and while the new management team is not fully in place, the due diligence team disbands or goes on to another deal, taking its knowledge of the acquired company with it. To avoid a vacuum, companies are increasingly turning to dedicated integration managers, supported by transition teams, to guide the process immediately after the deal is concluded.

Integration managers are transition specialists. Their role is to make sure that timelines are followed and that key decisions are taken while removing bottlenecks and making sure that speed of integration is maintained. They help to engineer the short-term successes that are essential to create positive energy around the merger. They should also communicate key messages across the new organization and identify new value-adding opportunities.[30]

An important aspect of the job is helping the acquired company to understand how the new owner operates and what it can offer in terms of capabilities. The integration manager can help the firm take advantage of the owner's resources, forge social connections, and help with essential but intangible aspects, such as interpreting a new language and ways-of-doing-things. This is important because, outside the acquisition team, few people will be familiar with the other organization.

The integration manager is also the information "gatekeeper" between the two sides, protecting the acquired business from the eager embrace of an owner who could unintentionally undermine the integration. New information requirements must be submitted in a very specific format, and reports can be embedded in incomprehensible jargon—indeed, corporate HR is often the guilty party here. When Nokia acquires small hi-tech venture companies, one of the rules is that all requests for information from the parent go to the integration manager, who decides whether and how the unit should comply with the request.

What skills does the integration manager need? First of all, deep knowledge of the parent company—where to get information, whom to talk to, how the informal system works. Flexible leadership style is also important—being tough about deadlines, yet a good listener and able to relate to people at different levels in the organization. Other preferred traits are comfort with ambiguity, emotional and cultural intelligence, and the willingness to take risks.[31] These jobs are often stepping stones into corporate leadership roles.

The Responsibilities of the Transition Team

In most acquisitions, integration teams and task forces support the integration manager. Since many of these teams are expected to start work on the first day after the deal is closed, the identification of potential members should be part of the due diligence process. HR professionals are often key members of the team.

The specific charter of the transition team depends on the integration approaches we discussed earlier (stand-alone, absorption, best of both, and transformation). Prioritization is critical. Too many task forces and teams create coordination problems, conflict, and confusion. In the ill-fated DaimlerChrysler merger, the complexity of a transition structure involving over a hundred different projects was one of the reasons why its integration process rapidly came to a standstill.[32] Integration projects should focus on tasks with high benefits at low risk, leaving those with greater risk or lower benefits until later. As one experienced M&A manager stated, "We only attack things that will bring benefits to the business. We do not integrate just for the sake of integrating."

Another task is to spell out the logic of the new business model and translate it into operational targets. This is important in international acquisitions, where big-picture statements from the corporate center may mean little in a different national and business context. The transition team can also serve as a role model for how the new organization should act. By facilitating personnel exchanges, the transition team can help both sides to develop a better understanding of each other's capabilities.

It is important that the transition team has authority. One of the factors undermining Daimler's (partial) acquisition of Mitsubishi Motors was that local Japanese employees perceived the mostly German integration managers as transients and ignored many of their decisions. Why? The locals were keenly aware that the team was not empowered to make independent decisions—most had to be approved in Stuttgart—so there was no need to take them seriously.[33]

As many successful acquirers have learned, integration teams are most effective when members come from both companies. A good example is Air France/KLM, where mixed integration teams were credited with the success of this airline merger relative to others in that industry.[34] People who are suited for a transition team usually have a mix of functional and interpersonal competences (including cross-cultural skills), backed up by strong analytical skills. Having an ability to accept responsibility without full authority and being effective in mobilizing resources across organizational boundaries are especially important. Consequently, these roles provide good development opportunities for those with high potential.

Moving with Speed

When executives are asked what they learned from their M&A experiences, they often say, "We should have moved faster, we should have done in nine months what it took us a year to do." GE, for example, has cut the 100-day process back to 60–75 days because it learned how to move faster and developed the tools to do so. Speed is essential: during the integration process insufficient attention is being paid to what really counts—the customers. According to GE:

> Decisions about management structure, key roles, reporting relationships, layoffs, restructuring, and other career-affecting aspects of the integration should be made, announced, and implemented as soon as possible after the deal is signed, within days if possible. Creeping changes, uncertainty, and anxiety that last for months are debilitating and immediately start to drain value from an acquisition.[35]

A survey of European acquisitions of US high-technology firms in Silicon Valley reported that speed of integration was a key driver of successful post-merger integration—but also one of the most problematic.[36] The understanding of "fast" by European acquirers (usually large, established companies with entrenched routines and procedures) was very different from Silicon Valley norms. This created confusion, frustration, and ultimately a loss of market opportunities.

Restructuring is often an essential step in realizing the necessary synergies. Restructuring should not be confused with integrating, but the rule is similar: it should be done *early, fast, and only once.* One problem jeopardizing the success of many acquisitions, motivated by good intentions, has been a tendency to restructure slowly to avoid excessively painful human change. But while time is spent helping people to adjust, competitors come along and take away the business.

A Japanese HR executive with extensive M&A experience with foreign firms in Japan was unambiguous in her assessment: "When you're changing something, you must do it all in one go, as quickly as possible. It becomes much harder to make small changes later on, when you would have to renegotiate every small detail. If you don't compromise at first, it will be better in the long run."[37]

Sometimes, foreign acquirers' fear of cultural backlash slows down the process. In another foreign-acquired company in Japan, the implementation of several elements of performance-based global HR policies was suspended for two years to give employees a chance to adapt. In retrospect, the company's local CEO thinks this may have been overcautious. "I think perhaps the grace period could have been a bit shorter. Some people got too comfortable for their own good. I think I may have been a bit too lenient because foreign companies are always criticized for being too harsh, for being vultures."[38]

The other dimension of speed is the focus on delivering quick, visible wins, such as new sales generated through a joint effort, or improvements based on shared practices. It is important to take time to celebrate each success and to communicate the accomplishments to the whole organization. A quick win can motivate target employees by offering tangible proof that the merger or acquisition was a step in the right direction, and shows that their efforts are appreciated.

Yet speed can also have unintended consequences. Bad decisions made under pressure could be avoided if time were spent on a judicious review of the issues. Conversely, good decisions meet resistance when no time is made to explain the new business logic. Again, the optimal speed depends on the strategic intent behind the acquisition and the desired end-state of the new organization.[39] An absorption strategy generally requires more urgency than a best-of-both approach. When the objective of the acquisition is to acquire intellectual capital, the pace of change must be particularly carefully calibrated to minimize the risk of alienating talent, as we will discuss later. Also, it has been argued that successful cross-border acquirers from emerging economies whose aim is to obtain competencies and technologies essential to their global strategies do not see a quick integration as top priority.[40]

People Challenges

Post-merger integration is a change process. All the lessons of change management apply to post-merger integration, including the importance of establishing a vision for the future, the need to restructure to remove resistance and empower champions, and management of the learning process by measuring progress against milestones. Several people challenges impacting the integration process merit particular attention—communication, retaining talent, and managing the process of cultural change.

Communication

In cross-border acquisitions, where cultural differences may intensify tensions due to misunderstandings and distance, the quality of communication is critical. But there are two additional objectives that have to be taken into account in the design of the communication process. One aim of communication is to alleviate the anxiety and stress that accompany every acquisition; another is to provide feedback to top management about the progress of integration and any potential roadblocks.

The need for flawless communication starts on the day the deal is announced. Top management has to express clearly the rationale for the acquisition, the synergies sought, and the degree of integration required.[41] It should also clarify its intentions for the organizational architecture. Although the transition teams can work out the details, the message to shareholders and the public has to be consistent with the message to employees in both the target and acquiring company.

This happens far less often than it should. In the survey of European acquisitions in Silicon Valley cited earlier, every single acquired unit reported lack of clarity about its role in the combined organization.[42] What is the intended end state or vision behind the new organization? Will one side dominate? Will it be the best of both, or will a transformation be attempted? Consistent and coherent communication helps to build morale and reassure those unsettled by the changes.

It is imperative to communicate a *clear vision* of how the acquisition or merger will create value. A well-articulated communication campaign conveys to the workforce that the leadership has a clear vision of where to take the acquisition.[43] Being open and honest about difficult issues is a must. The hard truth may not go down well, but the consequences are easier to handle than the alienation and mistrust that stem from lack of candor.

Effective communication during the integration is a two-way process, from the company to the employees and from the employees back to top management. Irrespective of the chosen road to integration, it is important to monitor progress in order to surface hidden issues and concerns that may create conflict. This is particularly important in cross-border deals where misinterpretations of the language can quickly poison the atmosphere and create confusion. The ability to react when false rumors spread is essential. Feedback must be obtained on how people in the acquired company feel about the integration process so that something can be done before unhappy staff walks away.

Retaining Talent

Many acquired businesses lose key employees soon after a merger, a major contributing factor in failed acquisitions. Research evidence from US acquisitions indicates that the probability of executives leaving increases significantly when their firm is acquired by a foreign multinational. About 75 percent of the firms' top management leaves by the fifth year, with a majority departing during the first two years.[44]

Given these statistics, it is not surprising that when the Chinese company Lenovo acquired IBM's PC division, the board of Lenovo's controlling shareholder allowed the company to proceed with the deal if, and only if, it could retain IBM's senior executives to manage the merged enterprise.[45] But the talent that Lenovo wanted was not limited to senior executives. When the deal closed, the company offered a job to every IBM employee worldwide, with no obligation to relocate or accept a pay cut.

When insufficient attention is paid to retaining talent, and especially if staff cuts are expected, employees often leave—and the best will exit first. After a deal is announced, and well before the actual closing, headhunters inevitably move in to pick off promising managers who are unsure about their career opportunities with the new and distant owner. For employees confronted with the uncertainties of a new organization, a firm job offer from another company looks attractive. Retention of key employees is therefore crucial to achieving acquisition goals in both short-term integration tasks and long-term business performance.

The first step is to know exactly who the talented people are and why they are essential to the new organization. Obtaining this information is not easy. The typical top-down cascading talent identification process often yields flawed results, since local managers may be protective of their people and unable to be objective about what they offer to the new organization. One of the biggest obstacles in international acquisitions is the difference in performance measures and standards.

The initial talent map needs to be refined quickly, through feedback from direct superiors, peers and subordinates, past performance reviews, personal interviews, formal skill assessments, and direct evaluation of performance during the integration period. While multiple sources of assessment are desirable, the quest for precision may slow down the process too much, increasing uncertainty and the risk of defection.

Fast and open communication is another element of success in retaining talent. Cisco's integration team holds small group sessions with all acquired employees on day one to discuss expectations and answer questions. Often, members of the integration team were themselves brought into Cisco through previous acquisitions. They understand what the newly merged employees are going through, so their messages are invested with additional credibility.

A complementary building block for talent retention is providing inducements for employees to stay. Companies often offer stock options, retention bonuses, or other incentives to employees who stay through the integration or until a specific merger-related project is completed.[46] However, even the most elaborate financial incentives cannot substitute for a one-on-one relationship with executives in the acquiring firm. High-potential employees in most companies are used to senior-level attention and without a similar treatment from the acquiring company they question their future and are more likely to depart. Distance may be an obstacle, but it cannot be used as an excuse. Meetings and informal sessions in the early days of the acquisition, if not before the closing, can go a long way toward building the foundations for long-term relationships. When BP-Amoco acquired Arco, it quickly organized Key Talent Workshops—two-day events in which senior BP executives networked with Arco's high-potential employees.[47]

Building the New Culture

The new organization will have a culture, whether by default or design, that may be marked by enduring conflict or may imply acceptance of shared destiny. The process of building a new culture can take a long time; sometimes hankering after the old ways can drag on for a decade. In most cases, this does not help the company move forward. This is the main reason why companies with strong cultures, like GE or Cisco, impose their culture onto the company they acquire. Indeed, they see their success as originating from their culture and the practices built on it. However, while the directions and expectations are clear, full cultural integration takes longer than changing the operating system.

For the integration to happen, desired values and behavioral norms have to be translated into action, guiding the process of culture building or cultural assimilation after an acquisition. Take the French company AXA as an example of the latter. AXA grew via acquisitions from being a local player in the French insurance industry to becoming a top global financial services institution. It makes no pretensions that its acquisitions are mergers of equals, acting quickly to AXA-ize the cultures of the firms it acquires.

Managers from acquired companies commented that one of AXA's most helpful assimilation tools is the company's 360-degree feedback process. The AXA values are encoded in this instrument, and to accelerate the process of cultural integration all managers and professionals in the acquired company go through 360-degree workshops. For most of the managers, this is the first time that they will have been exposed to such a multifaceted assessment, and they find the rigor of the approach reinforces the credibility of AXA as a highly professional organization. It makes the desired culture and values concrete, identifies personal needs for improvement, and leads to follow-up coaching in the AXA way.

The process of integration is not over in 100 days. To assimilate the new employees into the parent firm, the development of common tools, practices, and processes continues. Corporate education and long-term management exchanges are tools that help diffuse the shared culture, as well as the promotion of individuals who embody the values and norms of the desired culture.

M&A AS AN ORGANIZATIONAL CAPABILITY

For many companies, implementing mergers and acquisitions is still a formidable challenge. Yet there is little doubt that companies that master the art of international acquisitions will gain significant market advantage. Many emerging global firms, such as Arcelor-Mittal, CEMEX, and SABMiller view organizational competence in making international acquisitions as one of the supporting pillars of their business strategies.

Why is it so difficult for many multinationals to learn how to acquire successfully? Much of the problem stems from the fact that mergers and acquisitions are never identical. Firms need to disentangle what applies to specific situations and what know-how can be reused. M&A processes consist of a large number of inter-dependent actions and events taking place within two unique merging organizations, which in turn operate within a changing environment. It is therefore difficult for firms to draw valid conclusions about the relationship between decisions and actions taken and their outcomes.[48]

One practical issue to consider is whether it is better to have many individuals involved in acquisitions in order to gain and share wide experience, or to rely on a team of experts. Some companies create a special acquisition unit that is involved in every transaction, which creates a desirable pool of expertise. On the other hand, acquisition competence is increasingly seen as an indispensable generalist skill. This is the GE position, and because HR is one of the functions with a guaranteed seat at any GE acquisitions, smart young employees seek out HR jobs to have a shot at joining the acquisition team.

Managers who have extensive experience in international acquisitions should be viewed as valuable resource for the organization. Part of HR's responsibility is to ensure that it knows who and where they are so they can be mobilized quickly when required. From the employees' point of view, participation in a cross-border acquisition team is a good way to put to use skills accumulated during past international assignments. There is a significant overlap in the behavioral competences required by expatriates and integration team members; both roles demand emotional maturity, cultural empathy, tolerance for ambiguity, and skills in interpersonal communication.

Research evidence shows that the more companies invest in reflecting on their experiences and in codifying their learning in M&A due diligence and integration manuals, the better they perform.[49] The development of tools helps facilitate and speed up the cross-border acquisition process, from due diligence to integration. There is a qualitative difference in the approach to learning here. Acquisition "best practice" books present scenarios and suggest roadmaps for managers to follow. In contrast, acquisition tool kits provide managers with lists of issues and questions to address at each stage in the acquisition, broad guidelines on what to consider, simple and concise instruments, and sources of advice inside and outside the firm.

In repetitive acquisitions, the best practice approach may be sufficient, although most international acquisitions are one of a kind. In all cases, a feedback loop recording what worked, what did not, and what can be added, is essential. However, perhaps the most critical feature is that it should allow the people involved in the process to find the right answers for themselves. All deals are different, so flexibility in arriving at solutions is important.

In acquisitions, learning never stops. Auditing the whole integration process and incorporating any learning into the core planning blueprint completes the cycle—so that the next acquisition can be done even better.

NOTES

* Many of the ideas expressed in this reading are drawn from our recent book (Evans et al., 2011).

1. According to a Conference Board study (1997), the major reasons for M&A were "to achieve competitive size" (61 percent of responding firms) and to gain market share (57 percent).

2. "The Case Against Mergers," *The Economist*, January 1997, pp. 4–7; Kearney, 1999; KPMG, 1999.

3. King et al., 2004. According to a KPMG study published in 2006, 31 percent of deals created value and 26 percent reduced value. Dobbs et al. (2006) reported similar outcomes.

4. The premium is the acquisition price minus the stock exchange value of the target before the deal is announced. The premium tends to vary from a few percent to more than 50 percent.

5. Bleeke et al., 1993; KPMG, 1999; Larsson and Finkelstein, 1999; Bertrand and Zitouna, 2008.

6. Morosini et al., 1998; Vermeulen and Barkema, 2001; Björkman et al., 2007.

7. Morosini et al., 1998; Björkman et al., 2007.

8. Killing, 2003. Haspeslagh and Jemison (1991) offer a well-known alternative framework for examining different types of M&A integration.

9. Killing, 2003.

10. Killing, 2003.

11. Vaara et al., 2003. See also Vaara (2003) for a discussion of how cross-border integration issues can easily become politicized.

12. Killing, 2003.

13. Kay and Shelton, 2000. A study published by Towers Perrin and SHRM Foundation (2002) reported similar results.

14. Marsh et al., 2008, p. 46 (www.mercer.com).

15. KPMG, 1999, p. 15.

16. Schmidt, 2002.

17. Hitt et al., 2001, p. 111.

18. "Renault Steers Forward," *Wall Street Journal Europe*, February 15, 2001, p. 31.

19. Chu, 1996.

20. Schmidt, 2002.

21. Marsh et al., 2008.

22. Angwin, 2001.

23. One frequently used assessment tool is the Denison Culture Survey developed by Dan Denison (Denison et al., 2000). For an example of an internally developed instrument, see "Merging Cultures Evaluation Index" (MCEI) described in Marks and Mirvis (1998), pp. 65–6.

24. Chakrabarti et al., 2009.

25. Stahl and Voigt, 2008.

26. Stahl and Voigt, 2008.

27. Many companies are turning to outside vendors to assure the fairness and objectivity of this process.

28. Sitkin and Pablo, 2005; Fubini et al., 2007.

29. Pucik, 2008.

30. Ashkenas et al., 1998; Ashkenas and Francis, 2000.

31. Ashkenas and Francis, 2000.

32. For contrasting interpretations of the Daimler-Chrysler post-merger integration, see Morosini and Steger (2004) and Vlasic and Stertz (2000).

33. Froese and Goeritz, 2007.

34. Del Canho and Engelfrit, 2008.

35. Ashkenas et al., 1998.

36. Inkpen et al., 2000.

37. Pucik, 2008.

38. Pucik, 2008.

39. Homburg and Bucerius, 2006.

40. Kumar, 2009.

41. According to research conducted by Krug and Hegerty (2001), the decision of top managers in an acquired company to stay rather than leave following an acquisition is positively associated with their positive perceptions of the merger announcement.
42. Inkpen et al., 2000.
43. Marks and Mirvis, 1998, p. 74.
44. Krug and Hegerty, 1997.
45. Harding and Rouse, 2007.
46. Retention bonus guidelines provide desirable consistency, specifying eligibility, amount, performance criteria, etc. Their effect depends, however, on employees' expectations as well as on labor and tax legislation in the countries involved.
47. Corporate Leadership Council, 2000.
48. Levitt and March, 1988; Zollo and Winter, 2002.
49. Zollo and Singh, 2004; Fubini et al., 2007.

REFERENCES

Angwin, D. (2001). "Mergers and acquisitions across European borders: National perspectives on preacquisition due diligence and the use of professional advisers." *Journal of World Business* 36(1): 32–57.

Ashkenas, R.N., L.J. DeMonaco, and S.C. Francis (1998). "Making the deal real: How GE Capital integrates acquisitions." *Harvard Business Review* (January–February): 165–78.

Ashkenas, R.N. and S.C. Francis (2000). "Integration managers: Special leaders for special times." *Harvard Business Review* (November–December): 108–16.

Bertrand, O., and H. Zitouna (2008). "Domestic versus cross-border acquisitions: Which impact on the target firms' performance?" *Applied Economics* 40(17): 2221–38.

Björkman, I., G.K. Stahl, and E. Vaara (2007). "Cultural differences and capability transfer in cross-border acquisitions: The mediating roles of capability complementarity, absorptive capacity, and social integration." *Journal of International Business Studies* 38(4): 658–72.

Bleeke J., D. Ernst, J. Isono, and D.D. Weinberg (1993). "Succeeding at cross-border mergers and acquisitions." In *Collaborating to compete: Using strategic alliances and acquisitions in the global marketplace*, Eds. J. Bleeke and D. Ernst. New York: Wiley.

Chakrabarti, R., S. Gupta-Mukherjee, and N. Jayaraman (2009). "Mars–Venus marriages: Culture and cross-border M&A." *Journal of International Business Studies* 40(2): 216–35.

Chu, W. (1996). "The human side of examining a foreign target." *Mergers and Acquisitions* 30(4): 35–9.

Corporate Leadership Council (2000). *M&A talent management: Identification and retention of key talent during mergers and acquisitions*. Washington, DC: Corporate Executive Board Washington, DC.

Del Canho, D. and J. Engelfriet (2008). "Flying higher together." *Business Strategy Review* 19(1): 34–7.

Denison D., H.-J. Cho, and J. Young (2000). "Diagnosing organizational cultures: Validating a model and method." Working paper 2000–9. IMD, Lausanne.

Dobbs, R., M. Goedhart, and H. Suonio (2006). "Are companies getting better at M&A?" *McKinsey Quarterly* (December): www.mckinseyquarterly.com/ (online only).

Economist Intelligence Unit (2008). *M&A beyond borders: Opportunities and risks*. Marsh, Mercer and Kroll.

Evans, P., V. Pucik, and I. Björkman (2011): *The global challenge: International human resource management*, 2nd ed. Boston, MA: McGraw-Hill.

Froese, F.J. and L.G. Goeritz (2007). "Integration management of Western acquisitions in Japan." *Journal of Asian Business & Management* 6(1): 95–114.

Fubini, D., C. Price, and M. Zollo (2007). *Mergers: Leadership, performance and corporate health*. New York: Palgrave Macmillan.

Harding, D. and T. Rouse (2007). "Human due diligence." *Harvard Business Review* (April): 124–31.

Haspeslagh, P.C. and D.B. Jemison (1991). *Managing acquisitions: Creating value through corporate renewal.* New York: Free Press.

Hitt, M.A., J.J. Harrison, and R.D. Ireland (2001). *Mergers & acquisitions: A guide to creating value for stakeholders.* New York: Oxford University Press.

Homburg, C. and M. Bucerius (2006). "Is speed of integration really a success factor of mergers and acquisitions? An analysis of the role of internal and external relatedness." *Strategic Management Journal* 27(4): 347–67.

Inkpen, A.C., A.K. Sundaram, and K. Rockwood (2000). "Cross-border acquisitions of U.S. technology assets." *California Management Review* 42(3): 50–71.

Kay, I.T. and M. Shelton (2000). "The people problems in mergers." *McKinsey Quarterly* 4: 29–37.

kearney, a.t. (1999). "corporate marriage: Blight or bliss? A monograph on post-merger integration". Chicago: A.T. Kearney.

Killing, J.P. (2003). "Improving acquisition integration: Be clear on what you intend, and avoid 'best of both' deals." *Perspectives for Managers,* no. 97. Lausanne: IMD.

King, D.R., D.R. Dalton, C.M. Daily, and J.G. Covin (2004). "Meta-analyses of postacquisition performance: Indications of unidentified moderators." *Strategic Management Journal* 25(2): 187–200.

KPMG (1999). *Mergers and acquisitions: A global research report - Unlocking shareholder value.* Report, KPMG, New York.

Krug, J. and W.H. Hegerty (1997). "Postacquisition turnover among U.S. top management teams: An analysis of the effect of foreign versus domestic acquisition of U.S. targets." *Strategic Management Journal* 18(8): 667–75.

Krug, J. and W.H. Hegerty (2001). "Predicting who stays and leaves after an acquisition: A study of top managers in multinational firms." *Strategic Management Journal* 22(2): 185–96.

Kumar, N. (2009). "How emerging giants are rewriting the rules of M&A." *Harvard Business Review* (May): 115–21.

Larsson, R., and S. Finkelstein (1999). "Integrating strategic, organizational, and human resource perspectives on mergers and acquisitions: A case survey of synergy realization." *Organization Science* 10(1): 1–26.

Levitt, B. and J.G. March (1988). "Organizational learning." *Annual Review of Sociology* 14: 319–38.

Marks, M.L. and P.H. Mirvis (1998). *Joining forces: Making one plus one equal three in mergers, acquisitions, and alliances.* San Francisco, CA: Jossey-Bass.

Morosini, P., S. Shane, and H. Singh. (1998). "National cultural distance and cross-border acquisition performance." *Journal of International Business Studies* 29(1): 137–58.

Morosini, P. and U. Steger (2004). "Global mergers and acquisitions: Why do so many fail? How to make them successful." In *Managing complex mergers,* Eds. P. Morosini and U. Steger. London: Financial Times/Pearson Education.

Pucik, V. (2008). "Post-merger integration process in Japanese M&A: The voices from the frontline." In *Advances in mergers and acquisitions,* vol. 7, Eds. G.L. Cooper and S. Finkelstein. Bingley, UK: JAI Press.

Schmidt, J.A., Ed. (2002). *Making mergers work.* Alexandria, VA: Towers Perrin and SHRM Foundation.

Sitkin, S.B. and A.L. Pablo (2005). "The neglected importance of leadership in M&As." In *Mergers and acquisitions: Managing culture and human resources,* Eds. G.K. Stahl and M.E. Mendenhall. Stanford, CA: Stanford University Press.

Stahl, G.K. and A. Voigt. (2008). "Do cultural differences matter in mergers and acquisitions? A tentative model and examination." *Organization Science* 19(1): 160–76.

Vaara, E. (2003). "Post-acquisition integration as sensemaking: Glimpses of ambiguity, confusion, hypocrisy, and politicization." *Journal of Management Studies* 40(4): 859–94.

Vaara, E., J. Tienari, and I. Björkman (2003). "Global capitalism meets national spirit." *Journal of Management Inquiry* 12(4): 377–93.

Vermeulen, G.A.M., and H.G. Barkema (2001). "Learning through acquisitions." *Academy of Management Journal* 44(3): 457–76.

Vlasic, B. and B.A. Stertz (2000). *Taken for a ride: How Daimler-Benz drove off with Chrysler.* New York: Wiley.

Zollo, M. and H. Singh (2004). "Deliberate learning in corporate acquisitions: Postacquisition strategies and integration capability in U.S. bank mergers." *Strategic Management Journal* 25(13): 1233–56.

Zollo, M. and S.G. Winter (2002). "Deliberate learning and the evolution of dynamic capabilities." *Organization Science* 13(3): 339–51.

Philippe Lasserre

A MARRIAGE OF REASON: RENAULT AND NISSAN'S GLOBAL STRATEGIC ALLIANCE

O N MARCH 27, 1999, Mr Louis Schweitzer, CEO of Renault, and Mr Yoshikazu Hanawa, CEO of Nissan Motor Co., announced that they had signed an agreement for a total partnership "which will create the fourth largest automobile manufacturer in the world, while providing growth and profitability to the two partners."

The Renault Nissan agreement was closed after eight months of negotiations. Over 100 people on both sides were involved in this process. Renault was aware of the dangers of cultural stereotypes and prejudices and approached the negotiations with great sensitivity. The Japanese daily Asahi acknowledged this by mentioning that "Renault has done everything in order to avoid hurting the pride of Nissan and to avoid appearing as their 'savior'."

According to the agreement, Renault invested Y605b ($5.1b) to acquire 36.8 percent of the shares of Nissan Motor Co. and the associated voting rights, and had the possibility to exercise an option to increase its equity share to 44.4 percent during the next five years at a pre-determined price. On its side Nissan had the possibility to become a shareholder of Renault. It was also agreed that Mr Carlos Ghosn, who was formerly executive vice president of Renault, would become the new COO of Nissan and join its board of directors. All the VPs of Nissan would directly report to him. In addition, two other French top-level managers would become part of Nissan top management. Mr Patrick Pelata, currently director of development and vehicle engineering, would become executive vice president, product planning and strategy, and would join the board of Nissan as well, and Mr Thierry Moulonguet, who was director for investments of Renault, would become managing director, deputy CFO of Nissan. Finally, Mr Yoshikazu Hanawa, CEO of Nissan Motor Co., was offered a position on the board of directors of Renault.

The agreement stated: "The ties that Renault and Nissan are setting up will allow the two companies to develop synergies that will benefit both of them. These synergies will cover procurement, product strategy and research. Common platforms and common mechanical components will be co-developed. The synergies will also include geographical complementarities. Renault and Nissan expect to save $3.3b from these synergies only for the 2000-2002 period."

The announcement of the alliance generated a lot of skepticism among business observers and analysts, since Nissan was nearly bankrupt and Renault, being essentially concentrated in Europe, was considered as a weak player in the global car industry. However, eighteen months later Nissan had returned to profitability and the first signs of synergistic relationships with Renault were benefiting both companies. Against all odds, Carlos Ghosn, accompanied by a group of 20 French executives, had managed to turn around a dying giant. In 2008, the alliance, with 5.8 million cars, ranked 5th among the global automobile companies. In spite of the fact that in early 2009 the two companies were confronted with a drastic drop in sales due to the global financial crisis, the effects of the crisis have been moderated by the benefits accruing from the alliance.

STRATEGIC AND CAPABILITIES FITS

When Schweitzer and his team considered the alliance with Nissan and engaged in serious strategic, operational and financial due diligence in collaboration with some of Nissan's executives, they were convinced that a potential marriage between the two companies made a lot of sense both from the strategic as well as the capabilities fits.

From a strategic point of view Renault was looking for a partner that would give it the global scope for competitiveness in the car industry. Renault was essentially a European player with some productive assets in Latin America. It did not have significant presence in the US and in Asia. According to what Carlos Ghosn said later, "if you want to survive in the car industry you need to be global." Nissan on its side was financially in trouble and needed a rescuer in order to be able to stand again in the industry. So both partners had a strong strategic agenda that they could not fulfill alone. Renault did not have the means to become global and Nissan could not survive without a strong cash and management infusion: they had to ally. Subsequent alliances accomplished by Renault provide an overall coherent picture on the strategy Renault is pursuing to expand internationally. Currently, Renault's other most important alliances are with Dacia and Samsung Motors. Renault acquired a 73 percent stake in the Romanian car producer and plans to develop a €5,000 car for the Eastern markets. In view of the potential of the Asian market, the Renault Nissan alliance could benefit a lot from the development of the low-price car in emerging Asian markets. Renault's Samsung alliance fits well into the strategy since it is rooted in the technical partnership between Samsung and Nissan.

From a capabilities fit point of view, both firms were complementary. On the market side, Renault's business was concentrated in Europe while Nissan generated a large portion of its revenues in Asia-Pacific and in the US. Renault believed that through the alliance, it could take "advantage of the geographical synergies of the new group." In its 1999 annual report, Renault estimated that "Nissan helped Renault return to Mexico and expand in Japan and the Asia-Pacific region, while Renault supported Nissan in Europe and the Mercosur countries."

Renault's strength in R&D lies in its design know-how, a skill that Nissan needs desperately to attract style-conscious (more demanding) car consumers. Nissan, on the other hand, possesses strong engineering capacities, something that Renault is lagging behind, especially in larger displacement engines for increasingly popular models such as pick-up trucks and SUVs/4WDs. In the sourcing stage, Nissan has a heavy layer of integrated supply chains that is more of a liability than an asset. Having carried out the streamlining of its supply chain recently, Renault is suited to bring in its expertise and experience in supply chain rationalization.

In the manufacturing process, both firms bring their own factories into the alliance. In the regions where only one firm has factories, the other firm can begin manufacturing, especially when the alliance begins producing uniform platforms. In the regions where both companies have factories, the alliance can achieve cost savings through closing one of the factories. In addition, Nissan can contribute its high productivity practices to the alliance, while Renault can take advantage of Nissan's overcapacity in some regions.

CULTURAL AND ORGANIZATIONAL DISTANCES

As generally presumed in inter-continental alliance cases, there are a number of differences between Renault and Nissan such as language, decision-making process, communication patterns, accountability, and labor-management relations. Probably the most pronounced difference is the individualistic nature of the French company versus the group orientation of the Japanese company. In a typical French company, decisions are made either by majority or by someone with a position of authority whereas in Japan, decisions are made based on consensus and through bottom-up processes. Similarly, Renault as a French company puts responsibilities and accountabilities in the hands of individuals and rewards individuals accordingly whereas Nissan assigns responsibilities and accountabilities to groups and rewards groups as a whole.

However, the two companies have a number of similarities: they are both large and bureaucratic organizations with very hierarchical structures; they are both mature companies with long histories; many of their employees are former civil servants or graduates of elite schools and do not have entrepreneurial talents; they both have permanent employment systems; and finally due to excess weights and inefficiencies generated by the organizations, they both suffered from increased competition in the auto industry.

Probably the most important cultural divide was due to the fact that Renault as a company was not considered as a strong player in the auto industry while Nissan on its side was among the leading global brands. As a consequence for Nissan's staff, it could be considered as humiliation to be rescued by a second-league player.

THE CHALLENGES OF TURNAROUND AND INTEGRATION

The analysis of the various types of fit revealed a strong coherency at the strategic and capabilities levels but a lot of uncertainties at the cultural and organizational levels. *In fine*, the quality and effectiveness of the alliance had to be found in the implementation, i.e. how Renault could turn Nissan around with an appropriate non-aggressive and respectful style. The leadership team in charge of implementation was confronted with a double challenge. First, Nissan's turnaround was an absolute necessity. Overloaded by debts, increasingly losing market share, and accumulating losses, the Japanese giant was technically on the verge of bankruptcy. Any future benefits of the alliance would not materialize unless Nissan recovered from economic and financial distress. The second challenge that motivated the partners, and Renault in particular, was to create a synergistic collaboration leading to some sort of economies of scale, speed, and innovation for both partners. The leadership issues associated with each of those challenges were of a different nature and had to be treated differently.

RESCUING NISSAN

The Nissan rescue demanded quick mobilization energies in order to rapidly implement the necessary changes that would re-establish positive cash flow, marketing energy, and dynamism, in a quasi-static corporation in an emotional and cultural context that was not a priori favorable.

When, in May 1999, Carlos Ghosn arrived in Tokyo, according to his own words, "people were scared."[1] He had the reputation of being a "cost killer" and all stakeholders, including employees, dealers, suppliers, and local authorities, were afraid that he would disturb the Japanese social architecture by applying ready-made Western solutions. The case was even worsened by the fact that Renault, as a second-tier player in the global automobile industry, did not enjoy a positive image among the concerned populations. So the typical stressful tension that is exhibited in nearly all post-merger situations was amplified by a suspicion of anticipated cross-cultural mismanagement. As indicated in one of the talks given by Ghosn himself, "my first objective was to create the right atmosphere."

It has been argued that what matters in the first phase of a post-merger integration[2] is to create an emotional context conducive to collaboration and action. For Ghosn, the challenges were first to show that he was coming without any preconceived idea and that the solutions would have to be found from within Nissan itself. Second, he had to design an organisation through which quick positive results could emerge from the work done at the middle- and lower-management levels. Third, in order to generate trust, he had to show a significant degree of commitment to the task, and finally he had to demonstrate respect for the people who were in charge of implementing the change, and avoid any cultural stereotyping.

Ghosn's first action was to visit sites himself in order to interview employees, dealers, and suppliers, asking them two simple questions: "What do you think is wrong? What do you think are the solutions?" This simple step was designed to signal to Nissan's stakeholders that he was not coming with ready-made solutions and that the final solutions would eventually come from concerted actions.

The second significant step was to create nine cross-functional teams (CFTs) in various operational areas[3] in order to generate operational decisions and actions in various areas, based on the active participation of employees at the middle level with a very lean participation of Renault people. The team would report regularly to an Alliance Committee composed of Renault and Nissan executives. Obviously, Ghosn had some ideas about the problems confronting Nissan and about some needed changes to be implemented but according to him, "if I had tried simply to impose the changes from the top, I would have failed. Instead, I decided to use as the centre-piece of the turnaround effort a set of cross-functional teams." This practice of cross-functional teams had already been used by Ghosn in previous assignments and is considered as standard practice in mergers, acquisitions, or strategic alliances; however, what matters is not the design but the way mutual trust and desire for action are induced in those teams. Teams were supervised by an alliance committee composed of senior executives from Renault and Nissan. The teams "were given three months to review the company's operations and to come up with recommendations for returning Nissan to profitability and for uncovering opportunities for future growth."[4] The benefits of such teams are to generate "quick-wins" that have the double advantage of contributing to rapid operational improvements as well as creating a winning, motivating mindset among team members.

In addition, participative management involving both Nissan and Renault professionals was a way to bridge some of the potential cultural gaps. The first significant outcome of the cross-company teams was to produce a blueprint for what became the Nissan Revival Plan announced on October 18, 1999. Exhibit 1 outlines the main contents of the plan. In the plan, Ghosn made three commitments: (a) return to profitability for the fiscal year 2000, (b) achieve a consolidated operating profit of 4.5 percent of sales by fiscal year 2002, and (c) reduce net debt from 1.4 trillion yen to less than 700 billion yen by 2002.

When the Nissan Revival Plan was announced to the press, it came as a shock for the Japanese society, since part of the plan included the closure of factories, the reduction in the number of dealers, and the dismantling of the supplier system typical of Japanese vertical keiretsu. Most observers agreed that the announced measures were needed but did not believe that they could be implemented. The plan needed to be supported by a strong symbolic signal and this was where the demonstration of commitment came into place. To show his strong commitment to the results of Nissan, Carlos Ghosn publicly said that if any one of these three commitments was not reached by March 2003, he would resign from his position as well as all of the executive committee.

"I did not do that by calculation but it happens that in the Japanese history there are stories of commitment: they have samurais that commit seppuku if they fail. My commitment to resign if the results were not there was reminiscent of Japanese history and that people would say 'this guy is coming to Japan, he has nothing to do with the mess, but he is committing suicide if he does not deliver; let's give him the benefit of the doubt'."[5]

EXHIBIT 1. Main contents of the Nissan revival plan

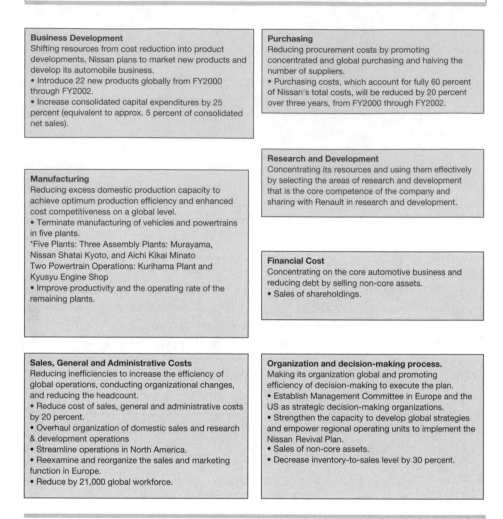

Business Development
Shifting resources from cost reduction into product developments, Nissan plans to market new products and develop its automobile business.
• Introduce 22 new products globally from FY2000 through FY2002.
• Increase consolidated capital expenditures by 25 percent (equivalent to approx. 5 percent of consolidated net sales).

Purchasing
Reducing procurement costs by promoting concentrated and global purchasing and halving the number of suppliers.
• Purchasing costs, which account for fully 60 percent of Nissan's total costs, will be reduced by 20 percent over three years, from FY2000 through FY2002.

Manufacturing
Reducing excess domestic production capacity to achieve optimum production efficiency and enhanced cost competitiveness on a global level.
• Terminate manufacturing of vehicles and powertrains in five plants.
*Five Plants: Three Assembly Plants: Murayama, Nissan Shatai Kyoto, and Aichi Kikai Minato Two Powertrain Operations: Kurihama Plant and Kyusyu Engine Shop
• Improve productivity and the operating rate of the remaining plants.

Research and Development
Concentrating its resources and using them effectively by selecting the areas of research and development that is the core competence of the company and sharing with Renault in research and development.

Financial Cost
Concentrating on the core automotive business and reducing debt by selling non-core assets.
• Sales of shareholdings.

Sales, General and Administrative Costs
Reducing inefficiencies to increase the efficiency of global operations, conducting organizational changes, and reducing the headcount.
• Reduce cost of sales, general and administrative costs by 20 percent.
• Overhaul organization of domestic sales and research & development operations
• Streamline operations in North America.
• Reexamine and reorganize the sales and marketing function in Europe.
• Reduce by 21,000 global workforce.

Organization and decision-making process.
Making its organization global and promoting efficiency of decision-making to execute the plan.
• Establish Management Committee in Europe and the US as strategic decision-making organizations.
• Strengthen the capacity to develop global strategies and empower regional operating units to implement the Nissan Revival Plan.
• Sales of non-core assets.
• Decrease inventory-to-sales level by 30 percent.

The last but not the least significant step was to avoid any cultural stereotyping, and demonstrating respect for the people who were in charge of implementing the change. Although the literature on mergers and acquisitions finds that the performance impact of cultural differences in M&A yields mixed results, both positive and negative,[6] it was important for Renault managers assigned to Nissan to understand the cultural sensitivity of Nissan's staff, given the significant cultural distance between Renault, a French company, and Nissan, a traditional Japanese one, although both were part of the automobile industry and both had a relative bureaucratic legacy. The point is that no major alliance of this magnitude (implying the control by a foreign firm and personnel) had ever happened in Japan. Empirical evidence has shown that Japanese society has traditionally strongly resisted Western-style, imported management styles.

In addition, as mentioned earlier, Renault lacked the recognition of being a successful global player; hence the attitude of avoiding any potential arrogance that would have ruined all effort at recovery. Ghosn was very concerned about a potential cultural clash and was very careful to adopt a collaborative approach based on cultural compromise and not cultural dominance. As he mentioned in one of his talks, "What is important is to insist on what is similar and not on what is different." Hence, the involvement of Nissan personnel in decisions, and during group works, decisions would be "based on data and agnostic; no preconceived idea, no preconceived dogma."[7] Eventually the combination of the four factors mentioned led to the successful achievement of the Nissan Revival Plan, one year ahead of time in 2001.

ACHIEVING SYNERGIES

Even before the successful completion of the Nissan Revival Plan, eleven cross-company teams (CCTs) were formed, focusing on all elements of the value chain and looking for leveraging potential synergies. Those areas covered the adoption of common platforms, the transfer of engines and components from one company to the other, the common sourcing of components, the adjustment of plant capacities across the world, and common management of specific projects and subsidiaries. The working methodology was similar to the cross-functional teams but with a time horizon that was less tense. The objective was to really achieve a level of integration that would contribute to each company without sacrificing their autonomy. The same principles of transparency, data-driven results, and respect of the other party were applied to the functioning of the teams that still exist today.

When asked why the Nissan Renault collaboration was not structured as a merger, Ghosn answered that he did not see the advantage of a merger since the two companies had strong brands in their respective markets, and it would be a brand dilution to merge, even if the brands themselves would stay separate. Obtaining synergies where it is useful and makes economic sense while at the same time keeping intact the identity and autonomy of the two partners was a model much more efficient than a straight merger. The cross company teams identified synergies that would materialize in the area of joint purchasing, common platforms, exchange of engines and other parts between companies, joint R&D and common logistics as well as new development and joint marketing in territories where neither Renault nor Nissan are well represented.

MAKING THE ALLIANCE WORK: THE CHALLENGE OF CONTINUITY

The ultimate objective of the alliance was to create an entity capable of sustaining long-term competitive advantages in the global marketplace. Once Nissan recovered, the second stage was to finalize the proper organizational and governance mechanisms to achieve the needed synergies, while preserving the identity of each company.

In March 2002, Renault increased its participation in Nissan to 44.3 percent while two months later Nissan took a stake of 15 percent in Renault's capital.

At the same time, the alliance structure was institutionalized with the creation of Renault-Nissan BV, a strategic management company incorporated in the Netherlands. This company was owned 50 percent by Renault and 50 percent by Nissan, and has for its task to decide on the long- and short-term plans, the validation of products, the commonalities in products and power trains, and on the principles of financial policies. In addition, this company is supervising the joint subsidiaries that are created in smaller countries, as well as the Renault-Nissan Joint Purchasing Organization and the Renault-Nissan Information services. This strategic management company is governed by an alliance board made of three Renault executives and three from Nissan, plus the president, Carlos Ghosn. In addition, a certain number of senior executives from both companies are assisting the board. However, the two companies, Nissan and Renault, are fully responsible for their marketing and operational strategies within the framework set up by the alliance committee. The cross-functional teams and the cross-company teams plus some ad hoc joint task forces are still active and are reporting to a steering committee, which in turn reports to the alliance board.

Through 2009, the results have been significant in term of cost savings, particularly in the domain of purchasing and in terms of product rationalization and exchange of components across the two companies. Some joint development, particularly in new capacities investment, that were planned to be done in Morocco have been put on hold because of the global financial crisis that undermined the automobile industry. But rather than loosening the ties between partners, the crisis has reinforced their cooperation in cost reduction as well as their joint decision to participate actively in a new generation of electric cars. In 2005, Carlos Ghosn became CEO of Renault while keeping his function as president and CEO of Nissan and CEO of Nissan US. While this triple responsibility facilitated homogeneity in direction, it put a lot of pressure on Ghosn's managerial ability. When, in 2007, results at Nissan were not as high as expected, some critics raised concerns about a potential dilution in strategic direction due to the stretch put on the "global chairman." Eventually, Ghosn abandoned the executive leadership of Nissan US but was still adamant about maintaining his dual function at Renault and Nissan. For him, this was essential to make the complex alliance mechanisms work properly.

In the middle of the financial crisis, Ghosn declared, "while synergistic relationships have been fruitful when the two companies were profitable and growing, today we have to move faster. Seeking synergies is no longer optional but mandatory."[8] He announced that an additional €1.5 billion of additional free cash flow has been identified, which is to be divided between the two companies.

CONCLUSIONS

In one of his talks, Ghosn mentioned, "it is important in an alliance such as Renault-Nissan to create the right atmosphere, because the atmosphere creates the synergies. I am not sure that the synergies create the right atmosphere."[9] By this rhetorical comparison, he wanted to re-affirm the prevalence of the emotional context over the technical or economical contents in a stressful situation. In the case of Renault-Nissan, what Ghosn did was not unusual: the activation of integration teams and the setting

---

EXHIBIT 2. Synergies achieved over the 2003–2008 period in the Renault-Nissan alliance

---

Purchasing

Renault-Nissan Purchasing Organization (RNPO) defines worldwide purchasing strategy by product family and selects the best suppliers project by project consistent with the partner companies' quality, cost and delivery time objectives. Economies of scale are sought by combining Renault and Nissan order volumes and by developing component standardization.

By April 2008, RNPO was covering 90 percent of Renault and Nissan purchases, with employees drawn from both companies using shared processes and tools.

Interchangeable Components Policy (ICP)

ICP consists of using same parts or fittings on different models, across several platforms and segments of the Renault-Nissan Alliance. Expanding the scope of common platforms by designing components that can be used for different platforms or segments, this offers greater scope for vehicle and market differentiation. Several engines and transmissions and power trains have been transferred from Renault to Nissan or from Nissan to Renault.

Capacity Utilization

Production of Renault vehicles in Nissan factories in Mexico, production of a compact van in Nissan's Barcelona plant commercialized by Nissan and Renault under different name (double badging). Development of a press tooling manufacturing plant in Romania by Renault for the benefit of both companies.

Joint Development

Creation of a joint venture in India with Bajaj to produce a low-cost vehicle. Opening of a joint Renault Nissan technology centre in Chennai. Joint project to manufacture cars in Morocco (Nissan stopped its commitment to that project as a consequence of the 2009 financial crisis).

Environmental Solutions

The Alliance invests across a wide range of technologies, including Electric Vehicles (EV), Fuel Cell, Hybrid technologies and improvement of current diesel/gasoline engines or transmissions.

The Renault Nissan alliance commits to become the global leader in zero-emission vehicles and to launch the first mass-marketed electric vehicles. Renault-Nissan signed in January 2008 a Memorandum of Understanding with Israel and announced in March 2008 its second deployment with Dong Energy in Denmark.

Source: Alliances Facts and Figures 2008, Renault-Nissan Booklet available at www.renault.com/en/groupe/.

up of a new direction are considered standard practices. Other alliances or mergers such as Chrysler and Daimler have used similar instruments with a far less successful outcome. What matters is not what is done but how it is done. The success of the alliance was determined primarily by the ability of the leadership team coming from both companies to establish trust and respect, as well as providing the means for lower-level staff to work jointly towards well-understood goals.

NOTES

1.   Video talk from Carlos Ghosn, July 2008, available on http://knowledge.insead.edu/.
2.   Haspeslagh, Philippe and David B. Jemison, *Managing Acquisitions: Creating Value Through Corporate Renewal*. The Free Press, NY, 1991.
3.   Carlos Ghosn, "Saving the Business Without Losing the Company," *Harvard Business Review*, January 2002, pp. 37–45.
4.   Extract from Ghosn" Saving the business," op. cit.
5.   Video talk from Carlos Ghosn, July 2008, available on http://knowledge.insead.edu/.
6.   Günter K. Stahl and Andreas Voigt, "Impact Of Cultural Differences on Merger And Acquisition Performance: A Critical Research Review and an Integrative Model," *Advances in Mergers and Acquisitions*, vol. 4, 51–83, 2005
7.   Those comments were made in a public speech held in Tokyo in November 2000.
8.   Le Figaro "Synergies Maximales entre Renault et Nissan," May 29, 2009.
9.   Video talk, INSEAD forum, Tokyo, November 2000.

Kathrin Köster and Günter K. Stahl

LENOVO–IBM: BRIDGING CULTURES, LANGUAGES, AND TIME ZONES

(A) AN AUDACIOUS DEAL

"Cultural integration is still one of the biggest challenges . . . We face the combined effect of different corporate cultures and the difference between the cultures of the East and the West."

Orr and Xing, 2007[1]

ON TUESDAY, DECEMBER 20, 2005, the public learned of the departure of Steve Ward, the CEO of Lenovo. He had lasted just eight months in the position before he was replaced by William Amelio, a former Dell executive.[2] The move came as China's Lenovo, despite its difficult start, seemed poised to become the world's leading PC maker.

Just 12 months prior, on December 8, 2004, Yang Yuanqing, who was then Lenovo's CEO, announced his intention to purchase IBM's PC division for US$1.75 billion—an unprecedented move for a company based in an emerging market (for a timeline of the deal, see Appendix A1). The radical deal would transform Lenovo from a company that sold exclusively in China into a major global player. Furthermore, IBM's PC division accounted for three times the sales that Lenovo earned, so the announcement seemed less like a merger and more like David was trying to swallow Goliath.

THE LONG MARCH FROM LEGEND TO LENOVO

Prior to 2004, Lenovo had been known as Legend, a company established by Liu Chuanzhi, a graduate of the Xi'an Military Communications Engineering College. In 1984, he and a few colleagues spun off Legend from the state-owned Chinese Academy of Sciences, which provided seed money of US$25,000 that the young entrepreneurs used to set up shop in a ramshackle building in "Swindler's Alley," Beijing's electronics black market. Very quickly, Liu Chuanzhi realized that differentiation through innovation was the only way forward. The Legend brand thus developed an add-on card that allowed Chinese applications to run on English-language operating systems; it catapulted China into the PC age. For this innovation, Legend received one of China's highest honors, a National Science Technology Progress Award.

In contrast with its main competitor, Great Wall, Legend was not well connected to or protected by government authorities. For example, the company was refused a license to manufacture in China. But with innovation as its watchword, Legend came up with the idea of entering into a joint venture in Hong Kong, in which capacity it would also build motherboards and PCs and thereby outmaneuver its better-connected Chinese rivals. It was not until 1990 that Liu Chuanzhi could realize his dream to build PCs in his home country, though.

In 1994, Legend went public to raise capital in Hong Kong and thus be able to compete with foreign computer manufacturers, whose products had been flooding the Chinese markets since the beginning of the 1990s. Before its competitors, Legend introduced a Pentium PC in China; this first-mover advantage contributed greatly to its status as the leading PC maker on the Chinese market.

Although Legend diversified into a few non-core businesses, such as IT services, the PC business remained the center of its operations. During the mid-1990s, a young manager, Yang Yuanqing, stood out for his work in this division. An unusually bright engineer with a strong desire for clarity and precision, Yang had been hired straight out of school and, like many of the company's high flyers, had been promoted at a very young age. A forceful personality and firm believer in discipline and centralized decision-making, the young Yang Yuanqing prompted descriptions such as acutely intelligent, tough, and decisive,[3] as well as autocratic in his leadership and abrasive. Yet Yang also proved a visionary, with a sharp eye for promising innovations and new business opportunities. In retrospect, observers noted that his arrival at the company was a true turning point in Legend's history (Appendix A2 provides a description of Yang Yuanqing).

With Liu, Yang shared the conviction that to achieve ambitious goals, Legend needed to attract China's best and brightest and then imbue them with the Legend spirit. Newcomers had to "fit the mold," and the company went to great lengths to instill the right mindset, values, and work ethic.

Legend's vice president Du Jianhua described the desired corporate culture, as well as required changes in management practices and individual behavior, using the "1-2-3-4-5 formula:"[4]

1. Adopt one common culture and vision that all Legend employees and managers share.
2. Require dual attitudes from employees. That is, Legend employees were expected to treat customers with the utmost respect and care, in line with the motto, "the customer is the emperor," and go the extra mile to meet customers' needs. Legend's definition of "customers" included internal customers, suppliers, dealers, and distributors, so employees also were warned not to offend or exploit

these members of the extended Legend family. The second employee characteristic the company prioritized was frugality. Every employee needed to be aware that Legend was a profit-maximizing organization, with the motto "Save money, save energy, save time."

3. Concentrate on three fundamental leadership tasks: build the management team, determine the strategy, and lead the troops. These tasks, reflecting the philosophy of Sunzi, constituted not only the capabilities that leaders needed to possess but also the recommended approach to managing people. Thus, management was to instill discipline and obedience in the rank-and-file staff and ensure employees strictly adhered to company rules and policies. Only in case of an emergency or crisis that might cause severe damage to the company could employees act according to their own judgment.

4. Adhere to four commandments: (1) don't abuse your position to line your own pockets; (2) don't accept bribes; (3) don't take any second job outside the company; and (4) don't discuss your salary with anybody in the company. These rules defined minimum requirements; employees also were expected to meet additional standards of conduct. In a management meeting in August 1997, Yang described the ideal Legend employee as follows: accurate, careful, and meticulous when it comes to details; able to analyze the root causes of problems and come up with practicable solutions; able to effectively communicate and cooperate with others; and marked by relentless self-discipline. At Legend, such military-like discipline was strictly enforced and backed by stiff penalties for misbehavior. Only under pressure and with clear rules and accountabilities, Yang was convinced, would employees perform and thrive. Employees had to clock in and out; if they came late to a meeting, they had to stand for one minute behind their chair. If they were seen outside the office building without a plausible explanation, they had to accept a pay deduction.

5. Consider five changes. As the twentieth century drew to a close, Legend's top management perceived a need to move away from hierarchical control toward a more participative style of leadership that encouraged people to take ownership and responsibility of their performance. Strict lines of authority and top-down control, Yang and Liu came to realize, would prevent Legend from responding to market needs and trends and achieving international significance. Thus the company faced the significant challenge of delegating responsibility broadly and promoting an entrepreneurial spirit, as well as leadership at all levels. Five changes in behavior and skills would be needed to implement Legend's new management model, which Yang introduced in 1998. Specifically, managers were expected to:

    (i)   work toward meeting goals and objectives rather than blindly following a supervisor's instructions;

    (ii)   develop from a people-oriented into a task-oriented manager;

    (iii) do what needs to be done to respond to the needs of the customer;

    (iv)   think in terms of numbers and specify concrete, quantifiable objectives to be achieved; and

    (v)   become more inquisitive and open-minded.

These management principles and rules aimed to impart a greater performance orientation and cultivate a culture of accountability throughout the company. They also were designed to reflect the company's core values: customer service, innovative and entrepreneurial spirit, accuracy and truth-seeking, trustworthiness, and integrity.

To instill these values, Legend's top managers decided to adopt Western-style performance management and human resource (HR) practices. It was among the first Chinese companies to introduce a stock option program for managers. It also implemented a forced ranking, or "rank and yank," system that required managers to identify the top and bottom 10 percent of performers, similar to the appraisal system introduced by Jack Welch at General Electric. This prompted some observers to conclude that Legend was not a "typical" Asian company.[5]

In 2001, when Yang was appointed CEO and Liu took on the chairman role, Legend also began globalizing. Yang and Liu had become convinced that growth opportunities in China were limited by the increasingly fierce competition in the Chinese market. To pursue opportunities outside China, they established a new vision for Legend, namely, to join the *Fortune* 500 and become the first global Chinese player. But the name Legend was already copyright-protected outside of China, so the company renamed itself Lenovo—"Le" from Legend and "novo" to indicate a new start. Also, in 2004, Lenovo announced its decision to become the worldwide partner of the International Olympic Committee, as the computer equipment provider for the 2006 Winter Olympics in Turin, Italy, and the 2008 Beijing Olympic Games.

THE IBM OPPORTUNITY: ACQUIRING AN AMERICAN ICON

IBM, an icon of corporate America, was founded in 1911 as The Computer-Tabulating-Recording Company. After its geographical expansion into Europe, South America, Asia, and Australia, the company took the new name International Business Machines, or IBM, under the leadership of Sir Thomas J. Watson Sr., the head of the organization from 1915 to 1956. A self-made man with no higher-level education, he reportedly stated: "The trouble with every one of us is that we don't think enough. We don't get paid for working with our feet; we get paid for working with our heads" (Forbes, 1948).[6] The slogan "THINK" was thus a mantra for IBM; it was also the motto above the door of the IBM schoolhouse where all new hires, usually fresh from college, had to undergo 12 weeks of education and orientation.[7]

The beliefs of Sir Watson not only prompted the company's innovativeness but also had long-term impacts on the attitudes and behaviors of its workforce. Watson emphasized impeccable customer service and insisted on dark-suited, white-shirted, alcohol-abstinent salesmen. With fervor, he instilled company pride and loyalty through job security for every worker, company sports teams, family outings, and a company band. Employees received comprehensive benefits and were convinced of their own superior knowledge and skills.[8]

IBM also prided itself on shaping the entire computer industry. With the advent of high-performing integrated circuits, "Big Blue"—a corporate nickname that recognized IBM's army of blue-suited salesmen and blue logo—could launch the System/360 processors that enabled it to lead the market with high profit margins and few competitive threats for decades. This position changed with the rise of UNIX and the age of personal computing, though. In 1986, IBM developed the first laptop, which weighed 12 pounds; by 1992, it was promoting the ThinkPad, the first notebook computer with a 10.4-inch color display that used Thin Film transistor technology.

Despite its pioneering entries into the PC market, IBM did not make its PC business a top priority and surrendered control of its highest-value components, namely, the operating system and the microprocessor, to Microsoft and Intel, respectively. Critics widely attributed IBM's decline in the late 1980s and early 1990s to its failure to protect its technological lead; it became a follower rather than an innovator.[9] The once-dominant giant came close to collapse when its mainframe computer business, the primary growth engine of the 1970s and 1980s, ground to a halt.

But the CEO in what were arguably IBM's darkest hours brought the company back from the brink. When he took over in 1993, Louis Gerstner recognized that IBM's cherished values—customer service, excellence, and respect—had become a sort of rigor mortis, which turned them from strengths into liabilities. "Superior customer service" had come to mean servicing machines on the customers' premises; "excellence" had mutated into an obsession with perfectionism. The numerous required checks, approvals, and validations nearly paralyzed the decision-making process. Even the belief in respect for the individual had turned into an entitlement, such that employees could reap rich benefits without earning them.[10]

Under Gerstner's leadership, the company was recentralized and structured around processes. He introduced global customer relationship management, a complex web of processes, roles, and IT tools that affected tens of thousands of employees. It took IBM nearly a decade to remake itself into a comprehensive software, hardware, and services provider, but Big Blue's successful strategic repositioning increased the "we feeling" and strengthened what has been described as an almost cult-like culture.[11]

Thus, when Sam Palmisano took over as CEO in 2002, his challenge was to come up with a mandate for the next stage in the company's transformation. His primary aim was to get different parts of the company to work together so IBM could offer a bundle of "integrated solutions"—hardware, software, services, financing—at a single price. A set of shared values supported the change in strategy and ensured consistency across the globe:

1. Dedication to every client's success.
2. Innovation that matters—for our company and for the world.
3. Trust and personal responsibility in all relationships.[12]

These core values provided the basis for IBM's management system and a crucial orientation frame for its diverse workforce, which serves clients in more than 170 countries.

Along with these changes to the company's orientations and values, in 2004, it made another sharp break with its history: IBM would sell off its PC business. The move would affect 10,000 IBMers working in the PC business, which was part of the company's Personal Systems Group. Although this division contributed 13 percent of the company's overall turnover of US$96.3 billion in 2004, it also incurred losses from the PC business.[13]

THE GREAT LEAP FORWARD

When IBM announced its interest in selling its PC division, Lenovo jumped at the chance; for Lenovo, the IBM deal was a giant leap forward. It gave Lenovo access to the computer giant's technology and expertise, a foothold into the lucrative US and European markets, and worldwide brand recognition.

As a well-established brand worth an estimated US$53 billion,[14] IBM was globally present and enjoyed a reputation for high quality, innovation, and reliability. As part of the deal, Lenovo obtained the right to use the IBM brand name for five years. This agreement would help maintain customer loyalty and avoid the risk that customers would notice any major changes. IBM also committed to continuing to provide service for its PCs and laptops, a move aimed to dispel customers' service concerns. Moreover, Lenovo hoped to benefit from IBM's long experience in global marketing and sales. Lenovo's own sales channels were limited to China, where it maintained excellent relations with major distributors, mainly due to the organization's transparent rules and procedures. But IBM had sales, support, and delivery operations all around the world.

In addition, IBM's huge sales volume would help lower the company's component costs. In the PC industry, 70–80 percent of total revenues go to components, so economies of scale are key contributors to keeping costs low. Lenovo expected to realize annual savings of US$200 million just through larger purchasing volumes. The "new Lenovo" thus could tackle price-sensitive markets, such as India, and appeal more to small- and medium-sized enterprises around the world. Lenovo estimated that these markets offered growth opportunities of about US$1 billion.[15] Finally, Lenovo extended its product portfolio overnight, immediately offering a broad range of products and services to diverse customers.

The deal also seemed to make sense for IBM. Since its reinvention in the 1990s, IBM had been moving constantly toward becoming a software and integrated services provider. In 1993, revenues from the hardware business represented more than half of IBM's total revenues; by 2004, they were less than one-third.[16] With this strategic reorientation, the low-margin hardware business lost importance. In addition, IBM's PC division continued to be a source of ongoing profit drains. From 2001 to mid-2004, the unit accumulated losses of US$965 million, which imposed a major burden on the overall organization.[17] The Lenovo deal promised to stop this profit drain and pave the way into the lucrative Chinese market. Lenovo's well-developed distribution network provided inroads into China, especially those leading to new corporate customers of IBM's software and service solutions. Lenovo's existing relationships with regulatory bodies and potential corporate customers, as well as its well-established brand name, could help IBM gain footing and expand quickly in mainland China.

Thus, Lenovo–IBM would obtain a competitive advantage that its closest competitors, Hewlett-Packard and Dell, could not match. As one Lenovo executive recalled: "On paper this was pretty much a match made in heaven."[18] The challenge was to make it work in practice.

APPENDIX A1: TIMELINE FOR THE LENOVO–IBM MERGER

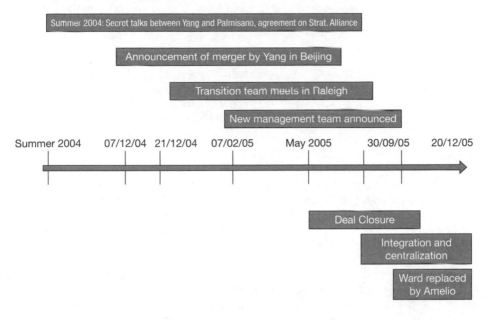

APPENDIX A2: YANG YUANQING: A PORTRAIT

> Yang's colleagues thought himself both strict with others and immodest about himself. For sure, he was honest and straightforward to the point of being blunt. Sometimes people were afraid to enter his office. Yang would eventually have to learn a more co-operative management style but for the moment there was no time.
>
> —Shan Feng and Janet Elfring, *The Legend Behind Lenovo*, unofficial corporate history

As chairman Yang centralized decision-making authority—in himself. He took full control of strategy, procurement, manufacturing, and marketing, which meant he was breaking virtually every management philosophy rule in the book. Yet it worked, perhaps because, as Yang himself recalled, "I could make quick decisions because I could look through all the functions. I knew the supply chain very well. I knew which components were in short supply. I knew when new [micro] processors were available. We could change our products, change our prices, respond quickly."

This agility combined with a willingness to make long-term investments. In 1997, Legend became the first Chinese company to implement an enterprise resource planning system provided by SAP, the German software company. Yang was determined to give his company a technology platform that at least equaled those of its global rivals. Thus, by the late 1990s, Legend was the best-selling PC brand in China. In 1999, it took 20 percent of the Chinese market. The combination of operational efficiency with PCs that had been designed specifically for the Chinese market proved difficult for its competitors to match.

In 2001, the distribution side of the business became Digital China, managed by Guo Wei, another young protégé of Liu. Yang became chief executive of the PC arm.

Sources

Sull, Donald N. (2005). *Made In China: What Western Managers Can Learn From Trailblazing Chinese Entrepreneurs*, Cambridge, MA: Harvard Business School Press.
Feng, Shan and Elfring, Janet. (2000). *The Legend Behind Lenovo: The Chinese IT Company that Dares to Succeed*, Hong Kong: Asia Publishing.

NOTES

1.   Orr, G. and Xing, J. (2007). When Chinese Companies go Global: An Interview with Lenovo's Mary Ma. *McKinsey on Finance,* 23, 18–22. Available on http://corporatefinance.mckinsey.com/knowledge/knowledgemanagement/mof.htm.
2.   Einhorn, B. (2005). Lenovo's New Boss: from Dell. *Business Week*, December 21, 2005. Available on www.businessweek.com/technology/content/dec2005/tc20051221_376268.htm.
3.   Ling, Z. (2006). *The Lenovo Affair: The Growth of China's Computer Giant and its Takeover of IBM-PC*. Singapore: Wiley & Sons.
4.   N.N. (2009). Lianxiang qiye wenhua yu guanli sixiang 12345, June 16, 2009. Available on http://oxford.icxo.com/htmlnews/2009/06/16/1389015.htm.
5.   London, S. (2005). The Making of a Multinational Part II: Your Rules and My Processes. *Financial Times,* November 10, 2005, p. 13.
6.   Bell, L. (1948). Thomas J. Watson, in Forbes, B. (ed.), *America's Fifty Foremost Business Leaders*. New York: Forbes & Son Publishing Company, p. 427.
7.   Weeks, J. (2004). *Culture and Leadership at IBM*. INSEAD case 10/2004–5239.
8.   Collins, J. & J. Porras (2002). *Built to Last: Successful Habits of Visionary Companies,* New York: HarperCollins.
9.   Mills, D. and Friesen, G. (1996). *Broken Promises - An Unconventional View of What Went Wrong at IBM*. Boston, MA: Harvard Business Press.
10. Gerstner, L. V. Jr. (2002). *Who Says Elephants Can't Dance? Inside IBM's Historic Turnaround*. London: HarperCollins.
11. Source: ibid.
12. Palmisano, S. (2004). *IBM Annual Meeting of Stockholders*. Providence: RI, April 27, 2004. Available on www.ibm.com/ibm/sjp/04-27-2004.html.
13. IBM (2004). IBM Annual Report 2004. Available on ftp://ftp.software.ibm.com/annual report/2004/.
14. Wolf, D. (2009). Lenovo: Amelio's Exit a Sign that IBM Integration Hitting the Rocks? Available on http://seekingalpha.com/article/118829-lenovo-amelio-s-exit-a-sign-that-ibm-intetration-hitting-the-rocks.
15. Source: ibid.
16. IBM (2004). IBM and Lenovo: New Leadership in Global PCs. Available on i.i.com.com/cnwk.1d/html/news/all_hands_presentation_final.ppt.
17. Pilzweger, M. (2006). IBM: PC-Sparte seit Jahren im Minus, *PC-Welt,* January 19, 2006. Available on www.pcwelt.de/news/IBM-PC-Sparte-seit-Jahren-im-Minus-18253.html.
18. Quelch, J. and Knoop, C.-I. (2006). *Lenovo: Building a Global Brand*. (Case No. 9-507-014). Boston, MA: Harvard Business School.

All interview excerpts were taken from Baumeister, B. (2009), Lenovo's acquisition of IBM's PC Division, unpublished master thesis, WU, Vienna, unless referenced otherwise.

(B) INTEGRATION CHALLENGES

POST-MERGER INTEGRATION

While the synergies between Lenovo and IBM looked great on paper, the roadblocks to making Lenovo–IBM the PC industry's world leader remained formidable. Not only would the process need to merge two companies with vastly different business models and cultures across 12 times zones, but the combined company needed to stay constantly competitive in the fast-paced PC industry. Michael Dell, the chairman of Lenovo's main rival, asserted: "It won't work."[19] Most observers agreed.

But Lenovo's top executives vowed to prove these skeptics wrong. Their vision for the new Lenovo was to create a computer powerhouse that would combine the best of both worlds and thereby reinvent the entire global PC industry. As Lenovo executives stated, "What Lenovo brings to the table is the best from East and West. From the original Lenovo we have the understanding of emerging markets, excellent efficiency and a focus on long-term strategy. From IBM we have deep insights into worldwide markets and best practices from Western companies."[20]

This best-of-both-worlds integration approach could work if the combination represented a partnership rather than a takeover. Lenovo's CEO Yang repeatedly stressed his perception of the IBM deal as a "marriage of equals," based on trust, respect, and compromise. Yang demonstrated his willingness to compromise right from the start: he stepped down as CEO to make way for IBM's Steve Ward, while he became chairman. Yang also accepted Ward's proposal to locate the new head-quarters in New York, rather than establishing dual headquarters in the US and China. Lenovo's new global headquarters took up the top floor of a nondescript office building outside the city; the IBM PC division's staff mainly continued to work out of their existing site in Raleigh, North Carolina.

Despite the seeming friendliness of the deal, cross-border problems soon emerged. Simple geographical distance was a major barrier: the flight from Beijing to New York took 13 hours and crossed 12 time zones. Without any direct flights from Beijing to Raleigh, North Carolina, that trip took an additional few hours. Making the trip, in either direction, for a day of meetings or workshops was not possible, and any gathering or information exchange had to be planned weeks in advance to make the trip worthwhile. The thousands of miles separating the company's main locations made exchanging information about best practices incredibly difficult. The regular business hours of New York and Beijing overlap only for three to four hours each day; if the company needed to include European colleagues, the opera-tion became nearly impossible—or required employees to arrive at the office at very odd hours.

Even as they racked up miles of travel and readjusted their alarm clocks, the management teams on both sides continued to view the deal as an opportunity to learn. They displayed a genuine and remarkable willingness to set aside their own egos and make decisions in the best interest of the combined company. As one former IBM executive recalled: "Where the Chinese approach worked best, we borrowed it, and where the IBM approach worked best, we borrowed that. Or maybe an outside approach. The point was to do the right thing . . . because the fundamental mission [was] to be seen as a global corporation, not a Western and not a Chinese company. And wherever we could get ideas or implement tools that advance that idea, we did."

This pragmatic and learning-oriented approach also featured what appeared to be an honest enthusiasm for creating something new and better. Ravi Marwaha, the Indian-Australian in charge of running Lenovo's worldwide sales, admitted, "I spent 36 years in IBM. I could easily have retired. Why am I here? Because it is exciting."[21] Another senior Lenovo executive explained, "We are the first of this kind in the world, and I think people are authentically and genuinely excited about being in a place that is very fresh, and young, and new . . . It is an experiment and something that has never been done before, and there is no company like us in the world."

Such enthusiasm might have been expected from Lenovo, given that it was Lenovo that had acquired IBM's PC business. But the general sense of excitement also seemed shared among the IBM PC executives, who had for years felt like the unpopular stepsister in their former company. That is, IBM considered hardware a peripheral business and thus made few investments in the PC division. With the merger, the PC division became a core business again, if for Lenovo.

This positive attitude spanned various levels of the organization. In the first days of the new Lenovo, people took creative steps to bridge their geographical distance. IBM sent camera teams to Raleigh and Beijing, to enable video greetings to various counterparts around the globe. In the call center in Raleigh, employees filmed themselves throwing their IBM badges into the trash. Frances O'Sullivan, the COO of Lenovo International, initiated a program called the "Trash Bin Project," which encouraged ex-IBMers to submit examples of what they had done in their previous work life but did not want to do in the new Lenovo.[22]

CREATING A STRUCTURE

The new Lenovo started with three separate business units: China PCs, China Cell Phones, and International Operations (former IBM PC division). In this sense, business continued much as usual for the IBMers, except that project teams formed to support different functions, such as sales, finance, and order management. The project teams consisted of former Lenovo and IBM managers and took the responsibility of preparing the further integration of the functions.

Yang Yuanqing announced a managerial restructuring on September 30, 2005. Top management jobs would be split approximately evenly between the Chinese and Western sides (see Appendix B1 for an overview). One-third of the board members would be from Hong Kong (where Lenovo is registered); another one-third would come from the US and Europe; and the rest would be from China.[23] This restructuring aimed to provide a framework for further integration, but it also was designed in accordance with Lenovo's goal of joining the league of global technology powerhouses, in that it provided a multinational management team spread across national boundaries and several time zones.

The new management structure then led to closer integration in functions such as supply chain management, planning and control, product development, and marketing. In support of its global supply chain, the company applied a unified IT system that enabled it to ship directly to 100 countries, usually with products configured to order.[24] In the wake of this integration, corporate headquarters moved from New York to Raleigh.

But the integration also meant some redundancies, especially in IBM's sales structure. Therefore, layoffs announced in March 2006 affected approximately 1,000 of the company's 21,400 employees. The cuts spread across company offices in the Americas, Asia-Pacific, and EMEA regions.[25]

UBIQUITOUS DIFFERENCES

The functions integrated, headquarters moved, and managerial responsibility was being shared. Yet without a common language and shared values, it would be impossible to form a unified, global management team.

A year before the acquisition, Lenovo had launched a major campaign to improve the English-language skills of its managers and employees. Most of the company's senior Chinese executives could speak some English, though not all were able to do so fluently or with sufficient ease to support effective working relationships. Few of the lower-level managers were fluent in English. Of the IBM managers, virtually no one had even rudimentary knowledge of Mandarin. These immense language barriers led to lengthy meetings and frequent misunderstandings. For example, one of the most senior executives did not speak English, so board meetings had to include a translator. Yet the company was determined that English would be its corporate language.

The language barriers seemed obvious from the start; less apparent were the widely divergent preferences regarding communication styles. Especially tricky were conference calls, which offered no visuals to help participants interpret the true meanings and nuances of others' verbal comments. Bill Matson, the HR Director of Lenovo, observed:

> IBM leaders would do most of the talking and the Lenovo leaders would do most of the listening. The Chinese, and Asian cultures in general, are much more silent in a conversation. They first think about what they want to say before they say it. And if you think about what you want to say before you say it, and you also translate it from your native language into English . . . you can understand that a 5-second or a 7-second gap in a conversation is not a long time. Yet, to a Western person, 5 seconds silence in a conversation seems like an eternity. So, often times what you would see in meetings is that the Western leaders would be filling in the gap in conversation, and therefore would dominate these discussions, and all too often would not spend as much time as they probably should have seeking out the perspectives and experiences of their Lenovo colleagues.

These differences in communication style were not just frustrating; they affected decision-making and problem-solving quality.

Therefore, the company instituted several programs designed to overcome such barriers. The "East Meets West" program taught the company's global executives about the foundations of both Chinese and American cultures. The "Lenovo Expression Worskhop" targeted the Chinese managers—typically, pragmatic, hands-on people who were not strong communicators, according to Western standards. One Chinese manager explained, "When Chinese people talk, we start from the background, and then we . . . talk about the present situation and the challenges that we are facing, and then we gather lots of supporting materials, so at the end we say 'OK, this is our proposal.' I guess this is different from what you call the Western approach: you have an executive summary at the very beginning, basically you tell what you want to tell on the first page." The program coached Chinese executives in Western communication and presentation styles, with the ultimate goal of facilitating mutual understanding and helping the staff members collaborate more effectively.

Beyond these differences, the variance in cultural norms and values became something of an issue; the US and China can be *worlds* apart, both literally and figuratively. In particular, their attitudes toward hierarchy and authority are widely divergent. As one former senior IBM executive observed, "Lenovo was a more hierarchically driven company . . . You didn't challenge authority quite as much, and the leadership was certainly revered . . . In IBM, you are probably a bit more process-oriented, a culture that is a bit more accepting of challenges and bottom-up kind of thinking." Another former IBM manager was surprised to receive, during his first meeting with his Chinese counterpart, gifts of a cell phone and a portable music player. He also noted a significantly greater level of attention to detail by his new Chinese colleagues.[26]

For the American managers, these differences were notable; for the Chinese delegates, they often verged on offensive. For example, Yang and several other Lenovo executives arrived at John F. Kennedy International Airport in New York for their first planning meeting and found no representatives of IBM waiting to greet them. In China, any such high-ranking guests would have found not only counterparts at the airport to greet them but also a limousine to whisk them away to their hotels.

The potential for offense was mitigated somewhat by the commonalities in the corporate cultures—both sides shared strong beliefs in innovation, personal responsibility, and responsiveness to customer needs. Both sides also talked about the need for commitment. However, on this topic, the interpretations were rather different: "in Lenovo, planning before you pledge, performing as you promise, delivering your commitment is really deeply ingrained in the culture. And when people sign up for a plan, they execute it. And that was probably not as effectively implemented in the old company [i.e. IBM's PC Division] that we bought."

These ubiquitous differences were not limited to the relationships between the two companies; they also influenced customer relationships. The deal had been tailored to minimize disruptions and offer service as usual to customers, but some refused to work with the new entity. The US State Department, citing fears of spyware in Lenovo computers, altered its use of some 14,000 PCs it had ordered from Lenovo.[27] The bias against the Chinese company also reared its head in some former IBM sites; in

Japan, the former IBM staff fiercely resisted the idea of Chinese ownership. The Japanese design team in particular expressed deep concerns about any attempts to change the look or feel of ThinkPad notebooks—a design inspired by a Japanese lunch box that had remained unchanged since 1992.

LEADERSHIP

A year into it, the "new" Lenovo could look back on some major achievements: it had launched its operations and brand in more than 65 countries, without any major disruptions to deliveries and support. No mass exodus of customers had occurred, as some had predicted. It managed to retain 98 percent of its employees. And it had gained global market share, including in BRIC countries, making it the world's third-largest PC manufacturer, behind Dell and HP (see Appendix B2 for an overview of global PC market shares).

Then, in December 2005, the skeptics felt a sense of vindication, because something had to be wrong: the American CEO Steve Ward resigned. Why did Ward last only eight months? Some guessed a personality clash with Yang Yuanqing—a man 10 years his junior who embraced a completely different style. Others speculated that Ward had been too accustomed to the "IBM way" and could not adapt to the new culture. Perhaps his departure marked the end of a power struggle between the Lenovo and former IBM executives, won by Yang. No one outside the company's top management team knew the answer for sure, which kept observers buzzing. Whether the IBM deal would help Lenovo become the global market leader in the PC industry remained uncertain, but this incident certainly raised questions about Lenovo's ability to build a strong multinational management team and successfully run a global business.

APPENDIX B1: "NEW" LENOVO'S EXECUTIVE TEAM

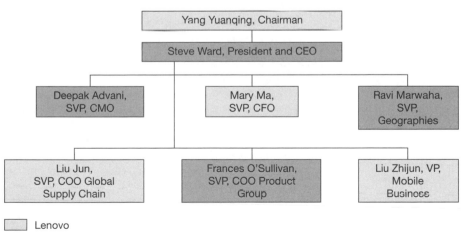

APPENDIX B2: LENOVO'S MARKET SHARE

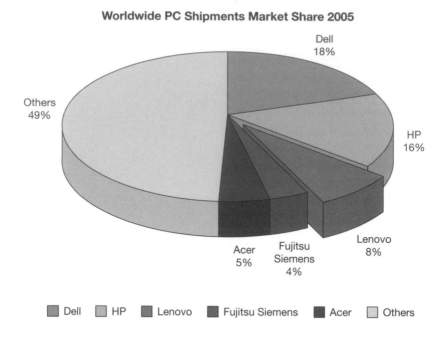

Worldwide PC Shipments Market Share 2005

Dell 18%
Others 49%
HP 16%
Acer 5%
Fujitsu Siemens 4%
Lenovo 8%

■ Dell   ■ HP   ■ Lenovo   ■ Fujitsu Siemens   ■ Acer   □ Others

Source: Adapted from Queech and Knoop (2006).

NOTES

19.   London, S. (2005). Lenovo: The Making of a Multinational Part I. A Global Power Made in China. *Financial Times*, November 9, 2005.

20.   Quelch J. and Knoop C.I. (2007) *Lenovo – Building a Global Brand*, Harvard Business School Case Study 9-508-703. Boston, MA: HBS Publishing. Available on http://etgstage. hbs.edu/lenovo/index.html, site of quotation: http://etgstage.hbs.edu/lenovo/heaven-brand. html.

21.   London, S. (2005). Lenovo: The Making of a Multinational Part I. A Global Power Made in China. *Financial Times*, 9 November, 2005.

22.   Hamm, S. and S. Wildstrom (2005). Turning Two Tech Teams into One, May 9, 2005, Information Technology Online Extra. Available on www.businessweek.com/print/magazine/ content/05_19/b3932116_mz063.htm?chan=gl.

23.   Liu, C. (2007). Lenovo: An Example of Globalization of Chinese Enterprises. *Journal of International Business Studies , 38*, pp. 573–577.

24.   Van Duijl, M. (2006). Lenovo: An Example of Chinese Globalization. Lenovo internal presentation delivered June 15, 2006 by EMEA and SVP president. Available on www.oecd. org./dataoecd/60/43/36929454.pdf.

25.   Ames, B. (2006). Lenovo to Lay Off 1,000, Move Headquarters to N.C. *Computerworld*, March 16, 2006. Available on www.computerworld.com/s/article/109604/Lenovo_to_lay_ off_1_000_move_headquarters_to_N.C.

26.   Tang, Y. (2006). We Are Trying Everyday To Make Lenovo A Global Brand: Interview with Deepak Advani. Available on http://english.peopledaily.com.cn/200606/19/eng 20060619_275249.html.

27.   Peng, M. (2009). *Global Business Update 2009*, Mason, OH: South-Western College Publisher.

Ingmar Björkman and Ming Zeng

GUANGDONG ELECTRONICS*

SITTING IN HIS OFFICE in a mid-sized city in Guangdong Province, China, Gunther Dane realized that he had inherited a difficult situation. It was late October 1998, and Dane was the new general manager of Guangdong Electronics Co. Ltd. (GE), a joint venture between Deutsche Elektro-Informatika (DEI), a huge German electronics company with a global presence, and Rural Red Star, a Chinese state-owned electronics company with 1,200 employees. Dane was a German expatriate.

Over the two months since his appointment as general manager in August 1998, Dane had learned that Guangdong Electronics was stumbling badly. The company was going to show a loss for 1998 and the latest forecasts indicated a 20 percent drop in sales when compared with the preceding year. The company had no formal sales planning and existing contracts received only haphazard follow up. Moreover, project management was virtually non-existent and was carried out with little, if any, documentation regarding resource planning, job responsibilities, and formal schedules. Now, as general manager, he had to decide what to do next. His first management group meeting was scheduled for November 5, 1998.

ESTABLISHING THE JOINT VENTURE

The agreement to establish GE was signed in 1991, and operations started the following year. It was DEI's first joint venture in the People's Republic of China. The company had operated for almost ten years in China with only a representative office in Beijing with a total of 25 employees. By 1991, it had carved out a relatively small niche market with modest sales. However, because the company viewed China as a potentially important market, corporate headquarters were encouraging an expansion of the operations in the country. Furthermore, several of its international competitors had already established local manufacturing units in China.

Operating in an industry that was tightly controlled by the Chinese government, the company viewed the establishment of a joint venture principally as a political move. The investment, its managers reasoned, would demonstrate to authorities that DEI was committed to China and was willing to transfer its technology to the country. If handled correctly, it was to be DEI's means to gain wider access to the Chinese market. Nonetheless, the managers had few concrete ideas about what products to manufacture in the joint venture.

In 1990, DEI started to search for a joint venture partner in the state-owned sector. Negotiations were undertaken in one of China's largest cities with the central ministry's support. However, the negotiations ended when the city government chose a Japanese company in DEI's place.

The Chinese authorities then suggested Rural Red Star as a suitable partner, even though it was not ideally located and its line of business was somewhat different from that of DEI. Nonetheless, as DEI was determined to establish a joint venture in China, Rural Red Star was accepted as the partner. DEI executives viewed the agreement as an important step towards enhancing their goodwill and relationships with the ministry in Beijing, and the Chinese vice minister agreed to attend the joint venture signing ceremony.

GE was established as a 50–50 joint venture. The chairman of the board was to come from the Chinese partner's organization—eventually, the president of Rural Red Star was appointed—while the deputy chairman was to come from the German firm. The contract also stated that the foreign partner was to appoint the GM, while the local partner held the right to appoint the deputy GM. The joint venture was going to start by importing products from DEI, but would soon start some kind of manufacturing. Hence, according to the plans that the partners had agreed upon, GE was to engage in sales, project implementation, customer service, customer training, and production. The venture was located on the premises of Rural Red Star, to which it paid rent.

THE EARLY DEVELOPMENT OF THE JOINT VENTURE

Two German managers arrived during the fall of 1992. Both had worked at DEI for several years. The general manager (GM) was a German in his 50s who had had a couple of years of international experience in the US. The other was a young engineer on his first overseas assignment. He was going to work with customer service and answer questions concerning future production. All local employees were transferred from the Chinese partner. Mr Chen, the deputy GM appointed by the Chinese partner, had been working in sales for Rural Red Star, which would be his principal function in GE. By the end of 1992, the company had 45 employees.

During 1994–96, DEI established several additional joint ventures in China. GE became a relatively small part of DEI's China business and received scant attention by top management, operating like "an unguided missile that people didn't pay attention to." The joint venture reported both to the product division in Germany and to DEI's China headquarters in Beijing; operating rather autonomously, the company was little integrated into DEI's China organization. Few corporate policies and practices that were implemented in the other DEI units were transplanted to GE, though its employees' technological knowledge of DEI product lines improved.

The culture of the joint venture remained "Chinese" rather than "Western." In fact, DEI's other joint ventures shared more of DEI's corporate culture than did GE. Within the joint venture, Chinese employees felt that "they should manage by themselves" and should avoid dealing much with DEI.

During 1992–96, the joint venture grew steadily both in terms of sales and number of employees. By the end of 1996, GE had 105 employees and net sales of close to 140 million yuan, approximately US$16 million. While small-scale manufacturing had begun, it never achieved economic feasibility and was closed down in 1997. In financial terms, the company was not quite living up to the profitability expectations of the parent organizations. Nonetheless, DEI benefited from supplying components to the joint venture. For Rural Red Star, GE had become a crucially important source of revenues through dividends, service fees, and rent. As a floundering state-owned enterprise, Rural Red Star was clearly unable to participate in financing the growth of the joint venture.

Herbert Klein, the immediate predecessor of Gunther Dane, was appointed in the summer of 1996. Klein, who was GE's third general manager, had previously worked as quality and factory manager in Germany. Up until the end of 1996, the joint venture had only two German expatriates: the GM and a German engineer working with customer service. Mr Chen continued to serve as deputy GM. In November 1996, DEI informed GE employees that on January 1, 1997, the financial statement of the joint venture would be consolidated into DEI's total operations. To develop compatible accounting and reporting procedures, the joint venture required a DEI financial controller. (The organizational chart of GE at the beginning of 1997 is presented in Exhibit 1.)

EXHIBIT 1. The Guangdong Electronics Organization in early 1997

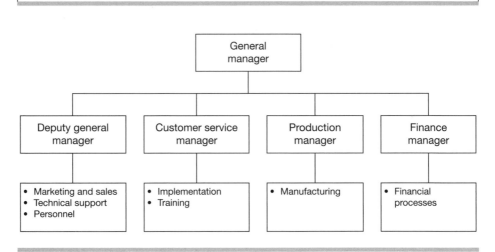

DEVELOPMENTS IN 1997

In 1997, GE received a large number of orders and its employees were busy filling them. However, employee relations in the company had begun to deteriorate.

First, there was the new financial controller, a British citizen and the first non-German expatriate in GE. Looking over the joint venture's books, he quickly realized that most financial procedures and tools were poorly developed and there was an urgent need to develop the financial planning and control processes. Unfortunately, his effort was undermined by a series of new problems. His wife, a Chinese woman from Shanghai who had been offered a job at GE, antagonized local Guangdong employees from the beginning; she was asked to resign. Then his relationship with the GM soured, until finally Klein fired him. During the fall of 1997, the company hired an interim expatriate financial controller, who tried to address the firm's most pressing concerns.

Second, Klein, who at that time served as GM, was not much involved in the day-to-day operations of the company. He spent relatively little time in the joint venture, preferring instead to travel within China and abroad; increasingly, he communicated with his managers through letters. Moreover, his relationship with Mr Chen and the chairman of the board gradually deteriorated.

In April 1997, Bernd Fischer, a new expatriate, arrived from Germany. His background at DEI was in production and he had visited GE a few times to help the company in the early stages of its attempts at manufacturing. Apart from a couple weeks of training in Germany, he had no experience with customer service, the area that he was appointed to manage. With little guidance from the GM concerning his responsibilities, he started to familiarize himself with the company's internal operations. It soon became clear to him that a number of things in the company badly needed improvement. For example, nobody knew the exact number of products in stock. While inventories were high, the "right" products were often out of stock. There was nobody in the company responsible for logistics.

Upon hearing Fischer's observations, Klein agreed that they should do something about these matters. Once contacted, the logistics department of DEI's product division suggested that GE adopt a sophisticated materials flow management program (STAR), which had been developed for use in the manufacturing operations in Germany. In spite of the fact that GE was shutting down its manufacturing operations, the head of the logistics department was convinced that the STAR program would be suitable for handling logistics issues in China as well. During the fall of 1997, Klein decided to implement STAR.

Logistics was not the only problem that Fischer identified. His overall impression was that "there were no procedures for doing anything, and very little documentation. Everything seemed ad hoc. The company was totally sales driven. And there were no formal project management tools in use." Perhaps the company could function without detailed procedures when it was smaller, he reasoned, but now they needed to do something about it. Fischer was not the first German to notice these problems, but the previous observers apparently had failed to do anything about them.

Klein discussed the issue with Fischer, whom he asked to make a presentation to the board of directors in June 1997 based on his observations. For starters, the board decided that an expatriate quality manager should be hired. Klein also suggested to the board that, by 1999, GE should fulfill the requirements for ISO 9002; because several Chinese customers recently had mentioned that their suppliers should have this certification, Mr Chen also supported the idea. Regarding other aspects of the company's operations, Klein pointed out a gap in human resource development, including both technical and general management skills. So far, he argued the company had no human resource (HR) manager; the board decided to appoint a local employee as HR manager.

Klein also formulated some ideas that he did not present at the board meeting. The salary system, for example, should be "totally updated." The yearly bonus obtained by the employees was currently linked only to sales, not to other relevant performance measures such as company profitability. More Germans should be brought in to develop the competence level in the company. Finally, DEI should acquire majority ownership of GE, and "take over and have a leading role in [GE's] overall development," including its full integration with DEI's other activities. Because Klein's views were in line with those of DEI's top executives in China, negotiations were initiated during the fall of 1997 to increase DEI's share of ownership. Klein neither discussed nor communicated his plans with his management team in GE.

During the summer and early fall, Fischer became convinced that there was a need to examine all existing sales contracts, a task that came to occupy a significant part of his time. The company signed some 300 contracts per year, most of which were very small. Unfortunately, Fischer found that the contracts did not contain enough information for the customer service department to devise plans. Some contracts contained no information about deadlines and no system existed to ensure that delivery commitments would be honored. Many contracts were written in Chinese, which violated company policy that they should be written in English as well. Indeed, some contracts were entirely missing. Perhaps most alarmingly, Fischer learned, the GE contract template contained clauses that stipulated stiff penalties for late deliveries, including discounts of up to 1 percent per day delayed. When asked about this, Chinese employees advised him not to worry about the content of the contract "as they had good relationships with the buyers [who] therefore would not demand any compensation." Fischer was not reassured, however, especially since the company consistently failed to meet delivery deadlines. Looking back, his first six months had been very frustrating.

In October, a German expert from the quality department visited GE. The purpose of the visit was to audit Rural Red Star as a potential supplier of some simple components to GE, an initiative that Fischer had spearheaded earlier by obtaining design drawings for the products. Upon approval as a supplier, which made Mr Chen "very happy," Fischer asked the quality expert to examine other operations at GE. The German expert found serious quality management problems, which led him to recommend that his boss in Germany, quality manager Rudolf Steiner, visit GE himself.

Steiner arrived in November and made a number of alarming observations regarding quality management. In the discussion that followed, he bluntly asked Klein why they had not been rectified. The general manager replied: "this is China, everything is very difficult!" Despite their somewhat tense introduction, Klein agreed to take Steiner on as the quality manager of the company at the beginning of the next year. The idea was to use the ISO 9002 certificate as a spur to improve the entire operation of the company. Though Steiner had not personally implemented an ISO 9002 project, he had worked as a quality manager in the parent organization; he estimated that it would take about two years to obtain the ISO 9002 certificate. The Chinese manager who had been in charge of production would serve as his assistant. German expatriates viewed the certificate as a good way to engage the Chinese partner and managers in a project that would lead to significant change.

FINANCE AND CONTROL

In 1998, Rudolf Steiner arrived with a new financial controller, Uli Beck. For both Germans, the beginning of their assignment brought unpleasant surprises.

Just before Beck arrived, Klein had told the expatriate interim controller that his services were no longer needed. This deprived Beck, who had left a position in an international accounting firm to take this job in China, of any introduction from his predecessor. When he examined his department in more detail, he was shocked at the number of errors he found. For instance, the 1997 accounts, which had boasted sound financial results, were revealed to be misleading: certain costs had simply been omitted.

Furthermore, though GE's lawyer had visited the company to instruct employees in contractual procedures, few changes had been made. Contracts tended to be incomplete, often still written exclusively in Chinese, which Klein had continued to sign in violation of company policy. In addition, oral commitments were often made to the buyers concerning delivery times. Even more seriously, one of the company's official stamps (the so-called "chop" routinely used in China to sign official company documents) was missing and it appeared that Rural Red Star had signed some of the deals in GE's name. It was only after strong pressure from Beck and Fischer that the stamp was returned to GE.

THE ISO 9002 PROJECT

When the new quality manager Rudolf Steiner arrived in China, he was informed that his assistant had left GE in order to return to the Rural Red Star organization. This reflected a lack of control in the joint venture's personnel issues about which Germans had long complained. In his place, a young Chinese-American, Patricia Gui, had been hired as his assistant. Ms Gui, whose husband worked in a US–Chinese joint venture in the same city, had graduated from a top US university with a degree in engineering, spoke fluent Mandarin, and appeared to be straightforward and direct in how she communicated with both the Germans and the Chinese. Nonetheless, she had very little practical experience. A local person was hired in March to provide further support in the quality department. Klein soon ordered Steiner to "speed up" the ISO 9002 certification process (Exhibit 2 summarizes some features concerning ISO certification).

To his astonishment, Steiner was asked immediately by the Chinese managers, "When will you give us the certificate?" The Chinese managers, he realized, understood neither the role he was going to play in the company nor the rigor that the ISO process would impose. In February, at his kick-off meeting with the managers, Steiner explained that their first tasks were to train the department heads in quality management and to document existing company practices. Nobody objected to this plan, which Patricia Gui was charged with implementing. As it turned out, the managers were unwilling to fully participate. Even those who showed up for meetings exhibited little interest, preferring to chat together or leaving frequently to take care of other tasks.

It was even more difficult to get the managers to document existing practices. Arguing that "the role of the quality manager is not to write them," Steiner refused to supply them himself. It fell to Ms Gui to meet with people in all the departments, but few cooperated. For example, Ms Gui provided a diagram of the overall marketing structure to the marketing manager and asked him to fill in the missing details; but somehow, he never got around to supplying them. The Germans in GE suggested various reasons why the local employees refused to cooperate in the documentation exercise, including:

- "They usually go against everything that the foreigners present."
- "They want to be free to do whatever they like."
- "They thought [Steiner] was brought here to do it."
- "They were not able to understand what this thing will do to their normal life."
- "They were not prepared for it."
- "He didn't know how to do it."
- "They were busy doing more important things and delegated it to their secretaries."

However, perhaps none of the Germans understood the real reason why local employees were reluctant to collaborate on this matter. As pointed out by customer service manager Fischer, "In the beginning it was often difficult to understand the concrete reasons why people didn't want to change. It's very important to know that they often had very concrete reasons, and it was not because people are lazy or unwilling to do new things!"

In May, Klein suddenly appointed Patricia Gui as the logistics manager, which Steiner learned after the fact. It was a serious blow for Steiner, who felt deeply disappointed to lose his assistant. Klein, he came to believe, was demonstrating how little he appreciated his work. From that moment on, the ISO 9002 project ran increasingly behind schedule. While employees had been promised a 100-yuan bonus upon the first successful internal audit, it was unclear whether this promise had provided any incentive for them to cooperate. The first task of Steiner's new assistant was to build a filing system for GE. He complained, however, that "[I] haven't come very far yet as people don't provide me with their files!"

EXHIBIT 2. The ISO 9000 series of quality standards

ISO 9000 was created by the International Organization for Standardization in 1987 to denote quality systems and standards. Although ISO certification began and initially grew mostly in Europe, by the late 1990s it was increasingly popular in both North America and Asia. In China, the government was encouraging companies to obtain ISO certification.

There are basically five standards associated with the ISO 9000 series:

1. ISO 9000
   Essentially a set of guidelines for the selection and use of the appropriate systems standards ISO 9001, 9002, and 9003
2. ISO 9001
   Model for quality assurance in design, development, production, installation, and servicing.
3. ISO 9002
   Model for quality assurance in production, installation, and servicing.
4. ISO 9003
   Model for quality assurance in final inspections and testing.
5. ISO 9004
   Guide for the application of various elements of a quality management system.

The ISO 9000 standards have 20 elements concerning how well the company's quality system operates (see, for example, R.B. Chase and N.J. Aquilano: *Production and Operations Management: Manufacturing and Services.* Irwin, Chicago, 1995). The company, not ISO, determines what quality standards to assure. Hence, the series are dealing with the management of quality systems rather than with the quality of the company's products and services.

The following activities are often parts of the process leading up the certification:

- assignment of responsibility;
- training of key people;
- assessment of existing practices and procedures;
- documentation of practices and procedures;
- implementation of procedures;
- internal audit and/or outside party pre-assessment;
- formal independent assessment; and
- certification and registration.

THE STAR PROGRAM

A project team from Germany arrived in February 1998 to install the STAR program and train employees in the system. The objective was to create an integrated logistics system, in which the STAR program would monitor stock levels and transmit product orders to Germany. In addition, the program would be supported by the price quotation system, PREIS, which generated equipment lists with prices. For the experts arriving from Germany, it was an exciting pilot project—nowhere else had the two programs been integrated. To do so made lots of sense: data from the price quotation system could boost the efficiency with which the ordering process would be handled. Furthermore, the logistics department in Germany believed that the experience in GE would prove useful in a new manufacturing joint venture that DEI was planning to establish in China.

Unfortunately, the project did not proceed according to expectations. Because Patricia Gui was not yet serving as logistics manager, GE had no logistics department and thus nobody in the organization had responsibility for the project. An additional problem was that the programs' computer language had never been used in China— it was impossible to find anybody there who could work with the program itself. Program documentation was also written in German, and the program would neither accept entries in, nor print, Chinese characters. Moreover, despite numerous attempts to train them, the sales staff found it "too complicated;" customers did as well. Finally, the program had been developed for production management, and thus was apparently unsuitable for a company devoted solely to sales and service. Eight months after the arrival of the project team, the STAR program could only be used to place orders in Germany. In retrospect, the German manager in charge commented that: "we tried to copy [the program] 100 percent in China—it wasn't a very good idea, and I'm not sure whether I think it's suitable there."

In order for the STAR system to work, the company's sales force had to use PREIS, a system that DEI used in a number of countries. To persuade them to do so became the task of Davi Mann, the fifth manager to arrive from Germany.

SALES AND MARKETING

Mann had previously worked as an international sales manager. When he signed his contract, Klein had told Mann that his main task was going to be to "help bring 'the DEI Way' to the company." His job title was "sales manager," with three sales team managers reporting directly to him. However, the local marketing manager was soon transferred to the training department, which added marketing management to his job title.

One of Mann's first challenges was to convince people to use the new sales contract templates. He began by telling the sales managers that they had to start using DEI templates in China, "as it's company procedure" and also because it included clauses that were regarded as necessary safeguards for the company. However, he made little progress with GE's sales people. While many were evasive in their answers, some told him directly that, because "customers refuse to read so many pages," the contract template was a useless handicap to their sales. Mann was not certain whether or not that was the main reason for their reluctance.

Mann later revised some of the clauses and tried a shorter version of the contract. This time, however, he began by discussing the matter with Chen. It's "the only way to get things done," he said. "They always check with him anyway before they do it." During the fall of 1998, sales people started to use the new template. However, it was still unclear whether the contracts included all necessary information, such as promises made to buyers during the negotiation process.

ISO 9002 added a few requirements to contracting procedures. Before contracts were signed, representatives of all the relevant departments should meet together to review them. For GE, this meant that sales and marketing, product competence center, customer service, and finance and control should meet. However, such a meeting had taken place only once, with the largest project signed by GE to date. In this meeting, managers noted that not only was the timetable too tight, but penalties for delivery delays were too severe. However, the sales people reassured everybody that the company would not need to pay: they had good relationships with buyers, whom, they said, they would keep happy. Because there was some pressure from DEI China to accept the project as well, eventually the contract was signed.

Another major challenge for Mann was to change the way in which project offers were made. The Controller Uli Beck also pushed him to work on this. So far, sales people included only the direct costs of the products in their calculations; other costs tended to be added at a later stage and thus were rarely included in their calculations. This also meant that GE signed contracts without knowing the real sales margins. What was needed, Mann thought, was a tool to calculate total project costs, which included after-sales services, agent commissions, finance charges according to pay-back conditions, kick-backs, and the like.

After six months into his job, Mann was beginning to have trouble handling all of the issues that came his way. The sales teams were still functioning on a rather ad hoc basis, without formal plans for their activities, that is, how to identify customers, how to qualify customers as well as gauge their prospects for winning a certain contract, how to make bids, and how to follow up on project implementation. They also seemed to spend too much time trying to win small contracts. As it turned out, the only sales team likely to meet its sales budget for 1998 was the group focusing on large projects.

Mann hoped to systematize the activities of the sales teams. But he knew that it would be a "very big change for the [sales people] from traveling and running around" to sitting in headquarters to "plan activities, write reports, etc. It's new terminology and a new way of thinking." Furthermore, communication across units was sporadic at best. It appeared that employees found it very difficult to think and work in terms of processes; their focus seemed to be entirely on the on-going activities of their own unit.

KLEIN LEAVES THE COMPANY

During the spring of 1998, morale in the company plummeted. Carrying out an old threat, Klein canceled the existing bonus scheme for the local employees, eliminating all the bonuses they had earned during the last six months. Enraged by this action, the sales people went on strike. When Klein refused to discuss the matter, it fell to Beck to negotiate with local employees. Although the issue was not entirely settled, the sales people did return to their jobs. Klein then decided to specify the size of the contracts that certain employees were allowed to sign. According to the new regulations, only he could sign major contracts, while the signatures of both deputy GM Chen and Mann would be required for medium-sized contracts. When he heard that he was not any more allowed to sign contracts by himself, Chen angrily refused to sign any contracts at all. Chen stopped working almost entirely, preferring to read business books during working hours instead. There were virtually no management meetings, which Chen would have refused to attend anyway. As contact dwindled between the German expatriates in GE and Rural Red Star, financial controllers became the only viable channel of communication. On the initiative of Rural Red Star, Beck regularly met his Chinese counterpart for informal discussions.

Klein, employees knew, had serious personal problems. He was consuming large quantities of alcohol. His relationship with the other Germans had become so bad that a fistfight broke out during a company outing that all employees witnessed. Gradually, Beck became the informal leader of the company. As people in DEI's China headquarters received information about the situation in GE, Fischer was asked to write a report to DEI's Controller in the China headquarters on the situation.

While there were sporadic attempts to negotiate with the Chinese partner concerning a change in the equity distribution, they proceeded only slowly. A decision, enshrined in a new contract, was finally reached: DEI would become the majority shareholder. The contract contained other important changes, including a provision that mandated DEI to appoint the chief controller, while Rural Red Star was responsible for naming an assistant controller. Regardless of the profitability of the company, the local partner would be paid a specified dividend.

At a board meeting in May 1998, the new contract was formally approved. There was also an informal meeting between one of DEI's board members and Fischer. During this meeting, Fischer was promised that action would be taken within two weeks. In reality, three months of virtual paralysis ensued. Then finally, employees were informed that Klein was going to be replaced by Gunther Dane.

THE NEW GM ARRIVES

In late August 1998, a management meeting took place. Klein chaired the meeting, introducing Gunther Dane, the new GM, to the management group. Dane had been offered the job in July. The message that he received from DEI's top executives was that: "There are some problems [in GE], go there and fix it!" After some hesitation, he accepted the position. By October, Dane had finally managed to finish most of

EXHIBIT 3. The Guangdong Electronics Organization in November 1998

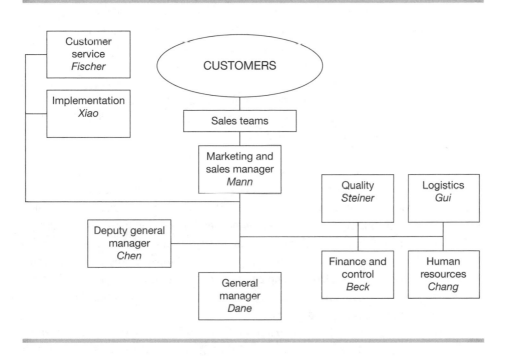

his ongoing tasks in Beijing and moved permanently to GE. However, he gave no indication how long he was willing to serve as the company's general manager.

Like all his predecessors, Dane was German. But he had already spent three years in China, based at the headquarters in Beijing. During this period he had visited GE a number of times, and had developed a good relationship with Mr Chen, now his deputy GM. The employees immediately noticed that Dane engaged in many more face-to-face interactions than his predecessor had done. Dane asked questions, listened, and discussed solutions with people in the company (See Exhibit 3 for the organizational structure of the company at the end of October 1998). His approach, to both German and local managers, was very personal.

LOOKING TO THE FUTURE

Now fully installed in his new office, Dane recognized a number of fundamental challenges. In addition to the managerial problems he had inherited, the company's products were not on the central government's list of "approved" and "suggested" products. There was also a new "buy local campaign." Already, local competitors had offered a number of good, yet cheaper products. In addition, the local Chinese firms had considerably more sales people at their disposal. Confirming the new GM's fears, the controller Uli Beck reported that sales lagged behind target and costs were rising. Finally, there was always the question of whether customers would start to demand penalties for late deliveries. Mr Chen had told him that at least one customer was likely to do so. With several other projects running behind schedule, Dane wondered whether more would demand the penalty payments to which they were entitled under contract. With a new building about to be constructed, GE's financial situation appeared increasingly precarious.

Nonetheless, Dane knew that GE stood on solid ground. The company's sales force appeared to have built a reliable network of customer relationships, and, in spite of some delays in the deliveries, the company enjoyed a good reputation. Many of the employees were competent and skillful, and their English skills had improved. Moreover, DEI's majority ownership had simplified decision-making.

Perhaps the most pressing question was what to do about the internal management of GE. The bonus system remained a divisive question. GE also needed to develop the HR function from the ground up. With the ISO 9002 project apparently stalled, Rudolf Steiner, the quality manager, had announced that he would return to Germany in December. In addition, customer service manager Bernd Fischer, the German with the longest tenure, planned to leave the company around then. On the technical front, STAR continued to suffer from technical problems that the logistics department had worked very hard to solve, including the Chinese character issue; PREIS also functioned in a less than satisfactory manner.

Further food for thought came from a quality audit report that was written by a DEI expert group following their visit to GE in October. The purpose of their visit had been to monitor GE's progress in the pursuit of the ISO 9002 benchmark standards and to suggest areas for improvement. In their report, the quality experts observed:

> Visions and long range plans of [GE] were not available. There is no evidence available that quality planning in general is done; [there appear to be] no defined processes, few documented procedures, and no defined objectives and targets; no evidence [emerged] that management is reviewing customer satisfaction, achievement of objectives, audit results, etc. [GE's] quality manual is not yet available, and many procedures have not been documented.

The summary of the report is reproduced in Exhibit 4.

Dane knew that morale in the joint venture would have to improve. He believed that he could motivate Chen again, but what kind of role should he give Chen in the management of the company? Up to now, GE appeared to be split between two "camps" in the firm, with Chinese employees on one side and German expatriates on the other. Patricia Gui seemed to be an outsider in both groups. Did he need to try to change this situation, and if so, how?

Dane's first management meeting would take place next week. What should he do?

> **EXHIBIT 4.** Summary of the report made by the quality audit group in October 1998

[GE] has no issued performance objectives. It seems that the organization is managed case by case, department by department.

Customer needs are not a self-evident goal. There are no defined processes [regarding how] to meet customer requirements.

The people in [GE] know their tasks and responsibilities; they have skills to do the tasks required by their departments.

There are many deficiencies to rectify before the third party certification to ISO 9002 can be achieved. The non-conformities recorded could have been divided into numerous detailed non-conformities. However, it is important to plan the objectives and business processes before the specific elements of quality management can be implemented.

The audit covered all elements of ISO 9002. For this reason the auditors recommend that the next audit covering the whole organization should be in 1999.

NOTE

* This case was written by Ingmar Bjorkman, Visiting Professor of International Management at INSEAD, France & Professor at the Hanken School of Economics, Finland, and Ming Zeng, Assistant Professor of Asian Business at INSEAD. It is intended to be used a basis for class discussion rather than to illustrate effective or ineffective handling of a situation. The identity of the companies and persons involved has been disguised.

PART 5

Global Business Ethics, Corporate Social Responsibility, and Management of Diversity

Thomas Donaldson

WHEN IS DIFFERENT JUST DIFFERENT, AND WHEN IS DIFFERENT WRONG?*

WHEN WE LEAVE HOME and cross our nation's boundaries, moral clarity often blurs. Without a backdrop of shared attitudes, and without familiar laws and judicial procedures that define standards of ethical conduct, certainty is elusive. Should a company invest in a foreign country where civil and political rights are violated? Should a company go along with a host country's discriminatory employment practices? If companies in developed countries shift facilities to developing nations that lack strict environmental and health regulations, or if those companies choose to fill management and other top-level positions in a host nation with people from the home country, whose standards should prevail?

Even the best-informed, best-intentioned executives must rethink their assumptions about business practice in foreign settings. What works in a company's home country can fail in a country with different standards of ethical conduct. Such difficulties are unavoidable for businesspeople who live and work abroad.

VALUES IN TENSION

But how can managers resolve the problems? What are the principles that can help them work through the maze of cultural differences and establish codes of conduct for globally ethical business practice? How can companies answer the toughest question in global business ethics: What happens when a host country's ethical standards seem lower than the home country's?

COMPETING ANSWERS

One answer is as old as philosophical discourse. According to cultural relativism, no culture's ethics are better than any other's; therefore, there are no international rights and wrongs. If the people of Indonesia tolerate the bribery of their public officials, so what? Their attitude is no better or worse than that of people in Denmark or Singapore who refuse to offer or accept bribes. Likewise, if Belgians fail to find insider trading morally repugnant, who cares? Not enforcing insider-trading laws is no more or less ethical than enforcing such laws.

The cultural relativist's creed — when in Rome, do as the Romans do — is tempting, especially when failing to do as the locals do means forfeiting business opportunities. The inadequacy of cultural relativism, however, becomes apparent when the practices in question are more damaging than petty bribery or insider trading.

In the late 1980s, some European tanneries and pharmaceutical companies were looking for cheap waste-dumping sites. They approached virtually every country on Africa's west coast from Morocco to the Congo. Nigeria agreed to take highly toxic polychlorinated biphenyls. Unprotected local workers, wearing thongs and shorts, unloaded barrels of PCBs and placed them near a residential area. Neither the residents nor the workers knew that the barrels contained toxic waste.

We may denounce governments that permit such abuses, but many countries are unable to police transnational corporations adequately even if they want to. And, in many countries, the combination of ineffective enforcement and inadequate regulations leads to behavior by unscrupulous companies, which is clearly wrong. A few years ago, for example, a group of investors became interested in restoring the SS United States, once a luxurious ocean liner. Before the actual restoration could begin, the ship had to be stripped of its asbestos lining. A bid from a US company, based on US standards for asbestos removal, priced the job at more than $100 million. A company in the Ukranian city of Sevastopol offered to do the work for less than $2 million. In October 1993, the ship was towed to Sevastopol.

A cultural relativist would have no problem with that outcome, but I do. A country has the right to establish its own health and safety regulations, but in the case described above, the standards and the terms of the contract could not possibly have protected workers in Sevastopol from known health risks. Even if the contract met Ukranian standards, ethical businesspeople must object. Cultural relativism is morally blind. There are fundamental values that cross cultures, and companies must uphold them. (For an economic argument against cultural relativism, see the box "The Culture and Ethics of Software Piracy," p. 386.)

ETHICS AWAY FROM HOME

At the other end of the spectrum from cultural relativism is ethical imperialism, which directs people to do everywhere exactly as they do at home. Again, an understandably appealing approach, but one that is clearly inadequate. Consider the large US computer products company that in 1993 introduced a course on sexual harassment in its Saudi Arabian facility. Under the banner of global consistency, instructors used the same approach to train Saudi Arabian managers that they had used with US managers: the participants were asked to discuss a case in which a manager makes sexually explicit remarks to a new female employee over drinks in a bar. The instructors failed to consider how the exercise would work in a culture with strict conventions governing relationships between men and women. As a result, the training sessions were ludicrous. They baffled and offended the Saudi participants, and the message to avoid coercion and sexual discrimination was lost.

The theory behind ethical imperialism is absolutism, which is based on three problematic principles. Absolutists believe that there is a single list of truths, that they can be expressed only with one set of concepts, and that they call for exactly the same behavior around the world.

The first claim clashes with many people's belief that different cultural traditions must be respected. In some cultures, loyalty to a community – family, organization, or society – is the foundation of all ethical behavior. The Japanese, for example, define business ethics in terms of loyalty to their companies, their business networks, and their nation. Americans place a higher value on liberty than on loyalty; the US tradition of rights emphasizes equality, fairness, and individual freedom. It is hard to conclude that truth lies on one side or the other, but an absolutist would have us select just one.

The second problem with absolutism is the presumption that people must express moral truth using only one set of concepts. For instance, some absolutists insist that the language of basic rights provide the framework for any discussion of ethics. That means, though, that entire cultural traditions must be ignored. The notion of a right evolved with the rise of democracy in post-Renaissance Europe and the US, but the term is not found in either Confucian or Buddhist traditions. We all learn ethics in the context of our particular cultures, and the power in the principles is deeply tied to the way in which they are expressed. Internationally accepted lists of moral principles, such as the United Nations' Universal Declaration of Human Rights, draw on many cultural and religious traditions. As philosopher Michael Walzer has noted, "There is no Esperanto of global ethics."

The third problem with absolutism is the belief in a global standard of ethical behavior. Context must shape ethical practice. Very low wages, for example, may be considered unethical in rich, advanced countries, but developing nations may be acting ethically if they encourage investment and improve living standards by accepting low wages. Likewise, when people are malnourished or starving, a government may be wise to use more fertilizer in order to improve crop yields, even though that means settling for relatively high levels of thermal water pollution.

When cultures have different standards of ethical behavior – and different ways of handling unethical behavior – a company that takes an absolutist approach may find itself making a disastrous mistake. When a manager at a large US specialty-products company in China caught an employee stealing, she followed the company's practice and turned the employee over to the provincial authorities, who executed him. Managers cannot operate in another culture without being aware of that culture's attitudes toward ethics.

If companies can neither adopt a host country's ethics nor extend the home country's standards, what is the answer? Even the traditional litmus test – what would people think of your actions if they were written up on the front page of the newspaper? – is an unreliable guide, for there is no international consensus on standards of business conduct.

BOX 1. The Culture and Ethics of Software Piracy

Before jumping on the cultural relativism bandwagon, stop and consider the potential economic consequences of a when-in-Rome attitude toward business ethics. Take a look at the current statistics on software piracy: In the US, pirated software is estimated to be 35 percent of the total software market, and industry losses are estimated at $2.3 billion per year. The piracy rate is 57 percent in Germany and 80 percent in Italy and Japan; the rates in most Asian countries are estimated to be nearly 100 percent.

There are similar laws against software piracy in those countries. What, then, accounts for the differences? Although a country's level of economic development plays a large part, culture, including ethical attitudes, may be a more crucial factor. The 1995 annual report of the Software Publishers Association connects software piracy directly to culture and attitude. It describes Italy and Hong Kong as having "'first world' per capita incomes, along with 'third world' rates of piracy." When asked whether one should use software without paying for it, most people, including people in Italy and Hong Kong, say no. But people in some countries regard the practice as *less* unethical than people in other countries do. Confucian culture, for example, stresses that individuals should share what they create with society. That may be, in part, what prompts the Chinese and other Asians to view the concept of intellectual property as a means for the West to monopolize its technological superiority.

What happens if ethical attitudes around the world permit large-scale software piracy? Software companies won't want to invest as much in developing new products, because they cannot expect any return on their investment in certain parts of the world. When ethics fail to support technological creativity, there are consequences that go beyond statistics – jobs are lost and livelihoods jeopardized.

Companies must do more than lobby foreign governments for tougher enforcement of piracy laws. They must cooperate with other companies and with local organizations to help citizens understand the consequences of piracy and to encourage the evolution of a different ethic toward the practice.

BALANCING THE EXTREMES: THREE GUIDING PRINCIPLES

Companies must help managers distinguish between practices that are merely different and those that are wrong. For relativists, nothing is sacred and nothing is wrong. For absolutists, many things that are different are wrong. Neither extreme illuminates the real world of business decision-making. The answer lies somewhere in between.

When it comes to shaping ethical behavior, companies must be guided by three principles:

- Respect for core human values, which determine the absolute moral threshold for all business activities.
- Respect for local traditions.
- The belief that context matters when deciding what is right and what is wrong.

Consider those principles in action. In Japan, people doing business together often exchange gifts – sometimes expensive ones – in keeping with long-standing Japanese tradition. When US and European companies started doing a lot of business in Japan, many Western businesspeople thought that the practice of gift giving might be wrong rather than simply different. To them, accepting a gift felt like accepting a bribe. As Western companies have become more familiar with Japanese traditions, however, most have come to tolerate the practice and to set different limits on gift giving in Japan than they do elsewhere.

Respecting differences is a crucial ethical practice. Research shows that management ethics differ among cultures; respecting those differences means recognizing that some cultures have obvious weaknesses – as well as hidden strengths. Managers in Hong Kong, for example, have a higher tolerance for some forms of bribery than their Western counterparts, but they have a much lower tolerance for the failure to acknowledge a subordinate's work. In some parts of the Far East, stealing credit from a subordinate is nearly an unpardonable sin.

People often equate respect for local traditions with cultural relativism. That is incorrect. Some practices are clearly wrong. Union Carbide's tragic experience in Bhopal, India provides one example. The company's executives seriously underestimated how much on-site management involvement was needed at the Bhopal plant to compensate for the country's poor infrastructure and regulatory capabilities. In the aftermath of the disastrous gas leak, the lesson is clear: companies using sophisticated technology in a developing country must evaluate that country's ability to oversee its safe use. Since the incident at Bhopal, Union Carbide has become a leader in advising companies on using hazardous technologies safely in developing countries.

Some activities are wrong no matter where they take place. But some practices that are unethical in one setting may be acceptable in another. For instance, the chemical EDB, a soil fungicide, is banned for use in the US. In hot climates, however, it quickly becomes harmless through exposure to intense solar radiation and high soil temperatures. As long as the chemical is monitored, companies may be able to use EDB ethically in certain parts of the world.

DEFINING THE ETHICAL THRESHOLD: CORE VALUES

Few ethical questions are easy for managers to answer. But there are some hard truths that must guide managers' actions, a set of what I call *core human values*, which define minimum ethical standards for all companies.[1] The right to good health and the right to economic advancement and an improved standard of living are two core human values. Another is what Westerners call the Golden Rule, which is recognizable in every major religious and ethical tradition around the world. In Book 15 of his *Analects,* for instance, Confucius counsels people to maintain reciprocity, or not to do to others what they do not want done to themselves.

Although no single list would satisfy every scholar, I believe it is possible to articulate three core values that incorporate the work of scores of theologians and philosophers around the world. To be broadly relevant, these values must include elements found in both Western and non-Western cultural and religious traditions. Consider the examples of values in the box "What Do These Values Have in Common?" below.

At first glance, the values expressed in the two lists seem quite different. Nonetheless, in the spirit of what philosopher John Rawls calls *overlapping consensus,* one can see that the seemingly divergent values converge at key points, Despite important differences between Western and non-Western cultural and religious traditions, both express shared attitudes about what it means to be human. First, individuals must not treat others simply as tools; in other words, they must recognize a person's value as a human being. Next, individuals and communities must treat people in ways that respect people's basic rights. Finally, members of a community must work together to support and improve the institutions on which the community depends. I call those three values *respect for human dignity, respect for basic rights,* and *good citizenship.*

Those values must be the starting point for all companies as they formulate and evaluate standards of ethical conduct at home and abroad. But they are only a starting point. Companies need much more specific guidelines, and the first step to developing those is to translate the core human values into core values for business. What does it mean, for example, for a company to respect human dignity? How can a company be a good citizen?

BOX 2. What Do These Values Have in Common?

Non-Western	*Western*
Kyosei (Japanese): Living and working together for the common good.	Individual liberty
Dharma (Hindu): The fulfillment of inherited duty.	Egalitarianism
Santutthi (Buddhist): The importance of limited desires.	Political participation
Zakat (Muslim): The duty to give alms to the Muslim poor.	Human rights

I believe that companies can respect human dignity by creating and sustaining a corporate culture in which employees, customers, and suppliers are treated not as means to an end but as people whose intrinsic value must be acknowledged, and by producing safe products and services in a safe workplace. Companies can respect basic rights by acting in ways that support and protect the individual rights of employees, customers, and surrounding communities, and by avoiding relationships that violate human beings' rights to health, education, safety, and an adequate standard of living. And companies can be good citizens by supporting essential social institutions, such as the economic system and the education system, and by working with host governments and other organizations to protect the environment.

The core values establish a moral compass for business practice. They can help companies identify practices that are acceptable and those that are intolerable – even if the practices are compatible with a host country's norms and laws. Dumping pollutants near people's homes and accepting inadequate standards for handling hazardous materials are two examples of actions that violate core values.

Similarly, if employing children prevents them from receiving a basic education, the practice is intolerable. Lying about product specifications in the act of selling may not affect human lives directly, but it too is intolerable because it violates the trust that is needed to sustain a corporate culture in which customers are respected.

Sometimes it is not a company's actions but those of a supplier or customer that pose problems. Take the case of the Tan family, a large supplier for Levi Strauss. The Tans were allegedly forcing 1,200 Chinese and Filipino women to work 74 hours per week in guarded compounds on the Mariana Islands. In 1992, after repeated warnings to the Tans, Levi Strauss broke off business relations with them.

Many companies don't do anything with their codes of conduct; they simply paste them on the wall.

CREATING AN ETHICAL CORPORATE CULTURE

The core values for business that I have enumerated can help companies begin to exercise ethical judgment and think about how to operate ethically in foreign cultures, but they are not specific enough to guide managers through actual ethical dilemmas. Levi Strauss relied on a written code of conduct when figuring out how to deal with the Tan family. The company's Global Sourcing and Operating Guidelines, formerly called the Business Partner Terms of Engagement, state that Levi Strauss will "seek to identify and utilize business partners who aspire as individuals and in the conduct of all their businesses to a set of ethical standards not incompatible with our own." Whenever intolerable business situations arise, managers should be guided by precise statements that spell out the behavior and operating practices that the company demands.

Ninety percent of all *Fortune* 500 companies have codes of conduct, and 70 percent have statements of vision and values. In Europe and the Far East, the percentages are lower but are increasing rapidly. Does that mean that most companies have what they need? Hardly. Even though most large US companies have both statements of values and codes of conduct, many might be better off if they didn't. Too many companies don't do anything with the documents; they simply paste them on the wall to impress employees, customers, suppliers, and the public. As a result, the senior managers who drafted the statements lose credibility by proclaiming values and not living up to them. Companies such as Johnson & Johnson, Levi Strauss, Motorola, Texas Instruments, and Lockheed Martin, however, do a great deal to make the words meaningful. Johnson & Johnson, for example, has become well known for its Credo Challenge sessions, in which managers discuss ethics in the context of their current business problems and are invited to criticize the company's credo and make suggestions for changes. The participants' ideas are passed on to the company's senior managers. Lockheed Martin has created an innovative site on the Web and on its local network that gives employees, customers, and suppliers access to the company's ethical code and the chance to voice complaints.

Codes of conduct must provide clear direction about ethical behavior when the temptation to behave unethically is strongest. The pronouncement in a code of conduct that bribery is unacceptable is useless unless accompanied by guidelines for gift giving, payments to get goods through customs, and "requests" from intermediaries who are hired to ask for bribes.

Motorola's values are stated very simply as "How we will always act: [with] constant respect for people [and] uncompromising integrity." The company's code of conduct, however, is explicit about actual business practice. With respect to bribery, for example, the code states that the "funds and assets of Motorola shall not be used, directly or indirectly, for illegal payments of any kind." It is unambiguous about what sort of payment is illegal: "the payment of a bribe to a public official or the kickback of funds to an employee of a customer." The code goes on to prescribe specific procedures for handling commissions to intermediaries, issuing sales invoices, and disclosing confidential information in a sales transaction – all situations in which employees might have an opportunity to accept or offer bribes.

Codes of conduct must be explicit to be useful, but they must also leave room for a manager to use his or her judgment in situations requiring cultural sensitivity. Host-country employees shouldn't be forced to adopt all home-country values and renounce their own. Again, Motorola's code is exemplary. First, it gives clear direction: "Employees of Motorola will respect the laws, customs, and traditions of each country in which they operate, but will, at the same time, engage in no course of conduct which, even if legal, customary, and accepted in any such country, could be deemed to be in violation of the accepted business ethics of Motorola or the laws of the United States relating to business ethics." After laying down such absolutes, Motorola's code then makes clear when individual judgment will be necessary. For example, employees may sometimes accept certain kinds of small gifts "in rare circumstances, where the refusal to accept a gift" would injure Motorola's "legitimate business interests." Under certain circumstances, such gifts "may be accepted so long as the gift inures to the benefit of Motorola" and not "to the benefit of the Motorola employee."

Striking the appropriate balance between providing clear direction and leaving room for individual judgment makes crafting corporate values statements and ethics codes one of the hardest tasks that executives confront. The words are only a start.

A company's leaders need to refer often to their organization's credo and code and must themselves be credible, committed, and consistent. If senior managers act as though ethics don't matter, the rest of the company's employees won't think they do, either.

Many activities are neither good nor bad but exist in *moral free space.*

CONFLICTS OF DEVELOPMENT AND CONFLICTS OF TRADITION

Managers living and working abroad who are not prepared to grapple with moral ambiguity and tension should pack their bags and come home. The view that all business practices can be categorized as either ethical or unethical is too simple. As Einstein is reported to have said, "Things should be as simple as possible – but no simpler." Many business practices that are considered unethical in one setting may be ethical in another. Such activities are neither black nor white but exist in what Thomas Dunfee and I have called *moral free space.*[2] In this gray zone, there are no tight prescriptions for a company's behavior. Managers must chart their own courses – as long as they do not violate core human values.

Consider the following example. Some successful Indian companies offer employees the opportunity for one of their children to gain a job with the company once the child has completed a certain level in school. The companies honor this commitment even when other applicants are more qualified than an employee's child. The perk is extremely valuable in a country where jobs are hard to find, and it reflects the Indian culture's belief that the West has gone too far in allowing economic opportunities to break up families. Not surprisingly, the perk is among the most cherished by employees, but in most Western countries, it would be branded unacceptable nepotism. In the US, for example, the ethical principle of equal opportunity holds that jobs should go to the applicants with the best qualifications. If a US company made such promises to its employees, it would violate regulations established by the Equal Employment Opportunity Commission. Given this difference in ethical attitudes, how should US managers react to Indian nepotism? Should they condemn the Indian companies, refusing to accept them as partners or suppliers until they agree to clean up their act?

Despite the obvious tension between nepotism and principles of equal opportunity, I cannot condemn the practice for Indians. In a country such as India that emphasizes clan and family relationships and has catastrophic levels of unemployment, the practice must be viewed in moral free space. The decision to allow a special perk for employees and their children is not necessarily wrong – at least for members of that country.

How can managers discover the limits of moral free space? That is, how can they learn to distinguish a value in tension with their own from one that is intolerable? Helping managers develop good ethical judgment requires companies to be clear about their core values and codes of conduct. But even the most explicit set of guidelines cannot always provide answers. That is especially true in the thorniest ethical dilemmas, in which the host country's ethical standards not only are different but also seem lower than the home country's. Managers must recognize that when countries have different ethical standards, there are two types of conflict that commonly arise. Each type requires its own line of reasoning.

In the first type of conflict, which I call a *conflict of relative development*, ethical standards conflict because of the countries' different levels of economic development. As mentioned before, developing countries may accept wage rates that seem inhumane to more advanced countries in order to attract investment. As economic conditions in a developing country improve, the incidence of that sort of conflict usually decreases. The second type of conflict is a *conflict of cultural tradition*. For example, Saudi Arabia, unlike most other countries, does not allow women to serve as corporate managers. Instead, women may work in only a few professions, such as education and health care. The prohibition stems from strongly held religious and cultural beliefs; any increase in the country's level of economic development, which is already quite high, is not likely to change the rules.

To resolve a conflict of relative development, a manager must ask the following question: would the practice be acceptable at home if my country were in a similar stage of economic development? Consider the difference between wage and safety standards in the US and in Angola, where citizens accept lower standards on both counts. If a US oil company is hiring Angolans to work on an offshore Angolan oil rig, can the company pay them lower wages than it pays US workers in the Gulf of Mexico? Reasonable people have to answer yes if the alternative for Angola is the loss of both the foreign investment and the jobs.

Consider, too, differences in regulatory environments. In the 1980s, the government of India fought hard to be able to import Ciba-Geigy's Entero Vioform, a drug known to be enormously effective in fighting dysentery but one that had been banned in the US because some users experienced side effects. Although dysentery was not a big problem in the US, in India, poor public sanitation was contributing to epidemic levels of the disease. Was it unethical to make the drug available in India after it had been banned in the US? On the contrary, rational people should consider it unethical not to do so. Apply our test: would the US, at an earlier stage of development, have used this drug despite its side effects? The answer is clearly yes.

If a company declared all gift giving unethical, it wouldn't be able to do business in Japan.

But there are many instances when the answer to similar questions is no. Sometimes a host country's standards are inadequate at any level of economic development. If a country's pollution standards are so low that working on an oil rig would considerably increase a person's risk of developing cancer, foreign oil companies must refuse to do business there. Likewise, if the dangerous side effects of a drug treatment outweigh its benefits, managers should not accept health standards that ignore the risks.

When relative economic conditions do not drive tensions, there is a more objective test for resolving ethical problems. Managers should deem a practice permissible only if they can answer no to both of the following questions: is it possible to conduct business successfully in the host country without undertaking the practice? And: is the practice a violation of a core human value? Japanese gift giving is a perfect

BOX 3. The Problem with Bribery

Bribery is widespread and insidious. Managers in transnational companies routinely confront bribery even though most countries have laws against it. The fact is that officials in many developing countries wink at the practice, and the salaries of local bureaucrats are so low that many consider bribes a form of remuneration. The US Foreign Corrupt Practices Act defines allowable limits on petty bribery in the form of routine payments required to move goods through customs. But demands for bribes often exceed those limits, and there is seldom a good solution.

Bribery disrupts distribution channels when goods languish on docks until local handlers are paid off, and it destroys incentives to compete on quality and cost when purchasing decisions are based on who pays what under the table. Refusing to acquiesce is often tantamount to giving business to unscrupulous companies.

I believe that even routine bribery is intolerable. Bribery undermines market efficiency and predictability, thus ultimately denying people their right to a minimal standard of living. Some degree of ethical commitment – some sense that everyone will play by the rules – is necessary for a sound economy. Without an ability to predict outcomes, who would be willing to invest?

There was a US company whose shipping crates were regularly pilfered by handlers on the docks of Rio de Janeiro. The handlers would take about 10 percent of the contents of the crates, but the company was never sure which 10 percent it would be. In a partial solution, the company began sending two crates – the first with 90 percent of the merchandise, the second with 10 percent. The handlers learned to take the second crate and leave the first untouched. From the company's perspective, at least knowing which goods it would lose was an improvement.

Bribery does more than destroy predictability; it undermines essential social and economic systems. That truth is not lost on businesspeople in countries where the practice is woven into the social fabric. CEOs in India admit that their companies engage constantly in bribery, and they say that they have considerable disgust for the practice. They blame government policies in part, but Indian executives also know that their country's business practices perpetuate corrupt behavior. Anyone walking the streets of Calcutta, where it is clear that even a dramatic redistribution of wealth would still leave most of India's inhabitants in dire poverty, comes face to face with the devastating effects of corruption.

example of a conflict of cultural tradition. Most experienced businesspeople, Japanese and non-Japanese alike, would agree that doing business in Japan would be virtually impossible without adopting the practice. Does gift giving violate a core human value? I cannot identify one that it violates. As a result, gift giving may be permissible for foreign companies in Japan even if it conflicts with ethical attitudes at home. In fact, that conclusion is widely accepted, even by companies such as Texas Instruments and IBM, which are outspoken against bribery.

Does it follow that all non monetary gifts are acceptable or that bribes are generally acceptable in countries where they are common? Not at all. (See the box "The Problem with Bribery" opposite.) What makes the routine practice of gift giving acceptable in Japan are the limits in its scope and intention. When gift giving moves outside those limits, it soon collides with core human values. For example, when Carl Kotchian, president of Lockheed in the 1970s, carried suitcases full of cash to Japanese politicians, he went beyond the norms established by Japanese tradition. That incident galvanized opinion in the US Congress and helped lead to passage of the Foreign Corrupt Practices Act. Likewise, Roh Tae Woo went beyond the norms established by Korean cultural tradition when he accepted $635.4 million in bribes as president of the Republic of Korea between 1988 and 1993.

GUIDELINES TOR ETHICAL LEADERSHIP

Learning to spot intolerable practices and to exercise good judgment when ethical conflicts arise requires practice. Creating a company culture that rewards ethical behavior is essential. The following guidelines for developing a global ethical perspective among managers can help.

Treat Corporate Values and Formal Standards of Conduct as Absolutes

Whatever ethical standards a company chooses, it cannot waver on its principles either at home or abroad. Consider what has become part of company lore at Motorola. Around 1950, a senior executive was negotiating with officials of a South American government on a $10 million sale that would have increased the company's annual net profits by nearly 25 percent. As the negotiations neared completion, however, the executive walked away from the deal because the officials were asking for $1 million for "fees." CEO Robert Galvin not only supported the executive's decision but also made it clear that Motorola would neither accept the sale on any terms nor do business with those government officials again. Retold over the decades, this story demonstrating Calvin's resolve has helped cement a culture of ethics for thousands of employees at Motorola.

Design and Implement Conditions of Engagement for Suppliers and Customers

Will your company do business with any customer or supplier? What if a customer or supplier uses child labor? What if it has strong links with organized crime? What if it pressures your company to break a host country's laws? Such issues are best not left for spur-of-the-moment decisions. Some companies have realized that. Sears, for instance, has developed a policy of not contracting production to companies that use prison labor or infringe on workers' rights to health and safety. And BankAmerica has specified as a condition for many of its loans to developing countries that environmental standards and human rights must be observed.

Allow Foreign Business Units to Help Formulate Ethical Standards and Interpret Ethical Issues

The French pharmaceutical company Rhône-Poulenc Rorer has allowed foreign subsidiaries to augment lists of corporate ethical principles with their own suggestions. Texas Instruments has paid special attention to issues of international business ethics by creating the Global Business Practices Council, which is made up of managers from countries in which the company operates. With the overarching intent to create a "global ethics strategy, locally deployed," the council's mandate is to provide ethics education and create local processes that will help managers in the company's foreign business units resolve ethical conflicts.

In Host Countries, Support Efforts to Decrease Institutional Corruption

Individual managers will not be able to wipe out corruption in a host country, no matter how many bribes they turn down. When a host country's tax system, import and export procedures, and procurement practices favor unethical players, companies must take action.

Many companies have begun to participate in reforming host-country institutions. General Electric, for example, has taken a strong stand in India, using the media to make repeated condemnations of bribery in business and government. General Electric and others have found, however, that a single company usually cannot drive out entrenched corruption. Transparency International, an organization based in Germany, has been effective in helping coalitions of companies, government officials, and others work to reform bribery-ridden bureaucracies in Russia, Bangladesh, and elsewhere.

Exercise Moral Imagination

Using moral imagination means resolving tensions responsibly and creatively. Coca Cola, for instance, has consistently turned down requests for bribes from Egyptian officials but has managed to gain political support and public trust by sponsoring a project to plant fruit trees. And take the example of Levi Strauss, which discovered in the early 1990s that two of its suppliers in Bangladesh were employing children under the age of 14 – a practice that violated the company's principles but was tolerated in Bangladesh. Forcing the suppliers to fire the children would not have ensured that the children received an education, and it would have caused serious hardship for the families depending on the children's wages. In a creative arrangement, the suppliers agreed to pay the children's regular wages while they attended school and to offer each child a job at age 14. Levi Strauss, in turn, agreed to pay the children's tuition and provide books and uniforms. That arrangement allowed Levi Strauss to uphold its principles and provide long-term benefits to its host country.

Many people think of values as soft; to some they are usually unspoken. A South Seas island society uses the word *mokita*, which means, "the truth that everybody knows but nobody speaks." However difficult they are to articulate, values affect how we all behave. In a global business environment, values in tension are the rule rather than the exception. Without a company's commitment, statements of values and codes of ethics end up as empty platitudes that provide managers with no foundation for behaving ethically. Employees need and deserve more, and responsible members of the global business community can set examples for others to follow. The dark consequences of incidents such as Union Carbide's disaster in Bhopal remind us how high the stakes can be.

NOTES

* Thomas Donaldson is a professor at the Wharton School of the University of Pennsylvania in Philadelphia, where he teaches business ethics. He wrote *The Ethics of International Business* (Oxford University Press, 1989) and is the coauthor, with Thomas W. Dunfee, of *Business Ethics as Social Contracts*, to be published by the Harvard Business School Press in the fall of 1997.

1.   In other writings, Thomas W. Dunfee and I have used the term *hypernorm* instead of *core human value*.
2.   Thomas Donaldson and Thomas W. Dunfee, "Toward a Unified Conception of Business Ethics: Integrative Social Contracts Theory," *Academy of Management Review*, April 1994; and "Integrative Social Contracts Theory: A Communitarian Conception of Economic Ethics," *Economics and Philosophy*, Spring 1995.

Judith White and Susan Taft

FRAMEWORKS FOR TEACHING AND LEARNING BUSINESS ETHICS WITHIN THE GLOBAL CONTEXT:* BACKGROUND OF ETHICAL THEORIES**

IN OUR GRADUATE AND UNDERGRADUATE organizational behavior and management classes, we have students from around in the world, yet throughout our teaching experience, we have not yet found a comprehensive theoretical approach to teaching and learning business ethics within a global context. Although many good models exist for teaching ethics from a domestic perspective (e.g. Liedtka, 1992; Mallinger, 1997; Piper et al., 1993), increasingly the business ethics challenges found both in the US and abroad involve understanding ethical dilemmas from the perspective of non-US stakeholders. In examining textbooks and journal articles, we find an increasing number of international business issues and cases but few tools to explore and understand the ethical challenges embedded in these issues. Following our interest in business ethics, global issues, and multi-culturalism, we developed a model to use in teaching and learning business ethics that addresses the global context.

We offer here a summary of several major traditional and contemporary philosophical and psychological approaches to ethical conduct to be used in business, along with five recognized sets of ethical guidelines from the twentieth century that are currently used in a global context. The different theoretical approaches, along with the guidelines, offer faculty and students an expanded means of exploring and solving ethical problems that honor a wide array of national, cultural, and ethnic contexts and differences. Additionally, we provide examples of corporate codes of conduct from particular corporations.

THE PHILOSOPHICAL TRADITIONS OF ETHICAL REASONING

Whether teaching organizational behavior, business and society, business ethics, human resources management, or general management, educating management students involves providing frameworks to approach ethical issues and dilemmas. Traditionally, these come from Western philosophy and psychology and are based on the ideas of Aristotle, Kant, Hume, Locke, Mill, Rawls, MacIntyre, Kohlberg, Noddings, and Gilligan. Some of these frameworks focus on processes or methods of making decisions or taking action, whereas other approaches are concerned almost exclusively with the consequences of actions and/or decisions. This separation of ends from means is an example of the Western way of thinking that is conditioned to divide into dualities.

As a foundation for teaching ethics in a global context, we offer here a brief summary of the main philosophical and psychological perspectives on ethical reasoning. To provide an orienting framework of ethics theory, we begin with a discussion of both Western and non-Western ethical frameworks, including those of Confucianism, Buddhism, and Native American traditions.

From the Western perspective, ethics have been divided into two main categories: teleological and deontological. *Teleological* or consequentialist approaches to ethics emphasize the consequences or results of an action or decision; whether actions are right or wrong depends on whether harm or good results from the action. Teleological theories, including utilitarianism, egoism, and care, claim that acts do not have intrinsic value but should be judged on the basis of the consequences they produce and on how they affect others.

Utilitarianism is based on the eighteenth-century ideas of Jeremy Bentham's belief in empiricism and the work of John Stuart Mill (Rosenstad, 1997; Velasquez, 1998), and is founded on the importance of basing knowledge on objective, physical evidence. Utilitarianism, as a teleological approach, takes a societal perspective on costs and benefits of ethical choice, suggesting that an action should be evaluated according to how much good or harm it causes and should consider the effects on all parties. Utilitarianism is meant to promote the welfare of all persons by minimizing harm and maximizing benefits, that is, using the criterion of achieving the greatest good for the greatest number, thus taking precedence over concerns of duties, rights, or justice. An example of a utilitarian-driven public policy decision would be to change US health care policy from a system that provides services primarily to insured individuals, leaving more than 43 million people without basic care, to a system that provides fundamental health and illness services to everyone.

Ethical *egoism* (Fritzsche, 1997), a teleological perspective, focuses on the maximization of an individual's own self-interest; however, it also can apply to the self-interest of an organization. In either case, decisions based on egoism are made to provide the most satisfactory consequences to the individual or organization making the decision or taking an action, regardless of the consequences to others. *Enlightened self-interest* takes into consideration the long-term and the welfare of others, considering direct and indirect consequences of an acton all relevant stakeholders during a period of time. As an example, a large company in a small town considers laying off a majority of its employees but can see the effects on the other local stake-holders, such as small businesses, social service agencies, and city services, and suspects its own future might be compromised as a consequence of the effects of the layoffs. When the company's management concludes that more damage will be done than benefits gained from the layoffs, and decides to postpone or minimize the layoffs, it is demonstrating enlightened self-interest.

The *ethic of care*, associated with the work of Gilligan (1982, 1987) and Noddings (1984), is both teleological and deontological. The ethic of care maintains that essential to ethical behavior are the basic principles of being responsible toward others, maintaining a relationship with others, minimizing harm to others, and considering both one's own and the others' feelings and emotions. When using the ethic of care to decide or act, one considers the specific context and/or circumstances surrounding the situation, assuming that every situation is unique and calls for a situation-specific solution and an individualized response rather than relying on abstract, universal, and generalized principles, rules, laws, or policies. Summarizing Gilligan's concept of care, White (1994) suggests care is

> a positive and essential aspect of moral maturity that calls for the avoidance of harm and the preservation of relationships . . . a morality of responsiveness to the needs of others, a strength valuable to developing relationships among people and in community and essential for survival . . . People who use a morality of care are concerned with outcomes; who will be harmed and what will happen to the relationship . . . Solutions to ethical dilemmas are inclusive, transforming the identity through the experience of relationship.
>
> (pp. 634–635)

The ethic of care has established a presence among the various frameworks of ethical reasoning in business (Derry, 1989; Dobson and White, 1995; White, 1994), previously having been attributed primarily to the domestic and personal rather than public arena. Some examples of applications of the ethic of care in the work-place include (a) a supervisor who bends rigid human resources policies and grants flex time to an employee to care for her sick child; (b) a human resources manager who, in the interests of developing a multicultural management team, bends the selection criteria set by the dominant white male management group and instead advocates for and hires a Latina who is capable of performing well in the position, if not entirely meeting the stated criteria; (c) a small US handicraft importer who invests in families in Southeast Asia by providing cottage industry production work, using protective clothing and equipment for the adults, and paying for their children's school fees rather than hiring the children for production.

The *deontological* approach to ethics—known as the categorical imperative, or nonconsequentialist approach—is often attributed to Immanuel Kant, and claims that certain actions in themselves are intrinsically good or bad or right or wrong, and are not to be judged by their results. A moral person makes an ethical decision based on what is right, using moral principles or rules, regardless of circumstances or consequences. A moral person acts according to a perceived duty, asking, "What is my duty or obligation in this situation?" Kant put forth the categorical imperative: every person should act only on those principles that he or she would prescribe as universal laws, applied to everyone, assuming that what is right for one person is right for all persons. Rights, justice, truth-telling, and virtue ethics all are deontological forms of ethical reasoning.

The *rights perspective*, associated with the ideas of Locke, Kant, Mill, and Rawls, is founded on a movement throughout history to overcome basic social injustice and/or constraints on personal freedom. Human rights, also referred to as natural rights, include those rights contained in the Bill of Rights of the US Constitution (1791) or the Universal Declaration of Human Rights of the United Nations (1948; see Appendix), delineating fundamental and unconditional rights to be respected because they are based on universal tenets in nature. Human rights are universal rights that individuals are born with, regardless of status, intelligence, or nationality. For example, the Universal Declaration of Human Rights of the United Nations states that everyone has the right to life, liberty, and security of person; no one shall be held in slavery or servitude; and no one shall be subjected to torture or to cruel, inhuman, or degrading treatment or punishment. Basic rights of one kind can override rights of another kind; for example, employees' right to a safe work environment overrides employers' right to cut costs and ignore safety in the workplace. Human rights may be based on moral principles and/or a legal system of rights, and whereas we may judge certain acts as immoral, the laws may permit such acts (Smith et al., 1988). Here are two examples: (a) in the US during the period from the sixteenthth to the nineteenth centuries, whites had the legal right to own slaves; (2) in the US, until 1920, women were prohibited by law from voting. Rights are aligned with justice and often asserted to overcome or correct some fundamental injustice. The US legal system demonstrates that rights serve justice, and justice takes rights into account.

A *justice* approach to ethics uses universal principles such as reciprocity and equality of human rights and respect for the dignity of all human beings as individual persons. Persons, situations, and dilemmas are to be judged in a fair, objective, equitable, and impartial manner, not, contrary to an ethic of care, swayed by circumstances. In a system of justice, individuals have moral autonomy within the context of a social contract and are expected to use reason to discern which principles should be followed. Society provides a hierarchy of rules, rights, and obligations that protect the infringement of individual rights. Systems of justice in society, and the grievance process in organizations, aim to incorporate these ideals. There are three types of justice principles:

- *Distributive justice* is a way to distribute benefits and burdens so that equals will be treated equally and nonequals will be treated unequally. The allocation of benefits and burdens may include equal shares to each person based on need, effort, merit, or social contribution (Fritzsche, 1997). An example is equal pay for equal work, including compensating women and men equally when performing the same job.

- *Retributive justice* is for the punishment of wrongdoing, proven through due process. The severity of the punishment is to be in proportion to the magnitude of the wrongdoing. A conviction of corporate executives for knowingly leaking toxic chemicals into ground water would lead to some form of retributive justice.
- *Compensatory justice* is concerned with compensating the injured party equal to the loss that was suffered. When compensation cannot be adequately provided, for example, in the case of lost life, property, or proprietary information, then compensation is for a fair estimate of damage. An example is the multibillion-dollar settlement paid by tobacco companies to states and individuals for the loss of life and damage to health caused from cigarettes.

Virtue ethics, grounded in the Western philosophy of Aristotle (384–322 BCE) and the Eastern philosophies of the Buddha (ca 500 BCE) and Confucius (ca 551–479 BCE), prescribes living one's life and behaving according to recognized virtues. Virtue, among other things, includes living in moderation, according to the "Golden Mean," or in Buddhism, the "Middle Way." It does not depend on rules or principles but rather motives and actions of people who are intent on doing the right thing at all times. Acting with virtue ethics depends on qualities, traits, or dispositions internal to an individual, or those qualities, traits, or dispositions that a person strives to have or be. Virtue ethics is based on being, emotion, and reason where one's actions are an expression of one's virtues. How to be virtuous is primarily prescribed or proscribed by one's culture, religion, and life circumstances.

Philosophers and spiritual leaders have preached their preferred virtues. Aristotle claimed that moral virtue involved both emotion and reason, including charity, courage, truthfulness, friendliness, modesty, and righteous indignation—or having a sense of justice (Rosenstad, 1997). St Thomas Aquinas believed in both the intellectual virtues of wisdom, justice, temperance, and fortitude, and the religious virtues of faith, hope, and charity, claiming that virtue is learned, not innate. Confucianism teaches that one should cultivate the virtues of patience, sincerity, obedience, and knowledge. Buddhism teaches that the right path to a moral life involves practicing compassion, forgiveness, nonharming of others, honesty, generosity, and equanimity, along with other practices. In all traditions, virtue focuses on moral character, asking questions such as, "What kind of person should I be?" "What kind of character should I have?" The aim of moral life is to develop moral virtues or general dispositions. The virtues provide criteria for evaluating individual actions, social institutions, and practices (Velasquez, 1998). With an internal locus of control, an individual facing a moral or ethical dilemma exercises personal judgment rather than applying universal rules.

A practical contemporary criterion for ethical conduct is the "light of day" test. This involves an assessment of how friends, family, and work associates would react to one's behavior if they were to know of it (Mallinger, 1997). One asks, "How would I feel if my actions were publicized on the front page of the newspaper?" The measure of ethical conduct would be the receipt of positive regard by valued others.

Native American approaches to ethics share similarities with Eastern perspectives in their emphasis on valuing relationships between individuals and maintaining community. Although there are more than 200 separate Native American tribal groups in the US (Young et al., 1987), we take the liberty to generalize about one of the more prevalent ethical traditions. Like Asian cultures, many Native Americans value community and group solidarity, so the dispute resolution process seeks to maintain relationships and restore harmony among disputing parties (Jack and Jack, 1989), congruent with the ethic of care. This Native American tradition emphasizes connection and harmony with others, including nature and animals, acknowledging interdependence and emphasizing cooperation. Defeat of another destroys the relationship and severs the community (Deloria, 1983).

The ethical approaches described up to this point provide us with a number of possible avenues for lecture content and student reflection and discussion (Table 1). Are there, for example, universal ethical laws that we can say should apply to everyone, everywhere, without qualification? In the realms of human rights and justice, we can identify ideal universal principles: freedom, respect, due process, truth, and equality of opportunity. Once such ethical principles are identified, however, a valuable line of inquiry is, why are these ethical approaches not practiced universally? Where in the world are there deviations from ideal principles? What are the cultural explanations for these deviations? Are the deviations ever acceptable?

Table 1. Summary of Frameworks for Ethical Reasoning

Approach	Description
Teleological approaches:	Actions are right or wrong based on their consequences.
• Utilitarianism	Actions are ethically sound when they produce the greatest good for the greatest number.
• Egoism	Acting consistently with one's own (or organization's) self-interest is ethical, with individual consequences taking priority, regardless of the consequences to others; may take the form of enlightened self-interest.
• Ethic of Care	Acting responsibly and responsively toward others, attending to the other's well-being, and not harming others; also fits with deontological approaches as a duty toward others. Similar to some Eastern and Native American perspectives.
Deontological approaches:	Actions are based on obligations; they are intrinsically good or bad in themselves, regardless of the consequences.
• Rights perspective	Fundamental rights are accorded to human beings of all circumstances and backgrounds, such as the right to life, liberty, security of person, and freedom from enslavement.
• Justice perspective	Demands respect for the dignity of every individual through the application of objective and impartial decisions, or actions; benefits, and punishments are allocated by society based on equality of rights among all human beings. Includes distributive, retributive, and compensatory types of justice.
• Virtue ethics	Actions flowing from the disposition and internal qualities of individuals who consistently strive to lead a moral life (e.g., ethical behavior via honesty, courage, modesty, compassion, integrity, andcharity). Core of Buddhist, Confucian, and many Native American ethical traditions.
• Ethic of care	(see above)

A second line of thinking in the classroom might be whether ethical behavior is best expressed by the pursuit of virtue or enacted through individual thought and conduct. Or should societies enforce ethical principles publicly through laws, processes of justice, and political mandates? What is the right balance between individual and societal behavior needed to create ethical environments? Should the guiding principles be concerned with universal laws, regardless of consequences, or should universal laws always be malleable in light of unknown or unpredictable consequences? The US ambivalence regarding mandatory sentencing for criminals committing crimes with guns, for example, represents the ethical tension of universal law versus appropriately designed individual punishments.

TWENTIETH-CENTURY ETHICAL PERSPECTIVES IN THE GLOBAL CONTEXT

In addition to the philosophical ethical traditions discussed above, recent guidelines on a global scale translate philosophy into meaningful business practice. The guidelines originated in corporate or political contexts and from particular activities or problems that called for the development of countervening principles, such as the abridgment of human rights or the threat of destruction to the environment. Of obvious relevance to global interorganizational relationships, these capture the attention of the business student. Here, we summarize some of these guidelines, offering principles teachers can use in working with business students (see Table 2). The complete texts of these principles are found in the Appendix.

Table 2. Eastern and Western Approaches to an Ethical Life

Approaches	What Matters
Western approaches	
• Teleological (utilitarianism, egoism, ethic of care, light of day)	Consequences to self, others, or society
Deontological (human rights, justice, virtue, ethic of care)	Intrinsically good (or bad) universal laws; individual character
Eastern approaches	
• Confucianism	A moral life: qualities, disposition, and character
• Buddhism	internal to the individual that are sought, learned, and practiced throughout life
Native American	Moral virtues: generosity, kindness, caring, compassion, understanding, restraint, honesty, mindfulness, nonharming, equanimity, forgiveness
	• Concern for continuity of relationships and strength of community
	• Preference for harmony over truth, peace over Justice
	• Justice through cooperation
	• Connection and interdependence with all living things; consequences to self, others, community

UNITED NATIONS UNIVERSAL DECLARATION OF HUMAN RIGHTS

The UN Universal Declaration of Human Rights was adopted by the General Assembly in 1948 (Schulz, 2001). It takes a deontological perspective, promoting justice and human rights worldwide. The declaration proclaims that no one shall be held in slavery or servitude, subjected to inhuman or degrading treatment or punishment, or subjected to arbitrary arrest, detention, or exile. It goes on to proclaim that everyone has the right to life, liberty, and security of person; is entitled to equal protection against any discrimination in violation of the declaration; and has the right to work, to free choice of employment, to just and favorable conditions of work, and to protection against unemployment as a result of discrimination. It includes the right to equal pay for equal work and to just and favorable remuneration ensuring for all persons and their families an existence worthy of human dignity, supplemented, if necessary, by other means of social protection. The declaration proclaims the right to form and join trade unions for the protection of workers' interests and the right to rest and leisure, including the reasonable limitation of working hours and periodic holidays with pay. Everyone has the right to a standard of living adequate for the health and well-being of him- or herself and of his or her family, including food, clothing, housing, and medical care and necessary social services, and the right to security in the event of unemployment, sickness, disability, widowhood, old age, or other lack of livelihood

Table 3. Twentieth-Century Ethical Guidelines[a]

- United Nations Universal Declaration of Human Rights: Adopted in 1948, proclaims the rights of peoples worldwide to freedom, protection, security, just working arrangements, and a reasonable standard of living.

- CERES Principles: Ten voluntary principles that commit signatories to protection of the biosphere, sustainable use of natural resources, conservation, reduction of wastes, production of safe products, timely informing of the public regarding any health or safety dangers, and other environmental goals.

- The Caux Principles: Formed by an organization of business leaders from Europe, Japan, and the United States in 1986, these principles promote the sacredness of each person (human dignity) and the value of working together for the common good.

- The Global Sullivan Principles: Originally developed in the 1970s, eight principles for corporate social responsibility related to justice, human rights, tolerance, and equal opportunity in global operations.

- International Labour Organization's (ILO) Core Labor Conventions: Adopted in 1982, seven core conventions have been ratified by varying numbers of ILO member-nations. These include freedom of association and protection of the right to organize, equal pay for equal work, abolition of forced labor, elimination of discrimination in access to employment, and the abolition of child labor.

- Individual Corporate Codes of Conduct

---

a. The above guidelines are available from the Web sites of the respective organizations or from the authors upon request.

in circumstances beyond his control. The universal application of these principles, however, is far from reality.

Throughout the world, from Nike's sweatshops in Vietnam and Indonesia (Post et al., 2002; Varley, 1998), to forced adult and child labor in Burma, to the trading of children for work on the cocoa plantations in western Africa, we see ongoing corporate violations of these universal human rights. In the US, these rights are violated in areas of agriculture, garment manufacturing, prison labor, and electronics assembly. Throughout the US, from the skilled crafts and trades to white-collar professions in academe, health care, and financial services, episodes of discrimination based on race, gender, and age continue. Nevertheless, the Universal Declaration of Human Rights serves as an agreed-upon global-scale ideal for human behavior toward other humans. It underscores the rights of workers to a decent quality of life *before* the right to profit or, its extreme, greed.

International human rights groups, labor organizations, religious groups, and related nongovernmental organizations have confronted governments and corporations through actions such as direct appeals to executives and government officials, stockholder resolutions, boycotts, protest demonstrations, and negotiations, urging corporations and governments to end abuses, take the higher moral ground, and comply with human rights guidelines. Examples include work of the Interfaith Center on Corporate Responsibility with corporate executives and its work developing and presenting shareholder resolutions at annual shareholder meetings; demonstrations at the World Trade Organization meetings or Nike corporate headquarters; consumer boycotts of PepsiCo products and fast food services; and direct-mail campaigns to both governments and corporate directors and executives. US foreign relations and trade with China and the case of Unocal in Burma both exemplify the difficulty of implementing corporate social responsibility principles. China and Burma have committed widespread violations of human rights, yet US and other corporations continue to operate and do business in these countries (Schulz, 2001).

THE CERES PRINCIPLES

The Coalition for Environmentally Responsible Economies (CERES) is a nonprofit coalition of socially responsible investors, foundations, public pension funds, labor unions, and environmental, religious, and public interest groups. The ten voluntary principles, teleological in orientation, commit signatory firms to the protection of the biosphere, sustainable use of natural resources, energy conservation, risk reduction, and other environmental goals. The CERES Principles apply only to business conduct in a single area of a company's operations: its environmental activities. Bethlehem Steel, Polaroid, General Motors, Sun Oil, and the Calvert Social Investing (Mutual) Fund have endorsed the CERES Principles (Lesser, 2000). An example of a recent CERES project is its Green Hotel Initiative that seeks to increase green lodging and meeting options by catalyzing market supply and demand. This multistakeholder effort—involving business, the hotel industry, nongovernmental organizations, labor, academia, and environmental advocates—encourages environmentally responsible hotel services and encourages meeting planners and travel buyers to stimulate the hotel market (CERES, n.d.).

THE CAUX PRINCIPLES

The Caux Round Table, begun in 1986, is an organization of business leaders from Europe, Japan, and the US. Its original purpose was to focus on the development of constructive economic and social relationships between participant countries; their "urgent joint responsibilities toward the rest of the world . . . focused attention on the importance of global corporate responsibility in reducing social and economic threats to world peace and stability" (*Caux Round Table*, n.d., para. 2, 3). The Caux Round Table's Principles for Business have at their core two basic ethical ideals: *kyosei* and human dignity. The Japanese concept of kyosei refers to living and working together for the common good, while the Caux Round Table's concept of human dignity refers to the sacredness of each person as an end, not as a means to the fulfillment of others' purposes. The Caux Principles combine elements of the ethic of care (between participant countries) and those of both human rights and virtue ethics.

THE GLOBAL SULLIVAN PRINCIPLES

The human rights perspective is advanced as well by the Rev. Leon Sullivan, who authored a set of principles in the 1970s designed to guide companies in improving the lives of Blacks in South Africa. In 1999, Rev. Sullivan developed a set of guidelines for corporate social responsibility for companies in their operations around the world. Specifically, the objectives of the Global Sullivan Principles are

> to support economic, social, and political justice by companies where they do business; to support human rights and to encourage equal opportunity at all levels of employment, including racial and gender diversity on decision making committees and boards; to train and advance disadvantaged workers for technical, supervisory and management opportunities; and to assist with greater tolerance and understanding among peoples; thereby, helping to improve the quality of life for communities, workers and children with dignity and equality.
>
> (Sullivan, 1997, para. 1)

Among the many corporations that have endorsed the Global Sullivan Principles are Fannie Mae, British Airways, American Airlines, Chevron, DaimlerChrysler, Pfizer, Hershey Foods, and Tata Industries of India.

INTERNATIONAL LABOUR ORGANIZATION'S LABOR CONVENTIONS

The International Labour Organization (ILO) was created in 1919 as a tripartite organization of government, business, and union representatives from 174 nations. Since then, it has adopted 177 lengthy labor "conventions" or standards. Seven of these are considered fundamental human rights, addressing issues such as forced labor, freedom of association, the right of collective bargaining, equal pay for men and women, discrimination in the workplace, and the minimum age for employment. As of 1996, only 27 ILO member-nations had ratified all 7 core conventions, and 12 had not ratified any of the 7. The United States had ratified only 1. Certain countries have refused to ratify conventions because they may be in opposition to national laws. Other countries with very low standards, such as Burma, have ratified conventions that they do not honor (Varley, 1998). In 2001, the ILO called for governments, including the United States, to impose a ban on all imports coming from Burma because the military government of Burma imposes a 5 percent export tax on all exports. Most goods produced in Burma, including clothing imported to the US and elsewhere, are manufactured with the use of forced labor and child labor, whereas the building of roads, energy, and water systems also are under the direct control of the military junta, which does not recognize basic human rights of free speech, free association, freedom of religion, free press, and freedom to unionize. A current bill under consideration in the US Senate is Bill 926, asking Congress to implement the ILO call for a ban on imports from Burma (International Labour Organization, n.d.).

CORPORATE CODES OF CONDUCT

Companies such as Anheuser-Busch, Disney, Dayton Hudson, Federated Department Stores, Levi Strauss, Ford Motor Company, Gap, Home Depot, Kmart, Liz Claiborne, JCPenney, Sears, Roebuck, and Wal-Mart have standards for vendors, contractors, manufacturers, and employees, usually in the form of ethical standards or codes of ethical conduct. These standards cover issues including a safe and healthy workplace, absence of forced or compulsory labor, nondiscrimination, absence of coercion and harassment, working conditions, fair wages, banning of child labor, protection of the environment, and ethical conduct (Varley, 1998). A good example is the social responsibility policies of Gap Inc., a company that makes none of its own clothes but works with thousands of factories in more than 50 countries. Upholding fair labor standards, environmental protection, and charitable giving are part of the organization's statement of social responsibility (Gap Inc., n.d.).

As our students encounter increasingly complex ethical situations in global business, we are challenged to learn more about teaching and learning business ethics. Our current global context provides dynamic opportunities to examine and apply diverse philosophical and psychological perspectives in approaching ethical dilemmas and problems. In this reading, we have presented traditional and contemporary Western and non-Western frameworks and theories to assist faculty as they help students understand and resolve ethical issues and quandaries in our global business environment.

APPENDIX 1: RECOMMENDED CASES FOR TEACHING ETHICS IN A GLOBAL CONTEXT

1. **On employee-employer relations:** Velasquez, M. (1998). The Gap, Inc. In *Business ethics: Concepts and cases* (4th ed., pp. 486–493). Upper Saddle River, NJ: Prentice Hall.

2. **On ethical principles:** Velasquez, M. (1998). Pepsi's Burma connection. In *Business ethics: Concepts and cases* (4th ed., pp. 159–163). Upper Saddle River, NJ: Prentice Hall.
3. **On ethical relativism:** Post, J., Lawrence, A., & Weber, J. (2002). Salt Lake City and the Olympics bribery scandal. In *Business and Society* (10th ed., pp. 515–523). New York: McGraw-Hill Irwin.
4. **On moral responsibility of corporations:** Bowie, N., & Lenway, S. (1998). H. B. Fuller in Honduras: Street children and substance abuse. In D. Adams & E. Maine (Eds.), *Business ethics for the 21st century* (pp. 58–68). Mountain View, CA: Mayfield. Two different shorter versions of the case are published in Beauchamp, T., & Bowie, N. (1993). *Ethical theory and business* (4th ed., pp. 101–103). Upper Saddle River, NJ: Prentice Hall; and Velasquez, M. (1998). *Business ethics concepts and cases* (4th ed., pp. 58–63). Upper Saddle River, NJ: Prentice Hall.
5. **On diversity:** Ellement, G., Maznevski, M., & Lane, H. (1999). Ellen Moore (A): Living and working in Bahrain. In T. Donaldson & P. Wehane (Eds.), *Ethical issues in business* (6th ed., pp. 325–337). Upper Saddle River, NJ: Prentice Hall.

NOTES

* In this reading, we provide a summary of several major traditional and contemporary philosophical and psychological perspectives on ethical conduct for businesses, along with five different sets of internationally accepted ethical guidelines for corporations operating anywhere in the world. We include examples of corporate codes of conduct from particular multinational corporations. Our orienting framework of ethics theory is expanded to include a discussion of both Western and non-Western frameworks, including those of Confucianism, Buddhism, and Native American traditions, allowing faculty and students to explore ethical problems that honor a wide array of national, cultural, and ethnic contexts and differences.

** This reading is the initial product of work on teaching global ethics that began with a presentation at OBTC in June 1997 at Case Western Reserve University by Gail Ambuske, Susan Taft, and Judith White. The authors would like to thank the reviewers, whose advice greatly improved the structure, content, and focus of the final manuscript. Please send proofs and all correspondence regarding this manuscript to Judith White, School of Business, University of Redlands, 1200 East Colton Avenue, Redlands, CA 92373; phone: (909) 748–6255; fax: (909) 335–5125; email: judith_white@redlands.edu.

REFERENCES

Caux Round Table principles for business. (n.d.). Retrieved January 4, 2004, from www.itcilo.it/english/actrav/telearn/global/ilo/code/caux.htm#Section%201.20Preamble.

CERES. (n.d.). *Our work: The CERES principles.* Retrieved January 4, 2004, from www.ceres.org/our_work/principles.htm.

Deloria, V. (1983). *American Indians, American justice.* Austin, TX: University of Texas.

Derry, R. (1989). An empirical study of moral reasoning among managers. *Journal of Business Ethics, 8,* 855–862.

Dobson, J., & White, J. (1995). Toward the feminine firm: An extension to Thomas White. *Business Ethics Quarterly, 5,* 463–478.

Fritzsche, D. J. (1997). *Business ethics: A global and managerial perspective*. San Francisco, CA: McGraw-Hill.

Gap Inc. (n.d.). *Social responsibility*. Retrieved January 4, 2004, from www.gapinc.com/social_resp/social_resp.htm.

Gilligan, C. (1982). *In a different voice*. Cambridge, MA: Harvard University Press.

Gilligan, C. (1987). Moral orientation and moral development. In E. F. Kittay & D. T. Meyers (Eds.), *Women and moral theory*. Totowa, NY: Rowman & Littlefield.

International Labour Organization. (n.d.). *Fundamental ILO conventions*. Retrieved January 4, 2004, from www.ilo.org/public/english/standards/norm/whatare/fundam/index.htm.

Jack, R., & Jack, D. C. (1989). Moral vision and professional decisions: The changing values of women and men lawyers. New York: Cambridge University Press.

Lesser, L. (2000). *Business, public policy, and society*. Orlando, FL: The Dryden Press.

Liedtka, J. (1992). Wounded but wiser: Reflections on teaching ethics to MBA students. *Journal of Management Education, 16*(4), 405–416.

Mallinger, M. (1997). Decisive decision making: An exercise using ethical frameworks. *Journal of Management Education, 21*(3), 411–417.

Noddings, N. (1984). *Caring: A feminine approach to ethics and moral education*. Berkeley, CA: University of California Press.

Piper, T. R., Gentile, M. C., & Parks, S. D. (1993). *Can ethics be taught?* Boston, MA: Harvard Business School.

Post, J., Lawrence, A., & Weber, J. (2002). *Business and society* (10th ed.). Boston, MA: McGraw-Hill Irwin.

Rosenstad, N. (1997). *The moral of the story: An introduction to ethics* (2nd ed.). Mountain View, CA: Mayfield.

Schulz, W. (2001). *In our own best interest: How defending human rights benefits us all*. Boston, MA: Beacon Press.

Smith, J. E., Forbes, J. B., & Extejt, M. M. (1988). Ethics in the organizational behavior course. *The Organizational Behavior Teaching Review, 13*(1), 85–95.

Sullivan, L. H. (1997). *Global Sullivan principles of social responsibility*. Retrieved January 4, 2004, from www.globalsullivanprinciples.org/Index.htm.htm

United Nations. (1948). *Universal declaration of human rights*. Retrieved January 4, 2004, from www.un.org/Overview/rights.html

Varley, P. (Ed). (1998). *The sweatshop quandary: Corporate responsibility on the global frontier*. Washington, DC: Investor Responsibility Research Center.

Velasquez, M. (1998). *Business ethics, concepts and cases* (4th ed.). Upper Saddle River, NJ: Prentice Hall.

White, J. (1994). Individual characteristics and social knowledge in ethical reasoning. *Psychological Reports, 75*, 627–649.

Young, T. J., LaPlante, C. & Robbins, W. (1987). Indians before the law: An assessment of contravening cultural/legal ideologies. *Quarterly Journal of Ideology, 11*, 59–70.

Loriann Roberson and
Carol T. Kulik*

STEREOTYPE THREAT AT WORK**

EXECUTIVE OVERVIEW

MANAGING DIVERSITY in organizations requires creating an environment where all employees can succeed. This reading explains how understanding "stereotype threat"—the fear of being judged according to a negative stereotype—can help managers create positive environments for diverse employees. While stereotype threat has received a great deal of academic research attention, the issue is usually framed in the organizational literature as a problem affecting performance on tests used for admission and selection decisions. Further, articles discussing stereotype threat usually report the results of experimental studies and are targeted to an academic audience. We summarize 12 years of research findings on stereotype threat, address its commonplace occurrence in the workplace, and consider how interventions effective in laboratory settings for reducing stereotype threat might be implemented by managers in organizational contexts. We end the reading with a discussion of how attention to stereotype threat can improve the management of diversity in organizations.

Ongoing demographic trends (increasing percentages of African Americans, Hispanics, and Asians in the American workforce, an aging population, expanding female labor force participation) have made diversity a fact of organizational life. When these trends were first identified in the mid-1980s, they were heralded as an opportunity for organizations to become more creative, to reach previously untapped markets, and in general to achieve and maintain a competitive advantage (Cox, 1994; Robinson and Dechant, 1997; Thomas and Ely, 1996).

However, employee diversity does not *necessarily* boost creativity, market share, or competitive advantage. In fact, research suggests that left unmanaged, employee diversity is more likely to damage morale, increase turnover, and cause significant communication problems and conflict within the organization (Jackson et al., 1991;

Jehn et al., 1999; Tsui et al., 1992; Zenger and Lawrence, 1989). Thus, "managing diversity" has become a sought-after managerial skill, and concerns about effective diversity management have spawned an industry of diversity training programs, diversity videos, and diversity consultants. But despite several decades of effort and millions of dollars invested, the evidence suggests that organizations continue to do a poor job of managing diversity. A recent comprehensive report concluded that organizations rarely are able to leverage diversity and capitalize on its potential benefits (Hansen, 2003; Kochan et al., 2003). What's the problem? Are we missing a key piece of the diversity management puzzle?

Most of the attention in the diversity management literature has been focused on the organizational decision maker—the manager who is prejudiced against certain groups and who allows these prejudices to influence how he or she treats employees. These individual-level prejudices become institutionalized—meaning, they become embodied in organizational policies and practices that systematically disadvantage some employees. In their efforts to reduce discrimination, organizations are increasingly concerned about hiring non-prejudiced managers, redesigning biased selection, appraisal, and promotion procedures, and generally eradicating stereotypes from managerial decision making (Greengard, 2003; Rice, 1996). If we eliminate stereotypes from organizational decision-making, the logic goes, we'll create an organization where all employees can flourish and advance.

Unfortunately, even if an organization were successful in hiring only non-prejudiced managers and eliminating stereotypes from its formal decision-making, stereotypes would still exist in broader society. As a result, every employee walking through the door of the organization knows the stereotypes that *might* be applied to him or her and wonders whether organizational decision makers and co-workers will endorse those stereotypes. Here, we discuss the effects of these stereotypes, and highlight an important aspect of diversity management that has not received much attention by diversity or management scholars: stereotype threat, the fear of being judged and treated according to a negative stereotype about members of your group (Steele et al., 2002). Research on stereotype threat has shown that societal stereotypes can have a negative effect on employee feelings and behavior, making it difficult for an employee to perform to his or her true potential. Research has also indicated that stereotype threat can result in employees working harder, but not better. When stereotype threat is present, performance declines. Therefore, a non-prejudiced manager who uses objective performance indicators as a basis for decision-making risks underestimating the employee's true ability. When an organizational context contains the conditions that create stereotype threat, nontraditional employees experience additional barriers to success despite the good intentions of everyone involved. Therefore, stereotype threat places certain demands on the manager of diverse employees—demands to create conditions that minimize the occurrence of stereotype threat, so that all employees can perform effectively.

Stereotype threat has been discussed almost exclusively as an issue for high stakes testing, particularly in educational arenas. For example, we're all familiar with the opportunities that hang on scores from tests such as the Scholastic Aptitude Test (SAT), the Graduate Record Examination (GRE) and the Graduate Management

Achievement Test (GMAT): without the "right" scores, a student won't be able to get into the best college for his or her chosen field. In 1999, PBS aired a documentary concluding that stereotype threat was suppressing the standardized test performance of African American students (Chandler, 1999). These effects on high stakes tests are important, but stereotype threat is not limited to African-American students taking large-scale standardized academic tests. It is also present in the everyday, routine situations that are a part of all jobs. Thus, knowledge of stereotype threat and its corrosive effects on performance is needed to understand the work experience of members of stereotyped groups and to manage diversity more effectively in the organization. In this reading, we answer the following questions: What is stereotype threat and what are its effects? How can stereotype threat be reduced?

We begin with a short review of the concept and the research evidence. We then describe the conditions that increase the risk of stereotype threat. Because these conditions regularly occur in the workplace, stereotype threat is also likely to be a common part of many people's work experience. Finally, we present strategies for reducing stereotype threat from the academic research literature, and consider if and how those strategies might be applied in organizations. We also discuss how attention to stereotype threat adds value to current organizational approaches to managing diversity.

STEREOTYPE THREAT AT WORK

Every job involves being judged by other people, whether you are giving a sales presentation to clients, representing your work team at a meeting, or showing your boss your work for some informal feedback. Being evaluated can raise anxieties for anyone. Apprehension in these kinds of situations is a common phenomenon, and in fact, a little anxiety can even boost performance (Cocchiara and Quick, 2004; Reio and Callahan, 2004; Yerkes and Dodson, 1908). But anxieties can be heightened for those employees who are members of a negatively stereotyped group, especially when they are performing a kind of task on which, according to the stereotype, members of their group do poorly. Consider these statements by people who are members of stereotyped groups:

From a marketing manager: "You can see in someone's eyes when you are first introduced that you're dead in the water just because you're seen as old." Many older workers refer to "the look" on someone's face as they are introduced. A 57 year old accounts supervisor recounted that on meeting someone face to face for the first time, she was told with a tone of disappointment, "Oh, you have such a young voice on the phone" (Blank and Shipp, 1994).

From a White loan officer (concerned about being perceived as racist or sexist): "I'm always worried about how I was heard. How will I be interpreted? Did I say the wrong thing?" (Blank and Shipp, 1994).

From a Black manager: "I felt Whites had a lot of negative ideas about Blacks. I felt evaluated when I asked questions. Asking questions became painful for me" (Dickins and Dickins, 1991).

From an overweight worker: "I work extra hard because I know the stereotype, and I feel I need to prove myself. I work harder than most of my coworkers who do the same job. Yet my (skinny, size-10) boss continually talks about me behind my back to my coworkers – she says that I'm lazy and that I don't take any initiative, and who knows what else. She sees me for maybe half an hour out of the work week, which is hardly enough time to judge me on my work . . . It doesn't matter that I know the job inside-out, or that my customer-service skills are top-notch. It doesn't matter that I'm on time and do any stupid little task that I'm asked. All that matters is the width of my ass" (Personal blog, 2005).

The individuals quoted here are members of different identity groups, but they all voice a common concern: the fear of being seen and judged according to a negative stereotype about their group, and the concern that they might do something that would inadvertently confirm the negative stereotype (Steele, 1997; Steele et al., 2002). These individuals are experiencing "stereotype threat."

Stereotype threat describes the psychological experience of a person who, while engaged in a task, is aware of a stereotype about his or her identity group suggesting that he or she will not perform well on that task. For example, a woman taking a math test is familiar with the common stereotype that "girls aren't good at math." Or a Black faculty member preparing his case for promotion is aware that some people believe that Blacks are intellectually inferior. This awareness can have a disruptive effect on performance—ironically resulting in the individual confirming the very stereotype he or she wanted to disconfirm (Kray et al., 2001). Anyone can experience anxiety while performing a task with important implications (a test to get into graduate school or a presentation to a big client), but stereotype threat places an additional burden on members of stereotyped groups. They feel "in the spotlight," where their failure would reflect negatively not only on themselves as individuals, but on the larger group to which they belong. As singer and actress Beyoncé Knowles said in an interview with Newsweek in 2003: "It's like you have something to prove, and you don't want to mess it up and be a negative reflection on Black women" (quoted in Smith, 2004, p. 198).

In the first (and now classic) study on stereotype threat, Claude Steele and Joshua Aronson (1995) asked Black and White students to take a very difficult test. The test was composed of items from the verbal section of the Graduate Record Examination, and it was deliberately designed to tax students' ability. For some students, this test was described simply as a laboratory problem-solving task. However, for other students, the test was described as a "genuine test of your verbal abilities and limitations." The important difference between these two descriptions was that race stereotypes were irrelevant in the "laboratory task" version—there was no reason for a Black participant to expect race to impact his or her performance, or to think that other people might expect race to have an impact. However, in the scenario where the test was described as a genuine test of abilities and limitations (the stereotype threat condition), the racial stereotype (that Blacks lack intellectual ability) was relevant, and the researchers predicted that Black participants would be both aware of the stereotype and want to avoid confirming it.

When Steele and Aronson examined the results, they found that White students' performance was largely unaffected by the test instructions—the White students performed about equally well whether the test had been described as an ability test or as a laboratory problem-solving task. However, the instructions made a big difference in the performance of Black students. They performed less well in the ability test condition than in the problem-solving condition—even though the test was equally difficult in both conditions. In fact, after Steele and Aronson controlled for pre-study differences in ability (measured by the students' SAT scores), they found that Black and White students in the laboratory problem-solving condition performed about the same—but Black students underperformed relative to Whites in the ability test condition (Steele and Aronson, 1995).

This basic experimental design, in which researchers compare the performance of two groups (one group is negatively stereotyped, the other is not) in two task conditions (one condition presents the task as stereotype-relevant, the other does not), has been replicated many times over the last twelve years with consistent results. The negatively stereotyped group underperforms when the stereotype is seen as relevant to the task. This research is summarized in Table 1.

As the table shows, the stereotype threat phenomenon has been documented in a large number of groups, across a wide range of diversity dimensions, and in many different performance domains. In the top (unshaded) part of the table, the "Who was affected?" column includes the people we generally think of as disadvantaged in the workplace due to negative stereotypes—racial and ethnic minorities, members of lower socio-economic classes, women, older people, gay and bisexual men, and people with disabilities. The academic literature sometimes describes members of these groups as "stigma conscious" (Aronson et al., 1999). That means that members of these groups can be very aware of the social stereotypes other people associate with their group. Since the relevant stereotype is very likely to come to mind, concerns about stereotype confirmation are easily aroused. As a result, very subtle contextual variations (a slight wording difference in the way a test is described, for example) may be enough to make the stereotype salient and disrupt performance.

But research has shown that this phenomenon does not apply only to people in disadvantaged groups. In fact, the bottom (shaded) part of Table 1 shows that even members of high status groups can experience stereotype threat. For example, we don't normally think of White men as being disadvantaged in the workplace. White men generally enjoy more hiring opportunities, higher salaries, and more organizational status than women or members of racial minority groups with comparable education and ability (Hite, 2004; Parks-Yancy, 2006). However, even high-status groups have some negative stereotypes associated with them, and one of the stereotypes most strongly associated with the White group is the belief that Whites are racist (Frantz et al., 2004). The research suggests that many Whites are chronically concerned with not appearing racist (and inadvertently confirming the stereotype). Therefore, task situations that are described as dependent on racial attitudes can trigger stereotype threat in Whites (and result in participants looking more prejudiced than they might actually be) (Frantz et al., 2004).

Further, members of any group may experience stereotype threat when their identity group is negatively compared with another group. For example, comparative stereotypes suggest that Whites have less mathematical ability than Asians, men are less effective in processing affective (emotional) information than women, and White men have less athletic prowess than Black men. These negative comparisons can induce stereotype threat, and members of the target group demonstrate the short-term performance detriments associated with stereotype threat, as the studies listed in the table have found. One conclusion that can be drawn from looking at the table is that stereotype threat can affect all of us because each of us is a member of at least one group about which stereotypes exist. If you think about the stereotypes that could be applied to your own social group, you might recall situations where you personally experienced stereotype threat. If you think about the stereotypes that could apply to your employees, you can also identify the situations where they might be vulnerable to stereotype threat.

The research referred to in the table has decisively shown that stereotype threat has a negative impact on short-term performance. But an unresolved question is *why* does stereotype threat have this negative impact? Researchers have suggested several different answers to this question (the literature calls these answers "mediating" explanations), but there is no consensus on which is the "right" answer. The dominant explanation has to do with anxiety (Aronson et al., 1998), but there is still some disagreement over how anxiety affects performance. One argument suggests that anxiety increases a person's motivation and effort. Stereotype threatened participants are very motivated to perform well, and sometimes they try *too* hard or are too cautious in performing (Cadinu et al., 2003). For example, Steele and Aronson (1995) found that the Black participants in their research spent too much time trying to answer a small number of problems. They worked too hard on getting the right answer, and they disadvantaged themselves by not answering enough questions. Another argument proposes the opposite—that anxiety decreases a person's motivation and effort (Cadinu et al., 2003). The explanation is that stereotype threatened participants lose confidence that they can perform well, and in a self-fulfilling way this undermines performance. Given that the evidence thus far is still mixed and unclear, we will have to wait for further research to provide a more definitive answer to the *why* question. However, research has clearly identified the conditions under which stereotype threat is more and less likely to occur. This brings us to the next section of our reading.

CONDITIONS FOR STEREOTYPE THREAT

We've seen that the content of stereotypes about groups includes beliefs about the abilities of group members to perform certain kinds of tasks. Stereotype threat will only occur for those tasks associated with the stereotype. But simply being *asked* to perform a stereotype-relevant task is not enough to create stereotype threat. Research has identified two additional conditions needed for stereotype threat to emerge: task difficulty and personal task investment. In addition, the context can influence the perceived relevance of the stereotype for performance of the task or job. We have diagrammed these conditions, and the stereotype threat process, in Figure 1.

Table 1. Examples of stereotype threat[1]

Who was affected?	How did the researchers create stereotype threat?	What stereotype was activated?	What happened?
Black students	Told the students that they were about to take a very difficult test that was a "genuine test of your verbal abilities and limitations"	"Blacks lack intellectual ability"	The students performed less well on the test
Latino students	Told the students that they were about to take a very difficult mathematical and spatial ability test that would provide a "genuine test of your actual abilities and limitations"	"Latinos lack intellectual ability"	The students performed less well on the test
Low socio-economic status (SES) students	Asked the students to provide background information including their parents' occupation and education, then told them they were about to take a difficult test that would "assess your intellectual ability for solving verbal problems"	"Low SES students lack intellectual ability"	The students attempted to solve fewer problems and had fewer correct answers on the test
Women	Reminded the women that "previous research has sometimes shown gender differences" in math ability, then asked them to take a test that "had shown gender differences in the past"	"Women have weak math ability"	The women performed more poorly on the math test
Older individuals (60 years and older)	Gave the older people a series of memory tests and presented them with a list of "senile" behaviors ("can't recall birthdate") too quickly for conscious awareness. Then researchers gave the older people the memory tests a second time	"Older people have bad memory"	The older people had a significant decline in memory performance from pretest to posttest
Gay and bisexual men	Asked the men to indicate their sexual orientation on a demographic survey, then videotaped the participants while they engaged in a "free play" activity with children	"Gay men are dangerous to young children"	Judges rated the men as more anxious and less suitable for a job at a daycare center
People with a head injury history	Told participants that a "growing number" of neuro-psychological studies find that individuals with head injuries "show cognitive deficits on neuropsychological tests," then gave participants a series of tests assessing memory and attention	"Persons with a head injury history experience a loss of cognitive performance"	The participants performed worse on tests of general intellect, immediate memory, and delayed memory

Group	Manipulation	Stereotype	Outcome
Whites	Told participants that a "high proportion of Whites show a preference for White people" before asking them to complete the IAT (implicit attitude test) that would measure their "unconscious racial attitudes toward Blacks and Whites"	"Whites are racist"	The participants had a larger IAT effect (the difference in response time between incompatible and compatible trials), suggesting a preference for White faces
White students	Gave the students a packet of newspaper articles emphasizing a "growing gap in academic performance between Asian and White students" before asking them to take a very challenging math test	"White students have less mathematical ability than Asian students"	The students solved fewer problems on the math test
Men	Reminded participants that "it is a well-known fact that men are not as apt as women to deal with affect . . . and to process affective information as effectively" then asked them to indicate whether a series of words were "affective" or not	"Men are less capable than women in dealing with affective (emotional) information"	The men made more errors on the task
White men	Told the men that they would be engaged in a golf task that measured their "natural athletic ability." The men completed a demographic survey that included a question about their racial identity, then took the test	"White men have less athletic prowess than Black men"	The men made more strokes (performed worse) on the golf task

[1] The research summarized in this table include the following articles: Steele, C. M., & Aronson, J. (1995). Stereotype threat and the intellectual test performance of African Americans. *Journal of Personality and Social Psychology*, 69, 797–811; Gonzales, P. M., Blanton, H., & Williams, K. J. (2002). The effects of stereotype threat and double-minority status on the test performance of Latino women. *Personality and Social Psychology Bulletin*, 28, 659–670; Croize, J., & Claire, T. (1998). Extending the concept of stereotype threat to social class: The intellectual underperformance of students from low socioeconomic backgrounds. *Personality and Social Psychology Bulletin*, 24, 588–594; Spencer, S. J., Steele, C. M., & Quinn, D. M. (1999). Stereotype threat and women's math performance. *Journal of Experimental Social Psychology*, 35, 4–28; Bosson, J. K., Haymovitz, E. L., & Pinel, E. C. (2004). When saying and doing diverge: The effects of stereotype threat and self-reported versus non-verbal ability. *Journal of Experimental Social Psychology*, 40, 247–255; Suhr, J. A., & Gunstad, J. (2002). "Diagnosis threat": The effect of negative expectations on cognitive performance in head injury. *Journal of Clinical and Experimental Neuropsychology*, 24, 448–457; Frantz, C. M., Cuddy, A. J. C., Burnett, M., Ray, H., & Hart, A. (2004). A threat in the computer: The race implicit association test as a stereotype threat experience. *Personality and Social Psychology Bulletin*, 30, 1611–1624; Aronson, J., Lustina, M. J., Good, C., Keough, K., Steele, C. M., & Brown, J. (1999). When White men can't do math: Necessary and sufficient factors in stereotype threat. *Journal of Experimental Social Psychology*, 35, 29–46; Leyens, J., Desert, M., Croizet, J., & Darcis, C. (2000). Stereotype threat: Are lower status and history of stigmatization preconditions of stereotype threat? *Personality and Social Psychology Bulletin*, 26, 1189–1199; Stone, J., Lynch, C. I., Sjomeling, M., & Darley. J. M. (1999). Stereotype threat effects on Black and White athletic performance. *Journal of Personality and Social Psychology*, 77, 1213–1227.

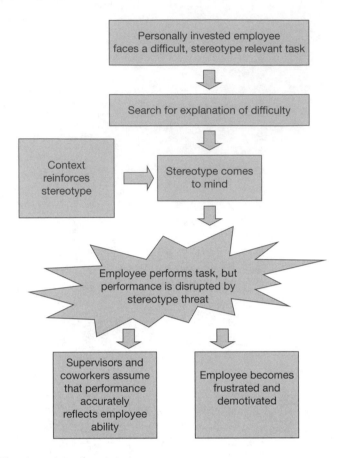

Figure 1. The stereotype threat process

STEREOTYPE RELEVANCE OF THE TASK: WHAT DOES IT TAKE TO PERFORM WELL?

Stereotype threat is situation specific, felt in situations where one can be "judged by, treated and seen in terms of, or self-fulfill a negative stereotype about one's group" (Spencer et al., 1999, p. 6). These situations occur when doing well on the task requires an ability on which, according to the stereotype, the person performing the task has a deficit. In the studies we have reviewed, the stereotype relevance of the task has often been created by telling participants that the task is a direct "test" of the stereotyped ability. So, for example, math tests have been used to create a stereotype relevant task for women and verbal or cognitive ability tests used to create stereotype relevant tasks for African Americans and Hispanics. But stereotype relevance isn't limited to standardized tests. Laura Kray and her colleagues surveyed participants to show that negotiation tasks are stereotype relevant for women. The researchers found that people believed that good negotiators were "assertive and concerned with personal gain" *and* that "men are more likely to be assertive than women" (Kray et al., 2002). Therefore, it logically follows that "men are better nego-tiators than women."

Research has shown that in our society many people believe successful managers have attributes more similar to those of men and Whites than to those of women, Hispanics, or African Americans (Chung-Herrera and Lankau, 2005; Heilman et al., 1989; Tomkiewicz et al., 1998). But beliefs about the traits necessary for jobs can also be organization specific. The potential for stereotype threat exists any time employees' beliefs about the particular traits needed for good job performance are linked to stereotypes about groups.

TASK DIFFICULTY: WHY IS THIS SO HARD?

Stereotype threat is most likely to influence performance on very difficult tasks—those that are at the limits of a person's abilities (Steele et al., 2002). On easier tasks, stereotype threat doesn't have much negative effect. According to psychologist Claude Steele, experiencing frustration with task accomplishment is an important trigger for stereotype threat (Steele et al., 2002). On a simple task there is little frustration—the person is doing well and knows it. But with a difficult task, pro-gress is not so smooth. People who experience frustration with a task try to explain their difficulty to themselves: "Why Is this so hard? Is this job just impossible? Am I not working hard enough? Am I having a bad day?" They also think about how others (co-workers, supervisors) will explain their difficulty: "Will they think I'm not working hard enough?" But when the person is a member of a stereotyped group, the stereotype is also likely to come to mind as a potential explanation that others might use: "Will they think the stereotype is true? It's going to look like the stereotype *is* true."

A negative dynamic operates between task difficulty and stereotype threat. When a task is difficult, stereotype threat evokes concern over performance. But this concern also has a greater *impact* on the performance of difficult tasks. Difficult jobs require concentration and focus; all of one's cognitive/mental resources must be directed toward accomplishing the work. If some of those resources are diverted towards worrying about one's skills and how one will be viewed by others, performance decre-ments occur (Beilock and Carr, 2005; Verbeke and Bagozzi, 2000). Thus, difficult tasks trigger stereotype threat, and also are most affected by it.

In work settings then, difficult, complex, and challenging tasks are where stereotype threat is most likely to occur. This creates a dilemma for managers. Task difficulty is not just a fact in many (especially professional) jobs, it is a desired condition. For years, job design experts have recommended that every job contain some challenging aspects to increase job involvement and avoid boredom and skill atrophy (Greenberg, 1996; Hackman and Oldham, 1980). In fact, giving demanding assignments to new hires is sometimes recommended as a good way to develop employees. Early demanding experiences predict later career success (Habermas and Bluck, 2000). In many organizations, "stretch" assignments (assignments for which an employee is not yet fully qualified, "stretching" the employee's skills and abilities)

(McCauley et al., 1995) are used as developmental tools throughout a person's tenure (Noe, 1999). Stretch assignments are needed for skill development, but managers must be aware of the extra potential for stereotype threat these assignments might involve for stereotyped employees, and counteract this risk. (We discuss how managers might do this later in the reading.)

In addition, tasks that are new and unfamiliar to the person performing them may be more at risk for stereotype threat than routine, familiar ones. New employees in particular are likely to find task accomplishment challenging as they learn their responsibilities. Thus, managers also must be aware of the higher potential for stereotype threat for their new hires.

PERSONAL TASK INVESTMENT: HOW IMPORTANT IS THIS TO WHO I AM?

Personal task investment refers to how important doing well on the task is to the individual's self esteem and identity. Some employees strongly identify with a particular skill or competency as a part of who they are. We often hear people say, "I'm good with people," or "I'm a techie." For these people, the skill is a part of how they define themselves. For such invested people, doing well in that task domain is important for their self-esteem and for feeling good about themselves. Researchers have argued that people who are personally invested in the task would be most influenced by stereotype threat because they are the ones who really care about their performance (Steele, 1997; Steele et al., 2002). If you want your work performance to say something about you personally, then the prospect of being viewed in terms of a negative stereotype is most disturbing. Studies have consistently confirmed this. Those invested in the task are more negatively affected by stereotype threat than those without such personal task investment.

What does this mean, practically? People tend to be invested in tasks they are good at (Steele, 1997). So the heavy impact of stereotype threat on the personally invested means that "the most capable members of stereotyped groups tend to be the most adversely affected in their performance by stereotype threat" (Kray et al., 2002, p. 388). This carries an important reminder for managers: the employees who care about their work and really want to do well are generally the ones that a manager is least likely to worry about since they are the ones he or she thinks will succeed on their own, and thus don't need coaxing, coaching, or extra attention. Yet, these are the people *most* likely to be affected by stereotype threat, and therefore, most in need of a manager's efforts to address and reduce it. For example, a manager might think that because the talented Hispanic salesperson graduated at the top of his class, he's already proven that stereotypes don't apply to him and isn't bothered by them. Or that the efficient accountant who earned her CPA despite caring for four children no longer worries about not being taken seriously by male managers. But it's exactly these employees, the ones who have made a big investment in their work, who might be most likely to suffer the effects of stereotype threat.

THE CONTEXT: IS THIS A PLACE WHERE STEREOTYPES OPERATE?

We've seen that the most important condition for stereotype threat is stereotype relevance: stereotype threat only occurs when the stereotype seems relevant to performing the task (Steele et al., 2002). In the academic research described earlier, stereotype relevance was created by the way the researchers described the tasks in a laboratory setting. In work settings, the relevance of the stereotype for performance can also be signaled and reinforced by the diversity (or the lack of diversity) of people who are currently performing the job. Rosabeth Moss Kanter used the term "token" to describe individuals who are different from others on a salient demographic dimension—race, sex, or age (Kanter, 1977). Kanter and others have shown that tokens feel very "visible"—that they stand out from the rest of the group. In addition, those in the majority are more likely to view tokens in terms of their distinguishing characteristic: as *the* woman or *the* Asian. Because everyone (the tokens and the tokens' colleagues) is more aware of group memberships under these conditions, associated stereotypes are more likely to come to mind (Niemann and Dovidio, 1998). In addition, the numerical differences reinforce the relevance of the stereotype for performance in the setting. Consider the solitary woman in a team of software engineers. Being the "only one" suggests that the stereotype about women lacking quantitative skills is true, and therefore sex is relevant to job performance. After all, the reasoning goes, if "those people" were good at this kind of job, wouldn't we see more of them performing it? Two studies have provided evidence of the link between token status and stereotype threat. In one, laboratory experimenters found that token women showed lower performance than non-tokens only on a math task (a stereotyped domain) and not on a verbal task (a non stereotyped domain) (Inzlicht and BenZeev, 2003). In the other, field researchers found that Black managers who were tokens in their work group reported higher levels of stereotype threat than non-tokens (Roberson et al., 2003).

Thus, group representation can raise the relevance of the stereotype for performance. Work situations involving lone members of a social or demographic group are common. For example, in the field research described above, 18 percent of the Black managers were tokens in their work group (Roberson et al., 2003). Managers need to be aware of this effect of the environment and find ways to neutralize it.

In summary, these conditions make stereotype threat more likely for members of negatively stereotyped groups:

- The employee is invested in doing well, on:
- A difficult, stereotype relevant task, where:
- The context reinforces the stereotype.

When stereotype threat occurs, performance is disrupted. But the effects of stereotype threat go beyond short-term performance decrements. The Black managers who experienced stereotype threat in the field research said that they spent more time monitoring their performance (for example, by comparing themselves to peers) and were more likely to discount performance feedback that they received from the organization (Roberson et al., 2003). So, for example, a Black employee who is regularly exposed to stereotype threat about his intellectual ability might dismiss performance feedback from his White manager that would have helped him to meet organizational performance expectations and get on the promotion "fast track."

But maybe these responses are functional. If your manager holds a negative stereotype about you, maybe you *should* discount feedback from that person (or at least, take it with a large grain of salt). If you can't trust your manager, monitoring the performance of your peers might yield more credible information with which to assess your performance. And if stereotype threat causes people to work harder, couldn't that be a positive benefit? Earlier, we quoted Beyoncé Knowles as feeling like she had "something to prove." Beyoncé has clearly been able to channel those feelings in a positive way in order to become a successful performer. Maybe a strong motivation to disprove a negative stereotype about your group can increase persistence and determination to succeed. Research on achievement goals has shown that a desire to prove one's ability can be a powerful form of motivation (Elliott and Harackiewicz, 1996), most effective in improving performance and persistence on simple tasks that are familiar to the performer (Steele-Johnson et al., 2000; Vandewalle, 2001). If you know *how* to perform a task, this kind of motivation can help you to perform better. But remember the Black students in Steele and Aronson's research—the ones who spent a lot of time answering very few questions? Those students were very motivated, but they were working on very complex, challenging problems and their efforts did not pay off. This kind of motivation often works for you, but it can work against you.

Questions about whether employee responses to stereotype threat can be functional or potentially beneficial indicate that we need to know a lot more about the long-term consequences of repeated exposure to stereotype threat. To answer these questions, research has to study stereotype threat over time in real-world organizational settings. So far, the research suggests that repeated exposure to stereotype threat may have serious, and primarily negative, side effects. Stereotype threat is accompanied by physiological reactions such as an increase in blood pressure, leading researchers to speculate that long-term exposure to stereotype threat conditions might contribute to chronic health problems such as hypertension (Blascovich et al., 2001). Stereotype threat is also associated with lower job satisfaction (Niemann and Dovidio, 1998; Roberson et al., 2003). Researchers have further suggested that repeated, regular exposure to stereotype threat may lead a person to disengage (or "disidentify") with the performance domain (Steele, 1997). That solo female in your engineering group may begin to think that an alternative career path might be preferable. This leads one to wonder whether long-term exposure to stereotype threat could be one cause of turnover for women and racial/ethnic minorities in professional and managerial jobs. Indeed, some studies have found that members of these groups leave jobs at a higher rate than White men (Hom et al., 2007).

Fortunately, research on the conditions under which stereotype threat is most likely to occur also provides information about reducing the risk of stereotype threat.

Recent studies have directly examined ways to reduce or eliminate stereotype threat by changing the conditions that produce the effect—in essence, interrupting the process. These studies are important because they point to some steps that can be taken by managers to lessen the possibility that stereotype threat operates for their employees. We now turn to specific strategies for reducing the likelihood of stereotype threat.

INTERRUPTING THE STEREOTYPE THREAT PROCESS: STRATEGIES FOR REDUCING STEREOTYPE THREAT

We have mentioned that stereotype threat effects are strongest for people who are highly identified with the task domain. Researchers fear that over time, stereotyped people may find one way to reduce stereotype threat themselves—by disidentifying with the affected task domain. In other words, they break the psychological connection between their performance and their self-esteem so that doing well on that kind of task is less important. This is the only solution under the individual's control, but it is also perhaps the worst solution, costly for both the individual who gives up a valued part of the self, and for the organization that loses an engaged and motivated employee. Here we describe some alternatives to this worst-case scenario—other strategies for reducing stereotype threat. These strategies, demonstrated to be effective in laboratory studies, all involve changing the conditions for stereotype threat. The strategies, and the points in the process at which they intervene, are shown in Figure 2.

PROVIDE A SUCCESSFUL TASK STRATEGY

We know that stereotype threat influences people only on very difficult tasks—those at the outer limits of ability and skill. Evidence suggests that stereotype threatened people seek to distance themselves from the stereotype by acting opposite to it (Aronson, 2002). They often put their noses to the grindstone, work harder and longer to prove the stereotype wrong—to show it does not apply to them. In the original study by Steele and Aronson, stereotype threatened Black students worked harder and more diligently at the task, expending more effort than the unthreatened. Unfortunately, working harder and more carefully didn't increase performance. The task they were working on was extremely difficult, right at the outer limit of their abilities. Effort *alone* couldn't boost performance—what the students needed was an effective strategy for solving the problems.

A recent study provided stereotype threatened participants with a strategy to successfully counteract the stereotype. In a negotiation task, women were explicitly told about gender stereotypes suggesting that women are less assertive than men and tend not to act in their own self-interest; these characteristics reduce their effectiveness in negotiations. The women in the study were able to counteract the stereotype by acting particularly assertively when making opening offers to their partners, and this strategy improved their performance in the negotiation. However, the women acted this way only when they were *explicitly* told about gender's effect on

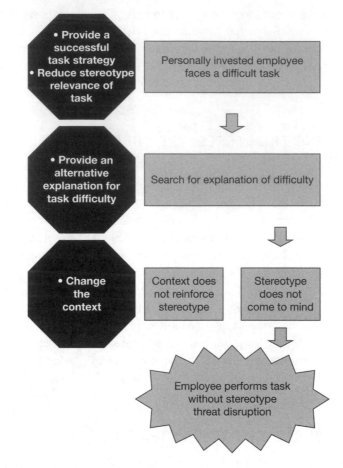

Figure 2. Interrupting the stereotype threat process

negotiation. The women already knew how to act assertively—all they needed to perform successfully was a cue that this context was one in which acting assertively was a good strategy (Kray et al., 2001).

This research suggests that one way to reduce stereotype threat is to teach affected employees behavioral strategies for improving performance and counteracting negative stereotypes. This intervention addresses task difficulty—one of the conditions for stereotype threat. Having good strategies available to cope with challenges makes the task seem less difficult and less frustrating. This research suggests that when using stretch assignments, managers should set goals, and also help employees develop strategies towards attaining them. The "sink or swim" attitude toward stretch assignments common in many organizations can be particularly detrimental for stereotype threatened individuals. If managers discuss and suggest task strategies to employees, stereotype threat should be reduced.

REDUCE THE STEREOTYPE RELEVANCE OF THE TASK

We also know that stereotype threat happens when the stereotype is relevant to the task; when performance on a task is believed to reflect an ability or trait that differentiates stereotyped and nonstereotyped groups (e.g. women and men; Blacks and Whites). Several studies have eliminated stereotype threat effects by refuting or diminishing the stereotype relevance of the task. In one study, researchers asked men and women to take a difficult math test composed of items from the GRE exam. All participants were told that they were taking the math test as part of an effort to develop new testing procedures for the university. Half of the participants were also informed that this particular test had been shown not to produce gender differences —that men and women performed equally well. The other half was not given any information about gender differences. The researchers predicted that stereotype threat would operate when there was no information given about gender differences, because when labeled simply as a "math test," the gender stereotype that "women can't do math" would be relevant. However, being told explicitly that there were no gender differences would reduce the relevance of the stereotype to the task, and hence reduce stereotype threat. By presenting the test as one with no gender differences, the stereotype would be irrelevant to interpreting performance on the test. These results were confirmed: women underperformed relative to men in the "no information" (stereotype relevant) condition, but performed equally to men in the "no gender difference" (stereotype irrelevant) condition (Spencer et al., 1999).

Another study reduced the stereotype relevance of the task in a slightly different way, by emphasizing characteristics shared by both groups. Male and female college students participated in a negotiation exercise. For half of the participants, researchers made gender stereotypes relevant by saying that the most effective negotiators are "rational and assertive" rather than "emotional and passive" (cueing gender stereotypes). For the other half, researchers eliminated the relevance of the gender stereotype for performance. They told this half of the participants that "rational and assertive" people do better than "emotional and passive" individuals. But then they added, "people who are in competitive academic environments, like you, do exceptionally well in the negotiation. This is true for men and women alike." This description highlighted characteristics important for performance that are shared by both men and women, diminishing the stereotype relevance of the task. This strategy was also successful in decreasing stereotype threat and gender differences in performance (Kray et al., 2001).

These studies show that reducing the stereotype relevance of the task—one of the conditions for stereotype threat—is effective in removing stereotype threat. But is this a realistic strategy in organizations? In the laboratory, it is possible to label an unfamiliar task as one showing group differences or not. It is easy to manipulate participants' beliefs about whether a task reflects group differences when those participants have no prior experience with the task. The situation is different with real world tasks or jobs where employees and co-workers may have strong opinions about the types of people who do well in various jobs or roles. Consider technical or mathematical tasks. Belief in gender differences on such tasks is widespread (Brown and Josephs, 1999), so when faced with a technical or mathematical task, a woman may not believe a manager who says it does not reflect gender differences. It might be more effective for managers instead to use the strategy in the second experiment. For example, rather than try to discredit gender differences, one could make gender differences irrelevant by stressing *common* characteristics of employees that are relevant for performing the task. This could be done by identifying characteristics important for task success that are unlinked to group stereotypes. Perhaps a manager could inform all employees that they were hired precisely because they have the skills needed to do well. For example, "We have such good hiring procedures—the people who we bring in, both men and women, have the skills to perform well."

PROVIDE AN ALTERNATIVE EXPLANATION FOR TASK DIFFICULTY

Task difficulty is a trigger for stereotype threat because people try to explain their difficulty to themselves: on a stereotype relevant task, where the context reinforces the stereotype, they are more likely to think of the stereotype as a potential explanation. The resulting anxiety and distress then disrupts performance. Several studies have shown that by giving an explanation for task difficulty *besides* the stereotype, stereotype threat can be reduced.

In one study, men and women students who came to the laboratory were told they would take a math test being developed by the psychology department for placement purposes. Immediately after this general description, half of the students were asked to begin the test, and were given 20 minutes to complete 20 problems. The other half was told that there would be a practice session before the test, administered on a computer. The experimenter explained that this would help them to "warm up," allowing a better assessment of their true ability level on the actual test. However, when the experimenter turned on the computer, the screen was unreadable (the computer had been rigged). After fiddling with the knobs and controls to no avail, the experimenter then announced that the students would have to take the test without the benefit of warming up, and this extenuating circumstance would be noted on their answer sheets. The researchers designed this study because they reasoned that being denied the "warm up" opportunity would provide a viable alternative to the gender stereotype as an explanation for any experienced task difficulty, reducing stereotype threat effects for women. Results confirmed this: men's performance was not affected by the test conditions. However, the performance of women was greatly affected. Women performed better on the math test when they were denied their "warm up" opportunity (Brown and Josephs, 1999).

In another study, researchers induced stereotype threat for White men by heightening the salience of the stereotype that Whites have less natural athletic ability than Blacks. The researchers then informed half of these participants that the lab space where they would perform athletic tasks had recently been renovated, and that the lab administration wanted "to know if the new changes made research participants feel tense or uneasy." Because of this concern, the participants would be asked to rate the lab space and its effects on their emotions after the experiment (Stone et al., 1999). This information provided participants with another explanation (the renovated lab space) for any anxiety they experienced during the task. White men who received this alternative explanation for poor performance performed better than those who did not.

Again, however effective these manipulations are in the laboratory, their feasibility for the work setting may be limited. Managers certainly shouldn't lie to their employees (as in the first study) to give them an excuse for task difficulty and poor performance. But managers could remind employees about real-life factors that might be constraining their performance (e.g. a difficult client, limited resources, or a tight deadline). Another feasible strategy for providing an alternative explanation comes from a third study. The experimenters induced stereotype threat for women using the usual setup—telling participants that they would be completing a standardized math test for a study of gender differences. One group received just these instructions. With another group, in addition to these instructions, the experimenters described the phenomenon of stereotype threat and said, "if you are feeling anxious while taking this test, this anxiety could be the result of these negative [gender] stereotypes that are widely known in society and have nothing to do with your actual ability to do well" (Johns et al., 2005: 176). These instructions had a positive effect on test performance. Women underperformed on the math test relative to men when given only the "math test" description. When stereotype threat was explained and offered as a possible cause of their anxiety, the performance of men and women was similar.

Telling people who might be affected by stereotype threat about the phenomenon has some advantages. Stereotype threat is real, and its effects on performance are well-documented. You might think that explicitly raising the issue of stereotype threat with a potentially affected employee might make matters worse by drawing attention to the stereotype—better to keep quiet and act like it doesn't exist. But instead the opposite appears to be true. Telling employees that you know stereotype threat can happen, and that they should be aware of it, gives them a different attribution for their difficulty and anxiety (it's not the stereotype, it's the stereotype *threat*).

CHANGE THE CONTEXT

The context is another condition that can affect the likelihood of stereotype threat. We discussed how one aspect of the context—the diversity of people performing the job—can reinforce or diminish the relevance of stereotypes. The research showing that tokens are more likely to experience stereotype threat also suggests a way to reduce stereotype threat: change the context by removing people from token situations.

This strategy may work in the laboratory, but how can managers realistically achieve this goal? In organizations, the composition of work groups is already constrained by employee skills, task interdependence, and other factors. Managers can't shuffle employees around based on their demographics to avoid token situations. However, several studies have changed the context using another strategy that does not involve changing the demographic make-up of the work group: presenting a role model who contradicts the stereotype. In one study, participants were administered a difficult math test by either a male or female experimenter. The experimenters gave identical instructions designed to accomplish two goals: (1) induce stereotype threat in the women by presenting the test as diagnostic of ability; and (2) create perceptions of the experimenter's competence in math. Scores on the math test showed that women underperformed relative to men only when the test was administered by a male experimenter. A follow-up study revealed that it was not the physical presence of the female experimenter, but rather her perceived competence that protected the women from stereotype threat. Seeing a woman who was competent in the math domain boosted women's beliefs in their own mathematical abilities and maintained their performance (Marx and Roman, 2002).

Other researchers found similar results when role models were presented in a different way. One study asked participants to read and critique four biographical essays. Half of the participants read essays concerning successful women in a variety of fields such as medicine and law. The other half read essays concerning successful corporations. Then all the participants completed a math test administered by a male experimenter. Results indicated that the role model manipulation reduced stereotype threat: Women scored worse than men on the test when they had read about successful corporations, but women scored at the same level as men when they had read about successful women (McIntyre et al., 2003).

These studies suggest that managers may be able to change the context for stereotyped employees by boosting the salience and visibility of role models. Note that in the "essay" study, the physical presence of a role model was not necessary — what was important was that the competence of the role model was salient. This strategy could be feasibly implemented in organizations. Managers can increase access to role models by encouraging employee participation in mentoring programs, professional associations, and employee network groups (Friedman and Holtom, 2002; Friedman et al., 1998). If managers maintain a diverse network of associates themselves, they can be more aware of potential role models for all of their employees, and attempt to connect people.

IMPLICATIONS FOR DIVERSITY MANAGEMENT

Would a greater focus on reducing stereotype threat add anything new to diversity management? We think it would. Existing diversity management programs tend to have two major objectives (Kellough and Naff, 2004): one goal is to change managers' *attitudes* — to reduce negative attitudes, stereotypes, and prejudice against members of different groups. Much diversity training is geared toward this goal. A second related goal is to change managers' *behaviors* — how they select, appraise, and develop employees (Brief and Barsky, 2000). For example, managers are encouraged, and often required, to specify explicit behavioral and performance standards for promotion or advancement, and to adhere to these in making decisions. These are important objectives. However, these objectives ignore two realities. First, changing attitudes and reducing stereotypes is a long-term endeavor. Stereotypes are embedded in the culture, and reinforced outside of the work setting (Brief, 1998). Until society changes, stereotypes about different groups will remain. Even if a particular manager is unprejudiced, others in the workgroup may not be, and employees may still feel stereotype threat. While we need to try to reduce stereotypes, in the foreseeable future we have to deal with existing attitudes, and try to reduce the *impact* of stereotypes on affected employees. Second, while increasing the objectivity of measurement and decisions is necessary, the presence of stereotype threat means that performance *itself* may convey biased information about a person's true ability. So the well-intentioned manager who relies on objective performance data without understanding the impact of stereotype threat will still unfairly underestimate performance. Focusing on stereotype threat takes these realities into account, and highlights two principles that are currently downplayed in most diversity management efforts:

1. **Acknowledge stereotypes and address them directly.** Unfortunately, the goal of eliminating stereotypes from organizational decision-making sometimes leads organizational members to deny their existence. People sometimes confuse stereotype awareness with stereotype endorsement (Adler, 2002). Yet research has shown that even unprejudiced people are familiar with the content of common stereotypes and can easily describe what prejudiced people believe about members of certain groups (Devine, 1989). Putting our strategies into action means that a manager has to honestly acknowledge the stereotypes that exist. The manager who acknowledges the existence and potential impact of stereotypes does not have to endorse or support those stereotypes. Only a manager who acknowledges stereotypes can acknowledge the opportunity for stereotype threat and take corrective action.

    The strategies for reducing stereotype threat further imply that managers should talk explicitly about stereotypes with their potentially threatened employees (Kray et al., 2001). Rarely are stereotypes directly named and described—particularly to the affected parties. Although many people (managers and subordinates alike) might see this as a risky step, explicit discussion about stereotypes can be useful in reducing their impact. If supervisors and subordinates trust one another, it can be a good strategy. David Thomas' comparison of successful and plateaued non-White executives demonstrated that successful executives found mentors early in their careers who were able to talk directly about race and the challenges it presented (Thomas, 2001; Thomas and Gabarro, 1999). Such openness about the existence of stereotypes and stereotype threat provides employees with alternative explanations for task difficulty and also may decrease concerns that they will be judged in light of the stereotype. Many managers would shy away from such a frank discussion, but the evidence says that evasion is not always helpful. Honest engagement of the problem and an exploration of action strategies to counteract perceptions can increase trust, reduce stereotype threat, and improve performance. How can managers be encouraged to take these risks? Perhaps diversity training should focus on providing managers with the skills and confidence to talk about stereotypes with their employees.

2. **Shift the focus from the manager to the environment.** Diversity management programs tend to focus on the manager as the target of change. Diversity training programs, for example, are designed to change managerial attitudes and behavior (Bendick et al., 2001). In contrast, the strategies for reducing stereotype threat focus on the *environment* as the target of change. In other words, changing the conditions that lead to stereotype threat. Managers need to attend to managing the environment and reducing the cues that signal to employees that stereotypes are operating.

Effective diversity management has always meant creating an environment where all can succeed (Cox, 1994; Thomas, 1991). Knowledge of stereotype threat increases our understanding of what that really means. It is more than being personally nonprejudiced and unbiased. It means actively reducing cues that limit the contributions of *all* employees. Only in this way can the benefits of diversity be realized.

NOTES

* Loriann Roberson (lr2356@columbia.edu) is Professor of Psychology and Education at Teachers College, Columbia University, in New York City.
Carol T. Kulik (carol.kulik@unisa.edu.au) is Research Professor of Human Resource Management at the School of Management, University of South Australia, Adelaide, Australia.

** We wish to thank Caryn Block and Benjamin Galvin for their helpful comments on an earlier draft of this reading, and Jeanne Tao for her assistance with the figures.

REFERENCES

Adler, N. J. (2002). *International dimensions of organizational behavior*, 4th edn. Cincinnati, OH: South-Western Publishing.

Aronson, J. (2002). Stereotype threat: Contending and coping with unnerving expectations. In J. Aronson (Ed.) *Improving academic achievement: Impact of psychological factors on education* (pp. 279–301). San Francisco, CA: Elsevier.

Aronson, J., Quinn, D. M., & Spencer, S. J. (1998). Stereotype threat and the academic under-performance of minorities and women. In Swim, J.K. & Stangor, C. (Eds.), *Prejudice: The target's perspective* (pp. 83–103). New York: Academic Press.

Aronson, J., Lustina, M. J., Good, C., Keough, K., Steele, C. M., & Brown, J. (1999). When White men can't do math: Necessary and sufficient factors in stereotype threat. *Journal of Experimental Social Psychology, 35,* 29–46.

Beilock, S. L., & Carr, T. H. (2005). When high-powered people fail: Working memory and "choking under pressure" in math. *Psychological Science, 16,* 101–105.

Bendick, M., Egan, M. L., & Lofhjelm, S. M. (2001). Workforce diversity training: From anti-discrimination compliance to organizational development. *Human Resource Planning, 24,* 10–36.

Blank, R., & Shipp, S. (1994). *Voices of diversity: Real people talk about problems and solutions in a workplace where everyone is not alike.* New York: AMACOM.

Blascovich, J., Spencer, S. J., Quinn, D., & Steele, C. (2001). African Americans and high blood pressure: The role of stereotype threat. *Psychological Science, 12,* 225–229.

Brief, A. P. (1998). *Attitudes in and around organizations.* Thousand Oaks, CA: Sage.

Brief, A. P., & Barsky, A. (2000). Establishing a climate for diversity: The inhibition of prejudiced reactions in the workplace. *Research in Personnel and Human Resources Management, 19,* 91–129.

Brown, R. P., & Josephs, R. A. (1999). A burden of proof: Stereotype relevance and gender differences in math performance. *Journal of Personality and Social Psychology, 76,* 246–257.

Cadinu, M., Maass, A., Frigerio, S., Impagliazzo, L., & Latinotti, S. (2003). Stereotype threat: The effect of expectancy on performance. *European Journal of Social Psychology, 33,* 267–285.

Chandler, M. (1999, October 4). *Secrets of the SAT* (FRONTLINE, #1802). New York and Washington, DC: Public Broadcasting Service.

Chung-Herrera, B. G., & Lankau, M. J. (2005). Are we there yet? An assessment of fit between stereotypes of minority managers and the successful-manager prototype. *Journal of Applied Social Psychology, 35,* 2029–2056.

Cocchiara, F. K., & Quick, J. C. (2004). The negative effects of positive stereotypes: Ethnicity-related stressors and implications on organizational health. *Journal of Organizational Behavior, 25,* 781–785.

Cox, T. H. Jr. (1994). *Cultural diversity in organizations: Theory, research, and practice.* San Francisco, CA: Berrett-Koehler.

Devine, P. G. (1989). Stereotypes and prejudice: Their automatic and controlled components. *Journal of Personality and Social Psychology, 56,* 5–18.

Dickins, F., & Dickens, J. B. (1991). *The Black manager: Making it in the corporate world.* New York: AMACOM.

Elliott, A. J., & Harackiewicz, J. M. (1996). Approach and avoidance achievement goals and intrinsic motivation: A mediational analysis. *Journal of Personality and Social Psychology, 70,* 461–475.

Frantz, C. M., Cuddy, A. J. C., Burnett, M., Ray, H., & Hart, A. (2004). A threat in the computer: The race implicit association test as a stereotype threat experience. *Personality and Social Psychology Bulletin, 30,* 1611–1614.

Friedman, R. A., & Holtom, B. (2002). The effects of network groups on minority employee turnover intentions. *Human Resource Management, 41,* 405–421.

Friedman, R. A., Kane, M., & Cornfield, D. B. (1998). Social support and career optimism: Examining the effectiveness of network groups among Black managers. *Human Relations, 51,* 1155–1177.

Greenberg, J. (1996). *Managing behavior in organizations: Science in service to practice.* Upper Saddle River, NJ: Prentice Hall.

Greengard, S. (2003). Gimme attitude. *Workforce, 82,* 56–60.

Habermas, T., & Bluck, S. (2000). Getting a life: The emergence of the life story in adolescence. *Psychological Bulletin, 12,* 748–769.

Hackman, J. R., & Oldham, G. R. (1980). *Work redesign.* Reading, MA: Addison-Wesley.

Hansen, F. (2003). Diversity's business case doesn't add up. *Workforce, 82,* 28–32.

Heilman, M. E., Block, C. J., Martell, R. F., & Simon, M. C. (1989). Has anything changed? Current characterizations of men, women, and managers. *Journal of Applied Psychology, 74,* 935–942.

Hite, L. M. (2004). Black and White women managers: Access to opportunity. *Human Resource Development Quarterly, 15,* 131–146.

Hom, P. W., Roberson, L., & Ellis, A. D. (2007). *Challenging conventional wisdom about who quits: Revelations from corporate America.* Manuscript submitted for publication, Arizona State University.

Inzlicht, M., & Ben Zeev, T. (2003). Do high-achieving female students underperform in private? The implications of threatening environments on intellectual processing. *Journal of Educational Psychology, 95,* 796–805.

Jackson, S. E., Brett, J. F., Sessa, V. I., Cooper, D. M., Julin, J. A., & Peyronnin, K. (1991). Some differences make a difference: Individual dissimilarity and group heterogeneity as correlates of recruitment, promotions, and turnover. *Journal of Applied Psychology, 76,* 675–689.

Jehn, K. A., Neale, M., & Northcraft, G. (1999). Why differences make a difference: A field study of diversity, conflict, and performance in workgroups. *Administrative Science Quarterly, 44*, 741–763.

Johns, M., Schmader, T., & Martens, A. (2005). Knowing is half the battle: Teaching stereotype threat as a means of improving women's math performance. *Psychological Science, 16*, 175–179.

Kanter, R. (1977). *Men and women of the organization*. New York: Basic Books.

Kellough, J. E., & Naff, K. C. (2004). Responding to a wake up call: An examination of Federal Agency Diversity Management Programs. *Administration & Society, 36*, 62–91.

Kochan, T., Bezrukova, K., Ely, R., Jackson, S., Joshi, A., Jehn, K., Leonare, J., Levine, D., & Thomas, D. (2003). The effects of diversity on business performance: Report of the diversity research network. *Human Resource Management, 42*, 3–21.

Kray, L. J., Thompson, L., & Galinsky, A. (2001). Battle of the sexes: Gender stereotype confirmation and reactance in negotiations. *Journal of Personality and Social Psychology, 80*, 942–958.

Kray, L. J., Galinsky, A. D., & Thompson, L. (2002). Reversing the gender gap in negotiations: An exploration of stereotype regeneration. *Organizational Behavior and Human Decision Processes, 87*, 386–409.

McCauley, C., Eastman, L., & Ohlott, P. (1995). Linking management selection and development through stretch assignments. *Human Resource Management, 34*, 93–115.

McIntyre, R. B., Paulson, R. M., & Lord, C. G. (2003). Alleviating women's mathematics stereotype threat through salience of group achievements. *Journal of Experimental Social Psychology, 39*, 83–90.

Marx, D. M., & Roman, J. S. (2002). Female role models: Protecting women's math test performance. *Personality and Social Psychology Bulletin, 28*, 1183–1193.

Niemann, Y. F., & Dovidio, J. F. (1998). Relationship of solo status, academic rank, and perceived distinctiveness to job satisfaction of racial/ethnic minorities. *Journal of Applied Psychology, 83*, 55–71.

Noe, R. A. (1999). *Employee training and development*. Boston, MA: Irwin McGraw-Hill.

Parks-Yancy, R. (2006). The effects of social group membership and social capital resources on career. *Journal of Black Studies, 36*, 515–545.

Personal blog. (2005, June 3). Available at: www.bigfatblog.com/archives/001607.php.

Reio, Jr., T. G., & Callahan, J. L. (2004). Affect, curiosity, and socialization-related learning: A path analysis of antecedents to job performance. *Journal of Business and Psychology, 19*, 3–22.

Rice, F. (1996). Denny's changes its spots. *Fortune, 133*, 133–138.

Roberson L., Deitch, E., Brief, A. P., & Block, C. J. (2003). Stereotype threat and feedback seeking in the workplace. *Journal of Vocational Behavior, 62*, 176–188.

Robinson, G., & Dechant, K. (1997). Building a business case for diversity. *Academy of Management Executive, 11*, 21–31.

Smith, J. L. (2004). Understanding the process of stereotype threat: A review of mediational variables and new performance goal directions. *Educational Psychology Review, 16*, 177–206.

Spencer, S. J., Steele, C. M., & Quinn, D. M. (1999). Stereotype threat and women's math performance. *Journal of Experimental Social Psychology, 35*, 4–28.

Steele, C. M. (1997). A threat in the air: How stereotypes shape intellectual identity and performance. *American Psychologist, 52*, 613–629.

Steele, C. M., & Aronson, J. (1995). Stereotype threat and the intellectual test performance of African Americans. *Journal of Personality and Social Psychology, 85*, 440–452.

Steele, C. M., Spencer, S. J., & Aronson, J. (2002). Contending with group image: The psychology of stereotype and social identity threat. *Advances in Experimental Social Psychology, 34*, 379–440.

Steele-Johnson, D., Beauregard, R. S., Hoover, P. B., & Schmidt, A. M. (2000). Goal orientation and task demand effects on motivation, affect, and performance. *Journal of Applied Psychology, 85*, 724–738.

Stone, J., Lynch, C. L., Sjomeling, M., & Darley, J.M. (1999). Stereotype threat effects on Black and White athletic performance. *Journal of Personality and Social Psychology, 77*, 1213–1227.

Thomas, D. A. (2001). The truth about mentoring minorities: Race matters. *Harvard Business Review, 79*, 98–107.

Thomas, D. A., & Ely, R. J. (1996). Making differences matter: A new paradigm for managing diversity. *Harvard Business Review, 74*, 79–91.

Thomas, D. A., & Gabarro, J. J. (1999). *Breaking through: The making of minority executives in corporate America*. Boston, MA: Harvard Business School Press.

Thomas, R. R. Jr. (1991). *Beyond race and gender: Unleashing the power of your total work force by managing diversity*. New York: AMACOM.

Tomkiewicz, J., Brenner, O. C., & Adeyemi-Bello, T. (1998). The impact of perceptions and stereotypes on the managerial mobility of African Americans. *Journal of Social Psychology, 138*, 88–92.

Tsui, A., Egan, T., & O'Reilly, C. (1992). Being different: Relational demography and organizational attachment. *Administrative Science Quarterly, 37*, 549–579.

Verbeke, W., & Bagozzi, R. (2000). Sales call anxiety: Exploring what it means when fear rules a sales encounter. *Journal of Marketing, 64*, 88–102.

Vandewalle, D. (2001). Goal orientation: Why wanting to look successful doesn't always lead to success. *Organizational Dynamics, 30*, 162–171.

Yerkes, R. M., & Dodson, J. D. (1908). The relation of strength of stimulus to rapidity of habit formation. *Journal of Comparative Neurology, 18*, 459–482.

Zenger, T., & Lawrence, B. (1989). Organizational demography: The differential effects of age and tenure distributions on technical communications. *Academy of Management Journal, 32*, 353–376.

Charlotte Butler and Henri-Claude de Bettignies

CHANGMAI CORPORATION*

D AVID MCLEOD HAD BEEN general manager of the All-Asia Paper Co. (AAP), part of the Changmai Corporation, for just two months. Previously, he had spent four years running a large and long-established pulp mill in South Africa. Bored by a job that had fallen into well-ordered routine, McLeod had eagerly responded to the challenge presented to him by Changmai's director of personnel, Barney Li: to take over as head of the five-year-old AAP pulp mill, one of the biggest in Southeast Asia, and double production within a year.

As Li explained, the ethnic Chinese owner of the Changmai group, Tommy Goh, was dissatisfied by the performance of the mill, then headed by a Malaysian expatriate and producing on average 21,500 tonnes of pulp per month. The mill contained state-of-the art equipment, which, Goh felt, was not being used to full capacity. He was therefore looking for an experienced Western manager to introduce a more professional approach and increase production. Time was of the essence, as Goh's instinct, which had never failed him yet, told him that the volatile paper industry was about to undergo one of its periodic surges. When this happened, Goh wanted to be able to take full advantage of the rise in pulp prices. Currently, the mill's production costs ran at US$200 per tonne of kraft pulp, for which the selling price was US$350 per tonne. If, as Goh anticipated, the price climbed again to its previous high of US$700 per ton, he stood to make a real killing.

McLeod, a highly qualified engineer, had a wide experience gained in some of the most sophisticated pulp mills in the world. A Scotsman by birth, he had begun his career in Scandinavia before moving on to Canada, the US and finally South Africa. For him, the opportunity to work in Asia was an added attraction. When he finally met Goh, in a hotel room in Hong Kong, he was impressed both by the man and by his knowledge of the industry.

At age 45, the entrepreneurial Goh was head of a diversified empire. Building new businesses was his life's blood, so, although rich and successful, he remained restless, always searching for the next big opportunity. Closest to him, apart from two family members working in the Changmai Group, were those dating from his early days in the tough world of street trading, where he made his first million by the age of 24. These people bore Goh unstinting loyalty.

Goh was a forceful personality, whose enthusiasm for what the mill could achieve made McLeod eager to get to work. His new boss, McLeod decided, was a man of some vision, clearly used to making fast decisions and seeing them implemented immediately. In meetings, Goh's impatience was signalled by the way he constantly checked his Rolex wristwatch, and barked orders to the young, smartly suited aide who relayed his chief's commands into a mobile phone. McLeod was surprised, therefore, when Goh invited him to lunch and then took him to a small backstreet restaurant that looked only one level up from a street stall, though the food was excellent. The incongruity of Goh, his aide and himself in such a setting while outside Roni, the waiting driver, leaned against the BMW eating a bowl of noodles, had struck McLeod forcefully. It was a memorable introduction to the cultural dissonances of this new world.

Goh's latest project was to build a rayon mill on the AAP site. Although the later chemical processes were different, pulp and rayon used the same wood and shared the initial production stages, so the synergies were obvious. To build the rayon mill, Goh had entered into a 50–50 joint venture with a Chicago-based US company whose representative, Dan Bailey, was permanently on site. McLeod was pleased to learn that he would find a fellow Westerner at AAP. Most of the workers on the site, said Li, were locals led by expatriate managers, mainly from the region.

Fired by his meeting with Goh, McLeod had gone to AAP full of energy and enthusiasm. His first sight of the mill was a rude shock. To his experienced eye, the five-year-old infant looked more like a battered old lady. On closer inspection, it was clear that, although the mill was indeed equipped with the most modem technology, its maintenance had been dangerously neglected. A dozen urgent repairs leapt to McLeod's eye following his first tour of the mill, and every succeeding day he discovered more. In the first few months, McLeod worked eighteen hours a day, often being called out in the middle of the night to deal with some urgent breakdown. The local employees he found willing, but completely untrained. Safety precautions were rudimentary, and McLeod was undecided about whether or not to try and impose Western standards. However, in a preliminary effort to raise standards he had regularly toured the site and pointed out the most glaring breaches of safety regulations to the offending superintendents.

Until today, McLeod had felt that, with effort and organisation, he could get the mill into shape and reach Goh's target. Then, at ten o'clock that morning, he had received a visit from Mr Lai, a government official from the Ministry of Safety and Environmental Control. McLeod knew that Lai had been inspecting the site for the past three days and had anticipated a reprimand from him, as, judged by Western environmental standards, the mill had several defects. On the other hand, thought McLeod, no accidents had occurred while Lai was on site, which was a good sign, and perhaps an indication that his emphasis on obeying safety rules was having an effect. So he was relieved when a beaming Mr Lai said how pleased he was with his inspection and invited McLeod to walk with him down to the river into which waste water from the mill was emptied after passing through the two-level treatment plant. Goh had been very proud of this feature of the mill, which, he had told McLeod, made environmental standards at AAP "the equal of those prevailing in Oregon." After primary treatment in a settling basin, the water passed through to a lagoon for secondary, bacteriological treatment in accordance with government standards. Only after two days of treatment in the lagoon was the water let out into the river.

As they walked along the muddy bank and discussed Lai's findings, only minor infringements were mentioned, from which McLeod inferred that local enforcement of environmental regulations was indeed less stringent than in the West. "So, all in all," Lai concluded, "I would say that I could put in a favourable A1 report on environmental standards at the mill except," he paused, "for two small problems that I'm sure can be easily resolved given goodwill on both sides. The first concerns the broken filter in the waste-water unit, which, I understand from your foreman, should be fixed in the near future. However in the meantime, as I saw for myself, the water coming through the outlet pipe is quite polluted. Such a pity for the villagers who live on the other bank and fish in the river, especially coming after the unfortunate incident last year when, as I understand it, the lagoon dam collapsed and untreated waste water poured into the river, just at this very bend. I hear that several shacks were washed away, and that the river was poisoned. The villagers have told me how angry they were when they found dead fish floating in the river. They say the compensation they received was very small, hardly anything in fact; and now, seeing the brown water coming out of the outlet pipe, they greatly fear a repeat of this shocking incident."

"Just imagine, Mr McLeod, if one of the local newspapers decided to write about their fears, about how the poor villagers and their simple fishing life were threatened by a rich and powerful company. Such publicity would be most unwelcome to AAP, not to mention Mr Goh. It might even harm his plans for future projects involving government concessions. How angry he would be in such a case – and I hear that his anger can be terrible indeed for those around him. You would have my very great sympathy." And the smooth brown face of Mr Lai had looked anxiously up at McLeod, apparently in genuine concern.

"My other small concern," continued Mr Lai, "is the mill's long-term safety record. Really, I am sorry to see that so many grave accidents have occurred; two deaths by falling from a height, and another from being caught and mangled by machinery in motion. Then there are several reports of serious burns and blisters to people working in the lime kiln, an operator blinded in one eye after iron chips flew out of the spinning tank and another who lost an arm when he slipped on to the roller conveyor. Plus, many other small accidents such as people being struck by falling objects or stepping on to nails with their bare feet. When you add up the number, Mr McLeod, the safety record does not look very harmonious."

"But do not look so worried, Mr McLeod," continued Lai. "I am sure we can find a solution if we put our heads together. I am returning to my hotel room in the village now, to write my report. It is my last task before I go on leave for a week.

My wife has won money on a lottery ticket and is going to use it to make a pilgrimage to Lourdes. As Christians, it has always been our dearest wish to visit Lourdes together one day. It would have meant so much to us. But, sad to say, this will not be. I cannot accompany her, as the lottery money will only pay for one person. So I must stay at home and look after our children," Lai sighed. "For someone like me on the salary of a humble government official, to visit Lourdes with my wife must remain just a dream. I was only just thinking to myself how wonderful it would be if I had a fairy godfather who could wave his wand, and make my dream come true."

McLeod felt sweat trickle down his back, not wholly because of the humid heat of the morning. The collapse of the lagoon dam, which had happened long before his arrival, he knew about. According to Goh, the contractors building the dam had cheated by using poor-quality cement. As a result, the dam had burst after a season of exceptionally heavy rains, with the consequences as recounted by Lai. However, Goh had assured McLeod that since then the lagoon had been rebuilt using the best-quality materials, and thoroughly tested. There was absolutely no possibility of such an incident being repeated. As for the filter, although it had been faulty for some time, the pollution that resulted from it was really very minor, as proved by the fact that the daily effluent readings of the water passing through the pipe still fell within the safety range specified by the Ministry. A new filter had been ordered but, unfortunately, had not yet arrived. With so many other things on his mind, it had not occurred to McLeod to associate the past lagoon collapse with the present fault in the waste unit and Lai's official inspection. Now he cursed himself for not having seen the potential danger of their being connected. As he was only too well aware, if the incident was resurrected by Lai and the gossip he had picked up, exaggerated by stories of the present pollution, was repeated into the wrong ears, then the effects could be catastrophic both for AAP and for the Changmai group. Inevitably, Goh had business rivals who would be only too pleased to have ammunition with which to attack him.

As for the safety record, McLeod wondered where Lai had got his information, as not all the examples he gave were familiar to him. McLeod had been strictly monitoring the accident figures since his arrival and, although there had been the usual crop of minor injuries inevitably associated with hi-tech machinery and an unskilled workforce, nothing major had occurred. Again, Lai must be using past history, for, as McLeod knew, in the early years of operations the mill's safety record had been very poor. As he tried vainly to think of a suitable reply, Lai turned to leave.

"You know where to find me," said Lai. "I will return to the Ministry tomorrow at nine thirty with my report, which I'm sure will be positive now we have had this little chat. I must say, I will be glad to get back to my family. We are quite worried about my eldest son. He has recently graduated from a small technical college in the south of England. It was a great sacrifice to send him, but we hoped that it would open up many opportunities for him. He is now a qualified mechanical engineer but so far has not been able to find a job that suited his talents. You know, it has occurred to me while touring this mill that here would be an ideal opening for my son. He would be very interested to work with your control distribution system. Computers have always fascinated him, and I'm sure he could very quickly learn to manage the system. What a good start it would be for him. Perhaps you have a suitable vacancy? If so, let me know tomorrow. Good day, Mr McLeod."

With a final beaming smile, Lai got into the company car that had been arranged for his use during his stay, and was driven off. His mind whirling, McLeod drove back to the office. This was the last thing he had expected. As he thought about what had passed, his shock was replaced by anger. How dare Lai try to blackmail him in this way? He would never give in to such demands. The thought of an inexperienced, unqualified person meddling in the computerised control distribution centre, one of the mill's most advanced features, made his hair stand on end. It was AAP's nerve centre, monitoring operations in all parts of the mill. Any breakdown there would be disastrous. Then he remembered Lai's comments about the damage that would be caused by a negative report that dug up the old scandal of the lagoon and hinted that history might repeat itself, or that highlighted AAP's early safety record, and the effects of all this on the villagers and on Goh. What was he going to do?

Just then, his thoughts were interrupted by a knock, and his secretary, Anna, rushed into the room. "Quick," she said, "accident in the chemical area. Many people hurt." Grabbing his hard hat, McLeod rushed from the room and drove over to the plant where a crowd was gathering. He cursed. The chemical plant had been one of the worst-maintained areas and he had been renovating it as fast as he could.

The supervisor, Mr Budi, met him. "It's not as bad as we first thought," said Budi. "There was a loose valve and some of the chlorine leaked. But one of the workers panicked and started shouting, and then everyone began rushing about yelling it was 'another Bhopal'. Only one person has been hurt because of the leak – he inhaled the gas and so burned his throat. His hands and eyes also need medical attention. Two others were trampled in the rush to get out, but I think that the guards are getting things under control." McLeod looked out of the window. The security guards were trying to disperse the crowd, with some success. "Luckily, it's nearly lunch time," continued Budi. "That should help." McLeod inspected the leak. As Budi said, it was minor. But, given the lack of training among the staff and the reluctance to wear safety clothing, any incident could fast become a full-scale disaster. "I'll go and see the injured men in the clinic," said McLeod, "and then get back to the office. Let me know if you need me."

Back in his office, McLeod added "safety drill" to the long list of jobs he had to tackle in the very near future. He knew he should phone Goh and tell him what had happened, but he didn't yet feel strong enough. On impulse, he decided to go over to see Dan Bailey on the rayon site. He needed to talk to someone, a fellow Westerner. As he drove up, however, he saw that Dan, too, was having problems. He was arguing with a man McLeod recognised as one of the local contractors whose gang was part of the construction team. As McLeod arrived, the contractor shrugged and walked off.

"What's up, Dan?" said McLeod, seeing the anger in Dan's face. "We've just had another man killed in a fall from the scaffolding," Bailey replied. "That makes ten since we started eight months ago. The man wasn't wearing boots, safety harness or a hard hat. I've told the contractors over and over again that they must provide the right equipment, it's even written into their contract. But they say 'yes, boss' and do nothing. They say they can't afford to, as Goh has negotiated such a tight contract. I spoke to Goh about it, but he says the workers don't belong to him, and that he cannot be held responsible for what the contractors do in his plant. His main concern is to get the mill finished fast and start production. Everyone squeezes everyone else, corners get cut, and as usual it's the poor at the bottom who pay for it. Have you seen the way they are living? There is no more room in the dormitories, so some containers have been temporarily converted by putting in wooden bunks. They have no running water, no electricity, they work up to their knees in mud in bare feet, and no one thinks anything of it. What a country!"

McLeod nodded in agreement. "The working conditions were the first thing that shocked me when I came to the site. I mentioned it to Goh, but he got really mad and told me the West had a nerve to try to interfere with other countries. He said to me, 'Look at your own history and see how you treated your workers in the past. Did any outsider tell you it was wicked? Look at conditions in your cities today – the drugs and violence, the crime and the homelessness – and then decide if you have a right to preach to others. I can't stand this Western pressure for labour rights in Asia, and your arguments about 'social dumping'. It's the same in China, where the Americans are always moaning about human rights. To us, trying to impose Western values seems just a dirty trick to protect your inefficient businesses. Don't condemn us before you take the beam out of your own eye." McLeod paused. "Goh must have learned that at mission school," he said with a smile. Then he went on to describe his encounter with Mr Lai.

Dan's reply was not comforting. "Sounds like you've got no choice, old buddy," he said. "But it just shows you how the attitude towards the enforcement of environmental standards, which is being monitored by powerful pressure groups, differs from the way safety legislation, which does not attract the same level of interest in the outside world, is more or less ignored. But if you think you've got problems, listen to this." Bailey lowered his voice. "You know that our CEO, Howard Hartford, is visiting from Chicago on his annual tour of our operations in the region. I spent yesterday morning with him in a meeting with Goh – it was quite a combat. Anyway, that evening, as I was leaving the office, Benny Burdiman, who's heading procurement for the rayon project, poked his head round the door, apologised for disturbing me and asked me to sign a form so he could go to town the next day and clear the new power boiler we've been expecting through customs. The form, from accounts, was a bill for 'R.S. Tax: US$35,000'. I was puzzled, as I thought everything had been paid for. I remembered authorising a cheque for the vendors a week ago. I hadn't a clue what this was for."

Bailey continued, "Well, you know what Benny is like. He has been with Goh from the beginning and is the sharpest negotiator in the region. He treated me like I was a backward child, and explained that the boiler was now in a bonded warehouse at the port. To get it, he had to give the director of customs a little present. He said it was quite normal, and that US $35,000 was the going rate. Apparently 'R.S. Tax' is a local joke – it stands for 'reliable service tax'. Accounts keeps a special budget to pay it. 'You'll get used to it', Benny said. Wanted me to sign at once, but I said, 'Now, hold on; I'll have to think about this. Let me get back to you tomorrow'."

"So what did you do?" asked McLeod.

"I dumped it straight in the CEO's lap," said Bailey, with some satisfaction. "You know how outspoken he has always been in the press about the decline of moral values in business. Well, I told him the whole story last night over dinner and said that, obviously, in the light of the circular he sent round to all operations six months ago, stating the company's commitment to conducting business round the world in a totally clean way and in the best traditions of US ethical business practice, backed by the threat of legal prosecution and instant dismissal for anyone contravening these standards, etc., etc., there was no way I could do what Benny wanted. Then I also reminded him how vital the boiler was for the plant, and how far we already are behind schedule, and how there are half a dozen other important items to be delivered in the very near future. He looked quite dazed."

"So what did he decide?" asked McLeod.

"Haven't heard from him yet," said Bailey. "But he promised to call me before he left this evening."

McLeod turned to go. "See you in the bar after work then, Dan. Can't wait to hear how it ends."

He returned to the office and, to his relief, the rest of the afternoon passed without incident. Standing at the guesthouse bar later, he reviewed his day: a near-riot and an attempt to blackmail him. Not quite what he had anticipated on taking the job. Still pondering his problems, McLeod took his drink over to a quiet corner but, within a few minutes, he was joined by Hari Tung, financial director of the Changmai Corporation, and a Frenchman, Thierry Dupont.

Born locally, Harvard-trained Hari Tung was a very smart young man who worked closely with Goh. Thierry Dupont, who worked for a French multinational, was one of the many vendors to the rayon project, on site to check the machinery his company had supplied. He was holding a bottle of champagne. "Come, my friends," said Thierry, "celebrate with me. I just heard that I have won a *very* lucrative contract for my firm with, let's say, a large conglomerate in a country not far from here. And you know what? I got it because of my 'corruption skills'. I outbid and outdid German and US, even Japanese competition to get it. It was hard work, requiring a lot of creativity, but it was worth it, and tonight I am so proud."

"Proud!" exclaimed McLeod. "You can't be serious! You are corrupt, and you have corrupted someone else. What is there to be proud of in that?"

"My friend," said Thierry, "thanks to this contract, my company back home will have work for the next two years. With 13 per cent unemployment in France, anyone who creates jobs is a hero. In my opinion, corruption is a small price to pay to give work to Europeans. And, of course, there will be a nice little promotion in it for me. Now, stop making a fuss and have a drink."

"But David has a point," said Hari in his perfect English. "By your actions you are corrupting others. And, if you think about it, that is not the only way that you in the West are helping to corrupt the people of this region. It is something that I and my friends, who are the fathers of young children, often argue about. Look at the Western values the young are absorbing while watching your films, full of sex and violence. What sort of heroes are they going to copy? I have always been glad to be part of a culture with such a strong sense of family. Take Mr Goh, whose family is extended to include all those who work for him. They know that the next generation will also find a place with him and so, secure in their 'iron rice bowl', they work together for the good of the group, not for the individual as I have seen people do in the West. But this sense of community is beginning to break down, and we Asians are allowing it to happen."

Hari continued, "Although we welcome the transfer of Western technological progress, we do not feel the same about your moral standards. As we see it, Western values are poisoning the local people who, in the end, we fear will be as morally bankrupt as people in your part of the world. You cannot stop the poison spreading. In every hotel, there is CNN showing the same images, encouraging the same materialist attitudes of want, want, want. Global products for global consumers, they claim. But where will it all end? Imagine, if each and every one of the 1.2 billion Chinese were to consume as much as Americans, it would mean 'goodbye, planet Earth'. It could not support that degree of consumption and the pollution that would go with it. And we would all be responsible."

"What absolute rubbish," said Thierry. "It will never happen. Come on, let's talk about something more cheerful. Leave morality to the professors. While there's business to be done and a buck to be made, why should we worry?"

NOTE

* This case was written by Charlotte Butler, Research Associate, and Henri-Claude de Bettignies, Professor at INSEAD. It is intended to be used as a basis for class discussion rather than to illustrate effective or ineffective handling of a situation.

Mark E. Mendenhall

OLIVIA FRANCIS

JIM MARKHAM DID NOT KNOW what to do. The more he tried to analyze the problem, the murkier it became. Normally, Jim felt confident in counseling his students – both past and present – but this time it was different. Olivia Francis had been one of the best students he had ever taught in the MBA program. She was intelligent and curious, one of those rare students whose thirst for knowledge was uppermost in her reasons for being in the program.

She had never disclosed much about her family or her past to him, but he knew from her student file and information sheet, and from bits and pieces of conversations with her, that she had come from a poor, somewhat impoverished neighborhood in St Louis and had earned her way through college on academic scholarships and part-time jobs. Upon graduation from the MBA program, she left the Midwest, taking a job with a prestigious consulting firm in Denver, and at the time he had felt sure she would travel far in her career. Perhaps that is why her phone call earlier that morning troubled him so much.

Awaiting him on his arrival to his office was a message on his answering machine from Olivia. He returned her call and wound up talking to her for an hour. The salient portions of their conversation began to run through his mind again. What had struck him initially were the range and the depth of her emotions. Never had he spoken to anyone before that had seethed with so much rage. After she had vented the rage, like air slowly being discharged from a balloon, she became almost apathetic, and her resignation to her situation almost frightened him – her only way out, as far as she could see, was to find another job. Jim could not recall ever being in a situation where he felt he had absolutely no control over what happened to him, where his input was meaningless to the resolution of a problem that he faced.

Olivia had stated that her first performance appraisal had been below average, and two weeks ago, her second appraisal was only average. She felt that she had worked hard on her part of the team's projects and believed her work was first rate. The only reason for the appraisals, as far as she could see, was that she was not White. She was the only African-American on the team – in the whole office for that matter. Jim believed her when she said that her work was excellent, for her work had always been excellent as a graduate student and as a research assistant. He had attempted to get her to analyze the situation further, but it was like pulling teeth; she seemed emotionally worn out and just wanted out.

"Surely they gave you more feedback about your performance on the first appraisal than that it was below average?" he remembered asking. All she would say is that they mentioned something about her attitude, not being a team player, that her work was technically exemplary, but that she was part of a team and that working with others was as critical as the nature of the work she did by herself. Olivia, however, stated that she felt that this was a smokescreen for the fact that she had been dumped on the office by a corporate recruiter with a diversity quota to fill, and that they were trying to get rid of her by using subjective criteria that she couldn't really defend herself against. The frustration came back to Jim as he remembered probing her for more information.

"What was the tone of your manager in the feedback session?"

"Condescending, false sincerity; there was a lot of talk on his part of 'my potential.' It was humiliating, actually."

"How do the other people in your team act toward you? Are they friendly, aloof, or what?"

"Oh, they're friendly on the surface – especially the project leader – but that's about as far as it goes."

"Is the project manager the person who gave you this feedback?"

"No, she is under the group manager. He is a long-time company guy. But obviously she gives him her evaluation and impressions of me, so I'm sure that they both pretty much see issues regarding me eye-to-eye."

"Tell me more about the group manager."

"Mr. Bresnan? I don't know much about him to tell you the truth. He oversees five project teams, and each project manager reports to him. He comes in and gives us a pep talk from time to time. Other than that, I've never had occasion to really interact with him. He's always cracking jokes, putting people at ease. Kind of a 'Theory Y' type – at least on the surface."

"Do you ever go to lunch as a group?"

"Yes, they go to lunch a lot and they invite me along, but all they talk about are things I don't find very interesting – they're kind of a shallow bunch."

"What do you mean, 'shallow'?"

"They couldn't care less about real issues – their discussions range from restaurants to social events around town to recent movies they've seen."

"Does the project manager go to these lunches?"

"Yes, she comes and even plans parties after work, too. Her husband is a movie producer. Nothing big, just documentaries and that type of thing, but they put on airs, if you what I mean. She is really gregarious and always wants to be of help to people, but she strikes me as putting on a front, a mask. Obviously she isn't really sincere in wanting to help everyone 'be the best that they can be' – that's one of her little slogans by the way – after all, look what happened to me."

"Why do you think they're prejudiced against you?"

"Well, the poor appraisals for one thing – those are completely unfounded. They do other less obvious things, too. Twice I've overheard some of them from behind cubicles relaxing and telling ethnic jokes.

"Is it just a few of them that do this? I can't believe all of them are racist."

"I don't know! I don't enter the cubicle and say, 'Hi everyone, tell a few more jokes!' But it isn't just one or two of them. Look, I obviously don't fit in, do I? It's lily-white in the office, and I'm not."

"What do they do that is work-related that bothers you?"

"Well, when project deadlines get closer their anxiety level increases. They run around the office, yell at secretaries ... it is like a volcano building up power to explode. They worry and agonize over the presentation to the client and have four or five trial presentation runs that everyone is required to go to. It's all so stupid."

"Why is that?"

"The clients always like what we produce, and with a few relatively small adjustments, our work is acceptable to the clients. So, it's as though all that wasted energy was needless. We could accomplish so much more if they would just settle down and trust their abilities."

"How do you act when they are like this?"

"I do my work. I respond to them rationally. I turn my part of the project in on time, and it is good work, Professor Markham. I guess I try to be the stabilizing force in the team by not acting as they do – I guess I just don't find the work pressures to be all that stressful."

"Why not?"

"Oh, I don't know really. Well maybe I do a little bit. I don't know if you know this or not, but my mother was a single parent with four kids. I was the oldest. She worked three jobs, and I looked after the kids when I came home from school. She worked hard to provide for us, so I would be in charge of the smaller kids sometimes upwards of nine o'clock at night. Doing your homework while taking care of a sick kid with the others listening to the television – that's stressful! These people at work, they don't know what stress is. Most of them are single, or if they are married they don't have any kids. They all seem very self-centered, like the universe revolves around them and their careers."

"What kind of behavior at work seems to get rewarded?"

"I guess doing good work doesn't. What seems to get rewarded is being white, being more or less competent, and being interested in insipid topics. Professor Markham, don't you know of any firms that are more enlightened that I can send my résumé to? I'm looking for a firm that will reward me for the work I do and not for who I am or am not."

*   *   *

Jim leaned back in his chair, pondering what to do next. He had promised Olivia that he would call her back in a day or two with some advice. He sensed that he didn't quite understand her problem — that there was more to it than what appeared on the surface — but he felt he didn't have enough data to analyze it properly. He decided to go for a walk around the neighborhood to clear his mind. As he opened the front door and gazed down his street, he suddenly realized for the first time that his neighborhood was lily-white.

Nicola Pless and Thomas Maak

LEVI STRAUSS & CO.: ADDRESSING CHILD LABOUR IN BANGLADESH

MATT WILSON[1] WAS DRIVING BACK from a factory close to Mymensingh in the administrative division of Dhaka. It was a September afternoon and the Jeep trip had been long and arduous. It was monsoon season in Bangladesh, the dirt tracks were muddy and Matt's vehicle got stuck several times. This was not the first time during the past weeks of travel when tropical downpours made driving quite difficult in Asia. Yet, as operations manager, he had to visit the ten suppliers in Chittagong and Dhaka. The purpose of the visits was to carry out the annual supplier assessments together with Kamir Rao, the regional advisor for South Asia. To get to the production sites, he had to drive through rural areas, where rice, mustard and tea are grown. From the jeep, he could see the workers in the paddy fields. Two-thirds of the Bangladeshi population of some 150 million work in the agricultural sector.[2] According to UNICEF, about 36 per cent of the population lives on less than a dollar a day.[3] He also thought he saw children working in the fields but then he could have been wrong. It is often difficult to tell a person's age in Bangladesh because people look younger due to malnutrition.

Matt had worked for Levi Strauss & Co. (LS&Co.) for eight years before moving to South East Asia. He had worked at the company headquarters in San Francisco, where he joined LS&Co. in 1997 after graduating from a top ten US business school. He joined LS&Co. because of the company's reputation as a good "corporate citizen" with a commitment to best business practices and its international presence (see Appendices 1 and 2). He soon got the opportunity to spread his wings in South Asia. With five years as operations manager in Bangladesh, he had built long-term relationships with most of LS&Co.'s suppliers in the garment industry. Since the 1980s, the garment industry had become the mainstay of Bangladesh's economy thanks to the country's rock-bottom labour costs. In fact, the industry contributes 75 per cent to the country's export earnings and employs over 3 million people, most of them women (90 per cent).[4] Back in the '80s, LS&Co. decided to expand its business internationally, both in sales markets and for sourcing its products.[5] Today they work with over 600 suppliers in 50 countries. It is these firms that produce LS& Co.'s branded garments.

This shift towards international suppliers has raised many thorny issues: Do suppliers meet LS&Co.'s' standards? What about child labour, environmental protection, health and safety, and human rights? These considerations led LS&Co. to draw up and introduce *Global Sourcing and Operating Guidelines* (see Appendix 3) in 1991, which were implemented the following year. These guidelines comprised two parts: the "Country Assessment Guidelines" and the "Business Partner Terms of Engagement" (TOE), which set specific standards for suppliers in areas such as: freedom of association; fair employment practices; workers' health and safety; and environmental management. In fact, LS&Co. was the first company to institute such a supplier code of conduct, thereby setting a standard for multinational companies.[6]

The company has conducted regular assessments since 1992 to ensure suppliers meet LS&Co.'s standards (TOE). The firm employs 20 factory assessors around the world. These staff are specially trained to assess and monitor compliance with the TOE code. This year, Matt had accompanied Kamir on most of the assessment visits to suppliers' factories in Bangladesh. It came as a shock when they discovered that two of the new suppliers were employing children under the minimum working age of 15. The two suppliers were actually offering very good working conditions by Bangladeshi standards: new factory buildings; safe machines and production equipment; a healthy, clean and safe environment for workers; and a staff canteen. Matt was also very pleased with the quality of products they delivered. Finding out that the two new suppliers were employing young children therefore came as a major disappointment.

However, he knew that the issue of underage labour is a complicated one in the country. While child labour violates International Labour Standards (ILO) as well as company guidelines, it is rife in Bangladesh and does not infringe local laws. According to UNICEF statistics, 13 per cent of children between the ages of 5 and 14 are involved in child labor activities.[7] Furthermore, many children born in the country are not issued birth certificates, a fact that makes it hard to determine their real age. In Bangladesh, whole families depend on a child's income. This places a great burden on kids. Not only are they deprived of schooling (which is often the only way out of the poverty trap) but they also have no say when it comes to where they work, the kind of jobs they do and their working conditions. Moreover, many of these children are cruelly exploited, run serious health risks and are paid a pittance (which is one of the reasons why employers prefer hiring children to adults). Put baldly, they have no rights. In fact, a great many children in Bangladesh grow up under conditions that can all too easily lead to exploitation and even prostitution (see Appendix 4).

Shortly after returning from the trip, Matt arranged a meeting with Kamir and the management team to address the suppliers' violations of ILO and TOE standards and to reach a decision on how best to deal with the situation. During the meeting, they discussed the situation in depth and identified the various stakeholders that would be affected by their decision. They also brainstormed different options for dealing with underage employees. Then they considered the challenge of reaching a solution that complied with international labour standards, reflected LS&Co.'s corporate values and met stakeholders' needs.

CASE DISCUSSION QUESTIONS

1. Who are the stakeholders that are affected by the management team's decision?
2. What are the management team's options?
3. Which solution would best suit Levi Strauss & Co.?

APPENDIX 1: MEMO BY THE PRESIDENT AND CEO JOHN ANDERSON ACCOMPANYING THE WORLDWIDE CODE OF BUSINESS CONDUCT[8]

TO: **Levi Strauss & Co. Employees Worldwide**

FROM: **John Anderson**

SUBJECT: **Worldwide Code of Business Conduct**

LS&CO. has a long and distinguished history of corporate citizenship, including our unwavering commitment to responsible business practices. Our values and strong belief in "doing the right thing" are the foundation of our success.

To ensure we provide our employees with a clear set of standards and guidance for conducting our business with integrity and the highest degree of compliance with the law, we established LS&CO.'s **Worldwide Code of Business Conduct**.

This code certainly does not cover every ethical or legal situation we may encounter in our business operations, but it does provide an excellent summary of important guidelines that define the way we choose to do business.

Our Worldwide Code of Business Conduct applies to all employees around the world; however, with a global footprint of more than 110 countries, we and our affiliates apply the code as appropriate in individual countries, consistent with local laws.

If you have any questions about the Worldwide Code of Business Conduct or how it should be applied in your location, please consult with your manager, Human Resources representative, the Legal department or the Chief Compliance Officer in San Francisco.

The integrity of our employees makes LS&CO. a great place to work. I encourage you to familiarize yourself with our Worldwide Code of Business Conduct and apply these standards to your work every day.

John Anderson
President and
Chief Executive Officer
Levi Strauss & Co.

APPENDIX 2: LEVI STRAUSS & CO. FACT SHEET[9]

Levi Strauss & Co. Fact Sheet

Founded in 1853 by Bavarian immigrant Levi Strauss, Levi Strauss & Co. (LS&CO.) is one of the world's largest brand-name apparel marketers with sales in more than 110 countries around the world. There is no other company with a comparable global presence in the jeans and casual pants markets. Our market-leading apparel products are sold under the **Levi's®, Dockers® and Signature by Levi Strauss & Co.™ brands**.

Company Profile

- FY 2008 Net Revenues: $4.4 billion
- Global presence: Three geographic divisions: Levi Strauss Americas (LSA), Levi Strauss Europe, Middle East and North Africa (LSEMA) and Asia Pacific Division (APD).
    - Regional headquarters located in San Francisco, Brussels and Singapore
    - Global sourcing headquarters in Singapore.
    - More than 5,000 registered trademarks in approximately 180 countries.
    - We derive approximately 40 percent of our net revenues and regional operating income from our European and Asia Pacific businesses.
- Retail distribution: LS&CO. products are sold through approximately 60,000 retail locations worldwide, including 260 company-operated stores and approximately 1,500 franchised stores around the world.
- Licensing: LS&CO. trademarks are licensed for products and accessories complementary to our core branded products and extend our brands into product categories that broaden the product range available to consumers and create compelling and distinctive brand looks, including:
    - Tops, sweaters, jackets, and outerwear
    - Kidswear
    - Footwear and hosiery
    - Loungewear and sleepwear
    - Belts, bags and wallets
    - Eyewear
    - Luggage and home bedding products
- Sourcing: We source our products primarily from independent manufacturers located throughout the world.
    - Contractors are located in approximately 45 countries around the world
    - No single country represents more than 20 percent of our production
- Employees: More than 11,400 worldwide
    - 4,700 in the Americas
    - 4,400 in Europe
    - 2,300 in Asia Pacific
- Ownership: The company is privately held by descendants of the family of Levi Strauss. Shares of company stock are not publicly traded. Shares of Levi Strauss Japan K.K., the company's Japanese affiliate, are publicly traded in Japan.

APPENDIX 2—*continued*

Levi Strauss & Co.

A Unique History

LS&CO.'s history and longevity are unique in the apparel industry: Levi's® jeans are the original, authentic and definitive jeans. In 1853, during the California Gold Rush, our founder, Levi Strauss, opened a wholesale dry goods business in San Francisco. That business became known as "Levi Strauss & Co." In 1873, Levi Strauss and Jacob Davis, a tailor, saw a consumer need for work pants that could hold up under rough conditions. They worked together and received a U.S. patent to make "waist overalls" with metal rivets at points of strain on the pants – and in so doing created the world's first jean. Levi Strauss & Co. brought these new workpants to market that year, and, in 1890, began using the lot number "501" to identify the product.

In 1986, we introduced the Dockers® brand of casual apparel, which was at the forefront of the business casual trend in the United States. In 2003, in response to the emergence and success of the mass channel, we launched the Levi Strauss Signature® brand of jeans and casual apparel for consumers who shop in the channel.

LS&CO.'s commitment to quality, innovation and corporate citizenship, manifested in many ways throughout our history, began with Levi Strauss and continues today.

Values and Vision

Four core values are at the heart of Levi Strauss & Co.:

- Empathy
- Originality
- Integrity
- Courage

These four values are linked. Our history demonstrates how these core values work together and are the source of our success. Generations of people have worn our products as a symbol of freedom and self-expression in the face of adversity, challenge and social change. The special relationship between our values, our consumers and our brands is the basis of our success and drives our core purpose. It is the foundation of who we are and what we want to become:

People love our clothes and trust our company.

We will market and distribute the most appealing and widely worn apparel brands.

Our products define quality, style and function.

We will clothe the world.

Corporate Citizenship

We believe that commercial success and corporate citizenship are closely linked. This principle is embedded in our 156-year experience and continues to anchor how we operate today.
For us, corporate citizenship includes a strong belief that we can help shape society through civic engagement and community involvement, responsible labor and workplace practices, philanthropy, ethical conduct, environmental stewardship and transparency. Our "profits through principles" business approach manifests itself in how we develop our business strategies and policies and make everyday decisions. Our history reflects our approach to corporate citizenship:

- In 1991, we were the first multinational apparel company to develop a comprehensive supplier code of conduct targeted toward ensuring that individuals making our products anywhere in the world would do so in safe and healthy working conditions and be treated with dignity and respect. For more information, see "Sourcing and Logistics – Sourcing Practices."

APPENDIX 2—*continued*

Levi Strauss & Co.

- Our commitment to equal opportunity and diversity predated the U.S. civil rights movement and federally mandated desegregation by two decades. We opened integrated factories in California in the 1940s. In 1960, we integrated our newly opened plants in the American South.

- In 1992, we became the first <u>Fortune 500</u> company to extend full medical benefits to domestic partners of employees, a practice now followed by many corporations and public agencies.

- We participate in public advocacy relating to trade policy. We believe that worker rights protections and enforcement measures should be an integral part of all bilateral, regional or multilateral trade negotiations. Since 2000, we have been a leader in publicly advocating this position.

- The Levi Strauss Foundation, a charitable foundation supported by us, focuses its core grantmaking primarily in three areas: AIDS/HIV prevention, building assets, and workers' rights in countries where we have a business presence.

- We support and encourage employee community involvement through volunteer activities, paid time off and grants by the Levi Strauss Foundation to nonprofit organizations we assist through our community activities.

- The Red Tab Foundation, a nonprofit organization created and largely funded by our employees, offers financial assistance to our employees and retirees who are unable to afford life's basic necessities.

APPENDIX 3: GLOBAL SOURCING AND OPERATING GUIDELINES[10]

Levi Strauss & Co. Global Sourcing and Operating Guidelines

Levi Strauss & Co.'s (LS&CO.) commitment to responsible business practices — embodied in our Global Sourcing and Operating Guidelines — guides our decisions and behavior as a company everywhere we do business. Since becoming the first multinational to establish such guidelines in 1991, LS&CO. has used them to help improve the lives of workers manufacturing our products, make responsible sourcing decisions and protect our commercial interests. They are a cornerstone of our sourcing strategy and of our business relationships with hundreds of contractors worldwide.

The Levi Strauss & Co. Global Sourcing and Operating Guidelines include two parts:

The Country Assessment Guidelines, which address large, external issues beyond the control of LS&CO.'s individual business partners. These help us assess the opportunities and risks of doing business in a particular country.

The Business Partner Terms of Engagement (TOE), which deal with issues that are substantially controllable by individual business partners. These TOE are an integral part of our business relationships. Our employees and our business partners understand that complying with our TOE is no less important than meeting our quality standards or delivery times.

Country Assessment Guidelines

The numerous countries where LS&CO. has existing or future business interests present a variety of cultural, political, social and economic circumstances.

The Country Assessment Guidelines help us assess any issues that might present concern in light of the ethical principles we have set for ourselves. The Guidelines assist us in making practical and principled business decisions as we balance the potential risks and opportunities associated with conducting business in specific countries. Specifically, we assess the following:

Health and Safety Conditions — must meet the expectations we have for employees and their families or our company representatives;

Human Rights Environment — must allow us to conduct business activities in a manner that is consistent with our Global Sourcing and Operating Guidelines and other company policies

Legal System — must provide the necessary support to adequately protect our trademarks, investments or other commercial interests, or to implement the Global Sourcing and Operating Guidelines and other company policies; and

Political, Economic and Social Environment — must protect the company's commercial interests and brand/corporate image. We do not conduct business in countries prohibited by U.S. laws.

Terms of Engagement

Our TOE help us to select business partners who follow workplace standards and business practices that are consistent with LS&CO.'s values and policies. These requirements are applied to every contractor who manufactures or finishes products for LS&CO. Trained assessors closely monitor compliance among our manufacturing and finishing contractors in more than 50 countries. The TOE include:

APPENDIX 3—*continued*

Levi Strauss & Co.

Ethical Standards
We will seek to identify and utilize business partners who aspire as individuals and in the conduct of all their businesses to a set of ethical standards not incompatible with our own.

Legal Requirements
We expect our business partners to be law abiding as individuals and to comply with legal requirements relevant to the conduct of all their businesses.

Environmental Requirements
We will only do business with partners who share our commitment to the environment and who conduct their business in a way that is consistent with LS&CO.'s Environmental Philosophy and Guiding Principles (See TOE Guidebook p.68).

Community Involvement
We will favor business partners who share our commitment to improving community conditions.

Employment Standards
We will only do business with partners who adhere to the following guidelines:

Child Labor
Use of child labor is not permissible. Workers can be no less than 15 years of age and not younger than the compulsory age to be in school. We will not utilize partners who use child labor in any of their facilities. We support the development of legitimate workplace apprenticeship programs for the educational benefit of younger people.

Prison Labor/Forced Labor
We will not utilize prison or forced labor in contracting relationships in the manufacture and finishing of our products. We will not utilize or purchase materials from a business partner utilizing prison or forced labor.

Disciplinary Practices
We will not utilize business partners who use corporal or other forms of mental or physical coercion.

Working Hours
While permitting flexibility in scheduling, we will identify local legal limits on work hours and seek business partners who do not exceed them except for appropriately compensated overtime. While we favor partners who utilize less than sixty-hour work weeks, we will not use contractors who, on a regular basis, require in excess of a sixty-hour week. Employees should be allowed at least one day off in seven.

Wages and Benefits
We will only do business with partners who provide wages and benefits that comply with any applicable law and match the prevailing local manufacturing or finishing industry practices.

Freedom of Association
We respect workers' rights to form and join organizations of their choice and to bargain collectively. We expect our suppliers to respect the right to free association and the right to organize and bargain collectively without unlawful interference. Business partners should ensure that workers who make such decisions or participate in such organizations are not the object of discrimination or punitive disciplinary actions and that the representatives of such organizations have access to their members under conditions established either by local laws or mutual agreement between the employer and the worker organizations.

Discrimination
While we recognize and respect cultural differences, we believe that workers should be employed on the basis of their ability to do the job, rather than on the basis of personal characteristics or beliefs. We will favor business partners who share this value.

APPENDIX 3—*continued*

Levi Strauss & Co.

<u>Health and Safety</u>
We will only utilize business partners who provide workers with a safe and healthy work environment. Business partners who provide residential facilities for their workers must provide safe and healthy facilities.

Evaluation and Compliance

All new and existing factories involved in the manufacturing or finishing of products for LS&CO. are regularly evaluated to ensure compliance with our TOE. Our goal is to achieve positive results and effect change by working with our business partners to find long-term solutions that will benefit the individuals who make our products and will improve the quality of life in local communities. We work on-site with our contractors to develop strong alliances dedicated to responsible business practices and continuous improvement.

If LS&CO. determines that a contractor is not complying with our TOE, we require that the contractor implement a corrective action plan within a specified time period. If a contractor fails to meet the corrective action plan commitment, Levi Strauss & Co. will terminate the business relationship.

APPENDIX 4: BANGLADESH: SHETRA'S STORY[11]: THE LIFE OF A SEXUALLY EXPLOITED CHILD IN BANGLADESH

The World Congress III against the Sexual Exploitation of Children, set for 25–28 November 2008 in Brazil, aims to promote international cooperation for more effective action on sexual exploitation. Here is one in a series of related stories.

BARISAL, Bangladesh, 19 November 2008 – a recent survey by UNICEF Bangladesh found the average age at which children became involved in commercial sexual exploitation was 13.

Although sexual abuse affects all strata of society, it remains a taboo that is not talked about in Bangladesh. As a result, many children who are being exploited as part of the commercial sex industry do not tell anyone.

The non-governmental organization Association of Voluntary Action for Society (AVAS) runs a drop-in centre here that is supported by UNICEF's HIV/AIDS programme. Through the drop-in centre, sex workers have access to condoms to prevent HIV infection, as well as other basic health services, counselling and HIV education.

Shetra's Story

Recently, a sexually exploited 13-year-old named Shetra was found in a hotel by a peer educator from AVAS. Here is her story, as told to UNICEF's Kathryn Seymour:

"My father died when I was six or seven, so my mother has always had to work to support us. When my mother goes to work, I look after my smallest sister, who is only 11 months old. My middle sister is eight.

"All four of us live in a rented house in Barisal, but the rent is very expensive. My mother often can't earn enough as a maid, and things are very difficult. Sometimes, we can't manage food or the rent for our house. Recently, I began to think that I really needed to earn some money to help us out, so I decided to go look for a job.

"For a short while, I got a job as a maid. My employer beat me and only gave me one meal a day, so I quit. Two months ago, I started as a sex worker.

"My mother doesn't know where I go when I leave to meet men. I tell her that I am going to visit a friend. When I give her the money afterwards and she asks me where it came from, I tell her that I got a job on the roads chipping bricks. This is the story I tell everyone.

How it Started

"I started as a sex worker because of one of our neighbours. He is close friends with my family, so I call him 'uncle', even though he is not my relative. One day, he called me and said that he had someone for me to meet at his house. When I got to his house, he introduced me to another man who he said I should also call 'uncle'.

"We went to a hotel together and that was my first time. It hurt a lot. Since then, two or three days a week I go to the hotel with this uncle. One time, he took me to his home when no one else was there. I've been to other hotels and sometimes to houses when the wives are away.

"Normally, the oldest men come to me. I think that they are mostly over 40 years old. My neighbour usually calls me when there is a man for me. I don't know if there are other girls that he calls, but there might be.

"I want to stop doing this, but I don't know how because my mother needs the money. I don't want to continue because then I know that I won't have an education, but I need to help feed my family."

NOTES

1. This case is a real-life example. However, names of places, people and biographical information are fictional. The number of assessors and suppliers contracted reflect an estimation. Bangladesh. (http://en.wikipedia.org/wiki/Bangladesh) Retrieved April 15, 2009.
2. UNICEF – Bangladesh – The big picture. (www.unicef.org/infobycountry/bangladesh_bangladesh_background.html) Retrieved April 15, 2009.
3. Bangladesh. (http://en.wikipedia.org/wiki/Bangladesh) Retrieved April 15, 2009.
4. Baron, D.P. 2003. *Business and its Environment*, 4th ed., New Jersey: Prentice Hall, p. 761.
5. Product Sourcing Practices (www.levistrauss.com/Citizenship/) Retrieved April 15, 2009.
6. Baron, D.P. 2003.
7. In their statistics, UNICEF defines child labour as the "Percentage of children aged 5 to 14 years of age involved in child labor activities at the moment of the survey [1999–2007]. A child is considered to be involved in child labor activities under the following classification: (a) children 5 to 11 years of age that during the week preceding the survey did at least one hour of economic activity or at least 28 hours of domestic work, and (b) children 12 to 14 years of age that during the week preceding the survey did at least 14 hours of economic activity or at least 42 hours of economic activity and domestic work combined." (www.unicef.org/infobycountry/stats_popup9.html) Retrieved April 15, 2009.
8. www.levistrauss.com/sites/default/files/librarydocument/2010/5/wwcoc-english_0.pdf.
9. www.levistrauss.com/library/levi-strauss-co-fact-sheet.
10. www.levistrauss.com/sites/default/files/librarydocument/2010/4/CitizenshipCodeOf Conduct.pdf.
11. www.unicef.org/infobycountry/bangladesh_46449.html.

LITERATURE AND SUGGESTED READINGS

Baron, D.P. 2003. *Business and its environment,* 4th ed., Upper Saddle River, NJ: Prentice Hall.
Donaldson, T., & Dunfee, T. (1999). *Ties that bind.* Boston, MA: Harvard Business School Press.
Freeman, R.E. 1984. *Strategic management: A stakeholder approach.* Boston, MA: Pitman Publishing.
Johnson, M. 1993. *Moral imagination: Implications of cognitive science for ethics.* Chicago, London: The University of Chicago Press.
Maak, T. & Pless, N.M. 2006a. Responsible leadership: A relational approach. In T. Maak & N. M. Pless (Eds.), *Responsible leadership*. London, New York: Routledge, 33–53.
Maak, T. & Pless, N.M. 2006b. Responsible leadership in a stakeholder society. A relational perspective. *Journal of Business Ethics*, 66(1), 99–115.

Pless, N.M. 2007. Understanding responsible leadership: Roles identity and motivational drivers. *Journal of Business Ethics,* 74(4), 437–456.

Pless, N.M. & Maak, T. 2005. Relational intelligence for leading responsibly in a connected world. In K.M. Weaver (Ed.), *Proceedings of the Sixty-fifth Annual Meeting of the Academy of Management,* Honolulu.

Werhane, P. 1999. *Moral imagination and management decision making.* New York, Oxford: Oxford University Press.

Index

Page numbers in *italics* denote a figure/table